ESSAYS FROM
CONTEMPORARY CULTURE

ESSAYS FROM CONTEMPORARY CULTURE

Third Edition

KATHERINE ANNE ACKLEY
UNIVERSITY OF WISCONSIN
AT STEVENS POINT

Harcourt Brace College Publishers

Fort Worth   Philadelphia   San Diego   New York   Orlando   Austin   San Antonio
Toronto   Montreal   London   Sydney   Tokyo

Publisher	Christopher P. Klein
Executive Editor	Michael Rosenberg
Acquisitions Editor	John Meyers
Developmental Editor	Diane Drexler
Art Director	Vicki Whistler
Production Manager	Diane Gray
Compositor	Publications Development Company of Texas

Cover illustration by Kevin Tolman

ISBN: 0-15-505302-7
Library of Congress Catalog Card Number: 97-71821

Address for orders: Harcourt Brace & Company, 6277 Sea Harbor Drive, Orlando, FL 32887-6777 1-800-782-4479

Address for editorial correspondence: Harcourt Brace College Publishers, 301 Commerce Street, Suite 3700, Fort Worth, TX 76102

Web site address: http://www.hbcollege.com

Harcourt Brace College Publishers may provide complimentary instructional aids and supplements or supplement packages to those adopters qualified under our adoption policy. Please contact your sales representative for more information. If as an adopter or potential user you receive supplements you do not need, please return them to your sales representative or send them to:

Attn: Returns Department, Troy Warehouse, 465 South Lincoln Drive, Troy, MO 63379

Printed in the United States of America

8 9 0 1 2 3 4 5 6   066   9 8 7 6 5 4 3 2

For my granddaughter Elizabeth Anne Schilling
and
my grandsons Lucas Konrad Schilling
and
Zackary Idir Yahi

PREFACE

What students read, think, and write about is inextricably linked with who they are and how they develop as responsible human beings in relation to their classmates, their families, and, eventually, the communities in which they live and work. *Essays from Contemporary Culture* is designed to encourage students to make informed opinions or observations about topics that matter to them in a variety of forums, such as expressive writing, classroom discussion, and formal essays. Many of the works are written from a particular viewpoint and are meant to be controversial. Such controversy is useful because it causes students to question what they read, to challenge writers' opinions with which they disagree, to explore their own thoughts, and to develop their own positions on important issues. The readings come from a variety of sources including newspapers, magazines, and books, and, although they vary in style, tone, and purpose, all in one way or another respond to a particular issue of importance in contemporary culture.

This third edition has undergone a number of changes in response to reviewers of the book who used the previous editions in the classroom. The number of total essays is increased from sixty-six to eighty-one. Of those, thirty-eight have been retained from the second edition and forty-three are new to this edition, most of which have been published in the 1990s. In addition, the number of chapters has been increased to ten, and most of the chapter titles have been changed. For instance, "Self-Perception" replaces "Living on the Outside," "Male-Female Relationships" replaces "Interpersonal Relationships," "Ethics, Morals, and Values" replaces "Acquiring Values," "Violence" replaces "Responding to Violence," and "Prejudice and Discrimination" replaces "Confronting Prejudice." The new chapters include "Insights," "Role Models," "Political Correctness," and "Popular Culture." This last chapter is subdivided into "Rap Music," "Hollywood and the Movies," and "Television."

I have broadened the range of rhetorical modes represented by the selections, including more representation of argument, analysis, and opinion, and I have included more writing suggestions that emphasize synthesis and argument. All of the writing topics have been moved to the end of each chapter (or section, in "Popular Culture"). A significant change is the addition of fiction to this edition. Six short stories by both frequently anthologized writers and new writers currently establishing themselves have been included. I have also increased the number of essays expressing opposing viewpoints on controversial topics: For instance, each section in the "Popular Culture" chapter has pieces by writers who hold differing opinions on the subject, and there are clustered readings on affirmative action, euthanasia, and speech codes and First Amendment issues. The number of minority and women writers remains high.

The selections in this textbook by and large represent contemporary responses to not only enduring social issues and the varieties of human experience but also to more recent phenomena such as affirmative action, political correctness, the devastating effects of the abuse of hard drugs, and rampant violent crime. While inequity in employment, demeaning or prejudicial speech, substance abuse, and crime have always been part of our society's problems, these are issues which have grown in importance in the 1990s. The contemporaneity of the readings, which address issues that students may have to face themselves, speaks to the relevance of this textbook to their lives beyond the classroom. Not all of the readings are written in a serious, weighty manner, however; many of them explore matters of interest and importance with humor and lightheartedness. A balance of gravity with levity helps keep these issues in their proper perspective.

Students are invited to read these essays, to think about them, and to respond to them. To assist in those purposes, each selection is followed by questions about their personal reactions to the piece and questions for class discussion. Students are asked for their personal reaction to the article first because subjective responses usually come before objective analyses of readings. Students would benefit by recording these personal responses in a journal, whether or not instructors ask students to share them in classroom discussion. After responding on a subjective level, students are asked to look back through the essay and answer questions about the author's purpose and meaning and the ways in which those are achieved. At the end of each chapter are writing suggestions that ask students to respond to individual writers, make connections between and among them, or write on some other topic related to the theme of the chapter.

The instructor's manual that accompanies this textbook begins with a general discussion of how to use the book, including ways to encourage students to participate in class and small group discussions. The manual also provides answers to the questions for discussion that follow each reading. Finally, for those instructors wishing to work on vocabulary, the instructor's manual includes a list of suggested vocabulary words for each of the readings.

I am grateful to the following reviewers for their work on the third edition of this book: Kirk Branch, University of Washington; Charlie Dee, Milwaukee Area Technical College; Marcia Huntington, Everett Community College; Sally Wood, De Anza College. I would also like to acknowledge the people who have contributed to the success of this book in past editions. Bruce L. Edwards, Bowling Green State University; L. Leyson, Fullerton College; Diane Maldonado, Community College of Allegheny County; David Moser, Butler County Community College; Brian O'Driscoll, Portland Community College; Peter Peterson, Shasta College; Mary Prindiville, University of Wisconsin-Green Bay; Margaret B. Racin, West Virginia University; Ajmal M. Razak, Ball State University; Uma Shrestha, Ball State University; Cindy Simpson, Fresno City College; Rosemarie Spight, Fresno City College; John Venne, Ball State University; and Susan R. Weintrob, Ball State University. All of their comments and suggestions continue to be a source of inspiration to me.

KATHERINE ANNE ACKLEY

CONTENTS

RHETORICAL TABLE OF CONTENTS

Note: Some essays appear in more than one category.

Comparison/Contrast

Definition

ESSAYS FROM CONTEMPORARY CULTURE

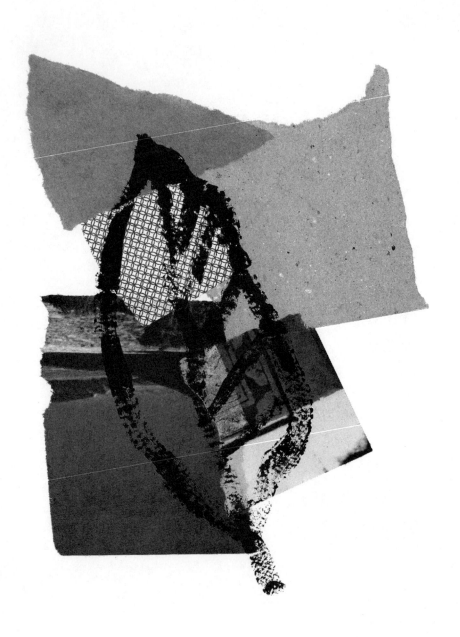

CHAPTER I

TRANSITIONS

Life is characterized by many transitions, such as the growth from childhood to adulthood, the change from high school to college, and the physical move from place to place. A transition can occur emotionally or psychology as well, such as when we achieve maturity or have a sudden insight that moves us from ignorance to knowledge. We make some of these transitions willingly; others we find difficult to make. But whether we welcome or resist transitions, they almost always affect us in significant ways.

This chapter opens with Jennifer Crichton's "'Who Shall I Be?' The Allure of a Fresh Start," a piece about the experience of students making the transition from high school to college. Using anecdotes about people she knows as well as personal experiences, Crichton explains how going away to college offers an opportunity to create an entirely new identity.

Several of the readings have to do with changes in physical location. In "Rootlessness," David Morris explains why he believes that Americans' tendency to move and change jobs frequently has bred "a costly instability in American life." He cites the effects on businesses and neighborhoods of the lack of connectedness among Americans and offers suggestions for restoring deeper roots among people. In contrast, Richard Ford thinks that moving is not so bad. In "An Urge for Going," Ford maintains that moving makes him feel "safe and in possession of [him]self."

For many people, a favorite retreat or particular place offers a way to escape everyday pressures or get away from the daily routine. For Susan Allen Toth in "Cabin Fever," the transition from city home to country cabin results in an enormous sense of release and a feeling of peace that is unmatched any place else. However, it sometimes happens that a place that holds wonderful memories for us is now gone, perhaps torn down or built over, or perhaps we have moved too far away to go there any more. In "White Breast Flats," Emilie Gallant describes a place filled with memories of her childhood and portrays a way of life that is long gone. Lynn Randall's ancestors' home was destroyed after they made their move against their will. In "Grandma's Story," Randall tells of the forced relocation of her grandparents and the bewilderment and insecurity that followed.

The last two readings are written from the perspective of an adult looking back on childhood and the growth, both intellectual and emotional, that resulted from growing up. In "Thinking as a Hobby," William Golding defines three grades of thinking as he recalls his own intellectual growth from childhood through adolescence to adulthood. Larry Watson's short story "Silence" features an event that happened when the narrator was eight years old and suggests that the transition from childhood to adulthood may carry with it some unresolved issues. Looking back as an adult on that memorable day, the narrator makes a painful realization.

"WHO SHALL I BE?" THE ALLURE OF A FRESH START

Jennifer Crichton

Jennifer Crichton has published articles in a number of national magazines. Her book, Delivery: A Nurse-Midwife's Story, *is a fictionalized account of life on the labor and delivery floor of a metropolitan hospital. She has also written* The Family Reunion Book, *a guide to planning and attending family reunions (1997). This essay was published in* Ms. *magazine in 1984.*

The student is a soul in transit, coming from one place en route to someplace else. Moving is the American way, after all. Our guiding principle is the fresh start, our foundation the big move, and nothing seduces like the promise of a clean slate.

"Do you realize how many people saw me throw up at Bob Stonehill's party in tenth grade? A lot of people," says my friend Anne. "How many forgot about it? Maybe two or three. Do you know how much I wanted to go someplace where nobody knew I threw up all over Bob Stonehill's living room in tenth grade? Very much. This may not seem like much of a justification for going away to college, but it was for me." Going away to college gives us a chance to rinse off part of our past, to shake off our burdensome reputations.

We've already survived the crises of being known, allowing how American high schools are as notoriously well-organized as totalitarian regimes, complete with secret police, punishment without trial, and banishment. High school society loves a label, cruelly infatuated with pinning down every species of student. Hilary is a klutz, Julie is a slut, and Michele a gossiping bitch who eats like a pig.

No wonder so many of us can't wait to be free of our old identities and climb inside a new skin in college. Even flattering reputations can be as confining as a pair of too-tight shoes. But identity is tricky stuff, constructed with mirrors. How you see yourself is a composite reflection of how you appear to friends, family, and lovers. In college, the fact that familiar mirrors aren't throwing back a familiar picture is both liberating and disorienting (maybe that's why so many colleges have freshman "orientation week").

"I guess you could call it an identity crisis," Andrea, a junior now, says of her freshman year. "It was the first time nobody knew who I was. I wasn't even anybody's daughter any more. I had always been the best and brightest—what was I going to do now, walk around the dorm with a sign around my neck saying 'Former High School Valedictorian'?"

For most of my college years, I was in hot pursuit of an identity crisis, especially after a Comparative Literature major informed me that the Chinese definition of "crisis" was "dangerous opportunity," with the emphasis on opportunity. On college applications, where there were blanks for your nickname, I carefully wrote "Rusty," although none of my friends (despite the fact that I have red hair) had ever, even for a whimsical moment, considered calling me that. I was the high-strung, sensitive, acne-blemished, antiauthoritarian, would-be writer. If I went through a day without some bizarre mood swing, people asked me what was wrong. I didn't even have the leeway to be the cheerful, smiling sort of girl I thought I might have it in me to be. My reputation seemed etched in stone, and I was pretty damn sick of it. As I pictured her, Rusty was the blithe spirit who would laugh everything off, shrug at perils as various as freshman mixers, bad grades, and cafeterias jammed with aloof strangers, and in general pass through a room with the vitality and appeal of a cool gust of wind.

But when I arrived at college, Rusty had vaporized. She was simply not in the station wagon that drove me up to campus. Much of college had to do with filling in the blanks, but changing myself would not be so easy, so predictable, so clichéd.

My parents, acting as anxious overseers on the hot, humid day I took my new self to college, seemed bound by a demonic ESP to sabotage my scarcely budding new identity. After a summer planning how I would metamorphose into the great American ideal, the normal teenage girl, I heard my mother tell my roommate, "I think you'll like Jenny—she's quite the oddball." Luckily, my roommate was saturated with all kinds of information the first day of college had flung at her, and the last thing she was paying attention to were the off-the-cuff remarks this oddball's mother was making. My unmarked reputation kept its sheen as it waited for me to cautiously build it up according to plan. My parents left without any further blunders, except to brush my bangs from my eyes ("You'll get a headache, Sweetheart") and foist on what had been a blissfully bare dormitory room an excruciatingly ugly lamp from home. As soon as the station wagon became a distant mote of dust on the highway, I pulled my bangs back over my eyes in my New Wave fashion of choice, tossed the ugly lamp in the nearest trash can, and did what I came to college to do. Anonymous, alone, without even a name, I would start over and become the kind of person I was meant to be: like myself, but better, with all my failures, rejections, and sexual indiscretions relegated to a history I hoped none of my new acquaintances would ever hear of.

Why was it, I wondered, when *any* change seemed possible that year, had it been so impossible in high school? For one thing, people know us well enough to see when we're attempting a change, and change can look embarrassingly like a public admission of weakness. Our secret desires, and the fact that we're not entirely pleased with ourselves, are on display. To change in public under the scrutiny of the most hypercritical witnesses in the world—other high school students—is to risk failure ("Look how cool she's trying to be, the jerk!") or succeeding but betraying friends in the process ("I don't understand her any more," they say, hurt and angry) or feeling so much like a fraud that you're forced to back down. And while we live at home, parental expectations, from the lovingly hopeful to the intolerably ambitious, apply the pressure of an invisible but very effective mold.

Jacki dressed in nothing but baggy Levis and flannel shirts for what seemed to be the endless duration of high school, even though she came to a sort of truce with her developing woman's body in eleventh grade and wasn't averse any longer to looking pretty. Looking good in college was a fantasy she savored because in high school, "I didn't want to make the attempt in public and then fail," she explains now, looking pulled together and chic. "I thought everyone would think I was trying to look good but I only managed to look weird. And I didn't want a certain group of girls who were very image-conscious to think they'd won some kind of victory either, that I was changing to please them.

"So I waited for college, and wore nice, new clothes right off the bat so nobody would know me any other way. I had set my expectations too high, though—I sort of thought that I'd be transformed into a kind of femme fatale or something. When I wasn't measuring up to what I'd imagined, I almost ditched the whole thing until I realized that at least I wasn't sabotaging myself any more. When I ran into a friend from high school, even though I had gotten used to the nice way I looked, I was scared that she could see right through my disguise. That's how I felt for a long time: a slobby girl just pretending to be pulled together."

12   At first, any change can feel uncomfortably like a pretense, an affectation. Dana had been a punked-out druggy in high school, so worried about being considered a grind that she didn't use a fraction of her considerable vocabulary when she was around her anti-intellectual friends. She promised herself to get serious academically in college, but the first night she spent studying in the science library, she recalls, "I half-expected the other kids to look twice at me, as if my fish-out-of-water feeling was showing. Of course, it wasn't. But it was schizophrenic at first, as if I were an imposter only playing at being smart. But when you do something long enough that thing becomes *you*. It's not playing any more. It's what you are."

Wanting to change yourself finds its source in two wellsprings: self-hatred and self-affirmation. Self-affirmation takes what already exists in your personality (even if slightly stunted or twisted) and encourages its growth. Where self-affirmation is expansive, self-hatred is reductive, negating one's own personality while appropriating qualities external to it and applying them like thick pancake makeup.

Joan's thing was to hang out with rich kids with what can only be described as a vengeance. She dressed in Ralph Lauren, forayed to town for $75 haircuts, and complained about the tackiness of mutual friends. But after a late night of studying, Joan allowed her self-control to slip long enough to tell me of her upbringing. Her mother was a cocktail waitress and Joan had never even found out her father's name. She and her mother had trucked about from one Western trailer park to another, and Joan always went to school dogged by her wrong-side-of-the-tracks background. That Joan had come through her hardscrabble life with such strong intellectual achievement seemed a lot more creditable—not to mention interesting—than the effortless achievements of many of our more privileged classmates.

Joan didn't think so, and, I suppose in fear I'd blow her cover (I never did), she cut me dead after her moment's indulgence in self-revelation. Joan was rootless and anxious, alienated not only from her background but, by extension, from herself, and paid a heavy psychic price. This wasn't change: this was lies. She scared me. But we learn a lot about friends from the kinds of masks they choose to wear.

After all, role-playing to some degree is the prerogative of youth. A woman of romance, rigorous academic, trendy New Waver, intense politico, unsentimental jock, by turn—we have the chance to experiment as we decide the kind of person we want to become. And a stereotypical role, adopted temporarily, can offer a refuge from the swirl of confusing choices available to us, by confining us to the limits of a type. Returning to my old self after playing a role, I find I'm slightly different, a little bit more than what I was. To contradict one's self is to transcend it.

As occasional fugitives from our families, we all sometimes do what Joan did. Sometimes you need a radical change in order to form an identity independent of your family, even if that change is a weird but transient reaction. My friend Lisa came from a family of feminists and academics. When she returned home from school for Thanksgiving, dressed as a "ditsy dame" straight out of a beach-blanket-bingo movie, she asked me, "How do you think I look? I've been planning this since tenth grade. Isn't it great?" Well, er, yes, it was great—not because she looked like a Barbie doll incarnate but because nobody would ever automatically connect her life with that of her parents again.

Another friend, Dan, went from a Southern military academy to a Quaker college in the North to execute his scheme of becoming a serious intellectual. The transformation went awry after a few months, partly because his own self was too likably irrepressible. It wouldn't lie down and play dead. "I kept running into myself like a serpent chasing its tail," as he puts it. But his openness to change resulted in a peculiar amalgamation of cultures whose charm lies in his realizing that, while he's of his background, he's not identical to it. Most of our personalities and bodies are just as stubbornly averse to being extinguished, even if the fantasy of a symbolic suicide and a renaissance from the ashes takes its obsessive toll on our thoughts now and again. But a blank slate isn't the same as a blank self, and the point of the blank slate that college provides is not to erase the past, but to sketch out a new history with a revisionist's perspective and an optimist's acts.

And what of my changes? Well, when I was friendly and happy in college, nobody gaped as though I had sprouted a tail. I learned to laugh things off as Rusty might have done, and there was one particular counterman at the corner luncheonette who called me Red, which was the closest I came to being known as Rusty.

What became of Rusty? Senior year, I stared at an announcement stating the dates that banks would be recruiting on campus, and Rusty materialized for the first time since freshman year. Rusty was a Yuppie now, and I pictured her dressed in a navy-blue suit, looking uneasily like Mary Cunningham, setting her sights on Citibank. I was still the high-strung, oversensitive, would-be writer (I'm happy to report my skin did clear up), but a little better, who left the corporate world to Rusty. For myself, I have the slate of the rest of my life to write on.

Personal Response

In what ways has college given you the opportunity for a "fresh start"? Have you made any changes in your behavior or appearance from when you were in high school? If so, explain what they are and why you have made them.

Questions for Discussion

1. What do you think Crichton means by the statement that "nothing seduces like the promise of a clean slate" (paragraph 1)? What major point does she make about the blank slate that college provides (paragraph 17)? In what sense can the fresh start of college be "both liberating and disorienting" (paragraph 4)?

2. According to Crichton, why is it so difficult to change in high school? Do you agree with her?

3. Comment on Crichton's statement that "we learn a lot about friends from the kinds of masks they choose to wear" (paragraph 14). How do the examples of Jacki, Dana, Joan, Lisa, and Dan each work to illustrate why college students want to change themselves and how they go about doing it?

4. What do you think Crichton means in paragraph 15 when she says, "To contradict one's self is to transcend it"?

5. What image of herself did Crichton hope to realize when she went to college? Why do you suppose that Crichton does not seem to mind that she did not essentially alter her personality when she was at college? Has she changed in any way?

ROOTLESSNESS

David Morris

David Morris is co-director of the Washington, DC, and Minneapolis-based Institute for Local Self-Reliance and an editorial columnist for the St. Paul Pioneer Press-Dispatch. He has written a book, The New City States *(1983), and is co-author with Karl Hess of* Neighborhood Power: The New Localism *(1975). A regular contributor to the* Utne Reader, *he wrote the following essay for the May/June 1990 issue of that magazine.*

Americans are a rootless people. Each year one in six of us changes residences; one in four changes jobs. We see nothing troubling in these statistics. For most of us, they merely reflect the restless energy that made America great. A nation of immigrants, unsurprisingly, celebrates those willing to pick up stakes and move on: the frontiersman, the cowboy, the entrepreneur, the corporate raider.

Rootedness has never been a goal of public policy in the United States. In the 1950s and 1960s local governments bulldozed hundreds of inner city neighborhoods, all in the name of urban renewal. In the 1960s and 1970s court-ordered busing forced tens of thousands of children to abandon their neighborhood schools, all in the interest of racial harmony. In the 1980s a wave of hostile takeovers shuffled hundreds of billions of dollars of corporate assets, all in the pursuit of economic efficiency.

Hundreds of thousands of informal gathering spots that once nurtured community across the country have disappeared. The soda fountain and lunch counter are gone. The branch library is an endangered species. Even the number of neighborhood taverns is declining. In the 1940s, 90 percent of beer and spirits was consumed in public places. Today only 30 percent is.

4   This privatization of American public life is most apparent to overseas visitors. "After four years here, I still feel more of a foreigner than in any other place in the world I have been," one well-traveled woman told Ray Oldenburg, the author of the marvelous new book about public gathering spots, *The Great Good Place* (1990, Paragon House). "There is no contact between the various households, we rarely see the neighbors and certainly do not know any of them."

The woman contrasts this with her life in Europe. "In Luxembourg, however, we would frequently stroll down to one of the local cafés in the evening and there pass a very congenial few hours in the company of the local fireman, dentist, bank employee, or whoever happened to be there at the time."

In most American cities, zoning laws prohibit mixing commerce and residence. The result is an overreliance on the car. Oldenburg cites the experience of a couple who had lived in a small house in Vienna and a large one in Los Angeles: "In Los Angeles we are hesitant to leave our sheltered home in order to visit friends or to participate in cultural or entertainment events because every such outing involves a major investment of time and nervous strain in driving long distances. In Vienna everything, opera, theaters, shops, cafés, are within easy walking distance."

Shallow roots weaken our ties in the neighborhood and workplace. The average blue-collar worker receives only seven days' notice before losing his or her job, only two days when not backed by a union. The *Whole Earth Review* unthinkingly echoes this lack of connectedness when it advises its readers to "first visit an electronics store near you and get familiar with the features—then compare price and shop mail order via [an] 800 number."

8   This lack of connectedness breeds a costly instability in American life. In business, when owners have no loyalty to workers, workers have no loyalty to owners. Quality of work suffers. Visiting Japanese management specialists point to our labor turnover rate as a key factor in our relative economic decline. In the pivotal electronics industry, for example, our turnover rate is four times that of Japan's.

American employers respond to declining sales and profit margins by cutting what they regard as their most expendable resource: employees. In Japan, corporate accounting systems consider labor a fixed asset. Japanese companies spend enormous amounts of money training workers. "They view that training as an investment, and they don't want to let the investment slip away," Martin K. Starr of

Columbia University recently told *Business Week*. Twenty percent of the work force, the core workers in major industrial companies, have lifetime job security in Japan.

Rootlessness in the neighborhood also costs us dearly. Neighborliness saves money, a fact we often overlook because the transactions of strong, rooted neighborhoods take place outside of the money economy.

- Neighborliness reduces crime. People watch the streets where children play and know who the strangers are.

- Neighborliness saves energy. In the late 1970s Portland, Oregon, discovered it could save 5 percent of its energy consumption simply by reviving the corner grocery store. No longer would residents in need of a carton of milk or a loaf of bread have to drive to a shopping mall.

- Neighborliness lowers the cost of health care. "It is cruel and unusual punishment to send someone to a nursing home when they are not sick," says Dick Ladd, head of Oregon's Senior Services. But when we don't know our neighbors we can't rely on them. Society picks up the tab. In 1987 home-based care cost $230 a month in Oregon compared to $962 per month for nursing home care.

Psychoanalyst and author Erich Fromm saw a direct correlation between the decline in the number of neighborhood bartenders and the rise in the number of psychiatrists. "Sometimes you want to go where everybody knows your name," goes the apt refrain of the popular TV show *Cheers*. Once you poured out your troubles over a nickel beer to someone who knew you and your family. And if you got drunk, well, you could walk home. Now you drive cross town and pay $100 an hour to a stranger for emotional relief.

12   The breakdown of community life may explain, in part, why the three best selling drugs in America treat stress: ulcer medication (Tagamet), hypertension (Inderal), tranquilizer (Valium).

American society has evolved into a cultural environment where it is ever harder for deep roots to take hold. What can we do to change this?

- **Rebuild walking communities.** Teach urban planners that overdependence on transportation is a sign of failure in a social system. Impose the true costs of the car on its owners. Recent studies indicate that to do so would raise the cost of gasoline by as much as $2 a gallon. Recently Stockholm declared war on cars by imposing a $50 a month fee for car owners, promising to increase the fee until the city was given back to pedestrians and mass transit.

- **Equip every neighborhood with a library, a coffeehouse, a diversified shopping district, and a park.**

- **Make rootedness a goal of public policy.** In the 1970s a Vermont land use law, for example, required an economic component to environmental impact statements. In at least one case, a suburban shopping mall was denied approval because it would undermine existing city businesses. In Berkeley, citizens voted two to one to permit commercial rent control in neighborhoods whose independently owned businesses were threatened by gentrification.

- **Reward stability and continuity.** Today, if a government seizes property it pays the owner the market price. Identical homes have identical value, even if one is home to a third-generation family, while the other is occupied by a new tenant. Why not pay a premium, say 50 percent above the current market price, for every 10 years the occupant has lived there? Forty years of residence would be rewarded with compensation four times greater than the market price. The increment above the market price should go not to the owner but to the occupant, if the two are not the same. By favoring occupants over owners, this policy not only rewards neighborliness, but promotes social justice. By raising the overall costs of dislocation, it also discourages development that undermines rootedness.

- **Prohibit hostile takeovers.** Japanese, German, and Swedish corporations are among the most competitive and innovative in the world. But in these countries hostile takeovers are considered unethical business practices or are outlawed entirely.

- **Encourage local and employee ownership.** Protecting existing management is not the answer if that management is not locally rooted. Very few cities have an ongoing economic campaign to promote local ownership despite the obvious advantages to the community. Employee ownership exists in some form in more than 5,000 U.S. companies, but in only a handful is that ownership significant.

- **And above all, correct our history books.** America did not become a wealthy nation because of rootlessness, but in spite of it. A multitude of natural resources across an expansive continent and the arrival of tens of millions of skilled immigrants furnished us enormous advantages. We could overlook the high social costs of rootlessness. This is no longer true.

Instability is not the price we must pay for progress. Loyalty, in the plant and the neighborhood, does not stifle innovation. These are lessons we've ignored too long. More rooted cultures such as Japan and Germany are now outcompeting us in the marketplace, and in the neighborhood. We would do well to learn the value of community.

Personal Response

Discuss your own sense of connectedness to or disconnectedness from your community or neighborhood. Do you feel strong ties to it? Do you plan to return to the place you grew up to establish your career or find a job, or do you intend to move somewhere else? Explain your answer.

Questions for Discussion

1. What examples of rootlessness does Morris give? How does Morris account for Americans' widespread acceptance of rootlessness as a way of life?

2. According to Morris, in what ways does rootlessness undermine the economy? How does rootlessness affect the quality of American lives? Do you agree with him on this point?

3. Morris implies that the Japanese way of running factories and businesses is better than the American way. Do you agree with him? Are there businesses in America that nurture employee welfare and build employee loyalty?

4. What is the effect of the repetition of the word "neighborliness" in paragraph 10?

5. Comment on the suggestions Morris makes for deepening roots and improving American business and community connectedness. Which do you think would be effective? Which do you think would be difficult to carry out?

AN URGE FOR GOING

Richard Ford

Richard Ford, who resides in New Orleans and Chinook, Montana, is a writer on the move, as he explains in this essay, which was first published in the February 1992 issue of Harper's Magazine. *He is a staff writer for the* New Yorker *and editor of* The Granta Book of the American. *His novel* Independence Day *won the 1995 Pulitzer Prize for fiction and the movie based on the book was nominated for an Academy Award in 1997.*

I've read someplace that in our descending order of mighty and important human anxieties, Americans suffer the death of a spouse, the loss of a house by fire, and moving to be the worst three things that can happen to us.

So far, I've missed the worst of these—the first, unspeakable, and my house up in flames. Though, like most of us, I've contemplated burning my house *myself*—prior to the spring fix-up season or during those grinding "on-the-market" periods when prices sag and interest rates "skyrocket" and I brood over the sign on my lawn bitterly demanding "make offer."

But moving. Moving's another matter. Moving's not so bad. I've done it a lot.

4   Twenty times, probably, in twenty years (I'm sure I've forgotten a move or two). And always for excellent reasons. St. Louis to New York, New York to California, California to Chicago, Chicago to Michigan, Michigan to New Jersey, New Jersey to Vermont, Vermont to Montana, Montana to Mississippi, Mississippi to Montana, Montana to Montana to here—New Orleans, land of dreamy dreams, where I doubt I'll stay much longer.

To speed the getaways I've sacrificed valuable mortgage points, valuable rent deposits, valuable realtors' commissions, valuable capital gains write-offs. I've blown off exterminator contracts, forsaken new paint jobs, abandoned antique mirrors, oil paintings, ten-speeds, armoires, wedding presents, snow chains, and—unintentionally—my grandfather's gold-handled cane engraved with his name.

What are my excellent reasons? No different from the usual, I imagine. I've just put more of mine into motion. My wife got a better job, I got a better job, I needed to leave a bad job. I began to hate the suburbs and longed for the country, I began to hate New York and longed for the Berkshires, I got frightened of becoming a Californian and longed for the Middle West, I longed to live again in the place where I was born, then later I couldn't stand to live in the place where I was born. I missed the West. I missed the South. I missed the East Coast. I missed my pals. I got sick of their company.

Longing's at the heart of it, I guess. Longing that overtakes me like a fast car on the freeway and makes me willing to withstand a feeling of personal temporariness. Maybe, on a decidedly reduced scale, it's what a rock star feels, or a chewing-gum heiress, celebs who keep houses all over the globe, visit them often, but never fully live in any: a sense that life's short and profuse and mustn't be missed.

In the past, when people have asked me why I've moved so often, I've answered that if you were born in Mississippi you either believed you lived in the vivid center of a sunny universe, or you believed as I did that the world outside of there was the more magical, exotic place and *that's* what you needed to see. Or else I've said it was because my father was a traveling salesman, and every Monday morning I would hear him whistling as he got ready to leave again: a happy weekend at home with his bag packed in the bedroom, then a happy work-week traveling, never seeming to suffer the wrench-pang of departure, never seeming to think life was disrupted or lonely.

I doubt now if either of those reasons is satisfactory. And, indeed, I'm suspicious of explanations that argue that any of us does anything because of a single reason, or two, or three.

Place, that old thorny-bush in our mind's backyard, is supposed to be important to us Southerners. It's supposed to hold us. But where I grew up was a bland, unadhesive place—Jackson, Mississippi—a city in love with the suburban Zeitgeist, a city whose inert character I could never much get interested in. I just never seemed like enough of a native, and Jackson just never meant as much to me as it did to others. Other places just interested me more.

My most enduring memories of childhood are mental snapshots not of my hometown streets or its summery lawns but of roads leading *out* of town. Highway 51 to New Orleans. Highway 49 to the delta and the coast. Highway 80 to Vicksburg and darkest Alabama. These were my father's customary routes, along which I was often his invited company—I and my mother together.

Why these should be what I now recollect most vividly, instead of, say, an odor of verbena or watermelons in a tub on the Fourth of July, I don't know, other than to conjecture that we were on the move a lot, and that it mattered to me that my parents were my parents and that they loved me, more than *where* they loved me.

Home—real home—the important place that holds you, always meant that: affection, love.

Once my wife and I were stranded with car trouble in the town of Kearney, Nebraska, on a blurry, hot midsummer day late in the '70s. And when we'd eaten our dinner in a little, home-cook place at the edge of town not far from the interstate, we walked out into the breezy, warm air and stood and watched the sun go down beyond the ocean of cornfields and the shining Platte River. And as the shadows widened on, my wife said to me, drowsily, "I've just gotten so sleepy now. I've got to go home and go to sleep." "Home?" I said. "How far is that from here?" "Oh, you know," she said and shook her head and laughed at the absurdity of that idea. "Just back to the motel. Where else?"

Oh, I've stayed places, plenty of times. I've owned "homes," three or four, with likable landscapes, pleasant prospects, safe streets, folksy friends nearby. I've held down jobs, paid millages, served on juries, voted for mayors. As with all of us, some part of me is a stayer. *Transient* is a word of reproach; *impermanence* bears a taint, a suspicion that the gentleman in question isn't quite . . . well . . . solid, lacks a certain depth, can't be fully *known,* possibly has messy business left on the trail somewhere—another county, something hushed up.

16

Other people's permanences are certainly in our faces all the time; their lengthy lengths-of-stay at one address, their many-layered senses of place, their store of lorish, insider blab. Their commitment. Yet I don't for a minute concede their establishment to be any more established than mine, or their self-worth richer, or their savvy regarding risk management and reality any more meticulous. They don't know any more than I do. In fact, given where they've been and haven't been, they probably know less.

"But you," they might say, "you only get a superficial view of life living this way, skimming the top layer off things the way you do." And my answer is: Memory always needs replenishing, and anyway you misunderstand imagination and how it thrives in us by extending partial knowledge to complete any illusion of reality. "We live amid surfaces, and the true art of life is to skate well on them," Emerson wrote.

One never moves without an uneasiness that staying is the norm and that what you're after is something not just elusive but desperate, and that eventually you'll fail and have to stop. But those who'll tell you what you *have to do* say so only because that's what they've done and are glad about it—or worse, are not so glad. Finally, I'll be the judge. It'll be on my bill, not theirs.

On the first night I ever spent in the first house I ever owned, I said to my wife as we were going to sleep on a mattress on the bedroom floor amid boxes and paper and disheveled furniture, "Owning feels a lot like renting, doesn't it? You just can't leave when you want to." This was in New Jersey, 15 years ago—a nice, brown three-story stucco of a vaguely Flemish vernacular, on a prizable double lot on a prizable oak-lined street named for President Jefferson—a home that cost $117,500, and that now probably runs above a half million if you could buy it, which you can't. This was a house I eventually grew to feel so trapped in that one night I got stirringly drunk, roared downstairs with a can of white paint, and flung paint on everything—all over the living room, the rugs, the furniture, the walls, my wife, even all over our novelist friend who was visiting and who hasn't been back since. I wanted, I think, to desanctify "the home," get the *joujou* out of permanence. And, in fact, in two months' time we were gone from there, for good.

20   Today, when people ask me, people who banked their fires and their equity, "Don't you wish you'd hung onto that house on Jefferson? You'd have it half paid for now. You'd be rich!" my answer is, "Holy Jesus no! Don't you realize I'd have had to *live* in that house all this time? Life's too short." It's an odd thing to ask a man like me.

It may simply and finally be that the way most people feel when they're settled is the way I feel when I move: safe and in possession of myself. So much so that when I'm driving along some ribbony highway over a distant and heat-miraged American landscape, and happen to spy, far across the median strip, a U-Haul van humping its cargo toward some pay dirt far away, its beetle-browed driver alone in the buzzing capsule of his own fears and hopes and silent explanations of the future, who I think of is . . . me. He's me. And my heart goes out to him. It's never a wasted effort to realize that what we do is what anybody does, all of us clinging to our little singularities, making it in the slow lane toward someplace we badly need to go.

Personal Response

Are your own sentiments about staying versus leaving closer to Ford's or to those who stay in one place permanently? Explain why you feel as you do.

Questions for Discussion

1. What contrasts does Ford draw between people on the move and people who stay in one place?

2. Discuss your understanding of Emerson's observation: "We live amid surfaces and the true art of life is to skate well on them" (paragraph 17).

3. How does Ford define "home"? Do you agree with that definition? Would you add to it in any way? Does home become more important at certain holidays or on special family occasions?

4. If you have read David Morris' "Rootlessness," how do you suppose Ford would respond to Morris' essay? What do you think Morris would say to Ford?

CABIN FEVER

Susan Allen Toth

Susan Allen Toth lives in Minneapolis, Minnesota, and teaches English at Macalaster College in St. Paul, Minnesota. She has published numerous essays, stories, and reviews. Her books include My Love Affair with England: A Traveler's Memoir *(1992) and the trilogy* Blooming: A Small-Town Girlhood *(1981),* Ivy Days: Making My Way Out East *(1984), and* How to Prepare for Your High-School Reunion and Other Mid-Life Musings *(1988). This essay first appeared in April 1989 in the* Minneapolis/St. Paul Magazine.

Sometimes when I am home, perhaps writing at my desk, or pausing at my bedroom door to decide whether to water plants or fold laundry or pick up books from the floor, or dashing to the ringing phone, I think of our cabin. I picture it, empty and silent, sunlight pouring through the large windows onto the wood floor. I let my mind walk slowly through its few rooms, noticing everything in place, swept and ready. Fresh wood lies by the stove, a clean towel hangs in the kitchen, a few magazines are neatly stacked on a low table. On the sofa is a small red cushion, plumped where I can put my head as I read. The house, I know, is waiting for me. Outside I can almost hear the wind whistling over the high-pitched roof and circling around the corners of the quiet bedroom.

In April, many Minnesotans are eager to open their cabins for the season. They have a form of 'cabin fever', not winter claustrophobia, but an intense longing to escape to a special place of one's own. It is so powerful it can feel like missing an absent lover. When travel or unavoidable obligation have kept me away too long, I get itchy and irritable. I start crossing off items on my calendar with fierce determination; no party, concert or meeting, I tell my husband with a fiery look in my eye, will keep me in town one more week. Since Wind Whistle, our place, is winterized, I have cabin fever all year.

I cannot really call Wind Whistle a cabin. It is actually a small house, designed by my architect husband, whose feeling for modernist forms and natural wood merged with my somewhat whimsical taste in colors. The result, with its yellow-shingled siding trimmed in green, pink and lavender, is quite idiosyncratic, and in my prejudiced eyes, wonderful. (Anyone who loves a cabin believes it is wonderful; owners passionately defend what might to someone else seem odd-shaped rooms or dim lighting or primitive plumbing.) Though Wind Whistle is not large, marble or magnificent, I call it my Taj Mahal, because James created it with such exuberance and love. Fortunately, unlike the Indian mogul's wife, I am still alive to enjoy it.

4   But the fact that Wind Whistle is definitely a house causes me some uneasiness. We do already have a house, a fairly new and pleasant one in south Minneapolis. Not long ago, I read an interview with a local social activist, whose protests in good causes I have long admired. She was quoted as saying that, although her husband wanted to build a vacation house on some land they owned in

another state, she wouldn't hear of it. It seemed wrong, she said, in a world where many people are homeless, to have two houses.

Drawn to many varieties of guilt, I tried this one on for size. It seemed, uncomfortably, to fit. So then I wondered if I would feel better if Wind Whistle were just a log cabin, with no running water, maybe not even a pump outside the door. Would that also be a moral affront? What about a cabin with a sink but no toilet? Or a toilet but no bathtub? If electric baseboards were not acceptable, was an old wood stove?

I often puzzle aloud with friends who, like me, are at the moment securely anchored in the middle class, about the moral level of consumption acceptable for a socially responsible person. I have found that most people have an intuitive but very clear set of standards about what is all right and what is too much. Those standards are wildly variable, usually depending upon income. For one friend, a $30 sweater is O.K., $50 is really stretching; for another, $75 doesn't seem unreasonable. Wandering through the Galleria or Conservatory, I can see many women who find $200 not excessive. And, of course, unloading a contribution at the Free Store at Nicollet and 31st, I am aware that for many, budgets don't allow for any new sweater at all.

Once, during the construction of Wind Whistle, I asked a friend who lives in a large, elegant house whether, though they can afford it, she ever worried about its cost. "Well," she said thoughtfully, "suppose I insisted that our family should give it up? Where do you think we should live? In a two-bedroom rambler outside the city? And why wouldn't *that* be too much? Should we give up a house entirely and move into a rented apartment? Instead of an apartment, why not a single room? Where do you decide to draw the line?"

8   I don't know. I haven't got answers for how other people ought to live. I do know that my husband and I are very fortunate to have a retreat. Wind Whistle means so much to me now that I cannot bear to think of giving it up. It is both an escape and a destination. Like many Minnesotans, I talk about "getting away" to my cabin. We run from the hectic daily pace of our lives, the intrusive telephone and doorbell, domestic responsibilities. But what are we getting away *to*?

Most of us get away to the country. (I don't happen to know anyone who escapes to a hideaway in Duluth or Rochester or Albert Lea, and in my circle, no one owns a retreat in London or Monte Carlo.) Many go to Minnesota's lakes, some to the woods or a river or a reclaimed farmstead on the prairie. Some drive an hour, others most of the day to get to "the cabin." My husband and I head 90 minutes south, down the Mississippi to Lake Pepin, where Wind Whistle is perched high on a bluff overlooking a dazzlingly wide expanse of water.

What I notice first at Wind Whistle is the quiet. Although we do have a telephone, the concept of "long distance" inhibits most callers, and it absolutely eliminates the army of pollsters, charitable solicitors and salespeople for siding, insulation, light bulbs and rug-cleaning services who regularly invade our house in Minneapolis. Although we have neighbors on the bluff, we seldom see them. All we hear are wind, thunder, rain and sleet; an occasional train; and on summer nights, the rustlings and cracklings of mysterious small animals who prowl the woods just outside our windows.

This surrounding quiet cushions me. I lean back against it, slowly relaxing. At Wind Whistle I am able to unroll and stretch out, as if I were a thin piece of much-written-on parchment that has been bound too tightly too long and cannot easily lie flat. At Wind Whistle, I do lie flat—or curled up on the sofa. No one around me is working; my husband may sketch or make notes on a project, but he doesn't make me feel I need to get up and busy myself at my keyboard. When I want to write, I do. Mostly I read, doze, play gin rummy with James and look out the windows.

12   Most days, in all weather, I walk on the dusty, seldom-traveled roads and paths that connect our edge of the woods to the meadows and small farms beyond. On these walks, I find myself drifting into thoughts so light and wispy they usually get buried under the steamroller of burdened days. One early winter morning in January at Wind Whistle, when the sun was warm and the wind almost balmy, I looked out on the frozen river through air so clear I could see the bends and curves of the opposite shoreline as if I were looking through an old-fashioned sharp-focused View-Master. High above, a bald eagle swept by, plunging and turning in the brilliant light that caught the white flash of its head and tail.

What I was thinking as I stood there I'm not sure. But suddenly two lines from an old-fashioned poem, the kind no one reads in school any more, floated to my mind and hung there, like the eagle hovering far overhead: "A boy's will is the wind's will, / And the thoughts of youth are long, long thoughts." When I was old enough to think myself a scholar, but still too young to have developed much understanding, I scorned such poetry as sentimental and meaningless. Now I know why it has lasted. What I seldom seem to have time for, I said to myself, is exactly that: long, long thoughts. Thoughts that start nowhere in particular, meander along like a twisting country road and pause at a wild rosebush or beside a trout stream covered with watercress. Thoughts that may not be deep, but are satisfyingly unbroken, flowing into one another like one of those streams.

In the distance, that morning on the bluff, I heard the faint whistle of a train. Trains run frequently on both sides of the river, chugging purposefully to and from Chicago with long strings of boxcars, but still singing the haunting song that used to draw me to the side of a track so I could watch the train flash by. Hearing a train whistle, I remember myself as a child, dreaming of strange cities, adventure and romance.

The sound of that whistle, slowly fading into the distance, also gives me a sense of space. The train goes on and on, past Wind Whistle, along the river, across the plains. Listening, I track it in my mind. That is another gift of a cabin: reminders of a larger world. Confined in the city, we easily forget what lies out there. I often see only the relentless spread of houses, office buildings and factories, and I picture 'development' as an armored and unappeasable dragon, eating up more and more land, belching smoke into an already hazy sky.

16   Speeding away from Minneapolis, beyond the encircling moats of freeways and scattered outposts of megamalls, I am always surprised how soon we are

released into the country. As fields ripple past, like a softly shaken blanket outside our window, I begin to loosen as if I were being shaken too. My vision, unlocked from its narrow focus, zooms into the distance. Looking at the horizon, I am reminded how this sky sweeps north, over forests, past thousands of lakes, toward glacier and tundra. I also remember that not too far to the west, mountains break the flatness of the plains and march towards the Pacific. Following the Mississippi along the Wisconsin border, I am aware that this great river snakes its way to the Gulf.

Driving past the long views across the flat lands south of the Twin Cities, then turning to wind between the soft hills near Miesville and New Trier, and finally passing beneath the bluffs of Red Wing, we see our cabin in its larger setting. The journey not only reminds me of space, it also gives me a gentle reprimand about time and mortality.

We do not make the mistake of thinking we own the land. Here on the bluff, surrounded by evidence of earlier dwellers—Indian names, a broken fence around land gone wild, an abandoned and crumbling barn—we know that we are as temporary as migrating birds who pause for a while before moving on. We also know we are city people, loving our bit of land but not belonging to it as those who work it do.

Because I love the wild beauty of our land, I want it to remain unspoiled. That is one of the ironies of cabin fever: No one wants anyone else to catch it. By building a house in the country, we are feeding the dragon.

20   A purist, who may well be right, would tell me that we should simply camp on our land, portaging in equipment, cleaning up after ourselves and leaving no trace of our stay. But when I think of Wind Whistle, waiting in silence for my next visit, each detail of the house is a familiar friend, often with a history. I look upwards toward the blue vaulted ceiling, watching a Japanese butterfly kite circle below the high painted beams, and I remember the day I found that kite in a museum shop. James looked it over, discussed it with me, finally approved. I think of the huge museum, the December weather outside, the noisy New York streets. I picture our master painter, Grant, carefully balancing on a tall ladder to hang the fragile paper kite.

I care intensely about what surrounds me indoors as well as out. Outdoors is wild and uncontrolled; inside, I like to feel familiar and secure. When I open the door of Wind Whistle, I am pleased that I find everything in its place. I know where the unopened box of Triscuits is stashed, what half-read book is holding its place on the bedside table, exactly where the old wool shirt is hanging on a closet hook. At home, waves of clutter sweep into the house on a daily tide, stranding packages, mail, newspapers, cassettes, coupons and folders on chairs, tables and stairsteps. Here at Wind Whistle, the beach remains relatively bare.

As I write these words, I am seated at my city desk, which is heaped with papers and unanswered mail. Thinking about Wind Whistle, I get lonely for it. I look out my window at pavement and wish I were gazing into the tangle of trees outside the window at Lake Pepin. If other Minnesotans share my kind of cabin fever, enough passion is raging in all of us to melt every snow of early spring.

Personal Response

Describe either your favorite retreat or a favorite possession and the memories associated with it.

Questions for Discussion

1. Explain what Toth means by "cabin fever."

2. Why does Toth feel guilty at times about owning Wind Whistle? Summarize why it is so important to her. How does Wind Whistle contrast with Toth's home in Minneapolis?

3. What does Toth find particularly appealing about the country? Do you have the same feeling about it that she does? What significance does a train whistle have for her?

4. According to Toth, why would it be a mistake to think that they own the land their cabin is on (paragraph 18)?

5. Discuss what you think is "the moral level of consumption for a socially responsible person" and Toth's comment that "most people have an intuitive but very clear set of standards about what is all right and what is too much" (paragraph 6). Do you have such a set of standards? Where do you draw the line on what level of consumption is acceptable for you personally?

WHITE BREAST FLATS

Emilie Gallant

Emilie Gallant is a Native American from the Piegan tribe. She was born in Alberta, Canada, and received her BEd from the University of Calgary, Alberta. The narrative reprinted here first appeared in A Gathering of Spirits: A Collection by North American Indian Women (1984), an anthology of drawings, poems, narratives, and other writings of Native American women.

As one grows older, and the past recedes swiftly as a bird, wings extended in the wind, there are people and places whose contours, caught through the clouds of memory, take on the dimensions of myth. For me, one such place is White Breast Flats on the Piegan Reserve in southwest Alberta where the plains give way to the foothills, the Rockies loom near, and the great obelisk Chief Mountain stands powerfully at the entrance to northern Montana. White Breast Flats is a name known only to a few. My grandfather, Otohkostskaksin (Yellow Dust), was the one who told me that name, and recently, when I read the name in a book, I felt a special joy. Seeing it in print, so many years and miles later, seemed to establish the place as fact, and it opened again the pages of that precious time in my past.

White Breast Flats was occupied solely by my grandparents, and on occasion by my mother. It was located on the first bottomland north of the Old Man River on the west end of the reserve, and the land that rose behind it—the valley wall I suppose you could call it—reached its highest point there, a half-mile from bottom to top, two miles in span. That valley wall was laced with a maze of foottrails, and there were bushes aplenty of saskatoon, whiteberries, gooseberries, chokecherries, and bullberries. There were also wild turnips and cactusberries there. All of these berries gave nourishment to my sisters, to my brother, and to me as we played or just wandered through.

The bottomland stretched from the base of the hill towards the river for a mile and a half at its farthest point and a quarter of a mile at its closest. The one-roomed log house my grandparents lived in was situated about a half a mile from the hill and about two hundred feet from the river. The Old Man has probably eaten away the spot where the house stood, for the bank crept a little closer each year. The trees there were of several varieties, but other than the willows, cottonwoods, chokecherry, saskatoon, and pussy willows, I am still unable to name the trees that made up the forest. Where there were no trees, the grasses grew wild and rampant, and I can still see fields of yellow and white sweet clover and the ever-present and venomous purple thistles which stabbed at us with their thorns every chance they got.

4   We were brought up to fear bears; and although I never saw a bear while I was growing up, I was always on the lookout for the one which I was sure was waiting for me to relax my guard. The most fearsome thing I ever saw was a snake. I was afraid of water, and the river bank we clambered down to reach the green, swirling currents was dotted with holes which I thought were the homes of deadly and poisonous snakes. My sisters were both strong swimmers and enjoyed swimming across the river, but I would churn inwardly with fear as I watched them splash and drift away, bantering and yelling with abandon. And there I would be, standing first on one dirt-caked rock with a dried-up water spider stuck to it, and moving to another, sometimes walking in the water up to my knees very cautiously and carefully, for the rocks were slippery. Sometimes a fish would awake and swim off suddenly, making my heart jump and my throat constrict with a scream I held in. The river was a malevolent thing to me, never friendly. I watched warily for the mythical water-being which I was convinced lived somewhere in the greenest, deepest part. It had to. Otherwise, where did all the foam come from which flecked the river's surface; it had to be the water-being's spittle.

One particular day, I was standing on the river's edge again, watching my two sisters, whom I resented and admired for their fearlessness, when I slipped and fell into the water. It was in the evening and the sun's last rays had turned the river into a golden, glinting, and somehow not so perilous place. I imagined that the water below the surface where the water-being lived was illuminated. In a matter of minutes the warmth of the day was exchanged for the coolness of the evening. My skin prickled with goosebumps from the chill, and I decided to put on my cotton dress until the two mermaids left the water. I picked up my dress and almost died with fright! A big snake slithered out of my dress. I screamed, and my mother, who had been washing and rinsing clothes some distance away, came running, and I got to ride her piggyback all the way home. I even had her throw my dress in the river, something I always remember, for we were very poor and could ill afford to throw clothing away.

There were plants that my grandmother would collect for her medicinal and everyday purposes. She would hang mint to dry in bunches from a line tied across the length of the room, close to the ceiling. I loved the smell of it, and although I didn't care for mint tea then, I do now. It's not only the taste that I enjoy; it's the remembering of moments of my childhood. Every so often I happen upon a cup of wild mint tea, and the bitterness of it, if the tea is made too strong, brings me back to my mother's house when I was probably five or six years old and deathly ill—or so I remember, because my grandmother was summoned. She was a medicine woman and had in her possession all kinds of herbs and roots with which she brought back to health anyone who was ailing. She came into the house on a cold, winter day, bundled up with shawls and blankets. The snowy wind whipped the log house until chinks of the limestone plaster were peeled off and swept away in the storm. My mother kept plugging up the cracks with rags to keep the snow from being blasted inside. The wet snow that stuck to my grandmother's wraps hissed as it hit the stove. She carried a flour sack, and from this she took out a bag made from fawn hide, spotted and with the little hooves on it. Inside the bag she had wrapped still other small bundles, and she took out something greasy and rubbed my chest. On top of that she placed a layer of dried leaves. Ritually she spat on these, and covered the leaves with a hot cloth. She gave me a drink of an awful-tasting brew, and I wouldn't have drunk it if she hadn't been the one to give it to me. She then chanted holy songs, her voice a little frail and weak at first but gaining strength and fullness until the sound was a soothing prayer. She had a sacred rattle made from rawhide and painted with red ochre; this she shook in time with the cadence of her voice. She closed her eyes as she sang, and as I watched her I saw that she had painted her face with the red ochre, and the hair that framed her face was tinted with it. After her song, she prayed that my health be restored and I be blessed with a long and happy life. From a little buckskin bag rubbed with the sacred red ochre, she took some paint that had the consistency of uncooked pastry but which became oily when she rubbed it in her hand. This she rubbed on my face and then she left, leaving some brew and plants for my mother to administer to me. She also left an orange in plain sight that I could have when I was well enough. Oranges during the Second World War were rare, and not seen unless at a feast.

Sometimes I can detect the smell of sweetgrass when there is none around. I've grown to know that is only my grandparents coming to visit me. Sweetgrass—an appropriate name for a special plant. Sweetgrass is the incense the old Indians used to honor the Creator, and the burning of it was a daily occurrence in my grandparents' home. Each morning my grandfather would get up and make the fire in the stove and as soon as the warmth made getting up comfortable, my grandmother would rise and they would pray together. He would burn incense to greet the Creator, and to give thanks for life and health of family and friends, and to ask for guidance in living the day, as well as for help in some special need. Then they shared a song between them and a smoke on their pipe from chunk tobacco.

8   A quarter of a mile east of the house and just where the woods began was a spring. This was where my grandfather got our drinking water. He used a wooden stoneboat to haul it. The stoneboat was constructed of two logs at the bottom; they were the runners, smooth and heavy. On top of them were wide planks of board, bolted onto the logs. The planks were so old I used to sit and scratch them with my fingernails and a papery, powdery substance would come off the wood. Grandfather would hitch up the team, and we children tagged along, jumping on and off the stoneboat with our dogs barking happily behind us until we reached the spring. He tied the team to a tree above the spring and carried two pails to bring the water back to the old metal-girded wooden barrel. He would make twenty or thirty trips until the barrel was full, and then he would put a canvas cover over it and tie the cover on with a rope. Once the water was brought home, my grandmother would have a drink of it first, then set about to making a pot of tea.

A slow-moving stream which leaked off the river and eased by the spring was a refrigerator for butter, meat, and the seasonal garden vegetables. The vegetables came from my grandfather's garden at the base of the hill. Everything grew in abundance there: carrots, rhubarb, turnips, onion, radishes, lettuce, potatoes, and sugar beets. It was neat and ordered, with its straight rows and well-tended mounds of earth. It was fascinating to watch the steam rising from the garden after my grandfather watered it or after a rainfall or shower. I thought a mysterious creature, perhaps a cousin of the water-being, inhabited the earth, and the steam was its breath just as the flecks of foam in the river were the water-being's spittle. I never hung around the garden alone.

The stream that adjoined the spring was the home of a thousand minnows. We would catch some in a jar and take them home, and although we fed them flies and bread, they always died. Long-legged water spiders glided silently around the stream and the little frogs of grey, green, or brown jumped noiselessly, even when they landed in the water. Only our big, clumsy dogs would ruin the silent stream with their panting, lolling tongues as they splashed in, sitting right in the water to have a drink. Then they would shake their wet bodies mightily until it seemed as though it was raining. Our shouts of anger and surprise would usually result in their jumping on us with friendly licks and muddy paws. Surprisingly, of all the dogs we had (it seems they were all shaggy) the only one I remember is Pete. Pete, the short-haired hound with long legs, a tail like a whip, and shiny ears, one of which would sometimes get stuck inside out or underside up, was blacker than the deepest badger-hole we dared to peep into, and he had white, laughing teeth and a rosy, wet tongue.

There was a faded, creaking ghost house on top of the hill. It had two stories and no windows or doors, just openings from which whitemen ghosts watched passersby. It used to belong to a white man I knew only as Inopikini, which means Long Nose. We would go to the ghost house in broad daylight, always in the protective company of my mother and grandmother. The wind was always blowing through the house, flapping wallpaper, rattling floorboards, shingles, and windowcasings. It was a wonderful, mysterious, scary place to go poking around in. It had lots of rooms, small ones and big ones. There were old curly shoes, clothing of all kinds, pieces of furniture, bits of toys, stray dishes, cracked cups without handles, and faded pictures still in their frames. We never took anything, because then Inopikini would haunt us until we returned what we had taken, or else, if he was a real mean ghost, he would twist our faces.

12   There was a trapdoor in one room which we never dared to open because we were sure something stayed down there, but we would stomp across it, each one stomping harder than the last but always with mother or grandmother in the room. After we verbally challenged the ghosts who had the guts to come out and meet us face to face, we would climax our visit by scaring only ourselves and stampede off in hysterical screams, our bodies prickling and our eyes wild with fear, not daring to look back lest we see Inopikini hot on our trail.

I always expected to see a tall, emaciated man with hair all over his skin and blood around his nostrils and perhaps little horns growing out of his head. He was always garbed, in my imagination, in the cracked, curly boots he left in his house and his body covered with the rags scattered about through the rooms.

Summer reminds me of my grandmother mashing cherries in her tipi, which was erected as soon as it was warm enough to sleep outside. My old grandmother used to herd us up the hill to dig for turnips and pick berries for some upcoming feast, but those were the times we wished berries didn't grow. It was always a hot day when we yearned to be down by the spring and we quarreled amongst ourselves and sneaked away.

On hot summer days when I wearied of playing or had nothing to do, I would go and ask my grandmother to check my head because it was itchy. She would put aside whatever she was doing and check my head, all the while telling me stories until I fell asleep. Sometimes when I didn't fall asleep soon enough for her, she would tell me to erase a cloud by rubbing my hands together and concentrating on that cloud. I demolished many a cloud. My grandmother was a tireless old woman who never rested. She was always busy beading, fixing deerskins, fixing berries (drying, mashing, sorting), repairing clothing, cooking, sweeping, washing clothes, and minding us kids. She would gather wood on a big piece of canvas and carry it home on her back or drag it behind her. Then she would sit at the woodpile and chop wood with her hatchet, which she also used for butchering the deer my grandfather killed.

16   I haven't been to White Breast Flats for a long time now, too long. The log house and outer buildings have long been dismantled and carried away for firewood, and the paths and roads are overcome by weeds. Only the descendants of the magpies, gophers, rabbits, and frogs have reclaimed their ancestral grounds. Perhaps a rusted wagon wheel or a skeletal haymower tells a hanging eagle that

people once lived here. White Breast Flats will not happen again; it only lives in the longings and hearts of Ippisuwahs, Piiksi Kiipipi Pahtskikaikana, and Itsinakaki, the grandchildren whose voices once rang clear and echoed through its secret places.

Personal Response

Freewrite for a few minutes about your own childhood. Did you have any fears such as Gallant's fear of bears (paragraph 4)? Do you have warm memories of your grandparents? Is there a place you used to go as a child that no longer exists?

Questions for Discussion

1. What do you think Gallant's purpose in writing this essay is?

2. Explain how people and places from the past "take on the dimension of myth" (paragraph 1).

3. What rituals associated with her tribe does Gallant mention?

4. Find passages that you feel are especially descriptive and comment on what makes them so.

5. Characterize Gallant's grandparents and their way of life.

GRANDMA'S STORY

Lynn Randall

Lynn Randall is a Native American from the Oglala tribe who lives in Pine Ridge Village, South Dakota. The following narrative appeared in A Gathering of Spirits: A Collection by North American Indian Women *(1984). In it, Randall recounts a story she heard her grandmother tell many times.*

She never told me the year nor the season it happened. I don't even know what it's called in the history books, or if it's even in the history books. All I know is what she told me, and that Grandma called it "The Bombing Range Days."

She lay in bed that day, a little longer than usual. With nine kids underfoot and one on the way, the peace and quiet of early morning hours were a luxury she seldom enjoyed. She thought about all the chores that needed to be done that day and the chores that were left over from yesterday. Mentally, she made a list assigning each child to a job. Still there were chores left to do. Chores that would probably be left over for tomorrow. Inwardly she groaned, rolling over and smothering any sound escaping into her pillow. Sighing wearily she got up to make cover. Stepping carefully over the bodies of her children sprawled all over the floor, she made her way into the kitchen. She put the last of the wood into the stove. As she poured the kerosene and lit the stove, she decided to let her husband sleep a while before asking him to fetch more wood for the afternoon meal. She put the coffee on the stove and started to mix the batter for pancakes.

The sun was barely warming the earth when the man came. Her husband had risen an hour ago and was out back chopping wood. The sound of the knocking frightened her; none of her friends or neighbors ever knocked. They always yelled by the gate, and she ran out to meet them. The knocking continued. Backing away from the door, she bumped against her eldest son. "Take it easy Mom, I'll get it," he assured her. The man at the door stood tall. He was dressed in a green hat. This was the dress of an Army man. She knew this and it frightened her more. "Where's your man?" he demanded of her. She could only nod towards the back. The man turned to leave and she followed. She listened in silent rage as the man told her husband they had until nightfall to get their belongings together and get out. "It isn't fair," she thought. "First they take all the good land away from us and put us here on this worthless tract of nothing-land: now they're taking that too." She listened on in new-found horror as the man explained what use the land would be to the Army. "New recruits need to be trained to fly and to know how to drop bombs. This worthless land will be perfect for this area of training. Tomorrow at eight o'clock, a squad of new recruits will be in for the first day of training." With that the man turned and left. She stared at her husband in shock and fear. Her husband's face reflected her own emotions. Together they quickly turned and ran toward the house, gathering objects as they ran.

4   Breathlessly she ran into the house shouting orders. Her oldest son, understanding immediately, ran out to help his father herd the cows together, heading them towards the boundary line. There wasn't much time and some would probably be lost or stolen before the day ended, but still they represented the food and money they would need later. The three oldest daughters started packing the household and personal items. The younger children were outside chasing and catching the hens and the old rooster, putting them in cardboard boxes, flour sacks, or whatever else would hold them. She ran out to hitch the team to the wagon. Almost immediately it began to fill. She started tearing apart the outhouse, throwing the planks down as she took them off. The wood was important, more useful than clothing, almost. Not paying attention to where she was walking, she stepped on a protruding nail. The nail was old and rusty. The pain was so great she found she couldn't stand on the foot for more than a few minutes. Sitting down, she cried in frustration, screaming at her children when they dared come close. Her husband, upon returning, found his wife sitting in the middle of a toilet, half-up half-down, crying her eyes out. He examined the wound, then bandaged it with an old sheet he found, soothing her as he worked. Lifting her gently, he put her in the already filled wagon.

Together they raced across the country to the boundary line. As they neared the line, she stared in shock at what she saw. Her friends and neighbors were all over, unloading their wagons in a pile next to the fence, then jumping back into their wagons and racing off for the next load. Unlike the friendly faces she was used to, their faces were grim and determined. Her husband finished unloading, then took her off the wagon, setting her down next to the load. He raced off in the direction of the house. She looked at the sun, it was sitting dangerously close to the west. She only hoped they had time to get everything of importance. Looking around she saw her neighbors' belongings all along the fence. The older women were clearing out spaces for the tents. Some of the children were gathering wood for the fires. Suddenly she realized her family hadn't eaten since last night and started searching through her stuff for pots and pans and food. Sending her young son off for some wood, she began preparing the evening meal.

It was well into the night when her husband returned with the last load. The coffee was hot, the soup long since done. She finished setting up the tent. Wearily she sat down, her leg throbbing in pain. Her swollen body ached with exhaustion. She watched as each of her children ate, then one by one crawled into the tent and to bed, till there was only herself and her husband. He hadn't said a word but only sat and stared into his coffee. Tears of frustration threatened her as she sat and looked at her husband. "What will happen now?" she asked. "Are we going to live on this hill, in this tent, the rest of our lives? Will we ever get to go back to our home?" He didn't answer her but only sat and stared into his cup. She looked at him for a while, then put her head down and cried.

For as long as I can remember I heard my grandma tell this story. Sometimes a friend would drop over and together they would tell tales of that day with horror or amusement, whatever mood they were in. I can never tell the story as she told it. Each time she told it, she would be able to raise some emotion in me. I would laugh with her or I would cry with her. She left us last summer.

Personal Response

How do you think you would react in circumstances similar to those experienced by Randall's grandmother and her family?

Questions for Discussion

1. Comment on the opening paragraph. Does it effectively introduce the narrative that follows? Did it spark your interest and make you want to keep reading?

2. What does "Grandma's Story" reveal about oppression?

3. Describe the living conditions of Grandma's family before and after the move. What do you think were the answers to Grandma's questions to her husband at the end of paragraph 6?

4. How did Grandma and her husband respond to the order to leave their home?

5. Although this is Grandma's story, it is being told by someone who has heard it many times. What details help characterize Grandma? How does Randall feel about her grandmother? How do you know?

THINKING AS A HOBBY
William Golding

William Golding was born in Cornwall, England, educated at Oxford University, and, after serving with the Royal Navy, spent his life teaching and writing. He died in 1993. His most famous work is Lord of the Flies *(1954), but he wrote many other novels, including* Pincher Martin *(1950),* The Spire *(1964),* The Pyramid *(1967),* Darkness Visible *(1979), and* Rites of Passage *(1980). Golding won the Nobel Prize for literature in 1983. "Thinking as a Hobby" first appeared in* Holiday *magazine in 1961.*

While I was still a boy, I came to the conclusion that there were three grades of thinking; and since I was later to claim thinking as my hobby, I came to an even stranger conclusion—namely, that I myself could not think at all.

I must have been an unsatisfactory child for grownups to deal with. I remember how incomprehensible they appeared to me at first, but not, of course, how I appeared to them. It was the headmaster of my grammar school who first brought the subject of thinking before me—though neither in the way, nor with the result, he intended. He had some statuettes in his study. They stood on a high cupboard behind his desk. One was a lady wearing nothing but a bath towel. She seemed frozen in an eternal panic lest the bath towel slip down any farther; and since she had no arms, she was in an unfortunate position to pull the towel up again. Next to her, crouched the statuette of a leopard, ready to spring down at the top drawer of a filing cabinet labeled A–AH. My innocence interpreted this as the victim's last, despairing cry. Beyond the leopard was a naked, muscular gentleman, who sat, looking down, with his chin on his fist and his elbow on his knee. He seemed utterly miserable.

Some time later, I learned about these statuettes. The headmaster had placed them where they would face delinquent children, because they symbolized to him the whole of life. The naked lady was the Venus of Milo. She was Love. She was not worried about the towel. She was just busy being beautiful. The leopard was Nature, and he was being natural. The naked, muscular gentleman was not miserable. He was Rodin's thinker, an image of pure thought. It is easy to buy small plaster models of what you think life is like.

4   I had better explain that I was a frequent visitor to the headmaster's study, because of the latest thing I had done or left undone. As we now say, I was not integrated. I was, if anything, disintegrated; and I was puzzled. Grownups never made sense. Whenever I found myself in a penal position before the headmaster's desk, with the statuettes glimmering whitely above him, I would sink my head, clasp my hands behind my back and writhe one shoe over the other.

The headmaster would look opaquely at me through flashing spectacles.

"What are we going to do with you?"

Well, what *were* they going to do with me? I would writhe my shoe some more and stare down at the worn rug.

8   "Look up, boy! Can't you look up?"

Then I would look up at the cupboard, where the naked lady was frozen in her panic and the muscular gentleman contemplated the hindquarters of the leopard in endless gloom. I had nothing to say to the headmaster. His spectacles caught the light so that you could see nothing human behind them. There was no possibility of communication.

"Don't you ever think at all?"

No, I didn't think, wasn't thinking, couldn't think—I was simply waiting in anguish for the interview to stop.

12   "Then you'd better learn—hadn't you?"

On one occasion the headmaster leaped to his feet, reached up and plonked Rodin's masterpiece on the desk before me.

"That's what a man looks like when he's really thinking."

I surveyed the gentleman without interest or comprehension.

16   "Go back to your class."

Clearly there was something missing in me. Nature had endowed the rest of the human race with a sixth sense and left me out. This must be so, I mused, on my way back to the class, since whether I had broken a window, or failed to remember Boyle's Law, or been late for school, my teachers produced me one, adult answer: "Why can't you think?"

As I saw the case, I had broken the window because I had tried to hit Jack Arney with a cricket ball and missed him; I could not remember Boyle's Law because I had never bothered to learn it; and I was late for school because I preferred looking over the bridge into the river. In fact, I was wicked. Were my teachers, perhaps, so good that they could not understand the depths of my depravity? Were they clear, untormented people who could direct their every action by this mysterious business of thinking? The whole thing was incomprehensible. In my earlier years, I found even the statuette of the Thinker confusing. I did not believe any of my teachers were naked, ever. Like someone born deaf, but bitterly determined to find out about sound, I watched my teachers to find out about thought.

There was Mr. Houghton. He was always telling me to think. With a modest satisfaction, he would tell me that he had thought a bit himself. Then why did he spend so much time drinking? Or was there more sense in drinking than there appeared to be? But if not, and if drinking were in fact ruinous to health—and Mr. Houghton was ruined, there was no doubt about that—why was he always talking about the clean life and the virtues of fresh air? He would spread his arms wide with the action of a man who habitually spent his time striding along mountain ridges.

20   "Open air does me good, boys—I know it!"

Sometimes, exalted by his own oratory, he would leap from his desk and hustle us outside into a hideous wind.

"Now boys! Deep breaths! Feel it right down inside you—huge draughts of God's good air!"

He would stand before us, rejoicing in his perfect health, an open-air man. He would put his hands on his waist and take a tremendous breath. You could hear the wind, trapped in the cavern of his chest and struggling with all the un-natural impediments. His body would reel with shock and his ruined face go white at the unaccustomed visitation. He would stagger back to his desk and col-lapse there, useless for the rest of the morning.

24   Mr. Houghton was given to high-minded monologues about the good life, sexless and full of duty. Yet in the middle of one of these monologues, if a girl passed the window, tapping along on her neat little feet, he would interrupt his discourse, his neck would turn of itself and he would watch her out of sight. In this instance, he seemed to me ruled not by thought but by an invisible and irre-sistible spring in his nape.

    His neck was an object of great interest to me. Normally it bulged a bit over his collar. But Mr. Houghton had fought in the First World War alongside both Americans and French, and had come—by who knows what illogic?—to a settled detestation of both countries. If either country happened to be prominent in current affairs, no argument could make Mr. Houghton think well of it. He would bang the desk, his neck would bulge still further and go red. "You can say what you like," he would cry, "but I've thought about this—and I know what I think!"

    Mr. Houghton thought with his neck.

    There was Miss Parsons. She assured us that her dearest wish was our wel-fare, but I knew even then, with the mysterious clairvoyance of childhood, that what she wanted most was the husband she never got. There was Mr. Hands—and so on.

28   I have dealt at length with my teachers because this was my introduction to the nature of what is commonly called thought. Through them I discovered that thought is often full of unconscious prejudice, ignorance and hypocrisy. It will lec-ture on disinterested purity while its neck is being remorselessly twisted toward a skirt. Technically, it is about as proficient as most businessmen's golf, as honest as most politicians' intentions, or—to come near my own preoccupation—as co-herent as most books that get written. It is what I came to call grade-three think-ing, though more properly, it is feeling, rather than thought.

    True, often there is a kind of innocence in prejudices, but in those days I viewed grade-three thinking with an intolerant contempt and an incautious mockery. I delighted to confront a pious lady who hated the Germans with the proposition that we should love our enemies. She taught me a great truth in dealing with grade-three thinkers; because of her, I no longer dismiss lightly a mental process which for nine-tenths of the population is the nearest they will ever get to thought. They have immense solidarity. We had better respect them, for we are outnumbered and surrounded. A crowd of grade-three thinkers, all shouting the same thing, all warming their hands at the fire of their own preju-dices, will not thank you for pointing out the contradictions in their beliefs. Man is a gregarious animal, and enjoys agreement as cows will graze all the same way on the side of a hill.

    Grade-two thinking is the detection of contradictions. I reached grade two when I trapped the poor, pious lady. Grade-two thinkers do not stampede easily, though often they fall into the other fault and lag behind. Grade-two thinking is a withdrawal, with eyes and ears open. It became my hobby and brought satisfaction and loneliness in either hand. For grade-two thinking destroys without having the power to create. It set me watching the crowds cheering His Majesty the King and asking myself what all the fuss was about, without giving me anything positive to put in the place of that heady patriotism. But there were compensations. To hear people justify their habit of hunting foxes and tearing them to pieces by claiming that the foxes liked it. To hear our Prime Minister talk about the great benefit we conferred on India by jailing people like Pandit Nehru and Gandhi. To hear American politicians talk about peace in one sentence and refuse to join the League of Nations in the next. Yes, there were moments of delight.

But I was growing toward adolescence and had to admit that Mr. Houghton was not the only one with an irresistible spring in his neck. I, too, felt the compulsive hand of nature and began to find that pointing out contradiction could be costly as well as fun. There was Ruth, for example, a serious and attractive girl. I was an atheist at the time. Grade-two thinking is a menace to religion and knocks down sects like skittles. I put myself in a position to be converted by her with an hypocrisy worthy of grade three. She was a Methodist—or at least, her parents were, and Ruth had to follow suit. But, alas, instead of relying on the Holy Spirit to convert me, Ruth was foolish enough to open her pretty mouth in argument. She claimed that the Bible (King James Version) was literally inspired. I countered by saying that the Catholics believed in the literal inspiration of Saint Jerome's *Vulgate*, and the two books were different. Argument flagged.

32 At last she remarked that there were an awful lot of Methodists, and they couldn't be wrong, could they—not all those millions? That was too easy, said I restively (for the nearer you were to Ruth, the nicer she was to be near to) since there were more Roman Catholics than Methodists anyway; and they couldn't be wrong, could they—not all those hundreds of millions? An awful flicker of doubt appeared in her eyes. I slid my arm round her waist and murmured breathlessly that if we were counting heads, the Buddhists were the boys for my money. But Ruth had *really* wanted to do me good, because I was so nice. She fled. The combination of my arm and those countless Buddhists was too much for her.

That night her father visited my father and left, red-cheeked and indignant. I was given the third degree to find out what had happened. It was lucky we were both of us only fourteen. I lost Ruth and gained an undeserved reputation as a potential libertine.

So grade-two thinking could be dangerous. It was in this knowledge, at the age of fifteen, that I remember making a comment from the heights of grade two, on the limitations of grade three. One evening I found myself alone in the school-hall, preparing it for a party. The door of the headmaster's study was open. I went in. The headmaster had ceased to thump Rodin's thinker down on the desk as an example to the young. Perhaps he had not found any more candidates, but the statuettes were still there, glimmering and gathering dust on top of the cupboard. I stood on a chair and rearranged them. I stood Venus in her bath towel on the filing cabinet, so that now the top drawer caught its breath in a gasp of sexy excitement. "A-ah!" The portentous Thinker I placed on the edge of the cupboard so that he looked down at the bath towel and waited for it to slip. Grade-two thinking, though it filled life with fun and excitement, did not make for content. To find out the deficiencies of our elders bolsters the young ego but does not make for personal security. I found that grade two was not only the power to point out contradictions. It took the swimmer some distance from the shore and left him there, out of his depth. I decided that Pontius Pilate was a typical grade-two thinker. "What is truth?" he said, a very common grade-two thought, but one that is used always as the end of an argument instead of the beginning. There is a still higher grade of thought which says, "What is truth?" and sets out to find it.

But these grade-one thinkers were few and far between. They did not visit my grammar school in the flesh though they were there in books. I aspired to them, partly because I was ambitious and partly because I now saw my hobby as an unsatisfactory thing if it went no further. If you set out to climb a mountain, however high you climb, you have failed if you cannot reach the top.

36   I *did* meet an undeniably grade-one thinker in my first year at Oxford. I was looking over a small bridge in Magdalen Deer Park, and a tiny mustached and hatted figure came and stood by my side. He was a German who had just fled from the Nazis to Oxford as a temporary refuge. His name was Einstein.

But Professor Einstein knew no English at that time and I knew only two words of German. I beamed at him, trying wordlessly to convey by my bearing all the affection and respect that the English felt for him. It is possible—and I have to make the admission—that I felt here were two grade-one thinkers standing side by side; yet I doubt if my face conveyed more than a formless awe. I would have given my Greek and Latin and French and a good slice of my English for enough German to communicate. But we were divided; he was as inscrutable as my headmaster. For perhaps five minutes we stood together on the bridge, undeniable grade-one thinker and breathless aspirant. With true greatness, Professor Einstein realized that any contact was better than none. He pointed to a trout wavering in midstream.

He spoke: "*Fisch.*"

My brain reeled. Here I was, mingling with the great, and yet helpless as the veriest grade-three thinker. Desperately I sought for some sign by which I might convey that I, too, revered pure reason. I nodded vehemently. In a brilliant flash I used up half of my German vocabulary. "*Fisch. Ja Ja.*"

40   For perhaps another five minutes we stood side by side. Then Professor Einstein, his whole figure still conveying good will and amiability, drifted away out of sight.

I, too, would be a grade-one thinker. I was irreverent at the best of times. Political and religious systems, social customs, loyalties and traditions, they all came tumbling down like so many rotten apples off a tree. This was a fine hobby and a sensible substitute for cricket, since you could play it all the year round. I came up in the end with what must always remain the justification for grade-one thinking, its sign, seal and charter. I devised a coherent system for living. It was a moral system, which was wholly logical. Of course, as I readily admitted, conversion of the world to my way of thinking might be difficult, since my system did away with a number of trifles, such as big business, centralized government, armies, marriage. . . .

It was Ruth all over again. I had some very good friends who stood by me, and still do. But my acquaintances vanished, taking the girls with them. Young women seemed oddly contented with the world as it was. They valued the meaningless ceremony with a ring. Young men, while willing to concede the chaining sordidness of marriage, were hesitant about abandoning the organizations which they hoped would give them a career. A young man on the first rung of the Royal Navy, while perfectly agreeable to doing away with big business and marriage, got as rednecked as Mr. Houghton when I proposed a world without any battleships in it.

Had the game gone too far? Was it a game any longer? In those prewar days, I stood to lose a great deal, for the sake of a hobby.

44   Now you are expecting me to describe how I saw the folly of my ways and came back to the warm nest, where prejudices are so often called loyalties, where pointless actions are hallowed into custom by repetition, where we are content to say we think when all we do is feel.

But you would be wrong. I dropped my hobby and turned professional.

If I were to go back to the headmaster's study and find the dusty statuettes still there, I would arrange them differently. I would dust Venus and put her aside, for I have come to love her and know her for the fair thing she is. But I would put the Thinker, sunk in his desperate thought, where there were shadows before him—and at his back, I would put the leopard, crouched and ready to spring.

Personal Response

What is your response to Golding's categories of thinkers? Do you think he is being too judgmental or even unfair when he places nine-tenths of the population in grade three (paragraph 29)?

Questions for Discussion

1. How effective do you find Golding's use of figurative language? Locate examples of similes and metaphors that you think make his abstract ideas concrete.

2. Why do you think Golding devotes so much time to describing his grade-school teachers? What evidence does Golding supply to explain why he reached the conclusion that he could not think at all?

3. Summarize the distinctive features of each of Golding's levels of thinkers. How does grade-three thinking differ from grade-two thinking? Why does Golding say that "grade-two thinking could be dangerous" and why does he call Pontius Pilate "a typical grade-two thinker" (paragraph 34)? What is it about Einstein that makes him a grade-one thinker?

4. In his narrative of his encounter with Einstein, Golding not only describes his example of an undeniable grade-one thinker but also humorously reveals something about himself. In what way is he making fun of himself? Where else does he do that?

5. How does Golding's rearranging the statuettes in the headmaster's office serve to "comment from the heights of grade two, on the limitations of grade three" (paragraph 34)? Why does Golding say in his conclusion that he would rearrange the statuettes differently now?

SILENCE

Larry Watson

Larry Watson teaches English at the University of Wisconsin at Stevens Point. His books include a chapbook of poetry, Leaving Dakota *(1984); two novels,* In a Dark Time *(1980) and* Montana 1948 *(1993), which won the Milkweed National Fiction Prize; and a collection of stories,* Justice *(1995). This short story appeared in* Cream City Review, *a publication of the University of Wisconsin at Milwaukee.*

I was eight years old when my father stole me, and on that day, I stopped speaking. I chose not to speak, yet once I made that decision, it gained its own power and was not easily unmade.

I remember still that sensation, of my tongue becoming a dry thickness in my mouth, of my throat dissolving into a tangle of slack muscles, and of silence itself, falling down from my brain like snow and smothering everything.

I was born in 1942, two years after my parents' marriage. At the time of my birth my father was in the Army and stationed in the Philippines, and my mother, to save on rent money, moved in with her father and mother. It was in my grandparents' house that I was born, in an upstairs bedroom of a white frame house in Pierce, a small town in western Wisconsin. That bedroom had been my mother's when she was a child, and she gave birth to me in her same, narrow childhood bed. The room still held some of the furniture, dolls, and toys of her girlhood, so into a child's world I was child born.

4   While my father was at war my mother stopped loving him. She did not fall in love with someone else, but in my father's absence she not only learned she could live without a husband—as she and so many women had to do—she went a step beyond and largely forgot about him altogether. Her task, at their initial separation, was to try to find some way not to think of her husband and the difficulty of their distance from each other, and at this she simply succeeded too well. Finally, when I was born I was not a reminder of her husband but another distraction, something else that kept her mind from him.

When my father came home in 1946, my mother had a new job (she was secretary and bookkeeper at a John Deere implement dealer), a new home (her old home actually), and a son she had for four years raised without a father. At his return, my half-forgotten father, like a large hand trying to squeeze into a small glove, had to try to fit into her—our—life.

Before long the impossibility of resuming a relationship in which one partner no longer loves the other declared itself. Less than two years after he returned from the war, my father moved out. The fault, as my mother always admitted freely, was hers, but laying blame in broken marriages does nothing to restore them. I remember only this about my father's leaving: he moved out with the same green footlocker with which he moved in, and I felt a vague relief when he was gone, as though a stranger had once again resumed his proper distance.

If my father would have resented me that would have been understandable. I had, after all, assumed a place at his wife's side while he was away, and he saw me only once during my infancy. My grandfather had more to do with my learning-to-walk, learning-to-talk years than my father did. My father, however, was incapable of feeling any bitterness toward his own child, and he was determined, in spite of the divorce, to have a normal relationship with his son. And there was the problem. My mother naturally was given custody of me, and my father had me for only one day a week and that was always Saturday. He lived in Eau Claire, fifty miles from us, and he was a salesman of office supplies, on the road Monday through Friday. Sunday was set aside for Sunday School and services at Mt. Olivet Lutheran Church, and for dinners with my grandparents. Only Saturday was left. My father wanted me to spend more time with him, for us to do more than go to a matinee or the park, have an ice cream, and hurry back to my grandparents, and it was all right with my mother that we do more together, except for one matter. She would not allow my father to keep me overnight. I don't know why she made that resolution, but about it she was intransigent. And, naturally, denied that, it became exactly what my father wanted most. "For *God's sake*, Irene," he would say, his voice shifting, within one sentence, from an angry demand to a plea, "for God's sake, we're only talking about one night." She always said no.

8   So, because there was one point these reasonable people could not be reasonable about, on a sunny August morning (not a Saturday) in 1950, my father in his black Buick pulled up to the curb in front of my grandparents' house. My mother was at work, and I was playing in the trickle of water that ran through the gutter.

I was a solitary child and small for my age, no bigger than many six-year-olds. The first fact made it easy for my father to find me alone; the second made it easy for him to do what he did next. He got out of his car quickly, bent down, and without a word, picked me up. His hat fell off, and when he picked it up he did it hastily, carelessly, crushing and ruining the perfect crease of the crown, the precise roll of the brim. I knew, from the rough way he treated his hat as well as from the speed with which he picked me up and put me in his car, that something was wrong, and that this was not something arranged or approved in advance.

Through the car window I looked to the house, hoping to see my grandmother or grandfather come out, but no one came. The Buick's scratchy grey wool upholstery was warm and smelled of oily office machines and stale cigarette smoke.

"I've got some calls to make, Lewis," my father said as he drove speedily away. "How about you coming along to help me out?"

12   I said nothing. Without knowing I had made the decision, I had made my commitment to silence, and the apparatus for speech was already shut down.

My father, nervous and guilty, talked so much as we drove out of town that he did not notice that I wasn't talking. "I'll bet sales pick up with you along," he said. "I'll bet you bring me good luck." He continued to chatter on about his work, going through his list of calls and mentioning how I was going to charm a secretary or supervisor so she would triple her usual order. One secretary, Miss Zeller, my father said, would probably forget about business altogether and propose marriage to me. I could do worse than Miss Zeller, he said with a wink.

To say I was frightened through all this would not have been accurate. Although I knew my father had done something wrong, and although I did not know him well enough from our Saturday afternoons together to be completely comfortable in his presence, I was not afraid. Still, though my father plainly meant me no harm, I was uneasy. I had been taken forcefully from my home, and I did not belong in that black car, driving through that bright, dry, yellow landscape. I was surrounded by the unfamiliar sights of corn and wheat fields and the strange smells of road dust and barnyards and cut hay, and I had no idea of how I might put order back in my life. When we are eight years old we have so little power in the adult world. What can we do? We can refuse to eat, drink, or go to sleep. Or we can refuse to speak.

I don't remember the names of the towns along the Minnesota-Wisconsin border where we stopped that day, but I do remember, in bits and pieces, some of the offices we visited. We climbed stairs, a narrow flight of some rickety steps over a shoe store and a wide set of stone steps leading up to the heavy metal doors of a county court house. We opened doors, a succession of them with windows of opaque glass on which were printed in gilt letters the names of lawyers or accountants. From one second story window I leaned against a radiator and looked down at a small main street and tried to pick out my father's car from the row of diagonally-parked cars below. In another office a big white-haired woman with a long jaw and peculiar little rimless glasses cautioned my father to "keep the armies away from that boy." In a tiny, airless office that smelled of cigar smoke and whiskey from the bar below, my father put a roll of paper into an adding machine for an accountant who was nearly blind. All day long my father delivered tightly-wrapped reams of paper, boxes of envelopes, and stacks of long legal pads. He looked inside typewriters, dictaphones, and adding machines that weren't working, he gave away blue pencils with his company's name printed in silver letters, and he raised the height of an office chair for a short typist.

16 And I met Miss Zeller. She was young and pretty and she had wavy dark hair that fell to her shoulders so neatly it looked like a thick black cloth. She gave me a stick of Beeman's gum from her desk drawer, and she shook my hand and said, "Your dad is lucky to have such a big helper."

It was strange that she called "dad" the man I always referred to as "father."

"Are you helping him carry some of his heavy machines?" she teased.

I nodded and stared at the floor but said nothing.

20 My father made a joke that excused me. "Sure, he does all the lifting. He's the strong, silent type."

When we left Miss Zeller's office my father put his hand on my shoulder and asked heartily, "What do you think? Didn't I say she was something? Didn't I say you could do worse?"

I was becoming angry at my father's pretense, how he continued to make believe that I was with him because I wanted to be. Be quiet, I thought, just be quiet; if you think Miss Zeller is so wonderful why don't you marry her—marry her and leave me alone.

At some time during the day my father noticed I wasn't talking. Or perhaps he noticed all along and finally chose to acknowledge it. I know from my own experience as a parent that I am seldom ignorant of what goes on in the lives of my children; I only choose to remain quiet about what I know. And since my father knew that his act was the cause of my silence, he must have thought long and hard before bringing up the subject. "You know," he said, "if you ever want to be a salesman, one thing you got to have is the gift of gab. If you're inclined to let the cat have your tongue you're going to have trouble turning over those sales."

24   It was the wrong tactic. I resented hearing any advice on how to be a salesman, or any presumption that I might want to be one. At eight I didn't know what I wanted to be, but on that day I knew I did not want to be in any way like the man who stole children from in front of their own home.

Later, my father tried to approach my silence from another side. "What I can't figure out is how you turned into such a shy one," he said. "Now me, me you've never been able to shut up, not now and not when I was a boy. My dad used to say I liked to yak more than old Mrs. Monka." No matter how hard he tried to convince me otherwise, I kept telling myself that my silence was not the result of my nature but of his sin. Of course, when I was eight I had a much clearer sense of what was sin and what was not.

After all the calls had been made, we stopped for dinner at a small roadside cafe in Whitman, Wisconsin. Neither my mother nor my grandparents ever took me to a restaurant because they thought it was wasteful and indulgent to pay others to prepare food which you were perfectly capable of fixing for yourself. So, sitting in the booth by the window and looking over at the slices of pie and cake in the glass case was a special experience, even under those circumstances.

When the waitress asked for our order, my father, having by now caught on to the rules of the game, ordered for me. He told the waitress that I wanted a hot roast beef sandwich, peas, and a glass of milk. I did not; I wanted a fried ham sandwich and an orange soda.

28   As soon as the waitress left, my father leaned across the table and spoke sternly to me. "Look, Lewis, this is nonsense. All I want is for you and me to spend some time together. You're my son. Now, I'm going to take you back to your mother in a day or two. In the meantime, let's get along."

When my father got angry his face would flush and a vein that ran straight down his forehead stood out like a piece of string. His anger frightened me, and perhaps if he had asked me a question instead of making a statement I would have spoken at that moment. I don't know. I turned and looked out the window at the cars and trucks speeding by the Whitman Cafe.

Try not talking for a long time. Try to go an entire day without speaking. After a time speech recedes even from your thoughts; you no longer talk to yourself, and your thinking becomes airy and wordless. You begin to doubt whether the mechanism works any more. Imagine what it is like for an eight-year-old boy. My father went to the restroom, and I picked up the menu. On the cover were the words "The Whitman Cafe: The Best Food," and I tried, just to see if my voice still worked, to say those words out loud. First I moved my lips only, but then I whispered, very softly, "The Whitman Cafe: The Best Food," over and over. But see for yourself; whispering, so much like our regular exhalations of breath, is not at all the same as talking.

After dinner, my father leaned back in the booth, lit a cigarette (after first tapping it on the crystal of his watch, a gesture that always fascinated and baffled me) and, uncharacteristically, for my father did almost everything with enthusiasm, watched with detachment. For a long time, his silence matched mine until finally he spoke: "Do you want cake or pie? Just tell me what kind you want and you can have a piece. But you have to tell me. You have to say it out loud."

32   I left the Whitman Cafe without dessert.

My father lived in a hotel in Eau Claire called The Kingsbury. He moved in after he left my grandparents' house, and he never got around to moving out of the hotel. He became friends with the owner who gave him a special rate. The hotel was small and the rooms had the same kind of furniture you might find in someone's home. In my father's room were lace curtains that blew in and out the open window on the warm night I was there, a single bed with a white chenille bedspread, a bureau, a bedside table, a dark green overstuffed chair, a floor lamp, and, in one corner, a metal two-drawer filing cabinet and typing table that belonged to my father. Two typewriters were on the floor. A picture of me, taken at a studio when I was five, was on the bureau next to a carton of Chesterfields.

While we were alone in the room my father tried to explain why he had taken me away. I remember little of what he said, but it was a stammering, incoherent speech designed to appeal to powers of reason that I did not have and to a love that I did not feel. Those were discoveries I made while my father talked to me. He kept saying, "Do you understand? You do understand, don't you?" I kept shaking my head. As he spoke my father gripped my shoulders with hands that were always ink-stained from handling typewriter ribbons. I remember the pressure of his hands better than his words.

After the futile attempt to make clear his motives, my father gave up and told me it was time to get ready for bed. From a grocery bag he brought out a new pair of pajamas and a tooth brush he had bought for me. The pajamas were white, starchy cotton with blue piping and much too big for me, but I put them on. I sat on the edge of the bed, and then I was scared. I wondered if I *was* going to go home again. The prospect of sleeping in a strange bed in new pajamas made the idea of home recede, the way a train station seems to pull away from you as you stand outside on the platform of the train's last car.

36   At about 9:00 I was lying awake in bed, unable to sleep, and my father was sitting in the chair smoking when someone knocked on the door and called out, "Frank? It's Bob Wirth. Are you in there?"

When he heard the man's voice, my father's head slumped forward so suddenly it was as if the muscles in his neck had been cut. He looked up and his face had the ashen, worn look of a man who has not slept for days. My father walked slowly to the door, opened it, and stood aside. The man outside looked in the room for me, and when he saw me said, "The boy's mother wants him back, Frank."

My father took another step back and a short, lean man in a dark suit walked over to the bed and looked down at me. "Get up and get dressed," he said. "You're going back to your mama. We'll go call your grandpa and he'll come get you." The man standing over me was, he announced, the Eau Claire County sheriff.

I went into the bathroom to dress, and while I was in there, I heard the sheriff say to my father, "Jesus, Frank, this was stupid. This wasn't something to go and do."

40   Tiredly, my father said, "It's a long story, Bob. Someday I'll tell you about it."

That my father and the sheriff were friends pleased and relieved me.

After I dressed, the sheriff told me he'd take me down to the lobby to wait for my grandfather. My father, who was sitting on the portion of the unmade bed where I had been lying, waved at me as I was leaving and called out, "So long for now, Lewis."

In the small, unsteady elevator we rode down to the lobby. There, the sheriff deposited me in an old worn leather club chair. The back of the chair was against a pillar, and the front was in full view of the desk and the night clerk. "Now you sit right here," the sheriff told me. "I'm going to call your people, and then I'm going back upstairs to have a word with your papa."

44   In less than an hour my grandfather arrived, and when he saw me, he asked one question: "Are you all right?"

I nodded yes.

I fell asleep in the car on the way home, and when we got back to Pierce, my grandfather carried me into the house and to my bed, the second time that day I was lifted in the arms of an adult.

When I awoke the next morning my mother was sitting in a chair in my bedroom. I knew instantly she had been there all night, and now, back in my room, I was embarrassed by her presence.

48   Her first question was the same as my grandfather's. "Are you all right?"

"Yes," I said out loud.

I never saw my father again after that night. His rights of custody were revoked by a judge who believed that no one, not even a parent, has the right to steal someone away against his will. My father made no attempt to fight this ruling, and his acquiesence was the result, I believe, of my behavior toward him that day. I believe that with my silence I killed his love for me.

My father eventually remarried. He married a widow from Eau Claire who had two sons, and one of the sons was an All-State basketball player who won an athletic scholarship to the University of Minnesota where he went on to receive an All-American honorable mention. I remember feeling an odd pride that my father was this boy's stepfather, and I also felt that by following this boy's career I was somehow staying in touch with my father. My father died of a heart attack in 1974.

52   Now this is the strange part. All of us grieve, at some time in our lives, for our lost childhood, but in the sameness of all the days of the past only the unusual day, the day different from all the other days, is likely to stand out in memory. And for me the day my father stole me is the day I remember best. As a result, when I wish I could be a boy again, I invariably, unwillingly, think of making business calls with my father. I miss those offices with their worn carpets and massive wooden desks. I miss the heavy black machines, the typewriters and dictaphones and adding machines. I miss the unsharpened pencils, the stacks of white paper, the smeary carbons and canary yellow legal pads, the embossed sheets of letter-head and the long envelopes. I miss my father.

Personal Response

The narrator Lewis tells of one memorable day from his childhood that stands out precisely because it is different from all the other days. Is there one day in particular from your childhood that you recall? What makes that day stand out from all the rest?

Questions for Discussion

1. What besides the boy's refusal to speak might the title "Silence" refer to?

2. Although we cannot know for sure because the story is told entirely from the son's point of view, how do you suppose the father sees his role as parent? How do you think he feels about his son?

3. What motivates the father to kidnap his son? Why does the son refuse to speak? Do you believe, as the eight-year-old Lewis did, that the boy's silence "killed his [father's] love" for his son (paragraph 50)? Are you sympathetic toward the father, the son, neither, or both?

4. In what ways is the relationship of the father and son in this story typical and in what ways is it atypical of father-son relationships in general?

5. Look closely at the concluding paragraph. Why does the narrator consider what he says there "the strange part"? Does it surprise you that he says he misses all of the places his father took him on that one day? Given the event he narrates and his feelings for his father when he was young, what do you make of his now saying, "I miss my father"?

Suggestions for Writing About TRANSITIONS

1. Write an essay explaining what you think is your most important transition to date and why you think it is so significant. For instance, describe a memorable experience you have had as a new college student and explain how your life

has changed as a result, or narrate the events surrounding a significant move you have made and the effects of that move on you.

2. Describe the image of yourself that you hope to have in college. Does it differ significantly from your old self, or is it the same? Have you undergone any changes at college in the way you act or in your appearance?

3. In "Rootlessness," David Morris contrasts the Japanese way of doing business with the American way, suggesting that the Japanese way is better. Write an essay in which you explain your position in relation to Morris' views on this issue. If possible, use the example of someone you know who has lost a job or had a bad employment experience.

4. If you have ever had an urge to pick up and leave everything behind you, as Richard Ford in "An Urge for Going" does, explain why you would like to leave, what you would hope to find, and how you think your life would be different.

5. Describe your own neighborhood in terms of the relationships among people who live there and your own ties to or disconnectedness from it.

6. Describe something you own that you would find unbearable to give up, as Susan Allen Toth does in "Cabin Fever."

7. Narrate a memory from your childhood that a particular smell, taste, or other stimulus always triggers, as Emilie Gallant does in "White Breast Flats."

8. Narrate your experience of returning to a place from your childhood, such as a former home or an old play area. How did your memory of the place contrast with the way it looked when you revisited it?

9. Analyze your own intellectual development in terms of the three levels William Golding describes in "Thinking as a Hobby."

10. Respond to the way in which William Golding categorizes thinkers in "Thinking as a Hobby" by explaining the extent to which you agree with his categories and why, using examples drawn from your own observations.

11. The narrator in Larry Watson's "Silence" says, "All of us grieve . . . for our lost childhood, but . . . only the unusual day, the day different from all the other days, is likely to stand out in memory" (paragraph 52). Write an essay describing the one day in your childhood that stands out in your memory and explain why it is significant.

12. Narrate or describe the circumstances that led to a moment of insight into your feelings for a loved one.

13. Describe a ritual you or your family carry out in special times such as celebration, illness, or family gatherings.

14. If your family no longer performs a ritual it once did or has stopped observing a particular holiday or religious custom, explain the change, why you think it occurred, and how you feel about it.

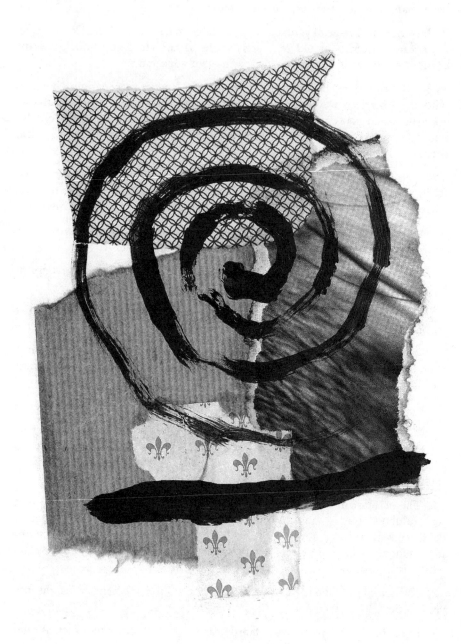

CHAPTER 2

INSIGHTS

This chapter contains selections that in one way or another describe insights their authors have had. The nature of these insights varies, but all have in common the narrators' seeing, recognizing, or understanding something. It may be recognition of a lesson or value about themselves or someone else, perhaps some new awareness of an important intangible aspect of their lives, or a general philosophical understanding of the larger pattern of things.

In the first selection, Frank Conroy, drawing on personal experience, shares his understanding of the ways in which insight happens in general. In "Think About It: Ways We Know, and Don't," Conroy distinguishes between two ways that education occurs and concludes that "understanding does not always mean resolution." For some things, he writes, never being sure of the answer is "our special fate, our inexpressibly valuable condition," but for others, insight comes with "a kind of click, a resolving kind of click." The remainder of the essays in the chapter illustrate the ways in which their writers have found both under-standing and resolution, many of them with the kind of click Conroy describes.

Pat Mora's "To Gabriela, a Young Writer" is in part about what it means to be a Mexican American and what it means to be a woman, but more impor-tantly, it is about what it means to be a writer. Addressing the thirteen-year-old daughter of a friend, Mora shares her insights into why she writes and how she goes about doing it well. Following Mora's essay, Amy Tan in "Mother Tongue" tells of certain insights she has had about the value of the various "Englishes" she speaks and the importance of her mother to her personally. Tan offers some sug-gestions about how to write effectively.

The next two essays are companion pieces and should be read together. Zoë Landale in "Remembering Karen" and Marjorie Simmins in "Trips from There to Here" write of the same person, their sister Karen who died of a drug over-dose. Without the other knowing, each sister wrote about her own experiences with Karen. But in the process of writing, each achieved insight not only into her sister Karen but also into herself.

The last two selections in this chapter illustrate that insight into something else can also mean insight into oneself. In "Shooting an Elephant," George Orwell recounts an incident in Burma when, as a British policeman there, he committed an act of unnecessary violence "solely to avoid looking a fool." Looking back on the incident, he realizes now that the experience gave him insight not only into the real nature of imperialism but also into his own character. Finally, Toni Cade Bambara's short story "The Lesson," told from the viewpoint of a street-tough, inner-city New York girl, focuses on insights several children have about the disparity between the rich and the poor as a result of a field trip to a very expensive Fifth Avenue toy store. This understanding of the chasm between what her family and friends can afford and what the rich parents of wealthy children can afford also leads the narrator to discover something important about herself.

THINK ABOUT IT: WAYS WE KNOW, AND DON'T

Frank Conroy

Frank Conroy has worked as a jazz pianist and writes often of American music. He currently directs the Iowa Writers' Workshop. His essays and stories have appeared in The New Yorker, Esquire, Harper's, *and* GQ. *Some of his short stories are collected in* Midair. *This essay was first published in* Harper's *in 1988.*

When I was sixteen I worked selling hot dogs at a stand in the Fourteenth Street subway station in New York City, one level above the trains and one below the street, where the crowds continually flowed back and forth. I worked with three Puerto Rican men who could not speak English. I had no Spanish, and although we understood each other well with regard to the tasks at hand, sensing and adjusting to each other's body movements in the extremely confined space in which we operated, I felt isolated with no one to talk to. On my break I came out from behind the counter and passed the time with two old black men who ran a shoeshine stand in a dark corner of the corridor. It was a poor location, half hidden by columns, and they didn't have much business. I would sit with my back against the wall while they stood or moved around their ancient elevated stand, talking to each other or to me, but always staring into the distance as they did so.

As the weeks went by I realized that they never looked at anything in their immediate vicinity—not at me or their stand or anybody who might come within ten or fifteen feet. They did not look at approaching customers once they were inside the perimeter. Save for the instant it took to discern the color of the shoes, they did not even look at what they were doing while they worked, but rubbed in polish, brushed, and buffed by feel while looking over their shoulders, into the distance, as if awaiting the arrival of an important person. Of course there wasn't all that much distance in the underground station, but their behavior was so focused and consistent they seemed somehow to transcend the physical. A powerful mood was created, and I came almost to believe that these men could see through walls, through girders, and around corners to whatever hyperspace it was where whoever it was they were waiting and watching for would finally emerge. Their scattered talk was hip, elliptical, and hinted at mysteries beyond my white boy's ken, but it was the staring off, the long, steady staring off, that had me hypnotized. I left for a better job, with handshakes from both of them, without understanding what I had seen.

Perhaps ten years later, after playing jazz with black musicians in various Harlem clubs, hanging out uptown with a few young artists and intellectuals, I began to learn from them something of the extraordinarily varied and complex riffs and rituals embraced by different people to help themselves get through life in the ghetto. Fantasy of all kinds—from playful to dangerous—was in the very air of Harlem. It was the spice of uptown life.

4   Only then did I understand the two shoeshine men. They were trapped in a demeaning situation in a dark corner in an underground corridor in a filthy subway system. Their continuous staring off was a kind of statement, a kind of dance. Our bodies are here, went the statement, but our souls are receiving nourishment from distant sources only we can see. They were powerful magic dancers, sorcerers almost, and thirty-five years later I can still feel the pressure of their spell.

The light bulb may appear over your head, is what I'm saying, but it may be a while before it actually goes on. Early in my attempts to learn jazz piano, I used to listen to recordings of a fine player named Red Garland, whose music I admired. I couldn't quite figure out what he was doing with his left hand, however; the chords eluded me. I went uptown to an obscure club where he was playing with his trio, caught him on his break, and simply asked him. "Sixths," he said cheerfully. And then he went away.

I didn't know what to make of it. The basic jazz chord is the seventh, which comes in various configurations, but it is what it is. I was a self-taught pianist, pretty shaky on theory and harmony, and when he said sixths I kept trying to fit the information into what I already knew, and it didn't fit. But it stuck in my mind—a tantalizing mystery.

A couple of years later, when I began playing with a bass player, I discovered more or less by accident that if the bass played the root and I played a sixth based on the fifth note of the scale, a very interesting chord involving both instruments emerged. Ordinarily, I suppose I would have skipped over the matter and not paid much attention, but I remembered Garland's remark and so I stopped and spent a week or two working out the voicings, and greatly strengthened my foundations as a player. I had remembered what I hadn't understood, you might say, until my life caught up with the information and the light bulb went on.

8   I remember another, more complicated example from my sophomore year at a small liberal-arts college outside Philadelphia. I seemed never to be able to get up in time for breakfast in the dining hall. I would get coffee and a doughnut in the Coop instead—a basement area with about a dozen small tables where students could get something to eat at odd hours. Several mornings in a row I noticed a strange man sitting by himself with a cup of coffee. He was in his sixties, perhaps, and sat straight in his chair with very little extraneous movement.

I guessed he was some sort of distinguished visitor to the college who had decided to put in some time at a student hangout. But no one ever sat with him. One morning I approached his table and asked if I could join him.

"Certainly," he said. "Please do." He had perhaps the clearest eyes I had ever seen, like blue ice, and to be held in their steady gaze was not, at first, an entirely comfortable experience. His eyes gave nothing away about himself while at the same time creating in me the eerie impression that he was looking directly into my soul. He asked a few quick questions, as if to put me at my ease, and we fell into conversation. He was William O. Douglas from the Supreme Court, and when he saw how startled I was he said, "Call me Bill. Now tell me what you're studying and why you get up so late in the morning." Thus began a series of talks that stretched over many weeks. The fact that I was an ignorant sophomore with literary pretensions who knew nothing about the law didn't seem to bother him. We talked about everything from Shakespeare to the possibility of life on other planets. One day I mentioned that I was going to have dinner with Judge Learned Hand. I explained that Hand was my girlfriend's grandfather. Douglas nodded, but I could tell he was surprised at the coincidence of my knowing the chief judge of the most important court in the country save the Supreme Court itself. After fifty years on the bench Judge Hand had become a famous man, both in and out of legal circles—a living legend, to his own dismay. "Tell him hello and give him my best regards," Douglas said.

Learned Hand, in his eighties, was a short, barrel-chested man with a large, square head, huge, thick, bristling eyebrows, and soft brown eyes. He radiated energy and would sometimes bark out remarks or questions in the living room as if he were in court. His humor was sharp, but often leavened with a touch of self-mockery. When something caught his funny bone he would burst out with explosive laughter—the laughter of a man who enjoyed laughing. He had a large repertoire of dramatic expressions involving the use of his eyebrows—very useful, he told me conspiratorially, when looking down on things from behind the bench. (The court stenographer could not record the movement of his eyebrows.) When I told him I'd been talking to William O. Douglas, they first shot up in exaggerated surprise, and then lowered and moved forward in a glower.

"*Justice* William O. Douglas, young man," he admonished. "*Justice* Douglas, if you please." About the Supreme Court in general, Hand insisted on a tone of profound respect. Little did I know that in private correspondence he had referred to the Court as "The Blessed Saints, Cherubim and Seraphim," "The Jolly Boys," "The Nine Tin Jesuses," "The Nine Blameless Ethiopians," and my particular favorite, "The Nine Blessed Chalices of the Sacred Effluvium."

12 Hand was badly stooped and had a lot of pain in his lower back. Martinis helped, but his strict Yankee wife approved of only one before dinner. It was my job to make the second and somehow slip it to him. If the pain was particularly acute he would get out of his chair and lie flat on the rug, still talking, and finish his point without missing a beat. He flattered me by asking for my impression of Justice Douglas, instructed me to convey his warmest regards, and then began talking about the Dennis case, which he described as a particularly tricky and difficult case involving the prosecution of eleven leaders of the Communist party.

He had just started in on the First Amendment and free speech when we were called into dinner.

William O. Douglas loved the outdoors with a passion, and we fell into the habit of having coffee in the Coop and then strolling under the trees down toward the duck pond. About the Dennis case, he said something to this effect: "Eleven Communists arrested by the government. Up to no good, said the government; dangerous people, violent overthrow, etc., First Amendment, said the defense, freedom of speech, etc." Douglas stopped walking. "Clear and present danger."

"What?" I asked. He often talked in a telegraphic manner, and one was expected to keep up with him. It was sometimes like listening to a man thinking out loud.

"Clear and present danger," he said. "That was the issue. Did they constitute a clear and present danger? I don't think so. I think everybody took the language pretty far in Dennis." He began walking, striding along quickly. Again, one was expected to keep up with him. "The F.B.I. was all over them. Phones tapped, constant surveillance. How could it be clear and present danger with the F.B.I. watching every move they made? That's a ginkgo," he said suddenly, pointing at a tree. "A beauty. You don't see those every day. Ask Hand about clear and present danger."

I was in fact reluctant to do so. Douglas's argument seemed to me to be crushing—the last word, really—and I didn't want to embarrass Judge Hand. But back in the living room, on the second martini, the old man asked about Douglas. I sort of scratched my nose and recapitulated the conversation by the ginkgo tree.

"What?" Hand shouted. "Speak up, sir, for heaven's sake."

"He said the F.B.I. was watching them all the time so there couldn't be a clear and present danger," I blurted out, blushing as I said it.

A terrible silence filled the room. Hand's eyebrows writhed on his face like two huge caterpillars. He leaned forward in the wing chair, his face settling, finally, into a grim expression. "I am astonished," he said softly, his eyes holding mine, "at Justice Douglas's newfound faith in the Federal Bureau of Investigation." His big, granite head moved even closer to mine, until I could smell the martini. "I had understood him to consider it a politically corrupt, incompetent organization, directed by a power-crazed lunatic." I realized I had been holding my breath throughout all of this, and as I relaxed, I saw the faintest trace of a smile cross Hand's face. Things are sometimes more complicated than they first appear, his smile seemed to say. The old man leaned back. "The proximity of the danger is something to think about. Ask him about that. See what he says."

I chewed the matter over as I returned to campus. Hand had pointed out some of Douglas's language about the F.B.I. from other sources that seemed to bear out his point. I thought about the words "clear and present danger," and the fact that if you looked at them closely they might not be as simple as they had first appeared. What degree of danger? Did the word "present" allude to the proximity of the danger, or just the fact that the danger was there at all—that it wasn't an anticipated danger? Were there other hidden factors these great men were weighing of which I was unaware?

But Douglas was gone, back to Washington. (The writer in me is tempted to create a scene here—to invent one for dramatic purposes—but of course I can't do that.) My brief time as a messenger boy was over, and I felt a certain frustration, as if, with a few more exchanges, the matter of *Dennis v. United States* might have been resolved to my satisfaction. They'd left me high and dry. But, of course, it is precisely because the matter did not resolve that has caused me to think about it, off and on, all these years. "The Constitution," Hand used to say to me flatly, "is a piece of paper. The Bill of Rights is a piece of paper." It was many years before I understood what he meant. Documents alone do not keep democracy alive, nor maintain the state of law. There is no particular safety in them. Living men and women, generation after generation, must continually remake democracy and the law, and that involves an ongoing state of tension between the past and the present which will never completely resolve.

Education doesn't end until life ends, because you never know when you're going to understand something you hadn't understood before. For me, the magic dance of the shoeshine men was the kind of experience in which understanding came with a kind of click, a resolving kind of click. The same with the experience at the piano. What happened with Justice Douglas and Judge Hand was different, and makes the point that understanding does not always mean resolution. Indeed, in our intellectual lives, our creative lives, it is perhaps those problems that will never resolve that rightly claim the lion's share of our energies. The physical body exists in a constant state of tension as it maintains homeostasis, and so too does the active mind embrace the tension of never being certain, never being absolutely sure, never being done, as it engages the world. That is our special fate, our inexpressibly valuable condition.

Personal Response

In your own words, explain what Conroy means by "resolving kind of click" (paragraph 22). If you have ever experienced such a "click," write about what happened.

Questions for Discussion

1. What does Conroy mean by the "magic dance" of the shoeshine men? How did Red Garland's saying the word "sixths" to Conroy later strengthen Conroy's foundation on the piano? What do Conroy's experiences with the shoeshine men and with what happened to him at the piano illustrate one "way of knowing"?

2. Comment on Conroy's effectiveness in describing Justice Douglas and Judge Hand. Do you have a clear image of both of them? Do you think he portrays one of them more vividly than the other? If so, which one?

3. How do the viewpoints of Judge Hand and Justice Douglas differ on the Dennis case? What does Judge Hand mean when he says that the Constitution and the Bill of Rights are pieces of paper (paragraph 21)?

4. What lesson about education—about the "ways of knowing"—does Conroy
   learn from his experience with Justice Douglas and Judge Hand?

TO GABRIELA, A YOUNG WRITER

Pat Mora

*Pat Mora, who holds BA and MA degrees in English from the University of
Texas at El Paso, has published three books of poetry,* Chants *(1984);* Bor-
ders *(1986); and* Communion *(1991); a children's book,* A Birthday Bas-
ket for Tia *(1992); and a collection of essays,* Nepantla: Essays from the
Land in the Middle *(1993), from which this selection is taken.*

The enthusiasm and curiosity of young writers is a source of energy. In one
sense, we are all fledgling writers. With each new piece, we embark on the mysterious process again, unsure if we can describe or evoke what is in our minds
and hearts. Sometimes it is difficult to convince those under thirty that the
struggle never ends, that art is not about formulas. Maybe that continuing risk
lures us. Luckily, octogenarians such as movie director Akira Kurosawa or Mexican painter Rufino Tamayo show us that we need never retire, and that what we
have to share near the end of our lives may be far more lyrical than our early efforts in any art form. A sad truth about art is that it is unlinked to virtue.
Wretches can write well while saints produce pedestrian passages.

I like to share what little I know, to encourage beginning writers. When a
friend asked if I'd give her thirteen-year-old daughter some advice, I wrote her.

DEAR GABRIELA,

Your mother tells me that you have begun writing poems and that you wonder
exactly how I do it. Do you perhaps wonder why I do it? Why would anyone sit
alone and write when she could be talking to friends on the telephone, eating
mint chocolate chip ice cream in front of the TV, or buying a new red sweater
at the mall?

And, as you know, I like people. I like long, slow lunches with my friends. I
like to dance. I'm no hermit, and I'm not shy. So why do I sit with my tablet and
pen and mutter to myself?

4   There are many answers. I write because I'm a reader. I want to give to others what writers have given me, a chance to hear the voices of people I will
never meet. Alone, in private. And even if I meet these authors, I wouldn't hear
what I hear alone with the page, words carefully chosen, woven into a piece unlike any other, enjoyed by me in a way no other person will, in quite the same
way, enjoy them. I suppose I'm saying that I love the privateness of writing and
reading. It's delicious to curl into a book.

I write because I'm curious. I'm curious about me. Writing is a way of finding out how I feel about anything and everything. Now that I've left the desert
where I grew up, for example, I'm discovering how it feels to walk on spongy fall

leaves and to watch snow drifting *up* on a strong wind. I notice what's around me in a special way because I'm a writer, and then I talk to myself about it on paper. Writing is my way of saving my feelings.

I write because I believe that Mexican Americans need to take their rightful place in U.S. literature. We need to be published and to be studied in schools and colleges so that the stories and ideas of our people won't quietly disappear. Although I'm happy when I finish the draft of a poem or story, deep inside I always wish I wrote better, that I could bring more honor and attention to those like the *abuelitas,* grandmothers, I write about. That mix of sadness and pleasure occurs in life, doesn't it?

Although we don't discuss it often because it's depressing, our people have been and sometimes still are viewed as inferior. Maybe you have already felt hurt when someone by a remark or odd look said to you: you're not like us, you're not one of us, speaking Spanish is odd, your family looks funny.

8   Some of us decide we don't want to be different. We don't want to be part of a group that is often described as poor and uneducated. I remember feeling that way at your age. I spoke Spanish at home to my grandmother and aunt, but I didn't always want my friends at school to know that I spoke Spanish. I didn't like myself for feeling that way. I sensed it was wrong, but I didn't know why. Now, I know.

I know that the society we live in and that the movies, television programs, and commercials we see all affect us. It's not easy to learn to judge others fairly, not because of the car they drive, the house they live in, the church they attend, the color of their skin, the language they speak at home. It takes courage to face the fact that we all have ten toes, get sleepy at night, get scared in the dark. Some families, some cities, some states, and even some countries foolishly convince themselves that they are better than others. And then they teach their children this ugly lie. It's like a weed with burrs and stickers that pricks people.

How are young women who are African American, Asian American, American Indian, Latinas, or members of all the other ethnic groups supposed to feel about themselves? Some are proud of their cultural roots. But commercials are also busy trying to convince us that our car, clothes, and maybe even our family are not good enough. It's so hard today to be yourself, your many interesting selves, because billboards and magazines tell you that beautiful is being thin, maybe blonde, and rich, rich, rich. No wonder we don't always like ourselves when we look in the mirror.

There are no secrets to good writing. Read. Listen. Write. Read. Listen. Write. You learn to write well by reading wonderful writing and by letting those words and ideas become part of your blood and bones. But life is not all books. You become a better writer by listening—to yourself and to all the colors, shapes, and sounds around you. Listen with all of your senses. Listen to wrinkles on your *tia's,* your aunt's, face.

12   Writers write. They don't just talk about writing just as dancers don't just talk about dancing. They do it because they love it and because they want to get better and better. They practice and practice to loosen up just as you practiced and practiced when you were learning to talk. And because you practiced, you don't talk the way you did when you were three.

Do you know the quotation that says that learning to write is like learning to ice-skate? You must be willing to make a fool of yourself. Writers are willing to try what they can't do well so that one day they can write a strong poem or novel or children's book.

After a writer gains some confidence, she begins to spend more and more time revising, just as professional ice-skaters create and practice certain routines until they have developed their own, unique style. You probably don't like rewriting now. I didn't either until a few years ago.

How or why a book or poem starts varies. Sometimes I hear a story I want to save, sometimes it's a line or an idea. It would be as if you saw someone dance and you noticed a step or some special moves and for a few days you didn't actually try the steps, but off and on you thought about them. Maybe you even feel the moves inside you. And then one day you just can't stand it anymore and you turn on the music and begin to experiment. You don't succeed right away, but you're having fun even while you're working to get the rhythm right. And slowly you loosen up, and pretty soon you forget about your feet and arms, and you and the music are just moving together. Then the next day you try it again, and maybe alter it slightly.

16   My pen is like that music. Usually I like to start in a sunny spot with a yellow, lined tablet and a pen. I have a number of false starts like you did dancing. I'm working but having fun. Alone. The first line of a poem is sometimes a hard one because I want it to be an interesting line. It may be the only line a reader will glance at to decide whether to read the whole piece. I'm searching for the right beginning. I play a little game with myself. (This game works with any kind of writing.) I tell myself to write any line no matter how bad or dull, because I can later throw it away. If I sit waiting for the perfect line, I might never write the poem. I'm willing to make a fool of myself. So I start, usually slowly. I write a few lines, read them aloud, and often start again. I keep sections I like and discard the uninteresting parts. The next day I read my work and try to improve it. I'm trying to pull out of myself the poem or story that's deep inside. It's important not to fall in love with the words you write. Pick your words or phrases, and then stand back and look at your work. Read it out loud.

You and I are lucky to be writers. So many women in history and even today who could be much better writers than I am have not had that private pleasure of creating with words. Maybe their families think writing is a waste of time, maybe they don't believe in themselves, maybe they have to work hard all day and then have to cook and clean and take care of their children at night, maybe they've never been taught to read and write.

I hope that you develop pride in being Mexican American and that you discover what you have to say that no one else can say. I hope that you continue writing, Gabriela.

Personal Response

Did this selection give you any insights into what to do to help your own writing?

Questions for Discussion

1. What reasons does Mora give for why she writes? Discuss which, if any, are your reasons for writing.

2. In paragraphs 8 to 12, Mora discusses the subject of image, beginning with the way in which Mexican Americans are viewed by many people. She writes, "How are young women who are African American, Asian American, American Indian, Latinas, or members of all the other ethnic groups supposed to feel about themselves?" (paragraph 12). Does she stray from her central purpose in this section? If not, explain how this section is related to her advice on writing.

3. Discuss the advice Mora gives for achieving good writing. What process does she follow when writing creatively? Do you find her advice useful? What other advice can you offer for producing good writing?

4. Discuss what you would tell a thirteen-year-old about writing. Does it matter that Mora's audience is only thirteen years old?

MOTHER TONGUE

Amy Tan

Amy Tan was born in Oakland, California, not long after her parents emigrated from China. Her novel The Joy Luck Club *(1989), told in the voices of four Chinese women and their California-born daughters, was on the* New York Times *best seller list for nine months and was subsequently made into a movie. Her second novel,* The Kitchen God's Wife *was published in 1991 and her third novel,* The Hundred Secret Senses, *was published in 1995. "Mother Tongue" was published in the* Threepenny Review *in 1990.*

I am not a scholar of English or literature. I cannot give you much more than personal opinions on the English language and its variations in this country or others.

I am a writer. And by that definition, I am someone who has always loved language. I am fascinated by language in daily life. I spend a great deal of my time thinking about the power of language—the way it can evoke an emotion, a visual image, a complex idea, or a simple truth. Language is the tool of my trade. And I use them all—all the Englishes I grew up with.

Recently, I was made keenly aware of the different Englishes I do use. I was giving a talk to a large group of people, the same talk I had already given to half a dozen other groups. The nature of the talk was about my writing, my life, and my book, *The Joy Luck Club*. The talk was going along well enough, until I remembered one major difference that made the whole talk sound wrong. My mother was in the room. And it was perhaps the first time she had heard me give a lengthy speech, using the kind of English I have never used with her. I was saying things like "The intersection of memory upon imagination" and "There is an aspect of my fiction that relates to thus-and-thus"—a speech filled with carefully wrought grammatical phrases, burdened, it suddenly seemed to me, with nominalized forms, past perfect tenses, conditional phrases, all the forms of standard English that I had learned in school and through books, the forms of English I did not use at home with my mother.

4   Just last week, I was walking down the street with my mother, and I again found myself conscious of the English I was using, the English I do use with her. We were talking about the price of new and used furniture and I heard myself saying this: "Not waste money that way." My husband was with us as well, and he didn't notice any switch in my English. And then I realized why. It's because over the twenty years we've been together I've often used that same kind of English with him, and sometimes he even uses it with me. It has become our language of intimacy, a different sort of English that relates to family talk, the language I grew up with.

So you'll have some idea of what this family talk I heard sounds like, I'll quote what my mother said during a recent conversation which I videotaped and then transcribed. During this conversation, my mother was talking about a political gangster in Shanghai who had the same last name as her family's, Du, and how the gangster in his early years wanted to be adopted by her family, which was rich by comparison. Later, the gangster became more powerful, far richer than my mother's family, and one day showed up at my mother's wedding to pay his respects. Here's what she said in part:

"Du Yusong having business like fruit stand. Like off the street kind. He is Du like Du Zong—but not Tsung-ming Island people. The local people call putong, the river east side, he belong to that side local people. That man want to ask Du Zong father take him in like become own family. Du Zong father wasn't look down on him, but didn't take seriously, until that man big like become a mafia. Now important person, very hard to inviting him. Chinese way, came only to show respect, don't stay for dinner. Respect for making big celebration, he shows up. Mean gives lots of respect. Chinese custom. Chinese social life that way. If too important won't have to stay too long. He come to my wedding. I didn't see, I heard it. I gone to boy's side, they have YMCA dinner. Chinese age I was nineteen."

You should know that my mother's expressive command of English belies how much she actually understands. She reads the *Forbes* report, listens to *Wall Street Week,* converses daily with her stockbroker, reads all of Shirley MacLaine's books with ease—all kinds of things I can't begin to understand. Yet some of my friends tell me they understand 50 percent of what my mother says. Some say they understand 80 to 90 percent. Some say they understand none of it, as if she were speaking pure Chinese. But to me, my mother's English is perfectly clear, perfectly natural. It's my mother tongue. Her language, as I hear it, is vivid, direct, full of observation and imagery. That was the language that helped shape the way I saw things, expressed things, made sense of the world.

8   Lately, I've been giving more thought to the kind of English my mother speaks. Like others, I have described it to people as "broken" or "fractured" English. But I wince when I say that. It has always bothered me that I can think of no other

way to describe it other than "broken," as if it were damaged and needed to be fixed, as if it lacked a certain wholeness and soundness. I've heard other terms used, "limited English," for example. But they seem just as bad, as if everything is limited, including people's perceptions of the limited English speaker.

I know this for a fact, because when I was growing up, my mother's "limited" English limited *my* perception of her. I was ashamed of her English. I believed that her English reflected the quality of what she had to say. That is, because she expressed them imperfectly her thoughts were imperfect. And I had plenty of empirical evidence to support me: the fact that people in department stores, at banks, and at restaurants did not take her seriously, did not give her good service, pretended not to understand her, or even acted as if they did not hear her.

My mother has long realized the limitations of her English as well. When I was fifteen, she used to have me call people on the phone to pretend I was she. In this guise, I was forced to ask for information or even to complain and yell at people who had been rude to her. One time it was a call to her stockbroker in New York. She had cashed out her small portfolio and it just so happened we were going to go to New York the next week, our very first trip outside California. I had to get on the phone and say in an adolescent voice that was not very convincing, "This is Mrs. Tan."

And my mother was standing in the back whispering loudly, "Why he don't send me check, already two weeks late. So mad he lie to me, losing me money."

12   And then I said in perfect English, "Yes, I'm getting rather concerned. You had agreed to send the check two weeks ago, but it hasn't arrived."

Then she began to talk more loudly. "What he want, I come to New York tell him front of his boss, you cheating me?" And I was trying to calm her down, make her be quiet, while telling the stockbroker, "I can't tolerate any more excuses. If I don't receive the check immediately, I am going to have to speak to your manager when I'm in New York next week." And sure enough, the following week there we were in front of this astonished stockbroker, and I was sitting there red-faced and quiet, and my mother, the real Mrs. Tan, was shouting at his boss in her impeccable broken English.

We used a similar routine just five days ago, for a situation that was far less humorous. My mother had gone to the hospital for an appointment, to find out about a benign brain tumor a CAT scan had revealed a month ago. She said she had spoken very good English, her best English, no mistakes. Still, she said, the hospital did not apologize when they said they had lost the CAT scan and she had come for nothing. She said they did not seem to have any sympathy when she told them she was anxious to know the exact diagnosis, since her husband and son had both died of brain tumors. She said they would not give her any more information until the next time and she would have to make another appointment for that. So she said she would not leave until the doctor called her daughter. She wouldn't budge. And when the doctor finally called her daughter, me, who spoke in perfect English—lo and behold—we had assurances the CAT scan would be found, promises that a conference call on Monday would be held, and apologies for any suffering my mother had gone through for a most regrettable mistake.

I think my mother's English almost had an effect on limiting my possibilities in life as well. Sociologists and linguists probably will tell you that a person's developing language skills are more influenced by peers. But I do think that the language spoken in the family, especially in immigrant families which are more insular, plays a large role in shaping the language of the child. And I believe that it affected my results on achievement tests, IQ tests, and the SAT. While my English skills were never judged as poor, compared to math, English could not be considered my strong suit. In grade school I did moderately well, getting perhaps B's, sometimes B-pluses, in English and scoring perhaps in the sixtieth or seventieth percentile on achievement tests. But those scores were not good enough to override the opinion that my true abilities lay in math and science, because in those areas I achieved A's and scored in the ninetieth percentile or higher.

16   This was understandable. Math is precise; there is only one correct answer. Whereas, for me at least, the answers on English tests were always a judgment call, a matter of opinion and personal experience. Those tests were constructed around items like fill-in-the-blank sentence completion, such as "Even though Tom was _____ , Mary thought he was _____ ." And the correct answer always seemed to be the most bland combinations of thoughts, for example, "Even though Tom was shy, Mary thought he was charming," with the grammatical structure "even though" limiting the correct answer to some sort of semantic opposites, so you wouldn't get answers like, "Even though Tom was foolish, Mary thought he was ridiculous." Well, according to my mother, there were very few limitations as to what Tom could have been and what Mary might have thought of him. So I never did well on tests like that.

The same was true with word analogies, pairs of words in which you were supposed to find some sort of logical, semantic relationship—for example, "*Sunset is to nightfall* as _____ is to _____ ." And here you would be presented with a list of four possible pairs, one of which showed the same kind of relationship: *red is to stoplight, bus is to arrival, chills is to fever, yawn is to boring.* Well, I could never think that way. I knew what the tests were asking, but I could not block out of my mind the images already created by the first pair, "*sunset is to nightfall*"—and I would see a burst of color against a darkening sky, the moon rising, the lowering of a curtain of stars. And all the other pairs of words—red, bus, stoplight, boring—just threw up a mass of confusing images, making it impossible for me to sort out something as logical as saying: "A sunset precedes nightfall" is the same as "a chill precedes a fever." The only way I would have gotten that answer right would have been to imagine an associative situation, for example, my being disobedient and staying out past sunset, catching a chill at night, which turns into feverish pneumonia as punishment, which indeed did happen to me.

I have been thinking about all this lately, about my mother's English, about achievement tests. Because lately I've been asked, as a writer, why there are not more Asian Americans represented in American literature. Why are there few Asian Americans enrolled in creative writing programs? Why do so many Chinese students go into engineering? Well, these are broad sociological questions I can't begin to answer. But I have noticed in surveys—in fact, just last week—that Asian students, as a whole, always do significantly better on math achievement tests than in English. And this makes me think that there are other Asian-American students whose English spoken in the home might also be described as "broken" or "limited." And perhaps they also have teachers who are steering them away from writing and into math and science, which is what happened to me.

Fortunately, I happen to be rebellious in nature and enjoy the challenge of disproving assumptions made about me. I became an English major my first year in college, after being enrolled as pre-med. I started writing nonfiction as a freelancer the week after I was told by my former boss that writing was my worst skill and I should hone my talents toward account management.

20   But it wasn't until 1985 that I finally began to write fiction. And at first I wrote using what I thought to be wittily crafted sentences, sentences that would finally prove I had mastery over the English language. Here's an example from the first draft of a story that later made its way into *The Joy Luck Club,* but without this line: "That was my mental quandary in its nascent state." A terrible line, which I can barely pronounce.

Fortunately, for reasons I won't get into today, I later decided I should envision a reader for the stories I would write. And the reader I decided upon was my mother, because these were stories about mothers. So with this reader in mind—and in fact she did read my early drafts—I began to write stories using all the Englishes I grew up with: the English I spoke to my mother, which for lack of a better term might be described as "simple": the English she used with me, which for lack of a better term might be described as "broken"; my translation of her Chinese, which could certainly be described as "watered down"; and what I imagined to be her translation of her Chinese if she could speak in perfect English, her internal language, and for that I sought to preserve the essence, but neither an English nor a Chinese structure. I wanted to capture what language ability tests can never reveal: her intent, her passion, her imagery, the rhythms of her speech, and the nature of her thoughts.

Apart from what any critic had to say about my writing, I knew I had succeeded where it counted when my mother finished reading my book and gave me her verdict: "So easy to read."

Personal Response

In what ways does your own language change according to situation and audience? For instance, do you use the same language with your parents, teachers, and employer as you do with friends and peers? Does your "family talk" (paragraph 4) differ from the way you talk to others?

Questions for Discussion

1. How is the term "mother tongue" generally used? In what sense(s) is Tan using it?

2. Tan says that she uses "all the Englishes [she] grew up with." What does she mean by that rather unusual word "Englishes"? How does her use of the word reflect Tan's central point about language?

3. Look again at Tan's transcription of her mother's language in paragraph 6. How would you describe that English? Does either the term "broken" or "limited" describe it? What do those terms imply to you?

4. Tan gives examples of situations in which she had to speak for her mother in order for her mother to be understood. What other examples can you give of situations in which non-native speakers of English might not be able to communicate with native speakers? What could be done to help non-native speakers in such situations?

5. What connections does Tan make between the English her mother speaks and the possibility that her own life choices might have been limited? What connection does she make between the language of her own family and the under-representation of Asian Americans in American literature and creative writing programs?

6. What insight about language and writing do Tan's last three paragraphs illustrate?

REMEMBERING KAREN

Zoë Landale

Zoë Landale has published two books, Harvest of Salmon *(1976), about her commercial fishing experience, and a book of poetry,* Burning Stone *(1993). Her work has been published in many anthologies and literary journals, and she has won several awards for her writing. This essay was one of three finalists in a "creative nonfiction" competition sponsored by a Canadian literary magazine. Because authors' names were blacked out, the judge of that contest, writer Andreas Schroeder, had no idea who the author was, other than that she was Karen's older sister. Several months later, when Schroeder was conducting a writers' clinic, he was astonished to find himself reading an essay written from an entirely different perspective, that of Karen's younger sister Marjorie Simmins. Struck by the coincidence of these two sisters, within a few months of each other and without the other's knowledge, writing about an experience that had devastated their family years before, Schroeder sent the essays to* Saturday Night, *a magazine published in Toronto, Ontario. The essays appeared together in the May 1993 issue of that magazine.*

I open the front door at Mum's to a blue-uniformed cop and I think: *Karen.* There is no other reason for him to be here. What has she done this time? Skipped out on an ambulance bill? Mum shouldn't be responsible any more, damn it. Isn't it just like Karen to wreck Christmas! I can't figure out where the policeman's questions are leading. It must take a good three minutes before he comes out with it: Karen is dead.

Dead? The world splinters into multiple thin cold lines. That's what he says. I don't believe him. She's sold her ID . . . it wouldn't be the first time.

By this time the cop is standing in the front hallway, and Mum is crying in the living room. Aunt Anne has her arms around her and is encouraging her to ventilate. Aunt Anne is big on ventilating. It comes from her time as an art therapist at Warrendale, an institution famous for its work with schizophrenic, autistic, and generally disturbed kids. John Brown, who founded Warrendale, has a centre in Vancouver. We once tried to get Karen in. No level of government would pay for her treatment. It would have cost us $7,000 a year.

4   Mum is sitting on the rust-coloured couch and going on and on about the last time she saw Karen, just three days ago when Dad came over from Victoria to take her out to the AA Christmas dinner. Mum had accused her of being stoned and Karen said no, she wasn't, it was the heels of her boots making her wobble. Now that's all Mum can think of, what an awful person she was to have thought Karen was stoned when it was the HEELS ON HER BOOTS. If she'd had Karen's HEELS fixed maybe this wouldn't have happened.

She must've been in a bad way for Mum to have caught on.

Thank goodness Aunt Anne is here.

Poor Aunt Anne, to have come all the way from Toronto for this.

8   I take the cop back to the kitchen. He is young, with a regulation moustache, dark and bushy. The stripes on his pants seem awfully yellow. They remind me of a wasp, there is that edge of irritation, of menace, in the colour. He asks and asks me questions. Who *cares* what Karen's real birthday is? It is either December 16 or December 18, but we always celebrate it on December 1 so she can get two sets of presents just like everyone else.

The cop cares. I have to ask Mum. December 18 it is. Back in the shabby kitchen, its ancient linoleum shining with Mop & Glo, I plug in the kettle to make tea. We have to pull ourselves together. I offer everyone, including the cop, tea and aspirin on a tray. I have been well trained. This is what one does in a crisis.

I take my own advice, two aspirin and a cup of tea. I am surprised when the cop refuses both. If I had to cope with a situation like this, I'd need tea, the stronger the better. Maybe not the aspirin: he *is* on duty.

I wonder, vaguely, what the cop thinks of the kitchen. Back in the sixties, Dad had it painted white with Easter-egg-purple trim. There are five doors, back, pantry, hall, basement, and dining-room, so it makes for a lot of purple. What I mind are the kitchen counters, made from tiny tiles that have permanent mildew between them.

12   It is beginning to sink in that very probably Karen is dead. Someone is. Someone died of an overdose in the Blue Boy hotel down on the South-East Marine, where Dad had paid for a room for Karen. Of course it could've been Lana . . . any of Karen's junkie friends.

"What did Karen die from?" I ask, finally.

"Mandrax," the cop says. He sees my frown. "They're a kind of barbiturate." And there's more about the assistant manager knocking on Karen's door, but I'm thinking about Mum getting phoned up by little old ladies who lived on tree-lined streets, "Excuse me, but I think this is your daughter I found lying unconscious," and how Karen is known by name at every emergency department in the whole Lower Mainland, and that she can't really be dead now.

That'd be too easy. Any moment she'll come in, laughing, though she's supposed to stay away from here for good. Very very funny. Like the blackmail she twisted out of at least one of her girlfriends' boyfriends. First of all she slept with the guy, then she came to him and said she was pregnant, that'd be $500 for an abortion. Right now. Then she wouldn't have to tell.

16   "So she'd be twenty," the police officer says.

"That's right." My math, as always, is weak, and in times of need deserts me completely. If he says twenty, twenty it is. I'm twenty-two, so he must be right.

"She just turned twenty," he repeats, as if he finds it incredible.

"She's been on drugs since she was eleven," I say. Harshly. That's nine years of hell, buddy boy. You have no idea of the kind of shit that went on in this house. Ever try to keep a full-grown person in her room? What do you do when she won't stay, come roaring up from the basement, time after time after time, so stoned she can't speak, but ready, willing, and determined to wreck the house?

20   Think about it. I do. I'd sworn I wouldn't ever spend another Christmas in this house but I had agreed to come back for tonight's Boxing Dinner because Aunt Anne was here and Mum finally, I couldn't believe it, FINALLY, said Karen couldn't come.

She couldn't come back for Christmas. She couldn't come back to live. Imagine! After me telling Mum for years that having Karen in the house was destroying my younger brother and sister, and Mum giving Karen fifteen more chances: "I really think she's changed, Zoë, this time will be different." Mum, the one-more-chance-forever Mum, didn't believe any more that things were going to change.

"When was the last time you saw her?"

I have to think. "A year and a half." I'd cut her venomous presence out of my heart. I had had no middle sister for years. This cop knew nothing. I'd have thought he'd have seen a few horrifying things by now, enough to stop being surprised. "She's been over in Victoria for the last year in the psychiatric wing of the Royal Jubilee Hospital."

24   "She was discharged and wanted to come back to Vancouver. Dad brought her over and took her out for Christmas dinner," I explain. "AA had some big do. Mum finally said she couldn't come back here. Dad got Karen a room at the Blue Boy so she could think about what she wanted to do."

The cop is so earnest, so straight. How can he understand all the horrible Christmases we've had with Karen stoned, black make-up smeared under her eyes, throwing fits, throwing scenes, throwing gravy, picking up and heaving the big dragon pitcher our great-grandmother painted, ugly as sin and two feet tall; if it had caught Geoffrey as it was meant to, it would've brained him. Mum was heartbroken about the pitcher. Perhaps it had never occurred to her before that Karen could be dangerous. But wait a minute, she'd once gone after someone with a bicycle chain that had a padlock on the end; who was that, Mum?

At one point during the questions, the cop brings me a box of Kleenex, there's always one on top of the fridge. I don't need Kleenex. Why should I cry for Karen? I'm not a hypocrite.

At last the police officer finishes. I walk him to the front door. "Thank you," I say.

28 He looks straight at me, not one of his pieces of paper. "This is the hardest part of the job, you know, no-one enjoys it."

I nod, blankly. It isn't until the next week that I realize he'd misunderstood. I meant thank you for being nice, for bringing me Kleenex. I am used to thinking of cops as blue insects.

Someone had to tell Dad. Mum in still crying in the living room. Hasn't she had enough ventilation by now? I call. Dad is back in Victoria. "Pull out a chair," I order. "Sit down." I listen to the words plop out, heavy and dark, but aren't I being practical too? I could imagine his knees giving way. I am sitting down. I have to.

"I'm sitting down," he says, sounding curious, and I am sorry, he thinks this may be fun. When I tell him, his "Oh my God!" wheeze echoes in my own gut and I think, I was right to tell him to sit. I watch the scratched black surface of the kitchen table, its jumble of papers, pens, the address book with Dad's number.

32 Someone has to identify Karen. Conde, my then husband, offered but the cop said no, it should be a blood relative. That meant me. It would haunt Mum for the rest of her days, I wouldn't even think of asking her. My brother and sister are too young. Besides, I didn't love Karen, so it might as well be me. Conde's offer makes a small warm spot I hug to myself, the only one in this dreary day.

After dinner (it is five o'clock by the time the policeman leaves), Conde and I drive down to the morgue. We are to go to the Coroner's Court, the cop said, the old brick building on East Cordova Street. He was surprised I knew where it was. (Murder mysteries are good for something. I'd long ago noticed the name engraved on it.) It is foggy and cold. No-one is about. It is Boxing Day after all. The Christmas lights on stores create ghostly pools of red and blue in the mist.

I am quite certain it won't be Karen. I'm sure she's sold her ID.

At the mortuary, a young man wearing a white lab coat leads us along acres of corridors to a waiting room where Conde and I sit on wooden benches until the young man is finally ready for us.

36 I can't get my breath.

We walk into a room filled with stainless-steel drawers. It's like a giant filing cabinet. One of the drawers has been pulled out. On it is a sheet cover . . . the young man walks ahead of us, pulls aside a corner of the sheet.

Karen.

My hand goes out to touch, involuntarily. The young man blocks it. Karen. You asked us all to spell it "Karin." I wouldn't do it. Such a simple thing to ask! I never saw the scar that bisects your bottom lip before. Your lips are blue and thin. I'd forgotten your hair was such a pretty colour, bronzy, but it's all matted. It needs brushing.

40 "Yes, that's my sister." The young man spins me around, out of the room while I feel as if I am still reaching out, still startled by the absolute whiteness of

Karen's face. Blazing white, with whatever made Karen, Karen gone. I under-stand now what is meant by "dead."

You really did it this time, girl. I will not cry. Karen is dead. I should be glad.

I can't get to sleep until after two in the morning. I see Mum and Anne shoot glances at one another at breakfast time when they ask me how I am, but really, it's not that Karen died, I just had trouble falling asleep. I didn't love her. I won't pretend.

There was no note. It could have been an overdose like the other times. It could have been that finally Karen was dumped into the world like a cat no-one wanted, to look after herself. None of her friends would put up with her. She went to stay with Lana once. Lana had had to phone Mum's in the middle of the night to beg us to come and get Karen. I was out of that one. Conde went down with Mum and covered himself in glory. I seem to remember that Karen was wandering about Lana's place with no top on, smashing things, stoned out of her mind. To this day, Mum is grateful to Conde for getting Karen out of there and home.

44   Karen get a job?

Karen have kids?

It relieved me to no end that Karen wouldn't be having children. She had pre-tended to be pregnant so often as part of her various scams (always swore with heart-wrenching sincerity *this* time it was true), I had grown quite upset thinking about the awful life any child of hers would have. She'd undoubtedly have given the baby to Mum to raise, then come back and caused horrendous scenes, run away with the child, begged for money....

Ah, Karen. As a family we have carried you about with us from the day of your death. Guilt. Mum and Dad were flattened with it for years. It had been up to them as parents ... if only ... if only. They wished they'd done ... *Star light star bright, first star I see tonight.*

48   Our sister, Marjorie, still dreams about you. I hated what you did to her, the malicious power you held, the way you made her jump, played on her fears. When she was little, you'd make up stories about animals for her. Nice, except all the animals would die. Marjorie would cry, but you'd never make them come back to life again.

I had nightmares for ten years after you died, Karen. In the dreams, you'd still be alive and coming after me. You'd put on weight in hospital. I incorporated that into my dreams, a heavier you, but with the same almost-waist-length hair, the white face, black eyeliner above and beneath your eyes à la Cher all those years ago, or Cleopatra on TV. Your slack, open bottom lip that let me know you were stoned, and I was in for it.

It took us years, as a family, before we got past talking about you every time any of us were together. What could we have done differently? Were there places we could have got help for you and hadn't tried? We did try. Although it would be more honest to say that Mum did. Every year, it seemed, Conde and I would sit down with Mum when we came back from that season's fishing and try to Straighten Things Out. No problem was impossible to solve if approached logi-cally. We'd come up with lots of ideas. Mum would either have tried them already, or would try them only to find out one more time that things wouldn't pan out.

Was it our fault, the way you turned out? Psychiatrists like to suggest that a family will pick one member, usually a middle child like you, onto whom they foist all their craziness. Knowing that, if it's true, could we have acted differently? Our failings still beat us about the head. Failure to love you. The withering away of belief in what you said. Failure to care, finally, what damage you did, as long as it was not our curtains you pulled down, our white walls smeared with blood from your cut wrists. We'd stopped jumping when you screamed.

52   Why can't I remember some good things? You were a wonderful actor. You could imitate anyone, do gestures, accents. I remember sitting in the kitchen nook, crying with laughter as you told a story about something that had happened to you. You could make us all laugh.

Lana came to your funeral. She was the only one of your friends to turn up. Me, I felt like punching her, she'd been hanging around doing drugs with you in the days before you died. I think it was Lana who insisted the assistant manager open the door. Once again an ambulance was called, again your stomach was pumped out, but this time you didn't revive. Dad was kind to Lana, who slunk in, a small figure in black, sobbing at the beginning of the service. He pointed out to me afterwards that Lana was the only person there who cried. I've liked her much better ever since, or her memory at least. I've never seen her again.

I don't know if I ever cried for you.

Wait, maybe I did. Conde and I had to go pick up what the police called "your effects." It didn't sound too terrible. We went down to the main police station, identified ourselves, and waited at a counter. An officer came back with a duffel bag, a knapsack, I can't remember now, and that was *all*. Then he opened an envelope that contained your "valuables"—five dollars and a watch. He checked them off against a list. The stuff in the knapsack we got to take home and sort out on our own. I pressed the nails of one hand hard into the other, below counter level so no-one could see. That was when tears came and I choked them back. Control, control, but I saw through a haze of sadness so deep it was almost anger.

56   It was so little. You'd had so little. Was that all you'd left to mark your life?

My real farewell to you came ten years afterwards. Garney, my second husband, and I were living up at Sechelt. Our house had a great tangle of blackberry behind it, out of which we'd hacked a yard, and there were several vacant lots to the east, which were bush. So looking out the windows, we had the illusion of being adrift in a sea of green. I was in the living room one sunny morning. It was early spring. I could hear hummingbirds zipping by the window, see magenta salmonberry flowers, the fresh crinkle of unfolding leaves. The sun was so warm I had the window open to let in some air. And I heard you laugh. I'd forgotten you ever laughed.

What really surprised me was that I was glad to hear you. It was like watching you eat toast. You ate it piled with more butter than anyone I've ever known. The flavour of you was unmistakable.

You laughed, and went out the window.

60   What a blessing! The sound swung me, released me. I was given you back again, all of you, not just your dead face, which I will see as long as I am alive,

but a Karen who laughed, who made jokes, who in spite of everything remains sister.

Personal Response

What is your reaction to Landale's tough stance on her sister's behavior? Do you think you might behave the same in similar circumstances?

Questions for Discussion

1. How do you account for Landale's apparently cold reaction to the news of Karen's death, that is, not only her inability to cry but her refusal to do so? What details suggest that she was not as unemotional about her sister's death as she claims to have been?

2. What does it tell you about Landale that she was the one who called her father about Karen's death and that she was the one who went to the morgue to identify Karen's body?

3. Why did Landale cry for her sister?

4. Explain what Landale means in paragraph 47 when she writes, "As a family we have carried you [Karen] about with us from the day of your death. Guilt." Why does the family feel guilty about a woman so obviously self-destructive as Karen?

5. Explain what it was that was "given back again" to Landale (last paragraph).

TRIPS FROM THERE TO HERE

Marjorie Simmins

Marjorie Simmins holds a B.A. in English literature from the University of British Columbia and is a full-time freelance writer. Her areas of special interest and expertise include the British Columbia commercial fishing industry and horses. As the younger sister of Karen in the previous essay, Simmins saw Karen from a point of view quite different from that of Zoë Landale.

When I think about Karin, I remember bacon and marmalade sandwiches and chocolate milk, the kind that comes out of the carton thick and sweet. And fried pork chops and baked potatoes with sour cream, her favourite dinner, back in the days when she was allowed to eat with us. I don't remember who banished her from the dinner table or when, but I remember why.

Throwing up. Anything that went down when she was stoned came flying back up within minutes. We tolerated this vomiting, even accommodated it: we always made sure she had the outside chair in our kitchen nook. That way, when she felt sick, she could run to the bathroom without tripping all over us.

Sometimes she wasn't fast enough to make it to the bathroom. The back door would smash open and we'd hear food splatter onto the cement walkway below the veranda. We kept a garden hose coiled at the side of the house.

First memories of my sister always come from the sound of raised voices and the feeling of dread in my stomach. I used to run to the bathroom upstairs, the farthest corner away from the noise. I'd turn on the tap and hum as I brushed my teeth trying to block out the yells from downstairs. I knew she wouldn't hurt me—I was too young to have anything she wanted—but she hurt the others with a bewildering and relentless accuracy. I couldn't stand watching the fights and I couldn't prevent them, so I created my own territory with her, the safest one I could think of: sister as shadow. I decided to be friends with her, to move beside her, where I could keep her in my peripheral vision.

4   Karin went through a magician phase; maybe sorceress is a better word. She used to put on performances in her incense-sweet bedroom in the basement. She had special clothes for these occasions, harem pants and gauzy scarfs that she wrapped around her red-gold hair. Sometimes she would make things disappear and other times she'd open cupboard doors just by looking at them. A neighbour who watched one of these shows couldn't resist trying to destroy Karin's illusions.

"Look," she said, "she's using a string to pull the door open! I can see it, can't you?"

Karin's eyes searched the darkened room, looking for mine. Speak up, guard the magic.

"Mrs. Williams, you're wrong. There's no string. This is real magic." I glared at her. The show concluded to loud applause.

8   Cats loved Karin, loved the way she rubbed their wet noses and hypnotized them with soft words and fishy treats. Some days I felt like a cat, gut-happy and mind-stroked with gentle words and promises. As long as I protected her—accepted her choices and her rules—the anger never came my way. I didn't know how else to protect myself.

We used to play horses out in the back yard. We'd take our horse collection—plastic and china figures—and set up a farm in the rock garden. Usually we chose the spot where the water faucet was hidden by a low, thick azalea bush. There were flat rocks beneath the faucet. When it rained, or when the faucet was left on a steady drip, the rocks held a shallow pool of water. We called this the pond and took the horses to swim there. I could play for hours, but Karin eventually got bored and the game would end with a ritualistic drowning of the horses. Hands that had moments earlier created bridles out of elastic bands and gently braided silky manes and tails would now seize the small animals and shove their heads under the water, making them gurgle and scream. I could sense the mood change, could see impatience in the movement of her fingers—but the vibrancy of her imagination was irresistible. In the garden of our make-believe world, death was a temporary condition; I knew I would play with her again the next day, when the sorceress pulled us up from the chill waters to start a new game.

Karin's eyes were dark blue, with a silver star around the iris. She plucked her eyebrows thin and wore heavy eyeliner. Pale skin, with a few freckles scattered over a finely shaped nose. Her stride was short, almost bouncy. In nearly all of her photographs she has her head tilted to one side—her expression a strange blend of coyness and misery.

I don't remember when her blue eyes started going grey every day. Around the same time she started taking her meals in the TV room. It was a relief to eat quiet dinners; I even started enjoying spaghetti again. But I was uneasy with the separation—and disliked cutting her off from the rest of the family. The nonoffenders would exchange news of the day, pass the butter, salt, and pepper around the table, and I'd be worrying if she wanted more food, or if she'd nodded out over her plate. As soon as I could I'd join her in the den.

12   We'd watch TV together, sprawled out on the couch, me leaning on her side with a pillow underneath my elbow. Her cigarette ash would burn longer and longer and without thinking I'd reach over and bump her arm over the ashtray.

"Karin, watch your smoke."

We started to find burn holes everywhere. The couch, the pillowcases, the bed sheets. She always seemed to wake up just before the smoke turned to flames.

Karin kept her methadone bottles in the refrigerator. She lined them up tidily, on the right-hand side of the door, nestled in with the Velveeta cheese. The methadone was mixed with orange juice, which masked the bitter taste a little bit. Karin told me never to touch them. But I did. I was curious about those white-capped bottles, even jealous of their daily importance. After everyone was asleep I'd sneak down to the kitchen and pull a bottle out. Sometimes I'd just smell the stuff, and wonder what she felt like when she drank it. One night I took a tiny slurp, then, terrified she'd know I had tried it, I filled the missing half-inch with water and ran back to bed. I lay awake a long time, wondering when I'd get smashed. I fell asleep with a trace of orange-sweet drug juice on my lips.

16   The year we bought Coqeyn, I recorded the event in my journal: "Over the weekend we bought a horse. He is an Arabian and Karin and I are going to look after it." Every twelve-year-old girl's dream come true. A living, breathing horse, to ride and love.

Coqeyn scared me. Mostly because I was sure we'd lose him, the moment our reflection in his purple-brown eyes became steady. Vet bills, board bills, and my mother teaching day school and night school to provide for us. I'd watch Mum disappear into her bedroom for a twenty-minute rest before dinner and hate the horse for filling the house with dragging steps and exhaustion. But Coqeyn was going to save the day: he was going to make Karin permanently straight and functioning. Like magic.

Karin's all-time straight record in seven years was three months. Straight from heroin and barbiturates. She drank the methadone every day, although at one point she weaned herself down to a quarter of a bottle, selling the other three-quarters to buy things for the horse. The endless supply of methadone came from the Narcotic Addiction Foundation, on Broadway at Oak, where we went each day after school. On the bus down there Karin would drink Coke, to fill her bladder for the sample she had to give to the doctors. Some days her bladder wouldn't cooperate. She'd park herself by the water fountain in the foundation's foyer and drink until the twinge in her gut felt certain.

"Okay, I'm ready." I'd watch her disappear into the bathroom, followed by a woman in a white lab coat. Minutes later, she'd return, smiling and giggling, jerking her thumb at the full sample bottle carried by the nurse: "Success!" Then she'd line up with the other junkies to get her methadone for the week. They always made her drink a cup of methadone before she left. She'd throw back her head, toss the liquid down, and make a major production of swallowing it. Actually, she didn't swallow any, but kept it in her mouth until we left the building from the back entrance. If I felt like teasing her, I'd poke her in the ribs, trying to make her laugh and spit the liquid out of her chipmunk cheeks. She'd shake her head, look furious, but I knew it was like the horses in the pond—no permanent damage done.

20   In the lane behind the foundation she'd take out one of her bottles and spit the methadone into it. She spat it out fast, discreet; you'd think she was stopping to cough and delicately wipe her mouth. We'd walk another half-block and sell the topped-up bottle to the first junkie with cash.

Karin loved Coqeyn as much as she loved smack. We groomed our horse, one on either side, until our arms ached. We read horse magazines and made plans to truck Coqeyn into the Interior, where we could go for long rides into the mountains. He would be an endurance horse, a jumper, a hunter—he was going to do it all and we were going to have a roomful of ribbons and trophies to gloat over. We took riding lessons, sold methadone, and bought expensive tack. Summer 1972: Jethro Tull *(Thick as a Brick),* paisley T-shirts, Export "A" cigarettes, and the barn, every day, all day.

There were triumphs in those years. The first time we won a ribbon at a recognized show I cried so hard I could hardly see where I was going as I ran over the bumpy hogfuel to meet Karin coming out of the ring.

"It's only a sixth place, Marjorie," she protested as I grabbed onto her gloved hand and squeezed it hard.

24   "But a ribbon, Karin! A rosette!"

She dismounted, leaned against Coqeyn's sweat-darkened shoulder. "Next time we'll do better."

Doing better. The words throbbed under our skins as the boundaries between us blurred. Doing better this week, only lied once about no bombers in the house. Found a rainbow assortment in her jewellery box, flushed them down the toilet. Doing better, though, no clouds in her eyes for three days. Relax, play the twin game: Levi jeans, blue ski jackets, black boots, velvet hunt caps, long hair in braids. Walk close, shoulders touching, steps synchronized. No one can tell us apart. You protect me and I'll protect you.

These periods—the quiet, symbiotic ones—vanished. One week we were inseparable; the next I was a Siamese twin, slowly ripping my body away from hers. We all tried to keep out of her way, to hide from the cruel taunts, the thievery, the broken dishes. My brother hid by going out with his friends; he spent nearly all his time at parties or in bars and pool halls. I used to ask him, as he was leaving, where he was going. The fringes on his leather jacket would swing as he shrugged his shoulders. "Out," he'd say, "going out." The door would slam behind him and I'd be left standing in the hallway, wondering where I could go. In six more months I would seek out all of Geoffrey's haunts and claim them as my own, but before then I spent many evenings walking around the back lanes behind our house.

28   Sometimes she'd still be up when I returned.

"Where have you been? I'm making a milkshake, would you like some?" Maybe she felt guilty or ashamed; maybe she just wanted to keep me on her side. I'd watch her pour the milkshake and accept the glass timidly. We'd go to the TV room and before I had a sip from my glass I'd wait, knowing she'd either spill hers or demand the rest of mine.

Her eyes and her moods were dead giveaways. Easy to know when she was high. When she got really affectionate, I knew it would be a back-lane night.

"Oh, Marjorie, I feel so good today. I'm so glad we're friends, aren't you? I love you, little sister, I love you so much." Words like those coiled every muscle in my body for flight. Karin's love always careened into anger.

32   Eventually even the horse wasn't safe. When Karin started coming to the barn stoned, I knew that I had to complete my separation from her. If I didn't, I'd find myself explaining not just a broken dish, or a missing wallet, but a death.

The final break came. I was in the feed room, mixing up a steaming bran mash. Karin burst in the door, eyes as wide as they could be when she was that high. Her face was white and sweaty, her words so slurred that at first I couldn't make out what she was saying.

"Come quick. It's in his stall, the cigarette, right by the door, I can't find it, hurry, hurry—come!"

He's gonna burn. He's gonna rear up in a box of flames and cook like a pig in a bonfire. Fear for Coqeyn made my heart lurch, but stronger than the fear was the pattern of hiding Karin's mistakes. No one would know what had happened, not if I moved quickly. I wanted to hit that pasty, out-of-focus face, but I just told her to get a wheelbarrow and start shovelling out the stall. I led Coqeyn out, tied him to a post. Stepped back inside the stall and glanced back over my shoulder to see who could see me. No one around. I tipped over the three-foot-high water bucket in the corner where she said she'd dropped the cigarette. All this time Karin was babbling and weaving, getting in my way. My hands, sticky with warm molasses, shook so much I could barely hold the shovel.

36   "Get out of my way. Get the fuck out of here." New and raw words I hurled at her, words that had nothing to do with the cigarette and a lot to do with the twin feeling its air supply being choked off. Breathe, little sister, breathe hard and fast.

Her expression was terrifying—dead straight and stoned to the limit. Of all her unusual abilities, this was the one that frightened me most. While anyone else would have fallen flat with the amount of chemicals she pumped into her body, small Karin staggered on, even casting aside, for a few minutes, the total effect of the drugs she had taken. "Thought I was a goner, sister/brother dear?" she'd sneer at Geoffrey and me, when we'd crouch beside her, deciding whether or not to call an ambulance. "Not yet, motherfuckers."

I concentrated on cleaning out the stall. By now I wasn't even scared about the cigarette. More was coming. Every hair standing up on my arms was preparing me for it.

When I came back from soaking the chips with water I found Karin tightening the girth on Coqeyn's saddle. The bridle was already on.

40   "What are you doing?" I kept my voice low and prayed she couldn't hear the pleading note beneath it.

"Gonna ride in the ring." As she spoke she lost her balance and caught at the bridle to steady herself. Coqeyn, jabbed in the mouth from this motion, threw up his head and took several quick steps backwards.

"Stand still, you bastard." She kneed him hard under the girth.

"Stop it!" I was shouting now, didn't care who heard me. "Leave him alone."

44   "Why? This bother you?" she asked, eyes for one instant clear and sober. "Watch, it gets better."

She took the bridle in both hands and jerked it down with all her weight. I could feel that iron cut down as though the bit were in my own mouth. I sucked in cold night air and howled. Coqeyn lunged, I lunged, Karin laughed. I pushed her down onto the tarmac and felt her rise up against my arm strong as a tidal wave. Fluid strength, like water all around us, and me twisting, kicking, punching to keep my head from going under.

I lost the fight. And I never walked shoulder to shoulder with Karin again.

That autumn I started grade nine. School was something that passed between hours of wondering whether Karin had died that day. Her eyes looked like grey cauliflowers now, with hardly any colour in them at all. She overdosed so many times that I got used to seeing her face blue. I distanced myself from my hands when they slapped the breath into her. She hurt herself, horribly, when she was stoned—gashes, bruises—but I didn't help her anymore. I ate my meals in the kitchen with the rest of the family and afterwards I retreated to my room.

48   One morning I came downstairs and found her passed out, with her eyes open, in the chair beside the front door. I stepped close to her, to see if she was breathing. It was a quarter to nine; if I didn't hurry, I'd be late for school. I couldn't bring myself to touch her. I imagined that she was a corpse that would suddenly reach out and crush my body into the deathland behind those unblinking eyes. Geoffrey walked into the hall, saw me staring at her slumped figure.

"She alive?"

"I can't tell. I think so. Wouldn't her eyes be closed if she was dead?"

"Maybe, don't know. Let's get out of here."

52   We walked up Dunbar Street towards the bus stop. Geoffrey's strides were long and fast; I took two for each one of his. Suddenly aware of our mismatched steps, he slowed down, until our shoulders brushed together. He reached into his jacket pocket and took out a Bar Six chocolate bar.

"Want some?"

"Yeah, sure."

Karin died a year later, in a room at the Blue Boy hotel. On Christmas Day. Unlike the china and plastic horses, she would stay dead.

56   I didn't ride for about eight years. Barns, with their cold cement floors and draughty corridors, felt like tombs. The smell of molasses made me sick. And when I saw young women with long hair and blue ski jackets walking close together, I'd stretch out my arms and feel oceans of empty air on either side of my body.

    My hair is short now. I wear a purple and black Gore-Tex jacket when I ride in the rain. Black leather chaps, too; Karin would have loved them. Since my sister died, I have travelled in Europe, Canada, the United States, and the West Indies. I have lived on boats, in downtown high-rises. I went to university and worked, as a waitress, a driver, an editor. Men, for days and daze, and two, loved unconditionally. I kissed/kiss them, remembering Karin's precise explanation of the perfect kiss.

    Last year I even dated a brother of one of her lovers. I met him, in one of those small-world situations, and wanted to be near him, because his brother had loved Karin. A tall and strange order to fill, and he only five feet eight inches, and a mind more focused on gains and losses.

    "Yeah," he said, "Kevin did heroin, but he's been clean for years. Your sister didn't make it, eh?"

60   "Where was your brother when Karin died?" (First date, the Holiday Inn on Broadway, him figuring out my income-tax return, me scanning his face for one flicker of shared memory.)

    "I don't know. Maybe they weren't friends any more. Besides, drugs weren't really a problem for Kevin. He hasn't used in years. He's married now, has a kid, and works as an actor—very talented. Why are you so hung up on the past?"

    "He wasn't at her memorial service." (Only saw Lana, ward-of-the-state Lana, crying and gibbering with fear because Karin was the smart one and why were her ashes in an urn when all the dummies were still living?)

    "Really? I wouldn't know. Now listen, do you want to get some money back—or a lot of money back?"

64   I wanted to sleep beside him, reach out for a dream fragment of his brother, my sister. I wanted to remember, for a moment, soft rubber tied around my fourteen-year-old arm and the sharp press of an empty needle against a blue, untravelled vein. Karin? Where do I stick this thing? Right in the vein? Or beside it, or under it, or in any part of my arm that is willing? Does the needle have to have heroin in it, or will water from the basement sink give me a rush?

    Couldn't do it—needles belonged to Karin. I watched her, though, and tied her arm when I couldn't stand her bad moods any more. She wore a lingering perfume called Omar's Delight, which she bought from a store on 4th Avenue. She smelled sweet, as I leaned close to watch her perfect aim with the needle.

Personal Response

What aspect of this essay impressed you the most? Is there any particular part of it that struck you as especially painful or poignant?

Questions for Discussion

1. Explain as best you can why Marjorie felt so protective of her older sister Karen. When did Simmins' attitude toward her sister change?

2. Trace the various stages of the relationship between Marjorie and Karen. How does Simmins feel about her sister now, a decade after Karen's death?

3. If you have read Zoë Landale's "Remembering Karen," compare Simmins' memories of Karen with Landale's.

4. In paragraph 48 of Zoë Landale's "Remembering Karen," she writes: "I hated what you did to [our sister Marjorie]." Does Simmins seem to resent Karen's influence on her when she was very young to the same degree that her sister Zoë Landale does?

5. How did Karen's behavior affect Simmins' brother?

SHOOTING AN ELEPHANT

George Orwell

George Orwell is the pseudonym of Eric Blair (1903–1950). Born in Bengal, India, he was brought up in England and educated at Eton. He served five years as a British policeman in Burma, with a growing disgust for the goals and values of British imperialism, before returning to England to become a writer. In 1936, he fought with the Loyalists in the Spanish Civil War. Orwell is best known for Animal Farm *(1945) and* 1984 *(1949), novels that reflect his hatred of totalitarianism and his sympathy for the oppressed. "Shooting an Elephant" is from his book* Shooting an Elephant and Other Essays *(1950).*

In Moulmein, in lower Burma, I was hated by large numbers of people—the only time in my life that I have been important enough for this to happen to me. I was subdivisional police officer of the town, and in an aimless, petty kind of way anti-European feeling was very bitter. No one had the guts to raise a riot, but if a European woman went through the bazaars alone somebody would probably spit betel juice over her dress. As a police officer I was an obvious target and was baited whenever it seemed safe to do so. When a nimble Burman tripped me up on the football field and the referee (another Burman) looked the other way, the crowd yelled with hideous laughter. This happened more than once. In the end the sneering yellow faces of young men that met me everywhere, the insults hooted after me when I was at a safe distance, got badly on my nerves. The young Buddhist priests were the worst of all. There were several thousands of them in the town and none of them seemed to have anything to do except stand on street corners and jeer at Europeans.

All this was perplexing and upsetting. For at that time I had already made up my mind that imperialism was an evil thing and the sooner I chucked up my job and got out of there the better. Theoretically—and secretly, of course—I was all for the Burmese and all against their oppressors, the British. As for the job I was doing, I hated it more bitterly than I can perhaps make clear. In a job like that you see the dirty work of Empire at close quarters. The wretched prisoners huddling in the stinking cages of the lock-ups, the gray, cowed faces of the long-term convicts, the scarred buttocks of the men who had been flogged with bamboos—all these oppressed me with an intolerable sense of guilt. But I could get nothing into perspective. I was young and ill educated and I had had to think out my problems in the utter silence that is imposed on every Englishman in the East. I did not even know that the British Empire is dying, still less did I know that it is a great deal better than the younger empires that are going to supplant it. All I knew was that I was stuck between my hatred of the empire I served and my rage against the evil-spirited little beasts who tried to make my job impossible. With one part of my mind I thought of the British Raj as an unbreakable tyranny, as something clamped down, in *saecula saeculorum,* upon the will of prostrate peoples; with another part I thought that the greatest joy in the world would be to drive a bayonet into a Buddhist priest's guts. Feelings like these are the normal by-products of imperialism; ask any Anglo-Indian official, if you can catch him off duty.

One day something happened which in a roundabout way was enlightening. It was a tiny incident in itself; but it gave me a better glimpse than I had had before of the real nature of imperialism—the real motives for which despotic governments act. Early one morning the sub-inspector at a police station at the other end of the town rang me up on the 'phone and said that an elephant was ravaging the bazaar. Would I please come and do something about it? I did not know what I could do, but I wanted to see what was happening and I got on to a pony and started out. I took my rifle, an old .44 Winchester and much too small to kill an elephant, but I thought the noise might be useful *in terrorem*. Various Burmans stopped me on the way and told me about the elephant's doings. It was not, of course, a wild elephant, but a tame one which had gone "must." It had been chained up, as tame elephants always are when their attack of "must" is due, but on the previous night it had broken its chain and escaped. Its mahout, the only person who could manage it when it was in that state, had set out in pursuit, but had taken the wrong direction and was now twelve hours' journey away, and in the morning the elephant had suddenly reappeared in town. The Burmese population had no weapons and were quite helpless against it. It had already destroyed somebody's bamboo hut, killed a cow and raided some fruit-stalls and devoured the stock; also it had met the municipal rubbish van and, when the driver jumped out and took to his heels, had turned the van over and inflicted violences upon it.

4   The Burmese sub-inspector and some Indian constables were waiting for me in the quarter where the elephant had been seen. It was a very poor quarter, a labyrinth of squalid bamboo huts, thatched with palm-leaf, winding all over a steep hillside. I remember that it was a cloudy, stuffy morning at the beginning of the rains. We began questioning the people as to where the elephant had gone and, as usual, failed to get any definite information. That is invariably the case in

the East; a story always sounds clear enough at a distance, but the nearer you get to the scene of events the vaguer it becomes. Some of the people said that the elephant had gone in one direction, some said that he had gone in another, some professed not even to have heard of any elephant. I had almost made up my mind that the whole story was a pack of lies, when we heard yells a little distance away. There was a loud, scandalized cry of "Go away, child! Go away this instant!" and an old woman with a switch in her hand came round the corner of a hut, violently shooing away a crowd of naked children. Some more women followed, clicking their tongues and exclaiming; evidently there was something that the children ought not to have seen. I rounded the hut and saw a man's dead body sprawling in the mud. He was an Indian, a black Dravidian coolie, almost naked, and he could not have been dead many minutes. The people said that the elephant had come suddenly upon him round the corner of the hut, caught him with its trunk, put its foot on his back and ground him into the earth. This was the rainy season and the ground was soft, and his face had scored a trench a foot deep and a couple of yards long. He was lying on his belly with arms crucified and head sharply twisted on one side. His face was coated with mud, the eyes wide open, the teeth bared and grinning with an expression of unendurable agony. (Never tell me, by the way, that the dead look peaceful. Most of the corpses I have seen looked devilish.) The friction of the great beast's foot had stripped the skin from his back as neatly as one skins a rabbit. As soon as I saw the dead man I sent an orderly to a friend's house nearby to borrow an elephant rifle. I had already sent back the pony, not wanting it to go mad with fright and throw me if it smelt the elephant.

The orderly came back in a few minutes with a rifle and five cartridges, and meanwhile some Burmans had arrived and told us that the elephant was in the paddy fields below, only a few hundred yards away. As I started forward practically the whole population of the quarter flocked out of the houses and followed me. They had seen the rifle and were all shouting excitedly that I was going to shoot the elephant. They had not shown much interest in the elephant when he was merely ravaging their homes, but it was different now that he was going to be shot. It was a bit of fun to them, as it would be to an English crowd; besides they wanted the meat. It made me vaguely uneasy. I had no intention of shooting the elephant—I had merely sent for the rifle to defend myself if necessary—and it is always unnerving to have a crowd following you. I marched down the hill, looking and feeling a fool, with the rifle over my shoulder and an ever-growing army of people jostling at my heels. At the bottom, when you got away from the huts, there was a metalled road and beyond that a miry waste of paddy fields a thousand yards across, not yet ploughed but soggy from the first rains and dotted with coarse grass. The elephant was standing eight yards from the road, his left side toward us. He took not the slightest notice of the crowd's approach. He was tearing up bunches of grass, beating them against his knees to clean them, and stuffing them into his mouth.

I had halted on the road. As soon as I saw the elephant I knew with perfect certainty that I ought not to shoot him. It is a serious matter to shoot a working elephant—it is comparable to destroying a huge and costly piece of machinery—and obviously one ought not to do it if it can possibly be avoided. And at that distance, peacefully eating, the elephant looked no more dangerous than a cow. I thought then and I think now that his attack of "must" was already passing off; in which case he would merely wander harmlessly about until the mahout came back and caught him. Moreover, I did not in the least want to shoot him. I decided that I would watch him for a little while to make sure that he did not turn savage again, and then go home.

But at that moment I glanced round at the crowd that had followed me. It was an immense crowd, two thousand at the least and growing every minute. It blocked the road for a long distance on either side. I looked at the sea of yellow faces above the garish clothes—faces all happy and excited over this bit of fun, all certain that the elephant was going to be shot. They were watching me as they would watch a conjurer about to perform a trick. They did not like me, but with the magical rifle in my hands I was momentarily worth watching. And suddenly I realized that I should have to shoot the elephant after all. The people expected it of me and I had got to do it; I could feel their two thousand wills pressing me forward, irresistibly. And it was at this moment, as I stood there with the rifle in my hands, that I first grasped the hollowness, the futility of the white man's dominion in the East. Here was I, the white man with his gun, standing in front of the unarmed native crowd—seemingly the leading actor of the piece; but in reality I was only an absurd puppet pushed to and fro by the will of those yellow faces behind. I perceived in this moment that when the white man turns tyrant it is his own freedom that he destroys. He becomes a sort of hollow, posing dummy, the conventionalized figure of a sahib. For it is the condition of his rule that he shall spend his life in trying to impress the "natives," and so in every crisis he has got to do what the "natives" expect of him. He wears a mask, and his face grows to fit it. I had got to shoot the elephant. I had committed myself to doing it when I sent for the rifle. A sahib has got to act like a sahib; he has got to appear resolute, to know his own mind and do definite things. To come all that way, rifle in hand, with two thousand people marching at my heels, and then to trail feebly away, having done nothing—no, that was impossible. The crowd would laugh at me. And my whole life, every white man's life in the East, was one long struggle not to be laughed at.

8   But I did not want to shoot the elephant. I watched him beating his bunch of grass against his knees with that preoccupied grandmotherly air that elephants have. It seemed to me that it would be murder to shoot him. At that age I was not squeamish about killing animals, but I had never shot an elephant and never wanted to. (Somehow it always seems worse to kill a *large* animal.) Besides, there was the beast's owner to be considered. Alive, the elephant was worth at least a hundred pounds; dead, he would only be worth the value of his tusks, five pounds, possibly. But I had got to act quickly. I turned to some experienced-looking Burmans who had been there when we arrived, and asked them how the elephant had been behaving. They all said the same thing: he took no notice of you if you left him alone, but he might charge if you went too close to him.

It was perfectly clear to me what I ought to do. I ought to walk up to within, say, twenty-five yards of the elephant and test his behavior. If he charged, I could shoot; if he took no notice of me, it would be safe to leave him until the mahout came back. But also I knew that I was going to do no such thing. I was a poor shot with a rifle and the ground was soft mud into which one would sink at every step. If the elephant charged and I missed him, I should have about as much chance as a toad under a steamroller. But even then I was not thinking particularly of my own skin, only of the watchful yellow faces behind. For at that moment, with the crowd watching me, I was not afraid in the ordinary sense, as I would have been if I had been alone. A white man mustn't be frightened in front of "natives"; and so, in general, he isn't frightened. The sole thought in my mind was that if anything went wrong those two thousand Burmans would see me pursued, caught, trampled on, and reduced to a grinning corpse like that Indian up the hill. And if that happened it was quite probable that some of them would laugh. That would never do. There was only one alternative. I shoved the cartridges into the magazine and lay down on the road to get a better aim.

The crowd grew very still, and a deep, low, happy sigh, as of people who see the theater curtain go up at last, breathed from innumerable throats. They were going to have their bit of fun after all. The rifle was a beautiful German thing with cross-hair sights. I did not then know that in shooting an elephant one would shoot to cut an imaginary bar running from ear-hole to ear-hole. I ought, therefore, as the elephant was sideways on, to have aimed straight at his ear-hole; actually I aimed several inches in front of this, thinking the brain would be further forward.

When I pulled the trigger I did not hear the bang or feel the kick—one never does when a shot goes home—but I heard the devilish roar of glee that went up from the crowd. In that instant, in too short a time, one would have thought, even for the bullet to get there, a mysterious, terrible change had come over the elephant. He neither stirred, nor fell, but every line of his body had altered. He looked suddenly stricken, shrunken, immensely old, as though the frightful impact of the bullet had paralyzed him without knocking him down. At last, after what seemed a long time—it might have been five seconds, I dare say—he sagged flabbily to his knees. His mouth slobbered. An enormous senility seemed to have settled upon him. One could have imagined him thousands of years old. I fired again into the same spot. At the second shot he did not collapse but climbed with desperate slowness to his feet and stood weakly upright, with legs sagging and head drooping. I fired a third time. That was the shot that did for him. You could see the agony of it jolt his whole body and knock the last remnant of strength from his legs. But in falling he seemed for a moment to rise, for as his hind legs collapsed beneath him he seemed to tower upward like a huge rock toppling, his trunk reaching skyward like a tree. He trumpeted, for the first and only time. And then down he came, his belly toward me, with a crash that seemed to shake the ground even where I lay.

I got up. The Burmans were already racing past me across the mud. It was obvious that the elephant would never rise again, but he was not dead. He was breathing very rhythmically with long rattling gasps, his great mound of a side

12

painfully rising and falling. His mouth was wide open—I could see far down into caverns of pale pink throat. I waited a long time for him to die, but his breathing did not weaken. Finally I fired my two remaining shots into the spot where I thought his heart must be. The thick blood welled out of him like red velvet, but still he did not die. His body did not even jerk when the shots hit him, the tortured breathing continued without a pause. He was dying, very slowly and in great agony, but in some world remote from me where not even a bullet could damage him further. I felt that I had got to put an end to that dreadful noise. It seemed dreadful to see the great beast lying there, powerless to move and yet powerless to die, and not even to be able to finish him. I sent back for my small rifle and poured shot after shot into his heart and down his throat. They seemed to make no impression. The tortured gasps continued as steadily as the ticking of a clock.

In the end I could not stand it any longer and went away. I heard later that it took him half an hour to die. Burmans were bringing dahs and baskets even before I left, and I was told they had stripped his body almost to the bones by the afternoon.

Afterward, of course, there were endless discussions about the shooting of the elephant. The owner was furious, but he was only an Indian and could do nothing. Besides, legally I had done the right thing, for a mad elephant has to be killed, like a mad dog, if its owner fails to control it. Among the Europeans opinion was divided. The older men said I was right, the younger men said it was a damn shame to shoot an elephant for killing a coolie, because an elephant was worth more than any damn Coringhee coolie. And afterward I was very glad that the coolie had been killed; it put me legally in the right and it gave me a sufficient pretext for shooting the elephant. I often wondered whether any of the others grasped that I had done it solely to avoid looking a fool.

Personal Response

What do you think of Orwell's shooting the elephant simply to save face? Do you think you would have done the same, under the circumstances?

Questions for Discussion

1. In what way is the shooting of the elephant "enlightening" (paragraph 3) for Orwell?

2. This essay is written from the perspective of a mature writer looking back on something that happened to him many years before. What is Orwell's attitude toward what he did at age 19? Does he attempt to excuse his behavior? Is he sympathetic toward or critical of his "young and ill educated" self (paragraph 2)?

3. What is the British Raj (paragraph 2)? What does Orwell learn about "the nature of imperialism" (paragraph 3)? What evidence of its evils does Orwell give?

4. In paragraph 2, Orwell says he has mixed feelings toward the Burmese. On the one hand, he "was all for the Burmese and all against their oppressors, the British." On the other hand, he "thought that the greatest joy in the world would be to drive a bayonet into a Buddhist priest's guts." Explain why he has these ambivalent feelings.

5. Orwell's essay contains some graphic descriptions of two deaths, the coolie's and the elephant's. Which death does Orwell devote more attention to? Why? What does he mean in his concluding paragraph when he writes, "And afterward I was very glad that the coolie had been killed"?

6. Orwell says in paragraph 8 that he did not want to shoot the elephant. It seemed to him "that it would be murder to shoot him." Why, then, does Orwell shoot the elephant? Explain as fully as possible the dilemma of the situation Orwell finds himself in.

THE LESSON

Toni Cade Bambara

Toni Cade Bambara grew up in Harlem and in Bedford Stuyvesant, New York City, and earned degrees from Queens College and City College of New York. After graduating, she worked as a welfare investigator, community organizer, and freelance writer. Her books include Tales and Stories of Black Folks *(1971); two collections of short stories,* Gorilla, My Love *(1972) and* The Sea Birds Are Still Alive *(1977); and the novel* The Salt Eaters *(1980). "The Lesson" is from* Gorilla, My Love.

Back in the days when everyone was old and stupid or young and foolish and me and Sugar were the only ones just right, this lady moved on our block with nappy hair and proper speech and no makeup. And quite naturally we laughed at her, laughed the way we did at the junk man who went about his business like he was some big-time president and his sorry-ass horse his secretary. And we kinda hated her too, hated the way we did the winos who cluttered up our parks and pissed on our handball walls and stank up our hallways and stairs so you couldn't halfway play hide-and-seek without a goddamn gas mask. Miss Moore was her name. The only woman on the block with no first name. And she was black as hell, cept for her feet, which were fish-white and spooky. And she was always planning these boring-ass things for us to do, us being my cousin, mostly, who lived on the block cause we all moved North the same time and to the same apartment then spread out gradual to breathe. And our parents would yank our heads into some kinda shape and crisp up our clothes so we'd be presentable for travel with Miss Moore, who always looked like she was going to church, though she never did. Which is just one of things the grownups talked about when they talked behind her back like a dog. But when she came calling with some sachet she'd sewed up or some gingerbread she'd made or some book, why then they'd all be too embarrassed to turn her down and we'd get handed over all spruced up. She'd been to college and said it was only right that she should take responsibility for the young ones' education, and she not even related by marriage or blood. So they'd go for it. Specially Aunt Gretchen. She was the main gofer in the family. You got some ole dumb shit foolishness you want somebody to go for, you send for Aunt Gretchen She been screwed into the go-along for so long, it's a blood-deep natural thing with her. Which is how she got saddled with me and Sugar and Junior in the first place while our mothers were in a la-de-da apartment up the block having a good ole time.

So this one day Miss Moore rounds us all up at the mailbox and it's puredee hot and she's knockin herself out about arithmetic. And school suppose to let up in summer I heard, but she don't never let up. And the starch in my pinafore scratching the shit outta me and I'm really hating this nappy-head bitch and her goddamn college degree. I'd much rather go to the pool or to the show where it's cool. So me and Sugar leaning on the mailbox being surly, which is a Miss Moore word. And Flyboy checking out what everybody brought for lunch. And Fat Butt already wasting his peanut-butter-and-jelly sandwich like the pig he is. And Junebug punchin on Q.T.'s arm for potato chips. And Rosie Giraffe shifting from one hip to the other waiting for somebody to step on her foot or ask her if she from Georgia so she can kick ass, preferably Mercedes'. And Miss Moore asking us do we know what money is, like we a bunch of retards. I mean real money, she say, like it's only poker chips or monopoly papers we lay on the grocer. So right away I'm tired of this and say so. And would much rather snatch Sugar and go to the Sunset and terrorize the West Indian kids and take their hair ribbons and their money too. And Miss Moore files that remark away for next week's lesson on brotherhood, I can tell. And finally I say we oughta get to the subway cause it's cooler and besides we might meet some cute boys. Sugar done swiped her mama's lipstick, so we ready.

So we heading down the street and she's boring us silly about what things cost and what our parents make and how much goes for rent and how money ain't divided up right in this country. And then she gets to the part about we all poor and live in the slums, which I don't feature. And I'm ready to speak on that, but she steps out in the street and hails two cabs just like that. Then she hustles half the crew in with her and hands me a five-dollar bill and tells me to calculate 10 percent tip for the driver. And we're off. Me and Sugar and Junebug and Flyboy hangin out the window and hollering to everybody, putting lipstick on each other cause Flyboy a faggot anyway, and making farts with our sweaty armpits. But I'm mostly trying to figure how to spend this money. But they all fascinated with the meter ticking and Junebug starts laying bets as to how much it'll read when Flyboy can't hold his breath no more. Then Sugar lays bets as to how much it'll be when we get there. So I'm stuck. Don't nobody want to go for my plan, which is to jump out at the next light and run off to the first bar-b-que we can find. Then the driver tells us to get the hell out cause we there already. And the meter reads eight-five cents. And I'm stalling to figure out the tip and Sugar say give him a dime. And I decide he don't need it bad as I do, so later for him. But then he tries to take off with Junebug foot still in the door so we talk about his mama something ferocious. Then we check out that we on Fifth Avenue and everybody dressed up in stockings. One lady in a fur coat, hot as it is. White folks crazy.

4   "This is the place," Miss Moore say, presenting it to us in the voice she uses at the museum. "Let's look in the windows before we go in."

"Can we steal?" Sugar asks very serious like she's getting the ground rules squared away before she plays. "I beg your pardon," say Miss Moore, and we fall out. So she leads us around the windows of the toy store and me and Sugar screamin, "This is mine, that's mine, I gotta have that, that was made for me, I was born for that," till Big Butt drowns us out.

"Hey, I'm goin to buy that there."

"That there? You don't even know what it is, stupid."

8   "I do so," he say punchin on Rosie Giraffe. "It's a microscope."

"Whatcha gonna do with a microscope, fool?"

"Look at things."

"Like what, Ronald?" ask Miss Moore. And Big Butt ain't got the first notion. So here go Miss Moore gabbing about the thousands of bacteria in a drop of water and the somethinorother in a speck of blood and the million and one living things in the air around us is invisible to the naked eye. And what she say that for? Junebug go to town on that "naked" and we rolling. Then Miss Moore ask what it cost. So we all jam into the window smudgin it up and the price tag say $300. So then she ask how long'd take for Big Butt and Junebug to save up their allowances. "Too long," I say. "Yeh," adds Sugar, "outgrown it by that time." And Miss Moore say no, you never outgrow learning instruments. "Why, even medical students and interns and," blah, blah, blah. And we ready to choke Big Butt for bringing it up in the first damn place.

12   "This here costs four hundred eighty dollars," say Rosie Giraffe. So we pile up all over her to see what she pointin out. My eyes tell me it's a chunk of glass cracked with something heavy, and different-color inks dripped into the splits, then the whole thing put into a oven or something. But for $480 it don't make sense.

"That's a paperweight made of semi-precious stones fused together under tremendous pressure," she explains slowly, with her hands doing the mining and all the factory work.

"So what's a paperweight?" asks Rosie Giraffe.

"To weigh paper with, dumbbell," say Flyboy, the wise man from the East.

16   "Not exactly," say Miss Moore, which is what she say when you warm or way off too. "It's to weigh paper down so it won't scatter and make your desk untidy." So right away me and Sugar curtsy to each other and then to Mercedes who is more the tidy type.

"We don't keep paper on top of the desk in my class," say Junebug, figuring Miss Moore crazy or lyin one.

"At home, then," she say. "Don't you have a calendar and a pencil case and a blotter and a letter-opener on your desk at home where you do your homework?"

And she know damn well what our homes look like cause she nosys around in them every chance she gets.

"I don't even have a desk," say Junebug. "Do we?"

20   "No. And I don't get no homework neither," say Big Butt.

"And I don't even have a home," say Flyboy like he do at school to keep the white folks off his back and sorry for him. Send this poor kid to camp posters, is his specialty.

"I do," says Mercedes. "I have a box of stationery on my desk and a picture of my cat. My godmother bought the stationery and the desk. There's a big rose on each sheet and the envelopes smell like roses."

"Who wants to know about your smelly-ass stationery," say Rosie Giraffe fore I can get my two cents in.

24   "It's important to have a work area all your own so that . . . "

"Will you look at this sailboat, please," say Flyboy, cuttin her off and pointin to the thing like it was his. So once again we tumble all over each other to gaze at this magnificent thing in the toy store which is just big enough to maybe sail two kittens across the pond if you strap them to the posts tight. We all start reciting the price tag like we in assembly. "Handcrafted sailboat of fiberglass at one thousand one hundred ninety-five dollars."

"Unbelievable," I hear myself say and am really stunned. I read it again for myself just in case the group recitation put me in a trance. Same thing. For some reason this pisses me off. We look at Miss Moore and she lookin at us, waiting for I dunno what.

"'Who'd pay all that when you can buy a sailboat set for a quarter at Pop's, a tube of glue for a dime, and a ball of string for eight cents? I must have a motor and a whole lot else besides," I say. "My sailboat cost me about fifty cents."

28   "But will it take water?" say Mercedes with her smart ass.

"Took mine to Alley Pond Park once," say Flyboy. "String broke, Lost it. Pity."

"Sailed mine in Central Park and it keeled over and sank. Had to ask my father for another dollar."

"And you got the strap," laugh Big Butt. "The jerk didn't even have a string on it. My old man wailed on his behind."

32   Little Q.T. was staring hard at the sailboat and you could see he wanted it bad. But he too little and somebody'd just take it from him. So what the hell. "This boat for kids, Miss Moore?"

"Parents silly to buy something like that just to get all broke up," say Rosie Giraffe.

"That much money it should last forever," I figure.

"My father'd buy it for me if I wanted it."

36   "Your father, my ass," say Rosie Giraffe getting a chance to finally push Mercedes.

"Must be rich people shop here," say Q.T.

"You are a very bright boy," say Flyboy. "What was your first clue?" And he rap him on the head with the back of his knuckles, since Q.T. the only one he could get away with. Though Q.T. liable to come up behind you years later and get his licks in when you half expect it.

"What I want to know is," I says to Miss Moore though I never talk to her, I wouldn't give the bitch that satisfaction, "is how much a real boat costs? I figure a thousand'd get you a yacht any day."

40   "Why don't you check that out," she says, "and report back to the group?" Which really pains my ass. If you gonna mess up a perfectly good swim day least you could do is have some answers. "Let's go in," she say like she got something up her sleeve. Only she don't lead the way. So me and Sugar turn the corner to where the entrance is, but when we get there I kinda hang back. Not that I'm scared, what's there to be afraid of, just a toy store. But I feel funny, shame. But what I got to be shamed about? Got as much right to go in as anybody. But somehow I can't seem to get hold of the door, so I step away for Sugar to lead. But she hangs back too. And I look at her and she looks at me and this is ridiculous. I mean, damn, I have never ever been shy about doing nothing or going nowhere. But then Mercedes steps up and then Rosie Giraffe and Big Butt crowd in behind and shove, and next thing we all stuffed into the doorway with only Mercedes squeezing past us, smoothing out her jumper and walking right down the aisle. Then the rest of us tumble in like a glued-together jigsaw done all wrong. And people lookin at us. And it's like the time me and Sugar crashed into the Catholic church on a dare. But once we got in there and everything so hushed and holy and the candles and the bowin and the handkerchiefs on all the drooping heads, I just couldn't go through with the plan. Which was for me to run up to the altar and do a tap dance while Sugar played the nose flute and messed around in the holy water. And Sugar kept givin me the elbow. Then later teased me so bad I tied her up in the shower and turned it on and locked her in. And she'd be there till this day if Aunt Gretchen hadn't finally figured I was lyin about the boarder takin a shower.

Same thing in the store. We all walkin on tiptoe and hardly touchin the games and puzzles and things. And I watched Miss Moore who is steady watchin us like she waitin for a sign. Like Mama Drewery watches the sky and sniffs the air and takes note of just how much slant is in the bird formation. Then me and Sugar bump smack into each other, so busy gazing at the toys, 'specially the sailboat. But we don't laugh and go into our fat-lady bump-stomach routine. We just stare at that price tag. Then Sugar run a finger over the whole boat. And I'm jealous and want to hit her. Maybe not her, but I sure want to punch somebody in the mouth.

"Watcha bring us here for, Miss Moore?"

"You sound angry, Sylvia. Are you mad about something?" Givin me one of them grins like she tellin a grown-up joke that never turns out to be funny. And she's lookin very closely at me like maybe she plannin to do my portrait from memory. I'm mad, but I won't give her that satisfaction. So I slouch around the store bein very bored and say, "Let's go."

44   Me and Sugar at the back of the train watchin the tracks whizzin by large then small then gettin gobbled up in the dark. I'm thinking about this tricky toy

I saw in the store. A clown that somersaults on a bar then does chin-ups just cause you yank lightly as his leg. Cost $35. I could see me askin my mother for a $35 birthday clown. "You wanna who that costs what?" she'd say, cocking her head to the side to get a better view of the hole in my head. Thirty-five dollars could buy new bunk beds for Junior and Gretchen's boy. Thirty-five dollars and the whole household could go visit Granddaddy Nelson in the country. Thirty-five dollars would pay for the rent and the piano bill too. Who are these people that spend that much for performing clowns and $1,000 for toy sailboats? What kinda work they do and how they live and how come we ain't in on it? Where we are is who we are, Miss Moore always pointin out. But it don't necessarily have to be that way, she always adds then waits for somebody to say that poor people have to wake up and demand their share of the pie and don't none of us know what kind of pie she talkin about in the first damn place. But she ain't so smart cause I still got her four dollars from the taxi and she sure ain't gettin it. Messin up my day with this shit. Sugar nudges me in my pocket and winks.

Miss Moore lines us up in front of the mailbox where we started from, seem like years ago, and I got a headache for thinkin so hard. And we lean all over each other so we can hold up under the draggy-ass lecture she always finishes us off with at the end before we thank her for borin us to tears. But she just looks at us like she readin tea leaves. Finally she say, "Well, what did you think of F.A.O. Schwartz?"

Rosie Giraffe mumbles, "White folks crazy."

"I'd like to go there again when I get my birthday money," says Mercedes, and we shove her out the pack so she has to lean on the mailbox by herself.

48   "I'd like a shower. Tiring day," say Flyboy.

Then Sugar surprises me by sayin, "You know, Miss Moore, I don't think all of us here put together eat in a year what that sailboat costs." And Miss Moore lights up like somebody goosed her. "And?" she say, urging Sugar on. Only I'm standin on her foot so she don't continue.

"Imagine for a minute what kind of society it is in which some people can spend on a toy what it would cost to feed a family of six or seven. What do you think?"

"I think," says Sugar pushing me off her feet like she never done before, cause I whip her ass in a minute, "that this is not much of a democracy if you ask me. Equal chance to pursue happiness means an equal crack at the dough, don't it?" Miss Moore is besides herself and I am disgusted with Sugar's treachery. So I stand on her foot one more time to see if she'll shove me. She shuts up, and Miss Moore looks at me, sorrowfully I'm thinkin. And somethin weird is going on, I can feel it in my chest.

52   "Anybody else learn anything today?" lookin dead at me. I walk away and Sugar has to run to catch up and don't even seem to notice when I shrug her arm off my shoulder.

"Well, we got four dollars anyway," she says.

"Uh hunh."

"We could go to Hascombs and get half a chocolate layer and then go to the Sunset and still have plenty money for potato chips and ice-cream sodas."

"Uh hunh."

56

"Race you to Hascombs," she say.

We start down the block and she gets ahead which is O.K. by me cause I'm going to the West End and then over to the Drive to think this day through. She can run if she want to and even run faster. But ain't nobody gonna beat me at nuthin.

Personal Response

What is your response to Sylvia's language? Does her language influence the way you view her?

Questions for Discussion

1. Discuss Sylvia's character. What does her very first sentence reveal about her, for instance? What does her running commentary on Miss Moore, their field trip, and the other children indicate about her? What do you think of the behavior of the rest of the children?

2. What is the lesson that Miss Moore wants to teach the children? Do the children learn what she wants them to? Could she have taught them the same lesson without taking them to the toy store?

3. Discuss the character of Miss Moore. What difference does it make that she is not from the neighborhood? How do you think she views the children, their parents, and the neighborhood?

4. Note Sylvia's mounting anger from the moment the children enter the toy store. What is she angry about?

5. What, if anything, does Sylvia learn? What does she mean by her concluding statement, "Ain't nobody gonna beat me at nuthin"?

Suggestions for Writing About INSIGHTS

1. Tell about an occasion on which you experienced "the resolving kind of click" Frank Conroy writes of in "Think About It."

2. If you have ever met someone famous, as Frank Conroy did, write an essay about the experience, including what you learned from that person.

3. With Pat Mora's "To Gabriela, a Young Writer" and Amy Tan's "Mother Tongue" in mind, write a paper analyzing your own writing, including what

you have learned about the writing process and how you apply it in your own work.

4. Do an analysis of Amy Tan's "Mother Tongue" and Toni Cade Bambara's "The Lesson," specifically focusing on what they say or imply about the power of language and its potential to limit or enhance one's opportunities in life.

5. Drawing on Zoë Landale's "Remembering Karen" and Marjorie Simmins' "Trips from There to Here," narrate an account of your own experience, or that of someone you know, with drug use or abuse. Or, explain the effects of drug use or alcoholism on your own family or friends.

6. Write a letter to either Zoë Landale or Marjorie Simmins in which you respond to her essay about her sister.

7. Write an essay analyzing the degree to which alcohol or drug abuse is a problem in the high school you attended or in your community.

8. Drawing on Frank Conroy's "Think About It," Toni Cade Bambara's "The Lesson," and your own experiences, define education.

9. In the manner of George Orwell's "Shooting an Elephant," describe an event or incident that happened many years ago and about which you have different feelings now. Tell what you did then and explain your view of it now.

10. Like George Orwell in "Shooting an Elephant," narrate an incident in which you did something you thought was wrong because you did not want to look foolish or lose face in front of others. Describe not only what you did but also your feelings after the incident.

11. If you have ever made a decision to do something at a time when other people thought it was inappropriate, write an essay telling what the decision was, why you made it, and whether you now think it was the right thing to do.

12. Write an analysis of Toni Cade Bambara's "The Lesson" in terms of what it suggests about the contrast between wealth and poverty in American society. Conclude by stating your own views on that contrast.

13. Do an analysis of the insights described in the selections in this chapter. What do they have in common? Taken as a whole, does any specific definition of "insight" or "lesson" or "self-knowledge" emerge from the selections?

14. Narrate an incident or event that taught you something about yourself, about another person (such as an authority figure, a parent, a relative, or a friend), or about an institution or organization (such as the police, a school, a church, or a club).

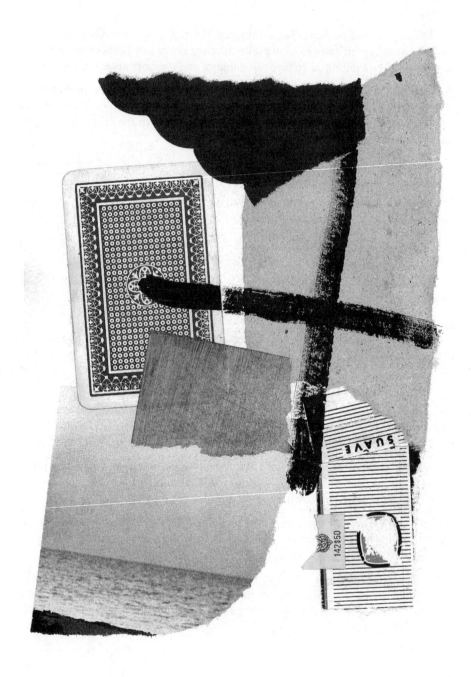

CHAPTER 3

SELF-PERCEPTION

How we perceive ourselves is influenced by a number of factors. Often much of the image we project reflects a perception of ourselves that is strongly tied to the expectations of others rather than to a clear understanding or acceptance of ourselves. Thus, a discussion of self-perception must usually include a consideration of self-knowledge and self-identity as well, for the way we see ourselves is strongly linked with how well we know ourselves. Many of the writers in this section discuss the profound influence of the ways in which others see us on self-image. If their perceptions are rooted in stereotypes based on our ethnic or cultural background, socioeconomic level, difference from the norm, or physical ability, then we may have a tremendous struggle with self-image, as some of the selections demonstrate.

In "You're Short, Besides!" Sucheng Chan explains the obstacles she had to overcome because of her physical handicap as well as her ethnic background. Like Chan, Nancy Mairs in "On Being a Cripple" describes the problems she faces in her struggle with a chronic debilitating illness. Noel Perrin's "The Androgynous Male" explains his perception of himself in terms of the ways in which he does not meet traditional sex-role expectations for men in American society. Brent Staples in "Just Walk on By: A Black Man Ponders His Power to Alter Public Space" also addresses the matter of America's definition of manhood, but he is more interested in the way in which his skin color alone affects the behavior of people around him.

Like Staples, three other writers in this chapter address the matter of skin color and its effect on self-perception. In "Race Without Face," Edward Iwata explains that his "hatred of Oriental facial features" and his "desire to do well in a white world" led him to resort to cosmetic surgery in an effort to create a new face. Similarly, Richard Rodriguez in "Complexion" explores the subject of skin color in terms of his family's experiences, their perception of him, and the effects of his skin color on others. What Edward Iwata says of Asian Americans could certainly apply in a broad sense to all of us: to be true to ourselves means refusing to conform to stereotypes and instead defining our own personalities and images. Zora Neale Hurston in "How It Feels to Be Colored Me" indicates that she has refused to conform and has forged her own identity. On the subject of skin color, her tone is different from that of Staples, Iwata, and Rodriguez. Hurston's essay is a powerful tribute to her strong sense of self and to her conviction that skin color is finally not as important as other characteristics that influence how others perceive us.

The chapter ends with the story of someone who has a positive perception not only of herself and her ethnic background but also of her religion. Grace Paley's "The Loudest Voice" portrays a fictional Jewish girl's confident exuberance as she reads the narrative of an elementary school Christmas pageant, more mindful of her pride in being selected for her loudest voice than she is of the controversy over Jewish children taking part in a Christian event.

YOU'RE SHORT, BESIDES!

Sucheng Chan

Sucheng Chan is professor of history and director of Asian-American Studies at the University of California, Santa Barbara. She is the author of three books, The Bittersweet Soil: The Chinese in California Agriculture, 1860–1910, *which won three awards;* Asian Californians; *and* Asian Americans: An Interpretive History. *She has also edited four books and written dozens of articles. This 1989 essay is from* Making Waves: An Anthology of Writings By and About Asian American Women.

When asked to write about being a physically handicapped Asian American woman, I considered it an insult. After all, my accomplishments are many, yet I was not asked to write about any of them. Is being handicapped the most salient feature about me? The fact that it might be in the eyes of others made me decide to write the essay as requested. I realized that the way I think about myself may differ considerably from the way others perceive me. And maybe that's what being physically handicapped is all about.

I was stricken simultaneously with pneumonia and polio at the age of four. Uncertain whether I had polio of the lungs, seven of the eight doctors who attended me—all practitioners of Western medicine—told my parents they should not feel optimistic about my survival. A Chinese fortune teller my mother consulted also gave a grim prognosis, but for an entirely different reason: I had been stricken because my name was offensive to the gods. My grandmother had named me "grandchild of wisdom," a name that the fortune teller said was too presumptuous for a girl. So he advised my parents to change my name to "chaste virgin." All these pessimistic predictions notwithstanding, I hung onto life, if only by a thread. For three years, my body was periodically pierced with electric shocks as the muscles of my legs atrophied. Before my illness, I had been an active, rambunctious, precocious, and very curious child. Being confined to bed was thus a mental agony as great as my physical pain. Living in war-torn China, I received little medical attention; physical therapy was unheard of. But I was determined to walk. So one day, when I was six or seven, I instructed my mother to set up two rows of chairs to face each other so that I could use them as I would parallel bars. I attempted to walk by holding my body up and moving it forward with my arms while dragging my legs along behind. Each time I fell, my mother gasped, but I badgered her until she let me try again. After four nonambulatory years, I finally walked once more by pressing my hands against my thighs so my knees wouldn't buckle.

My father had been away from home during most of those years because of the war. When he returned, I had to confront the guilt he felt about my condition. In many East Asian cultures, there is a strong folk belief that a person's physical state in this life is a reflection of how morally or sinfully he or she lived in previous lives. Furthermore, because of the tendency to view the family as a single unit, it is believed that the fate of one member can be caused by the behavior of another. Some of my father's relatives told him that my illness had doubtless been caused by the wild carousing he did in his youth. A well-meaning but somewhat simple man, my father believed them.

4

Throughout my childhood, he sometimes apologized to me for having to suffer retribution for his former bad behavior. This upset me; it was bad enough that I had to deal with the anguish of not being able to walk, but to have to assuage his guilt as well was a real burden! In other ways, my father was very good to me. He took me out often, carrying me on his shoulders or back, to give me fresh air and sunshine. He did this until I was too large and heavy for him to carry. And ever since I can remember, he has told me that I am pretty.

After getting over her anxieties about by constant falls, my mother decided to send me to school. I had already learned to read some words of Chinese at the age of three by asking my parents to teach me the sounds and meaning of various characters in the daily newspaper. But between the ages of four and eight, I received no education since just staying alive was a full-time job. Much to her chagrin, my mother found no school in Shanghai, where we lived at the time, which would accept me as a student. Finally, as a last resort, she approached the American School which agreed to enroll me only if my family kept an *amah* (a servant who takes care of children) by my side at all times. The tuition at the school was twenty U.S. dollars per month—a huge sum of money during those years of runaway inflation in China—and payable only in U.S. dollars. My family afforded the high cost of tuition and the expense of employing a full-time *amah* for less than a year.

We left China as the Communist forces swept across the country in victory. We found an apartment in Hong Kong across the street from a school run by Seventh-Day Adventists. By that time I could walk a little, so the principal was persuaded to accept me. An *amah* now had to take care of me only during recess when my classmates might easily knock me over as they ran about the playground.

After a year and a half in Hong Kong, we moved to Malaysia, where my father's family had lived for four generations. There I learned to swim in the lovely warm waters of the tropics and fell in love with the sea. On land I was a cripple; in the ocean I could move with the grace of a fish. I liked the freedom of being in the water so much that many years later, when I was a graduate student in Hawaii,

I became greatly enamored with a man just because he called me a "Polynesian water nymph."

8   As my overall health improved, my mother became less anxious about all aspects of my life. She did everything possible to enable me to lead as normal a life as possible. I remember how once some of her colleagues in the high school where she taught criticized her for letting me wear short skirts. They felt my legs should not be exposed to public view. My mother's response was, "All girls her age wear short skirts, so why shouldn't she?"

The years in Malaysia were the happiest of my childhood, even though I was constantly fending off children who ran after me calling, *"Baikah! Baikah!"* ("Cripple! Cripple!" in the Hokkien dialect commonly spoken in Malaysia). The taunts of children mattered little because I was a star pupil. I won one award after another for general scholarship as well as for art and public speaking. Whenever the school had important visitors my teacher always called on me to recite in front of the class.

A significant event that marked me indelibly occurred when I was twelve. That year my school held a music recital and I was one of the students chosen to play the piano. I managed to get up the steps to the stage without any problem, but as I walked across the stage, I fell. Out of the audience, a voice said loudly and clearly, "Ayah! A *baikah* shouldn't be allowed to perform in public." I got up before anyone could get on stage to help me and, with tears streaming uncontrollably down my face, I rushed to the piano and began to play. Beethoven's "Für Elise" had never been played so fiendishly fast before or since, but I managed to finish the whole piece. That I managed to do so made me feel really strong. I never again feared ridicule.

In later years I was reminded of this experience from time to time. During my fourth year as an assistant professor at the University of California at Berkeley, I won a distinguished teaching award. Some weeks later I ran into a former professor who congratulated me enthusiastically. But I said to him, "You know what? I became a distinguished teacher by *limping* across the stage of Dwinelle 155!" (Dwinelle 155 is a large, cold classroom that most colleagues of mine hate to teach in.) I was rude not because I lacked graciousness but because this man, who had told me that my dissertation was the finest piece of work he had read in fifteen years, had nevertheless advised me to eschew a teaching career.

12   "Why?" I asked.

"Your leg . . ." he responded.

"What about my leg?" I said, puzzled.

"Well, how would you feel standing in front of a large lecture class?"

16   "If it makes any difference, I want you to know I've won a number of speech contests in my life, and I am not the least bit self-conscious about speaking in front of large audiences. . . . Look, why don't you write me a letter of recommendation to tell people how brilliant I am, and let *me* worry about my leg!"

This incident is worth recounting only because it illustrates a dilemma that handicapped persons face frequently: those who care about us sometimes get so protective that they unwittingly limit our growth. This former professor of mine had been one of my greatest supporters for two decades. Time after time, he had written glowing letters of recommendation on my behalf. He had spoken as he did because he thought he had my best interests at heart; he thought that if I got a desk job rather than one that required me to be a visible, public person, I would be spared the misery of being stared at.

Americans, for the most part, do not believe as Asians do that physically handicapped persons are morally flawed. But they are equally inept at interacting with those of us who are not able-bodied. Cultural differences in the perception and treatment of handicapped people are most clearly expressed by adults. Children, regardless of where they are, tend to be openly curious about people who do not look "normal." Adults in Asia have no hesitation in asking visibly handicapped people what is wrong with them, often expressing their sympathy with looks of pity, whereas adults in the United States try desperately to be polite by pretending not to notice.

One interesting response I often elicited from people in Asia but have never encountered in America is the attempt to link my physical condition to the state of my soul. Many a time while living and traveling in Asia people would ask me what religion I belonged to. I would tell them that my mother is a devout Buddhist, that my father was baptized a Catholic but has never practiced Catholicism, and that I am an agnostic. Upon hearing this, people would try strenuously to convert me to their religion so that whichever God they believed in could bless me. If I would only attend this church or that temple regularly, they urged, I would surely get cured. Catholics and Buddhists alike have pressed religious medallions into my palm, telling me if I would wear these, the relevant deity or saint would make me well. Once while visiting the tomb of Muhammad Ali Jinnah in Karachi, Pakistan, an old Muslim, after finishing his evening prayers, spotted me, gestured toward my legs, raised his arms heavenward, and began a new round of prayers, apparently on my behalf.

20 In the United States adults who try to act "civilized" towards handicapped people by pretending they don't notice anything unusual sometimes end up ignoring handicapped people completely. In the first few months I lived in this country, I was struck by the fact that whenever children asked me what was the matter with my leg, their adult companions would hurriedly shush them up, furtively look at me, mumble apologies, and rush their children away. After a few months of such encounters, I decided it was my responsibility to educate these people. So I would say to the flustered adults, "It's okay, let the kid ask." Turning to the child, I would say, "When I was a little girl, no bigger than you are, I became sick with something called polio. The muscles in my leg shrank up and I couldn't walk very well. You're much luckier than I am because now you can get a vaccine to make sure you never get my disease. So don't cry when your mommy takes you to get a polio vaccine, okay?" Some adults and their little companions I talked to this way were glad to be rescued from embarrassment; others thought I was strange.

Americans have another way of covering up their uneasiness: they become jovially patronizing. Sometimes when people spot my crutch, they ask if I've had a skiing accident. When I answer that unfortunately it is something less glamorous than that, they say, "I bet you *could* ski if you put your mind to it!" Alternately, at parties where people dance, men who ask me to dance with them get almost belligerent when I decline their invitation. They say, "Of course you can dance if you *want* to!" Some have given me pep talks about how if I would only develop the right mental attitude, I would have more fun in life.

Different cultural attitudes toward handicapped persons came out clearly during my wedding. My father-in-law, as solid a representative of middle America as could be found, had no qualms about objecting to the marriage on racial grounds, but he could bring himself to comment on my handicap only indirectly. He wondered why his son, who had dated numerous high school and college beauty queens, couldn't marry one of them instead of me. My mother-in-law, a devout Christian, did not share her husband's prejudices, but she worried aloud about whether I could have children. Some Chinese friends of my parents, on the other hand, said that I was lucky to have found such a noble man, one who would marry me despite my handicap. I, for my part, appeared in church in a white lace wedding dress I had designed and made myself—a miniskirt!

How Asian Americans treat me with respect to my handicap tells me a great deal about their degree of acculturation. Recent immigrants behave just like Asians in Asia; those who have been here longer or who grew up in the United States behave more like their white counterparts. I have not encountered any distinctly Asian American pattern of response. What makes the experience of Asian American handicapped people unique is the duality of responses we elicit.

24 Regardless of racial or cultural background, most handicapped people have to learn to find a balance between the desire to attain physical independence and the need to take care of ourselves by not overtaxing our bodies. In my case, I've had to learn to accept the fact that leading an active life has its price. Between the ages of eight and eighteen, I walked without using crutches or braces but the effort caused my right leg to become badly misaligned. Soon after I came to the United States, I had a series of operations to straighten out the bones of my right leg; afterwards though my leg looked straighter and presumably better, I could no longer walk on my own. Initially my doctors fitted me with a brace, but I found wearing one cumbersome and soon gave it up. I could move around much more easily—and more important, faster—by using one crutch. One orthopedist after another warned me that using a single crutch was a bad practice. They were right. Over the years my spine developed a double-S curve and for the last twenty years I have suffered from severe, chronic back pains, which neither conventional physical therapy nor a lighter work load can eliminate.

The only thing that helps my backaches is a good massage, but the soothing effect lasts no more than a day or two. Massages are expensive, especially when one needs them three times a week. So I found a job that pays better, but at which I have to work longer hours, consequently increasing the physical strain on my body—a sort of vicious circle. When I was in my thirties, my doctors told me that if I kept leading the strenuous life I did, I would be in a wheelchair by the time I was forty. They were right on target: I bought myself a wheelchair when I was forty-one. But being the incorrigible character that I am, I use it only when I am *not* in a hurry!

It is a good thing, however, that I am too busy to think much about my handicap or my backaches because pain can physically debilitate as well as cause depression. And there are days when my spirits get rather low. What has helped me is realizing that being handicapped is akin to growing old at an accelerated rate. The contradiction I experience is that often my mind races along as though I'm only twenty while my body feels about sixty. But fifteen or twenty years hence, unlike my peers who will have to cope with aging for the first time, I shall be full of cheer because I will have already fought, and I hope won, that battle long ago.

Beyond learning how to be physically independent and, for some of us, living with chronic pain or other kinds of discomfort, the most difficult thing a handicapped person has to deal with, especially during puberty and early adulthood, is relating to potential sexual partners. Because American culture places so much emphasis on physical attractiveness, a person with a shriveled limb, or a tilt to the head, or the inability to speak clearly, experiences great uncertainty—indeed trauma—when interacting with someone to whom he or she is attracted. My problem was that I was not only physically handicapped, small, and short, but worse, I also wore glasses and was smarter than all the boys I knew! Alas, an insurmountable combination. Yet somehow I have managed to have intimate relationships, all of them with extraordinary men. Not surprisingly, there have also been countless men who broke my heart—men who enjoyed my company "as a friend," but who never found the courage to date or make love with me, although I am sure my experience in this regard is no different from that of many able-bodied persons.

28   The day came when my backaches got in the way of having an active sex life. Surprisingly that development was liberating because I stopped worrying about being attractive to men. No matter how headstrong I had been, I, like most women of my generation, had had the desire to be alluring to men ingrained into me. And that longing had always worked like a brake on my behavior. When what men think of me ceased to be compelling, I gained greater freedom to be myself.

I've often wondered if I would have been a different person had I not been physically handicapped. I really don't know, though there is no question that being handicapped has marked me. But at the same time I usually do not *feel* handicapped—and consequently, I do not *act* handicapped. People are therefore less likely to treat me as a handicapped person. There is no doubt, however, that the lives of my parents, sister, husband, other family members, and some close friends have been affected by my physical condition. They have had to learn not to hide me away at home, not to feel embarrassed by how I look or react to people who say silly things to me, and not to resent me for the extra demands my condition makes on them. Perhaps the hardest thing for those who live with handicapped people is to know when and how to offer help. There are no guidelines applicable to all situations. My advice is, when in doubt, ask, but ask, in a way that does not smack of pity or embarrassment. Most important, please don't talk to us as though we are children.

So, has being physically handicapped been a handicap? It all depends on one's attitude. Some years ago, I told a friend that I had once said to an affirmative action compliance officer (somewhat sardonically since I do not believe in the head count approach to affirmative action) that the institution which employs me is triply lucky because it can count me as nonwhite, female and handicapped. He responded, "Why don't you tell them to count you four times? . . . Remember, you're short, besides!"

Personal Response

In the opening paragraph, Chan writes: "I realized that the way I think about myself may differ considerably from the way others perceive me." How do you think others see you? Do you think that others see you differently from the way you see yourself? Explain your answer.

Questions for Discussion

1. Chan devotes much space to contrasting Eastern and Western beliefs, practices, and ways of viewing her. Outline the contrasts she identifies.

2. Characterize Chan's attitude toward herself.

3. Explain what it was about the piano recital when Chan was twelve that was so significant that "it marked [her] indelibly" (paragraph 10). What does that experience tell you about her?

4. Discuss the various obstacles Chan has faced. Which of them are directly related to her handicap? Which of them might anyone, handicapped or not, have to face? How do you think you might face such obstacles if Chan's circumstances were your own?

ON BEING A CRIPPLE

Nancy Mairs

Nancy Mairs was born in California, grew up in New England, and now lives in Tucson, Arizona. A teacher and writer, she has a PhD in English from the University of Arizona and has published an award-winning collection of poems, In All the Rooms of the Yellow House, *and two collections of essays,* Carnal Acts *(1990) and* Plaintext *(1986), from which "On Being a Cripple" is taken.*

To escape is nothing. Not to escape is nothing.
—Louise Bogan

The other day I was thinking of writing an essay on being a cripple. I was thinking hard in one of the stalls of the women's room in my office building, as I was shoving my shirt into my jeans and tugging up my zipper. Preoccupied, I flushed, picked up my book bag, took my cane down from the hook, and unlatched the door. So many movements unbalanced me, and as I pulled the door open I fell over backward, landing fully clothed on the toilet seat with my legs splayed in front of me: the old beetle-on-its-back routine. Saturday afternoon, the building deserted, I was free to laugh aloud as I wriggled back to my feet, my voice bouncing off the yellowish tiles from all directions. Had anyone been there with me, I'd have been still and faint and hot with chagrin. I decided that it was high time to write the essay.

First, the matter of semantics. I am a cripple. I choose this word to name me. I choose from among several possibilities, the most common of which are "handicapped" and "disabled." I made the choice a number of years ago, without thinking, unaware of my motives for doing so. Even now, I'm not sure what those motives are, but I recognize that they are complex and not entirely flattering. People—crippled or not—wince at the word "cripple," as they do not at "handicapped" or "disabled." Perhaps I want them to wince. I want them to see me as a tough customer, one to whom the fates/gods/viruses have not been kind, but who can face the brutal truth of her existence squarely. As a cripple, I swagger.

But, to be fair to myself, a certain amount of honesty underlies my choice. "Cripple" seems to me a clean word, straightforward and precise. It has an honorable history, having made its first appearance in the Lindisfarne Gospel in the tenth century. As a lover of words, I like the accuracy with which it describes my condition: I have lost the full use of my limbs. "Disabled," by contrast, suggests any incapacity, physical or mental. And I certainly don't like "handicapped," which implies that I have deliberately been put at a disadvantage, by whom I can't imagine (my God is not a Handicapper General), in order to equalize chances in the great race of life. These words seem to me to be moving away from my condition, to be widening the gap between word and reality. Most remote is the recently coined euphemism "differently abled," which partakes of the same semantic hopefulness that transformed countries from "undeveloped" to "underdeveloped," then to "less developed," and finally to "developing" nations. People have continued to starve in those countries during the shift. Some realities do not obey the dictates of language.

Mine is one of them. Whatever you call me, I remain crippled. But I don't care what you call me, so long as it isn't "differently abled," which strikes me as pure verbal garbage designed, by its ability to describe anyone, to describe no one. I subscribe to George Orwell's thesis that "the slovenliness of our language makes it easier for us to have foolish thoughts." And I refuse to participate in the degeneration of the language to the extent that I deny that I have lost anything in the course of this calamitous disease; I refuse to pretend that the only differences between you and me are the various ordinary ones that distinguish any one person from another. But call me "disabled" or "handicapped" if you like. I have long since grown accustomed to them; and if they are vague, at least they hint at the truth. Moreover, I use them myself. Society is no readier to accept crippledness than to accept death, war, sex, sweat, or wrinkles. I would never refer to another person as a cripple. It is the word I use to name only myself.

I haven't always been crippled, a fact for which I am soundly grateful. To be whole of limb is, I know from experience, infinitely more pleasant and useful than to be crippled; and if that knowledge leaves me open to bitterness at my loss, the physical soundness I once enjoyed (though I did not enjoy it half enough) is well worth the occasional stab of regret. Though never any good at sports, I was a normally active child and young adult. I climbed trees, played hopscotch, jumped rope, skated, swam, rode my bicycle, sailed. I despised team sports, spending some of the wretchedest afternoons of my life, sweaty and humiliated, behind a field-hockey stick and under a basketball hoop. I tramped alone for miles along the bridle paths that webbed the woods behind the house I grew up in. I swayed through countless dim hours in the arms of one man or another under the scattered shot of light from mirrored balls, and gyrated through countless more as Tab Hunter and Johnny Mathis gave way to the Rolling Stones, Creedence Clearwater Revival, Cream. I walked down the aisle. I pushed baby carriages, changed tires in the rain, marched for peace.

When I was twenty-eight I started to trip and drop things. What at first seemed my natural clumsiness soon became too pronounced to shrug off. I consulted a neurologist, who told me that I had a brain tumor. A battery of tests, increasingly disagreeable, revealed no tumor. About a year and a half later I developed a blurred spot in one eye. I had, at last, the episodes "disseminated in space and time" requisite for a diagnosis: multiple sclerosis. I have never been sorry for the doctor's initial misdiagnosis, however. For almost a week, until the negative results of the tests were in, I thought that I was going to die right away. Every day for the past nearly ten years, then, has been a kind of gift. I accept all gifts.

Multiple sclerosis is a chronic degenerative disease of the central nervous system, in which the myelin that sheathes the nerves is somehow eaten away and scar tissue forms in its place, interrupting the nerves' signals. During its course, which is unpredictable and uncontrollable, one may lose vision, hearing, speech, the ability to walk, control of bladder and/or bowels, strength in any or all extremities, sensitivity to touch, vibration, and/or pain, potency, coordination of movements—the list of possibilities is lengthy and, yes, horrifying. One may also lose one's sense of humor. That's the easiest to lose and the hardest to survive without.

8 In the past ten years, I have sustained some of these losses. Characteristic of MS are sudden attacks, called exacerbations, followed by remissions, and these I have not had. Instead, my disease has been slowly progressive. My left leg is now so weak that I walk with the aid of a brace and a cane; and for distances I use an Amigo, a variation on the electric wheelchair that looks rather like an electrified kiddie car. I no longer have much use of my left hand. Now my right side is weakening as well. I still have the blurred spot in my right eye. Overall, though, I've been lucky so far. My world has, of necessity, been circumscribed by my losses, but the terrain left me has been ample enough for me to continue many of the activities that absorb me: writing, teaching, raising children and cats and plants and snakes, reading, speaking publicly about MS and depression, even playing bridge with people patient and honorable enough to let me scatter cards every which way without sneaking a peek.

Lest I begin to sound like Pollyanna, however, let me say that I don't like having MS. I hate it. My life holds realities—harsh ones, some of them—that no right-minded human being ought to accept without grumbling. One of them is fatigue. I know of no one with MS who does not complain of bone-weariness; in a disease that presents an astonishing variety of symptoms, fatigue seems to be a common factor. I wake up in the morning feeling the way most people do at the end of a bad day, and I take it from there. As a result, I spend a lot of time *in extremis* and, impatient with limitation, I tend to ignore my fatigue until my body breaks down in some way and forces rest. Then I miss picnics, dinner parties, poetry readings, the brief visits of old friends from out of town. The offspring of a puritanical tradition of exceptional venerability, I cannot view these lapses without shame. My life often seems a series of small failures to do as I ought.

I lead, on the whole, an ordinary life, probably rather like the one I would have led had I not had MS. I am lucky that my predilections were already solitary, sedentary, and bookish—unlike the world-famous French cellist I have read about, or the young woman I talked with one long afternoon who wanted only to be a jockey. I had just begun graduate school when I found out something was wrong with me, and I have remained, interminably, a graduate student. Perhaps I would not have if I'd thought I had the stamina to return to a full-time job as a technical editor; but I've enjoyed my studies.

In addition to studying, I teach writing courses. I also teach medical students how to give neurological examinations. I pick up freelance editing jobs here and there. I have raised a foster son and sent him into the world, where he has made me two grandbabies, and I am still escorting my daughter and son through adolescence. I go to Mass every Saturday. I am a superb, if messy, cook. I am also an enthusiastic laundress, capable of sorting a hamper full of clothes into five subtly differentiated piles, but a terrible housekeeper. I can do italic writing and, in an emergency, bathe an oil-soaked cat. I play a fiendish game of Scrabble. When I have the time and the money, I like to sit on my front steps with my husband, drinking Amaretto and smoking a cigar, as we imagine our counterparts in Leningrad and make sure that the sun gets down once more behind the sharp childish scrawl of the Tucson Mountains.

12   This lively plenty has its bleak complement, of course, in all the things I can no longer do. I will never run again, except in dreams, and one day I may have to write that I will never walk again. I like to go camping, but I can't follow George and the children along the trails that wander out of a campsite through the desert or into the mountains. In fact, even on the level I've learned never to check the weather or try to hold a coherent conversation: I need all my attention for my wayward feet. Of late, I have begun to catch myself wondering how people can propel themselves without canes. With only one usable hand, I have to select my clothing with care not so much for style as for ease of ingress and egress, and even so, dressing can be laborious. I can no longer do fine stitchery, pick up babies, play the piano, braid my hair. I am immobilized by acute attacks of depression, which may or may not be physiologically related to MS but are certainly its logical concomitant.

These two elements, the plenty and the privation, are never pure, nor are the delight and wretchedness that accompany them. Almost every pickle that I get into as a result of my weakness and clumsiness—and I get into plenty—is funny as well as maddening and sometimes painful. I recall one May afternoon when a friend and I were going out for a drink after finishing up at school. As we were climbing into opposite sides of my car, chatting, I tripped and fell, flat and hard, onto the asphalt parking lot, my abrupt departure interrupting him in mid-sentence. "Where'd you go?" he called as he came around the back of the car to find me hauling myself up by the door frame. "Are you all right?" Yes, I told him, I was fine, just a bit rattly, and we drove off to find a shady patio and some beer. When I got home an hour or so later, my daughter greeted me with "What have you done to yourself?" I looked down. One elbow of my white turtleneck with the green froggies, one knee of my white trousers, one white kneesock were bloodsoaked. We peeled off the clothes and inspected the damage, which was nasty enough but not alarming. That part wasn't funny: The abrasions took a long time to heal, and one got a little infected. Even so, when I think of my friend talking earnestly, suddenly, to the hot thin air while I dropped from his view as though through a trap door, I find the image as silly as something from a Marx Brothers movie.

I may find it easier than other cripples to amuse myself because I live propped by the acceptance and the assistance and, sometimes, the amusement of those around me. Grocery clerks tear my checks out of my checkbook for me, and sales clerks find chairs to put into dressing rooms when I want to try on clothes. The people I work with make sure I teach at times when I am least likely to be fatigued, in places I can get to, with the materials I need. My students, with one anonymous exception (in an end-of-the-semester evaluation), have been unperturbed by my disability. Some even like it. One was immensely cheered by the information that I paint my own fingernails; she decided, she told me, that if I could go to such trouble over fine details, she could keep on writing essays. I suppose I became some sort of bright-fingered muse. She wrote good essays, too.

The most important struts in the framework of my existence, of course, are my husband and children. Dismayingly few marriages survive the MS test, and why should they? Most twenty-two- and nineteen-year-olds, like George and me, can vow in clear conscience, after a childhood of chickenpox and summer colds, to keep one another in sickness and in health so long as they both shall live. Not many are equipped for catastrophe: the dismay, the depression, the extra work, the boredom that a degenerative disease can insinuate into a relationship. And our society, with its emphasis on fun and its association of fun with physical performance, offers little encouragement for a whole spouse to stay with a crippled partner. Children experience similar stresses when faced with a crippled parent, and they are more helpless, since parents and children can't usually get divorced. They hate, of course, to be different from their peers, and the child whose mother is tacking down the aisle of a school auditorium packed with proud parents like a Cape Cod dinghy in a stiff breeze jolly well stands out in a crowd. Deprived of legal divorce, the child can at least deny the mother's disability, even her existence, forgetting to tell her about recitals and PTA meetings, refusing to accompany her to stores or church or the movies, never inviting friends to the house. Many do.

But I've been limping along for ten years now, and so far George and the children are still at my left elbow, holding tight. Anne and Matthew vacuum floors and dust furniture and haul trash and rake up dog droppings and button my cuffs and bake lasagne and Toll House cookies with just enough grumbling so I know that they don't have brain fever. And far from hiding me, they're forever dragging me by racks of fancy clothes or through teeming school corridors, or welcoming gaggles of friends while I'm wandering through the house in Anne's filmy pink babydoll pajamas. George generally calls before he brings someone home, but he does just as many dumb thankless chores as the children. And they all yell at me, laugh at some of my jokes, write me funny letters when we're apart—in short, treat me as an ordinary human being for whom they have some use. I think they like me. Unless they're faking. . . .

Faking. There's the rub. Tugging at the fringes of my consciousness always is the terror that people are kind to me only because I'm a cripple. My mother almost shattered me once, with that instinct mothers have—blind, I think, in this case, but unerring nonetheless—for striking blows along the fault-lines of their children's hearts, by telling me, in an attack on my selfishness, "We all have to make allowances for you, of course, because of the way you are." From the distance of a couple of years, I have to admit that I haven't any idea just what she meant, and I'm not sure that she knew either. She was awfully angry. But at the time, as the words thudded home, I felt my worst fear, suddenly realized. I could bear being called selfish: I am. But I couldn't bear the corroboration that those around me were doing in fact what I'd always suspected them of doing, professing fondness while silently putting up with me because of the way I am. A cripple. I've been a little cracked ever since.

Along with this fear that people are secretly accepting shoddy goods comes a relentless pressure to please—to prove myself worth the burdens I impose, I guess, or to build a substantial account of goodwill against which I may write drafts in times of need. Part of the pressure arises from social expectations. In our society, anyone who deviates from the norm had better find some way to compensate. Like fat people, who are expected to be jolly, cripples must bear their lot meekly and cheerfully. A grumpy cripple isn't playing by the rules. And much of the pressure is self-generated. Early on I vowed that, if I had to have MS, by God I was going to do it well. This is a class act, ladies and gentlemen. No tears, no recriminations, no faint-heartedness.

One way and another, then, I wind up feeling like Tiny Tim, peering over the edge of the table at the Christmas goose, waving my crutch, piping down God's blessing on us all. Only sometimes I don't want to play Tiny Tim. I'd rather be Caliban, a most scurvy monster. Fortunately, at home no one much cares whether I'm a good cripple or a bad cripple as long as I make vichyssoise with fair regularity. One evening several years ago, Anne was reading at the dining-room table while I cooked dinner. As I opened a can of tomatoes, the can slipped in my left hand and juice spattered me and the counter with bloody spots. Fatigued and infuriated, I bellowed, "I'm so sick of being crippled!" Anne glanced at me over the top of her book. "There now," she said, "do you feel better?" "Yes," I said, "yes, I do." She went back to her reading. I felt better. That's about all the attention my scurviness ever gets.

20   Because I hate being crippled, I sometimes hate myself for being a cripple. Over the years I have come to expect—even accept—attacks of violent self-loathing. Luckily, in general our society no longer connects deformity and disease directly with evil (though a charismatic once told me that I have MS because a devil is in me) and so I'm allowed to move largely at will, even among small children. But I'm not sure that this revision of attitude has been particularly helpful. Physical imperfection, even freed of moral disapprobation, still defies and violates the ideal, especially for women, whose confinement in their bodies as objects of desire is far from over. Each age, of course, has its ideal, and I doubt that ours is any better or worse than any other. Today's ideal woman, who lives on the glossy pages of dozens of magazines, seems to be between the ages of eighteen and twenty-five; her hair has body, her teeth flash white, her breath smells minty, her underarms are dry; she has a career but is still a fabulous cook, especially of meals that take less than twenty minutes to prepare; she does not ordinarily appear to have a husband or children; she is trim and deeply tanned; she jogs, swims, plays tennis, rides a bicycle, sails, but does not bowl; she travels widely, even to out-of-the-way places like Finland and Samoa, always in the company of the ideal man, who possesses a nearly identical set of characteristics. There are a few exceptions. Though usually white and often blonde, she may be black, Hispanic, Asian, or Native American, so long as she is unusually sleek. She may be old, provided she is selling a laxative or is Lauren Bacall. If she is selling a detergent, she may be married and have a flock of strikingly messy children. But she is never a cripple.

Like many women I know, I have always had an uneasy relationship with my body. I was not a popular child, largely, I think now, because I was peculiar: intelligent, intense, moody, shy, given to unexpected actions and inexplicable notions and emotions. But as I entered adolescence, I believed myself unpopular because I was homely: my breasts too flat, my mouth too wide, my hips too narrow, my clothing never quite right in fit or style. I was not, in fact, particularly ugly, old photographs inform me, though I was well off the ideal; but I carried this sense of self-alienation with me into adulthood, where it regenerated in response to the depredations of MS. Even with my brace I walk with a limp so pronounced that, seeing myself on the videotape of a television program on the disabled, I couldn't believe that anything but an inchworm could make progress humping along like that. My shoulders droop and my pelvis thrusts forward as I try to balance myself upright, throwing my frame into a bony S. As a result of contractures, one shoulder is higher than the other and I carry one arm bent in front of me, the fingers curled into a claw. My left arm and leg have wasted into pipe-stems, and I try always to keep them covered. When I think about how my body must look to others, especially to men, to whom I have been trained to display myself, I feel ludicrous, even loathsome.

At my age, however, I don't spend much time thinking about my appearance. The burning egocentricity of adolescence, which assures one that all the world is looking all the time, has passed, thank God, and I'm generally too caught up in what I'm doing to step back, as I used to, and watch myself as though upon a stage. I'm also too old to believe in the accuracy of self-image. I know that I'm not a hideous crone, that in fact, when I'm rested, well dressed, and well made up, I look fine. The self-loathing I feel is neither physically nor intellectually substantial. What I hate is not me but a disease.

I am not a disease.

24 And a disease is not—at least not singlehandedly—going to determine who I am, though at first it seemed to be going to. Adjusting to a chronic incurable illness, I have moved through a process similar to that outlined by Elizabeth Kübler-Ross in *On Death and Dying*. The major difference—and it is far more significant than most people recognize—is that I can't be sure of the outcome, as the terminally ill cancer patient can. Research studies indicate that, with proper medical care, I may achieve a "normal" life span. And in our society, with its vision of death as the ultimate evil, worse even than decrepitude, the response to such news is, "Oh well, at least you're not going to *die*." Are there worse things than dying? I think that there may be.

I think of two women I know, both with MS, both enough older than I to have served me as models. One took to her bed several years ago and has been there ever since. Although she can sit in a high-backed wheelchair, because she is incontinent she refuses to go out at all, even though incontinence pants, which are readily available at any pharmacy, could protect her from embarrassment. Instead, she stays at home and insists that her husband, a small quiet man, a retired civil servant, stay there with her except for a quick weekly foray to the supermarket. The other woman, whose illness was diagnosed when she was eighteen, a nursing student engaged to a young doctor, finished her training, married her doctor, accompanied him to Germany when he was in the service, bore three sons and a daughter, now grown and gone. When she can, she travels with her husband; she plays bridge, embroiders, swims regularly; she works, like me, as a symptomatic-patient instructor of medical students in neurology. Guess which woman I hope to be.

At the beginning, I thought about having MS almost incessantly. And because of the unpredictable course of the disease, my thoughts were always terrified. Each night I'd get into bed wondering whether I'd get out again the next morning, whether I'd be able to see, to speak, to hold a pen between my fingers. Knowing that the day might come when I'd be physically incapable of killing myself, I thought perhaps I ought to do so right away, while I still had the strength. Gradually I came to understand that the Nancy who might one day lie inert under a bedsheet, arms and legs paralyzed, unable to feed or bathe herself, unable to reach out for a gun, a bottle of pills, was not the Nancy I was at present, and that I could not presume to make decisions for that future Nancy, who might well not want in the least to die. Now the only provision I've made for the future Nancy is that when the time comes—and it is likely to come in the form of pneumonia, friend to the weak and the old—I am not to be treated with machines and medications. If she is unable to communicate by then, I hope she will be satisfied with these terms.

Thinking all the time about having MS grew tiresome and intrusive, especially in the large and tragic mode in which I was accustomed to considering my plight. Months and even years went by without catastrophe (at least without one related to MS), and really I was awfully busy, what with George and children and snakes and students and poems, and I hadn't the time, let alone the inclination, to devote myself to being a disease. Too, the richer my life became, the funnier it seemed, as though there were some connection between largesse and laughter, and so my tragic stance began to waver until, even with the aid of a brace and a cane, I couldn't hold it for very long at a time.

28   After several years I was satisfied with my adjustment. I had suffered my grief and fury and terror, I thought, but now I was at ease with my lot. Then one summer day I set out with George and the children across the desert for a vacation in California. Part way to Yuma I became aware that my right leg felt funny. "I think I've had an exacerbation," I told George. "What shall we do?" he asked. "I think we'd better get the hell to California," I said, "because I don't know whether I'll ever make it again." So we went on to San Diego and then to Orange, up the Pacific Coast Highway to Santa Cruz, across to Yosemite, down to Sequoia and Joshua Tree, and so back over the desert to home. It was a fine two-week trip, filled with friends and fair weather, and I wouldn't have missed it for the world, though I did in fact make it back to California two years later. Nor would there have been any point in missing it, since in MS, once the symptoms have appeared, the neurological damage has been done, and there's no way to predict or prevent that damage.

The incident spoiled my self-satisfaction, however. It renewed my grief and fury and terror, and I learned that one never finishes adjusting to MS. I don't know now why I thought one would. One does not, after all, finish adjusting to life, and MS is simply a fact of my life—not my favorite fact, of course—but as ordinary as my nose and my tropical fish and my yellow Mazda station wagon. It may at any time get worse, but no amount of worry or anticipation can prepare me for a new loss. My life is a lesson in losses. I learn one at a time.

And I had best be patient in the learning, since I'll have to do it like it or not. As any rock fan knows, you can't always get what you want. Particularly when you have MS. You can't, for example, get cured. In recent years researchers and the organizations that fund research have started to pay MS some attention even though it isn't fatal; perhaps they have begun to see that life is something other than a quantitative phenomenon, that one may be very much alive for a very long time in a life that isn't worth living. The researchers have made some progress toward understanding the mechanism of the disease: It may well be an autoimmune reaction triggered by a slow-acting virus. But they are nowhere near its prevention, control, or cure. And most of us want to be cured. Some, unable to accept incurability, grasp at one treatment after another, no matter how bizarre:

megavitamin therapy, gluten-free diet, injections of cobra venom, hypothermal suits, lymphocytopharesis, hyperbaric chambers. Many treatments are probably harmless enough, but none are curative.

The absence of a cure often makes MS patients bitter toward their doctors. Doctors are, after all, the priests of modern society, the new shamans, whose business is to heal, and many an MS patient roves from one to another, searching for the "good" doctor who will make him well. Doctors too think of themselves as healers, and for this reason many have trouble dealing with MS patients, whose disease in its intransigence defeats their aims and mocks their skills. Too few doctors, it is true, treat their patients as whole human beings, but the reverse is also true. I have always tried to be gentle with my doctors, who often have more at stake in terms of ego than I do. I may be frustrated, maddened, depressed by the incurability of my disease, but I am not diminished by it, and they are. When I push myself up from my seat in the waiting room and stumble toward them, I incarnate the limitation of their powers. The least I can do is refuse to press on their tenderest spots.

32   This gentleness is part of the reason that I'm not sorry to be a cripple. I didn't have it before. Perhaps I'd have developed it anyway—how could I know such a thing?—and I wish I had more of it, but I'm glad of what I have. It has opened and enriched my life enormously, this sense that my frailty and need must be mirrored in others, that in searching for and shaping a stable core in a life wrenched by change and loss, change and loss, I must recognize the same process, under individual conditions, in the lives around me. I do not deprecate such knowledge, however I've come by it.

All the same, if a cure were found, would I take it? In a minute. I may be a cripple, but I'm only occasionally a loony and never a saint. Anyway, in my brand of theology God doesn't give bonus points for a limp. I'd take a cure; I just don't need one. A friend who also has MS startled me once by asking, "Do you ever say to yourself, 'Why me, Lord?'" "No, Michael, I don't," I told him, "because whenever I try, the only response I can think of is 'Why not?'" If I could make a cosmic deal, who would I put in my place? What in my life would I give up in exchange for sound limbs and a thrilling rush of energy? No one. Nothing. I might as well do the job myself. Now that I'm getting the hang of it.

Personal Response

What do you think your response would be if you were faced with the kind of chronic debilitating illness that Mairs has?

Questions for Discussion

1. Mairs begins by stating her purpose: to write an essay "on being a cripple." But why did she want to write such an essay? What do you think she hoped to accomplish? How does the opening scene, which takes place in a public

toilet, lead Mairs to decide "it was high time to write the essay" (paragraph 1)? How is that setting—both a very private and a public space—appropriate for introducing her essay?

2. Look at paragraph 7, in which Mairs defines multiple sclerosis. Why do you think she uses medical terminology? What is the effect of the last sentence in that paragraph? What evidence is there that Mairs has not lost her sense of humor?

3. Summarize the effects, both positive and negative, that Mairs' illness has had on her. Why do you think Mairs prefer to identify with Caliban rather than Tiny Tim (paragraph 19)?

4. Why do you think Mairs goes into such detail about "today's ideal woman" (paragraph 20)? What connection is she making between that image and her own self concept?

5. In what ways are women "trained to display [themselves]" (paragraph 21)? Are men trained similarly to display themselves to others?

THE ANDROGYNOUS MALE

Noel Perrin

Noel Perrin teaches American literature at Dartmouth College and raises beef cattle on his farm in Vermont. His books include Vermont: In All Weathers *(1973) and three collections of his essays,* First Person Rural *(1978), Second Person Rural (1980), and* Third Person Rural *(1983). The essay reprinted here first appeared in the "On Men" column in the* New York Times Magazine *in 1984.*

The summer I was 16, I took a train from New York to Steamboat Springs, Colo., where I was going to be assistant horse wrangler at a camp. The trip took three days, and since I was much too shy to talk to strangers, I had quite a lot of time for reading. I read all of "Gone With the Wind." I read all the interesting articles in a couple of magazines I had, and then I went back and read all the dull stuff. I also took all the quizzes, a thing of which magazines were even fuller then than now.

The one that held my undivided attention was called "How Masculine/ Feminine Are You?" It consisted of a large number of inkblots. The reader was supposed to decide which of four objects each blot most resembled. The choices might be a cloud, a steam engine, a caterpillar and a sofa.

When I finished the test, I was shocked to find that I was barely masculine at all. On a scale of 1 to 10, I was about 1.2. Me, the horse wrangler? (And not just wrangler, either. That summer, I had to skin a couple of horses that died—the camp owner wanted the hides.)

4   The results of that test were so terrifying to me that for the first time in my life I did a piece of original analysis. Having unlimited time on the train, I looked at the

"masculine" answers over and over, trying to find what it was that distinguished real men from people like me—and eventually I discovered two very simple patterns. It was "masculine" to think the blots looked like man-made objects, and "feminine" to think they looked like natural objects. It was masculine to think they looked like things capable of causing harm, and feminine to think of innocent things.

Even at 16, I had the sense to see that the compilers of the test were using rather limited criteria—maleness and femaleness are both more complicated than *that*—and I breathed a huge sigh of relief. I wasn't necessarily a wimp, after all.

That the test did reveal something other than the superficiality of its makers I realized only many years later. What it revealed was that there is a large class of men and women both, to which I belong, who are essentially androgynous. That doesn't mean we're gay, or low in the appropriate hormones, or uncomfortable performing the jobs traditionally assigned our sexes. (A few years after that summer, I was leading troops in combat and, unfashionable as it now is to admit this, having a very good time. War is exciting. What a pity the 20th century went and spoiled it with high-tech weapons.)

What it does mean to be spiritually androgynous is a kind of freedom. Men who are all-male, or he-man, or 100 percent red-blooded Americans, have a little biological set that causes them to be attracted to physical power, and probably also to dominance. Maybe even to watching football. I don't say this to criticize them. Completely masculine men are quite often wonderful people: good husbands, good (though sometimes overwhelming) fathers, good members of society. Furthermore, they are often so unself-consciously at ease in the world that other men seek to imitate them. They just aren't as free as us androgynes. They pretty nearly have to be what they are; we have a range of choices open.

8   The sad part is that many of us never discover that. Men who are not 100 percent red-blooded Americans—say, those who are only 75 percent red-blooded—often fail to notice their freedom. They are too busy trying to copy the he-men ever to realize that men, like women, come in a wide variety of acceptable types. Why this frantic imitation? My answer is mere speculation, but not casual. I have speculated on this for a long time.

Partly they're just envious of the he-man's unconscious ease. Mostly they're terrified of finding that there may be something wrong with them deep down, some weakness at the heart. To avoid discovering that, they spend their lives acting out the role that the he-man naturally lives. Sad.

One thing that men owe to the women's movement is that this kind of failure is less common than it used to be. In releasing themselves from the single ideal of the dependent woman, women have more or less incidentally released a lot of men from the single ideal of the dominant male. The one mistake the feminists have made, I think, is in supposing that *all* men need this release, or that the world would be a better place if all men achieved it. It wouldn't. It would just be duller.

So far I have been pretty vague about just what the freedom of the androgynous man is. Obviously, it varies with the case. In the case I know best, my own, I can be quite specific. It has freed me most as a parent. I am, among other things, a fairly good natural mother. I like the nurturing role. It makes me feel good to see a child eat—and it turns me to mush to see a 4-year old holding a glass with both small hands, in order to drink. I even enjoyed sewing patches on the knees of my daughter Amy's Dr. Dentons when she was at the crawling stage. All that pleasure I would have lost if I had made myself stick to the notion of the paternal role that I started with.

12   Or take a smaller and rather ridiculous example. I feel free to kiss cats. Until recently it never occurred to me that I would want to, though my daughters have been doing it all their lives. But my elder daughter is now 22, and in London. Of course, I get to look after her cat while she is gone. He's a big, handsome farm cat named Petrushka, very unsentimental, though used from kittenhood to being kissed on the top of the head by Elizabeth. I've gotten very fond of him (he's the adventurous kind of cat who likes to climb hills with you), and one night I simply felt like kissing him on the top of the head, and did. Why did no one tell me sooner how silky cat fur is?

Then there's my relation to cars. I am completely unembarrassed by my inability to diagnose even minor problems in whatever object I happen to be driving, and don't have to make some insider's remark to mechanics to try to establish that I, too, am a "Man With His Machine."

The same ease extends to household maintenance. I do it, of course. Service people are expensive. But for the last decade my house has functioned better than it used to because I've had the aid of a volume called "Home Repairs Any Woman Can Do," which is pitched just right for people at my technical level. As a youth, I'd as soon have touched such a book as I would have become a transvestite. Even though common sense says there is really nothing sexual whatsoever about fixing sinks.

Or take public emotion. All my life I have easily been moved by certain kinds of voices. The actress Siobhan McKenna's, to take a notable case. Give her an emotional scene in a play, and within 10 words my eyes are full of tears. In boyhood, my great dread was that someone might notice. I struggled manfully, you might say, to suppress this weakness. Now, of course, I don't see it as a weakness at all, but as a kind of fulfillment. I even suspect that the true he-men feel the same way, or one kind of them does, at least, and it's only the poor imitators who have to struggle to repress themselves.

16   Let me come back to the inkblots, with their assumption that masculine equates with machinery and science, and feminine with art and nature. I have no idea whether the right pronoun for God is He, She or It. But this I'm pretty sure of. If God could somehow be induced to take that test, God would not come out macho, and not feminismo, either, but right in the middle. Fellow androgynes, it's a nice thought.

Personal Response

To what extent are you and your friends "androgynous"? To what extent do you feel limited to or free from traditional sex-role expectations? How do you feel about men who are only "75 percent red-blooded Americans"?

Questions for Discussion

1. How does Perrin define the purely masculine personality? What does he see as its limitations?

2. Perrin says that men who are not "100 percent red-blooded Americans" fail to notice their freedom because they are too busy trying to copy he-men. How does he account for this "frantic imitation" (paragraph 8)?

3. What examples of his own behavior does Perrin give to define androgyny?

4. Summarize the point Perrin makes in his final paragraph.

5. Perrin makes the statement that "there is a large class of men and women both . . . who are essentially androgynous" (paragraph 6). Given his definition of the androgynous male, how do you think he would define the androgynous female?

JUST WALK ON BY: A BLACK MAN PONDERS HIS POWER TO ALTER PUBLIC SPACE

Brent Staples

Brent Staples, who holds a PhD in psychology from the University of Chicago, is an editorial writer for the New York Times. *His memoir,* Parallel Time: Growing Up in Black and White, *was published in 1994. The essay reprinted here first appeared in* Ms. *magazine in 1986.*

My first victim was a woman—white, well dressed, probably in her early twenties. I came upon her late one evening on a deserted street in Hyde Park, a relatively affluent neighborhood in an otherwise mean, impoverished section of Chicago. As I swung onto the avenue behind her, there seemed to be a discreet, unimflammatory distance between us. Not so. She cast back a worried glance. To her, the youngish black man—a broad six feet two inches with a beard and billowing hair, both hands shoved into the pockets of a bulky military jacket—seemed menacingly close. After a few more quick glimpses, she picked up her pace and was soon running in earnest. Within seconds she disappeared into a cross street.

That was more than a decade ago. I was twenty-two years old, a graduate student newly arrived at the University of Chicago. It was in the echo of that terrified woman's footfalls that I first began to know the unwieldy inheritance I'd come into—the ability to alter public space in ugly ways. It was clear that she thought herself the quarry of a mugger, a rapist, or worse. Suffering a bout of insomnia, however, I was stalking sleep, not defenseless wayfarers. As a softy who is scarcely able to take a knife to a raw chicken—let alone hold it to a person's throat—I was surprised, embarrassed, and dismayed all at once. Her flight made me feel like an accomplice in tyranny. It also made it clear that I was indistinguishable from the muggers who occasionally seeped into the area from the surrounding ghetto. That first encounter, and those that followed, signified that a vast, unnerving gulf lay between nighttime pedestrians—particularly women—and me. And I soon gathered that being perceived as dangerous is a hazard in itself. I only needed to turn a corner into a dicey situation, or crowd some frightened, armed person in a foyer somewhere, or make an errant move after being pulled over by a policeman. Where fear and weapons meet—and they often do in urban America—there is always the possibility of death.

In that first year, my first away from my hometown, I was to become thoroughly familiar with the language of fear. At dark, shadowy intersections in Chicago, I could cross in front of a car stopped at a traffic light and elicit the *thunk, thunk, thunk, thunk* of the driver—black, white, male, or female—hammering down the door locks. On less traveled streets after dark, I grew accustomed to but never comfortable with people who crossed to the other side of the street rather than pass me. Then there were the standard unpleasantries with police, doormen, bouncers, cab drivers, and others whose business it is to screen out troublesome individuals *before* there is any nastiness.

4 I moved to New York nearly two years ago and I have remained an avid night walker. In central Manhattan, the near-constant crowd cover minimizes tense one-on-one street encounters. Elsewhere—visiting friends in SoHo, where sidewalks are narrow and tightly spaced buildings shut out the sky—things can get very taut indeed.

Black men have a firm place in New York mugging literature. Norman Podhoretz in his famed (or infamous) 1963 essay, "My Negro Problem—And Ours," recalls growing up in terror of black males; they "were tougher than we were, more ruthless," he writes—and as an adult on the Upper West Side of Manhattan, he continues, he cannot constrain his nervousness when he meets black men on certain streets. Similarly, a decade later, the essayist and novelist Edward Hoagland extols a New York where once "Negro bitterness bore down mainly on other Negroes." Where some see mere panhandlers. Hoagland sees "a mugger who is clearly screwing up his nerve to do more than just *ask* for money." But Hoagland has "the New Yorker's quick-hunch posture for broken-field maneuvering," and the bad guy swerves away.

I often witness that "hunch posture," from women after dark on the warren-like streets of Brooklyn where I live. They seem to set their faces on neutral and, with their purse straps strung across their chests bandolier style, they forge ahead as though bracing themselves against being tackled. I understand, of course, that the danger they perceive is not a hallucination. Women are particularly vulnerable to street violence, and young black males are drastically overrepresented among the perpetrators of that violence. Yet these truths are no solace against the kind of alienation that comes of being ever the suspect, against being set apart, a fearsome entity with whom pedestrians avoid making eye contact.

It is not altogether clear to me how I reached the ripe old age of twenty-two without being conscious of the lethality nighttime pedestrians attributed to me. Perhaps it was because in Chester, Pennsylvania, the small, angry industrial town where I came of age in the 1960s, I was scarcely noticeable against a backdrop of gang warfare, street knifings, and murders. I grew up one of the good boys, had perhaps a half-dozen fist fights. In retrospect, my shyness of combat has clear sources.

8   Many things go into the making of a young thug. One of those things is the consummation of the male romance with the power to intimidate. An infant discovers that random flailings send the baby bottle flying out of the crib and crashing to the floor. Delighted, the joyful babe repeats those motions again and again, seeking to duplicate the feat. Just so, I recall the points at which some of my boyhood friends were finally seduced by the perception of themselves as tough guys. When a mark cowered and surrendered his money without resistance, myth and reality merged—and paid off. It is, after all, only manly to embrace the power to frighten and intimidate. We, as men, are not supposed to give an inch of our lane on the highway; we are to seize the fighter's edge in work and in play and even in love; we are to be valiant in the face of hostile forces.

Unfortunately, poor and powerless young men seem to take all this nonsense literally. As a boy, I saw countless tough guys locked away; I have since buried several, too. They were babies, really—a teenage cousin, a brother of twenty-two, a childhood friend in his mid-twenties—all gone down in episodes of bravado played out in the streets. I came to doubt the virtues of intimidation early on. I chose, perhaps even unconsciously, to remain a shadow—timid, but a survivor.

The fearsomeness mistakenly attributed to me in public places often has a perilous flavor. The most frightening of these confusions occurred in the late 1970s and early 1980s when I worked as a journalist in Chicago. One day, rushing into the office of a magazine I was writing for with a deadline story in hand, I was mistaken for a burglar. The office manager called security and, with an ad hoc posse, pursued me through the labyrinthine halls, nearly to my editor's door. I had no way of proving who I was. I could only move briskly toward the company of someone who knew me.

Another time I was on assignment for a local paper and killing time before an interview. I entered a jewelry store on the city's affluent Near North Side. The proprietor excused herself and returned with an enormous red Doberman pinscher straining at the end of a leash. She stood, the dog extended toward me, silent to my questions, her eyes bulging nearly out of her head. I took a cursory look around, nodded, and bade her good night. Relatively speaking, however, I never fared as badly as another black male journalist. He went to nearby Waukegan, Illinois, a couple of summers ago to work on a story about a murderer who was born there. Mistaking the reporter for the killer, police hauled him from his car at gunpoint and but for his press credentials would probably have tried to book him. Such episodes are not uncommon. Black men trade tales like this all the time.

12   In "My Negro Problem—And Ours," Podhoretz writes that the hatred he feels for blacks makes itself known to him through a variety of avenues—one being his discomfort with that "special brand of paranoid touchiness" to which he says blacks are prone. No doubt he is speaking here of black men. In time, I

learned to smother the rage I felt at so often being taken for a criminal. Not to do so would surely have led to madness—via that special "paranoid touchiness" that so annoyed Podhoretz at the time he wrote the essay.

I began to take precautions to make myself less threatening. I move about with care, particularly late in the evening. I give a wide berth to nervous people on subway platforms during the wee hours, particularly when I have exchanged business clothes for jeans. If I happen to be entering a building behind some people who appear skittish, I may walk by, letting them clear the lobby before I return, so as not to seem to be following them. I have been calm and extremely congenial on those rare occasions when I've been pulled over by the police.

And on late-evening constitutionals along streets less traveled by, I employ what has proved to be an excellent tension-reducing measure: I whistle melodies from Beethoven and Vivaldi and the more popular classical composers. Even steely New Yorkers hunching toward nighttime destinations seem to relax, and occasionally they even join in the tune. Virtually everybody seems to sense that a mugger wouldn't be warbling bright, sunny selections from Vivaldi's *Four Seasons*. It is my equivalent of the cowbell that hikers wear when they know they are in bear country.

Personal Response

How do you feel about Staples' decision to change his own behavior in public in order to accommodate other people's fear of him? Would you be willing to do the same? Why or why not?

Questions for Discussion

1. Why does Staples use the word "victim" in his opening paragraph? In what sense is that white woman a "victim"? Who else might be considered a victim? Is Staples himself a victim? Explain your answer.

2. How is Staples able to "alter public space in ugly ways" (paragraph 2)? What do you think he means by "ugly"?

3. What does Staples mean by "the language of fear" (paragraph 3)? How does he feel about his effect on other people? Is he angry? sympathetic? outraged? Does he consider their fear unfair or irrational? Find specific passages to support your answer. Is his experience entirely a racial issue? If not, what else accounts for the fear he elicits from other people?

4. In paragraphs 8 and 9, Staples explains a definition of manhood that he chose early in life not to embrace. What is that definition and why did he reject it?

5. What is Staples' image of himself? How does it differ from the image that others have of him?

RACE WITHOUT FACE

Edward Iwata

Edward Iwata is a business writer for the San Francisco Examiner. *He has worked as a freelance journalist, writing about the media, racial issues, Asian American culture, and the Pacific Rim for such publications as the* Los Angeles Times, Newsweek Japan, *and* Editor and Publisher. *He is also a former co-director of Stanford University's Okada House, a residence hall and community center that offers programs on Asian American topics. "Race Without Face" first appeared in the May 1991 issue of the* San Francisco Focus.

I would soon discover I was different from white people.

A cosmetic surgeon was about to cut into my face that gray winter morning. Hot lights glared as I lay on the operating table. Surgical tools clattered in containers, sharp metal against metal. I felt like a lamb awaiting a shearing of its wool.

Shivering from the air-conditioned chill, I wondered if I'd made a mistake. Had my hatred of Oriental facial features, fanned by my desire to do well in a white world, blinded me so easily?

4   An instant before the anesthetic numbed my brain cells, I felt the urge to cry out. I imagined ripping off my gown and sprinting to freedom. But at that point, even wetting my cracked lips was hard to do.

"I trust you implicitly," I said, as a supplicant might beseech a priest.

Oddly, I imagined seeing, as if peering through a bloody gauze, the contours of two faces rushing toward me. One face was twisted into sadness. The other glowed with a look akin to pride. One white, one yellow; one white, one yellow. I did not know which was which.

A month earlier in her Beverly Hills medical office, the surgeon said she planned to taper the thick, round tip of my nose. She also wanted to build up my flat bridge with strips of cartilage.

8   "Oriental noses have no definition," she said, waving a clipboard like an inspector on an auto assembly line.

While she was at it, she suggested, why not work on the eyes, also? They looked dark and tired, even though I was twenty years old then. A simple slash along my eyelids would remove the fat cells that kept my eyes from springing into full, double-lidded glory.

Why not? I had thought. Didn't I want to distance myself from the faceless, Asian masses? I hated the pale image in the mirror. I hated the slurs hurled at me that I couldn't shut out. I hated being a gook, a Nip.

It's a taboo subject, but true: many people of color have, at some point in their youths, imagined themselves as Caucasian, the Nordic or Western European ideal. Hop Sing meets Rock Hudson. Michael Jordan magically transformed into Robert Redford.

12   For myself, an eye and nose job—or *blepharoplasty* and *rhinoplasty* in sur-
geons' tongue—would bring me the gift of acceptance. The flick of a scalpel
would buy me respect.

To make the decision easier, a close friend loaned me $1500. I didn't tell my
parents or anyone else about it.

The surgery was quick and painless. My friend drove me at dawn to the medical clinic. At 7 A.M. sharp, the surgeon, a brusque Hispanic woman, swept into
the office and rushed past us.

The next time I saw her, she was peering down at me and penciling lines on
my face to guide her scalpel. A surgeon's mask and cap hid her own face; I saw
only a large pair of eyes plotting the attack on my epidermis and cartilage. While
I shivered, a nurse and an anesthesiologist laughed and gossiped.

16   "You have beautiful lashes, Edward," the surgeon said. It seemed like an odd
thing to notice at that moment.

I tumbled into darkness. My last memory was a deep desire to yell or strike
out, to stab the surgeon and her conspirators with their knives.

The surgeon went for my eyes first. Gently, she cut and scooped out the fat
cells that lined my upper eyelid. That created a small furrow, which popped open
my eyes a bit and created double lids, every Asian model's dream.

Ignoring the blood, she then slit the upper inside of my nostril. Like a short-
order cook trimming a steak, she carved the cartilage and snipped off bits of bone
and tissue. Soon she was done. After a coffee break or lunch, she would move on
to the next patient.

20   Later that day, I was wheeled out of a bright recovery room. My head and
limbs felt dull and heavy, as if buried in mud. A draft swept up my surgical gown
and chilled my legs. Although my face was bound in bandages, I felt naked. Without warning, a sharp sense of loss engulfed me, a child away from home who is
not sure why he aches so.

"Eddie, what did you do?" asked my mother when I next saw her. Then, her
voice shaking, "Why did you do this? Were you ashamed of yourself?" As if struck
by a lance, my legs weakened, my body cleaved. I was lost, flailing away in shadows, but I shrugged off her question and said something lame. I didn't sense at the
time that whatever had compelled me to scar my face could also drive me farther
from home.

One week passed before I was brave enough to take my first look in the mirror. I stood in the bathroom, staring at my reflection until my feet got sore.

Stitch marks scarred my face like tracks on a drug addict's arm. My haggard
eyes were rounder; my nose smaller and puggy. In the glare of the bathroom
light, my skin seemed pale and washed out, a claylike shade of light brown. I
looked like a medical illustration from a century ago, when doctors would have
measured my facial angle and cranium size for racial intelligence.

24   I wanted to claw my new face.

The image I pictured in the mirror was an idealized Anglo man, an abstraction. I
didn't realize at the time that my flaws were imagined, not real. I felt compelled

to measure up to a cultural ideal in a culture that had never asked me what my ideal was.

Indeed, to many Anglos, the males of our culture are a mystery. Most whites know us only through the neutered images: Japanese salarymen. Sumo wrestlers. Sushi chefs. We're judged by our slant of eye and color of skin. We're seen only as eunuchs, as timid dentists and engineers. Books and movies portray us as ugly and demonic. We're truly a race of Invisible Men.

Clearly, Asian-American men have been psychologically castrated in this country. Our history is one of emasculation and accommodation. Japanese Americans, for the most part, filed quietly into the internment camps. Proud Cantonese immigrants were trapped in their Chinatown ghettoes and bachelor societies by poverty and discrimination.

28   In the corporate arena, Asian-American men find their cultural values and strengths overshadowed by ego-driven, back-slapping, hypercompetitive whites. And, while socially we may be more "acceptable" than blacks and Hispanics, we are not acceptable enough to run legislatures, schools, corporations. Our women may be marriage material for whites, but our men are still seen as gooks. On the street, we're cursed or spat upon—even killed—because of our looks.

It cannot be denied, either, that we're regarded as kowtowing wimps not only by whites, but by a lot of Asian-American women—even those with racial and ethnic pride. Privately, they confess they see a lack of strong Asian-American men who fit an ideal of manhood: virile and sensitive, intelligent and intuitive, articulate and confident.

Of course, we must share part of the blame. Many of us grow up swallowing the stereotypes, accepting the role white society imposes on us. And aside from a handful of us in politics, law, the media, education, and the arts, the rest of us are too reserved and opinionless in the white world.

Simone de Beauvoir wrote that a woman "insinuates herself into a world that has doomed her to passivity." The same could have been said of too many Asian-American men, including myself.

32   I recall an episode four years ago when a former boss and I lunched at a Thai restaurant. I thought I deserved a promotion—new status, new duties, a bigger paycheck—real fast. He disagreed. Between bites of curry chicken, I was startled to hear this executive label me in words used for "docile" Asian men and "uppity" blacks.

"You're a quiet, reserved kind of guy," he said, waving his hands in the air. A few bites later, he veered the other way and portrayed me as a "cocky, arrogant young reporter . . . with a chip on your shoulder."

I was confused. Was I an obedient employee, or a hard-charging militant? And how could I be both? I ate my rice and said little. My face flushed with anger. Later that day, I left work early, fantasizing about a bloody, *ninja*-style revenge.

Why didn't I fight back? Instead of sitting silently, why didn't I challenge his superficial view of me?

36   Part of it was cultural. Our Eastern values are living, breathing elements in our lives, not topics we study in Zen Buddhism class. Regardless of how assimilated we

may be, these values rise to claim our attention at unpredictable moments. So while I fancied myself a strong-minded journalist, I still felt shackled by cultural bonds, afraid of arguing back. It was the whole *deference* thing, this Asian habit of respecting authority to a fault.

I yearned for my boss's acceptance. I was blinded by my desire to fit in as a man, a journalist, a corporate player. In Japan, this could be called *ittaikan*, a longing for oneness with a person or a group. Readers of the Japanese psychiatrist Takeo Doi might think of it as *amae*, a passive dependency on another's love or kindness.

And so, by others and by ourselves, we're rendered impotent. I wasn't a limp lover. But outside my home or bedroom, I often felt powerless—desexed like a baby chick. It was as if I didn't exist. Employers didn't acknowledge my work. Professors in college rebuffed my remarks in the classroom. Maître d's ignored my presence in restaurants. I felt voiceless, faceless.

A friend of mine, a San Francisco lawyer in her thirties, was thrilled to meet a liberal Japanese man from Tokyo after years of dating Asian Americans. Several of her boyfriends had been bright and sensitive, but they lacked what she called "male energy"—a strength of purpose and destiny, a vision of one's goals in life.

40 "It's almost a samurai spirit that Asian-American men somehow lost in white society, as if they'd been neutered," she said. "Even though I'm a career woman, sometimes I want a man to take the lead, while I play the mothering role . . . Reconnecting with a strong, decisive Asian male has been an eye-opener."

My friend's opinion is not unusual. Unfortunately, some Asian-American men, scared of the nerd label, charge blindly in the opposite direction, aping Western notions of kick-ass masculinity: Rambo. Mike Tyson. Michael Milken. They become obsessed with the art of war, obsessed with competition. It's yet another stereotype, and equally damaging.

One example, a hot item in our community, is an all-male calendar, featuring pinups of Asian-American hunks. While the men photographed are all respected, the beefcake images they project are caricatures of the white physical ideal: the well-oiled, muscular body, the chiseled face, the hint of male power and violence. They're like minorities in beauty pageants who look more like the blond Miss America prototype than their own race.

"How warped that sense of manhood and beauty is," observes King-Kok Cheung, a literary scholar at UCLA. "In some ways, our internal oppression as Asians is greater than white oppression. We need to understand that anyone who is comfortable with himself is attractive."

44 Probably the biggest blow to my young psyche occurred at my predominantly white high school. My advanced English class boasted students who were versed in Petrarchan sonnets before I had learned to read baseball box scores. Even so, as a teenager I saw myself as a maverick writer in the manner of Jack Kerouac or Jack London. Mrs. Worthy, our strict teacher, showed me otherwise.

"Mr. Iwata, I'd like you to work on 'A Book Is Like a Frigate' by Emily Dickinson," she said, assigning homework. "That shouldn't be too difficult to handle, even for you."

I still get chills when I recall my classmates shifting in their seats, their blue and green eyes staring at me. To Mrs. Worthy, I was the slow, quiet Asian boy who sat by the window, waiting for the school bus to dump me back in the inner city.

Outside the classroom, media images confused me even more. Nowhere—from racist children's books to great literature to movies with evil Jap soldiers—did I see my reflection in the larger world. Unlike students today, I had no Asian or Asian-American heroes, no cultural icons, to lead the way.

48 In sociological jargon, I was an Assimilationist, a Marginal Man, Stranger. Like many Asian Americans, I craved admiration and acceptance, mostly from whites. I worshiped Anglo models of success, the middle-class ethos carried to extremes.

But contrary to our shining image as model minorities, I learned I had *not* arrived. All the hard work and schooling and cosmetic surgery in the world couldn't change the way I looked, or the way I was perceived. I could not erase my skin color, no matter how hard I tried. My status in the white professional world was illusory; it did not transcend the harsh realities of race and class.

In my search for acceptance, I modeled myself after whites, especially in college—in speech and diction, style and dress, body language and eye contact. I thought I was a failure when no white coeds danced with me at a frat party. At beer busts, I avoided Asian-American women because they looked like the girls in my old neighborhood, with their moon faces and *daikon* (white radish) legs.

Before that, I used to hang with Hispanic buddies from East L.A. I was a *vato,* an esé, a buddha brother. And before that, I played basketball and dodged gangs in Crenshaw, a black and Asian neighborhood in Los Angeles. I wasn't cool, but I could fake it. When black classmates called me "nigger" or "homes" (short for "homeboy"), I smiled inside. Another mask.

52 At the same time, I fought the tug of family and culture. Seeking a place beyond my ken, I left Crenshaw to live on campus as a college freshman. I saw my new world as a stage ripe for rebellion.

My courses—journalism, literature, history—disappointed my parents. They hoped I would study medicine or business, like all good Japanese-American kids.

I was studying, all right: the science of interviewing accident victims for newspaper stories. Themes of Dionysian abandon, from Blake to Lord Byron. My literary hero was James Joyce, whose modernist art promised to transport me to Arabys unknown. I had not yet begun to study myself.

My bid for a cultural identity, a sense of manhood, quickened as my mother and father retired, and as Dad's health worsened. Clearly, a strong impulse pushed me to step up and fill their vacuum, to carry on a family legacy in some way.

56 My parents, Phillip and Midori, and sixteen relatives spent the years during World War II at Manzanar, the internment camp eight miles from the town of Independence in the Mojave Desert. When I was a kid, Mom never talked about

Manzanar. Instead, she wove harmless tales for my brother, my sister, and me. The stories protected us from the truth.

Dad, a strong silent type, claimed he never cared about the political quest for redress—the twenty thousand dollars due each Japanese American interned during the war. Interviewing him for the first story I did on Manzanar was not easy. "You don't have to write about this, do you?" he asked. Speaking to him the next time was even harder. "I told you I'm not a good person to interview," he snapped. "Talk to Mom again."

His reticence was understandable. Conservative Japanese Americans hide their private faces in public. *Nomen no yo,* their ancestors said. *The face is like a Noh mask.* My mother and father calmly accepted their fates.

Like many Japanese Americans, my parents veiled the past and whitewashed their memories. They believed the government line that Uncle Sam sent them to the concentration camps for their own good, for their safety. The camps also gave them postwar opportunities by spreading them across the great land, they were told.

60   In truth, the internment was a horror for families, a civil rights disaster, the death of the old Japanese-American culture. For the men, the sense of powerlessness must have been devastating.

In my parents' desire to hide the past, I sensed a reflection of my own self-hate. Like most *sansei* (third generation), I ignored or never sought out the tragic facts of that era. As a student, I never read about the camps. As a young journalist, I picked up shards of history, but never the whole dark tale.

But after much cajoling, I persuaded my folks to join me on a pilgrimage to Manzanar in 1988. Only tumbleweeds, stone ruins, and barbed wire remained at the windy, desolate site. Nonetheless, the pilgrimage was a glimpse into a forgotten world, a gateway to the past. The ghosts were powerful. But I found no neat, easy answers.

There was no stopping now. The next spring, we flew to Japan. While trade wars dominated the news in Tokyo, my parents and I journeyed into the rural heart of our ancestral homeland.

64   For the first time, we met the Iwata and Kunitomi clans, who still live on the rice farms in Wakayama and Okayama that our families have owned since the eighteenth century. Among other revelations, I learned that the head of the Iwata family, my father's cousin, shared my Japanese name, Masao ("righteous boy").

Seated on a *tatami* floor at the Iwata homestead, we enjoyed sukiyaki and country-style vegetables we hadn't eaten since my grandmothers died several years ago. The *gohan* (steamed rice) was the lightest and sweetest we had ever tasted. Masao smiled broadly as he served the hot food, its steam rising toward the small family altar in the corner of the dining room.

At one point, I noticed Masao staring at Dad. His steady gaze was rude by Japanese standards. But apparently struck by the family resemblance, Masao couldn't avert his eyes from Dad's face. With their wavy hair and thick eyebrows, their dark skin and rakish grins, they could have been brothers.

I'm not a misty-eyed romantic longing for an ancestral past. Peering for gods in mountain shrines and temple ruins is not my idea of good journalism. Still, this was my flesh and blood seated in an old farmhouse on that warm spring night. I thought of a line from *No-No Boy*, a novel of World War II by John Okada: "If he was to find his way back to that point of wholeness and belonging, he must do so in the place where he had begun to lose it." Here was my point of origin, where my family began. As we scooped bowlfuls of rice into our hungry selves, a light rain wet the furrows of black soil in the field outside.

68   For me, Japan brought to the surface cultural conflicts and competing values. Even though I was as American as teriyaki chicken, the old Buddhist and Confucian values reached me in southern California. *Giri* (obligation). *Omoiyari* (empathy). *Oyakoko* (filial piety). The Japanese, in fact, have a phrase unique to them: "*Jubun ga nai*," or "to have no self." They rarely use the first-person pronoun when they speak. Loyal samurai who followed their feudal barons to the grave had little over some Japanese-American kids.

Those values gave me strength—and also confused the hell out of me. The issue of personal independence and family ties was the most painful. How was I to pursue my goals, forge an identity, yet honor my parents without question? And if I chose filial piety, how was I to keep the bond strong without sacrificing my hard-won, American-style autonomy?

A Zen *koan* asks, "What was your face like before you were born?" I cannot know for sure how deeply the culture of my ancestors touches me, but I know I will never again see myself as a scarred, hollow man lost in the shadows, beating back death.

Japan freed my spirit and gave rise to an atavistic pride I had never known. The past, I realized, could be cradled like an heirloom found in an old trunk in the attic. I was a player in a family history that spanned the reigns of emperors, from feudal Japan to the modern Heisei Era, Year One—the year of my first visit to Japan. And my story would add a few scenes to that unfolding narrative.

72   After Manzanar and Japan, I began to see my surgery in a new slant of light. Like the victims of internment, I started coming to terms with my real and emotional scars.

Obviously, the surgery had been a rebellion against my "Japaneseness" and the traditional values of my parents. It was psychic surgery, an act of mutilation, a symbolic suicide. It was my self-hatred finding a stage.

Like many Asian Americans, I'm searching for a new cultural character and destiny.

Certainly, we need to change many of our past goals. While much is known of our drive toward the American dream, little is written of our worship of materialism, our narcissism, our obsession with showing that we've *arrived*. We're brilliant students of what historian Richard Hofstadter called "status politics," the effort to enhance one's social standing.

76   Somewhere between Asia and an "A+" in Achievement, we lost our way. The trappings of style and success—a fancy degree, a prestigious job, a Mercedes

in every garage—have become more important than the accomplishments. Instead, the images we impress upon white society and other Asian Americans are paramount. We have become the "racial bourgeoisie," a term coined by legal scholar Mari Matsuda. The hard work may bring "success," but this kind of success will not set us free.

The numbers reflect the reality. They tell a sad story, especially in education, supposedly our stronghold. Asian Americans held 3.1 percent of administrative and management jobs in California colleges and universities, according to an analysis of 1980 census data by Amado Cabezas and Gary Kawaguchi of UC Berkeley's Ethnic Studies Department. Even more startling were the income figures. Asian-American faculty and staff were paid salaries *40 to 70 percent* of the mean annual income of white men. And this is only in one field.

A century ago, sugar plantation owners in Hawaii counted Asian laborers as part of their business supplies. Today, we're still regarded similarly: as bodies to fill affirmative-action goals, as background in movies. Even worse, we gladly accept what society imposes on us, so anxious are we to measure up to its standards of "success."

There is so much cultural brainwashing to undo, and so much to learn about our place in this country.

80   Many of us will not tolerate the status quo anymore. The *Miss Saigon* controversy reflects our rising anger. It's *our* March on Washington, *our* Stonewall gay riot, *our* Jackson, Mississippi. In other recent shows of strength, we've rallied around the racial killings of Asian Americans. Our congressional and community leaders won redress payments for the internment of Japanese Americans. And more Asian Americans are filling seats in public office.

But where do we go next? And how do we define our community, if at all?

Clearly, we need new visions, new models. Elaine Kim, a UC Berkeley dean and ethnic studies scholar, says our community defies easy branding. The boundaries of Asian America are changing, fusing, changing again. "We're much more than white versus nonwhite, suburbanites versus urban people of color, East versus West, tradition versus modernity," she argues. "We're creating our culture every day."

Slowly and surely, a strong Asian-American culture is coming of age. It's a bold culture, unashamed and true to itself. It's a culture with a common destiny, *a community of the mind and soul.* And it's taking many forms—in plays and films, in literature and journalism, in history and the social sciences, in professional groups and political caucuses. We can certainly start by realizing we don't need to parrot anyone else's notions of success and beauty. "We're not slaves to culture, but agents of culture, agents of change," says King-Kok Cheung. Instead of conforming to prefabricated images and stereotypes, we must define our own successes, our own personalities, our own images.

84   We must not vanish completely into the suburbs, nor must we isolate ourselves in our close-knit but ethnocentric Asian communities. Instead, we must find a new common ethos, a new aesthetic, a new psychology.

This new Asian American must transcend, yet embrace, our differences. It must value collective ethnic pride, yet respect individualism. It must honor equality of race and gender, and bury our hypocritical racism, sexism, and homophobia. And it must not hide behind moral self-righteousness or ideological rigidity, which poisons the radical left and fundamentalist right.

Our artists and scholars and educators, for the most part, create positive images, but we need many more; we cannot wait for Hollywood. Role models in all fields are important. Parents must teach their kids inner strength, not outer conformity. We must build more bridges with whites and others in a meaningful sense, not merely for show.

And as for Asian-American manhood? For Buddha's sake, let's use our imagination. The Lone Ranger and Bruce Lee are dead. We don't need to outgun or measure up to anyone. We can return to the original meaning of compete, which comes from the Latin word *competere,* "to come together." Manhood now is a destructive, stereotyped, behavioral trap. Asian Americans must recast our concept of masculinity, sculpting it into a larger definition of humanity.

88   For our role models, we can look to the past. The Japanese *bushido* ethic, the samurai spiritual and martial philosophy, is one. The scholarly Sage-King and Superior Man of Confucian thought is another, as is the Greek concept of *areté*— virtue in thought and action. All prized a male beauty and an ethos of strength and serenity, action and calmness, yin and yang.

To be sure, more Asian-American men are refusing to lock themselves into narrow roles and models. Rick Yuen, for example, a dean at Stanford, often finds himself caring for his two children and deferring to his wife, San Francisco Community College board member Mabel Teng, on many family and career decisions. "I start with the basic assumption that we're men and women of equal standing," he says simply.

In the literary arts, playwrights David Henry Hwang and Philip Gotanda and poet David Mura explore themes of ethnic manhood and sexuality. In the social arena, gay Asians are starting to emerge, attacking the layer upon layer of racism and homophobia they face in the straight and gay worlds.

On a recent trip to Los Angeles, I stumbled across an irresistible metaphor for our culture. A journalist friend, Brenda Sunoo of the *Korea Times,* had invited me to join her family at a concert of young Asian-American musicians, all amateurs.

92   The concert was a romp in culture-bending and blending. There were Korean rappers. A Japanese folksinger. A Filipino multimedia artist. When the rap dancers blew a tricky move and fell to the ground, drawing laughs, they hid their faces in their hands in embarrassment. Another singer, his set delayed by technical problems, repeatedly thanked the audience for its patience.

The performers seemed much like Asian America: shy but daring; apologetic but confident; imitative yet novel. "There's no blueprint for us," said Brenda. "Our history is being written now. Our individual choices will make us unique."

We've barely started to explore the beauty of our culture. With a little luck, the new Asian America will be a choral celebration, not an aria sung to an elite few. This will keep us from fading into white society as admired but bleached Americans.

We're trying to change the cultural paradigm, image by image. We have to. For it is how we see each other that will ultimately transform the world. How we see each other, and how we see ourselves.

96   So where does this all lead me? Do I feel more whole in my newfound identity? Have I tossed the masks slapped on me by society, my family, myself? Do I know why I cut off my nose to spite my race?

Yes, to all of the above. Now I see my image and others in a less harsh light. I know one's slant of eye and color of skin are bogus issues. For beyond acculturation, beyond racial identity, is the larger question of *kokoro*—Japanese for heart and soul. Make no mistake: I've learned I *am* different from white people. Not better, not worse, but distinct. The faces rushing toward me in my presurgical daze were neither white nor yellow. They were mine.

Personal Response

Iwata writes that he "cut [his] nose to spite [his] race" (paragraph 96). Have you ever changed something about yourself to spite others? Would you consider plastic surgery to change any feature of your appearance? What do you do to alter your appearance?

Questions for Discussion

1. Why did Iwata decide to have cosmetic surgery? What did he hope to change? Did he get what he hoped for by having the surgery? Did he get anything that he hadn't expected as a result of the surgery?

2. In what ways was Iwata's surgery "psychic surgery, an act of mutilation, a symbolic suicide" (paragraph 73)?

3. Summarize the common image Iwata believes that others, especially whites, have of Asian American men. How much blame does Iwata attribute to Asians for perpetuating that image? Why was Iwata so passive when discriminated against? Does he seem to be passive now?

4. How did Iwata's trips to Manzanar and Japan clarify his feelings about himself and what he hopes for his culture? Summarize the changes in image, the "new cultural character," Iwata wants Asian Americans to make. What positive developments does he already see in the Asian-American community?

5. Define the term "cultural brainwashing" (paragraph 79) and then discuss what it means not only for Asian Americans but for other groups as well. Does the majority group also undergo cultural brainwashing? Where does the brainwashing come from?

COMPLEXION

Richard Rodriguez

Richard Rodriguez was born in San Francisco, the son of Mexican immigrants. He earned a BA and an MA at Stanford University and a PhD in English from the University of California at Berkeley. A lecturer and a writer, he publishes frequently in magazines such as The American Scholar, Saturday Review, *and* Harper's. *In 1982, Rodriquez published* Hunger of Memory, *a collection of autobiographical essays in which he describes the conflicts and challenges of growing up in an immigrant household in America. This selection is an excerpt from a chapter of* Hunger of Memory.

Regarding my family, I see faces that do not closely resemble my own. Like some other Mexican families, my family suggests Mexico's confused colonial past. Gathered around a table, we appear to be from separate continents. My father's face recalls faces I have seen in France. His complexion is white—he does not tan; he does not burn. Over the years, his dark wavy hair has grayed handsomely. But with time his face has sagged to a perpetual sigh. My mother, whose surname is inexplicably Irish—Moran—has an olive complexion. People have frequently wondered if, perhaps, she is Italian or Portuguese. And, in fact, she looks as though she could be from southern Europe. My mother's face has not aged as quickly as the rest of her body; it remains smooth and glowing—a cool tan—which her gray hair cleanly accentuates. My older brother has inherited her good looks. When he was a boy people would tell him that he looked like Mario Lanza, and hearing it he would smile with dimpled assurance. He would come home from high school with girlfriends who seemed to me glamorous (because they were) blonds. And during those years I envied him his skin that burned red and peeled like the skin of the *gringos*. His complexion never darkened like mine. My youngest sister is exotically pale, almost ashen. She is delicately featured, Near Eastern, people have said. Only my older sister has a complexion as dark as mine, though her facial features are much less harshly defined than my own. To many people meeting her, she seems (they say) Polynesian. I am the only one in the family whose face is severely cut to the line of ancient Indian ancestors. My face is mournfully long, in the classical Indian manner; my profile suggests one of those beak-nosed Mayan sculptures—the eaglelike face upturned, open-mouthed, against the deserted, primitive sky.

"We are Mexicans," my mother and father would say, and taught their four children to say whenever we (often) were asked about our ancestry. My mother and father scorned those "white" Mexican-Americans who tried to pass themselves off as Spanish. My parents would never have thought of denying their ancestry. I never denied it: My ancestry is Mexican, I told strangers mechanically. But I never forgot that only my older sister's complexion was as dark as mine.

My older sister never spoke to me about her complexion when she was a girl. But I guessed that she found her dark skin a burden. I knew that she suffered for being a "nigger." As she came home from grammar school, little boys came up behind her and pushed her down to the sidewalk. In high school, she struggled in the adolescent competition for boyfriends in a world of football games and proms, a world where her looks were plainly uncommon. In college, she was afraid and scornful when dark-skinned foreign students from countries like Turkey and India found her attractive. She revealed her fear of dark skin to me only in adulthood when, regarding her own three children, she quietly admitted relief that they were all light.

4   That is the kind of remark women in my family have often made before. As a boy, I'd stay in the kitchen (never seeming to attract any notice), listening while my aunts spoke of their pleasure at having light children. (The men, some of whom were dark-skinned from years of working out of doors, would be in another part of the house.) It was the woman's spoken concern: the fear of having a dark-skinned son or daughter. Remedies were exchanged. One aunt prescribed to her sisters the elixir of large doses of castor oil during the last weeks of pregnancy. (The remedy risked an abortion.) Children born dark grew up to have their faces treated regularly with a mixture of egg white and lemon juice concentrate. (In my case, the solution never would take.) One Mexican-American friend of my mother's who regarded it a special blessing that she had a measure of English blood, spoke disparagingly of her husband, a construction worker, for being so dark. "He doesn't take care of himself," she complained. But the remark, I noticed, annoyed my mother, who sat tracing an invisible design with her finger on the tablecloth.

There was affection too and a kind of humor about these matters. With daring tenderness, one of my uncles would refer to his wife as *mi negra*. An aunt regularly called her dark child *mi feito* (my little ugly one), her smile only partially hidden as she bent down to dig her mouth under his ticklish chin. And at times relatives spoke scornfully of pale, white skin. A *gringo's* skin resembled *masa*—baker's dough—someone remarked. Everyone laughed. Voices chuckled over the fact that the *gringos* spent so many hours in summer sunning themselves. ("They need to get sun because they look like *los muertos*.")

I heard the laughing but remembered what the women had said, with unsmiling voices, concerning dark skin. Nothing I heard outside the house, regarding my skin, was so impressive to me.

In public I occasionally heard racial slurs. Complete strangers would yell out at me. A teenager drove past, shouting, "Hey, Greaser! Hey, Pancho!" Over his shoulder I saw the giggling face of his girlfriend. A boy pedaled by and announced matter-of-factly, "I pee on dirty Mexicans." Such remarks would be said so casually that I wouldn't quickly realize that they were being addressed to me. When I did, I would be paralyzed with embarrassment, unable to return the insult. (Those times I happened to be with white grammar school friends, *they* shouted back. Imbued with the mysterious kindness of children, my friends would never ask later why I hadn't yelled out in my own defense.)

8   In all, there could not have been more than a dozen incidents of name-calling. That there were so few suggests that I was not a primary victim of racial

abuse. But that, even today, I can clearly remember particular incidents is proof of their impact. Because of such incidents, I listened when my parents remarked that Mexicans were often mistreated in California border towns. And in Texas. I listened carefully when I heard that two of my cousins had been refused admittance to an "all-white" swimming pool. And that an uncle had been told my some man to go back to Africa. I followed the progress of the southern black civil rights movement, which was gaining prominent notice in Sacramento's afternoon newspaper. But what most intrigued me was the connection between dark skin and poverty. Because I heard my mother speak so often about the relegation of dark people to menial labor, I considered the great victims of racism to be those who were poor and forced to do menial work. People like the farmworkers whose skin was dark from the sun.

After meeting a black grammar school friend of my sister's, I remember thinking that she wasn't really "black." What interested me was the fact that she wasn't poor. (Her well-dressed parents would come by after work to pick her up in a shiny green Oldsmobile.) By contrast, the garbage men who appeared every Friday morning seemed to me unmistakably black. (I didn't bother to ask my parents why Sacramento garbage men always were black. I thought I knew.) One morning I was in the backyard when a man opened the gate. He was an ugly, square-faced black man with popping red eyes, a pail slung over his shoulder. As he approached, I stood up. And in a voice that seemed to me very weak, I piped, "Hi." But the man paid me no heed. He strode past to the can by the garage. In a single broad movement, he overturned its contents into his larger pail. Our can came crashing down as he turned and left me watching, in awe.

"*Pobres negros*," my mother remarked when she'd notice a headline in the paper about a civil rights demonstration in the South. "How the *gringos* mistreat them." In the same tone of voice she'd tell me about the mistreatment her brother endured years before. (After my grandfather's death, my grandmother had come to America with her son and five daughters.) "My sisters, we were still all just teenagers. And since *mi pápa* was dead, my brother had to be the head of the family. He had to support us, to find work. But what skills did he have! Twenty years old. *Pobre*. He was tall, like your grandfather. And strong. He did construction work. 'Construction!' The *gringos* kept him digging all day, doing the dirtiest jobs. And they would pay him next to nothing. Sometimes they promised him one salary and paid him less when he finished. But what could he do? Report them? We weren't citizens then. He didn't even know English. And he was dark. What chances could he have? As soon as we sisters got older, he went right back to Mexico. He hated this country. He looked so tired when he left. Already with a hunchback. Still in his twenties. But old-looking. No life for him here. *Pobre*."

Dark skin was for my mother the most important symbol of a life of oppressive labor and poverty. But both my parents recognized other symbols as well.

My father noticed the feel of every hand he shook. (He'd smile sometimes—marvel more than scorn—remembering a man he'd met who had soft, uncalloused hands.)

My mother would grab a towel in the kitchen and rub my oily face sore when I came in from playing outside. "Clean the *grasa* off of your face!" (*Greaser!*)

Symbols: When my older sister, then in high school, asked my mother if she could do light housework in the afternoons for a rich lady we knew, my mother was frightened by the idea. For several weeks she troubled over it before granting conditional permission: "Just remember, you're not a maid. I don't want you wearing a uniform." My father echoed the same warning. Walking with him past a hotel, I watched as he stared at a doorman dressed like a Beefeater. "How can anyone let himself be dressed up like that? Like a clown. Don't you ever get a job where you have to put on a uniform." In summertime neighbors would ask me if I wanted to earn extra money by mowing their lawns. Again and again my mother worried: "Why did they ask *you*? Can't you find anything better?" Inevitably, she'd relent. She knew I needed the money. But I was instructed to work after dinner. ("When the sun's not so hot.") Even then, I'd have to wear a hat. *Un sombrero de* baseball.

(*Sombrero.* Watching gray cowboy movies, I'd brood over the meaning of the broad-rimmed hat—that troubling symbol—which comically distinguished a Mexican cowboy from real cowboys.)

16   From my father came no warnings concerning the sun. His fear was of dark factory jobs. He remembered too well his first jobs when he came to this country, not intending to stay, just to earn money enough to sail on to Australia. (In Mexico he had heard too many stories of discrimination in *los Estados Unidos*. So it was Australia, that distant island-continent, that loomed in his imagination as his "America.") The work my father found in San Francisco was work for the unskilled. A factory job. Then a cannery job. (He'd remember the noise and the heat.) Then a job at a warehouse. (He'd remember the dark stench of old urine.) At one place there were fistfights; at another a supervisor who hated Chinese and Mexicans. Nowhere a union.

His memory of himself in those years is held by those jobs. Never making money enough for passage to Australia; slowly giving up the plan of returning to school to resume his third-grade education—to become an engineer. My memory of him in those years, however, is lifted from photographs in the family album which show him on his honeymoon with my mother—the woman who had convinced him to stay in America. I have studied their photographs often, seeking to find in those figures some clear resemblance to the man and the woman I've known as my parents. But the youthful faces in the photos remain, behind dark glasses, shadowy figures anticipating my mother and father.

They are pictured on the grounds of the Coronado Hotel near San Diego, standing in the pale light of a winter afternoon. She is wearing slacks. Her hair falls seductively over one side of her face. He appears wearing a double-breasted suit, an unneeded raincoat draped over his arm. Another shows them standing together, solemnly staring ahead. Their shoulders barely are touching. There is to their pose an aristocratic formality, an elegant Latin hauteur.

The man in those pictures is the same man who was fascinated by Italian grand opera. I have never known just what my father saw in the spectacle, but he has told me that he would take my mother to the Opera House every Friday night—if he had money enough for orchestra seats. ("Why go to sit in the balcony?") On Sundays he'd don Italian silk scarves and a camel's hair coat to take his new wife to the polo matches in Golden Gate Park. But one weekend my father stopped going to the opera and polo matches. He would blame the change in his life on one job—a warehouse job, working for a large corporation which today advertises its products with the smiling faces of children. "They made me an old man before my time," he'd say to me many years later. Afterward, jobs got easier and cleaner. Eventually, in middle age, he got a job making false teeth. But his youth was spent at the warehouse. "Everything changed," his wife remembers. The dapper young man in the old photographs yielded to the man I saw after dinner: haggard, asleep on the sofa. During "The Ed Sullivan Show" on Sunday nights, when Roberta Peters or Licia Albanese would appear on the tiny blue screen, his head would jerk up alert. He'd sit forward while the notes of Puccini sounded before him. ("Un bel dì.")

20 By the time they had a family, my parents no longer dressed in very fine clothes. Those symbols of great wealth and the reality of their lives too noisily clashed. No longer did they try to fit themselves, like paper-doll figures, behind trappings so foreign to their actual lives. My father no longer wore silk scarves or expensive wool suits. He sold his tuxedo to a second-hand store for five dollars. My mother sold her rabbit fur coat to the wife of a Spanish radio station disc jockey. ("It looks better on you than it does on me," she kept telling the lady until the sale was completed.) I was six years old at the time, but I recall watching the transaction with complete understanding. The woman I knew as my mother was already physically unlike the woman in her honeymoon photos. My mother's hair was short. Her shoulders were thick from carrying children. Her fingers were swollen red, toughened by housecleaning. Already my mother would admit to foreseeing herself in her own mother, a woman grown old, bald and bowlegged, after a hard lifetime of working.

In their manner, both my parents continued to respect the symbols of what they considered to be upper-class life. Very early, they taught me the *propio* way of eating *como los ricos*. And I was carefully taught elaborate formulas of polite greeting and parting. The dark little boy would be invited by classmates to the rich houses on Forty-fourth and Forty-fifth streets. "How do you do?" or "I am very pleased to meet you," I would say, bowing slightly to the amused mothers of classmates. "Thank you very much for the dinner; it was very delicious."

I made an impression. I intended to make an impression, to be invited back. (I soon realized that the trick was to get the mother or father to notice me.) From those early days began my association with rich people, my fascination with their secret. My mother worried. She warned me not to come home expecting to have the things my friends possessed. But she needn't have said anything. When I went to the big houses, I remembered that I was, at best, a visitor to the world I saw there. For that reason, I was an especially watchful guest. I was my parents' child. Things most middle-class children wouldn't trouble to notice, I studied. Remembered to see: the starched black and white uniform worn by the maid who opened the door; the Mexican gardeners—their complexions as dark as my own. (One gardener's face, glassed by sweat, looked up to see me going inside.)

"Take Richard upstairs and show him your electric train," the mother said. But it was really the vast polished dining room table I'd come to appraise. Those nights when I was invited to stay for dinner, I'd notice that my friend's mother rang a small silver bell to tell the black woman when to bring in the food. The father, at his end of the table, ate while wearing his tie. When I was not required to speak, I'd skate the icy cut of crystal with my eye; my gaze would follow the golden threads etched onto the rim of china. With my mother's eyes I'd see my hostess's manicured nails and judge them to be marks of her leisure. Later, when my schoolmate's father would bid me goodnight, I would feel his soft fingers and palm when we shook hands. And turning to leave, I'd see my dark self, lit by chandelier light, in a tall hallway mirror.

Personal Response

Were you ever the object of teasing or cruel remarks about a physical characteristic? If so, describe the experience.

Questions for Discussion

1. How would you describe Rodriguez's relationship with his family? Why do you think Rodriguez was so impressed by what the women in his family said about dark skin? What is Rodriguez's attitude toward his own skin color?

2. Locate and discuss the symbols that are important to Rodriguez's parents.

3. What connection does Rodriguez make between skin color and poverty?

4. What do the stories of their work experiences in America reveal about the lives of Rodriguez's uncle and father? What connection does Rodriguez draw between those experiences and the color of their skin?

5. What ideas from earlier in the essay do the concluding sentences refer to? What is the implication of Rodriguez's seeing "his dark self, lit by chandelier light" (paragraph 23)?

HOW IT FEELS TO BE COLORED ME

Zora Neale Hurston

Zora Neale Hurston (1903–1960) was born in the small all-black town of Eatonville, Florida, and educated at Howard University, Barnard College, and Columbia University. Barnard's only black student, she received a degree in anthropology in 1928. After gathering material in her hometown of Eatonville, Hurston edited a collection of black folklore, Mules and Men *(1935). She went on to write short stories, drama, essays, and novels, of which* Their Eyes

Were Watching God (1937) is perhaps her best known. Her autobiography,
Dust Tracks on a Road, was published in 1942. "How It Feels to Be Colored
Me" was published in The World Tomorrow in 1928.

I am colored but I offer nothing in the way of extenuating circumstances except
the fact that I am the only Negro in the United States whose grandfather on the
mother's side was not an Indian chief.

I remember the very day that I became colored. Up to my thirteenth year I
lived in the little Negro town of Eatonville, Florida. It is exclusively a colored
town. The only white people I knew passed through the town going to or coming from Orlando. The native whites rode dusty horses, the Northern tourists
chugged down the sandy village road in automobiles. The town knew the Southerners and never stopped cane chewing when they passed. But the Northerners
were something else again. They were peered at cautiously from behind curtains
by the timid. The more venturesome would come out on the porch to watch
them go past and got just as much pleasure out of the tourists as the tourists got
out of the village.

The front porch might seem a daring place for the rest of the town, but it
was a gallery seat for me. My favorite place was atop the gate-post. Proscenium
box for a born first-nighter. Not only did I enjoy the show, but I didn't mind the
actors knowing that I liked it. I usually spoke to them in passing. I'd wave at
them and when they returned my salute, I would say something like this:
"Howdy-do-well-I-thank-you-where-you-goin'?" Usually automobile or the
horse paused at this, and after a queer exchange of compliments, I would probably "go a piece of the way" with them, as we say in farthest Florida. If one of
my family happened to come to the front in time to see me, of course negotia-
tions would be rudely broken off. But even so, it is clear that I was the first
"welcome-to-our-state" Floridian, and I hope the Miami Chamber of Commerce will please take notice.

During this period, white people differed from colored to me only in that
they rode through town and never lived there. They liked to hear me "speak
pieces" and sing and wanted to see me dance the parse-me-la, and gave me gen-
erously of their small silver for doing these things, which seemed strange to me
for I wanted to do them so much that I needed bribing to stop. Only they didn't
know it. The colored people gave no dimes. They deplored any joyful tendencies
in me, but I was their Zora nevertheless. I belonged to them, to the nearby hotels, to the county—everybody's Zora.

But changes came in the family when I was thirteen, and I was sent to school
in Jacksonville. I left Eatonville, the town of the oleanders, as Zora. When I dis-
embarked from the river-boat at Jacksonville, she was no more. It seemed that I
had suffered a sea change. I was not Zora of Orange County any more. I was
now a little colored girl. I found it out in certain ways. In my heart as well as in
the mirror, I became a fast brown—warranted not to rub nor run.

But I am not tragically colored. There is no great sorrow dammed up in my
soul, nor lurking behind my eyes. I do not mind at all. I do not belong to the

sobbing school of Negrohood who hold that nature somehow has given them a lowdown dirty deal and whose feelings are all hurt about it. Even in the helter-skelter skirmish that is my life, I have seen that the world is to the strong regardless of a little pigmentation more or less. No, I do not weep at the world—I am too busy sharpening my oyster knife.

Someone is always at my elbow reminding me that I am the granddaughter of slaves. It fails to register depression with me. Slavery is sixty years in the past. The operation was successful and the patient is doing well, thank you. The terrible struggle that made me an American out of a potential slave said, "On the line!" The Reconstruction said "Get set!"; and the generation before said "Go!" I am off to a flying start and I must not halt in the stretch to look behind and weep. Slavery is the price I paid for civilization, and the choice was not with me. It is a bully adventure and worth all that I have paid through my ancestors for it. No one on earth ever had a greater chance for glory. The world to be won and nothing to be lost. It is thrilling to think—to know that for any act of mine, I shall get twice as much praise or twice as much blame. It is quite exciting to hold the center of the national stage, with the spectators not knowing whether to laugh or to weep.

8   The position of my white neighbor is much more difficult. No brown specter pulls up a chair beside me when I sit down to eat. No dark ghost thrusts its leg against mine in bed. The game of keeping what one has is never so exciting as the game of getting.

I do not always feel colored. Even now I often achieve the unconscious Zora of Eatonville before the Hegira. I feel most colored when I am thrown against a sharp white background.

For instance at Barnard. "Beside the waters of the Hudson" I feel my race. Among the thousand white persons, I am a dark rock surged upon, and over-swept, but through it all, I remain myself. When covered by the waters, I am; and the ebb but reveals me again.

Sometimes it is the other way around. A white person is set down in our midst, but the contrast is just as sharp for me. For instance, when I sit in the drafty basement that is The New World Cabaret with a white person, my color comes. We enter chatting about any little nothing that we have in common and are seated by the jazz waiters. In the abrupt way that jazz orchestras have, this one plunges into a number. It loses no time in circumlocutions, but gets right down to business. It constricts the thorax and splits the heart with its tempo and narcotic harmonies. This orchestra grows rambunctious, rears on its hind legs and attacks the tonal veil with primitive fury, rending it, clawing it until it breaks through to the jungle beyond. I follow those heathen—follow them exultingly. I dance wildly inside myself; I yell within, I whoop; I shake my assegai above my head, I hurl it true to the mark yeeeeooww! I am in the jungle and living in the jungle way. My face is painted red and yellow and my body is painted blue. My pulse is throbbing like a war drum. I want to slaughter something—give pain, give death to what, I do not know. But the piece ends. The men of the orchestra wipe their lips and rest their fingers. I creep back slowly to the veneer we call civilization with the last tone and find the white friend sitting motionless in his seat, smoking calmly.

12   "Good music they have here," he remarks, drumming the table with his fingertips.

Music. The great blobs of purple and red emotion have not touched him. He has only heard what I felt. He is far away and I see him but dimly across the ocean and the continent that have fallen between us. He is so pale with his whiteness then and I am *so* colored.

At certain times I have no race, I am *me*. When I set my hat at a certain angle and saunter down Seventh Avenue, Harlem City, feeling as snooty as the lions in front of the Forty-Second Street Library, for instance. So far as my feelings are concerned, Peggy Hopkins Joyce on the Boule Mich with her gorgeous raiment, stately carriage, knees knocking together in a most aristocratic manner, has nothing on me. The cosmic Zora emerges. I belong to no race nor time. I am the eternal feminine with its string of beads.

I have no separate feeling about being an American citizen and colored. I am merely a fragment of the Great Soul that surges within the boundaries. My country, right or wrong.

16   Sometimes, I feel discriminated against, but it does not make me angry. It merely astonishes me. How *can* any deny themselves the pleasure of my company? It's beyond me.

But in the main, I feel like a brown bag of miscellany propped against a wall. Against a wall in company with other bags, white, red and yellow. Pour out the contents, and there is discovered a jumble of small things priceless and worthless. A first-water diamond, an empty spool, bits of broken glass, lengths of string, a key to a door long since crumbled away, a rusty knife-blade, old shoes saved for a road that never was and never will be, a nail bent under the weight of things too heavy for any nail, a dried flower or two still a little fragrant. In your hand is the brown bag. On the ground before you is the jumble it held—so much like the jumble in the bags, could they be emptied, that all might be dumped in a single heap and the bags refilled without altering the content of any greatly. A bit of colored glass more or less would not matter. Perhaps that is how the Great Stuffer of Bags filled them in the first place—who knows?

Personal Response

Explain your response to Hurston's assessment of being black in white America.

Questions for Discussion

1. In one word, characterize Hurston's tone in this essay and then, for class discussion, see how many of your classmates came up with the same or a synonymous word. What passages in particular express this tone?

2. Why do you think Hurston does not tell the details about how she "became colored" on her trip from Eatonville to Jacksonville? Why are the details of that trip not important to the purpose of her essay?

3. Hurston makes some references to people, things, and events that she assumes her readers will recognize. Because the essay was written in 1928, however, you may not know that Peggy Hopkins Joyce (paragraph 14) was an American beauty and fashion-setter of the 1920s. The Boule Mich (paragraph 14) is the Boulevard Saint-Michel, a fashionable street in Paris, and an assegai (paragraph 11) is a light spear used by tribesmen in southern Africa. What are "the terrible struggle" and the "Reconstruction" Hurston refers to in paragraph 7? What is the Hegira (paragraph 9)?

4. Explain what Hurston means in paragraph 8 when she says that her white neighbor is in a worse position than she is. What does she mean when she says that "the game of keeping what one has is never so exciting as the game of getting" (paragraph 8)?

5. What does Hurston mean when she refers to herself as "the Cosmic Zora" (paragraph 14)? How important does she think skin color is? What does she believe is truly important about each human being?

THE LOUDEST VOICE

Grace Paley

Grace Paley was born in New York into a family of socialist Russian Jews and grew up listening to the tales her parents, aunts, and uncles told her. These stories inspired her to become a writer. She has published two collections of short stories, The Little Disturbances of Man *(1959), which won her immediate critical acclaim, and* Enormous Changes at the Last Minute *(1974). "The Loudest Voice" is from* The Little Disturbances of Man.

There is a certain place where dumbwaiters boom, doors slam, dishes crash; every window is a mother's mouth bidding the street shut up, go skate somewhere else, come home. My voice is the loudest.

There, my own mother is still as full of breathing as me and the grocer stands up to speak to her. "Mrs. Abramowitz," he says, "people should not be afraid of their children."

"Ah, Mr. Bialik," my mother replies, "if you say to her or her father 'Ssh,' they say, 'In the grave it will be quiet.' "

"From Coney Island to the cemetery," says my papa. "It's the same subway; it's the same fare."

I am right next to the pickle barrel. My pinky is making tiny whirlpools in the brine. I stop a moment to announce: "Campbell's Tomato Soup. Campbell's Vegetable Beef Soup. Campbell's S–c–otch Broth . . ."

"Be quiet," the grocer says, "the labels are coming off."

"Please, Shirley, be a little quiet," by mother begs me.

8   In that place the whole street groans: Be quiet! Be quiet! but steals from the happy chorus of my inside self not a tittle or a jot.

There, too, but just around the corner, is a red brick building that has been old for many years. Every morning the children stand before it in double lines which must be straight. They are not insulted. They are waiting anyway.

I am usually among them. I am, in fact, the first, since I begin with "A."

One cold morning the monitor tapped me on the shoulder. "Go to Room 409, Shirley Abramowitz," he said. I did as I was told. I went in a hurry up a down staircase to Room 409, which contained sixth-graders. I had to wait at the desk without wiggling until Mr. Hilton, their teacher, had time to speak.

12   After five minutes he said, "Shirley?"

"What?" I whispered.

He said, "My! My! Shirley Abramowitz! They told me you had a particularly loud, clear voice and read with lots of expression. Could that be true?"

"Oh, yes," I whispered.

16   "In that case, don't be silly; I might very well be your teacher someday. Speak up, speak up."

"Yes," I shouted.

"More like it," he said. "Now, Shirley, can you put a ribbon in your hair or a bobby pin? It's too messy."

"Yes!" I bawled.

20   "Now, now, calm down." He turned to the class. "Children, not a sound. Open at page 39. Read till 52. When you finish, start again." He looked me over once more. "Now, Shirley, you know, I suppose, that Christmas is coming. We are preparing a beautiful play. Most of the parts have been given out. But I still need a child with a strong voice, lots of stamina. Do you know what stamina is? You do? Smart kid. You know, I heard you read 'The Lord is my shepherd' in Assembly yesterday. I was very impressed. Wonderful delivery. Mrs. Jordan, your teacher, speaks highly of you. Now listen to me, Shirley Abramowitz, if you want to take the part and be in the play, repeat after me, 'I swear to work harder than I ever did before.' "

I looked to heaven and said at once, "Oh, I swear." I kissed my pinky and looked at God.

"That is an actor's life, my dear," he explained. "Like a soldier's, never tardy or disobedient to his general, the director. Everything," he said, "absolutely everything will depend on you."

That afternoon, all over the building, children scraped and scrubbed the turkeys and the sheaves of corn off the schoolroom windows. Goodbye Thanksgiving. The next morning a monitor brought red paper and green paper from the office. We made new shapes and hung them on the walls and glued them to the doors.

24   The teachers became happier and happier. Their heads were ringing like the bells of childhood. My best friend Evie was prone to evil, but she did not get a

single demerit for whispering. We learned "Holy Night" without an error. "How wonderful!" said Miss Glacé, the student teacher. "To think that some of you don't even speak the language!" We learned "Deck the Halls" and "Hark! The Herald Angels." . . . They weren't ashamed and we weren't embarrassed.

Oh, but when my mother heard about it all, she said to my father: "Misha, you don't know what's going on there. Cramer is the head of the Tickets Committee."

"Who?" asked my father. "Cramer? Oh yes, an active woman."

"Active? Active has to have a reason. Listen," she said sadly, "I'm surprised to see my neighbors making tra-la-la for Christmas."

28 My father couldn't think of what to say to that. Then he decided: "You're in America! Clara, you wanted to come here. In Palestine the Arabs would be eating you alive. Europe you had pogroms. Argentina is full of Indians. Here you got Christmas. . . . Some joke, ha?"

"Very funny, Misha. What is becoming of you? If we came to a new country a long time ago to run away from tyrants, and instead we fall into a creeping pogrom, that our children learn a lot of lies, so what's the joke? Ach, Misha, your idealism is going away."

"So is your sense of humor."

"That I never had, but idealism you had a lot of."

32 "I'm the same Misha Abramovitch, I didn't change an iota. Ask anyone."

"Only ask me," says my mama, may she rest in peace. "I got the answer."

Meanwhile the neighbors had to think of what to say too.

Marty's father said: "You know, he has a very important part, my boy."

36 "Mine also," said Mr. Sauerfeld.

"Not my boy!" said Mrs. Klieg. "I said to him no. The answer is no. When I say no! I mean no!"

The rabbi's wife said, "It's disgusting!" But no one listened to her. Under the narrow sky of God's great wisdom she wore a strawberry-blond wig.

Every day was noisy and full of experience. I was Right-hand Man. Mr. Hilton said: "How could I get along without you, Shirley?"

40 He said: "Your mother and father ought to get down on their knees every night and thank God for giving them a child like you."

He also said: "You're absolutely a pleasure to work with, my dear, dear child."

Sometimes he said: "For God's sake, what did I do with the script? Shirley! Shirley! Find it."

Then I answered quietly: "Here it is, Mr. Hilton."

44 Once in a while, when he was very tired, he would cry out: "Shirley, I'm just tired of screaming at those kids. Will you tell Ira Pushkov not to come in till Lester points to that star the second time?"

Then I roared: "Ira Pushkov, what's the matter with you? Dope! Mr. Hilton told you five times already, don't come in till Lester points to that star the second time."

"Ach, Clara," my father asked, "what does she do there till six o'clock she can't even put the plates on the table?"

"Christmas," said my mother coldly.

48   "Ho! Ho!" my father said. "Christmas. What's the harm? After all, history teaches everyone. We learn from reading this is a holiday from pagan times also, candles, lights, even Chanukah. So we learn it's not altogether Christian. So if they think it's a private holiday, they're only ignorant, not patriotic. What belongs to history, belongs to all men. You want to go back to the Middle Ages? Is it better to shave your head with a secondhand razor? Does it hurt Shirley to learn to speak up? It does not. So maybe someday she won't live between the kitchen and the shop. She's not a fool."

I thank you, Papa, for your kindness. It is true about me to this day. I am foolish but I am not a fool.

That night my father kissed me and said with great interest in my career, "Shirley, tomorrow's your big day. Congrats."

"Save it," my mother said. Then she shut all the windows in order to prevent tonsillitis.

52   In the morning it snowed. On the street corner a tree had been decorated for us by a kind city administration. In order to miss its chilly shadow our neighbors walked three blocks east to buy a loaf of bread. The butcher pulled down black window shades to keep the colored lights from shining on his chickens. Oh, not me. On the way to school, with both my hands I tossed it a kiss of tolerance. Poor thing, it was a stranger in Egypt.

I walked straight into the auditorium past the staring children. "Go ahead, Shirley!" said the monitors. Four boys, big for their age, had already started work as propmen and stagehands.

Mr. Hilton was very nervous. He was not even happy. Whatever he started to say ended in a sideward look of sadness. He sat slumped in the middle of the first row and asked me to help Miss Glacé. I did this, although she thought my voice too resonant and said, "Show-off!"

Parents began to arrive long before we were ready. They wanted to make a good impression. From among the yards of drapes I peeked out at the audience. I saw my embarrassed mother.

56   Ira, Lester, and Meyer were pasted to their beards by Miss Glacé. She almost forgot to thread the star on its wire, but I reminded her. I coughed a few times to clear my throat. Miss Glacé looked around and saw that everyone was in costume and on line waiting to play his part. She whispered, "All right . . ." Then:

Jackie Sauerfeld, the prettiest boy in first grade, parted the curtains with his skinny elbow and in a high voice sang out:

"Parents dear
We are here
To make a Christmas play in time.
It we give
In narrative
And illustrate with pantomime."

He disappeared.

My voice burst immediately from the wings to the great shock of Ira, Lester, and Meyer, who were waiting for it but were surprised all the same.

60   "I remember, I remember, the house where I was born . . ."

Miss Glacé yanked the curtain open and there it was, the house—an old hayloft, where Celia Kornbluh lay in the straw with Cindy Lou, her favorite doll. Ira, Lester, and Meyer moved slowly from the wings toward her, sometimes pointing to a moving star and sometimes ahead to Cindy Lou.

It was a long story and it was a sad story. I carefully pronounced all the words about my lonesome childhood, while little Eddie Braunstein wandered upstage and down with his shepherd's stick, looking for sheep. I brought up lonesomeness again, and not being understood at all except by some women everybody hated. Eddie was too small for that and Marty Groff took his place, wearing his father's prayer shawl. I announced twelve friends, and half the boys in the fourth grade gathered round Marty, who stood on an orange crate while my voice harangued. Sorrowful and loud, I declaimed about love and God and Man, but because of the terrible deceit of Abie Stock we came suddenly to a famous moment. Marty, whose remembering tongue I was, waited at the foot of the cross. He stared desperately at the audience. I groaned, "My God, my God, why hast thou forsaken me?" The soldiers who were sheiks grabbed poor Marty to pin him up to die, but he wrenched free, turned again to the audience, and spread his arms aloft to show despair and the end. I murmured at the top of my voice, "The rest is silence, but as everyone in this room, in this city—in this world—now knows, I shall have life eternal."

That night Mrs. Kornbluh visited our kitchen for a glass of tea.

64   "How's the virgin?" asked my father with a look of concern.

"For a man with a daughter, you got a fresh mouth, Abramovitch."

"Here," said my father kindly, "have some lemon, it'll sweeten your disposition."

They debated a little in Yiddish, then fell in a puddle of Russian and Polish. What I understood next was my father, who said, "Still and all, it was certainly a beautiful affair, you have to admit, introducing us to the beliefs of a different culture."

68   "Well, yes," said Mrs. Kornbluh. "The only thing . . . you know Charlie Turner—that cute boy in Celia's class—a couple others? They got very small parts or no part at all. In very bad taste, it seemed to me. After all, it's their religion."

"Ach," explained my mother, "what could Mr. Hilton do? They got very small voices; after all, why should they holler? The English language they know from the beginning by heart. They're blond like angels. You think it's so important they should get in the play? Christmas . . . the whole piece of goods . . . they own it."

I listened and listened until I couldn't listen any more. Too sleepy, I climbed out of bed and kneeled. I made a little church of my hands and said, "Hear, O Israel . . ." Then I called out in Yiddish, "Please, good night, good night. Ssh." My father said, "Ssh yourself," and slammed the kitchen door.

I was happy. I fell asleep at once. I had prayed for everybody: my talking family, cousins far away, passersby, and all the lonesome Christians. I expected to be heard. My voice was certainly the loudest.

Personal Response

What do you think of the Jewish Shirley Abramowitz's participating in a Christian celebration? What do you think of Miss Glacé's comment about her students and their cultural background?

Questions for Discussion

1. Explain Shirley's parents' differing views on her participation in the Christmas program. What do you think each parent wants Shirley to learn? What does their reaction to Shirley's starring role say about them? Do you side more with her mother's position or her father's on Shirley's participation? Explain your answer.

2. What point does Mrs. Kornbluh make when she comments on Mr. Hilton's casting Christian children in small roles? What motivated Mr. Hilton to make the casting decisions he did? What does Shirley's mother mean when she says, "Christmas . . . the whole piece of goods . . . they own it" (paragraph 69)?

3. How does Shirley feel about her loud voice? Why do some people object to it? How do you view Shirley?

4. What do you think Shirley means when she says, "I am foolish but I am not a fool" (paragraph 49). What does her narrative suggest about the kind of woman she would grow up to be?

5. What do you think Shirley means when she prays for "all the lonesome Christians" (paragraph 71)?

Suggestions for Writing About SELF-PERCEPTION

1. Respond to this statement by Sucheng Chan in "You're Short, Besides!": "Perhaps the hardest thing for those who live with handicapped people is to know when and how to offer help."

2. Referring to the experiences described in Sucheng Chan's "You're Short, Besides!" and Nancy Mairs' "On Being a Cripple," describe a person you know who has overcome or adjusted to a disability. Use very specific details to convey fully a sense of that person and the difficulties of the disability.

3. With Sucheng Chan's "You're Short, Besides!" and Nancy Mairs' "On Being a Cripple" in mind, write an essay on the use of euphemisms, such as those for dying, bodily functions, or certain occupations, citing examples and exploring possible reasons why people often prefer to use euphemisms. Relate your discussion of euphemisms to the subject of self-perception.

4. With Richard Rodriguez's "Complexion" in mind, narrate a personal experience with being the victim of name-calling or other verbal abuse. What were the circumstances of the incident? How did you respond to it? How did you feel afterwards?

5. Either support or argue against Noel Perrin's contention in "The Androgynous Male" that androgynous people are freer than those who adhere to traditional sex-role expectations.

6. Noel Perrin in "The Androgynous Male" says that the world would not necessarily be a better place if all men were androgynous (paragraph 10). Write an essay in which you either support or argue against his statement that we also need men who are "100 percent red-blooded Americans."

7. Brent Staples in "Just Walk on By: A Black Man Ponders His Power to Alter Public Space" writes from the point of view of a black man who is frightening to many people, particularly white women. Explore possible reasons for the apprehension of the woman in paragraph 1 of his essay and the actions she took in response to it. Or, if you have been in the position of the "victim" Staples describes, narrate that experience and discuss reasons for your own behavior.

8. Brent Staples wrote "Just Walk on By: A Black Man Ponders His Power to Alter Public Space" in 1986 about something he experienced over a decade before that. Write an essay in which you explain why, using examples drawn from personal experience or other sources, that either much has changed or much has not changed since Staples' experience in the mid-1970s.

9. Write an essay addressed to Zora Neale Hurston in which you explain to her what race relations are like in America now or the importance that skin color has in determining how people are treated.

10. Drawing on Brent Staples' "Just Walk on By: A Black Man Ponders His Power to Alter Public Space," Edward Iwata's "Race Without Face," Richard Rodriguez's "Complexion," and Zora Neale Hurston's "How It Feels to Be Colored Me," discuss the phenomenon of "cultural brainwashing" (Iwata, paragraph 79).

11. Keeping in mind what the writers in this chapter say about key events or incidents in their lives that taught them something about themselves, write about an experience you have had that taught you something about yourself.

12. If you have undergone a change in self-image, like Edward Iwata's in "Race Without Face," contrast your image of yourself before with your image of yourself now. How do you account for the change?

13. Write an essay on the subject of the relationship of self-image to established norms for appearance by taking into account any or all of the essays in this chapter. Consider such things as the need to conform, the ways in which "cultural brainwashing" works, and/or the factors affecting self-image.

14. Narrate an incident from your childhood in which other children were cruel or bullying to you, including your perception of the incident at the time and your perception of the incident now. Include a discussion of how the incident affected your self-image. Can you account for the other children's treatment of you? Do you feel differently about it now, looking back from the perspective of adulthood?

15. Explore the effects of a particular physical characteristic such as a prominent birth mark, skin color, racial background, birth defect, or the like, on your own life or the life of someone you know.

16. Narrate an experience in which you were very much aware of your difference—in skin color, political beliefs, religious beliefs, or some other noticeable way—from others around you. Explain the situation, how you differed from others, how you felt about yourself, and how you felt about the experience.

CHAPTER 4

ROLE MODELS

Role models are people who serve as positive examples of admirable behavior or action and who provide hope, inspiration, or incentive to others. They may be heroes as well, for the terms "role model" and "hero" are often used interchangeably. Certainly heroes can make excellent role models, and role models may be viewed as heroes by their admirers. People become heroes for feats of courage or nobility of purpose, such as in wartime, where heroism often involves sacrifice of life for the benefit of others. Heroes are also those who make special achievements or perform extraordinarily in their fields, such as scientists, entertainers, or athletes. They often become celebrities, widely known and admired for what they have done. But whether their fame is spread wide or limited to family and community, whether they serve the greater good of society or benefit much smaller populations, role models or heroes are those outstanding individuals whose character we praise and whom we would hope to pattern our own behavior or actions after.

The readings in this chapter indicate the various ways in which people can serve as role models. Professionals, no matter what their field, often influence others who would follow similar career paths. For instance, Russell Baker, in "Deems," explains how his interest in journalism was sparked by a man he both feared and admired. Several of the essays demonstrate that teachers often affect lives, as in Nicholas Gage's "The Teacher Who Changed My Life" and Roger Wilkins' "I Became Her Target." Gage tells how one teacher inspired him to find his voice as a writer and to make journalism his career, while Wilkins narrates how his eighth-grade teacher not only helped him gain self-confidence but also, in one memorable incident, broke down the barriers between him and his classmates that had been created by ignorance and stereotypes. In "*Italianità* in a World Made of Love and Need," Thom Tammaro names six teachers who gave him courage to break from the pattern of his family and community, teachers who, like the one Nicholas Gage describes, changed his life and greatly influenced who he is today. On the other hand, in "Lessons from Two Ghosts," Scott Fisher tells of the influence of a bad teacher as he explains how two college friends who were preparing to become teachers served as role models and continue to affect his own behavior as a teacher.

On the subject of cultural role models, Shanlon Wu explains in "In Search of Bruce Lee's Grave" that he had no Asian male role models when he was growing up, that is, not until he discovered Bruce Lee. His personal essay explores the effects of this glaring deficiency on the development of his own sense of self and raises the question of how to provide positive role models for minority populations.

While the entertainment industry may provide images for young people to emulate, often our role models come from our family or neighborhood. In "On Excellence," Cynthia Ozick, while defining "excellence" by contrasting her mother's ways of doing things with her own, clearly conveys her admiration for her mother and suggests the many ways in which her mother was a positive role model. Mary E. Wilkins Freeman's short story, "The Revolt of 'Mother,' " written about a century ago, portrays a woman struggling with the demands of two roles—wife and mother. While the story focuses on the mother, it also illustrates the role the father plays and, in doing so, explores the limitations of adhering to traditional sex roles and the possibilities of providing positive models of behavior within those roles.

ON EXCELLENCE

Cynthia Ozick

Cynthia Ozick is a highly acclaimed writer noted for the kind of serious, meticulous attention to her work that she describes in this essay. She has written three novels, Trust *(1966),* The Cannibal Galaxy *(1983), and* The Messiah of Stockholm *(1987), and her essays have been collected in* Art and Ardor *(1983) and* Metaphor and Memory *(1989). A* Cynthia Ozick Reader *(1955), edited by Elaine M. Kauver, is a collection of her poems, stories, and essays. The essay reprinted here first appeared in* Ms. *magazine in 1985.*

In my Depression childhood, whenever I had a new dress, my cousin Sarah would get suspicious. The nicer the dress was, and especially the more expensive it looked, the more suspicious she would get. Finally she would lift the hem and check the seams. This was to see if the dress had been bought or if my mother had sewed it. Sarah could always tell. My mother's sewing had elegant outsides, but there was something catch-as-catch-can about the insides. Sarah's sewing, by contrast, was as impeccably finished inside as out; not one stray thread dangled.

My uncle Jake built meticulous grandfather clocks out of rosewood; he was a perfectionist, and sent to England for the clockworks. My mother built serviceable radiator covers and a serviceable cabinet, with hinged doors, for the pantry. She built a pair of bookcases for the living room. Once, after I was grown and in a house of my own, she fixed the sewer pipe. She painted ceilings, and also landscapes; she reupholstered chairs. One summer she planted a whole yard of tall corn. She thought herself capable of doing anything, and did everything she imagined. But nothing was perfect. There was always some clear flaw, never visible head-on. You had to look underneath where the seams were. The corn thrived, though not in rows. The stalks elbowed one another like gossips in a dense little village.

"Miss Brrrroooobaker," my mother used to mock, rolling her Russian *rs,* whenever I crossed a *t* she had left uncrossed, or corrected a word she had mis- spelled, or became impatient with a *v* that had tangled itself up with a *w* in her speech. ("Vvventriloquist," I would say. "Vvventriloquist," she would obediently repeat. And the next time it would come out "wiolinist." Miss Brubaker was my high school English teacher, and my mother invoked her name as an emblem of raging finical obsession. "Miss Brrrroooobaker," my mother's voice hoots at me down the years, as I go on casting and recasting sentences in a tiny handwriting on monomaniacally uniform paper. The loops of my mother's handwriting—it was the Palmer Method—were as big as hoops, spilling generous splashy ebul- lience. She could pull off, at five minutes' notice, a satisfying dinner for 10 con- cocted out of nothing more than originality and panache. But the napkin would be folded a little off-center, and the spoon might be on the wrong side of the knife. She was an optimist who ignored trifles; for her, God was not in the details but in the intent. And all these culinary and agricultural efflorescences were ex- tracurricular, accomplished in the crevices and niches of a 14-hour business day. When she scribbled out her family memoirs, in heaps of dog-eared notebooks, or on the backs of old bills, or on the margins of last year's calendar, I would re- sist typing them; in the speed of the chase she often omitted words like "the," "and," "will." The same flashing and bountiful hand fashioned and fired ceramic pots, and painted brilliant autumn views and vases of imaginary flowers and ferns, and decorated ordinary Woolworth platters and lavish enameled gardens. But bits of the painted petals would chip away.

4   Lavish: my mother was as lavish as nature. She woke early and saturated the hours with work and inventiveness, and read late into the night. She was all profu- sion, abundance, fabrication. Angry at her children, she would run after us whirling the cord of the electric iron, like a lasso or a whip; but she never caught us. When, in the seventh grade, I was afraid of failing the Music Appreciation final exam because I could not tell the difference between "To a Wild Rose" and "Barcarolle," she got the idea of sending me to school with a gauze sling rigged up on my writ- ing arm, and an explanatory note that was purest fiction. But the sling kept slipping off. My mother gave advice like mad—she boiled over with so much passion for the predicaments of strangers that they turned into permanent cronies. She told inti- mate stories about people I had never heard of.

Despite the gargantuan Palmer loops (or possibly because of them), I have always known that my mother's was a life of—intricately abashing word!—ex- cellence: insofar as excellence means ripe generosity. She burgeoned, she pro- liferated; she was endlessly leafy and flowering. She wore red hates, and called herself a Gypsy. In her girlhood she marched with the suffragettes and for Mar- garet Sanger* and called herself a Red. She made me laugh, she was so varied: like a tree on which lemons, pomegranates, and prickly pears absurdly all hang together. She had the comedy of prodigality.

---

* (1883–1966). Leader in the American birth-control movement.

My own way is a thousand times more confined. I am a pinched perfection-ist, the ultimate fruition of Miss Brubaker; I attend to crabbed minutiae and am self-trammeled through taking pains. I am a kind of human snail, locked in and condemned by my own nature. The ancients believed that the moist track left by the snail as it crept was the snail's own essence, depleting its body little by little; the farther the snail toiled, the smaller it became, until it finally rubbed itself out. This is how perfectionists are. Say to us Excellence, and we will show you how we use up our substance and wear ourselves away, while making scarcely any progress at all. The fact that I am an exacting perfectionist in a narrow strait only, and nowhere else, is hardly to the point, since nothing matters to me so much as a comely and muscular sentence. It is my narrow strait, this snail's road: the track of the sentence I am writing now; and when I have eked out the wet sub-stance, ink or blood, that is its mark, I will begin the next sentence. Only in read-ing out sentences am I perfectionist; but then there is nothing else I know how to do, or take much interest in. I miter every pair of abutting sentences as scrupulously as Uncle Jake fitted one strip of rosewood against another. My mother's worldly and bountiful hand has escaped me. The sentence I am writing is my cabin and my shell, compact, self-sufficient. It is the burnished horizon—a merciless planet where flawlessness is the single standard, where even the in-most seams, however hidden from a laxer eye, must meet perfection. Here "ex-cellence" is not strewn casually from a tipped cornucopia, here disorder does not account for charm, here trifles rule like tyrants.

I measure my life in sentences, and my sentences are superior to my mother's, pressed out, line by line, like the lustrous ooze on the underside of the snail, the snail's secret open seam, its wound, leaking attar. My mother was too mettlesome to feel the force of a comma. She scorned minutiae. She measured her life according to what poured from the horn of plenty, which was her ample, cascading, elastic, susceptible, inexact heart. My narrower heart rides between the tiny horns of the snail, dwindling as it goes.

8   And out of this thinnest thread, this ink-wet line of words, must rise a visionary fog, a mist, a smoke, forging cities, histories, sorrows, quagmires, entan-glements, lives of sinners, even the life of my furnace-hearted mother: so much wilderness, waywardness, plenitude on the head of the precise and impeccable snail, between the horns.

Personal Response

Which approach to life does your own life resemble, Ozick's or her mother's? Ex-plain your answer.

Questions for Discussion

1. What do you think is Ozick's primary purpose in this essay? Is her goal to define an abstract concept, describe her mother's character, or explain her own approach to writing, or is it a combination of all of those purposes?

2. Find examples of both literal and figurative language that you think is especially effective. Where does Ozick use metaphor and simile, for instance?

3. Explain the difference between Ozick's way of doing things and her mother's. What is Ozick's attitude toward the differences between herself and her mother?

4. What does the fact that Ozick's mother marched with the suffragettes and for Margaret Sanger (paragraph 5) in her girlhood indicate about her mother's character?

5. How does Ozick define "excellence" in terms of her mother's nature and personality? How does her approach to writing define another form of excellence? What does Ozick mean in paragraph 6 when she says that she is "the ultimate fruition of Miss Brubaker"?

DEEMS

Russell Baker

Russell Baker was born in Virginia and worked as a newspaper reporter in both Baltimore and Washington, D.C., before becoming a columnist for the New York Times. Since 1962, his Pulitzer Prize–winning syndicated column, the "Observer," has entertained readers with humorous insights into and criticisms of social issues, politics, and culture. Among his eleven books are A Baker's Dozen (1964), So This Is Depravity (1980), and There's a Country in My Cellar (1990). He has written two memoirs, Growing Up (1982) and The Good Times (1989), from which the following is taken.

My mother started me in newspaper work in 1937 right after my twelfth birthday. She would have started me younger, but there was a law against working before age twelve. She thought it was a silly law, and said so to Deems.

Deems was boss of a group of boys who worked home delivery routes for the *Baltimore News-Post.* She found out about him a few weeks after we got to Baltimore. She just went out on the street, stopped a paperboy, and asked how he'd got his job.

"There's this man Deems . . ."

Deems was short and plump and had curly brown hair. He owned a car and a light gray suit and always wore a necktie and white shirt. A real businessman, I thought the first time I saw him. My mother was talking to him on the sidewalk in front of the Union Square Methodist Church and I was standing as tall as I could, just out of earshot.

"Now, buddy, when we get down there keep your shoulders back and stand up real straight," she had cautioned me after making sure my necktie was all right and my shirt clean.

Watching the two of them in conversation, with Deems glancing at me now and then, I kept my shoulders drawn back in the painful military style I'd seen in movies, trying to look a foot taller than I really was.

"Come over here, Russ, and meet Mister Deems," she finally said, and I did, managing to answer his greeting by saying, "The pleasure's all mine," which I'd heard people say in the movies. I probably blushed while saying it, because meeting strangers was painfully embarrassing to me.

8   "If that's the rule, it's the rule," my mother was telling Deems, "and we'll just have to put up with it, but it still doesn't make any sense to me."

As we walked back to the house she said I couldn't have a paper route until I was twelve. And all because of some foolish rule they had down here in Baltimore. You'd think if a boy wanted to work they would encourage him instead of making him stay idle so long that laziness got embedded in his bones.

That was April. We had barely finished the birthday cake in August before Deems came by the apartment and gave me the tools of the newspaper trade: an account book for keeping track of the customers' bills and a long, brown web belt. Slung around one shoulder and across the chest, the belt made it easy to balance fifteen or twenty pounds of papers against the hip. I had to buy my own wire cutters for opening the newspaper bundles the trucks dropped at Wisengoff's store on the corner of Stricker and West Lombard streets.

In February my mother had moved us down from New Jersey, where we had been living with her brother Allen ever since my father died in 1930. This move of hers to Baltimore was a step toward fulfilling a dream. More than almost anything else in the world, she wanted "a home of our own." I'd heard her talk of that "home of our own" all through those endless Depression years when we lived as poor relatives dependent on Uncle Allen's goodness. "A home of our own. One of these days, Buddy, we'll have a home of our own."

12   That winter she had finally saved just enough to make her move, and she came to Baltimore. There were several reasons for Baltimore. For one, there were people she knew in Baltimore, people she could go to if things got desperate. And desperation was possible, because the moving would exhaust her savings, and the apartment rent was twenty-four dollars a month. She would have to find a job quickly. My sister Doris was only nine, but I was old enough for an after-school job that could bring home a few dollars a week. So as soon as it was legal I went into newspaper work.

The romance of it was almost unbearable on my first day as I trudged west along Lombard Street, then south along Gilmor, and east down Pratt Street with the bundle of newspapers strapped to my hip. I imagined people pausing to admire me as I performed this important work, spreading the news of the world, the city, and the racetracks onto doorsteps, through mail slots, and under doorjambs. I had often gazed with envy at paperboys; to be one of them at last was happiness sublime.

Very soon, though, I discovered drawbacks. The worst of these was Deems. Though I had only forty customers, Deems sent papers for forty-five. Since I was billed for every paper left on Wisengoff's corner, I had to pay for the five extra copies out of income or try to hustle them on the street. I hated standing at streetcar stops yelling, "Paper! Paper!" at people getting off trolleys. Usually, if my mother wasn't around to catch me, I stuck the extras in a dark closet and took the loss.

Deems was constantly baiting new traps to dump more papers on me. When I solved the problem of the five extras by getting five new subscribers for home delivery, Deems announced a competition with mouth-watering prizes for the newsboys who got the most subscribers. Too innocent to cope with this sly master of private enterprise, I took the bait.

16   "Look at these prizes I can get for signing up new customers," I told my mother. "A balloon-tire bicycle. A free pass to the movies for a whole year."

The temptation was too much. I reported my five new subscribers to help me in the competition.

Whereupon Deems promptly raised my order from forty-five to fifty papers, leaving me again with the choice of hustling to unload the five extras or losing money.

I won a free pass to the movies, though. It was good for a whole year. And to the magnificent Loew's Century located downtown on Lexington Street. The passes were good only for nights in the middle of the week when I usually had too much homework to allow for movies. Still, in the summer with school out, it was thrilling to go all the way downtown at night to sit in the Century's damask and velvet splendor and see MGM's glamorous stars in their latest movies.

20   To collect my prize I had to go to a banquet the paper gave for its "honor carriers" at the Emerson Hotel. There were fifty of us, and I was sure the other forty-nine would all turn out to be slicksters wised up to the ways of the world, who would laugh at my doltish ignorance of how to eat at a great hotel banquet. My fear of looking foolish at the banquet made me lie awake nights dreading it and imagining all the humiliating mistakes I could make.

I had seen banquets in movies. Every plate was surrounded by a baffling array of knives, forks, and spoons. I knew it would be the same at the Emerson Hotel. The Emerson was one of the swankiest hotels in Baltimore. It was not likely to hold down on the silverware. I talked to my mother.

"How will I know what to eat what with?"

The question did not interest her.

24   "Just watch what everybody else does, and enjoy yourself," she said.

I came back to the problem again and again.

"Do you use the same spoon for your coffee as you do for dessert?"

"Don't worry about it. Everybody isn't going to be staring at you."

28   "Is it all right to butter your bread with the same knife you use to cut the meat?"

"Just go and have a good time."

Close to panic, I showed up at the Emerson, found my way to the banquet, and was horrified to find that I had to sit beside Deems throughout the meal. We probably talked about something, but I was so busy sweating with terror and rolling my eyeballs sidewise to see what silverware Deems was using to eat with that I didn't hear a word all night. The following week, Deems started sending me another five extras.

Now and then he also provided a treat. One day in 1938 he asked if I would like to join a small group of boys he was taking to visit the *News-Post* newsroom. My mother, in spite of believing that nothing came before homework at night, wasn't cold-hearted enough to deny me a chance to see the city room of a great metropolitan newspaper. I had seen plenty of city rooms in the movies. They were glamorous places full of exciting people like Lee Tracy, Edmund Lowe, and Adolphe Menjou trading wisecracks and making mayors and cops look like saps. To see such a place, to stand, actually stand, in the city room of a great newspaper and look at reporters who were in touch every day with killers and professional baseball players—that was a thrilling prospect.

32   Because the *News-Post* was an afternoon paper, almost everybody had left for the day when we got there that night. The building, located downtown near the harbor, was disappointing. It looked like a factory, and not a very big factory either. Inside there was a smell compounded of ink, pulp, chemicals, paste, oil, gasoline, greasy rags, and hot metal. We took an elevator up and came into a long room filled with dilapidated desks, battered telephones, and big blocky typewriters. Almost nobody there, just two or three men in shirt-sleeves. It was the first time I'd ever seen Deems look awed.

"Boys, this is the nerve center of the newspaper," he said, his voice heavy and solemn like the voice of Westbrook Van Voorhis, the *March of Time* man, when he said, "Time marches on."

I was confused. I had expected the newsroom to have glamour, but this place had nothing but squalor. The walls hadn't been painted for years. The windows were filthy. Desks were heaped with mounds of crumpled paper, torn sheets of newspaper, overturned paste pots, dog-eared telephone directories. The floor was ankle deep in newsprint, carbon paper, and crushed cigarette packages. Waist-high cans overflowed with trash. Ashtrays were buried under cigarette ashes and butts. Ugly old wooden chairs looked ready for the junk shop.

It looked to me like a place that probably had more cockroaches than we had back home on Lombard Street, but Deems was seeing it through rose-colored glasses. As we stood looking around at the ruins, he started telling us how lucky we were to be newsboys. Lucky to have a foot on the upward ladder so early in life. If we worked hard and kept expanding our paper routes we could make the men who ran this paper sit up and notice us. And when men like that noticed you, great things could happen, because they were important men, the most important of all being the man who owned our paper: Mr. Hearst Himself, William Randolph Hearst, founder of the greatest newspaper organization in America. A great man, Mr. Hearst, but not so great that he didn't appreciate his newsboys, who were the backbone of the business. Many of whom would someday grow up and work at big jobs on this paper. Did we realize that any of us, maybe all of us, could end up one of these days sitting right here in this vitally important room, the newsroom, the nerve center of the newspaper?

36   Yes, Deems was right. Riding home on the streetcar that night, I realized I was a lucky boy to be getting such an early start up the ladder of journalism. It

was childish to feel let down because the city room looked like such a dump instead of like city rooms in the movies. Deems might be a slave driver, but he was doing it for my own good, and I ought to be grateful. In *News Selling*, the four-page special paper Mr. Hearst published just for his newsboys, they'd run a piece that put it almost as beautifully as Deems had.

YOU'RE A MEMBER OF THE FOURTH ESTATE was the headline on it. I was so impressed that I put the paper away in a safe place and often took it out to read when I needed inspiration. It told how "a great English orator" named Edmund Burke "started a new name for a new profession—the Fourth Estate . . . the press . . . NEWSPAPER MEN."

And it went on to say:

"The Fourth Estate was then . . . and IS now . . . a great estate for HE-men . . . workers . . . those who are proud of the business they're in!"

40   (Mr. Hearst always liked plenty of exclamation marks, dots, and capital letters.)

"Get that kick of pride that comes from knowing you are a newspaper man. That means something!"

"A newspaper man never ducks a dare. YOU are a newspaper man. A salesman of newspapers . . . the final cog in the immense machine of newspaper production—a SERVICE for any man to be proud of."

"So throw back the chest. Hit the route hard each day. Deliver fast and properly. Sell every day. Add to your route because you add to the NEWSPAPER field when you do. And YOU MAKE MONEY DOING IT. It is a great life—a grand opportunity. Don't boot it—build it up. Leave it better than when you came into it."

44   "It is a great life." I kept coming back to that sentence as I read and reread the thing. No matter how awful it got, and it sometimes got terrible, I never quit believing it was a great life. I kept at it until I was almost sixteen, chest thrown back, delivering fast and properly, selling every day and adding to my route. At the end I'd doubled its size and was making as much as four dollars a week from it.

A few months after he took us down to see the city room, Deems quit. My mother said he'd found a better job. Later, when I thought about him, I wondered if maybe it wasn't because he hated himself for having to make life hell for boys. I hoped that wasn't the reason because he was the first newspaperman I ever knew, and I wanted him to be the real thing. Hard as nails.

Personal Response

Deems says of his first day as a newspaper boy that "the romance of it was almost unbearable" (paragraph 13). Did you have a similar response to your first job? Write about your first job, especially your feelings about it when you first began.

Questions for Discussion

1. What conclusions can you draw about Deems' character on the basis of the young Baker's perception of him? What was it about Deems that Baker admired? How did Deems inspire the young Baker?

2. Describe Baker's mother. What part did she play in putting Baker on his career path?

3. In what ways was the young Baker influenced by what he saw in the movies?

4. What contrasts does Baker make between the romanticized images he saw in the movies and reality? How did the visit to the *News-Post* newsroom serve both to dispel his illusions and inspire Baker to pursue journalism as a career? Why do you think William Randolph Hearst was such a strong determining influence in Baker's life?

ITALIANITÀ IN A WORLD MADE OF LOVE AND NEED

Thom Tammaro

Thom Tammaro is a professor of multidisciplinary studies at Moorhead (Minnesota) State University. He is author of Minnesota Suite *(1987, rpt. 1995), a chapbook of poems; editor of* Roving Across Fields: A Conversation with William Stafford and Uncollected Poems 1942–1982 *(1983); editor, with Mark Vinz, of* Inheriting the Land: Contemporary Voices from the Midwest *(1993); and* Imagining Home: Writing from the Midwest *(1995), which won the Critics' Choice Award for 1995 and a 1996 Minnesota Book Award. When the Italians Came to My Home Town *(1995) is his latest collection of poems. The essay reprinted here is from* Two Worlds Walking: Short Stories, Essays, and Poetry by Writers with Mixed Heritages *(1994).*

> *Amore e eruduzione annobiliscono la vita*
> *Love and learning ennoble life*
> Italian Proverb

I am an Italian-American, the grandson of three Italian immigrants who, upon arriving in this country in the early 1900s from their south central Italian village of Sepino near Campobasso (described in one recent guidebook as the "Akron of Italy") in Molise, walked through the Great Hall at Ellis Island. Like thousands before them who did not know the language of the new world, they stood mute in front of customs and immigration officials. But with papers in order and, perhaps, with the help of a bilingual staff worker, they eventually found their way to the steel mills of western Pennsylvania. My fourth grandparent, my paternal grandmother, was American-born. However, she returned with her mother and father to their Italian village shortly after her birth, where she lived most of her childhood and early adolescence until the family returned once again to western Pennsylvania. I do not know why they came to the United States, though I have no reason to think their reasons were any different from more than two million others who made the journey from their Italian homeland to the U.S. in the first decade of the 1900s: economic, social, political, health, and, for some, sheer adventure.

I was born, raised, schooled, and churched in an Italian-American neighborhood and culture. From a map I once sketched of the three-square-block neighborhood of my childhood, I recognized only fourteen non-Italian households from among the 107 families living there. Thirty-three of the Italian households were three-generational. Not until I studied a map of Italy, some time during high school, did I realize that many of my friends and neighbors carried the name of their Italian village with them in their American surnames: the Costas, the Ferraras, the Gardas, the Genovas, the Melfis, the Riccios, the Tarantos, the Venezis. Even my surname carries the name of the river that flows through my ancestral village.

Forty-eight first cousins and aunts and uncles lived within walking distance of my house, all within a mile radius of the Tammaro and DeTullio homesteads. We lived a kind of village life then. My father's ten brothers and sisters and my mother's eight brothers and sisters provided me with a bevy of blood-cousin playmates. Back doors were always open: for uncles and aunts, who dropped by to visit, found no one home, then helped themselves to coffee and biscotti; for cousins who looked for a cool glass of water to quench their thirst from a hard day of play; for a neighbor, who left a tomato, bell pepper, or freshly cut flowers on the kitchen table; and for the insurance man, who knew where my father kept the quarterly premium when he came around to collect and found no one at home. . . .

4   Only when I ventured from my neighborhood did I hear people speak *without* Italian accents. Later, in my late twenties, I would lament the failure of my grandparents and parents to preserve the Italian language in their households, though I do understand their strong desire to drop any hints of the Old Country, if not in their accents, at least in the accents of their children and grandchildren. Even though my grandparents did not permit Italian to be spoken in their houses, I absorbed enough Italian from the surrounding neighborhood culture so years later on the train from Rapallo to Genoa, to my surprise, I could carry on what I think was an intelligible conversation with a wonderful Italian woman who knew no English. Words came flooding back to me from some long forgotten reservoir of memory, though sometime I wonder if Signora Fermenti's bright laughter that sweltering July afternoon was really caused by the silly and outrageous combination of words I struggled to string together.

By the time I was enrolled in a Catholic school kindergarten in 1956, only a few of my classmates spoke with an Italian accent, their parents being recent immigrants. Most of us were second and third generation Italian-Americans, whose vowels and stresses had long been smoothed and Americanized. By the time I graduated from eighth grade, the once prominent accents of my Italian-speaking classmates had vanished, their talk stripped of any residue of their native language. A sure sign that American education had triumphed. . . .

Within my family and the neighborhood where I grew up, I remember few, if any, models of professionalism—no doctors, no lawyers, no dentists, no CPAs, CEOs, or MBAs or PhDs. We were low-to-middle class Italian blue-collar steel mill laborers. I remember an old immigrant saying that goes something like this: "They told us the streets of America were paved with gold, but when we got there we discovered that the streets were paved with bricks, and we did the paving!" To me, becoming a doctor or lawyer or CPA was as distant from my reality as the homeland of many of my neighbors. We were the ones paving the streets, so to speak. My father's second-oldest brother was an exception. He attended Pittsburgh's Carnegie Institute of Technology (now Carnegie-Mellon) from 1936–1940 on a football scholarship. He quarterbacked the team in their 1940 New Year's Day Sugar Bowl appearance against TCU. Upon graduation that same year with an engineering degree, he worked as an engineer until his retirement at the same steel fabricating plant—four blocks from the Tammaro homestead—where my father and uncles worked as laborers. Had he not been able to throw or run with a football with some skill, attending college would have been an economic impossibility for him in 1936.

The centrality of the family in the Italian-American experience is difficult to deny. In the May 15, 1983, cover story for *The New York Times Magazine,* Stephen B. Hall writes: "Inherited responsibilities, moral as well as economic and practical, were so overwhelming that second generation Italians grew up with a heightened sense of familial responsibility that occasioned unusual anxiety when it comes to separation from family." Sons felt a natural obligation to follow in their father's footsteps to the mills; daughters were destined to follow their mother's path that often led to the house rather than away from it. And guilt often followed those who decided otherwise. Census Bureau data from the late 1970s show that educational levels among individuals with two Italian parents rank near the bottom among ethnic groups, as opposed to individuals with one Italian parent.

8   For many of the Italians in my neighborhood, survivalism was a way of life. Motivation beyond that which allowed for week-to-week survival was difficult to find. Children grew up with a constricted view of the future, with horizons extended not much further than the chain link fences that surrounded the mills. Where I grew up, most second and third generation Italian-Americans were content with supporting a family with jobs that offered good pay and benefits, usually jobs in the steel mills and their off-shoot industries. Paycheck-to-paycheck living became the gauge against which I measured the good life. This short-sightedness is something I still struggle with today. And the good life meant the basics: food on your table, a roof over your head, and clothes on your back. And maybe a little left over, but not much. It was mainly about providing for your family. Does anyone have the right to ask for more? This survival mentality is consistent with what I have read about immigrants from the *mezzagiorno* or middle region of Italy—the region from which most of my family and neighbors emigrated. My childhood horizon extended to the three square blocks of my neighborhood. I don't remember families having such luxuries as "savings accounts for college," since college was never really thought of as being part of our future. I saw many relatives and neighbors return from their daily work indifferent and numbed by that which made their lives possible. Until I was fifteen or sixteen, I believed that people were not supposed to enjoy or find reward and satisfaction in their life's

work. If those workers found enjoyment and satisfaction in their work, they certainly did not express it to anyone. So, at an early age, I understood that whatever my life's work was to be, I was not supposed to enjoy it. I understood it as one of life's irrevocable tenets.

But there are always forces working their magic on you, whether or not you are conscious of them. For me, those forces, that magic, came in the form of three women, all English teachers at my high school. And I am forever grateful to them. Like a child in a fairy tale who journeys through dark forests or under mountains guided by benevolent feminine forces, I was guided by these women who recognized my desire to move beyond the constricted view of the future from which they, too, had emerged. How wonderful that they had come back to help others along the same journey! Each woman, in her own way, offered me a new measure of possibility: Ms. DeMark, who offered unconditional support and nurturing of my newly found love of writing—how I admired her strength and courage to live by a creed that claimed books and language as equally vital to life as jobs and money; Ms. Gibbons, who listened carefully to my talk about writing but, more importantly, challenged me to get it down on paper, which taught me that words on paper were commitments; and Mrs. Ionta, who taught me that the job of poems and stories—mine as well as others'—was not complete until something changed inside.

The way these women moved through the world, the way they thought and talked and envisioned the world, their vitality and liveliness, their joy in their own lives, their "differentness," suggested possibilities I had never imagined. Being in the presence of these women was their gift to me. Perhaps that is the gift of the true teacher: to invite you into their world and suggest possibilities where limitations rule.

And so I accepted their invitations; I followed and trusted their guidance. Because of them, I believed I could step from the patterns of my ancestors and culture and make my own way. And perhaps I could step from those patterns because one April afternoon in 1968 we read Robert Frost's poem "Two Tramps in Mud Time," a poem I'm sure rooted in my unconscious but only revealed its meaning to me many years later. It is a poem about work and the proper relationship to it. The woodchopper who speaks in the poem suspects that the two tramps coming along might be after his job. The last stanza, I think, not only resolves the woodchopper's dilemma about his relationship to his work, but also suggests Frost's bold assertion about his own life's work—writing and poetry:

> But yield who will to their separation,
> My object in living is to unite
> My avocation and my vocation
> As my two eyes make one in sight.
> Only where love and need are one,
> And the work is play for mortal stakes,
> Is the deed ever really done
> For Heaven and the future's sake.

12   With these words impressed in my mind—and with parents who knew that college was now affordable to their son because of President Kennedy's plan to create a "democracy of opportunity" by providing guaranteed student loans at low interest rates to the needy, I left the neighborhood. But early in my freshman year of college, I discovered the true meaning of an old Italian proverb, *Chi lascia la via vecchia per la nuova, sa quel che perde e non squel che trova:* "Whoever forsakes the old way for the new knows what he is leaving but not what he will find."

In 1969 it would have been easy for me to walk directly from high school into the steel mills, as my younger brother did a few years later, and make $18,000 or $20,000 a year, for those were the boom years in the smoke stack communities that spilled out along the Ohio and Beaver Rivers of the industrial valley of western Pennsylvania. I could have stayed in those towns, made "good money," as they used to say, got married, fathered children, owned a home and cars, and planned hunting and fishing trips and two-week summer vacations. Instead I delayed those dreams and in the early summer of 1969 found myself speeding north on Interstate 79, in search of the Albion-Edinboro Exit and one of Pennsylvania's people's colleges.

Like my immigrant grandparents before me, I was journeying to a new world. But I was an immigrant on a different voyage. I arrived with my blue collar tucked beneath my khakis and cotton shirts. I was only an hour or two away from home, ninety-three miles if I correctly remember the odometer, but distance cannot always be measured by time or miles. What I found waiting for me at college was a world like no other I had known. I might as well have been a million miles away from the blast furnaces and open hearths of U.S. Steel and Jones & Laughlin, around which the lives of friends and families revolved as they toiled through the long days and nights of their lives; for I toiled near another fire then, one that burned deep and bright and does so still today.

Arriving at college with a vision of the future that didn't include steel mills or union strikes in the winter, I, like so many other first-generation college students, found myself a stranger in a strange land. Lacking the social graces that come with two or three generations of middle class breeding and finishing, I stumbled through my first years of college, stumbled not academically, but emotionally, socially, and psychologically. I lacked the savvy that comes from having parents and siblings who before me moved through the new, strange rituals and codes of academic culture and then passed along that savvy to me—through a kind of cultural osmosis—so I, too, could feel at home and move nimbly through that privileged class.

16   In her intelligent and important book *Errors and Expectations,* the late Mina Shaughnessy, a wonderful educator, speaking of underprepared students, wrote: "college both beckons and threatens them, offering to teach them useful ways of thinking about the world, promising to improve the quality of their lives, but threatening at the same time to take them from their distinctive ways of interpreting the world, to assimilate them into a culture of academia without acknowledging their experiences as outsiders." And somewhere Freud writes that moving up two steps in the social class hierarchy results in neurosis. I certainly recognize neurosis during my early college days. After fifteen years of university

teaching, I know that underpreparation means more than academic underpreparation. I understand how emotional, social, cultural, and psychological underpreparation camouflages intellect and potential. Perhaps this accounts for part of the high attrition rate among first-generation college students? In many ways, we are all underprepared—outsiders if you will. We come to whatever new experiences before us at once excited by the prospects that lie ahead, yet threatened by those very forces that can liberate us.

So how do we journey through dark forests and venture across forbidden zones? How do we reconcile that which at once beckons and threatens? Perhaps this is what true education of the Self is all about. In the dark forest of college and graduate school, once again I was guided—but this time by three male English professors, each of whom led me through intellectual territories where my father did not travel. Again, I am grateful for their mentoring, for their showing me new measures of possibility, for their recognition of my struggles (which later I discovered were once their own struggles) in this new world. They provided a kind of safety zone against the threats of stepping from old world limitations to new world possibilities. I am grateful to Professors Carothers, Heffernan, and Koontz for their good counsel, for their open hearts and their generosity of spirit and intellect.

I consider myself fortunate that between the ages of fifteen and thirty I found a wonderful balance of feminine and masculine guides. Looking back at those years, what I remember above all else about those three women and three men who guided me along my journey was the intensity with which they lived and loved their lives. At the center of their lives, each possessed a love, a passion if you will, for their life's work: teaching literature and writing poetry. And I do not think it is a coincidence that nearly twenty-five years along the journey, I, too, teach literature and writing and write poetry. Remember Frost: *Only where love and need are one, / And the work is play for mortal stakes, / Is the deed ever really done.*

We all possess the power to guide. And now as someone teaching writing and literature to others, I hope to give back the gift that was given to me: to offer my students new measures of possibility; to guide the lost stranger along his or her own way; to help others find a passion to place at the center of their lives, for I truly believe that one passion often leads to other passions. If we can make choices in our lives, striving to keep love and need as one, perhaps we can unite our avocation with our vocation, as Frost says, and come from our jobs not numbed or indifferent but singing the vital song of our lives. "To be a person, identical with myself," the developmental psychologist Erik Erikson writes, "presupposes a basic trust in one's origins—and the courage to emerge from them." Escape was once a word I used to characterize my dissociation from my origins. But it is not a word I use now. It is not so much escape as it is emergence, for we can never really escape those origins. It is not so much rejection as it is acceptance and recognition of how something can be at once nourishing and vital as well as starving and suffocating.

20   In their book *Ethnicity and Family Therapy,* Giordanno and McGoldritch say that to understand the second and third generation Italian-American we must think that most "trimmed their sails of personal ambition simply to avoid conflict

with parents." Moving away from the codes, rituals, mores, patterns, and habits of one's native culture toward those of another is often misunderstood as a rejection or forsaking of that culture. The old bugaboos of "What's the matter? Your father's way of life not good enough for you?" and "What's the matter? You too good for us?" often echo in the minds of those who light out on their own to discover new ways of seeing or thinking. This was certainly true for me. And yet, to some degree, it was that very same independence and spirit that drove so many Italian immigrants to this new world in search of the *via nuova,* which they often found radically different from the lives of their parents and grandparents.

The image of my grandparents standing mute before customs and immigration officials in the Great Hall at Ellis Island because they did not know the language is a stark juxtaposition to the image of their grandson standing in front of his university classroom, talking to and teaching students about the liberation that comes with expressing one's private self and thoughts through language. And while I do not think they could have imagined that life for one of their grandchildren, I am sure they would appreciate and take joy in the irony. How often I have wished they were alive to witness the fruits of their labor.

Italianità is a term used by Italian-American writers, scholars, and critics to characterize the varied ways in which their Italian culture and heritage filters into their life and work. It is a term whose definition is painted with broad strokes, as it should be, for who can truly and surely pin down the ways in which anyone's culture seeps into one's life and work? *Italianità* is the cultural collective that colors and shapes experience, in all of its hues and tones, some bright and lively, others muted and subtle. It is the trickle down theory of heritage; it is the residue of culture that clings to us long after we have moved away from it. The great Russian painter Marc Chagall wrote in his journal "Every painter is born somewhere . . . a certain aroma of his birthplace clings to his work." Is that not true for non-painters as well? We come to discover it is with us, more often than not, and in ways more intricate than simple. It is the way we explain ourselves to others and, most importantly, to ourselves. It is at once the real and mythic identity we have accumulated. *Italianità* is Ariadne's thread that leads us out of the dark cave of our cultural ignorance to recover the light of our own heritage.*

Those living *italianità* often embrace the baggage of origin—sometimes heavy and burdensome—of who and what they are and where they come from. Family and place: two aspects of culture we must face if and when we ask ourselves the question "Who am I?" As an Italian American, I live with and accept those tensions that drive my life: of *la via vecchia* and *via nuova,* the old ways and the new; of *l'ordine della famiglia* and *strano paese,* of the ways of the family and the strange ways of the new land. It has not always been easy. However, I would not exchange

---

* In her pioneering *The Dream Book: An Anthology of Writings by Italian American Women* (NY: Schocken Books, 1985), Helen Barolini introduces the term in her "Preface." An extended discussion of *italianità* can be found in the "Introduction" to the book *From the Margin: Writings from Italian Americans,* a wonderful anthology of Italian-American writing edited by Anthony J. Tamburri, Paolo A. Giordano, and Fred L. Gardaphé (Purdue University Press, 1991).

those experiences of childhood and adolescence for any other in the world. I cherish and value *italianità* and trust in all its goodness; but I also understand its other dimension and try to recognize when it is at work in my life. Once boundaries are drawn, once limits are created, once restrictions are enforced, narrowness of mind and behavior soon follows. And it is narrowness of mind and behavior that restricts and devalues—ourselves as well as others. And that is something I work to avoid in all my actions. In the larger sense, we are all immigrants on the journey. When we find and create our own new world, let it be a world made of love and need.

Personal Response

Discuss whether your experience in going to college is similar to or different from Tammaro's when he writes: "What I found waiting for me at college was a world like no other I had known" (paragraph 14)?

Questions for Discussion

1. Discuss your understanding of the title of this essay in your own words and then locate the passages in which Tammaro explains the word *Italianità* and the references to love and need. Do you share his view that "family and place" are "two aspects of culture we must face if and when we ask ourselves the questions 'Who am I?'" (paragraphs 22–23). Does your own career goal reflect both "love and need"?

2. How do the introductory paragraphs in which Tammaro describes his family and neighborhood relate to his discussion of the teachers who became his role models?

3. What do the six role models Tammaro names have in common? Have you had teachers with any of the qualities Tammaro mentions? If so, describe them and why you believe they make good role models.

4. Respond to Tammaro's comment in paragraph 19 that "we all possess the power to guide." Do you agree with him?

5. What distinctions does Tammaro make between escape and emergence, rejection and acceptance? How do those distinctions relate to his discussion of the relation of avocation to vocation and of making choices about our lives?

THE TEACHER WHO CHANGED MY LIFE

Nicholas Gage

Nicholas Gage wrote of the 1948 torture and murder of his mother by Communist guerrillas in Greece in his best-selling book Eleni *(1983). He is also author of* The Bourlotas Fortune *(1975);* Hellas, a Portrait of Greece

(1987); and A Place for Us *(1989), in which he tells how he and his sisters adjusted to life in the United States. This essay, adapted from that book, appeared in* Parade *magazine in December 1989.*

The person who set the course of my life in the new land I entered as a young war refugee—who, in fact, nearly dragged me onto the path that would bring all the blessings I've received in America—was a salty-tongued, no-nonsense schoolteacher named Marjorie Hurd. When I entered her classroom in 1953, I had been to six schools in five years, starting in the Greek village where I was born in 1939.

When I stepped off a ship in New York Harbor on a gray March day in 1949, I was an undersized 9-year-old in short pants who had lost his mother and was coming to live with the father he didn't know. My mother, Eleni Gatzoyiannis, had been imprisoned, tortured and shot by Communist guerrillas for sending me and three of my four sisters to freedom. She died so that her children could go to their father in the United States.

The portly, bald, well-dressed man who met me and my sisters seemed a foreign, authoritarian figure. I secretly resented him for not getting the whole family out of Greece early enough to save my mother. Ultimately, I would grow to love him and appreciate how he dealt with becoming a single parent at the age of 56, but at first our relationship was prickly, full of hostility.

4   As Father drove us to our new home—a tenement in Worcester, Mass.—and pointed out the huge brick building that would be our first school in America, I clutched my Greek notebooks from the refugee camp, hoping that my few years of schooling would impress my teachers in this cold, crowded country. They didn't. When my father led me and my 11-year-old sister to Greendale Elementary School, the grim-faced Yankee principal put the two of us in a class for the mentally retarded. There was no facility in those days for non-English-speaking children.

By the time I met Marjorie Hurd four years later, I had learned English, been placed in a normal, graded class and had even been chosen for the college preparatory track in the Worcester public school system. I was 13 years old when our father moved us yet again, and I entered Chandler Junior High shortly after the beginning of seventh grade. I found myself surrounded by richer, smarter and better-dressed classmates who looked askance at my strange clothes and heavy accent. Shortly after I arrived, we were told to select a hobby to pursue during "club hour" on Fridays. The idea of hobbies and clubs made no sense to my immigrant ears, but I decided to follow the prettiest girl in my class—the blue-eyed daughter of the local Lutheran minister. She led me through the door marked "Newspaper Club" and into the presence of Miss Hurd, the newspaper adviser and English teacher who would become my mentor and my muse.

A formidable, solidly built woman with salt-and-pepper hair, a steely eye and a flat Boston accent, Miss Hurd had no patience with layabouts. "What are all you goof-offs doing here?" she bellowed at the would-be journalists. "This is the Newspaper Club! We're going to put out a *newspaper.* So if there's anybody in this room who doesn't like work, I suggest you go across to the Glee Club now, because you're going to work your tails off here!"

I was soon under Miss Hurd's spell. She did indeed teach us to put out a newspaper, skills I honed during my next 25 years as a journalist. Soon I asked the principal to transfer me to her English class as well. There, she drilled us on grammar until I finally began to understand the logic and structure of the English language. She assigned stories for us to read and discuss; not tales of heroes, like the Greek myths I knew, but stories of underdogs—poor people, even immigrants, who seemed ordinary until a crisis drove them to do something extraordinary. She also introduced us to the literary wealth of Greece—giving me a new perspective on my war-ravaged, impoverished homeland. I began to be proud of my origins.

8   One day, after discussing how writers should write about what they know, she assigned us to compose an essay from our own experience. Fixing me with a stern look, she added, "Nick, I want you to write about what happened to your family in Greece." I had been trying to put those painful memories behind me and left the assignment until the last moment. Then, on a warm spring afternoon, I sat in my room with a yellow pad and pencil and stared out the window at the buds on the trees. I wrote that the coming of spring always reminded me of the last time I said goodbye to my mother on a green and gold day in 1948.

I kept writing, one line after another, telling how the Communist guerrillas occupied our village, took our home and food, how my mother started planning our escape when she learned that the children were to be sent to re-education camps behind the Iron Curtain and how, at the last moment, she couldn't escape with us because the guerrillas sent her with a group of women to thresh wheat in a distant village. She promised she would try to get away on her own, she told me to be brave and hung a silver cross around my neck, and then she kissed me. I watched the line of women being led down into the ravine and up the other side, until they disappeared around the bend—my mother a tiny brown figure at the end who stopped for an instant to raise her hand in one last farewell.

I wrote about our nighttime escape down the mountain, across the minefields and into the lines of the Nationalist soldiers, who sent us to a refugee camp. It was there that we learned of our mother's execution. I felt very lucky to have come to America, I concluded, but every year, the coming of spring made me feel sad because it reminded me of the last time I saw my mother.

I handed in the essay, hoping never to see it again, but Miss Hurd had it published in the school paper. This mortified me at first, until I saw that my classmates reacted with sympathy and tact to my family's story. Without telling me, Miss Hurd also submitted the essay to a contest sponsored by the Freedoms Foundation at Valley Forge, Pa., and it won a medal. The Worcester paper wrote about the award and quoted my essay at length. My father, by then a "five-and-dime-store chef," as the paper described him, was ecstatic with pride, and the Worcester Greek community celebrated the honor to one of its own.

12   For the first time I began to understand the power of the written word. A secret ambition took root in me. One day, I vowed, I would go back to Greece,

find out the details of my mother's death and write about her life, so her grand-children would know of her courage. Perhaps I would event track down the men who killed her and write of their crimes. Fulfilling that ambition would take me 30 years.

Meanwhile, I followed the literary path that Miss Hurd had so forcefully set me on. After junior high, I became the editor of my school paper at Classical High School and got a part-time job at the Worcester *Telegram and Gazette*. Although my father could only give me $50 and encouragement toward a college education, I managed to finance four years at Boston University with Scholarships and part-time jobs in journalism. During my last year of college, an article I wrote about a friend who had died in the Philippines—the first person to lose his life working for the Peace Corps—led to my winning the Hearst Award for College Journalism. And the plaque was given to me in the White House by President John F. Kennedy.

For a refugee who had never seen a motorized vehicle or indoor plumbing until he was 9, this was an unimaginable honor. When the Worcester paper ran a picture of me standing next to President Kennedy, my father rushed out to buy a new suit in order to be properly dressed to receive the congratulations of the Worcester Greeks. He clipped out the photograph, had it laminated in plastic and carried it in his breast pocket for the rest of his life to show everyone he met. I found the much-worn photo in his pocket on the day he died 20 years later.

In our isolated Greek village, my mother had bribed a cousin to teach her to read, for girls were not supposed to attend school beyond a certain age. She had always dreamed of her children receiving an education. She couldn't be there when I graduated from Boston University, but the person who came with my father and shared our joy was my former teacher, Marjorie Hurd. We celebrated not only my bachelor's degree but also the scholarships that paid my way to Columbia's Graduate School of Journalism. There, I met the woman who would eventually become my wife. At our wedding and at the baptisms of our three children, Marjorie Hurd was always there, dancing alongside the Greeks.

16   By then, she was Mrs. Rabidou, for she had married a widower when she was in her early 40s. That didn't distract her from her vocation of introducing young minds to English literature, however. She taught for a total of 41 years and continually would make a "project" of some balky student in whom she spied a spark of potential. Often these were students from the most troubled homes, yet she would alternately bully and charm each one with her own special brand of tough love until the spark caught fire. She retired in 1981 at the age of 62 but still avidly follows the lives and careers of former students while overseeing her adult stepchildren and driving her husband on camping trips to New Hampshire.

Miss Hurd was one of the first to call me on Dec. 10, 1987, when President Reagan, in his television address after the summit meeting with Gorbachev, told the nation that Eleni Gatzoyiannis' dying cry, "My children!" had helped inspire him to seek an arms agreement "for all the children of the world."

"I can't imagine a better monument for your mother," Miss Hurd said with an uncharacteristic catch in her voice.

Although a bad hip makes it impossible for her to join in the Greek dancing, Marjorie Hurd Rabidou is still an honored and enthusiastic guest at all family celebrations, including my 50th birthday picnic last summer, where the shish kebab was cooked on spits, clarinets and *bouzoukis* wailed, and costumed dancers led the guests in a serpentine line around our Colonial farmhouse, only 20 minutes from my first home in Worcester.

20   My sisters and I felt an aching void because my father was not there to lead the line, balancing a glass of wine on his head while he danced, the way he did at every celebration during his 92 years. But Miss Hurd was there, surveying the scene with quiet satisfaction. Although my parents are gone, her presence was a consolation, because I owe her so much.

This is truly the land of opportunity, and I would have enjoyed its bounty even if I hadn't walked into Miss Hurd's classroom in 1953. But she was the one who directed my grief and pain into writing, and if it weren't for her I wouldn't have become an investigative reporter and foreign correspondent, recorded the story of my mother's life and death in *Eleni* and now my father's story in *A Place for Us,* which is also a testament to the country that took us in. She was the catalyst that sent me into journalism and indirectly caused all the good things that came after. But Miss Hurd would probably deny this emphatically.

A few years ago, I answered the telephone and heard my former teacher's voice telling me, in that won't-take-no-for-an-answer tone of hers, that she had decided I was to write and deliver the eulogy at her funeral. I agreed (she didn't leave me any choice), but that's one assignment I never want to do. I hope, Miss Hurd, that you'll accept this remembrance instead.

Personal Response

Imagine that you are in Miss Hurd's English class and have been assigned to write about something from your own experience, perhaps something about which you have painful memories. What do you think you would write about? What details would you be sure to include?

Questions for Discussion

1. Nicholas Gage is a professional writer. Assess the quality of writing in this piece, which was intended for a general audience. What are its strengths and weaknesses? Do you think that Gage manages to convey a clear sense of chronology, despite the fact that his narrative covers a number of years in a brief space? Does he successfully describe his teacher, the subject of his essay?

2. What was it about Miss Hurd's teaching that inspired Gage to become a writer? What did Gage learn from his writing assignment that sparked his determination to write the life story of his mother?

3. What details about his father does Gage's narrative reveal? How, for example, did his father feel about Gage's accomplishments as a writer?

4. What details indicate the closeness between Marjorie Hurd Rabidou and her former pupil?

IN SEARCH OF BRUCE LEE'S GRAVE

Shanlon Wu

Shanlon Wu was born in America to Chinese immigrant parents. He holds a BA degree in English literature from Vassar College, an MFA in creative writing from Sarah Lawrence College, and a law degree from Georgetown University. Wu is a judicial clerk for the United States Court of Appeals for the Ninth Circuit and is working on a novel based on his first visit to China. "In Search of Bruce Lee's Grave" first appeared in the New York Times *in 1990.*

It's Saturday morning in Seattle, and I am driving to visit Bruce Lee's grave. I have been in the city for only a couple of weeks and so drive two blocks past the cemetery before realizing that I've passed it. I double back and turn through the large wrought-iron gate, past a sign that reads: "Open to 9 P.M. or dusk, whichever comes first."

It's a sprawling cemetery, with winding roads leading in all directions. I feel silly trying to find his grave with no guidance. I think that my search for his grave is similar to my search for Asian heroes in America.

I was born in 1959, an Asian-American in Westchester County, N.Y. During my childhood there were no Asian sports stars. On television, I can recall only that most pathetic of Asian characters, Hop Sing, the Cartwright family houseboy on "Bonanza." But in my adolescence there was Bruce.

4   I was 14 years old when I first saw "Enter the Dragon," the grandaddy of martial-arts movies. Bruce had died suddenly at the age of 32 of cerebral edema, an excess of fluid in the brain, just weeks before the release of the film. Between the ages of 14 and 17, I saw "Enter the Dragon" 22 times before I stopped counting. During those years I collected Bruce Lee posters, putting them up at all angles in my bedroom. I took up Chinese martial arts and spent hours comparing my physique with his.

I learned all I could about Bruce: that he had married a Caucasian, Linda; that he had sparred with Kareem Abdul-Jabbar; that he was a buddy of Steve McQueen and James Coburn, both of whom were his pallbearers.

My parents, who immigrated to America and had become professors at Hunter College, tolerated my behavior, but seemed puzzled at my admiration of an "entertainer." My father jokingly tried to compare my obsession with Bruce to his boyhood worship of Chinese folk-tale heroes.

"I read them just like you read American comic books," he said.

8   But my father's heroes could not be mine; they came from an ancient literary tradition, not comic books. He and my mother had grown up in a land where they belonged to the majority. I could not adopt their childhood and they were wise enough not to impose it upon me.

Although I never again experienced the kind of blind hero worship I felt for Bruce, my need to find heroes remained strong.

In college, I discovered the men of the 442d Regimental Combat Team, a United States Army all-Japanese unit in World War II. Allowed to fight only against Europeans, they suffered heavy casualties while their families were put in internment camps. The motto was "Go for Broke."

I saw them as Asians in a Homeric epic, the protagonists of a Shakespearean tragedy; I knew no Eastern myths to infuse them with. They embodied my own need to prove myself in the Caucasian world. I imagined how their American-born flesh and muscle must have resembled mine: epicanthic folds set in strong faces nourished on milk and beef. I thought how much they had proved where there was so little to prove.

12   After college, I competed as an amateur boxer in an attempt to find my self-image in the ring. It didn't work. My fighting was only an attempt to copy Bruce's movies. What I needed was instruction on how to live. I quit boxing after a year and went to law school.

I was an anomaly there: a would-be Asian litigator. I had always liked to argue and found I liked doing it in front of people even more. When I won the first-year moot court competition in law school, I asked an Asian classmate if he thought I was the first Asian to win. He laughed and told me I was probably the only Asian to even compete.

The law-firm interviewers always seemed surprised that I wanted to litigate. "Aren't you interested in Pacific Rim trade?" they asked.

16   "My Chinese isn't good enough," I quipped.

My pat response seemed to please them. It certainly pleased me. I thought I'd found a place of my own—a place where the law would insulate me from the pressure of defining my Asian maleness. I sensed the possibilities of merely being myself.

But the pressure reasserted itself. One morning, the year after graduating from law school, I read the obituary of Gen. Minoru Genda—the man who planned the Pearl Harbor attack. I'd never heard of him and had assumed that whoever did that planning was long since dead. But the general had been alive all those years—rising at 4 every morning to do his exercises and retiring every night by 8. An advocate of animal rights, the obituary said.

I found myself drawn to the general's life despite his association with the Axis powers. He seemed a forthright, graceful man who died unhumbled. The same paper carried a front-page story about Congress's failure to pay the Japanese-American internees their promised reparation money. The general, at least, had not died waiting for reparations.

20   I was surprised and frightened by my admiration for General Genda, by my still-strong hunger for images of powerful Asian men. That hunger was my vulnerability manifested, a reminder of my lack of place.

The hunger is eased this gray morning in Seattle. After asking directions from a policeman—Japanese—I easily locate Bruce's grave. The headstone is red granite with a small picture etched into it. The picture is very Hollywood—

Bruce wears dark glasses—and I think the calligraphy looks a bit sloppy. Two tourists stop but leave quickly after glancing at me.

I realize I am crying. Bruce's grave seems very small in comparison to his place in my boyhood. So small in comparison to my need for heroes. Seeing his grave, I understand how large the hole in my life has been, and how desperately I'd sought to fill it.

I had sought an Asian hero to emulate. But none of my choices quite fit me. Their lives were defined through heroic tasks—they had villains to defeat and wars to fight—while my life seemed merely a struggle to define myself.

24   But now I see how that very struggle has defined me. I must be my own hero even as I learn to treasure those who have gone before.

I have had my powerful Asian male images: Bruce, the men of the 442d and General Genda; I may yet discover others. Their lives beckon like fireflies on a moonless night, and I know that they—like me—may have been flawed by foolhardiness and even cruelty. Still, their lives were real. They were not houseboys on "Bonanza."

Personal Response

Are you sympathetic toward Wu in his search for positive Asian role models? Did you have any trouble finding heroes as you were growing up? Who were your childhood heroes?

Questions for Discussion

1. Wu begins by stating that his search for Bruce Lee's grave is like his "search for Asian American heroes in America" (paragraph 2). In the course of the essay, what else does Wu reveal that he is searching for? Does he find what he is looking for? Why do you think he cries at Bruce Lee's grave?

2. Wu gives three examples of powerful Asian role models. What appeals to Wu about each of them? Do the reasons Wu gives for admiring these men reflect your own reasons for admiring someone?

3. Why does Wu say that his father's heroes could not be his own (paragraph 8)? Do you think that your own parents' or guardians' heroes cannot be yours? Must different generations necessarily have different role models and heroes?

4. Wu twice mentions the houseboy on *Bonanza* (paragraphs 3 and 25) as being a "pathetic" media image of Asians. If you are familiar with the character of Hop Sing on *Bonanza,* discuss why he provides a pathetic image. Can you think of other negative portrayals of Asians in either television or the movies? What examples of positive media portrayals of Asians can you name?

5. In paragraph 11, Wu says that he "knew no Eastern myths" and thus the men he admired "embodied [his] own need to prove [himself] in a Caucasian world." His comment raises the issue of American education's almost

exclusive focus on Western traditions and the place of cultural diversity in the curriculum. Explore your views on this matter. Does American education have an obligation to teach about cultures outside the Western tradition? Has your own education reflected such a focus, or did you have exposure to other cultures and traditions as well?

I BECAME HER TARGET

Roger Wilkins

Roger Wilkins is a senior fellow at the Institute for Policy Studies in Washington, DC, Clarence J. Robinson Professor at George Mason University, and chairperson of the Pulitzer Prize Board. This essay first appeared in Newsday *in 1987.*

My favorite teacher's name was "Dead-Eye" Bean. Her real name was Dorothy. She taught American history to eighth graders in the junior high section of Creston, the high school that served the north end of Grand Rapids, Mich. It was the fall of 1944. Franklin D. Roosevelt was president; American troops were battling their way across France; Joe DiMaggio was still in the service; the Montgomery bus boycott was more than a decade away, and I was a 12-year-old black newcomer in a school that was otherwise all white.

My mother, who had been a widow in New York, had married my stepfather, a Grand Rapids physician, the year before, and he had bought the best house he could afford for his new family. The problem for our new neighbors was that their neighborhood had previously been pristine (in their terms) and they were ignorant about black people. The prevailing wisdom in the neighborhood was that we were spoiling it and that we ought to go back where we belonged (or alternatively, ought not intrude where we were not wanted). There was a lot of angry talk among the adults, but nothing much came of it.

But some of the kids, those first few weeks, were quite nasty. They threw stones at me, chased me home when I was on foot and spat on my bike seat when I was in class. For a time, I was a pretty lonely, friendless and sometimes frightened kid. I was just transplanted from Harlem, and here in Grand Rapids, the dominant culture was speaking to me insistently.

4   I can see now that those youngsters were bullying and culturally disadvantaged. I knew then that they were bigoted, but the culture spoke to me more powerfully than my mind and I felt ashamed for being different—a nonstandard person.

I now know that Dorothy Bean understood most of that and deplored it. So things began to change when I walked into her classroom. She was a pleasant-looking single woman, who looked old and wrinkled to me at the time, but who was probably about 40.

Whereas my other teachers approached the problem of easing in their new black pupil by ignoring him for the first few weeks, Miss Bean went right at me.

On the morning after having read our first assignment, she asked me the first question. I later came to know that in Grand Rapids, she was viewed as a very liberal person who believed, among other things, that Negroes were equal.

I gulped and answered her question and the follow-up. They weren't brilliant answers, but they did establish the facts that I had read the assignment and that I could speak English. Later in the hour, when one of my classmates had bungled an answer, Miss Bean came back to me with a question that required me to clean up the girl's mess and established me as a smart person.

8   Thus, the teacher began to give me human dimensions, though not perfect ones for an eighth grader. It was somewhat better to be an incipient teachers' pet than merely a dark presence in the back of the room onto whose silent form my classmates could fit all the stereotypes they carried in their heads.

A few days later, Miss Bean became the first teacher ever to require me to think. She asked my opinion about something Jefferson had done. In those days, all my opinions were derivative. I was for Roosevelt because my parents were and I was for the Yankees because my older buddy from Harlem was a Yankee fan. Besides, we didn't have opinions about historical figures like Jefferson. Like our high school building or old Mayor Welch, he just was.

After I had stared at her for a few seconds, she said: "Well, should he have bought Louisiana or not?"

"I guess so," I replied tentatively.

12   "Why?" she shot back.

Why! What kind of question was that, I groused silently. But I ventured an answer. Day after day, she kept doing that to me, and my answers became stronger and more confident. She was the first teacher to give me the sense that thinking was part of education and that I could form opinions that had some value.

Her final service to me came on a day when my mind was wandering and I was idly digging my pencil into the writing surface on the arm of my chair. Miss Bean impulsively threw a hunk of gum eraser at me. By amazing chance, it hit my hand and sent the pencil flying. She gasped, and I crept mortified after my pencil as the class roared. That was the ice breaker.

Afterward, kids came up to me to laugh about "Old Dead-Eye Bean." The incident became a legend, and I, a part of that story, became a person to talk to.

16   So that's how I became just another kid in school and Dorothy Bean became "Old Dead-Eye."

Personal Response

To what extent do you agree with Wilkins that prejudice comes in part from the stereotypes children are taught? Who teaches children stereotypes? What can be done to prevent or undo stereotyping?

Questions for Discussion

1. What purpose is served by the references to Franklin D. Roosevelt, Joe DiMaggio, and the Montgomery bus boycott in the first paragraph?

2. Wilkins narrates the events leading up to the incident of the eraser throwing in chronological order, but he also includes his perception of those events as an adult. Where does he shift to his adult perception? What purpose is served by doing so?

3. Explain what Wilkins means when he says that "the dominant culture was speaking to [him] insistently" (paragraph 3). What effect did that insistent "speaking" have on the young Wilkins?

4. How does Wilkins account for the reactions of the people in his new neighborhood to his family? What does Wilkins mean when he says that the youngsters who bullied him were "culturally disadvantaged" (paragraph 4)?

5. In what ways did Dorothy Bean give Wilkins "human dimensions" (paragraph 8)? What were those dimensions? Why does Wilkins call the eraser-throwing incident Miss Bean's "final service" (paragraph 14) to him?

6. Discuss the connection between prejudice and ignorance that Wilkins implies in his narrative. What do you think can be done to dispel such ignorance? What role might teachers and other professionals play in reducing the kind of ignorance that leads to prejudice?

LESSONS FROM TWO GHOSTS

Scott Fisher

Scott Fisher teaches English at Rock Valley College. For many years he also taught vocational automotive and aircraft technology. His freelance work includes technical and training print and video publications for the automotive industry, two books on Iowa history, a dozen magazine and journal articles, and a dozen short fiction pieces. He has won writing awards in technical publications, short fiction, nonfiction historical narrative, and personal essay. "Lessons from Two Ghosts" was first published in the June 14, 1996, issue of The Chronicle of Higher Education.

I know many educators who, like me, spend scores of extra hours planning, developing, and evaluating ideas and materials for their courses. I admire my colleagues for being so dedicated to their students and their profession. I wish I could say my reasons for my long hours were as altruistic. In fact, I often wish I had more time to read for pleasure, hike in the mountains, or go to more baseball games.

The truth is that there are ghosts in my office that force me to stay there and work, even when I'd rather be somewhere else. Oh, they let me go home and get enough rest and nourishment to sustain my body. But they know I'll be back, and they're always waiting for me when I unlock the door to my office. As Poe would have asked: "You think me mad?" Maybe I am.

I've known these ghosts—there are two of them—for about 25 years. That's longer than I've been teaching, although they really only started haunting me on my first day as a student teacher. Every day since then, they've been standing right behind or on either side of me. Heck, I knew them before they were ghosts. They were young men once, as I was.

4   Their names are (were) Pritchard and Simplett. We were classmates—freshmen—in the late '60s at a teachers' college in the Midwest. Pritchard was the kicker on our football team. He could make field goals from any angle, off any surface, in any temperature, in rain, show, or high winds. If the ball was inside the 30-yard line, Pritch could nail it dead center every time. He didn't miss a single field goal or extra point all season. I can testify to that, because I was his holder (I was too small and slow to start in any other position). We weren't a powerhouse team, by any means, but Pritchard's foot made the difference in some of our games.

Simplett and I were on the baseball team that year. He was an outstanding shortstop, with a rifle arm (excuse the cliché). He could go into the hole, drop to his knees, and fling a runner out at first base by two steps. I was a fourth-string catcher, used almost exclusively when the game was not in doubt and the coach didn't want to risk injury to any of his "good" players. That was also when Simp got his chance to pitch. He was magnificent—about one-third of the time. The other two-thirds, his blazing fastball had a mind of its own. Also, Simp had a little trouble reading his catcher's signs. He couldn't see too well from 60 feet away. That's why nobody wanted to catch for him. I tried everything—flashing the signs very slowly, wrapping white adhesive tape around my fingertips—but nothing worked. We finally agreed that he would just "throw 'em," and I'd try to "catch 'em," which worked out about as well as anything else. We didn't win many games, but we had fun.

Pritch, Simp, and I had a couple of other things in common besides sports. For one thing, we all liked to write. I liked research and writing historical narrative—essays on the Old West, sports teams of the 1930s, classic airplanes, that kind of thing.

Pritch was into fantasy. He could weave a wonderful tale, gripping readers with his spellbinding tales of planets and sorcerers, which he illustrated deftly with bizarre, intriguing drawings.

8   Simp was a poet. His mind worked in metaphor; even in the dugout he would call umpires the "traffic cops of the basepaths" and the pain of a batter's hands when the bat connected on a cold day "the sweet sting of spring." And he loved all kinds of music. He lived across the hall from me in the dorm, and on Thursday nights ("rave" nights, when it was okay to make a little more noise), he'd bring over his Country Joe McDonald records, and we'd sing along at the top of our offkey voices: "And it's one, two, three, what're we fightin' for? Don't ask me, I don't give a damn; next stop is Vietnam."

Just as I admired their athletic ability, I was in awe of my friends' talents and creativity, both in writing and in living. While I had to work for each ounce of strength, both on the athletic field and at the typewriter, Pritch and Simp had natural gifts. I was envious, but also proud to know them. Their talents inspired me to work harder to improve myself.

It may sound corny now, but those guys were preparing themselves to be skilled educators in every activity they pursued. They often helped out in the tutoring lab in the evenings and volunteered to coach elementary-school teams on weekends. They loved taking kids from the town on field trips to nearby farms or sporting events. I was amazed at how both of them could motivate even the shyest youngster. They were natural leaders and role models. Kids seemed to be drawn to them instinctively.

The only time all three of us were together regularly was in "Old Man" Rivers's (Professor Rivers, that is) English-composition class. Now, in retrospect, I can corroborate what we thought then: He was a complete jerk. He seemed to be about 160 years old, wore black suits, starched white shirts, bow ties, black wingtip shoes, and white socks. He was a fanatical Freudian and expected all our writing to reflect Freud's theories. Even though I did my best to work them into my narrative essays, short-story analyses, and research thesis, my papers always came back with a C, if I was lucky. Although I had been praised as a clear and insightful writer in high school, Old Man Rivers made it clear to me that I had no writing talent and that perhaps I should consider hiring a tutor or retaking the class in the summer.

12   I was too immature and unclear about my role as a future teacher to care all that much about what an eccentric English professor thought of me. But for Simp and Pritch it was different. They saw Professor Rivers for what he really was—a "scholarly bully," Simp called him. (Pritch's description was more profane, as I recall.) They often challenged (respectfully, at first) his weird interpretations of the stories, poems, and essays that we discussed in class. Of course, this did not please Rivers one bit, although their arguments made perfect sense to me.

Some of the more "intellectually needy" members of the class, including me, often tried to get some extra help from the old duffer, but he always was too busy to bother with "ignorant freshmen," especially if he was working on his latest textbook. He was particularly cool to us athletes, because he thought college sports were a waste of time and didn't like the fact that we had permission to miss classes when we had games at other colleges.

Most of us decided just to go with the flow, earn our solid C's, and get on with our lives. But Pritchard and Simplett were not about to go that route. They each spent hours preparing for the essays we had to write in class, looking up literary critical analysis that even doctoral candidates wouldn't want to read, just so they could prove their points with logic that Rivers couldn't refute. Yet Rivers was such a pedant that my two friends didn't stand a chance.

Those two guys spent all year—freshmen were stuck with Rivers for both semesters—trying to show him up. They each received D's the first semester, which threatened to put them on academic probation. By April, the situation had deteriorated to the point that they no longer even tried to suppress their snide comments in class. Pritch drew some hilarious, obscene sketches of Rivers expounding on Freudian aspects of fiction. And Simp concocted a tune about what a dirty old man Rivers was. Both of these creative scholarly works were published in the local forum—the men's bathroom in the athletic building.

16   Pritch and Simp each were called in by the dean at various times and told to knock it off. They were reminded that we "boys" were all I-A in the eyes of Uncle Sam, and that without their educational deferments, they would quickly find themselves in the military.

      But that wasn't enough of a threat for them, because they had very different ideas of what education was supposed to be. They continued to rebel against Old Man Rivers, and they continued to be reprimanded. In the end, they both failed Rivers's class the second semester and were placed on academic probation, with the understanding that they could make up the credits during summer session. But guess who taught all the summer composition classes?

      There was a lot I didn't quite grasp back then. I couldn't understand how a teacher at the college to which we were paying such high tuition could be so aloof and arrogant. I also couldn't understand how a published author of English textbooks could fail to recognize the talents of two gifted writers, right under his own nose. But neither could I understand why two intelligent guys would keep trying to buck the system when they knew Rivers wasn't going to change. Didn't they get it? They could just get through the class and pursue their own ideas after they graduated, with their own students.

      But they just laughed in disgust at any notion of compromise. Each of them, separately, refused to take the summer-school makeup course from Rivers and decided to head back to their respective hometowns. They planned to take their chances with the draft, maybe start again at another college the following year or when they got out of the service, should they be drafted.

20   Within 18 months, Pritchard and Simplett were dead. Pritch was blown apart by a land mine during an infantry patrol. A few months later, the Army helicopter in which Simp was riding crashed and burned, leaving no survivors.

      Of course, it's really not Old Man Rivers's fault that my friends died. It was just a cruel trick of timing. Still, I can't help thinking that by sticking around my office after hours, I might help some student stay on track. I feel the presence of my two old friends, and I see traits of theirs, such as their eagerness to ask challenging questions and explore opposing viewpoints, in a lot of my students. Some of them may go on to make a difference in young people's lives in a way in which my ghostly friends cannot. I hope they do.

      So I just keep plugging away, like a fourth-string catcher, giving extra help where I can. It's not because I'm a great humanitarian, or that I'm gifted or even dedicated.

      I'm just haunted.

Personal Response

Of the two responses to the arrogant and aloof professor Rivers, which do you think is closer to the way you imagine yourself responding in a similar situation, the author's or his friends'? Why?

Questions for Discussion

1. Summarize the characteristics of his two friends that Fisher most admires. What about them especially haunts him?

2. Fisher writes in paragraph 10 that Pritchard and Simplett were "natural teachers and role models." What characteristics of his friends does Fisher illustrate to define those terms? Do you agree with Fisher that those characteristics define "natural teacher" and "role model"?

3. Fisher says that his friends were "preparing themselves to be skilled educators" (paragraph 10). Discuss the characteristics you would expect a skilled educator to have. Have you had such a teacher?

4. Fisher says that his friends often challenged Professor Rivers, at first respectfully and then "with snide comments in class" (paragraph 15). Discuss the appropriateness of such behavior. In what circumstances do you think it appropriate to challenge teachers? Should it be done in class or privately?

5. Discuss the people you know who keep trying to "buck the system," as Pritchard and Simplett did. Do you admire such people or not? Explain your answer.

THE REVOLT OF "MOTHER"

Mary E. Wilkins Freeman

Mary E. Wilkins Freeman was a New England writer whose long, successful career began in the 1880s with the publication of her short stories in several prominent magazines. The stories collected in A Humble Romance and Other Stories *(1887) and* A New England Nun and Other Stories *(1891) are generally regarded as her best work. In 1926, the American Academy of Letters awarded her the William Dean Howells Gold Medal for Fiction, and that same year Freeman and Edith Wharton became the first women to be elected to the National Institute of Arts and Letters. By the time of her death in 1930, she had published twenty volumes of adult fiction, both novels and short stories, and six volumes of children's stories. "The Revolt of 'Mother'" was first published in 1891.*

"Father!"

"What is it?"

"What are them men diggin' over there in the field for?"

4   There was a sudden dropping and enlarging of the lower part of the old man's face, as if some heavy weight had settled therein; he shut his mouth tight, and went on harnessing the great bay mare. He hustled the collar on to her neck with a jerk.

"Father!"

The old man slapped the saddle upon the mare's back.

"Look here, father, I want to know what them men are diggin' over in the field for, an' I'm goin' to know."

8 "I wish you'd go into the house, mother, an' 'tend to your own affairs," the old man said then. He ran his words together, and his speech was almost as inarticulate as a growl.

But the woman understood; it was her most native tongue.

"I ain't goin' into the house till you tell me what them men are doin' over there in the field," said she.

The she stood waiting. She was a small woman, short and straight-waisted like a child in her brown cotton gown. Her forehead was mild and benevolent between the smooth curves of gray hair; there were meek downward lines about her nose and mouth; but her eyes, fixed upon the old man, looked as if the meekness had been the result of her own will, never of the will of another.

12 They were in the barn, standing before the wide open doors. The spring air, full of the smell of growing grass and unseen blossoms, came in their faces. The deep yard in front was littered with farm wagons and piles of wood; on the edges, close to the fence and the house, the grass was a vivid green, and there were some dandelions.

The old man glanced doggedly at his wife as he tightened the last buckles on the harness. She looked as immovable to him as one of the rocks in his pastureland, bound to the earth with generations of blackberry vines. He slapped the reins over the horse, and started forth from the barn.

"*Father!*" said she.

The old man pulled up. "What is it?"

16 "I want to know what them men are diggin' over there in that field for."

"They're diggin' a cellar, I s'pose, if you've got to know."

"A cellar for what?"

"A barn."

20 "A barn? You ain't goin' to build a barn over there where we was goin' to have a house, father?"

The old man said not another word. He hurried the horse into the farm wagon, and clattered out of the yard, jouncing as sturdily on his seat as a boy.

The woman stood a moment looking after him, then she went out of the barn across a corner of the yard to the house. The house, standing at right angles with the great barn and a long reach of sheds and out-buildings, was infinitesimal compared with them. It was scarcely as commodious for people as the little boxes under the barn eaves were for doves.

A pretty girl's face, pink and delicate as a flower, was looking out of one of the house windows. She was watching three men who were digging over in the field which bounded the yard near the road line. She turned quietly when the woman entered.

24 "What are they digging for, mother?" said she. "Did he tell you?"

"They're diggin' for—a cellar for a new barn."

"Oh, mother, he ain't going to build another barn?"

"That's what he says."

28   A boy stood before the kitchen glass combing his hair. He combed slowly and painstakingly, arranging his brown hair in a smooth hillock over his forehead. He did not seem to pay any attention to the conversation.

"Sammy, did you know father was going to build a new barn?" asked the girl.

The boy combed assiduously.

"Sammy!"

32   He turned, and showed a face like his father's under his smooth crest of hair. "Yes, I s'pose I did," he said, reluctantly.

"How long have you known it?" asked his mother.

"'Bout three months, I guess."

"Why didn't you tell of it?"

36   "Didn't think 'twould do no good."

"I don't see what father wants another barn for," said the girl, in her sweet, slow voice. She turned again to the window, and stared out at the digging men in the field. Her tender, sweet face was full of a gentle distress. Her forehead was as bald and innocent as a baby's, with the light hair strained back from it in a row of curl-papers. She was quite large, but her soft curves did not look as if they covered muscles.

Her mother looked sternly at the boy. "Is he goin' to buy more cows?" said she.

The boy did not reply; he was tying his shoes.

40   "Sammy, I want you to tell me if he's goin' to buy more cows."

"I s'pose he is."

"How many?"

"Four, I guess."

44   His mother said nothing more. She went into the pantry, and there was a clatter of dishes. The boy got his cap from a nail behind the door, took an old arithmetic from the shelf, and started for school. He was lightly built, but clumsy. He went out of the yard with a curious spring in the hips, that made his loose home-made jacket tilt up in the rear.

The girl went to the sink, and began to wash the dishes that were piled up there. Her mother came promptly out of the pantry, and shoved her aside. "You wipe 'em," said she; "I'll wash. There's a good many this mornin'."

The mother plunged her hands vigorously into the water, the girl wiped the plates slowly and dreamily. "Mother," said she, "don't you think it's too bad father's going to build that new barn, much as we need a decent house to live in?"

Her mother scrubbed a dish fiercely. "You ain't found out yet we're women-folks, Nanny Penn," said she. "You ain't seen enough of men-folks yet to. One of these days you'll find it out, an' then you'll know that we know only what men-folks think we do, so far as any use of it goes, an' how we'd ought to reckon men-folks in with Providence, an' not complain of what they do any more than we do of the weather."

48   "I don't care; I don't believe George is anything like that, anyhow," said Nanny. Her delicate face flushed pink, her lips pouted softly, as if she were going to cry.

"You wait an' see. I guess George Eastman ain't no better than other men. You hadn't ought to judge Father, though. He can't help it, 'cause he don't look at things jest the way we do. An' we've been pretty comfortable here, after all. The roof don't leak—ain't never but once—that's one thing. Father's kept it shingled right up."

"I do wish we had a parlor."

"I guess it won't hurt George Eastman any to come to see you in a nice clean kitchen. I guess a good many girls don't have as good a place as this. Nobody's ever heard me complain."

52   "I ain't complained either, mother."

"Well, I don't think you'd better, a good father an' a good home as you've got. S'pose your father made you go out an' work for your livin'? Lots of girls have to that ain't no stronger an' better able to than you be."

Sarah Penn washed the frying-pan with a conclusive air. She scrubbed the outside of it as faithfully as the inside. She was a masterly keeper of her box of a house. Her one living-room never seemed to have in it any of the dust which the friction of life with inanimate matter produces. She swept, and there seemed to be no dirt to go before the broom; she cleaned, and one could see no difference. She was like an artist so perfect that he had apparently no art. To-day she got out a mixing bowl and a board, and rolled some pies, and there was no more flour upon her than upon her daughter who was doing finer work. Nanny was to be married in the fall, and she was sewing on some white cambric and embroidery. She sewed industriously while her mother cooked, her soft milk-white hands and wrists showed whiter than her delicate work.

"We must have the stove moved out in the shed before long," said Mrs. Penn. "Talk about not havin' things, it's been a real blessin' to be able to put a stove up in that shed in hot weather. Father did one good thing when he fixed that stove-pipe out there."

56   Sarah Penn's face as she rolled her pies had that expression of meek vigor which might have characterized one of the New Testament saints. She was making mince-pies. Her husband, Adoniram Penn, liked them better than any other kind. She baked twice a week. Adoniram often liked a piece of pie between meals. She hurried this morning. It had been later than usual when she began, and she wanted to have a pie baked for dinner. However deep a resentment she might be forced to hold against her husband, she would never fail in sedulous attention to his wants.

Nobility of character manifests itself at loop-holes when it is not provided with large doors. Sarah Penn's showed itself to-day in flaky dishes of pastry. So she made the pies faithfully, while across the table she could see, when she glanced up from her work, the sight that rankled in her patient and steadfast soul—the digging of the cellar of the new barn in the place where Adoniram forty years ago had promised her their new house should stand.

The pies were done for dinner. Adoniram and Sammy were home a few minutes after twelve o'clock. The dinner was eaten with serious haste. There was never much conversation at the table in the Penn family. Adoniram asked a blessing, and they ate promptly, then rose up and went about their work.

Sammy went back to school, taking soft sly lopes out of the yard like a rabbit. He wanted a game of marbles before school, and feared his father would give him some chores to do. Adoniram hastened to the door and called after him, but he was out of sight.

60   "I don't see what you let him go for, mother," said he. "I wanted him to help me unload that wood."

Adoniram went to work out in the yard unloading wood from the wagon. Sarah put away the dinner dishes, while Nanny took down her curl-papers and changed her dress. She was going down to the store to buy some more embroidery and thread.

When Nanny was gone, Mrs. Penn went to the door. "Father!" she called.

"Well, what is it!"

64   "I want to see you jest a minute, father."

"I can't leave this wood nohow. I've got to git it unloaded an' go for a load of gravel afore two o'clock. Sammy had ought to helped me. You hadn't ought to let him go to school so early."

"I want to see you jest a minute."

"I tell ye I can't, nohow, mother."

68   "Father, you come here." Sarah Penn stood in the door like a queen; she held her head as if it bore a crown; there was that patience which makes authority royal in her voice. Adoniram went.

Mrs. Penn led the way into the kitchen, and pointed to a chair. "Sit down, father," said she; "I've got somethin' I want to say to you."

He sat down heavily; his face was quite stolid, but he looked at her with restive eyes. "Well, what is it, mother?"

"I want to know what you're buildin' that new barn for, father?"

72   "I ain't got nothin' to say about it."

"It can't be you think you need another barn?"

"I tell ye I ain't got nothin' to say about it, mother; an' I ain't goin' to say nothin'."

"Be you goin' to buy more cows?"

76   Adoniram did not reply; he shut his mouth tight.

"I know you be, as well as I want to. Now, father, look here"—Sarah Penn had not sat down; she stood before her husband in the humble fashion of a Scripture woman—"I'm goin' to talk real plain to you; I never have sence I married you, but I'm goin' to now. I ain't never complained, an' I ain't goin' to complain now, but I'm goin' to talk plain. You see this room here, father; you look at it well. You see there ain't no carpet on the floor, an' you see the paper is all dirty, an' droppin' off the walls. We ain't had no new paper on it for ten year, an' then I put it on myself, an' it didn't cost but ninepence a roll. You see this room, father; it's all the one I've had to work in an' eat in an' sit in sence we was married.

There ain't another woman in the whole town whose husband ain't got half the means you have but what's got better. It's all the room Nanny's got to have her company in; an' there ain't one of her mates but what's got better, an' their fathers not so able as hers is. It's all the room she'll have to be married in. What would you have thought, father, if we had had our weddin' in a room no better than this? I was married in my mother's parlor, with a carpet on the floor, an' stuffed furniture, an' a mahogany card-table. An' this is all the room my daughter will have to be married in. Look here, father!"

Sarah Penn went across the room as though it were a tragic stage. She flung open a door and disclosed a tiny bedroom, only large enough for a bed and bureau, with a path between. "There, father," said she—"there's all the room I've had to sleep in forty year. All my children were born there—the two that died, an' the two that's livin'. I was sick with a fever there."

She stepped to another door and opened it. It led into the small, ill-lighted pantry. "Here," said she, "is all the buttery I've got—every place I've got for my dishes, to set away my victuals in, an' to keep my milk-pans in. Father, I've been takin' care of the milk of six cows in this place, an' now you're goin' to build a new barn, an' keep more cows, an' give me more to do in it."

80

She threw open another door. A narrow crooked flight of stairs wound upward from it. "There, father," said she, "I want you to look at the stairs that go up to them two unfinished chambers that are all the places our son an' daughter have had to sleep in all their lives. There ain't a prettier girl in town nor a more ladylike one than Nanny, an' that's the place she has to sleep in. It ain't so good as your horse's stall; it ain't so warm an' tight."

Sarah Penn went back and stood before her husband. "Now, father," said she, "I want to know if you think you're doin' right an' accordin' to what you profess. Here, when we was married, forty year ago, you promised me faithful that we should have a new house built in that lot over in the field before the year was out. You said you had money enough, an' you wouldn't ask me to live in no such place as this. It is forty year now, an' you've been makin' more money, an' I've been savin' of it for you ever since, an' you ain't built no house yet. You've built sheds an' cow-houses an' one new barn, an' now you're goin' to build another. Father, I want to know if you think it's right. You're lodgin' your dumb beasts better than you are your own flesh an' blood. I want to know if you think it's right."

"I ain't got nothin' to say."

"You can't say nothin' without ownin' it ain't right, father. An' there's another thing—I ain't complained; I've got along forty year, an' I s'pose I should forty more, if it wa'n't for that—if we don't have another house. Nanny she can't live with us after she's married. She'll have to go somewheres else to live away from us, an' it don't seem as if I could have it so, noways, father. She wa'n't ever strong. She's got considerable color, but there wa'n't never any backbone to her. I've always took the heft of everything off her, an' she ain't fit to keep house an' do everything herself. She'll be all worn out inside of a year. Think of her doin' all the washin' an' ironin' an' bakin' with them soft white hands an' arms, an' sweepin'! I can't have it so, noways, father."

84   Mrs. Penn's face was burning; her mild eyes gleamed. She had pleaded her lit-tle cause like a Webster; she had ranged from severity to pathos; but her oppo-nent employed that obstinate silence which makes eloquence futile with mocking echoes. Adoniram arose clumsily.

"Father, ain't you got nothin' to say?" said Mrs. Penn.

"I've got to go off after that load of gravel. I can't stan' here talkin' all day."

"Father, won't you think it over, an' have a house built there instead of a barn?"

88   "I ain't got nothin' to say.

Adoniram shuffled out. Mrs. Penn went into her bedroom. When she came out, her eyes were red. She had a roll of unbleached cotton cloth. She spread it out on the kitchen table, and began cutting out some shirts for her husband. The men over in the field had a team to help them this afternoon; she could hear their halloos. She had a scanty pattern for the shirts; she had to plan and piece the sleeves.

Nanny came home with her embroidery, and sat down with her needlework. She had taken down her curl-papers, and there was a soft roll of fair hair like an aureole over her forehead; her face was as delicately fine and clear as porcelain. Suddenly she looked up, and the tender red flamed all over her face and neck. "Mother," said she.

"What say?"

92   "I've been thinking—I don't see how we're goin' to have any—wedding in this room. I'd be ashamed to have his folks come if we didn't have anybody else."

"Mebbe we can have some new paper before then; I can put it on. I guess you won't have no call to be ashamed of your belongin's."

"We might have the wedding in the new barn," said Nanny, with gentle pet-tishness. "Why, mother, what makes you look so?"

Mrs. Penn had started, and was staring at her with a curious expression. She turned again to her work, and spread out a pattern carefully on the cloth. "Nothin'," said she.

96   Presently Adoniram clattered out of the yard in his two-wheeled dump cart, standing as proudly upright as a Roman charioteer. Mrs. Penn opened the door and stood there a minute looking out; the halloos of the men sounded louder.

It seemed to her all through the spring months that she heard nothing but the halloos and the noises of saws and hammers. The new barn grew fast. It was a fine edifice for this little village. Men came on pleasant Sundays, in their meet-ing suits and clean shirt bosoms, and stood around it admiringly. Mrs. Penn did not speak of it, and Adoniram did not mention it to her, although sometimes, upon a return from inspecting it, he bore himself with injured dignity.

"It's a strange thing how your mother feels about the new barn," he said, confidentially, to Sammy one day.

Sammy only grunted after an odd fashion for a boy; he had learned it from his father.

100   The barn was all completed ready for use by the third week in July. Adoniram had planned to move his stock in on Wednesday; on Tuesday he received a letter

which changed his plans. He came in with it early in the morning. "Sammy's been to the post-office," said he, "an' I've got a letter from Hiram." Hiram was Mrs. Penn's brother, who lived in Vermont.

"Well," said Mrs. Penn, "what does he say about the folks?"

"I guess they're all right. He says he thinks if I come up country right off there's a chance to buy jest the kind of a horse I want." He stared reflectively out of the window at the new barn.

Mrs. Penn was making pies. She went on clapping the rolling-pin into the crust, although she was very pale, and her heart beat loudly.

104   "I dun' know but what I'd better go," said Adoniram. "I hate to go off jest now, right in the midst of hayin', but the ten-acre lot's cut, an' I guess Rufus an' the others can git along without me three or four days. I can't get a horse round here to suit me, nohow, an' I've got to have another for all that wood-haulin' in the fall. I told Hiram to watch out, an' if he got wind of a good horse to let me know. I guess I'd better go."

"I'll get out your clean shirt an' collar," said Mrs. Penn calmly.

She laid out Adoniram's Sunday suit and his clean clothes on the bed in the little bedroom. She got his shaving-water and razor ready. At last she buttoned on his collar and fastened his black cravat.

Adoniram never wore his collar and cravat except on extra occasions. He held his head high, with a rasped dignity. When he was all ready, with his coat and hat brushed, and a lunch of pie and cheese in a paper bag, he hesitated on the threshold of the door. He looked at his wife, and his manner was defiantly apologetic. "*If* them cows come to-day, Sammy can drive 'em into the new barn," said he; "an' when they bring the hay up, they can pitch it in there."

108   "Well," replied Mrs. Penn.

Adoniram set his shaven face ahead and started. When he had cleared the door-step, he turned and looked back with a kind of nervous solemnity. "I shall be back by Saturday if nothin' happens," said he.

"Do be careful, father," returned his wife.

She stood in the door with Nanny at her elbow and watched him out of sight. Her eyes had a strange, doubtful expression in them; her peaceful forehead was contracted. She went in, and about her baking again. Nanny sat sewing. Her wedding-day was drawing nearer, and she was getting pale and thin with her steady sewing. Her mother kept glancing at her.

112   "Have you got that pain in your side this mornin'?" she asked.

"A little."

Mrs. Penn's face, as she worked, changed, her perplexed forehead smoothed, her eyes were steady, her lips firmly set. She formed a maxim for herself, although incoherently with her unlettered thoughts. "Unsolicited opportunities are the guide-posts of the Lord to the new roads of life," she repeated in effect, and she made up her mind to her course of action.

"S'posin' I *had* wrote to Hiram," she muttered once, when she was in the pantry—"s'posin' I had wrote, an' asked him if he knew of any horse? But I didn't, an' father's goin' wa'n't none of my doin'. It looks like a providence." Her voice rang out quite loud at the last.

116 "What you talkin' about, mother?" called Nanny.

"Nothin'."

Mrs. Penn hurried her baking; at eleven o'clock it was all done. The load of hay from the west field came slowly down the cart track, and drew up at the new barn. Mrs. Penn ran out. "Stop!" she screamed—"stop!"

The men stopped and looked; Sammy upreared from the top of the load, and stared at his mother.

120 "Stop!" she cried out again. "Don't you put the hay in that barn; put it in the old one."

"Why, he said to put it in here," returned one of the hay-makers, wonderingly. He was a young man, a neighbor's son, whom Adoniram hired by the year to help on the farm.

"Don't you put the hay in the new barn; there's room enough in the old one, ain't there?" said Mrs. Penn.

"Room enough," returned the hired man, in his thick, rustic tones. "Didn't need the new barn, nohow, far as room's concerned. Well, I s'pose he changed his mind." He took hold of the horses' bridles.

124 Mrs. Penn went back to the house. Soon the kitchen windows were darkened, and a fragrance like warm honey came into the room.

Nanny laid down her work. "I thought father wanted them to put the hay into the new barn?" she said, wonderingly.

"It's all right," replied her mother.

Sammy slid down from the load of hay, and came in to see if dinner was ready.

128 "I ain't goin' to get a regular dinner to-day, as long as father's gone," said his mother. "I've let the fire go out. You can have some bread an' milk an' pie. I thought we could get along." She set out some bowls of milk, some bread, and a pie on the kitchen table. "You'd better eat your dinner now," said she. "You might jest as well get through with it. I want you to help me afterward."

Nanny and Sammy stared at each other. There was something strange in their mother's manner. Mrs. Penn did not eat anything herself. She went into the pantry, and they heard her moving dishes while they ate. Presently she came out with a pile of plates. She got the clothesbasket out of the shed, and packed them in it. Nanny and Sammy watched. She brought out cups and saucers, and put them in with the plates.

"What you goin' to do, mother?" inquired Nanny, in a timid voice. A sense of something unusual made her tremble, as if it were a ghost. Sammy rolled his eyes over his pie.

"You'll see what I'm goin' to do," replied Mrs. Penn. "If you're through, Nanny, I want you to go up-stairs an' pack up your things; an' I want you, Sammy, to help me take down the bed in the bedroom."

132 "Oh, mother, what for?" gasped Nanny.

"You'll see."

During the next few hours a feat was performed by this simple, pious New England mother which was equal in its way to Wolfe's storming of the Heights of Abraham. It took no more genius and audacity of bravery for Wolfe to cheer his wondering soldiers up those steep precipices, under the sleeping eyes of the enemy, than for Sarah Penn, at the head of her children, to move all their little household goods into the new barn while her husband was away.

Nanny and Sammy followed their mother's instructions without a murmur; indeed, they were overawed. There is a certain uncanny and superhuman quality about all such purely original undertakings as their mother's was to them. Nanny went back and forth with her light loads, and Sammy tugged with sober energy.

136   At five o'clock in the afternoon the little house in which the Penns had lived for forty years had emptied itself into the new barn.

Every builder builds somewhat for unknown purposes, and is in a measure a prophet. The architect of Adoniram Penn's barn, while he designed it for the comfort of four-footed animals, had planned better than he knew for the comfort of humans. Sarah Penn saw at a glance its possibilities. Those great box-stalls, with quilts hung before them, would make better bedrooms than the one she had occupied for forty years, and there was a tight carriage-room. The harness-room, with its chimney and shelves, would make a kitchen of her dreams. The great middle space would make a parlor, by-and-by, fit for a palace. Up stairs there was as much room as down. With partitions and windows, what a house would there be! Sarah looked at the row of stanchions before the allotted space for cows, and reflected that she would have her front entry there.

At six o'clock the stove was up in the harness-room, the kettle was boiling, and the table set for tea. It looked almost as home-like as the abandoned house across the yard had ever done. The young hired man milked, and Sarah directed him calmly to bring the milk to the new barn. He came gaping, dropping little blots of foam from the brimming pails on the grass. Before the next morning he had spread the story of Adoniram Penn's wife moving into the new barn all over the little village. Men assembled in the store and talked it over, women with shawls over their heads scuttled into each other's houses before their work was done. Any deviation from the ordinary course of life in this quiet town was enough to stop all progress in it. Everybody paused to look at the staid, independent figure on the side track. There was a difference of opinion with regard to her. Some held her to be insane; some, of a lawless and rebellious spirit.

Friday the minister went to see her. It was in the forenoon, and she was at the barn door shelling pease for dinner. She looked up and returned his salutation with dignity, then she went on with her work. She did not invite him in. The saintly expression of her face remained fixed, but there was an angry flush over it.

140   The minister stood awkwardly before her, and talked. She handled the pease as if they were bullets. At last she looked up, and her eyes showed the spirit that her meek front had covered for a lifetime.

"There ain't no use talkin', Mr. Hersey," said she. "I've thought it all over an' over, an' I believe I'm doin' what's right. I've made it the subject of prayer, an' it's betwixt me an' the Lord an' Adoniram. There ain't no call for nobody else to worry about it."

"Well, of course, if you have brought it to the Lord in prayer, and feel satisfied that you are doing right, Mrs. Penn," said the minister, helplessly. His thin graybearded face was pathetic. He was a sickly man; his youthful confidence had cooled; he had to scourge himself up to some of his pastoral duties as relentlessly as a Catholic ascetic, and then he was prostrated by the smart.

"I think it's right jest as much as I think it was right for our forefathers to come over from the old country 'cause they didn't have what belonged to 'em," said Mrs. Penn. She arose. The barn threshold might have been Plymouth Rock from her bearing. "I don't doubt you mean well, Mr. Hersey," said she, "but there are things people hadn't ought to interfere with. I've been a member of the church for over forty year. I've got my own mind an' my own feet, an' I'm goin' to think my own thoughts an' go my own ways, an' nobody but the Lord is goin' to dictate to me unless I've a mind to have him. Won't you come in an' set down? How is Mis' Hersey?"

144   "She is well, I thank you," replied the minister. He added some more perplexed apologetic remarks; then he retreated.

He could expound the intricacies of every character study in the Scriptures, he was competent to grasp the Pilgrim Fathers and all historical innovators, but Sarah Penn was beyond him. He could deal with primal cases, but parallel ones worsted him. But, after all, although it was aside from his province, he wondered more how Adoniram Penn would deal with his wife than how the Lord would. Everybody shared the wonder. When Adoniram's four new cows arrived, Sarah ordered three to be put in the old barn, the other in the house shed where the cooking-stove had stood. That added to the excitement. It was whispered that all four cows were domiciled in the house.

Towards sunset on Saturday, when Adoniram was expected home, there was a knot of men in the road near the new barn. The hired man had milked, but he still hung around the premises. Sarah Penn had supper all ready. There were brown-bread and baked beans and a custard pie; it was the supper that Adoniram loved on a Saturday night. She had on a clean calico, and she bore herself imperturbably. Nanny and Sammy kept close at her heels. Their eyes were large, and Nanny was full of nervous tremors. Still there was to them more pleasant excitement than anything else. An inborn confidence in their mother over their father asserted itself.

Sammy looked out of the harness-room window. "There he is," he announced, in an awed whisper. He and Nanny peeped around the casing. Mrs. Penn kept on about her work. The children watched Adoniram leave the new horse standing in the drive while he went to the house door. It was fastened. Then he went around to the shed. That door was seldom locked, even when the family was away. The thought how her father would be confronted by the cow flashed upon Nanny. There was a hysterical sob in her throat. Adoniram emerged from the shed and stood looking about in a dazed fashion. His lips moved; he was saying something, but they could not hear what it was. The hired man was peeping around a corner of the old barn, but nobody saw him.

148 Adoniram took the new horse by the bridle and led him across the yard to the new barn. Nanny and Sammy slunk close to their mother. The barn doors rolled back, and there stood Adoniram, with the long mild face of the great Canadian farm horse looking over his shoulder.

Nanny kept behind her mother, but Sammy stepped suddenly forward, and stood in front of her.

Adoniram stared at the group. "What on airth you all down here for?" said he. "What's the matter over to the house?"

"We've come here to live, father," said Sammy. His shrill voice quavered out bravely.

152 "What"—Adoniram sniffed—"what is it smells like cookin'?" said he. He stepped forward and looked in the open door of the harness-room. Then he turned to his wife. His old bristling face was pale and frightened. "What on airth does this mean, mother?" he gasped.

"You come in here, father," said Sarah. She led the way into the harness-room and shut the door. "Now, father," said she, "you needn't be scared. I ain't crazy. There ain't nothin' to be upset over. But we've come here to live, an' we're goin' to live here. We've got jest as good a right here as new horses an' cows. The house wa'n't fit for us to live in any longer, an' I made up my mind I wa'n't goin' to stay there. I've done my duty by you forty year, an' I'm goin' to do it now; but I'm goin' to live here. You've got to put in some windows and partitions; an' you'll have to buy some furniture.

"Why, mother!" the old man gasped.

"You'd better take your coat off an' get washed—there's the wash-basin—an' then we'll have supper."

156 "Why, mother!"

Sammy went past the window, leading the new horse to the old barn. The old man saw him, and shook his head speechlessly. He tried to take off his coat, but his arms seemed to lack the power. His wife helped him. She poured some water into the tin basin, and put in a piece of soap. She got the comb and brush, and smoothed his thin gray hair after he had washed. Then she put the beans, hot bread, and tea on the table. Sammy came in, and the family drew up. Adoniram sat looking dazedly at his plate, and they waited.

"Ain't you goin' to ask a blessin', father?" said Sarah.

And the old man bent his head and mumbled.

160 All through the meal he stopped eating at intervals, and stared furtively at his wife; but he ate well. The home food tasted good to him, and his old frame was too sturdily healthy to be affected by his mind. But after supper he went out, and sat down on the step of the smaller door at the right of the barn, through which he had meant his Jerseys to pass in stately file, but which Sarah designed for her front house door, and he leaned his head on his hands.

After the supper dishes were cleared away and the milkpans washed, Sarah went out to him. The twilight was deepening. There was a clear green glow in the sky. Before them stretched the smooth level of field; in the distance was a cluster of hay-stacks like the huts of a village; the air was very cool and calm and sweet. The landscape might have been an ideal one of peace.

Sarah bent over and touched her husband on one of his thin, sinewy shoulders. "Father!"

The old man's shoulders heaved: he was weeping.

164 "Why, don't do so, father," said Sarah.

"I'll—put up the—partitions, an'—everything you—want, mother."

Sarah put her apron up to her face; she was overcome by her own triumph.

Adoniram was like a fortress whose walls had no active resistance, and went down the instant the right besieging tools were used. "Why, mother," he said, hoarsely, "I hadn't no idee you was so set on't as all this comes to."

Personal Response

What is your opinion of Sarah Penn's revolt? Do you admire her for what she has done? How do you suppose you might have acted in similar circumstances?

Questions for Discussion

1. What are Sarah Penn's chief characteristics? What do her confrontations with her husband and the minister reveal about her character?

2. How do others—her children, her husband, the community, and the minister—view Sarah Penn's decision to move into the barn? What does she think of their opinions? How do you think Freeman wants readers to see Sarah Penn?

3. Describe the roles Sarah and Adoniram Penn play as "Mother" and "Father." How do those roles relate to their roles as husband and wife? Why do you think Freeman puts "Mother" in quotation marks in the title? By the end of the story, what have both Sarah and Adoniram learned about the roles they play?

4. What has Father taught Sammy about being a husband and father? What has Mother taught Nanny about being a wife and mother? By the end of the story, what have both Nanny and Sammy learned about those roles?

5. Discuss Sarah Penn's motives for her revolt. Are they selfish? What is her most compelling reason for it?

Suggestions for Writing About ROLE MODELS

1. Taking into consideration selected readings from this chapter, define "role model." Consider what common definitions of the term "role model" the

writers share, whether you disagree with the way in which any of them defines the term, and what you would add to the definition that emerges through these readings.

2. In "Lessons from Two Ghosts," Scott Fisher states his belief that his two friends were preparing to be skilled educators. Define "skilled educator" and illustrate your definition by using examples of teachers you have had. You might consider comparing two teachers, one whom you believe to be skilled, the other unskilled.

3. Nicholas Gage writes from his perspective as a Greco American, Shanlon Wu as an Asian American, Thom Tammaro as an Italian American, and Roger Wilkins an African American. Compare and contrast the views of these four writers of mixed heritage on the subject of American education or American culture. Include a statement about your own ethnic heritage and your position in relation to these writers on the subject of education or culture.

4. Compare Thom Tammaro's personal essay "*Italianità* in a World Made of Love and Need" with Mary E. Wilkins Freeman's story "The Revolt of 'Mother'" in terms of their treatment of the larger issues of breaking from traditional roles and the ways in which family and community figure into the decision to make that break.

5. If you have ever broken with tradition, explain what you did, why you did it, who, if anyone, inspired you, and what your family and/or friends thought of your decision.

6. Write an essay on Sarah Penn in "The Revolt of 'Mother'" in which you examine her actions and motivations and state whether you believe her to be an admirable role model.

7. Write an essay in which you illustrate by example this sentence from "The Revolt of 'Mother' ": "Nobility of character manifests itself at loop-holes when it is not provided with large doors" (paragraph 57). Take into consideration the context in which the statement occurs, explain what it means in terms of role models, and, if possible, apply it to the character of a real person you know. Another approach is to apply the statement to some of the people in the readings from this chapter, such as Russell Baker's "Deems," Cynthia Ozick's "On Excellence," Scott Fisher's "Lessons from Two Ghosts," and/or Roger Wilkins' "I Became Her Target."

8. Russell Baker ("Deems"), Cynthia Ozick ("On Excellence"), and Roger Wilkins ("I Became Her Target") all describe colorful or remarkable people who had a strong influence on them. Taking the descriptive techniques of Baker, Ozick, and Wilkins as models, write an essay describing a person whom you find colorful and/or admirable, such as a parent, friend, relative, teacher, or coach. Try to convey the characteristics of that person and to explain as precisely as possible what you like and admire about her or him.

9. Argue in support of or against the statement that America no longer has heroes.

10. Argue in support of or against the statement that American schools should teach about role models from minority groups.

11. Explain who your role models or heroes are and why.

12. Write an essay explaining how someone has had a strong effect on you, perhaps influencing you to see yourself differently, gain self-confidence, solve difficulties you were having, or determine goals for yourself.

13. Describe a person whom you admire for bravery or strength in a difficult time.

Última Corrida realizada em Arraiolos, na qual
participaram homens afeiçonados desta terra.

ARRAIOLOS

— ☆ —

Domingo, 11 de Julho e Segunda... de Julho de 1937

— ☆ —

Cavaleiros

SIMÃO DA VEIGA (Junior)

amadores

ASCO JARDIM (Valença)

AQUIM CAMARA M. MIRA

CHAPTER 5

MALE-FEMALE RELATIONSHIPS

The readings in this chapter explore some of the issues related to love, commitment, and marriage and how the differing attitudes of men and women affect relationships between the sexes. The topics discussed here include ways to eliminate barriers between men and women, the dangers of unprotected sex, societal expectations regarding marriage for both men and women, and the importance of commitment for making relationships work.

The chapter begins with a selection by Deborah Tannen, who has done extensive research into the different communication styles of men and women. "Sex, Lies, and Conversation" summarizes her findings about patterns of conversation between the sexes, notes the ways in which the different conversational styles of men and women affect relationships, and offers insights into how to overcome those difficulties.

Next, Carol Tavris in "Love Story" argues for an alternative vision of human love from the one that American society seems to accept and support. Beginning and ending the selection with the love story of Annie Oakley and Frank Butler, Tavris maintains that if men and women would respect the differences between them, they could achieve an abiding intimacy and long-lasting love. Similarly, Wendell Berry in "Men and Women in Search of Common Ground" searches for reasons why human relationships are now so impermanent and offers suggestions for how to make them permanent.

Shifting focus and tone, the next essay addresses a deadly risk for people engaging in unprotected sex. In fact, Robert C. Noble goes so far as to declare "There Is No Safe Sex." Noble, a doctor and professor of medicine with extensive experience working with AIDS, speaks from that perspective as well as from his perspective as a father.

The next two essays respond to the dim view society takes of men over forty who choose not to marry and of women in their early twenties who choose to marry. Ron Beathard maintains in his essay "Over Forty and Unmarried" that single men are widely misunderstood and even suspect, though the discrimination against them is benign, curious, and often amusing. Whereas Beathard's perspective is that of an older man who has chosen not to marry, Katherine Davis explores the dismay and even hostility that her decision to marry young gave rise to. In

"I'm Not Sick, I'm Just in Love," Davis explains how her decision to marry at age 23 caused a furor among her friends.

The chapter ends with Julie Showalter's short story "Vows," which features a couple who marry with the knowledge that love sometimes does not last and can even turn nasty and vindictive. The story explores the nature of commitment in light of that knowledge and affirms the possibilities for lasting love.

SEX, LIES, AND CONVERSATION
Deborah Tannen

Deborah Tannen is professor of linguistics at Georgetown University. Her book, You Just Don't Understand: Women and Men in Conversation *(1990), was widely discussed on television, in print, and among couples across the nation. This article first appeared in the* Washington Post *in 1990 with the subtitle "Why Is It So Hard for Men and Women to Talk to Each Other?"*

I was addressing a small gathering in a suburban Virginia living room—a women's group that had invited men to join them. Throughout the evening, one man had been particularly talkative, frequently offering ideas and anecdotes, while his wife sat silently beside him on the couch. Toward the end of the evening, I commented that women frequently complain that their husbands don't talk to them. This man quickly concurred. He gestured toward his wife and said, "She's the talker in our family." The room burst into laughter; the man looked puzzled and hurt. "It's true," he explained. "When I come home from work I have nothing to say. If she didn't keep the conversation going, we'd spend the whole evening in silence."

This episode crystallizes the irony that although American men tend to talk more than women in public situations, they often talk less at home. And this pattern is wreaking havoc with marriage.

The pattern was observed by political scientist Andrew Hacker in the late '70s. Sociologist Catherine Kohler Riessman reports in her new book *Divorce Talk* that most of the women she interviewed—but only a few of the men—gave lack of communication as the reason for their divorces. Given the current divorce rate of nearly 50 percent, that amounts to millions of cases in the United States every year—a virtual epidemic of failed conversation

4   In my own research, complaints from women about their husbands most often focused not on tangible inequities such as having given up the chance for a career to accompany a husband to his, or doing far more than their share of daily life—support work like cleaning, cooking, social arrangements and errands. Instead, they focused on communication: "He doesn't listen to me," "He doesn't talk to me." I found, as Hacker observed years before, that most wives want their husbands to be, first and foremost, conversational partners, but few husbands share this expectation of their wives.

In short, the image that best represents the current crisis is the stereotypical cartoon scene of a man sitting at the breakfast table with a newspaper held up in front of his face while a woman glares at the back of it, wanting to talk.

Linguistic Battle of the Sexes

How can women and men have such different impressions of communication in marriage? Why the widespread imbalance in their interests and expectations?

In the April issue of *American Psychologist,* Stanford University's Eleanor Maccoby reports the results of her own and others' research showing that children's development is most influenced by the social structure of peer interactions. Boys and girls tend to play with children of their own gender, and their sex-separate groups have different organizational structures and interactive norms.

8   I believe these systematic differences in childhood socialization make talk between women and men like cross-cultural communication, heir to all the attraction and pitfalls of that enticing but difficult enterprise. My research on men's and women's conversations uncovered patterns similar to those described for children's groups.

For women, as for girls, intimacy is the fabric of relationships, and talk is the thread from which it is woven. Little girls create and maintain friendships by exchanging secrets; similarly, women regard conversation as the cornerstone of friendship. So a woman expects her husband to be a new and improved version of a best friend. What is important is not the individual subjects that are discussed but the sense of closeness, of a life shared, that emerges when people tell their thoughts, feelings, and impressions.

Bonds between boys can be as intense as girls', but they are based less on talking, more on doing things together. Since they don't assume talk is the cement that binds a relationship, men don't know what kind of talk women want, and they don't miss it when it isn't there.

Boys' groups are larger, more inclusive, and more hierarchical, so boys must struggle to avoid the subordinate position in the group. This may play a role in women's complaints that men don't listen to them. Some men really don't like to listen, because being the listener makes them feel one-down, like a child listening to adults or an employee to a boss.

12   But often when women tell men, "You aren't listening," and the men protest, "I am," the men are right. The impression of not listening results from misalignments in the mechanics of conversation. The misalignment begins as soon as a man and a woman take physical positions. This became clear when I studied videotapes made by psychologist Bruce Dorval of children and adults talking to their same-sex best friends. I found that at every age, the girls and women faced each other directly, their eyes anchored on each other's faces. At every age, the boys and men sat at angles to each other and looked elsewhere in the room, periodically glancing at each other. They were obviously attuned to each other, often mirroring each other's movements. But the tendency of men to face away can give women the impression they aren't listening even when they are. A young woman in college was frustrated: Whenever she told her boyfriend she wanted to talk to him, he would lie down on the floor, close his eyes, and put his arm over his face. This signaled to her "He's taking a nap." But he insisted he was listening extra-hard. Normally, he looks around the room, so he is easily distracted. Lying down and covering his eyes helped him concentrate on what she was saying.

Analogous to the physical alignment that women and men take in conversation is their topical alignment. The girls in my study tended to talk at length about one topic, but the boys tended to jump from topic to topic. The second-grade girls exchanged stories about people they knew. The second-grade boys teased, told jokes, noticed things in the room and talked about finding games to play. The sixth-grade girls talked about problems with a mutual friend. The sixth-grade boys talked about 55 different topics, none of which extended over more than a few turns.

Listening to Body Language

Switching topics is another habit that gives women the impression men aren't listening, especially if they switch to a topic about themselves. But the evidence of the 10th-grade boys in my study indicates otherwise. The 10th-grade boys sprawled across their chairs with bodies parallel and eyes straight ahead, rarely looking at each other. They looked as if they were riding in a car, staring out the windshield. But they were talking about their feelings. One boy was upset because a girl had told him he had a drinking problem, and the other was feeling alienated from all his friends.

Now, when a girl told a friend about a problem, the friend responded by asking probing questions and expressing agreement and understanding. But the boys dismissed each other's problems. Todd assured Richard that his drinking was "no big problem" because "sometimes you're funny when you're off your butt." And when Todd said he felt left out, Richard responded, "Why should you? You know more people than me."

16   Women perceive such responses as belittling and unsupportive. But the boys seemed satisfied with them. Whereas women reassure each other by implying, "You shouldn't feel bad because I've had similar experiences," men do so by implying, "You shouldn't feel bad because your problems aren't so bad."

There are even simpler reasons for women's impression that men don't listen. Linguist Lynette Hirschman found that women make more listener-noise, such as "mhm," "uhuh," and "yeah," to show "I'm with you." Men, she found, more often give silent attention. Women who expect a stream of listener-noise interpret silent attention as no attention at all.

Women's conversational habits are as frustrating to men as men's are to women. Men who expect silent attention interpret a stream of listener-noise as overreaction or impatience. Also, when women talk to each other in a close, comfortable setting, they often overlap, finish each other's sentences and anticipate what the other is about to say. This practice, which I call "participatory listenership," is often perceived by men as interruption, intrusion and lack of attention.

A parallel difference caused a man to complain about his wife, "She just wants to talk about her own point of view. If I show her another view, she gets mad at me." When most women talk to each other, they assume a conversationalist's job is to express agreement and support. But many men see their conversational duty as pointing out the other side of an argument. This is heard as disloyalty by women, and refusal to offer the requisite support. It is not that women don't want to see other points of view, but that they prefer them phrased as suggestions and inquiries rather than as direct challenges.

20   In his book *Fighting for Life,* Walter Ong points out that men use "agonistic" or warlike, oppositional formats to do almost anything; thus discussion becomes debate, and conversation a competitive sport. In contrast, women see conversation as a ritual means of establishing rapport. If Jane tells a problem and June says she has a similar one, they walk away feeling closer to each other. But this attempt at establishing rapport can backfire when used with men. Men take too literally women's ritual "troubles talk," just as women mistake men's ritual challenges for real attack.

The Sounds of Silence

These differences begin to clarify why women and men have such different expectations about communication in marriage. For women, talk creates intimacy. Marriage is an orgy of closeness: you can tell your feelings and thoughts, and still be loved. Their greatest fear is being pushed away. But men live in a hierarchical world, where talk maintains independence and status. They are on guard to protect themselves from being put down and pushed around.

This explains the paradox of the talkative man who said of his silent wife, "She's the talker." In the public setting of a guest lecture, he felt challenged to show his intelligence and display his understanding of the lecture. But at home, where he has nothing to prove and no one to defend against, he is free to remain silent. For his wife, being home means she is free from the worry that something she says might offend someone, or spark disagreement, or appear to be showing off; at home she is free to talk.

The communication problems that endanger marriage can't be fixed by mechanical engineering. They require a new conceptual framework about the role of talk in human relationships. Many of the psychological explanations that have become second nature may not be helpful, because they tend to blame either women (for not being assertive enough) or men (for not being in touch with their feelings). A sociolinguistic approach by which male-female conversation is seen as cross-cultural communication allows us to understand the problem and forge solutions without blaming either party.

24   Once the problem is understood, improvement comes naturally, as it did to the young women and her boyfriend who seemed to go to sleep when she wanted to talk. Previously, she had accused him of not listening, and he had refused to change his behavior, since that would be admitting fault. But then she learned about and explained to him the differences in women's and men's habitual ways of aligning themselves in conversation. The next time she told him she wanted to talk, he began, as usual, by lying down and covering his eyes. When the familiar negative reaction bubbled up, she reassured herself that he really was listening. But then he sat up and looked at her. Thrilled, she asked why. He said, "You like me to look at you when we talk, so I'll try to do it." Once he saw their differences as cross-cultural rather than right and wrong, he independently altered his behavior.

Women who feel abandoned and deprived when their husband won't listen to or report daily news may be happy to discover their husbands trying to adapt once they understand the place of small talk in women's relationships. But if their husbands don't adapt, the women may still be comforted that for men, this is not a failure of intimacy. Accepting the difference, the wives may look to their friends or family for that kind of talk. And husbands who can't provide it shouldn't feel their wives have made unreasonable demands. Some couples will still decide to divorce, but at least their decisions will be based on realistic expectations.

In these times of resurgent ethnic conflicts, the world desperately needs cross-cultural understanding. Like charity, successful cross-cultural communication should begin at home.

Personal Response

How accurately do Tannen's conclusions about the different conversational styles of men and women reflect your own experiences?

Questions for Discussion

1. What evidence does Tannen supply to support her assertion in paragraph 2 that men's noncommunicativeness at home is "wreaking havoc with marriage"?

2. How does Tannen answer the questions she poses in paragraph 6: "How can women and men have such different impressions of communication in marriage? Why the widespread imbalance in their interests and expectations?"

3. Summarize the differences Tannen has identified between men's and women's conversation styles. How do these differences cause frustration for both men and women when communicating with members of the other sex? Besides those Tannen mentions, what other differences in the conversational practices of males and females have you observed?

4. How does Tannen account for the paradox in her opening paragraph about the talkative man who says his wife is "the talker"?

5. What solution does Tannen offer to the communication problems between men and women? What do you think of that solution?

LOVE STORY

Carol Tavris

Carol Tavris is a social psychologist, writer, and lecturer. She has written numerous articles and book reviews on many aspects of psychology for a wide variety of general interest magazines, such as Psychology Today, Discover, Harper's, New York, *and* Vogue. *Her books include* The Longest War:

Sex Differences in Perspective *(1984), co-edited by Carole Wade;* Anger: The Misunderstood Emotion *(1989); and* The Mismeasure of Woman *(1992), from which the following piece is excerpted.*

As a child, I was nuts about cowboys, guns, and Palomino ponies, and so when I first saw the musical *Annie Get Your Gun* I was in heaven. Annie Oakley was a woman who could ride, wear cowgirl outfits, and shoot. She became my hero at once. She sang "Anything you can do, I can do better," and she outshot her rival, Frank Butler. I loved Annie Oakley so much that I entirely blocked out the end of the musical, when she realizes that "You can't get a man with a gun." Annie deliberately blows her next competition with Butler, who of course then realizes he loves her after all. I couldn't understand why a woman would give up being the world's best sharpshooter (even for Frank Butler, who was definitely terrific), or why Frank Butler would love Annie only if she gave up sharpshooting.

I wish I had known then what I know now: In the real-life story of Annie Oakley and Frank Butler, she never had to make that choice. Annie did get her man with a gun. In 1875, as a teenager, she defeated Frank Butler in an arranged competition. "It was her first big match—my first defeat," wrote Butler. "The next day I came back to see the little girl who had beaten me, and it was not long until we were married."[1] For the next fifty years they worked and traveled together in Europe and America, Annie as featured sharpshooter in the Buffalo Bill Wild West show and Frank as her manager. They remained devoted, and Frank continued to express his affections for Annie in published love poems and interviews with the press. They died, within eighteen days of one another, in 1926.

"Why was the true love story of Annie Oakley and Frank Butler discarded as the basis for the musical?" asks writer Bonnie Kreps.[2] Because, she argues, the real story was not romantic enough—which is to say, it did not fit our myths of love. The strong silent hero does not rescue the poor weak lamb. The woman does not have to trade love for competence; she's allowed to have both. The man does not have to squeeze himself into some frozen mold of masculinity, competing with the woman over who does what better. Instead, he speaks, in a human voice, of his love and admiration for the "little girl who had beaten me." The true love story would never sell.

4   The feminization of love in America, the glorification of women's ways of loving, is not about the love between autonomous individuals. It celebrates a romantic, emotional love that promotes the myth of basic, essential differences between women and men. It supports the opposition of women's love and men's work. In so doing, it derails women from thinking about their own talents and aspirations, rewarding instead a narrowed focus on finding and keeping Mr. Right.[3]

---

[1] Butler's memoirs cited in Bonnie Kreps (1990), *Subversive thoughts, authentic passions* (San Francisco: Harper & Row, 1990), p. 78.

[2] Ibid., p. 79.

[3] See Dorothy C. Holland and Margaret A. Eisenhart (1991), *Educated in romance: Women, achievement, and college culture* (Chicago: University of Chicago Press), who studied college women at two southern schools over a

The stereotype of woman-as-love-expert blurs the similarity between the sexes in their human needs for love, intimacy, and attachment, *and* for autonomy and self-development.[4] It allows men's needs for attachment to remain covert and repressed, while women's needs become overt and exaggerated. It encourages women to overfocus on relationships and men to underfocus on them. As Francesca Cancian says, "When women are unhappy, they usually think they need more love; but the objective evidence suggests that they need more independence."[5] When men are unhappy, they usually think they need more success; but the objective evidence suggests that they need more time "to smell the flowers."

Women who live only for love will inevitably love too much. The need will become bottomless and unfillable, like the equally unquenchable thirst among some who live only for work, for more and more wealth. The trouble with romantic love, says Bonnie Kreps, is that it blinds women to the less charming realities of life with the Prince. Many women become what she calls a Reverse Sleeping Beauty: They kiss the Prince and promptly fall asleep. This is why so many of love's experts become, too easily, love's victims.

To move toward an alternative vision of human love, women and men would have to budge from their current certainty that their sex is the only one that knows how to love.

8   We would stop blaming women for everything that happens in the family and make men as accountable as women for the quality of family life. We would recognize that men's silences and absences have as deep and powerful an effect on the people around them as do the words and interventions of women.

We would value, as a society, the loving work that women and men do for one another. We would value, along with the ability to express feelings, productive work in the home and the physical care of others. We would acknowledge the ways men love, instead of assuming that they are helpless incompetents in the domains of feeling and the family.

We would break the polarity between the "male" model of stoicism and the "female" emotions it defends against. There is a place for stoicism. No one wants a firefighter to burst into tears at the sight of a fire, and in a crisis everyone should know how to behave without collapsing into puddles of anxiety. But there

---

period of several (recent) years. They found that peer pressure and patriarchal culture are sharply curtailing the aspirations and expectations of young women today. Many are entering college with high hopes and ambitions, and leaving with the single goal of catching the right husband.

[4] Studies of love, intimacy, grief, and attachment find no sex differences of any significance. Men and women are equally likely, for example, to have "secure" attachments or those marked by anxiety, ambivalence, and avoidance; see Phillip Shaver, Cindy Hazen, and Donna Bradshaw (1988), Love as attachment: The integration of three behavioral systems, in R. J. Sternberg and M. L. Barnes (Eds.), *The psychology of love* (New Haven, CT: Yale University Press). Paul Wright (1988) [Interpreting research on gender differences in friendship: A case for moderation and a plea for caution, *Journal of Social and Personal Relationships, 5,* 367–373] warns of the hazards of falsely dividing men and women into two exaggerated extremes, since the same kinds of experiences and exchanges take place to some degree in all close friendships.

[5] Francesca M. Cancian (1987), *Love in America: Gender and self-development* (Cambridge, England: Cambridge University Press), p. 81.

is also a place for feeling; empathy, remorse, regret, worry, sadness, and compassion are our links to other people and to the human condition.

None of this means, in my opinion, that women should try turning their husbands into their girlfriends, or that men should try to make their wives into one of the boys. Such efforts are bound to backfire, even when both participants know the other person's love language. One friend of mine told her lover, "Herb, I don't want you to do the male thing just now. I don't need advice. I've had a bad day, and I just want you to hold me and console me." He looked absolutely perplexed. "What good will that do?" he said.

12   Nor am I recommending some vague androgynous ideal, in which women have to give up their love of intimate chat and men have to give up teasing and kidding around. Instead, I am arguing for flexibility, the ability to speak both languages when required. I admit that narrow rules for a division of emotional labor are easier to follow. I think it will be as uncomfortable, even frightening, for women to modify their fondness for talk and risk independent action, when this is called for, as for men to modify their silences and risk vulnerability. It's much easier for women to focus on changing men, even if the results are few and puny, than to develop their own programs of self-development. It's much easier for men to withdraw into silence than to try to articulate the fears and losses that jeopardize masculine identity.

But perhaps we can begin by accepting the fact that neither sex has all the answers. Couples can regard each other as a source of charming anecdotes, a repository of a different kind of expertise, and a resource in emergencies. They can exchange help, knowledge, talents, stories, and experiences. An abiding intimacy, in contrast to the fleeting intimacy of momentary emotions, does not require that partners be the same. It requires a reciprocity of affection, power, and respect for differences—the basis of a love between equals, the love between Annie Oakley and Frank Butler.

Personal Response

To what degree does Tavris' analysis fit your personal view of men and women in love? If you are in love, how well does her analysis fit your relationship?

Questions for Discussion

1. What are the "myths of love" that Tavris refers to in paragraph 3? How does the movie version of the Annie Oakley/Frank Butler relationship support Tavris' point about such myths?

2. What does Tavris mean by "the feminization of love" (paragraph 4)? What does she see as its effects on male-female relationships?

3. Tavris calls for a "move toward an alternative vision of human love" (paragraph 7). State in your own words what Tavris believes we would have to do to achieve that alternative vision. Do you agree with her that such a vision of human love is achievable or even desirable?

MEN AND WOMEN IN SEARCH OF COMMON GROUND

Wendell Berry

Wendell Berry is a poet, novelist, essayist, and farmer who has published over a dozen books. His collections of essays include The Long-Legged Horse *(1969),* The Hidden Wound *(1970),* A Continuous Harmony *(1972),* The Unsettling of America *(1977),* The Gift of Good Land *(1981), and Standing by Woods *(1985). His book* What Are People For? *(1990) was issued on the twentieth anniversary of Earth Day and addresses his on-going concern with the future of the human race and his belief that we must change the way we live in order to avoid destruction. "Men and Women in Search of Common Ground" is from Berry's 1987 collection of essays,* Home Economics.

> The domestic joys, the daily housework
> or business, the building of houses—
> they are not phantasms . . . they have
> weight and form and location.
> Walt Whitman, *To Think of Time*

I am not an authority on men or women or any of the possible connections between them. In sexual matters I am an amateur, in both the ordinary and the literal senses of that word. I speak about them only because I am concerned about them; I am concerned about them only because I am involved in them; I am involved in them, apparently, only because I am a human, a qualification for which I deserve no credit.

I do not believe, moreover, that any individual *can* be an authority on the present subject. The common ground between men and women can only be defined by community authority. Individually, we may desire it and think about it, but we are not going to occupy it if we do not arrive there together.

That we have not arrived there, that we apparently are not very near to doing so, is acknowledged by the title of this symposium ["Men and Women in Search of Common Ground," a symposium at the Jung Institute of San Francisco]. And that a symposium so entitled should be held acknowledges implicitly that we are not happy in our exile. The specific cause of our unhappiness, I assume, is that relationships between men and women are now too often extremely tentative and temporary, whereas we would like them to be sound and permanent.

4   Apparently, it is in the nature of all human relationships to aspire to be permanent. To propose temporariness as a goal in such relationships is to bring them under the rule of aims and standards that prevent them from beginning. Neither marriage, nor kinship, nor friendship, no neighborhood can exist with a life expectancy that is merely convenient.

To see that such connections aspire to permanence, we do not have to look farther than popular songs, in which people still speak of loving each other "forever." We now understand, of course, that in this circumstance the word "forever" is not to be trusted. It may mean only "for a few years" or "for a while" or even "until tomorrow morning." And we should not be surprised to realize that if the word "forever" cannot be trusted in this circumstance, then the word "love" cannot be trusted either.

This, as we know, was often true before our own time, though in our time it seems easier than before to say "I will love you forever" and to mean nothing by it. It is possible for such words to be used cynically—that is, they may be *intended* to mean nothing—but I doubt that they are often used with such simple hypocrisy. People continue to use them, I think, because they continue to try to mean them. They continue to express their sexual feelings with words such as "love" and "forever" because they want those feelings to have a transferable value, like good words or good money. They cannot bear for sex to be "just sex," any more than they can bear for family life to be just reproduction or for friendship to be just a mutually convenient exchange of goods and services.

The questions that I want to address here, then, are: Why are sexual and other human relationships now so impermanent? And under what conditions might they become permanent?

8   It cannot be without significance that this division is occurring at a time when division has become our characteristic mode of thinking and acting. Everywhere we look now, the axework of division is going on. We see ourselves more and more as divided from each other, from nature, and from what our traditions define as human nature. The world is now full of nations, races, interests, groups, and movements of all sorts, most of them unable to define their relations to each other except in terms of division and opposition. The poor human body itself has been conceptually hacked to pieces and parceled out like a bureaucracy. Brain and brawn, left brain and right brain, stomach, hands, heart, and genitals have all been set up in competition against each other, each supported by its standing army of advocates, press agents, and merchants. In such a time, it is not surprising that the stresses that naturally, and perhaps desirably, occur between the sexes should result in the same sort of division with the same sort of doctrinal justification.

This condition of division is one that we suffer from and complain about, yet it is a condition that we promote by our ambitions and desires and justify by our jargon of "self-fulfillment." Each of us, we say, is supposed to "realize his or her full potential as an individual." It is as if the whole two hundred million of us were saying with Coriolanus:

> I'll never
> Be such a gosling to obey instinct, but stand
> As if a man were author of himself
> And knew no other kin. (V, iii, 34–37)

By "instinct" he means the love of family, community, and country. In Shakespeare's time, this "instinct" was understood to be the human norm—the definition of humanity, or a large part of that definition. When Coriolanus speaks these lines, he identifies himself, not as "odd," but as monstrous, a *danger* to family, community, and country. He identifies himself, that is, as an individual prepared to act alone and without the restraint of reverence, fidelity, or love. Shakespeare is at one with his tradition in understanding that such a person acted inevitably, not as the "author of himself," but as the author of tragic consequences both for himself and for other people.

The problem, of course, is that we are *not* the authors of ourselves. That we are not is a religious perception, but it is also a biological and a social one. Each of us has had many authors, and each of us is engaged, for better or worse, in that same authorship. We could say that the human race is a great coauthorship in which we are collaborating with God and nature in the making of ourselves and one another. From this there is no escape. We may collaborate either well or poorly, or we may refuse to collaborate, but even to refuse to collaborate is to exert an influence and to affect the quality of the product. This is only a way of saying that by ourselves we have no meaning and no dignity; by ourselves we are outside the human definition, outside our identity. "More and more," Mary Catharine Bateson wrote in *With a Daughter's Eye*, "it has seemed to me that the idea of an individual, the idea that there is someone to be known, separate from the relationships, is simply an error."

Some time ago I was with Wes Jackson, wandering among the experimental plots at his home and workplace, the Land Institute in Salina, Kansas. We stopped by one plot that had been planted in various densities of population. Wes pointed to a Maximilian sunflower growing alone, apart from the others, and said, "There is a plant that has 'realized its full potential as an individual.' " And clearly it had: It had grown very tall; it had put out many long branches heavily laden with blossoms— and the branches had broken off, for they had grown too long and too heavy. The plant had indeed realized its full potential as an individual, but it had failed as a Maximilian sunflower. We could say that its full potential as an individual *was* this failure. It had failed because it had lived outside an important part of its definition, which consists of *both* its individuality and its community. A part of its properly realizable potential lay in its community, not in itself.

12   In making a metaphor of this sunflower, I do not mean to deny the value or the virtue of a *proper* degree of independence in the character and economy of an individual, nor do I mean to deny the conflicts that occur between individuals and communities. Those conflicts belong to our definition, too, and are probably as necessary as they are troublesome. I do mean to say that the conflicts are not everything, and that to make conflict—the so-called "jungle law"—the basis of social or economic doctrine is extremely dangerous. A part of our definition is our common ground, and a part of it is sharing and mutually enjoying our common ground. Undoubtedly, also, since we are humans, a part of our definition is a recurring contest over the common ground: Who shall describe its boundaries, occupy it, use it, or own it? But such contests obviously can be carried too far,

so that they become destructive both of the commonality of the common ground and of the ground itself.

The danger of the phrase "common ground" is that it is likely to be meant as no more than a metaphor. I am *not* using it as a metaphor; I mean by it the actual ground that is shared by whatever group we may be talking about—the human race, a nation, a community, or a household. If we use the term only as a metaphor, then our thinking will not be robustly circumstantial and historical, as it needs to be, but only a weak, clear broth of ideas and feelings.

Marriage, for example, is talked about most of the time as if it were only a "human relationship" between a wife and a husband. A good marriage is likely to be explained as the result of mutually satisfactory adjustments of thoughts and feelings—a "deep" and complicated mental condition. That is surely true for some couples some of the time, but, as a general understanding of marriage, it is inadequate and probably unworkable. It is far too much a thing of the mind and, for that reason, is not to be trusted. "God guard me," Yeats wrote, "from those thoughts men think / In the mind alone . . ."

Yeats, who took seriously the principle of incarnation, elaborated this idea in his essay on the Japanese Noh plays, in which he says that "we only believe in those thoughts which have been conceived not in the brain but in the whole body." But we need a broader concept yet, for a marriage involves more than just the bodies and minds of a man and a woman. It involves locality, human circumstance, and duration. There is a strong possibility that the basic human sexual unit is composed of a man and a woman (bodies and minds), plus their history together, plus their kin and descendants, plus their place in the world with its economy and history, plus their natural neighborhood, plus their human community with its memories, satisfactions, expectations, and hopes.

16   By describing it in such a way, we begin to understand marriage as the insistently practical union that it is. We begin to understand it, that is, as it is represented in the traditional marriage ceremony, those vows being only a more circumstantial and practical way of saying what the popular songs say dreamily and easily: "I will love you forever"—a statement that, in this world, inescapably leads to practical requirements and consequences because it proposes survival as a goal. Indeed, marriage is a union much more than practical, for it looks both to our survival as a species and to the survival of our definition as human beings— that is, as creatures who make promises and keep them, who care devotedly and faithfully for one another, who care properly for the gifts of life in this world.

The business of humanity is undoubtedly survival in this complex sense—a necessary, difficult, and entirely fascinating job of work. We have in us deeply planted instructions—personal, cultural, and natural—to survive, and we do not need much experience to inform us that we cannot survive alone. The smallest possible "survival unit," indeed, appears to be the universe. At any rate, the ability of an organism to survive outside the universe has yet to be demonstrated. Inside it, everything happens *in concert;* not a breath is drawn but by the grace of an inconceivable series of vital connections joining an inconceivable multiplicity of created things in an inconceivable unity. But of course it is preposterous for a mere individual human to espouse the universe—a possibility that is purely mental, and productive of nothing but talk. On the other hand, it may be that our marriages, kinships, friendships, neighborhoods, and all our forms and acts of home-making are the rites by which we solemnize and enact our union with the universe. These ways are practical, proper, available to everybody, and they can provide for the safekeeping of the small acreages of the universe that have been entrusted to us. Moreover, they give the word "love" its only chance to mean, for only they can give it a history, a community, and a place. Only in such ways can love become flesh and do its worldly work. For example, a marriage without a place, a household, has nothing to show for itself. Without a history of some length, it does not know what it means. Without a community to exert a shaping pressure around it, it may explode because of the pressure inside it.

These ways of marriage, kinship, friendship, and neighborhood surround us with forbiddings; they are forms of bondage, and involved in our humanity is always the wish to escape. We may be obliged to look on this wish as necessary, for, as I have just implied, these unions are partly shaped by internal pressure. But involved in our humanity also is the warning that we can escape only into loneliness and meaninglessness. Our choice may be between a small, humansized meaning and a vast meaninglessness, or between the freedom of our virtues and the freedom of our vices. It is only in these bonds that our individuality has a use and a worth; it is only to the people who know us, love us, and depend on us that we are indispensable as the persons we uniquely are. In our industrial society, in which people insist so fervently on their value and their freedom "as individuals," individuals are seen more and more as "units" by their governments, employers, and suppliers. They live, that is, under the rule of the interchangeability of parts: What one person can do, another person can do just as well or a newer person can do better. Separate from the relationships, there is nobody to be known; people become, as they say and feel, nobodies.

It is plain that, under the rule of the industrial economy, humans, at least as individuals, are well advanced in a kind of obsolescence. Among those who have achieved even a modest success according to the industrial formula, the human body has been almost entirely replaced by machines and by a shrinking population of manual laborers. For enormous numbers of people now, the only physical activity that they cannot delegate to machines or menials, who will presumably do it more to their satisfaction, is sexual activity. For many, the only necessary physical labor is that of childbirth.

20   According to the industrial formula, the ideal human residence (from the Latin *residere*, "to sit back" or "remain sitting") is one in which the residers do not work. The house is built, equipped, decorated, and provisioned by other people, by strangers. In it, the married couple practice as few as possible of the disciplines of household or homestead. Their domestic labor consists principally of

buying things, putting things away, and throwing things away, but it is understood that it is "best" to have even those jobs done by an "inferior" person, and the ultimate industrial ideal is a "home" in which *everything* would be done by pushing buttons. In such a "home," a married couple are mates, sexually, legally, and socially, but they are not helpmates; they do nothing useful either together or for each other. According to the ideal, work should be done *away* from home. When such spouses say to each other, "I will love you forever," the meaning of their words is seriously impaired by their circumstances; they are speaking in the presence of so little that they have done and made. Their history together is essentially placeless; it has no visible or tangible incarnation. They have only themselves in view.

In such a circumstance, the obsolescence of the body is inevitable, and this is implicitly acknowledged by the existence of the "physical fitness movement." Back in the era of the body, when women and men were physically useful as well as physically attractive to one another, physical fitness was simply a condition. Little conscious attention was given to it; it was a by-product of useful work. Now an obsessive attention has been fixed upon it. Physical fitness has become extremely mental; once free, it has become expensive, an industry—just as sexual attractiveness, once the result of physical vigor and useful work, has now become an industry. The history of "sexual liberation" has been a history of increasing bondage to corporations.

Now the human mind appears to be following the human body into obsolescence. Increasingly, jobs that once were done by the minds of individual humans are done by computers—and by governments and experts. Dr. William C. DeVries, the current superstar of industrial heart replacement, can blithely assure a reporter that "the general society is not very well informed to make those decisions [as to the imposition of restraints on medical experiments on human patients], and that's why the medical society or the government who has a wider range of view comes in to make those decisions" (Louisville *Courier-Journal,* 3 Feb. 1985). Thus we may benefit from the "miracle" of modern medical science on the condition that we delegate all moral and critical authority in such matters to the doctors and the government. We may save our bodies by losing our minds, just as, according to another set of experts, we may save our minds by forsaking out bodies. Computer thought is exactly the sort that Yeats warned us against; it is made possible by the assumption that thought occurs "in the mind alone" and that the mind, therefore, is an excerptable and isolatable human function, which can be set aside from all else that is human, reduced to pure process, and so imitated by a machine. But in fact we know that the *human* mind is not distinguishable from what it knows and that what it knows comes from or is radically conditioned by its embodied life in this world. A machine, therefore, cannot be a mind or be like a mind; it can only *replace* a mind.

We know, too, that these mechanical substitutions are part of a long-established process. The industrial economy has made its way among us by a process of division, degradation, and then replacement. It is only after we have been divided against each other that work and the products of work can be degraded; it is only after work and its products have been degraded that workers can be replaced by machines. Only when thought has been degraded can a mind be replaced by a machine, or a society of experts, or a government.

24   It is true, furthermore, that, in this process of industrialization, what is free is invariably replaced by a substitute that is costly. Bodily health as the result of useful work, for instance, is or was free, whereas industrial medicine, which has flourished upon the uselessness of the body, is damagingly and heartlessly expensive. In the time of the usefulness of the body, when the body became useless it died, and death was understood as a kind of healing; industrial medicine looks upon death as a disease that calls for increasingly expensive cures.

Similarly, in preindustrial country towns and city neighborhoods, the people who needed each other lived close to each other. This proximity was free, and it provided many benefits that were either free or comparatively cheap. This simple proximity has been destroyed and replaced by communications and transportation industries that are, again, enormously expensive and destructive, as well as extremely vulnerable to disruption.

Insofar as we reside in the industrial economy, our obsolescence, both as individuals and as humankind, is fast growing upon us. But we cannot regret or, indeed, even know that this is true without knowing and naming those never-to-be-official institutions that alone have the power to reestablish us in our true estate and identity: marriage, family, household, friendship, neighborhood, community. For these to have an effective existence, they must be located in the world and in time. So located, they have the power to establish us in our human identity because they are not merely institutions in a public, abstract sense, like the organized institutions but are also private conditions. They are the conditions in which a human is complete, body and mind, because completely necessary and needed.

When we live within these human enclosures, we escape the tyrannical doctrine of the interchangeability of parts; in these enclosures, we live as members, each in its own identity necessary to the others. When our spouse or child, friend or neighbor is in need or in trouble, we do not deal with them by means of a computer, for we know that, with them, we must not think without feeling. We do not help them by sending a machine, for we know that, with them, a machine cannot represent us. We know that, when they need us, we must go and offer ourselves, body and mind, as we are. As members, moreover, we are useless and worse than useless to each other if we do not care properly for the ground that is common to us.

28   It is only in these trying circumstances that human love is given its chance to have meaning, for it is only in these circumstances that it can be borne out in deeds through time—"even," to quote Shakespeare again, "to the edge of doom"—and thus prove itself true by fulfilling its true term.

In these circumstances, in place and in time, the sexes will find their common ground and be somewhat harmoniously rejoined, not by some resolution of conflict and power, but by proving indispensable to one another, as in fact they are.

Personal Response

What have been your observations on relationships? Do you believe, as Berry argues, that they are now too often only tentative and temporary, or have the relationships of people you know been permanent and committed?

Questions for Discussion

1. Why is Berry critical of the concept of "self-fulfillment" (paragraph 9)? In what ways are we not the "authors of ourselves" (paragraph 10)? How does the example of the Maximilian sunflower (paragraph 11) illustrate that statement?

2. What does Berry mean when he says that "division has become our characteristic mode of thinking and acting" (paragraph 8)? In what ways does he mean that? What examples does he give?

3. How does Berry's definition of marriage differ from the way it is often regarded?

4. Explain what Berry means when he says that "the smallest possible 'survival unit,' indeed, appears to be the universe" (paragraph 17). What is his point here? In what ways are human relationships forms of bondage, according to Berry?

5. Summarize what Berry says about the impact of the industrial economy on humans. What does Berry think of the ideal human residence, according to the industrial formula (paragraph 20)?

6. What does Berry mean when he says in paragraph 21 that "the obsolescence of the body is inevitable"? In what way is the human mind "following the human body into obsolescence" (paragraph 22)?

THERE IS NO SAFE SEX

Robert C. Noble

Robert C. Noble is a doctor and professor of medicine at the University of Kentucky Medical Center. A specialist in infectious diseases, he works as an AIDS doctor with the poor. This essay first appeared in the April 1991 issue of Newsweek.

The other night on the evening news, there was a piece about condoms. Some-one wanted to provide free condoms to high-school students. A perky, fresh-faced teenage girl interviewed said everyone her age was having sex, so what was the big deal about giving out condoms? Her principal replied that giving out con-doms set a bad example. Then two experts commented. One was a lady who sat very straight in her chair, white hair in a tight perm, and, in a prudish voice, de-clared that condoms didn't work very well; teenagers shouldn't be having sex anyway. The other expert, a young, attractive woman, said that since teenagers were sexually active, they shouldn't be denied the protection that condoms af-forded. I found myself agreeing with the prude.

What do I know about all this? I'm an infectious-diseases physician and an AIDS doctor to the poor. Passing out condoms to teenagers is like issuing them squirt guns for a four-alarm blaze. Condoms just don't hack it. We should stop kidding ourselves.

I'm taking care of a 21-year-old boy with AIDS. He could have been the model for Donatello's David, androgynous, deep blue eyes, long blond hair, as sweet and gentle as he can be. His mom's in shock. He called her the other day and gave her two messages. I'm gay. I've got AIDS. His lover looks like a fellow you'd see in Sunday school; he works in a bank. He's had sex with only one per-son, my patient (*his* second partner), and they've been together for more than a year. These fellows aren't dummies. They read newspapers. You think condoms would have saved them?

4   Smart people don't wear condoms. I read a study about the sexual habits of college women. In 1975, 12 percent of college women used condoms when they had sexual intercourse. In 1989, the percentage had risen to only 41 percent. Why don't college women and their partners use condoms? They know about herpes. They know about genital warts and cervical cancer. All the public-health messages of the past 15 years have been sent, and only 41 percent of the college women use condoms. Maybe your brain has to be working to use one. In the heat of passion, the brain shuts down. You have to use a condom every time. *Every time.* That's hard to do.

I can't say I'm comforted reading a government pamphlet called "Condoms and Sexually Transmitted Diseases Especially AIDS." "Condoms are not 100 per-cent safe," it says, "but if used properly will reduce the risk of sexually transmitted diseases, including AIDS." *Reduce* the risk of a disease that is 100 percent fatal! That's all that's available between us and death? How much do condoms reduce the risk? They don't say. So much for Safe Sex. Safe Sex was a dumb idea anyway. I've noticed that the catchword now is "Safer Sex." So much for truth in advertis-ing. Other nuggets of advice: "If you know your partner is infected, the best rule is to void intercourse (including oral sex). If you do decide to have sex with an in-fected partner, you should *always* be sure a condom is used from start to finish, every time." Seems reasonable, but is it really helpful? Most folks don't know when their partner is infected. It's not as if their nose is purple. Lots of men and women with herpes and wart-virus infections are having sex right now lying their heads off to their sexual partners—that is, to those who ask. At our place we are taking care of a guy with AIDS who is back visiting the bars and having sex. "Well, did your partner use a condom?" I ask. "Did you tell him that you're infected with the virus?" "Oh, no, Dr. Noble," he replies, "it would have broken the mood." You bet it would have broken the mood. It's not only the mood that gets broken. "Condoms may be more likely to break during anal intercourse than during other types of sex. . . ." Condoms also break in heterosexual sex; one study shows a 4 percent breakage rate. "Government testing can *not* guarantee that condoms will always prevent the spread of sexually transmitted diseases." That's what the pamphlet says. Condoms are all we've got.

Nobody these days lobbies for abstinence, virginity or single lifetime sexual partners. That would be boring. *Abstinence and sexual intercourse with one mutually faithful uninfected partner are the only totally effective prevention strategies.* That's from another recently published government report. . . .

What am I going to tell my daughters? I'm going to tell them that condoms give a false sense of security and that having sex is dangerous. *Reducing* the risk is not the same as *eliminating* the risk. My message will fly in the face of all other media messages they receive. In the movie *The Tall Guy*, a nurse goes to bed with the "Guy" character on their first date, boasting that she likes to get the sex thing out of the way at the beginning of the relationship. His roommate is a nymphomaniac who is always in bed with one or more men. This was supposed to be cute. *Pretty Woman* says you can find happiness with a prostitute. Who are the people that write this stuff? Have the '80s passed and everyone forgotten sexually transmitted diseases? Syphilis is on the rise. Gonorrhea is harder to treat and increasing among black teenagers and adults. Ectopic pregnancies and infertility from sexually transmitted diseases are mounting every year. Giving condoms to high school kids isn't going to reverse all this.

8   That prim little old lady on TV had it right. Unmarried people shouldn't be having sex. Few people have the courage to say this publicly. Doctors can't fix most of the things you catch out there. There's no cure for AIDS. There's no cure for herpes or genital warts. Gonorrhea and chlamydial infection can ruin your chance of ever getting pregnant and can harm your baby if you do. That afternoon in the motel may leave you with an infection that you'll have to explain to your spouse. Your doctor can't cover up for you. Your spouse's lawyer may sue him if he tries. There is no safe sex. Condoms aren't going to make a dent in the sexual epidemics that we are facing. If the condom breaks, you may die.

Personal Response

Has this essay in any way made you rethink your attitude toward sex and the use of condoms? Explain your answer.

Questions for Discussion

1. Summarize in a phrase or sentence the controversial issue that is the subject of this essay. What is Noble's position on this issue? Where does he first explicitly state his position?

2. What qualifies Noble to write with authority on this issue? What audience do you think he wants to reach?

3. What opposing opinions does Noble address? How effectively do you think Noble refutes those opposing opinions?

4. Do you think Noble's argument is convincing? Does he present solid evidence, and is his reasoning sound?

OVER 40 AND UNMARRIED

Ron Beathard

Ron Beathard is a writer and columnist living in Harrison, Ohio. He wrote this essay for the "My Turn" column of the June 3, 1996, issue of Newsweek.

A few months ago, a major midwestern newspaper accepted an essay I had written on the topic of being over 40 and never married. The editor called and asked me to suggest a headline that would tie in with Valentine's Day, the date of publication. My subject, I explained, had nothing whatsoever to do with Valentine's Day, but since he had bought the column and paid for it, he could do with it as he pleased. And he did. The headline: MY AGING VALENTINE—ON AN OLDER MAN'S THOUGHTS NOT TURNING TO FANCY. Good Lord, I thought, that's me he's talking about. I was filled with woe.

The percentage of the population consisting of unmarried men over 40 has fluctuated between 3 and 6 percent over the years. No one knows why. Sociologists rarely study us, psychologists don't quiz us and politicians don't count us. For all we know, the fluctuation could be due to the length of the fur on autumn caterpillars. Or vice versa. We do know our numbers are increasing this decade and, according to forecasts, will continue to rise in the future. It is not for me to discuss why, but simply to explain who and what we are.

We are minority group, although we would never qualify for affirmative-action programs. The discrimination against us is benign and curious—and often amusing. ("Did you know he's never married?" "Is he gay?" "I don't think so." "There must be something wrong.") And: ("Have you ever tasted his lasagna?" "Delicious." "He'll make a great wife." Laughter.) Slightly suspect, we innocently create problems in a double-occupancy world. How does one divide an odd number into equal teams for golf, bridge or badminton? ("But I can't have five for dinner. It's not symmetrical." "Ask him to invite a friend." "What if he doesn't have any?")

4   Although a minority, we are accorded a high degree of social acceptability—higher than single women. We are bachelors; they are old maids. The men's magazines tell us we are forever young; the women's magazines tell them they are already old. The worst adjectives that are ever thrown at us are "confirmed" and "eccentric." Our biological clock has no hands. If we at the age of 60 sire a child, we are admired (snow on the roof but fire in the heart and all that); a mother at

that age is tabloid material. Aside from wistful thoughts of a son to teach our secrets of throwing sliders or engaging the girls, the paternal urge lacks the urgency of the maternal one. Besides, nowadays cryogenic sex makes coupling unnecessary.

My peers and I are not much into Robert Bly's "Iron John" male thing. Let others sit cross-legged around a fire, outfitted in Pendleton plaid. Taking a journey into the mythopoetic spirit of the male wilderness is best left to men described by Somerset Maugham in "The Moon and Sixpence": "There are men whom a merciful Providence has undoubtedly ordained to a single life [but] have flown in the face of its decrees. There is no object more deserving of pity than the married bachelor."

Having heeded Providence, we aging singles lack an immediate companion with whom to share the good times of a winning lottery ticket or the beauty of a starry night. Social activities are haphazard and precarious. Without a built-in partner, a night out or an afternoon in requires coordination and planning. But sometimes we get seeds that drop from the feeder. ("I have an extra ticket for Saturday night." "Ask Ron. I'm sure he's not busy.")

We have learned to cope with our solitary state. It takes a confident man to dine alone. The less self-assured pretend they are on the road traveling from important client to important CEO, and read an important business journal as if they just don't have the time to eat and socialize simultaneously. They can order water and service for two, glance impatiently at their watches every two minutes, then sigh to the waiter, "I guess she got tied up in court."

8   Having less need of diversion than other men, we tend to take up solitary hobbies and pastimes—reading, collecting, building something in the basement, exploring rivers and mountains, and asking more "why" and "what if" questions than most people. We tend to be introspective. In our homes there is no one with whom to chit and chat about the weather and the elections. Without time-consuming and weekend-filling household chores, family pleasures and social responsibilities, we talk to ourselves a great deal because there is no one we know as well.

However, we are not hermits. Weighty introspection does not preclude an occasional encounter with contemporary cultural icons: Pearl Jam and Barney, Rollerblading and line dancing, grungy and bungee. We do keep in touch. We try not to make stupid remarks like "I'm too old/mature for that." If we have to put limitations on ourselves, we'll do it tomorrow. Because there are few volleyball leagues, social clubs, newsletters or special days at the ballpark devoted exclusively to single men over 40, we are forced from our clique to enjoy the rewarding diversity of people.

Our married critics say that we are impractical and maintain a fantasy of perfection, that we shun family and parental involvement, that we are too self-centered to have children and—lowest of all—that we avoid commitment. Perhaps. We have many chances to get married; it's simply that we don't take any. But we understand the suspicions we arouse. We mention our mothers cautiously. We seem to raise Freudian eyebrows.

Contrary to popular opinion, the single life is not in direct opposition to family life. The two situations are not poles apart, not us-and-them or winners-and-losers. They are complementary. We make terrific uncles and great nice guys next door. We are serving and standing and waiting.

12   We aren't stylish, nor were we meant to be. Perhaps one brief day we will be in style, writing a best-selling confession or two, trotted out on talk shows, welcomed as the fifth dinner guest. Then after a few days we will go home quietly and continue to make our contributions to society.

Personal Response

Beathard writes that most people view single men over forty with surprise, curiosity, and humor. How did you view such men before reading this essay? Has your view changed in any way?

Questions for Discussion

1. Beathard says that he wants to explain "who and what [single men over forty] are" (paragraph 2). How successfully do you think he accomplishes that purpose? Do you now have a clearer understanding of Beathard and others like him?

2. Beathard devotes attention to the differences in the ways people perceive unmarried men and unmarried women. What contrasts in those perceptions does he identify? Do you agree with him? Can you add any other differences to those he names?

3. Beathard uses the terms "bachelor" and "old maid" in paragraph 4. What connotative values do those words have? Do people still use the phrase "old maid" to refer to unmarried women? At what age do men become "bachelors" and women "old maids"?

4. Discuss your understanding of the Somerset Maugham quotation that "there is no object more deserving of pity than the married bachelor" (paragraph 5).

I'M NOT SICK, I'M JUST IN LOVE

Katherine Davis

Katherine Davis works as an editorial assistant in New York City. She wrote this essay for the "My Turn" column of the July 24, 1996, issue of Newsweek.

A couple of months ago, I received a phone call from one of my college roommates. We hadn't spoken since our graduation from Barnard College a year ago, and we both had big news to share. Her boyfriend of five years had proposed. I was thrilled for her, but not surprised. Marriage seemed inevitable for two people who have been inseparable for as long as they have. I *was* surprised to hear that they won't be getting married for at least five years. She wants to concentrate on her career.

I, too, am engaged to be married. Unlike my friend, my big news included the start of wedding plans: designing a dress, invitations, menus, engagement parties and bridal showers. While I've probably picked up more copies of brides' magazines than The Economist lately, I also want to focus on my career. But since I decided to marry at the age of 23, I've been made to feel as if a career is no longer a viable option. Once I was viewed as a bright young woman with promise. Now I'm dismissed by acquaintances and strangers as being sentenced to an insignificant life. I *am* young, but no younger than women who married a generation ago. The distress and hostility I've encountered has more to do with changing attitudes toward the *role* of wife. When everyone is touting "family values," why does marriage have such a bad rap?

I certainly didn't plan on an early marriage. I didn't intend to get married, ever. I envisioned my future as a broadcast journalist, traveling, meeting international leaders and, more realistically, long days and deadlines—not a husband and kids. Friends predicted I'd be a real-life Murphy Brown: ambitious, self-serving and single.

4   My quest to become a reporter began at MTV News, where I interned during my last semester at college, and started working as a desk assistant upon graduation. That's where I met my fiancé. Eight years my senior, Wilson has spent most of his adult life abroad and is well versed in everything from Russian literature to motorcycle repair. We found common ground in our career ambitions and agreed to a get-together some night after work to discuss them. Then I avoided him. I convinced myself I was too busy with my senior thesis and job interviews. There was no room for another commitment.

Room *was* made. By the end of last year, we were in love—and engaged. At work, since we'd kept our relationship under wraps, the news of our engagement came as a shock. Wilson was treated to some pats on the back and a celebratory night on the town. Few congratulations were addressed to me, however. I received comments like "You're so young!" or "What about your career?" When I left MTV for print journalism, some co-workers assumed I'd quit to plan my wedding. Others made me feel, as a woman, I was ceding my place in the newsroom to Wilson. One suggested that I not mention my pending nuptials to prospective employers. It might suggest lack of motivation for hard work.

My plans also touched off panic among my girlfriends. It's a return of the domino theory and, to protect themselves, some have chosen not to sympathize with the enemy. I've been taunted that my days of "sowing my wild oats" are over and reproached for secretly wanting a baby right away. (There's even a bet I'll become pregnant by Jan. 31, 1998.) I've been accused of misrepresenting myself during college as someone trying to earn a MRS. degree rather than an education. When "feminist" friends hear that I am taking my husband's name, they act as if I'm forsaking "our" cause. One Saturday afternoon, a friend phoned and I admitted I was spending the day doing laundry—mine and his. Her voice resonated with such pity that I hung up.

New York City, where we live, breeds much of this antagonism toward marriage. I've read that half of Manhattan households consist of single people. Home to the worlds of "Friends" and "Seinfeld," marriage is sort of an anomaly here. One fifth of women in this town over the age of 45 have never been married. Manhattanites aren't exactly diving to catch the bouquet.

8   I've also experienced prejudice in my hometown in Colorado. At a local store's bridal registry, I walked in wearing a Columbia University sweatshirt and the consultant asked if I'd gone to school there. On hearing that I'd graduated 10 months earlier, she explained that she had a daughter my age. "But she is very involved in her career," she added, presuming that I, selecting a silverware pattern, was not.

Registering at another store brought my mother and me to tears. As I perused the housewares, my mom mistook my interest in cookware to be a sign of impending domesticity and wondered where she'd gone wrong. A former home-ec teacher, my mom always joked that my lowest grade in junior high was earned in her field of expertise. It's not funny when your career-bent daughter wants a Crockpot.

It's been difficult for my mom to watch her daughter choose a husband before establishing a career—as she once did. Throughout my education, she has seen the opportunities made available to me, some that weren't imaginable when she was young. She and my father strove to provide me with the skills to take advantage of these new avenues. In the process, she grew attached to the idea of my becoming a successful professional.

I have no intention of dropping my career goals for marriage. While I'm excited by the prospect of having children, motherhood will not necessarily be the defining feature of my life. And I'll be no worse a wife for having a career. My engagement has made me no less ambitious, hardworking—or a feminist.

12   During our conversation, my old roommate described her engagement ring, which sits in her jewelry box because she feels people treat her differently when she wears it. I thought she was being a bit foolish. Now I understand her insecurities. Presented with an array of career options, young women today are pressured to reject "traditional" roles.

Wilson and I are fortunate to have a relationship that allows us to be as committed to our professions as we are to each other. Soon I'll be his blushing bride. And my rosy complexion will be from exuberance—not embarrassment.

Personal Response

What are your thoughts about when you will marry? How do you think marriage will affect your career?

Questions for Discussion

1. Davis writes: "The distress and hostility I've encountered has more to do with changing attitudes toward the *role* of wife. . . . Young women today are

pressured to reject 'traditional' roles" (paragraphs 2 and 11). In what ways have attitudes toward the role of wife changed? What is the "traditional" role of women? What sex-role expectations are there for young women today? Is the attitude toward the role of husband changing? Are men pressured to reject traditional roles?

2. Davis says that her friends predicted that she would be "a real-life Murphy Brown." What other models of single women in key roles on television programs are there? Do they all fit the Murphy Brown pattern of being "ambitious, self-serving and single" (paragraph 3)?

3. Davis tells of the contrast in responses when her fiancé and she announced their engagement (paragraph 5). How does she account for those differences? Can you think of other reasons why the reactions of friends and co-workers would differ? Would the responses among your friends and co-workers be the same in similar circumstances? Where do expectations about age of marriage for men and women come from? Do you think it unreasonable to think a woman necessarily compromises her career by marrying young?

VOWS

Julie Showalter

Julie Showalter holds a PhD in literature from Ball State University. A writer whose stories have appeared in Other Voices, The Chicago Sun Times, *and* The Maryland Review, *she has read her work on National Public Radio and was a 1995 winner of a Glimmertrain new writer award. This story first appeared in the spring 1996 issue of* Other Voices, *a publication of the University of Illinois at Chicago.*

I was surprised that Adam wanted a wedding. He hadn't seemed to want to get married. But once we decided, he said of course there'll be a ceremony. Of course my parents will come. Of course your parents will come. Of course we'll invite our friends.

We'd lived together over two years, both damaged by previous divorces. Every few months he'd get angry and say, "Admit it, Jan, you really want to get married." My analyst said I should admit it because it was what I wanted, good girl from Missouri who didn't live with men unless she was married, no matter how many husbands she'd had. "Besides," he said, "the way Adam keeps bringing it up, I think he must want to get married too."

So, when he said it again, "Admit it. You're conventional. You want to get married," I said, "Yes, yes I am, yes I do."

4   We'd agreed from the start that he wasn't supposed to take care of me. I'd just come from a marriage where I'd been taken care of until I almost suffocated. And when Adam left his ex-wife, she said, "You promised to take care of me forever. I won't let you go so easy." So, we were agreed. We were independent

people with independent lives, independent careers, and independent check-books. And now we were going to get married.

I thought we could just sneak into it, go to City Hall on a lunch hour, tell our friends and family sometime later. But he wanted a wedding, said there had to be a wedding. I thought people would laugh. Here I was, thirty-four years old, twice divorced, and acting like I thought I could be a bride; like my promise to love, honor, and cherish meant something; like I could make a life-time commitment.

We found a minister who said, "About all anyone knows about Unitarians is that they'll marry anyone." After we laughed politely, he leaned forward, suddenly serious, assuming his spiritual-advisor role, "You two have to decide about your ceremony. I can't tell you what you want to promise each other. Only you can decide that."

Adam said, "We thought we'd go with the Dearly Beloved option."

8   The minister shook his head. "I don't do canned ceremonies. It has to come from your heart. You have to write it yourself."

As we left, Adam muttered, "Pompous asshole."

A small wedding in our home. Our parents, my daughter, a few close friends. Neither of us had met the other's parents. Twenty people at most. A simple ser-vice, a cake, coffee, some champagne. That's what we planned. Or what I planned, looking to him for approval.

Most of the time during the two months between our decision to marry and the wedding he seemed angry. When I suggested we call it off, he said no. "It's what you want," he said, "so we'll do it."

12   I wrote each invitation by hand. "Dear Ken and Bev, Please join us at our home for a celebration of our marriage," and so on. Then, two days after they were in the mail, I found a pebble in my left breast. I sat up in bed. "Feel this," I said, taking his hand. "What does this feel like to you?" Half asleep, he put his hand over my breast and squeezed. "No, here. Toward the top. There's some-thing there."

He sat up and pushed me down, his hands suddenly doctor's hands, both moving lightly over my breast like a blind man reading Braille. "It feels like a lump," he said. "It's probably nothing. Give Joel a call tomorrow." Adam and Joel had been interns together; one of the invitations had gone to him. Now I had to call him about my breast.

We lay there a while. I said, "It's too bad I didn't find this last month."

"Why?"

16   "Well, you're more or less trapped into marrying me now."

"That's the stupidest thing you've ever said." He rolled over presenting me with his back. We lay that way a long time, neither of us sleeping.

The next day I saw Joel who felt my breast and said, "I'm not impressed." Then he took me to see a surgeon—"best breast man in the city"—who said, "This is nothing. Don't worry. Come back in three weeks and I'll check it again." The follow-up appointment was scheduled for two days before the wedding.

When Adam got home from work, he said, "I'm glad things went well for you today. I know you were scared." He handed me a jewelry box—a gold watch. "It's a wedding gift, a little early." We didn't speak again of my fear, and we never mentioned his.

20   That night he held me while I slept. Twice I woke with a start. "There, there," he said, kissing my hair. "There, there."

His parents were due on Thursday before the wedding on Sunday. He'd arranged to get off early Thursday by scheduling patients until 9:00 Wednesday night. At 5:00 on Wednesday the phone rang. "This is your future mother-in-law. We can't find a parking place." I met them at the curb as they circled the block in their pickup. Adam's father didn't speak except to say, "I don't think this neighborhood looks safe."

With my ten-year-old daughter Rebecca, I tried to entertain them for the evening. It was difficult to find things to talk about because I didn't know how much they knew about me or how much Adam wanted them to know. I knew he didn't want them to know that he'd been involved with me while he was still married to Diane. I didn't think he wanted them to know I'd been married twice before. I settled on a position that made it look as if I'd sprung full-grown without a history into Adam's life about a year earlier. I hoped they wouldn't ask about Rebecca's father and that she wouldn't tell them she liked Adam more than my last husband. His mother said, "You just have to understand that I'm going to slip and call you Diane. It's been Adam and Diane for so long, it will take me some time to adjust."

By the time Adam got home, they were ready for bed.

24   On Thursday, Adam and I both managed to get off early. We got home at 3:00 to find his parents were gone. Two washed coffee cups and a carefully refolded morning paper were the only signs they'd been there. "Maybe they left a note," I said, but there was no note. Adam mixed two gin and tonics without speaking.

At 5:00 the phone rang. Adam answered it. Just then, from our third floor window I saw my mother getting out of a cab. As she started up the walk, Adam slammed down the phone. "God damn them to hell!" he said. I helped Mother get her luggage up the stairs. When I came back, Adam had gone to our bedroom. After fifteen minutes, I went in. He was lying on the bed in the dark, his arm thrown over his eyes. "They're at a motel," he said. "My mother said my father was too upset to stay with us. I don't know if they'll be back for the wedding." He didn't move.

I went back to Mother. "Adam's upset," I explained. "Some problems with his folks." He didn't come out all evening. Mother kept saying, "I just know this has something to do with me. I'm sure if I weren't here, everything would be fine."

The next day was full. Prenuptial agreement in the morning, breast check in the afternoon. Adam met my mother at breakfast. He was gracious and charming. Apologized for being under the weather the night before. I wanted to kill him.

28   When we arrived at his lawyer's office, the attorney asked, "Didn't you bring your own lawyer? Do you understand what you're signing?"

"I think so," I said as I signed away all rights present and future to Adam's earnings. We both had a history of being taken in a divorce. My first husband stole my daughter. My second stole my car. Adam's ex-wife got all the money, all the furniture, and alimony besides. She even got the stereo his parents bought him as a graduation gift from medical school. The agreement I signed stated specifically that the stereo in our condo belonged to Adam.

In exchange for the prenuptial agreement, I asked that we discontinue our separate household financial accounts. I was tired of "you owe me $2.47 for half of the pound of corned beef I bought at the White Hen last week." For two years I had kept these accounts, a running balance of who owed what to whom. Twice a month I would present the list to Adam saying, "I owe you $10.50," or "Your paying for dinner last night balances us out." He always appeared to think he'd been cheated. He'd ask, "Did you divide the dry cleaning bill or charge it all to me?" I was tired of keeping the list, of the real or imagined suspicion.

I was ready to stop hedging my bets and keeping score, ready to start trusting again. That's why I signed the agreement. That's why I wanted to get married.

32   That afternoon, the surgeon patted my shoulder. "This is nothing. Hasn't changed a bit. I wouldn't worry." Then he said, "I can tell you're not going to be able to relax until we take a real look at it. We can do a biopsy to set your mind at rest."

"Do you have any time available next Wednesday?" I asked. "My parents will be leaving on Tuesday. I'll just take one more vacation day."

Saturday afternoon my father arrived, bringing my nine-year-old niece with him. He thought adding Stephanie to the guest list would be a surprise for me and for Rebecca. My father, despite having three daughters, knew nothing about little girls and jealousy. As Rebecca announced, "I'm the bridesmaid. I'm the only bridesmaid. I get a bouquet," Stephanie kept saying, "I flew on the airplane with Grandpa. Just Grandpa and me." Over and over. Louder and louder.

Adam's parents appeared mid-afternoon, as if nothing had happened, as if they hadn't just disappeared for two days. The two mothers exchanged stories about what foolish / clumsy /difficult children Adam and I had been. The two fathers sat in the den and didn't talk.

36   Sunday, July 20. Wedding day. Adam woke to say, "You're really not going to write my vows. I can't believe you're not going to write my vows." I had written the ceremony as the minister had required, passing it by Adam for approval lest it be promising more than he intended to promise, saying more than he wanted to say. But I had not written his vows.

"Your vows are what you're promising to me," I said. "I can't write that."

It was the hottest day of the summer. Our window air conditioner hummed ominously. When we bought the condo, we knew to check things like electrical wiring. We even had an independent inspector look things over. "That's a good breaker box," he'd said, looking at the giant box containing twenty-four circuit breakers. He was right, it was a good box. Unfortunately, only two circuits were wired. One controlled the dining room chandelier, the other the rest of the seven-room apartment. In the six months we'd been there, we accommodated to the electrical system's idiosyncrasies. We'd shout, "Don't use your hair dryer. I'm starting the microwave." Now we were running the air conditioner and the apartment was filling with people who thought they could just walk in a room and flip a light switch willy-nilly, with no regard for consequences. We kept losing power in the rest of the apartment while the dining room chandelier blazed on.

People had been invited for 2:00. As each guest buzzed the buzzer, the two girls raced down the three flights of stairs. I had suggested that Rebecca introduce her cousin, hoping this official hostess role might make her feel special, make Stephanie feel like an honored guest. "This is my cousin Stephanie," she said to our friends. "She came unexpected."

40   The minister was late. His softball game had gone extra innings. Adam's father took Adam aside. "What kind of preacher plays baseball on Sunday?"

The ceremony I had written thanked our friends for helping us make note of a gradual change in our relationship, a relationship which had evolved into a marriage and would continue to evolve. In other words, this is no big deal. In other words, ye gods or irony, bad timing and cruel jokes who have controlled my life thus far, don't pay any attention to what's going on here.

I had memorized my vows, planned to say them looking into Adam's eyes. But when the time came, I went blank. The artfully crafted lines with appropriate quotations from Donne and Shakespeare were gone. I looked at the floor, I looked at the ceiling, I looked at Adam. "I love you," I said finally, my voice quavering. "I want to spend my life with you." Adam put his arm around me and squeezed. Family and guests sighed and sniffled.

Then Adam took his vows from his pocket. He read them quickly, too quickly for me to remember. I know he said he loved me, but they seemed to focus more on what he wasn't promising than what he was. "I can't promise forever," he said, "because I can't know what will happen. I love you now." Later, when my mother asked for a copy of the service, Adam's vows had disappeared.

44   We cut the cake; I made the coffee; we opened the champagne. As we were serving, Adam's parents said, "We need to head back to Missouri." They left. It was 3:15. I asked for more champagne.

Joel took me aside and said, "Don't worry about the biopsy. It's nothing. It's really just to set your mind at rest."

"Fine, I won't worry," I said.

Cheryl, Joel's girlfriend, took me aside. "I hope you're not worried. I had a biopsy six months ago and it was nothing. I worried a lot for nothing."

48   "Fine," I said, "I'm not worried. I'll not give it another thought." I smiled. "Any more champagne?" I asked.

Guests started leaving:

Joel and Cheryl had a long drive.

The Chious had a family gathering.

52 The Jamisons begged off. He was tired from the radiation treatments for his brain tumor. We didn't know until the next week that she was divorcing him.

The Baileys, who were separated but had arrived together, looked as if they'd go the distance. Then Laura got sick from too much champagne and Dave had to take her home.

There were thirteen of us left. I had made no provision for dinner, unable to plan beyond the cake, the coffee, the champagne. "Let's go to Costa Brava," Adam suggested. We grabbed six bottles of burgundy and set off.

Later, as we straggled back to the apartment, the oppressive heat seemed on the verge of breaking. Lightning flashed over the lake. I walked with my father. "I may have had too much wine," I said.

56 "That's OK," he said. "You're entitled. This is your big day."

Adam used to say that sooner or later he ended up cleaning up the vomit of every woman he'd ever been involved with. He said, "I think it was a particular virus that made the rounds while I was in school. First symptom—make a date with Adam Sherman; second symptom—mild nausea; third symptom—throw up where Adam has to clean it up." I always said that he'd never had to clean up after me and he never would. I could take care of myself.

On our wedding night, Adam held me while I threw up, helped me out of my wedding dress, and cleaned up the mess. In the living room the little girls explained to the remaining guests that ladies often got sick on their wedding nights. "It's part of the tradition," they said, those two little girls who would both end up pregnant and married, in that order, before they were eighteen.

I woke up the next morning wishing I could drop off the face of the earth. Surprisingly, no one was angry. "The heat," they said. "So much tension," they said. "Maybe a little too much wine," they said. "A combination," they said.

60 "How are you feeling, Hon Bun?" Adam asked. He was transformed. The angry, surly man I'd lived with the past two months was gone, and the loving, gentle fellow I'd fallen in love with had taken his place. It was as if he'd come through some terrible ordeal and was happy and surprised to be alive and in one piece.

On Wednesday, since it was no big deal, we agreed I'd just take a cab to the hospital. There was no reason to disrupt his day. I'd see him at home that evening.

I was in the waiting room trying to read when Adam appeared. "I finished rounds early and have a few minutes before I have to leave for outpatients. Thought I'd see how you were doing."

"I'm fine," I said. "I'm glad you came by, but don't mess up your schedule on my account."

64 "I have a few more minutes. I'll just get some work done here." We sat there, shoulders touching, both pretending to read. When they called my name, Adam said, "I'll wait around a little while longer. I don't have to leave until noon."

In the operating room, the surgeon joked with the nurses and with me. As he had promised, I felt some tugging, some pressure, but no pain. A tent of blue sheets kept me from seeing his face or what he was doing. We talked about Joel and other mutual friends as he worked.

He became silent. When he spoke again, we were no longer friends chatting. "How long have you had this?" he asked. His voice was flat.

"I noticed it three weeks ago," I said. "The night before I saw you the first time."

68   "Oh," he said.

There was no more banter in the room. Conversation was limited to commands like "Suction here" and replies like "Yes, Doctor."

Serious talk in serious voices.

Serious trouble.

72   I looked at the clock on the wall. It was 12:05. I said, "Could someone check to see if my husband's left yet? If he's still there, would you ask him to stay for a few more minutes, tell him that I'd like to talk to him. Could someone check right now. He may have already left."

A nurse went out. The clock flipped over to 12:07. He'd be gone. He was never late for his patients.

The nurse came back in. "He's here," she said. "He said not to worry. He said to tell you he'll be here. He promised."

Personal Response

What do you think of the relationship between Adam and Jan, of their wedding vows, and of the likelihood that their marriage will work?

Questions for Discussion

1. In what ways does the wife avoid committing to the marriage? When does she resolve her conflict about the marriage?

2. How does their knowledge that love sometimes does not last, that it can turn nasty and vindictive, affect Adam's and Jan's decision to marry and their willingness to trust one another?

3. Why does Jan sign a prenuptial agreement? How is that an act of trust?

4. What function do the man with the brain tumor and the wife who divorces him serve in relation to the matter of marriage and commitment?

5. How does Jan's finding the lump relate to the central issue of the story? Is her cancer the central issue? If not, what is?

Suggestions for Writing About
MALE-FEMALE RELATIONSHIPS

1. Do your own informal research on conversation patterns of men and women by observing conversations between men, between women, and between men and women. What conclusions can you draw? How do your conclusions relate to what Deborah Tannen writes in "Sex, Lies, and Conversation"?

2. Drawing on Deborah Tannen's "Sex, Lies, and Conversation" and Wendell Berry's "Men and Women in Search of Common Ground," explore reasons to account for why couples divorce. Can you offer explanations for the high divorce rate?

3. Carol Tavris in "Love Story" calls for a "move toward an alternative vision of human love" (paragraph 7). Explain how your vision of a love relationship compares with Tavris' and what you think men and women would have to do to achieve your vision.

4. Explain what Carol Tavris in "Love Story" means by the phrase "feminization of love" and your own position on the subject of the roles men and women play in relationships. For instance, do you think men and women see love and marriage differently?

5. With Deborah Tannen's "Sex, Lies, and Conversation" and Carol Tavris' "Love Story" in mind, compare or contrast men and women in an area other than communication style.

6. Explain your reasons for agreeing or disagreeing with Robert Noble's statement that "there is no safe sex."

7. Drawing on Ron Beathard's "Over Forty and Unmarried," Katherine Davis' "I'm Not Sick, I'm Just in Love," Carol Tavris' "Love Story," and Julie Showalter's "Vows," write an essay on cultural expectations for relationships between men and women. Explain whether your own view of relationships agrees with the commonly held cultural view.

8. Drawing on Wendell Berry's "Men and Women in Search of Common Ground," Julie Showalter's "Vows," and other relevant readings in this chapter, define what you believe is a successful marriage. Support your generalizations with specific examples, using a couple or couples you know who have successful marriages to illustrate what you mean.

9. Analyze the extent to which you think that messages from family, friends, or popular culture about marriage and career have limited or shaped your own behavior or plans for the future.

10. Analyze media messages about love, marriage, and commitment by focusing on one medium such as popular music, television, or the movies.

11. Use humor or satire to comment on some aspect of relationships between the sexes, such as meeting someone new, dating, or maintaining a relationship.

12. Based on what you have experienced or observed, contrast the attitudes of men and women on dating, sex, commitment, and/or marriage.

13. Argue for or against the distribution of free condoms to high school students.

14. Explain why a marriage or relationship you know of personally—your own, that of a friend, or even your parents'—did not last.

15. Explore the effects of divorce on the two people involved, on their family, and/or on their friends.

CHAPTER 6

POPULAR CULTURE

Broadly speaking, popular culture refers to the music, literature, arts, and media of a particular society and the ways in which those things reflect the current tastes, interests, and talents of its people. Thus, popular culture includes not only television, film, and music but also advertising, cartoons, newspapers, magazines, books, and virtually any other product you can think of that reveals something about people in a particular time and place.

Because the subject of popular culture covers such a wide range of topics, this chapter is divided into three sections, each focusing on a particular aspect of popular culture: rap music, Hollywood and the movies, and television. The essays in each of these sections reflect differing viewpoints on a particular controversy or offer different interpretations of a particular product of popular culture. Each section ends with suggestions for writing on that particular topic.

RAP MUSIC

Music is an integral part of popular culture. All kinds of music enjoy popularity in American culture, but certain kinds, especially those that young people listen to, seem to draw the attention of cultural critics more than other kinds of music do. For instance, rock and roll music has from its beginning in the 1950s been the object of heated critical debate, with arguments usually centered on its sexual content and the potential effect of such lyrics on audiences. This unit on music in popular culture focuses specifically on rap music, which has in recent years gained widespread public attention and prompted a host of opinions about its lyrics and the musicians who perform it. Of particular concern to critics are rap's violent lyrics, especially the way it links sexuality with violence, and the often violent lives of rap musicians themselves.

In this section on rap music, three writers comment on the cultural implications of rap music, focusing in particular on its meaning for black males and its effect on black women. In exploring the issues of gender, race, and class in relation to the lyrics of young black rappers, these writers raise some provocative and important questions. Michele Wallace in "When Black Feminism Faces the Music, and the Music Is Rap" maintains that the "glaringly sexist" lyrics of rap music reveal a blatant lack of respect "for the humanity of black women." Next, Tricia Rose in "Rap Music and the Demonization of Young Black Males" is concerned about what she believes is unfair press given to rap music, especially the message it sends about black males. Finally, Paul Delaney in "Gangsta Rappers vs. the Mainstream Black Community" also believes that the media play an important role in shaping the public's perception of musicians, in this case "gangsta rappers." Commenting on demeaning and unfair portrayals of blacks in the media, Delaney make a case for rap music as social commentary.

WHEN BLACK FEMINISM FACES THE MUSIC, AND THE MUSIC IS RAP

Michele Wallace

Michele Wallace is a feminist cultural critic. This commentary on rap music first appeared in the July 29, 1990, issue of the New York Times.

Like many black feminists, I look on sexism in rap as a necessary evil. In a society plagued by poverty and illiteracy, where young black men are as likely to be in prison as in college, rap is a welcome articulation of the economic and social frustrations of black youth.

In response to disappointments faced by poor urban blacks negotiating their future, rap offers the release of creative expression and historical continuity: it draws on precedents as diverse as jazz, reggae, calypso, Afro-Cuban, African and heavy-metal, and its lyrics include rudimentary forms of political, economic and social analysis.

But with the failure of our urban public schools, rappers have taken education into their own hands; these are oral lessons (reading and writing being low priorities). And it should come as no surprise that the end result emphasizes innovations in style and rhythm over ethics and morality. Although there are exceptions, like raps advocating world peace (the W.I.S.E. Guyz's "Time for Peace") and opposing drugs use (Ice-T's "I'm Your Pusher"), rap lyrics can be brutal, raw and, where women are the subject, glaringly sexist.

4   Given the genre's current cross-over popularity and success in the marketplace, including television commercials, rap's impact on young people is growing. A large part of the appeal of pop culture is that it can offer symbolic resolutions to life's contradictions. But when it comes to gender, rap has not resolved a thing.

Though styles vary—from that of the X-rated Ice-T to the sybaritic Kwaneé to the hyperpolitics of Public Enemy—what seems universal is how little male rappers respect sexual intimacy and how little regard they have for the humanity of the black woman. Witness the striking contrast within rap videos: for men, standard attire is baggy outsize pants; for women, spike heels and short skirts.

Videos often feature the ostentatious and fetishistic display of women's bodies. In Kool Moe Dee's "How Ya Like Me Now," women gyrate in tight leather with large revealing holes. In Digital Underground's video "Doowutchyalike," set poolside at what looks like a fraternity house party, a rapper in a clown costume pretends to bite the backside of a woman in a bikini.

As Trisha Rose, a black feminist studying rap, puts it, "Rap is basically a locker room with a beat."

The recent banning of the sale of 2 Live Crew's album "As Nasty as They Wanna Be" by local governments in Florida and elsewhere has publicized rap's treatment of women as sex objects, but it also made a hit of a record that contains some of the bawdiest lyrics in rap. Though such sexual explicitness in lyrics is rare, the assumptions about women—that they manipulate men with their bodies—are typical.

8   In an era when the idea that women want to be raped should be obsolete, rap lyrics and videos presuppose that women always desire sex, whether they know it or not. In Bell Biv De-Voe's rap-influenced pop hit single "Poison," for instance, a beautiful girl is considered poison because she does not respond affirmatively and automatically to a sexual proposition.

In "Yearning: Race, Gender, Cultural Politics" (Southend, 1990), Bell Hooks sees the roots of rap as a youth rebellion against all attempts to control black masculinity, both in the streets and in the home. "That rap would be anti-domesticity and in the process anti-female should come as no surprise," Ms. Hooks says.

At present there is only a small platform for black women to address the problems of sexism in rap and in their community. Feminist criticism, like many other forms of social analysis, is widely considered part of a hostile white culture. For a black feminist to chastise misogyny in rap publicly would be viewed as divisive and counterproductive. There is a widespread perception in the black community that public criticism of black men constitutes collaborating with a racist society.

The charge is hardly new. Such a reaction greeted Ntozake Shange's play "For Colored Girls Who Have Considered Suicide When the Rainbow Is Enuf," my own essays, "Black Macho and the Myth of the Superwoman," and Alice Walker's novel "The Color Purple," all of which were perceived as critical of black men. After the release of the film version of "The Color Purple," feminists were lambasted in the press for their supposed lack of support for black men; such critical analysis by black women has all but disappeared. In its place is "A Black Man's Guide to the Black Woman," a vanity-press book by Shahrazad Ali, which has sold more than 80,000 copies by insisting that black women are neurotic, insecure and competitive with black men.

12   Though misogynist lyrics seem to represent the opposite of Ms. Ali's world view, these are, in fact, just two extremes on the same theme: Ms. Ali's prescription for what ails the black community is that women should not question men about their sexual philandering, and should be firmly slapped across the mouth when they do. Rap lyrics suggest just about the same: women should be silent and prone.

There are those who have wrongly advocated censorship of rap's more sexually explicit lyrics, and those who have excused the misogyny because of its basis in black oral traditions.

Rap is rooted not only in the blaxploitation films of the 60's but also in an equally sexist tradition of black comedy. In the use of four-letter words and explicit sexual references, both Richard Pryor and Eddie Murphy, who themselves drew upon the earlier examples of Redd Foxx, Pigmeat Markham and Moms Mabley, are conscious reference points for the 2 Live Crew. Black comedy, in turn, draws on an oral tradition in which black men trade "toasts," stories in which dangerous bagmen and trickster figures like Stackolee and Dolomite sexually exploit women and promote violence among men. The popular rapper Ice Cube, in the album "Amerikkka's Most Wanted," is Stackolee come to life. In "The Nigga Ya Love to Hate," he projects an image of himself as a criminal as dangerous to women as to the straight white world.

Rap remains almost completely dominated by black males and this mind-set. Although women have been involved in rap since at least the mid-80's, record companies have only recently begun to promote them. And as women rappers like Salt-n-Pepa, Monie Love, M. C. Lyte, L. A. Star and Queen Latifah slowly gain more visibility, rap's sexism may emerge as a subject for scrutiny. Indeed, the answer may lie with women, expressing in lyrics and videos the tensions between the sexes in the black community.

16 Today's women rappers range from a high ground that doesn't challenge male rap on its own level (Queen Latifah) to those who subscribe to the same sexual high jinks as male rappers (Oaktown's 3.5.7). M. C. Hammer launched Oaktown's 3.5.7, made up of his former backup dancers. These female rappers manifest the worst-case scenario: their skimpy, skintight leopard costumes in the video of "Wild and Loose (We Like It)" suggest an exotic animalistic sexuality. Their clothes fall to their ankles. They take bubble baths. Clearly, their bodies are more important than rapping. And in a field in which writing one's own rap is crucial, their lyrics are written by their former boss, M. C. Hammer.

Most women rappers constitute the middle ground: they talk of romance, narcissism and parties. On the other hand, Salt-n-Pepa on "Shake Your Thang" uses the structure of the 1969 Isley Brothers song "It's Your Thing" to insert a protofeminist rap response: "Don't try to tell me how to party. It's my dance and it's my body." M. C. Lyte, in a dialogue with Positive K on "I'm Not Havin' It," comes down hard on the notion that women can't say no and criticizes the shallowness of the male rap.

Queen Latifah introduces her video, "Ladies First," performed with the English rapper Monie Love, with photographs of black political heroines like Winnie Mandela, Sojourner Truth, Harriet Tubman and Angela Davis. With a sound that resembles scat as much as rap, Queen Latifah chants "Stereotypes they got to go" against a backdrop of newsreel footage of the apartheid struggle in South Africa. The politically sophisticated Queen Latifah seems worlds apart from the adolescent, buffoonish sex orientation of most rap. In general, women rappers seem so much more grown up.

Can they inspire a more beneficent attitude toward sex in rap?

20   What won't subvert rap's sexism is the actions of men; what will is women speaking in their own voice, not just in artificial female ghettos, but with and to men.

Personal Response

Respond to Wallace's comment that the "glaringly sexist" lyrics of rap music reveal a blatant lack of respect "for the humanity of black women" (paragraph 5).

Questions for Discussion

1. Begin a discussion of Wallace's observation in paragraph 4 that pop culture "can offer symbolic resolutions to life's contradictions" by considering the "contradictions" Wallace thinks rap addresses. Next consider her comment that "when it comes to gender, rap has not resolved a thing" and why she feels that rap music fails on the issue of gender. Then explore your own views on Wallace's observations.

2. Wallace believes that "rap lyrics and videos presuppose that women always desire sex" (paragraph 8) and provides examples to support her point. Do you find her examples persuasive? Could the examples she provides be interpreted differently? Can you give examples of recent rap lyrics and videos that either support or refute her?

3. What problem does Wallace see with writing from her perspective as a black feminist critic on the matter of black male misogyny in rap lyrics? Do you agree with her on the nature of the problem?

4. When this piece was written in 1990, Wallace's remark that rap music is "almost completely dominated by black males" was accurate (paragraph 15). Is it still accurate? Can you think of additional women rappers?

5. Discuss Wallace's comment that "women rappers seem so much more grown up [than male rappers]" (paragraph 19) and her implied hope that women rappers will "inspire a more beneficent attitude toward sex in rap" (paragraph 20). Do you agree with her? Give examples to support your answer.

RAP MUSIC AND THE DEMONIZATION OF YOUNG BLACK MALES

Tricia Rose

Tricia Rose is assistant professor of history and African studies at New York University and author of Black Noise: Rap Music and Black Culture in Contemporary America. *This essay first appeared in* USA Today Magazine *in May 1994.*

In these times, when media-crafted frenzies are the bread and butter of television news, entertainment programming, and tabloid journalism, street crime has become the coal that fires the crisis boiler. The notion that violent crime has swung out of control in this country is less a matter of fact and more a matter of perception constructed by law-and-order budget managers and ratings-hungry media executives. In fact, according to the FBI's National Crime Survey, burglary, homicides, and other violent crimes have decreased steadily since the mid 1970s.

Crime and violence have become the central focus of popular attention not because more and more people are the victims of crime, but because more Americans vicariously experience more violence through repetition of tabloid, televised news, and other reality-based programming. Street crime is sexy copy because, more than other equally pressing and even more urgent crises in American urban communities, it can be fitted into presentational formats crucial for mass media news consumption.

First, street crime lends itself to personal portraits of loss and horror; second, unlike corporate or economic crimes against people, it has clearly identifiable victims *and* villains, even when no villain is caught; third, it takes just one or two gruesome acts to terrorize viewers; and fourth, most street crime is committed by the least powerful members of society, those most easily villified. Other violent criminals with greater economic resources are less vulnerable to categorical public censure. Since reporting these sorts of crime appears to be a matter of public service, it creates the illusion that the terms of the discussion automatically are in the best interests of the public.

4   In this whirlwind of produced, heightened, and repeated anxieties, it is essential to take a step back and distinguish between criminal acts and the social language used to talk about crime and to define criminals. It is important not to lose sight of the fact that these are not one in the same. In other words, crimes taking place are not the same thing as the perception of these crimes nor are they equivalent to the process of counting, naming, categorizing, and labeling criminal activity and ultimately criminalizing populations. (Think for a moment about the media explosion of child abuse cases and its relationship to the history of child abuse.)

These distinctions are not merely a matter of semantics. Understanding them allows people to see how the way they talk about a problem determines the solutions they deem logical and necessary. In other words, the terms of the discussion on crime in the public arena are helping set the direction of public policy.

In a still profoundly segregated and racially hierarchical society, popular public images and descriptions of poor black and Latino communities as hotbeds of crime, drugs, and violent behavior appear to be "mere descriptions" of the people and environments where crime takes place. These stories and pictures are not simply descriptive, however. They describe *some* elements of life in poor communities with a particular set of assumptions and consistently leave out and obscure descriptions of other parts.

The stories that frame violent street crimes deliberately omit information that would draw attention away from the sense of crisis produced by the depiction of an overwhelmingly horrible incident. "What," the stories often cry out, "would make a young person do such a thing?" Answers that might focus on the larger social picture—not flawed causal responses like poverty causes crime or there are more criminals so we need more prisons, but relational answers such as street crime is linked closely with unemployment and poverty—are deemed "excuses" by the logic of the story that surrounds it, not explanations.

8   The pity is that more information is not set forth about the conditions that foster such behaviors—the active municipal and corporate decisions that have exacerbated poverty, homelessness, and community instability. Relevant discourse could discourage current widespread public feelings of helplessness, bridge communities that do not currently see the similarities between them, and begin to lay the groundwork for a real examination of the vast and interdependent social forces and structures that have produced and transformed the face of street crime and destabilized the most fragile communities.

For all the public hue and cry about some categories of crime, rarely are Americans exposed to an informed exploration of the relationship between some kinds of crime and the extraordinary institutional violence done to the nation's poorest children of color. These include massive unemployment for them, their parents, and relatives; constant police harassment and violence against their peers, coupled with limited police efficacy against and in some cases complicity with the drug trade; routine arrests for "suspicious" behavior (anyone who is black and/or has lived in a poor black community knows that cops often equate suspicious behavior and black male bodies); appalling housing or none at all; limited access to legal or political redress; and dehumanizing state aid bureaucracies (such as demanding that welfare parents continually scour the listings for affordable apartments in order to keep their monthly rent coupons when the lowest market rentals cost two and three times more than their coupons can cover). This is topped off by economic shifts that have transformed the already bleak labor landscape in black urban communities into tenuous, low-pay, and dead-end service jobs.

Imagine how differently the same acts of violent street crime would read if they were coupled with stories that labeled these government-orchestrated institutional actions and neglects as acts of violence. What if these social policies that support the interests of the wealthy at the cruel expense of everyone else—especially the poor—were labeled acts of social violence? How then would Americans respond to the crime crisis? What policies would these criminal activities encourage?

Even more provocatively, what if we took a look at all crime (e.g., domestic violence, embezzlement, the savings and loan scandal, serial killers, real estate fraud, murder, arson, rape, etc.) and highlighted the most consistent common denominator—men—and decided that, to solve the problem, it was necessary somehow to change the behavior of men as a group regardless of race and class. How would this alter our understanding of the crime dilemma? Instead of exploring these relationships, we are treated to disproportionately high visibility of a relatively small number of violent offenders who are intended to inspire fear in us. Without any relationship between these aspects of so-called social order and behavior of society's least powerful, the "real" answer implied by the constructed irrationality of street crime or participation in the drug trade is already present in the story: These are not people; they are monsters.

Media Villification

12   The demonization of young black males in the popular media, by black and white leaders, and among law enforcement officials has been well-documented by a range of scholars and others. This portrayal of young black men as unhuman—or dangerously superhuman, like the police fantasies of Rodney King—is an important part of creating a moral justification for the perpetuation of brutal and dehumanizing state policies. The white American public, many of whom only tangentially know any young black men personally, has been inundated with images of young black men who appear fully invested in a life of violent crime, who have participated in drug-related gang shoot-outs and other acts of violence for "no apparent reason."

This last representation is crucial to the fear that current crime reporting encourages and to the work of demonizing. Such people are violent for no apparent reason; *they* are not like *us*. Isn't it reasonable to treat an animal like an animal? What rights and social obligations are extended to monsters?

Demonization is hard work. Making monsters out of a multitude of young people who struggle to survive under immense pressures involves drawing attention away from the difficulties they face, minimizing the abuses they suffer, and making their cultural activity seem a product or example of their status as dangerous creatures. "Representing" young black inner city males and "their ways" without considering black cultural literacy (especially hip hop) or devoting sufficient attention to larger structural forces and historical contextualization paves the way for readings of rap as the black monster's music. Adolescent and vernacular cultures always have tested the boundaries of acceptable speech, frequently exploring taboo and transgressive subjects. This is true of 18th-century English and Irish folk practices, the blues of the early 20th century, and rap today.

Most attacks on rap music offer profoundly shallow readings of its use of violent and sexist imagery and rely on a handful of provocative and clearly troubling songs or lyrics. Rarely is the genre described in ways that encompass the range of passionate, horrifying, and powerful storytelling in rap and gangsta rap. Few critics in the popular realm—there are some exceptions such as Robin D.G. Kelley, Maxine Waters (D.-Calif.), George Lipsitz, and Michael Dyson—have responded to rap's disturbing elements in a way that attempts to understand the logic and motivations behind these facets of its expressions.

16   The aesthetic complexity of some of the lyrics by prominent hardcore (some say gangsta) rappers such as Snoop Doggy Dog, Scarface from the Geto Boys, and Ice Cube and the genius of the best music that accompanies it almost always are overlooked completely in the attacks on rap, in part out of genuine

ignorance (similar dismissals have clung to the reception of all black American music, jazz included), and in part because exploring these facets of rap's lure would damage the process of creating easily identifiable villains.

Basically, reality is more complicated than the current crime debate allows. Who would we blame, if not rappers and their fans? Rap music has become a lightning rod for those politicians and law and order officials who are hell-bent on scape-goating it as a major source of violence instead of attending to the much more difficult and complicated work of transforming the brutally unjust institutions that shape the lives of poor people. Attacking rap during this so-called crisis of crime and violence is a facile smokescreen that protects the real culprits and deludes the public into believing that public officials are taking a bite out of crime. In the face of daunting economic and social conditions that are felt most severely by the young people they represent, rappers are cast as the perpetrators.

Some hardcore rap no doubt is producing images and ideas that I, among many others, find troubling and saddening. This is not to be interpreted as a denial or defense of rap's problematic elements. At the same time and in equal amounts, many rappers are able to codify the everyday experiences of demonized young black men and bear witness to the experiences they face, never see explained from their perspective, but know are true. Many a gangsta rap tale chronicles the experience of wandering around all day, trying to make order out of a horizon of unemployment, gang cultural occupation, the threat of violence from police and rival teens, and fragile home relationships.

Given this complexity in rap's story telling, how is it that most Americans only know about the most extremely violent passages? What does it mean to villify rap in the face of the profound social and economic dispossession that consumes poor communities today? How can a black leader like Rev. Calvin Butts make his media name on attacking a cultural form he exhibits so little knowledge about? How can black representatives, such as Rep. Cardiss Collins (D.-Ill.) and Sen. Carol Moseley-Braun (D.-Ill.), hold a series of Congressional and Senatorial hearings on gangsta rap under the Sub-committees on Commerce and Consumer Protection and Youth and Urban Crime, respectively, when life and death matters of social and political justice that face Chicago's black teens remain unscheduled for public scrutiny? These hearings are a form of empty moral grandstanding, a shameful attempt by politicians to earn political favors and ride the wave of public frenzy about crime while at the same time remaining unable and often unwilling to tackle the real problems that plague America's cities and their poorest black children.

20   Hip hop culture and rap music have become the cultural emblem for America's young black city kids, only a small percentage of which participate in street crimes. The more public opinion, political leaders, and policymakers criminalize hip hop as the cultural example of a criminal way of thinking, the more imaginary black monsters will surface. In this fearful fantasy, hip hop style (or whatever style young black men create and adopt) becomes a code for criminal behavior, and censuring the music begins to look more and more like fighting crime.

Personal Response

What do you think of Rose's charges against those who criticize rap music? Look again at the series of questions she asks in paragraph 19 and her allegation that Congressional and Senatorial hearings on rap music are "empty, moral grandstanding." What is your response to what she says there and elsewhere about the unfair press given to rap music?

Questions for Discussion

1. Discuss Rose's use of language to convey her position on her subject. For instance, look at the opening sentences and consider her use of words and phrases such as "media-crafted frenzies," "the bread and butter of television news," "the coal that fires the crisis boiler," "notion," and "ratings-hungry media executive." What do they tell you about her stance on the subject and her opinion of the media? Locate other sentences that you feel convey Rose's position particularly well.

2. What is the central purpose of this essay? What is Rose's position on the subject of rap lyrics? Where does she stand in relation to Michele Wallace in "When Black Feminism Faces the Music, And the Music Is Rap"?

3. What do you think of the reasons Rose gives to explain why "street crime is sexy copy" (paragraph 2) and of the distinction she believes must be made "between criminal acts and the social language used to talk about crime and to define criminals" (paragraph 4). What changes would Rose like to see in the media's representation of street crime and in the discussions about rap music?

4. How does Rose define "demonization"? Does she convince you that popular media "demonize" young black males?

5. Evaluate the strengths and weaknesses of Rose's argument. Does she provide convincing evidence? Does she support generalizations? Does she develop her argument logically and reasonably? Is she fair in her attacks on the media and others who she believes are too critical of rap music?

GANGSTA RAPPERS VS. THE MAINSTREAM BLACK COMMUNITY

Paul Delaney

Paul Delaney is chairman of the Department of Journalism at the University of Alabama at Tuscaloosa. His essay appeared in USA Today Magazine *in January 1995.*

Black Americans and other non-whites always have been, for good reason, extremely nervous about and sensitive to how whites perceive them. From the beginning, they imitated the dominant society in dress, dance, and culture—whether they took it seriously or mocked it. This was because blacks knew that those perceptions made a huge difference in their lives, determining their role and status—for example, which would be field or house slaves or who would rise to company vice presidency or fail.

The media play a vital role in shaping and perpetuating perceptions, helping people make up their minds on racial matters. That is why African-Americans so zealously have kept vigil on what the media say about them. On many occasions, it has seemed an overreaction. Such vigilance and sensitivity, at times, have been the subject of debate within the black community. At the turn of the century, there was deep division over the philosophies of Booker T. Washington and W. E. B. DuBois on how to proceed following the Supreme Court ruling in *Plessy v. Ferguson* that "separate but equal" facilities were constitutional. During the 1960s, there was a split between the moderates of the National Association for the Advancement of Colored People and the more militant organizations over the course of the civil rights movement.

There have been serious differences within the black community over social, cultural, and religious issues as well. Many a blues artist who started out singing in the church choir had to overcome strong family objections to performing "Satan's music." Adults in the 1950s complained about dirty and suggestive words in many doo-wop songs, such as the entire "Annie" series of recordings by Hank Ballard and the Midnighters, including "Work with Me Annie" and "Annie Had a Baby," and the group's "Sexy Ways." Meanwhile, of course, white parents had to contend with Elvis Presley and equally suggestive lyrics from the 1960s ("Having My Baby") and since.

4   Then came rap—gangsta rap, to be more precise. Defenders of rap are correct in one thing, that the music mirrors serious urban problems and may be a plea, a warning, to do something about them. Rap came along after the convergence of a host of powerful and sometimes conflicting phenomena: the civil rights movement, progress that resulted from it, and the ensuing backlash; sexual and women's liberation; hard-earned black successes in the media, especially on television and in the entertainment industry, and the fact that much of the exposure and success has been no better or worse than TV fare in general—that is, terminally stupid sitcoms and "new vaudeville"; the shallowness of much television programming in view of the medium's awesome power; justifiable concern for First Amendment rights vs. creativity and increasing violence and gratuitous sex; and the decreasing quality of news programming and the tabloidization of the print media.

Most important for blacks, TV's influence eventually came to overwhelm traditional sources of authority in the community—parents and neighbors, the church educators, and civil rights and community leaders. (This is not to say that influence did not extend to whites, but that its impact on an already embattled, insecure black community was more devastating.) Those sources of taste, decorum, mores, and habits—the full range of social behavior and codes—were overpowered by mass communication and modern American life. Were many, if not the majority, of black parents used to wield influence over what their children did and what personal and cultural and community forces would be emphasized, it is virtually impossible to do so nowadays.

There are other forces—the relationship between black consumers and television and blacks in and on television—that have put African-Americans in a box, a position that is nothing new. On the one hand, there is genuine pride in the fact that recent times have been good to and for blacks as stars, producers, directors, and in other jobs previously denied because of race. On the other hand, there is strong objection to many of the roles and images transmitted, particularly the messages of gangsta rappers portraying women as "bitches" and "hos" [whores], guns, violence, and hatred of police.

Headlines highlight the issues: "Must Blacks Be Buffoons?," *Newsweek* asked; "Black Life on TV: Realism or Stereotypes?," posed *The New York Times*. Have blacks come all the way from the Harlem Renaissance to the rights movement; from colored to Negro to black to African-American; from black and proud and "We shall overcome" to bitches and hos on the airwaves and over the counter in record stores?

8   Along the way, though, there was a significant shift in whites' feelings and responses to race. The Ronald Reagan and George Bush campaigns and administrations pandered to racism, details conveniently overlooked nowadays by many political and social commentators. Reagan set the stage for much of what followed in the 1980s and 1990s with his pandering-to-whites presidential campaign-opener in 1979 in—of all places—Philadelphia, Miss. Before then, Richard Nixon's "southern strategy" and Alabama Gov. George Wallace's racist fulminations had stirred the pot.

Nevertheless, no matter the grievances and their causes, there was no justification for gangsta rappers to go on a binge against women. Bushwick Bill of the Geto Boys defended his use of bitches and hos by explaining that he was brought up to think of women in those terms. When he told this to a workshop audience at the 1993 convention of the National Association of Black Journalists in Houston, several hundred women, joined by some male supporters, walked out.

"What arrested emotional development had led so many young black men to feel this way (or at any rate support those who do)?," asked William Raspberry, Pulitzer Prize-winning columnist of the *Washington Post*. "What self-contempt has led so many young black women to go along with it? What perversion of priorities has led the rest of us to ignore it for so long?"

(My own answer—without benefit of scientific studies or data, of which there seems to be none, but based on a career of covering social problems—is that a lot of it, indeed, is contempt for women. Such feelings are the result of being born to a struggling single or teen mother who had boyfriends in and out of their home and her bed, many times with children in the same room. This is something sons in particular find contemptible, and, I believe, leave terrible emotional scars and permanent resentment of women.)

12   Historically, blacks had no control over the way whites felt about them, but they did try to exercise a measure of control over the actions and activity of

their children and community. Hence, the concern about image and preventing those white perceptions of blacks from dominating black youth and the black community, as well as the battle against "Birth of a Nation," blackface comedy, and "Amos 'n' Andy."

Mel Watkins dealt with these and other issues in his book, *On the Real Side: Laughing, Lying, and Signifying—The Underground Tradition of African-American Humor That Transformed American Culture, From Slavery to Richard Pryor.* "While white society had geared itself to resist advances by blacks in employment, voting, housing, and union affiliation, there were fewer obstacles to blacks in publishing and entertainment," he wrote. (Whites have never objected to being entertained by blacks.) "There, they felt the battle for racial equality could best be fought by presenting a more complete view of black life and by demonstrating that blacks could make worthwhile contributions to higher culture."

His point is reminiscent of a sincere belief among some blacks a generation ago that integrated sports, both college and professional, would soften white attitudes about them and lead to their salvation. This view was prevalent, especially, among some sports editors, including the late Marion Jackson of the *Atlanta Daily World,* where I worked at the time. I disagreed totally and spent many hours arguing the point with him.

In his book, Watkins traces the development of black comedy, noting that black contributions largely were ignored and that only recently, since the 1960s, could white Americans tolerate being the brunt of biting humor by black comedians. Whites could accept those comics with "a less truculent, more polite middle-class demeanor," he notes. Eventually, the more abrasive style of Redd Foxx, Flip Wilson, and Richard Pryor, among others, changed that.

16   Today, there are gangsta rappers, with their in-your-face realism, putting on compact disc what previously was reserved for the privacy of the parlor, the street corner, or under-the-table record sales. This is what it boils down to: if playing the dozens were still on the corner; if calling women bitches and hos remained behind closed doors instead of becoming nightly offerings on cable and on CDs and blaring from loudspeakers of the car in the next lane or a block away—in your face, everybody!; if the electronic media were not so powerful and influential; if we were only back in the 1940s (as a lot of Americans wish); and if all the above and more were so, we would not be having this debate today.

It is fascinating that the flap over harsh language and gangsta rap rages mostly in the black community. Whites typically look on from the sidelines, like innocent bystanders. Yet, most of the financial benefits go to white record company owners, white marketing experts, white producers, etc., and more white kids buy and listen to rap music than do black youngsters. Many African-Americans are cynical about it, convinced that, when white youngsters grow up or tire of the music or it is time to get serious about life, they can pull the plug on rap, go back to the safety and security of suburbia and the family business or their own professional careers, and live happily ever after. Meanwhile, black kids remain glued to the ghetto.

Most African-Americans feel that gangsta rappers, vulgar comedians, and movie makers are doing a great disservice to the black cause. Performers such as Bill Cosby and Danny Glover have spoken out against them, but they had little effect until recently.

Pressure Builds

Things are beginning to change, though. Pressure finally is getting to the rappers. Snoop Doggy Dogg said on an MTV special that he looked forward to sitting down and talking to one of the most outspoken critics of the style, the Rev. Calvin Butts, pastor of New York's Abbysinian Baptist Church. He indicated that he would be willing to tone down his lyrics, that rappers would listen to leaders who lead. Bushwick Bill apologized to the audience in Houston in 1993. Political leaders are bringing pressure on performers, record company owners, and radio stations. Some stations have stopped airing gangsta rap, and a few black stations never did. The majority of blacks disagree with glorifying the rough lifestyle some gangsta rappers not only sing about, but lead, including the flashing of guns, abusing women, and other anti-social behavior.

20   While the courts will resolve the innocence or guilt in criminal charges several rappers are facing, the public already has made certain judgments. Gangsta rap may have run its course. The novelty seems to have worn off—you know how faddish we Americans are and what short attention spans we have. Still, there are those who feel that rap will make a lasting impression, much as doo-wop did, and they may be right.

Nevertheless, there is a softening of positions. On an MTV special, rapper Dr. Dre admitted that his motivation is strictly financial. "I'm no gangsta; I'm here to make money," he declared. Some female groups—Queen Latifah and Salt-n-Pepa, for example—are countering the macho men and urging women to demand respect.

In the area of comedy, the depiction of blacks on many TV shows is a real throwback to objectionable programs of the past, but social pressure—and not an assault on the First Amendment—most likely will temper them. At the same time, though, there is a growing debate about whether blacks are past the point of rejecting the likes of Amos 'n' Andy and other demeaning portrayals.

I personally do not think it is time yet, that the country is not ready. Still, it may be ready to debate the issue. As Watkins noted, it certainly is time to give black comedy its due. In that regard, gangsta rap may have been the wake-up call and opened up something that may turn out to be good.

Personal Response

Delaney suggests that "gangsta rap may have run its course," but then points out that "there are those who feel that rap will make a lasting impression . . . and they may be right" (paragraph 20). What is your opinion? Has rap music faded in importance and will it soon disappear? Or will rap music have a lasting influence? Explore your thinking on this subject.

Questions for Discussion

1. Summarize Delaney's position on the importance of the media in shaping attitudes and influencing behavior and then select specific statements from his essay for class or small group discussion. For instance, discuss his comments on the way in which blacks are portrayed in a television situation comedy or drama and whether you agree with him.

2. Review Delaney's personal opinion on the questions William Raspberry asks (paragraphs 10–11) and then discuss your own views on the issues both Delaney and Raspberry raise.

3. Delaney suggests that rap music developed as a result of a number of complex and powerful influences. Locate the reasons he names and discuss them in terms of whether you agree with him and whether you can add additional or different reasons to account for the development of rap music.

4. Delaney brings up the matter of media portrayals of blacks throughout his piece, referring, for instance, to "terminally stupid sitcoms and 'new vaudeville'" in paragraph 4 and "the likes of Amos 'n' Andy and other demeaning portrayals" in paragraph 22. Discuss this subject by using specific examples of images of blacks portrayed in current television situation comedies and dramas.

Suggestions for Writing About Rap Music

1. Respond to Michele Wallace's observations that rap music is sexist and even misogynistic, especially in regard to black women ("When Black Feminism Faces the Music, And the Music Is Rap"). Use examples from rap lyrics to support your position.

2. Taking into consideration the closing comments of Michele Wallace in "When Black Feminism Faces the Music, And the Music Is Rap," compare the lyrics of selected women rappers to those of selected male rappers.

3. Select a passage from Tricia Rose's "Rap Music and the Demonization of Young Black Males" and respond to it by exploring its significance in relation to rap music. For instance, consider her remark that America is "still a profoundly segregated and racially hierarchical society" (paragraph 6) or her reference to "the extraordinary institutional violence done to the nation's poorest children of color" (paragraph 9).

4. Paul Delaney states in his concluding paragraph of "Gangsta Rappers vs. the Mainstream Black Community" that he does not think that America is ready to reject demeaning portraits of blacks in popular entertainment. Write an opinion on that subject.

5. Compare and contrast the commentaries on rap music of Tricia Rose in "Rap Music and the Demonization of Young Black Males" and Paul Delaney in "Gangsta Rappers vs. the Mainstream Black Community." To what extent do

Rose and Delaney agree? In what ways are their positions similar and how are they different? What conclusions can you draw from their positions?

6. Summarize the position of each of the three authors in this section on the subject of rap music in order to determine where each stands on the issue and how their positions are similar or different. Draw your own conclusions on the subject, quoting or referring to material in the readings where appropriate.

7. Write your own commentary on the subject of sexism and/or misogyny in rap lyrics.

8. In "When Black Feminism Faces the Music, and the Music Is Rap," Michele Wallace writes that "a large part of the appeal of pop culture is that it can offer symbolic resolutions to life's contradictions" (paragraph 4). Select a particular performer or group and consider its music in relation to that statement. Does the music resolve contradictions? If so, what are the contradictions and what "symbolic resolutions" does the music offer?

9. Write an opinion essay on whether or not people are influenced by the music they listen to. Could listening to music about love and peace, for instance, alter a person's feelings about war? Do violent lyrics make people want to commit violence?

10. Write an analysis of rap music in the context of the recent murders of two well known gangsta rappers Tupac Shakur and the Notorious B.I.G. (Christopher Wallace). To what extent do you see a connection between the lyrics the musicians sang and their own deaths?

HOLLYWOOD AND THE MOVIES

Hollywood has been subject to criticism from the early days of the movie industry. In particular, discussion often centers on the relationship of movies to behavior, whether movies influence behavior or reflect it and to what degree film makers bear a moral obligation to society. In the 1920s, concern over the possible negative influence of Hollywood films was so great that the Hays Office censorship code was developed to monitor the content of movies. The ratings system evolved out of that perceived need to censor offensive content, especially material that would adversely affect young children. The PG-13 rating, for instance, came about because some movies with a PG rating were so violent that they terrified young children.

Although the issues keep re-emerging and are subject at times to rather heated, widespread debate, they remain largely unresolved. The essays in this section represent various perspectives on the subject of Hollywood and its impact on social norms and individual beliefs and behavior. The first two pieces are by noted critics of Hollywood, who find fault with much of what the movie and television industries produce. In "Political Entertainment," Michael Parenti argues that the entertainment industry has a profound influence on people and that its "class, racial, gender, and other political biases" shape what people believe. In "A Sickness in the Soul," Michael Medved laments the "empty material" in today's movies, suggesting that they are characterized by "sleaze and self-indulgence."

In the next selection, "Is God Really Dead in Beverly Hills? Religion and the Movies," Stanley Rothman answers the question in his title by reporting selected aspects of his extensive study of the portrayal of religion and religious characters in Hollywood films. The unit ends with a sharp criticism of those who would blame Hollywood for negatively influencing public morality and social mores. Christopher Sharrett in "Movies, Morality, and Conservative Complaints" explains what he sees as weaknesses or generalizations in the views of conservatives and offers his own perspective on the issue.

POLITICAL ENTERTAINMENT

Michael Parenti

Michael Parenti holds a PhD in political science from Yale University. He has taught at a number of colleges and universities and lectured widely on college campuses. His articles have appeared in The Nation, *the* New York Times, *and the* Los Angeles Times. *His books include* Power and the Powerless, Democracy for the Few, Inventing Reality: The Politics of the Mass Media, *and* The Sword and the Dollar: Imperialism, Revolution, and the Arms Race. *"Political Entertainment" is from the first chapter of Parenti's 1992 book* Make-Believe Media: The Politics of Entertainment.

Make-believe. The term connotes the playful fantasies of our childhood, a pleasant way of pretending. But in the world created by movies and television, make-believe takes on a more serious meaning. In some way or other, many people come to believe the fictional things they see on the big and little screens. The entertainment media are the make-believe media; they make us believe.

Today, very little of our make-believe is drawn from children's games, storytelling, folktales, and fables, very little from dramas and dreams of our own making. Instead we have the multibillion-dollar industries of Hollywood and television to fill our minds with prefabricated images and themes. Nor are these just idle distractions. I will argue that such images often have real ideological content. Worse still, they discourage any critical perception of the great and sometimes awful realities of our lives and sociopolitical system, implanting safe and superficial pictures in our heads. Even if supposedly apolitical in its intent, the entertainment industry is political in its impact.

How can we speak of Hollywood films and television shows as being "purely" entertainment when they regularly propagate certain political themes and carefully avoid others? To borrow Robert Cirino's phrase: "We're being more than entertained."[1] Hollywood and television are permeated with class, racial, gender, and other political biases. George Gerbner argues that all media carry a "hidden curriculum" of values and explanations about how things happen.[2] The sociologist Hal Himmelstein believes that through its settings, music, words, and stories, television has become "one of our society's principal repositories of ideology."[3] A leading communications critic, Herbert Schiller, writes that "one central myth dominates the world of fabricated fantasy; the idea that [media] entertainment and recreation are value-free, have no point of view, and exist outside . . . the social process."[4] Another critic, Erik Barnouw, concludes: "Popular entertainment is basically propaganda for the status quo."[5]

In accord with those observations, I will try to demonstrate in the chapters ahead that over the years, films and television programs have propagated images and ideologies that are supportive of imperialism, phobic anticommunism, capitalism, racism, sexism, militarism, authoritarian violence, vigilantism, and anti-working-class attitudes. More specifically, media dramas teach us that:

- Individual effort is preferable to collective action.

- Free enterprise is the best economic system in the world.

- Private monetary gain is a central and worthy objective of life.

- Affluent professionals are more interesting than blue-collar or ordinary service workers.

- All Americans are equal, but some (the underprivileged) must prove themselves worthy of equality.

- Women and ethnic minorities are not really as capable, effective, or interesting as White males.

- The police and everyone else should be given a freer hand in combatting the large criminal element in the United States, using generous applications of force and violence without too much attention to constitutional rights.

- The ills of society are caused by individual malefactors and not by anything in the socioeconomic system.

- There are some unworthy persons in our established institutions, but they usually are dealt with and eventually are deprived of their positions of responsibility.

- U.S. military force is directed only toward laudable goals, although individuals in the military may sometimes abuse their power.

---

[1] Robert Cirino, *We're Being More Than Entertained* (Honolulu: Lighthouse Press, 1977).

[2] George Gerbner, Larry Gross, and William Meldoy, eds., *Communications Technology and Social Policy* (New York: Wiley, 1973).

[3] Hal Himmelstein, *Television Myth and the American Mind* (New York: Praeger, 1984), p. 3.

[4] Herbert Schiller, *The Mind Managers* (Boston: Beacon Press, 1973), pp. 79–80.

[5] Erik Barnouw, "Television as a Medium," *Performance,* July/August 1972, cited in Schiller, *The Mind Managers,* p. 80.

- Western industrial and military might, especially that of the United States, has been a civilizing force for the benefit of "backward" peoples throughout the Third World.

- The United States and the entire West have long been threatened from abroad by foreign aggressors, such as Russians, Communist terrorists, and swarthy hordes of savages, and at home by unAmerican subversives and conspirators. These threats can be eradicated by a vigilant counterintelligence and by sufficient doses of force and violence.

The Hollywood director Cecil B. deMille once said that if you want to send a message use Western Union. Hollywood is strictly an entertainment business and not a purveyor of social messages or political causes, he maintained. In fact, Hollywood, like television, is very much in the business of sending political messages. Certainly not the kind of reformist or dissident messages that deMille objected to, but ones—like those listed above—with which he felt comfortable, so comfortable that he did not think they had political content.

What the media actually give us is something that is neither purely entertainment nor purely political. It is a hybrid that might be called "political entertainment." The entertainment format makes political propagation all the more insidious. Beliefs are less likely to be preached than assumed. Woven into the story line and into the characterizations, they are perceived as entertainment rather than as political judgments about the world. When racial subjugation is transmuted into an amusing Sambo and imperialist violence into an adventuresome Rambo, racism and imperialism are more likely to be accepted by viewers, who think they are merely being entertained. "Beliefs, attitudes, and values are more palatable and credible to an audience when they are molded and reinforced by characters and program plots than when they are preached by a newscaster or speaker for a particular cause."[6] To quote Schiller:

> For manipulation to be most effective, evidence of its presence should be non-existent. When the manipulated believe things are the way they are naturally and inevitably, manipulation is successful. In short, manipulation requires a false reality that is a continuous denial of its existence.
>
> It is essential, therefore, that people who are manipulated believe in the neutrality of their key social institutions. They must believe that government, the media, education, and science are beyond the clash of conflicting social interests.[7]

Seeing Is Believing

People are affected by social forces sometimes far removed from their immediate perceptions. They perceive only a relatively small portion of the influences

---

[6] Ralph Arthur Johnson, "World without Workers: Prime Time's Presentation of Labor," *Labor Studies Journal,* 5, Winter 1981, p. 200.

[7] Schiller, *The Mind Managers,* p. 11.

that play upon them. The modern mass society, people rely to a great extent on distant imagemakers for cues about a vast world. In both their entertainment and news shows, the media invent a reality much their own.[8] Our notion of what a politician, a detective, a corporate executive, a farmer, an African, or a Mexican-American is like; what rural or inner-city life should be; our anticipations about romantic experience and sexual attractiveness, crime and foreign enemies, dictators and revolutionaries, bureaucrats and protestors, police and prostitutes, workers and Communists, are all heavily colored by our exposure to the media.

8   Many of us have never met an Arab, but few of us lack some picture in our minds of what an Arab is supposed to be like. This image will be more a stereotype than a reality, and if drawn largely from the mass media, it is likely to be a rather defamatory stereotype.[9] As Walter Lippmann noted, stereotypic thinking "precedes reason," and "as a form of perception [it] imposes a certain character on the data of our senses."[10] When we respond to a real-life situation with the exclamation, "Just like in the movies," we are expressing recognition and even satisfaction that our media-created mental frames find corroboration in the real world.

The media images in our heads influence how we appraise a host of social realities, including our government's domestic and foreign policies. If we have "learned" from motion pictures and television dramas that our nation is forever threatened by hostile alien forces, then we are apt to support increased military spending and CIA interventions. If we have "learned" that inner-city denizens are violent criminals, then we are more apt to support authoritarian police measures and cuts in human services to the inner city. Remarking on the prevalence of media-induced stereotypes of African-Americans, Ellen Holly put it well:

> When I express concern for [the image of Black people] in the media, don't imagine for one moment that anything as shallow as a racial ego posture is involved. The way we are perceived by this society affects the most basic areas of our lives. When you apply for a job the interviewer in personnel reacts to you not only in terms of who you are but also in terms of who he *thinks* you are. There are countless images floating around in his head and many of them are traceable to the media. You may sit in front of him as a neatly dressed, intelligent female who would do an efficient job, but if he has been fed one stereotype too many he may look and see not you but Flip Wilson's "Geraldine" goofing on the job, painting her fingernails and calling up her boyfriend to chat on company time. If so, for all your qualifications, you're not the one who is going to get the job. . . .
>
> Again and again I have seen Black actors turned down for parts because they were told that they did not look the way a Black person should or sound the way a Black person should. What is this business of should? What kind of box are we being put into? I have seen Black writers told that the Black

---

[8] For a critical study of the news media, see Michael Parenti, *Inventing Reality: The Politics of the Mass Media* (New York: St. Martin's Press, 1986).

[9] Jack G. Shaheen, *The TV Arab* (Bowling Green, Ohio: Bowling Green State University Popular Press, 1984).

[10] Walter Lippmann, *Public Opinion* (New York: Macmillan, 1922), pp. 88–89.

characters they put down on a page were not believable because they were too intelligent.[11]

Audiences usually do some perceptual editing when watching a movie or TV program, projecting their own viewpoint upon the performance. But this editing is itself partly conditioned by the previously internalized images fed to audiences by the same media they are now viewing. In other words, rather than being rationally critical of the images and ideologies of the entertainment media, our minds—after prolonged exposure to earlier programs and films— sometimes become active accomplices in our own indoctrination.

We are probably far more affected by what we see than we realize. Jeffrey Schrank notes that 90 percent of the nation's adult viewers consider themselves to be "personally immune" to the appeals of TV advertisements, yet these viewers account for about 90 percent of all sales of advertised products.[12] While we might think it is always other people (less intelligent than ourselves) who are being manipulated by sales appeals and entertainment shows, the truth might be something else.

12   Another investigator, Jerry Mander, argues that media images are "irresistible," since our brains absorb them regardless of how we might consciously regard such images. Children believe that what they are seeing in the make-believe media is real. They have no innate capacity to distinguish between real and unreal images. Only as they grow older, after repeated assurances from their elders, do they begin to understand that the stories and characters on the big and little screens do not exist in real life. In other words, their ability to reject media images as unreal has to be learned.[13] The problem does not end there, however. Even as adults, when we *consciously* know that a particular movie or television program is fictional, we still "believe" it to some extent; that is, we still accumulate impressions that lead to beliefs about the real world. When drawing upon the images in our heads, we do not keep our store of media imagery distinct and separate from our store of real-world imagery. "The mind doesn't work that way," Mander concludes.[14]

It has been argued that the claims made about media influence can be unduly alarmist; it is not all a matter of our helpless brains being electronically pickled by the sinister media. Indeed, things can be overstated, but that is no excuse for dismissing the important impact the media do have. Consider some of the more troubling instances such as the "copycat" or "trigger" effects, when media exposure sparks imitative responses from viewers. One sociologist reports that suicides (along with auto fatalities and airplane accidents) increase significantly for a brief period immediately after news reports

---

[11] Ellen Holly, "The Role of Media in Programming of an Underclass," *Black Scholar,* January/February 1979, pp. 34–35. For a fuller discussion of African-Americans in the media, see Chapter Eight.

[12] Jeffrey Schrank, *Snap, Crackle, and Popular Taste* (New York: Delta, 1977), p. 84.

[13] Jerry Mander, *Four Arguments for the Elimination of Television* (New York: Quill, 1978), pp. 250–52.

[14] Ibid., p. 257; and passim; also Martin Large, *Who's Bringing Them Up? Television and Child Development* (Gloucester, UK: MHC Large, 1980).

about suicide.[15] Probably the most dramatic instance of copycat behavior was the rash of self-killings following the news that Marilyn Monroe had taken her life. Other incidents are worth pondering:

• After *The Deer Hunter* began playing in theaters in 1979, at least twenty-five viewers around the country reenacted the movie's Russian roulette scene and blew their brains out.

• NBC showed the film *The Doomsday Flight,* about a man who tries to extract a ransom from an airline after planting a bomb on one of its planes. Within a week, a dozen bomb threats were reported by the major airlines, a dramatic increase over the previous month.

• A woman in Boston's Roxbury district was doused with gasoline and burned to death shortly after the telecasting with the film *Fuzz,* which portrayed a similar act.

• A fourteen-year-old whiz kid in Syracuse committed a series of robberies fashioned after techniques he saw on "Mission Impossible." He was apprehended only after a friend informed the police.

• In Los Angeles, a maid caught a seven-year-old boy sprinkling ground glass into his family's dinner. He said he wanted to see if it would work as it did on television.[16]

For some viewers, it is less a matter of consciously imitating the media and more an inability to distinguish between the real world and make-believe. Some years ago it was reported that an actor who played a villainous character on "Secret Storm" was shot by an irate viewer. Eileen Fulton, who played the much-hated Lisa on "As the World Turns," was assaulted by an angry viewer who called her "a terrible woman."[17]

A half-century ago Orson Welles caused panic across the nation with his radio dramatization of an invasion from Mars. Thousands of people mistook the program for an actual newscast. Presumably, audiences have become more media-sophisticated since then. Yet such panic reactions are not unknown today. In 1983, for instance, NBC ran a made-for-television film *Special Bulletin* about peace activists who take hostages on a boat outside Charleston, South Carolina, and demand the dismantling of nuclear warheads. In the ensuing confrontation, the nuclear device on the boat—which the protestors are using as a threat—accidentally detonates, destroying Charleston and its environs. The movie was done with

---

[15] See the reports by David P. Phillips in *Science,* 196, June 24, 1977, pp. 1464–65; and in *Science,* 210, August 25, 1978, pp. 748–50.

[16] The example of *The Deer Hunter* is from Tim Lahaye, *The Hidden Censors* (Old Tappan, N.J.: Revell, 1984); all the other examples are from Schrank, *Snap, Crackle,* p. 29. For other instances of the relationship of trigger effect to violence, see the discussion in chapter ten: "Child Abuse."

[17] Schrank, *Snap, Crackle,* p. 154.

grainy film and a handheld camera to give it a documentary effect. However, the word "dramatization" was also flashed across a corner of the screen every few minutes. Obviously, the show's producers anticipated that many viewers might have difficulties telling fact from fiction. Indeed, despite the precaution of the repeatedly flashed message, the network was swamped with calls from concerned people who thought the explosion had really taken place. Perhaps many viewers simply did not know the meaning of "dramatization" or were so convinced by the documentary quality of the film as to place no significance on the word.

16   The more time people spend watching television and movies, the more their impressions of the world seem to resemble those of the make-believe media. Gerbner and Gross found that heavy TV users, having been fed abundant helpings of television crime and violence, are more likely to overestimate the amount of crime and violence that exists in real life. They are also more apt to overestimate the number of police in the United States and the percentage of persons with professional jobs. (Professionals and police are overrepresented on TV as opposed to other service and blue-collar employees.) "While television may not directly cause the results that have turned up in our studies, it certainly can confirm or encourage certain views of the world."[18]

Consider how media's advertisements influence consumption patterns. Bombarded by junk-food television commercials over the years, Americans, especially younger ones, changed their eating habits dramatically. Compared to the pre-TV days of the 1940s, per capita consumption of vegetables, fruits, and dairy products was down 20 to 25 percent by the mid-1970s, while consumption of cakes, pastry, soft drinks, and other snacks was up 70 to 80 percent.[19] Television advertising campaigns transformed "soda pop" from something consumed at ball games and picnics to a beverage drunk daily with almost every meal and between meals, complete with "family-size" bottles. In 1961, after years of television ads, annual softdrink consumption was up to 128 bottles per capita. By 1981, following a still more intense media blitz, it rose to 412.3 bottles per person.[20] This represented not only a dramatic increase in quantity, but a transformation in the social definition of the product itself—from an occasional indulgence to a national drink.

Along with commercials, entertainment shows influence consumption patterns. A salesman at Continental Gun Shop in Miami reported: "Everybody comes in and bugs me about that Bren 10mm semi [automatic] that guy uses in 'Miami Vice.'" The Bren sold like hotcakes at $885 each.[21] Manufacturers have become aware of the "product placement" opportunities in motion pictures: Jerry Lewis selling Dunkin' Donuts in *Hardly Working* (1981), Kevin Kline flashing his Nike shoes in *The Big Chill* (1983), Melanie Griffith drinking Coors beer in *Working Girl* (1988), to name a few. The producers of *E.T., The Extra-Terrestrial* (1982) received

---

[18] George Gerbner and Larry Gross, "The Scary World of TV's Heavy Viewer," *Psychology Today,* April 1976, p. 45.

[19] Catherine Larza and Michael Jacobson, eds., *Food for People Not for Profits* (New York: Ballantine, 1975), p. 165.

[20] *Washington Post,* February 1, 1983.

[21] *City Paper* (Washington, DC), May 10, 1985.

promotional help from Hershey Foods in exchange for featuring Reese's Pieces in the film. Sales of that candy product then shot up 70 percent.[22]

Regarding personal styles, people often take their cues from entertainment figures. One need only recall the Beatles imitators, the Madonna imitators, and the "Miami Vice" imitators (a day's growth of beard for that sexy, rugged look). There was the Calvin Klein jeans craze, the Cabbage Patch doll craze, the Michael Jackson craze, and other such hypes that were induced mostly by mass media. A study conducted by the National Institute of Mental Health finds that most adults and children treat television dramas and other fictional shows as valid guides for dealing with actual life situations, including family relations, friendships, and social, cultural, and political issues.[23] In sum, people are influenced by the media in the way they dress, talk, interrelate, spend their money, define social problems, identify with prominent personalities, and in the kinds of ideological images they embrace.

Personal Response

Can you think of ways in which your behavior has been directly influenced by something you saw in the movies or on television? For instance, have you ever bought something as a direct response to an advertisement or changed your hair or clothing style because of a movie?

Questions for Discussion

1. How does Parenti define "political entertainment"?

2. Look at the list of images and ideologies Parenti maintains that films and television programs propagate. Can you think of examples to support or refute any of them?

3. Parenti makes a charge that is often leveled by critics of the industry when he gives examples to suggest that "media exposure sparks imitative responses from viewers" (paragraph 13). What do you think of the examples he cites? Do they demonstrate convincingly that movies must bear some of the responsibility for the violent or aberrant behavior they influence? If so, what do you think the movie industry ought to do about the problem?

4. Discuss your position on Parenti's closing statement that people are influenced by the media in all kinds of ways. Can you give examples from personal observation or experience of any of the ways he says people are influenced?

---

[22] Leslie Goodman-Malamuth, "Hollywood Hucksters," *Public Citizen,* April 1986, p. 11; *New York Times,* January 13, 1989.

[23] Eli Rubinstein, George Comstock, and John Murray, eds., *Television in Day to Day Life: Patterns of Use* (Washington, DC: National Institute of Mental Health, n.d., circa 1975).

A SICKNESS IN THE SOUL

Michael Medved

Michael Medved is an honors graduate of Yale University and the author of seven nonfiction books. Before becoming cohost of Sneak Previews, *a weekly PBS program, in 1985, he worked as a screenwriter on several feature film projects. His comments on the media and society have appeared in many major publications. This selection is excerpted from his 1992 book* Hollywood vs. America: Popular Culture and the War on Traditional Values.

Even without the pronouncements of experts, ordinary Americans understand that Hollywood is in serious trouble. As a point of reference, ask yourself a simple question: when was the last time that you heard someone that you know say that movies—or TV, or popular music, for that matter—were better than ever? On the other hand, how recently have you listened to complaints about the dismal quality of the movies at the multiplex, the shows on the tube, or the songs on the radio?

In recent years, not even Jack Valenti, the well-paid cheerleader for the Motion Picture Association, can claim with a straight face that the movie business is scaling new artistic heights. David Puttnam, Oscar-winning producer of *Chariots of Fire* and former chairman of Columbia Pictures, reports, "As you move around Hollywood in any reasonably sophisticated group, you'll find it quite difficult to come across people who are proud of the movies that are being made." In December 1991, industry journalist Grover Lewis went even further when he declared in the pages of the *Los Angeles Times*: "The movies, which many of us grew up regarding as the co-literature of the age, have sunk to an abysmal low unimaginable only a few years ago."

In fact, nearly everyone associated with the industry acknowledges the obvious collapse in the caliber of today's films, and at the same time manages to blame someone else for the disastrous situation.

4   Jeffrey Katzenberg, production chief at the beleaguered Walt Disney Studios, shrugs his shoulders and cites inscrutable Higher Powers. "We're in the hands of the movie gods," he told the *Los Angeles Times*, "who will either shine down and give us good fortune or not. . . . That's part of what keeps people going in this business—the magical and mysterious nature of it."

Producer Gene Kirkwood *(Rocky)* offers a less "magical and mysterious" explanation for Hollywood's troubles, pointing his finger at the writers. "When you look at the writing that's around today, most of which is not very good, it makes you want to go back to the old films," he explains. One of the writers of those old films, Oscar-winner I. A. L. Diamond *(The Apartment)* in turn cites "the lawyers and agents who run the studios, and the subliterate subteenagers who form the bulk of the audience" for creating the present problems. Julia Phillips, the outspoken outcast who produced *The Sting,* specifically accuses Mike Ovitz, head of the Creative Artists Agency, who "first ruined movies, then sold out to the Japanese."

Film critic Michael Sragow manages to identify an even more nefarious and omnipotent culprit, blaming the industry's whole sorry mess on an over-the-hill Warner Brothers star who actually abandoned the movie business more than twenty years ago. Asserting that "American movies are still reaping the harvest of Ronald Reagan's reign of mediocrity and escapism," Sragow concluded in 1990 that it was actually the former President who "ate Hollywood's brain."

While searching for scapegoats, the entertainment industry ignores the obvious: that Hollywood's crisis is, at its very core, a crisis of values. It's not "mediocrity and escapism" that leave audiences cold, but sleaze and self-indulgence. What troubles people about the popular culture isn't the competence with which it's shaped, but the messages it sends, the view of the world it transmits.

8   Hollywood no longer reflects—or even respects—the values of most American families. On many of the important issues in contemporary life, popular entertainment seems to go out of its way to challenge conventional notions of decency. For example:

- Our fellow citizens cherish the institution of marriage and consider religion an important priority in life; but the entertainment industry promotes every form of sexual adventurism and regularly ridicules religious believers as crooks or crazies.

- In our private lives, most of us deplore violence and feel little sympathy for the criminals who perpetrate it; but movies, TV, and popular music all revel in graphic brutality, glorifying vicious and sadistic characters who treat killing as a joke.

- Americans are passionately patriotic, and consider themselves enormously lucky to live here; but Hollywood conveys a view of the nation's history, future, and major institutions that is dark, cynical, and often nightmarish.

- Nearly all parents want to convey to their children the importance of self-discipline, hard work, and decent manners; but the entertainment media celebrate vulgar behavior, contempt for all authority, and obscene language—which is inserted even in "family fare" where it is least expected.

As a working film critic, I've watched this assault on traditional values for more than a decade. Not only have I endured six or seven movies every week, year after year, but I've also received a steady stream of letters from moviegoers who are upset by one or another of Hollywood's excesses. At times, they blame me for failing to warn them ardently enough about avoiding a particular film; in other cases they are writing to express their pent-up frustration with an industry that seems increasingly out of control and out of touch. My correspondents frequently use words such as "disgusting" or "pathetic" to describe the sorry state of today's films. In 1989 a young woman from Westport, Connecticut, expressed these sentiments with memorable clarity. "The problem is that whenever I take a chance and go against my better judgment and venture back into a movie theater," she wrote, "I always feel like a worse person when I come out. I'm embarrassed for the people who made this trash, and I'm embarrassed for myself. It's like watching the stuff that I've just watched has made me a smaller human being. Isn't that sad?"

It *is* terribly sad, especially in view of the technical brilliance that turns up in so many of Hollywood's most recent productions. When people express their disappointment at the generally low level of contemporary films, they seldom indict the camera work, the editing, the set design, or even the acting. In fact, these components of moviemaking have reached a level of consistent competence—even artistry—that would be the envy of Hollywood's vaunted Golden Age. I regularly marvel at gorgeous and glowing visual images, captured on screen in the service of some pointless and heartless waste of celluloid, or sympathize with an ensemble of superbly talented performers, acting their hearts out, and trying to make the most of empty material that is in no way worthy of them. If Robert De Niro and Dustin Hoffman have failed to inspire the sort of devoted and consistent following once enjoyed by Jimmy Stewart or John Wayne, it is not because they are less capable as actors. What ails today's films has nothing to do with the prowess or professionalism of the filmmakers. The true sickness is in the soul.

Personal Response

This selection opens with Medved asking, "When was the last time that you heard someone that you know say that movies—or television, or popular music, for that matter—were better than ever?" He goes on to ask if you have heard people complain about "the dismal quality" of movies, television, and popular music. How would you answer those questions? Do you think movies, television, and popular music are "better than ever"? Or do you complain about their quality?

Questions for Discussion

1. Because this is a brief excerpt from one chapter of a book on the subject, there is little evidence to support Medved's contention that there is an "obvious collapse in the caliber of today's films" (paragraph 3). What evidence does he give in this short selection?

2. Look at the examples Medved lists in paragraph 8 of ways he believes "Hollywood no longer reflects—or even respects—the values of most American families" but even goes out of its way "to challenge conventional notions of decency." Can you support or refute any of his allegations with specific examples of movies?

3. Medved says that everyone in the entertainment industry "manages to blame someone else for the disastrous situation" (paragraph 3) and that the industry is "searching for scapegoats" (paragraph 7). Given Medved's allegations, does that shifting of blame surprise you? Discuss you own views on this blame-shifting.

4. Medved says that "Hollywood's crisis is, at its very core, a crisis of values. It's not 'mediocrity and escapism' that leaves audiences cold, but sleaze and self-indulgence" (paragraph 7). Drawing on examples of movies you have seen, discuss the values you see Hollywood films projecting.

IS GOD REALLY DEAD IN BEVERLY HILLS? RELIGION AND THE MOVIES

Stanley Rothman

Stanley Rothman is Mary Huggins Gamble Professor of Government Emeritus at Smith College and the director of the Center for the Study of Social and Political Change. He has authored or co-authored 14 books. His most recent books include Watching America: What Television Tells Us About Our Lives *(1991),* The Mass Media in Liberal Democratic Societies *(1992),* Giving for Social Change: Foundations of Public Policy and the American Political Agenda *(1994), and* Molding the Good Citizen: The Politics of High School History Texts *(1995). His latest books are* American Elites *(1996) and* Hollywood's America: Social and Political Themes in Motion Pictures *(1996). This essay is part of a larger study of motion pictures and social change in the United States and was published in* The American Scholar *in 1996.*

In recent years at least two films have treated the Christian religion and those who practice it with reasonable respect. *Black Robe* (1991), a film about Jesuit missionaries to the Indians in what is now Canada, treats a Jesuit priest, one of the major characters in the film, as a person of sincere humility and deep belief. On the other hand, the Hurons, the recipients of his mission, are all but destroyed as the result of his efforts to convert them. *Shadowlands* (1993), a fictional biography of C. S. Lewis, takes Lewis and his Christian beliefs seriously, though he is something of a maverick, and the Christian message he delivers periodically to audiences of middle-aged women is presented as thin and contrived. Theoretically, it will be less so in the future (as the picture ends) because, after a tragic loss, he, the Lewis of the movie, finally opens himself to life.

Other films, of course, have presented religion or religious characters in a positive light. On the whole, however, religious themes have played rather poorly in Hollywood movies for the past forty years. In their efforts to entertain large audiences, moviemakers have, since 1965, largely ignored traditional religious themes, dwelling on demonic forces or manifestations of the supernatural that bear little or no relationship to traditional Jewish or Christian stories. The parade of epic biblical films—such as those of Cecil B. De Mille—that packed the theaters before 1965 disappeared in the second half of the decade and have never returned.

Given the overwhelmingly non-religious orientations of Hollywood's contemporary artists, none of this is surprising. In spite of the fact that traditional religion is still important to the vast majority of Americans, recent movies are no longer concerned with traditional religious topics and biblical storytelling.

4   Most of the few notable exceptions—for example, Monty Python's *Life of Brian* (1979) and Martin Scorsese's *Last Temptation of Christ* (1988), have taken such satiric or radical directions that the Catholic church and other religious groups have sharply criticized them. Even when movies seem to present a favorable image of Western religious beliefs—as in *Oh God!* (1977), for example—the deity is seen, at best, from a Unitarian perspective, and representatives of older religious traditions, if not benighted, are given short shrift.

In *Hollywood vs. America,* the movie critic Michael Medved argues that, while movies concentrating on religious topics might still draw large audiences if they were more orthodox in outlook, filmmakers have emphasized irreverent accounts of the life of Christ, and these have usually "flopped resoundingly at the box office." The majority of movies depicting the afterlife or any kind of supernatural force seem to reflect a Hollywood preoccupation with satanic evil, religious satire, conflict between individuals and supernatural evil that lacks a religious referent, and interaction with benevolent or evil extraterrestrials. These newer box office hits are aimed at today's youth market, and their treatment of religion is obviously quite different from what Hollywood offered in the past.

A few yeas ago a *Time* magazine writer, arguing that Hollywood was becoming interested in religion again following such hits as *Field of Dreams* and *Ghost,* suggested that

> the preoccupation with the afterlife reflects the obsession of Los Angeles, the crystal-and-channeling capital of the country, where people can mention their past lives with the same seriousness as getting the car engine tuned. No doubt Shirley MacLaine's philosophical musings and Richard Gere's cassette-tape readings from the *Tibetan Book of the Dead* have permeated the collective unconscious of fortysomething producers forced to face mortality through the death of their parents and the tragic toll of colleagues who have died of AIDS.

Moviemakers have transformed customary religious storytelling in three important ways. First, they have reoriented religious movies toward the darker side of spiritual belief. Conventional religious beliefs are presented but only to provide a recognizable background against which evil can be made more compelling and powerful. Beginning with Roman Polanski's *Rosemary's Baby* (1968), Hollywood's new generation of filmmakers abandoned conventional religious stories and began churning out movies exhibiting a fascination with evil. A slew of movies about the devil or other demonic or magical forces at work on Earth sprang forth, bringing impressive returns from the new cineplexes operating in malls across the country. People sat in theaters, drive-ins, or more recently in their own living rooms, fascinated at the spectacle of demonic forces overtaking unfortunate victims for no apparent reason. The effect on audiences of such movies as *The Exorcist* (1974) was clearly substantial. Owing to their appealing imagery, such movies made for a number of box-office hits in the seventies. Special effects improved as audiences refined their appetite for the nightmarish amusement park rides that the new genre offered.

8   In the early seventies, a number of movies began to satirize the practices of organized religions as archaic and authoritarian, if not merely silly. Satire is perhaps the least prevalent of the themes, and the criticisms of religious practices or characters portrayed as religious are often fairly subtle. Fairly typical examples are *Tommy* (1975) and *The Witches of Eastwick* (1987); the latter comically sympathizes with the devil, and those who are aware of the presence of evil in the small town come to a bad end.

Using very sophisticated techniques, moviemakers have reformulated the natural and supernatural worlds, exploring different kinds of realities that include elements of religion, magic, mysticism, horror, science-fiction, and the occult, which have little or no connection with traditional religious orientations. In a number of these films, one finds increasing ambiguity in the portrayal of good and evil.

In these movies, evil is not always defeated by story's end, and this is not simply to leave an opening for sequels. The stories frequently make a point of demonstrating that evil is beyond control and that we can all become its helpless victims. In some of these movies, Hollywood presents a mixture of natural and supernatural occurrences in the same story, without drawing any clear lines between the two realms. In *The Golden Child* (1986), for example, the forces of good and evil are at play in the natural world and a select few individuals are empowered by them, influencing events both natural and supernatural. In *Beetlejuice* (1988) the afterlife is merely a ghostly and grotesque extension of natural existence in which the living and the dead are able to commingle. In the comedy *Ghostbusters* (1984), the line between the supernatural and natural is very thin, but the supernatural world has nothing to do with traditional religious beliefs. One finds the same pattern in such films as *The Shining* (1980) or *Poltergeist* (1982). The inability finally to defeat evil is further illustrated by the *Nightmare on Elm Street* or the *Friday the 13th* series of movies of the 1980s. Most of these films, while assuming the existence of the supernatural, have nothing to do with traditional Western religious themes.

A distinct variant of the supernatural films draws from the science fiction genre, presuming the existence of supernatural powers in outer space. *Star Wars* and *Close Encounters of the Third Kind* conjure up supernatural forces from the ruins of the religious sentiments of a bygone era in Hollywood. In these films, moviemakers have replaced God with less omnipotent forces. Nevertheless, the spectacle of brilliant alien technology, far more sophisticated than anything on Earth, does have some parallels to biblical accounts of celestial phenomena. Michael Pye and Lynda Myles, in their discussion of *Close Encounters*, observe:

> These wheels of light careening through the sky have their historic parallels: the visions of the prophet Ezekiel, the idea of the chariot of God, the mandals of Jung. The fiery clouds of biblical texts become the boiling clouds and blinding light of Spielberg's film. Intervention from above, bringing hope at last, is a constant theme at times of social crisis and change. Some God must save us, because we cannot save ourselves. And if God is an alien, with lights and wonder and color and music, then God is prettier than we thought.

12   Contemporary science fiction films are important to a discussion of Hollywood's treatment of religion because they do more than confront us with the possibility of other life forms. If this were the only message conveyed, the films would be less uplifting and entertaining. While sidestepping the issue of whether traditional beliefs about God and heaven have validity, at least some of these films comfort us with the thought that benevolent beings from outer space watch over us. In a sense, they suggest that although Western society, built around scientific and rational principles, must inevitably relinquish its hold on ancient biblical accounts of the meaning of life, we can nonetheless still hope for salvation from above.

This hope does not always require the moral virtue once expected of religious characters. It is Everyman's salvation. *Cocoon* (1985), like *Star Wars* and *Close Encounters,* conveys exactly this message. Regardless of the kind of lives they have led, the old folks in *Cocoon* will be taken by the aliens to a place where they'll never get any older and never die. For these lucky individuals salvation is no longer contingent upon predestination, faith, or good works, though it might require being in the right place at the right time.

Stanley Kubrick, alluding to the new trend among science fiction films in a discussion of *2001: A Space Odyssey* (1968), remarked: "The God concept is at the heart of the film." David Bowman becomes "an enhanced human being, a star child, a superhuman . . . returning to earth prepared for the next leap forward of man's evolutionary destiny." Kubrick's idiosyncratic view of religion retains only the scientific concepts of evolution and our experiences with space travel—and nothing divine or spiritual at all.

In a similar vein, Luke Skywalker of the *Star Wars* trilogy (1977, 1980, 1983) relies on a naturalistic kind of power derived from all living things in the universe, which is known simply as "The Force." The power of The Force transcends our ordinary conception of natural death because Ben (Obi-Wan Kenobe) continues to be seen as an apparition instructing Luke on how to use his power; The Force is not quite equivalent to a divine power either, however, since it originates in nature and therefore has a certain scientific plausibility. Ben explains: "It's an energy field created by all living things. It surrounds us, it penetrates us, it binds the galaxy together."

16   Of course, at least some science fiction movies, including such films as *Alien* (1979), deal with powerful evil forces that cannot be finally vanquished. Science fiction movies wrestle with many of the same issues that used to be dealt with in films emphasizing traditional religious beliefs.

What is it that makes Hollywood so averse to a more frequent and more positive treatment of traditional religion? Why, even in the face of what appears to be a strong market potential, have Hollywood writers, directors, and producers avoided this particular mainstream of Western beliefs? Do they hold a grudge against the institutions that have constrained their expression in the past? This, in part, is Michael Medved's argument. Constrained only by the demands of the marketplace, Hollywood producers, actors, and writers attack bourgeois American culture and religion because they hate both.

Perhaps. But one does not detect much open hostility to traditional religion in popular Hollywood movies—only, at worst, a decline in the sanctity of religion as a subject compelling interest on its own. While this indicates a disregard for religion as an important institution, lack of interest, rather than deep hostility, seems to be the rule. Because of their secular views, filmmakers may simply be so intrigued by other alternatives that they do not wish to return to earlier types of religious storytelling.

In any case, religion has fallen even further out of fashion than the Western, which is currently enjoying a modest comeback. To understand these recent trends in popular entertainment it is important first to document the changes that I have just described.

20   To talk usefully about the major themes of motion pictures it is necessary to analyze a representative sample of films. My colleagues at the Center for the Study of Social and Political Change and I sampled the ten top-grossing films for each year from 1946 to 1990, a total of 440 films. After completing the study, we took a sample of 21 of the ten top-grossing films for each year from 1990 to 1994. We did not include these in our statistical analysis but found few differences from earlier films. The actual number of films viewed for the period 1946 to 1990 was 159.

We maintain that choosing films viewed by large audiences gives us a better handle on the nature and role of the film industry than choosing a sampling of the total product of that industry. It is our considered opinion, incidentally, that a sample of the total production of Hollywood would have more strongly validated our hypotheses as to the changing nature of the film industry and its products than the sample we actually chose.

Rather than analyzing films as literary works, we conducted a systematic content analysis of social and political themes in them. Our goal was to develop methods for counting themes in motion pictures that would enable us to make supportable generalizations about them. College students were hired to view films and code themes. Initially, a select sample of films was coded by two persons. Only those categories or themes on which agreement was achieved 80 percent or more of the time were retained for further analysis. For some purposes our unit of analysis was the film as a whole. In general, however, we coded all the significant characters in each film.

Many of the themes were quite simple. To take materials of relevance to this essay, students were asked to count the number of films in which some version of the Jewish or Christian God appeared or in which some version of the devil was presented. They were also asked to count the number of persons in films who were identified as members of traditional religious groups, or as members of the clergy. They counted how frequently characters achieved their goals, and how the film evaluated their moral character (positively, negatively, or mixed).

24   There are weaknesses to this approach. Some more complicated themes in individual films can be missed, and, if not used with care, one can overstate the certainty of results. The method certainly gives no clues as to the subtlety of a given movie or any hint about whether or not it may be enjoyable.

Our systematic content analysis of movies that deal with religious themes is rather straightforward and supports our qualitative discussion. It served, indeed, as the basis for it.

Looking at the religious composition of characters, we find that the number of characters in movies actually identified as practicing one religion or another has declined dramatically since the 1940s. In the 1945 to 1956 decade, 19 percent of the characters in major motion pictures were Protestants, Catholics, Jews, or some other identifiable religion. Eighty-one percent were unknown, atheist, or agnostic.

In the second decade under study, the number of religious characters drops slightly lower, to 15 percent. In the third decade the figure drops to nine percent, and in the 1976 to 1990 period it declines even further, to about 4 percent whose religious orientation is identified in the movie. As we shall see, the proportion of films in which God or God's agents play a role also drops very sharply.

28   When we compare the small group of characters identified as Protestant, Catholic, or Jewish with all other characters, we find a consistent pattern. In the first two decades, the character ratings (positive, negative, mixed) of the major characters identified with these religions are somewhat more likely to be positive than those of persons not identified with them. In the first decade, 81 percent of these characters are rated positively compared with only 63 percent of non-religiously identified characters. In the second decade, positive ratings decline slightly, to 74 percent, but are still higher for religious than for non-religious characters, only 48 percent of whom are characterized positively. In the third decade, positive ratings among religiously identified characters decline to 67 percent, but they are still higher than those for non-religious characters, who remain at 48 percent positive characterization. In the fourth decade, however, religious characters nearly reach an equilibrium with non-religious characters, slipping to 56 percent positive, while positive ratings for non-religious characters rise slightly, to 52 percent. As compared to earlier decades, the declining number of religious characters are now no more likely than non-religious characters to be portrayed positively.

In the same vein, the percentages of religiously identified characters who fail to achieve their goals has risen during recent decades. This corresponds with our impression of a declining power of religion in predetermining the intentions, actions, and outcomes of religious characters. In the first decade, only 15 percent of the characters with religious ties are unsuccessful compared with 31 percent of non-religious characters. In the second decade, 26 percent fail to achieve their goals compared to 33 percent of non-religious characters. In the third decade, 23 percent of the religious fail to achieve their objectives compared to 33 percent of non-religious characters. The greatest change occurs in the most recent period. Now the number of religious characters who fail to achieve their goals rises to 36 percent compared to only 28 percent of non-religious defeated characters. Religious affiliation today actually seems to increase the likelihood that a character will fail to achieve her or his objectives.

Evaluating an even more narrow group of religious characters—religious workers, nuns, and missionaries—we find further evidence of the declining prestige of religious institutions in Hollywood movies. Among these, character ratings are, with only one exception, entirely positive in the first two decades, but they fall markedly in the last two. From 1946 to 1965, sixteen of seventeen religious workers are rated positively and the one exception (Dr. Hewitt, from *The Sandpiper*) receives a mixed rather than a negative rating. In the third decade, positive depictions decline to four out of seven, or only 57 percent positive. The remaining three (43 percent) are presented negatively. In the most recent decade, only three of six religious workers are presented positively, two are represented as negative characters, and one receives a mixed rating.

We find the same pattern in the presentation of attaining goals. In the first decade, either all the religious workers succeed in achieving their objectives or some of the issues remain unresolved. In the second decade, 86 percent score similarly. Since this was the era of biblical epics, a disproportionate number of religious characters are persecuted. Mitigating against this lower success rate is the image of Jews and Christians serving a higher purpose. We must also bear in mind that, in spite of their predicaments, these characters are still overwhelmingly presented in a positive fashion corresponding with their moral virtue.

32   In the third decade, though portrayals of religious workers are substantially less positive, 85 percent are still either successful or the outcome of their efforts is at least ambiguous. It is not until the most recent period that we find a precipitous decline. From 1976 to 1990, only 17 percent of the few religious workers in our sample meet with success. Whereas none of the religious workers are defeated in the first decade and only 14 percent fail to achieve their objectives in the second and third decades, 50 percent fail in the most recent period and in 33 percent the results are ambiguous. While somewhat more ambivalent character ratings emerge among religious workers in the second and third decades, they are still overwhelmingly successful in attaining their objectives until the most recent period, at which time the character ratings of religious workers continue to decline, and failure to achieve goals increases dramatically.

Overall, traditional religious figures in the movies have suffered a multiple decline. They were once presented very positively, consistent with the reverence for religious institutions mandated by the Hollywood Production Code. Since the mid-sixties, their reputation has become less exalted. The larger story of what has happened to religion in popular movies must be understood in light of a sharply diminished presence of religious characters. Yet, at the same time, the decline of traditional religion has been accompanied by the increasing presentation of alternate sources of supernatural events.

Our thematic analysis of films, designed to measure broader trends in motion pictures, suggests the magnitude of the shift from traditional religious to alternative supernatural themes. Supernatural events occur in only a few movies from 1946 to 1975 (nine movies, or 10 percent on average); however, in the 1976 to 1990 period alone, 14 movies (26 percent of the total movies coded for that period) had such events. Among such films, the trend is away from more traditional depictions of God and religion. In the first two decades, God is present in five of seven movies with supernatural events; in the period from 1966 to 1990, God is present in only two of sixteen.

Conversely, the devil is not present in any of the seven movies from the first two decades but is present in three of sixteen films in the two more recent periods. Even more interesting is the fact that extraterrestrials, absent from top-grossing movies over the thirty years from 1946 to 1976, are the source of supernatural events in five of the fourteen (36 percent) films in which such events occur from 1976 to 1990. Forty-three percent of the films involve supernatural forces that have no relationship to any of these categories. Magic, for good or ill, permeates the universe. Together these trends clearly demonstrate the decline of traditional depictions of God and religion, and a growing interest in movies that present supernatural events as demonic or extraterrestrial. Clearly, the development of space travel in the real world, as well as the increasing ability of Hollywood's technicians to simulate events in outer space, has also played a role in the growth of this genre.

36 In the movies of the studio era, religion was granted an especially high status; it was an institution upon which both heroic and ordinary characters relied for support. Religion held a special power over the lives of the faithful that was thought to enable them to accomplish or to endure things that others could not. Consequently, not only religious workers, but also other characters holding religious beliefs, were portrayed favorably more often than the non-religious. These characters were also more successful in achieving their objectives by story's end. Although religion itself may not have been at issue in many of these movies, its moral influence on the characters was clear and pronounced.

In biblical stories, the Judeo-Christian religious heritage is presented as the progress of humanity against barbarism and evil. God empowers various characters to protect and lead the righteous. Those who oppose God's plan meet with disaster. The power of religion over characters in more modern settings remained overwhelmingly positive in the studio days. Religion provides a source of strength to those who believe, and these believers make the world a better place. The Production Code and the Hollywood mogul's conservative control over the industry mandated this kind of representation, but, importantly, these movies were also harmonious with American religious sensibilities and remained very popular.

The elimination of censorship and other changes within the movie industry and American society in the sixties and seventies resulted in the replacement of these films with much more ambiguous representations of a declining number of religious characters. Perhaps even more significant, Hollywood movies now also express a much greater apprehension about the presence of evil in the world—satanic evil as well as other forms of supernatural evil. While the forces of evil have multiplied in recent years in popular movies, there has been less good in the world, either supernatural or human, to combat it. Characters seldom expect divine or supernatural intervention, or rely on the power of religious institutions to deliver them from supernatural evil. As a result, in many movies characters have much less control over their lives.

Hollywood's new mythos has freed characters in movies from much of the restraint imposed by religious customs, as it has freed them from other restraints on behavior, but this has left these characters vulnerable to unknown, usually uncontrollable evil. The supernaturalism that has replaced the authoritative religious storytelling of the past seems to reflect Hollywood's own agnostic torment. Having abandoned so much of religious tradition, Hollywood is unable to offer compelling and authoritative alternatives. The kinds of movies that have filled the void have not ignored religion altogether but instead have re-created it in such a way that it loses much of its previously affirmative value. Whether movies shape or merely reflect our collective hopes or fears about this life or the next, Hollywood has conjured up a predominantly nightmarish alternative to more traditional stories.

40   Part of this trend may be a matter of choice on the part of a secular motion picture industry. And yet one suspects there is something more going on, both in the choice of plots and in their popularity among mass audiences. In *The Uses of Enchantment: The Meaning and Importance of Fairy Tales* (1976), Bruno Bettelheim argues that the violence of fairy tales—and they can be very violent—serves a useful function. Children need to be assured that if they act at the behest of powerful, violent, anti-social impulses within them, they will be destroyed by the more powerful magical forces of good. In this way they come to identify with such forces and to turn their violent proclivities to socially responsible tasks. Self-control—the development of a superego—is thus fostered and children can become more or less comfortable with their impulses.

Insofar as we never fully succeed in mastering our violent anti-social drives, and insofar as the child continues to function within the adult, it can be argued that most human beings require some mythic structure if they are to function effectively as responsible adults. The myth of the inevitable triumph of good over evil may seem simpleminded to the sophisticated Hollywood producers and directors, who believe that they themselves do not need such myths. They are, in fact, little different from the audiences they serve. They cannot find a satisfactory substitute for religion, though they continue to try. Their failure is reflected in a plethora of films that document the triumph of evil, an evil which, as in *Alien,* often emerges from the bowels of the victim. One suspects that these themes are, at least partially, symbolic of a feared loss of control of the evil impulses within the self.

Personal Response

Rothman writes in his concluding paragraph that Hollywood producers and directors do not believe in "the myth of the inevitable triumph of good over evil" that provides the foundation of traditional religious beliefs. Do you believe in the triumph of good over evil? Explain why or why not.

Questions for Discussion

1. Summarize Rothman's study of selected Hollywood films by explaining which films he included and why, how the study was conducted, and what themes his researchers were looking for. What weaknesses and strengths of his approach does Rothman identify? Do you see any additional weaknesses or strengths?

2. What answer does Rothman give to the question posed in his title? State in your own words what he concludes about religion and the movies.

3. Rothman's study covers the forty-four-year period from 1946 to 1990. Working in small groups or brainstorming on your own, make a list of box office hits in the years since 1990. Then discuss, for those you have seen, whether you think the films on your list support the findings of Rothman's study.

4. How does Rothman account for the changes in Hollywood's portrayal of traditional religious themes? Can you think of other reasons to account for it?

5. Re-read Rothman's final paragraph and then respond to each point he makes. For instance, what do you think of his assumptions and the conclusion he draws from them in his opening sentence? What do you think of his comments about the "myth of the inevitable triumph of good over evil"? What do you make of his observation that Hollywood producers and directors make movies about the triumph of evil because such triumph is "symbolic of a feared loss of control of the evil impulses within the self"?

MOVIES, MORALITY, AND CONSERVATIVE COMPLAINTS

Christopher Sharrett

Christopher Sharrett is an associate professor of communications at Seton Hall University and associate mass media editor of USA Today. *This essay appeared in the September 1993 issue of* USA Today Magazine.

There has been renewed discourse lately about Hollywood's moral obligations to the public and the extent to which the sex and violence of feature films does violence to existing social morés. The most notable feature of the largely unremarkable debate is its lack of timeliness. Had it occurred at the heyday of Reaganism, when Jerry Falwell, Jimmy Swaggart, and their ilk were riding high in the media spectacle (and the nation was enjoying a bizarre somnambulism), these condemnations would be of a piece with the reaction of the 1980s. Neoconservative culture has not left the scene with the closing of the Reagan/Bush era, but the recent complaints about Hollywood's sins, particularly given the forward-looking Clinton moment, seem hopelessly anachronistic.

The renewed hand-wringing about movie morality has at its base a theory of communication enunciated more than 50 years ago by Harold Lasswell, who suggested a "hypodermic" notion of media, wherein communication processes are seen as something an individual or agency does to someone else. Like "impact" theories of art, this idea proceeds on the assumption that the public is a kind of *tabula rasa* (clean slate) upon which is inscribed all social, cultural, economic, political, and moral ideas. Such theories pay little attention to the role media have in reflecting ideas already circulating in society. According to this notion, "Hill Street Blues" and "Miami Vice" were different from "Dragnet" not because 1980s television necessarily reflected 1980s culture, but because TV producers decided to sabotage the time-honored and unshakable style and ideology of Jack Webb.

When John Hinckley shot Ronald Reagan, a few critics immediately seized on the assailant's preoccupation with the film "Taxi Driver." Such a focus exempts us from a more complex discourse about the root causes of violence or other anti-social conduct. When Ted Bundy blamed horror movies and pornography for his crimes, the New Right jumped on a bandwagon that a sociopath and pathological liar propped up for them, failing to notice that horror films and porn were rather tame when Bundy began his murderous career, and those things that impact a sociopath, abused from childhood, might have negligible effect on the rest of society.

4   The conservative criticism of cinema is and always has been involved in the pursuit of scapegoats. This criticism is little interested in systemic issues that very well may be involved in both the dominant ideology and moral code, as well as their built-in self-destruction. These critiques also look back to a halcyon, innocent age, a common inclination these days given the amount of nostalgia for the 1950s that saturates cultural production. Yearning for the innocence of childhood, always a cultural fixation, may be particularly difficult to overcome when our view of this golden age of serene suburban households constantly is returned to us through the prisms of the media, through "Father Knows Best" and the whipped-cream image of America in which Hollywood specialized during its overly sentimentalized studio system epoch.

Very often, criticism of the films Hollywood produces is combined with that of the behavior of its producers. A large bluenose alarmist faction became very upset in the 1920s with the Fatty Arbuckle scandal and similar tales of Hollywood Babylon, which had almost as much to do with the effectuation of the Hays Office censorship code as did the actual content of movies. Although we continue to thrive on scandal more than we revile it, similar processes occur in our reception of cultural products. Madonna's success as sex goddess, heir to Marilyn Monroe, etc., is as much involved in the minute off-screen chronicling of her antics and the promotion of various books, CDs, videos, and films. The quality, even the shock value, of these products is almost uniformly mediocre, leading to some very essential questions: If the show biz world is so out of step with American values and if, in fact, Hollywood is conspiring to rot our moral fiber, why do we keep buying? If the image of sexuality in "Basic Instinct" and "Body of Evidence" is so distant from audiences' tastes, why do they keep coming back for more?

I would agree with the neoconservatives that we could do with far fewer films along the lines of "Basic Instinct," although my position is that they simply are bad art with a retrograde view of gender relations; far too absurd, in my judgment, to have much consequence for human behavior. Hollywood, like the rest of our cultural outlets, feeds us rancid bowls of Fruit Loops because it is easy and safe to do so since we have become accustomed to such junk food and have failed, for a century or more, to ask anything else of our culture.

If the cinema is to be accused of anything, it is anesthetizing us, but here again, the blame lies squarely and solely with the consumer. It is not in the interest of the commercial media to do anything but move product in the quickest and most efficient way possible. Consequently, everything that might be termed "art" thoroughly is marginalized and moved to venues off the average consumer's beaten path. If Hollywood product seems more nihilistic and amoral, we might take note that Vietnam, Watergate, the Reagan/Bush years, and the relegation of the U.S. to debtor status with the collapse of its economy have given this nation a considerably more jaded palate than it had, say, in the 1950s. Accordingly, the culture mills must add more hot sauce, horseradish, and red pepper to such overcooked, leftover stews. It's time to look for new recipes, rather than lynch the woebegone, ignorant chef.

Personal Response

Do you share Sharrett's view that Hollywood, as well as the rest of popular culture, feeds the public "junk food" and that the movie industry is simply responding to the demands of the consumer when it produces "rancid bowls of Fruit Loops" (paragraphs 6–7)? Explain your answer.

Questions for Discussion

1. What criticisms does Sharrett make of conservatives' attacks on the movie industry?

2. Apply Sharrett's criticisms to the views of other writers in this unit whose essays you have read. What would he think of the complaints of Michael Parenti, Michael Medved, and/or Stanley Rothman about Hollywood movies? For instance, do any of those writers "look back to a halcyon, innocent age" (paragraph 4)? Do any of them combine a criticism of "the films Hollywood produces" with "the behavior of its producers" (paragraph 5)?

3. Respond to this question: "If the show biz world is so out of step with American values and if, in fact, Hollywood is conspiring to rot our moral fiber, why do we keep buying?" (paragraph 5).

4. Respond to this statement: "Hollywood, like the rest of our cultural outlets, feeds us rancid bowls of Fruit Loops because it is easy and safe to do so since we have become accustomed to such junk food and have failed, for a century

or more, to ask anything else of our culture" (paragraph 6). Make sure you consider all aspects of the statement.

5. Discuss Sharrett's comment in his concluding paragraph that "everything that might be termed 'art' thoroughly is marginalized and moved to venues off the average consumer's beaten path."

Suggestions for Writing About Hollywood and the Movies

1. Argue your own position on the subject of imitative responses to media images, taking into account the examples Michael Parenti cites in "Political Entertainment."

2. Michael Medved contends in "A Sickness in the Soul" that Hollywood movies promote sleaze and self-indulgence. Use examples to either support or refute his position.

3. Respond to any other specific issue or comment in either Michael Parenti's "Political Entertainment" or Michael Medved's "A Sickness in the Soul."

4. Christopher Sharrett's position on such films as *Basic Instinct* and *Body of Evidence* is that "they simply are bad art with a retrograde view of gender relations" ("Movies, Morality, and Conservative Complaints," paragraph 6). If you have seen either film—or one with a similar theme and similar depiction of sexuality—and have an opinion on its artistic quality and view of gender relations, write an essay explaining your views.

5. Explain your own belief on the subject of whether good triumphs over evil or vice versa, keeping in mind Stanley Rothman's observations in "Is God Really Dead in Beverly Hills?: Religion and the Movies." Give specific examples or illustrations where appropriate.

6. Compare and contrast the positions of Michael Parenti, Michael Medved, Stanley Rothman, and Christopher Sharrett on the subject of Hollywood's moral obligation to the public.

7. Explain your own perspective on some aspect of the subject of Hollywood, taking into account the views expressed by the writers in this unit. Focus on a specific issue about which you have formed an opinion after reading their views, refer to the other writers as a way of providing the context for your own essay, and then explain in detail your own position.

8. Conduct your own small version of Stanley Rothman's study of religion in Hollywood films ("Is God Really Dead in Beverly Hills? Religion and the Movies") by applying his methods to box office hits of the last year. View as many films as you have time for, count those aspects of the films that Rothman lists in paragraph 23, and explain your conclusions. Does your small study differ from or support Rothman's much larger study?

9. Examine one form of popular entertainment, such as rock videos, popular music, television shows, advertising, or movies, for the ways in which it promotes or fosters an attitude of acceptance of violence.

TELEVISION

Almost all Americans either own television sets or have access to them and are quite familiar with television programming and the range of viewing options available to them. In addition to the major networks, hundreds of other stations exist, vying with one another for audiences and sponsors. Not surprisingly, television, like other components of popular culture that have the potential for reaching vast numbers of people, has been subject to the scrutiny of critics from its inception. The readings in this unit on television have been selected to suggest the kind of analysis that television programming gives rise to and the nature of criticism leveled against it.

Two writers are interested in daytime television programming and the ways in which it reflects cultural values and attitudes. In her essay, "Soap Opera Men in the '90s: Signs of Fearful Times," based on research she did for a booklength study of television soap operas, Carol Traynor Williams assesses the ways in which men are portrayed in soaps. Joshua Gamson in "Do Ask, Do Tell" is interested in talk shows that provide a forum for homosexuals to articulate their experiences and feelings. He explores the ways in which homosexual guests are treated by both talk show hosts and audiences and assesses the implications of that treatment for both homosexual guests and viewers.

The other two selections in this unit address the subject of television sex and violence. John Davidson in "Menace to Society" reviews the negative criticism of media images of sex and violence that occurs especially during election years and suggests that the real "menace" when it comes to violent programming is not prime time network shows but Saturday morning children's shows. Similarly, objecting that complaining about sex and violence on prime time network television is "beating a dead horse," Joe Saltzman suggests in "Beating the Same Old Dead Horse" that popular culture provides a host of sources other than television for graphic sex and violence.

SOAP OPERA MEN IN THE '90s: SIGNS OF FEARFUL TIMES

Carol Traynor Williams

Carol Traynor Williams is a professor of humanities at Roosevelt University in Chicago. She is author of the book "It's Time for My Story": Soap Opera Sources, Structure, and Response (1992). This article, based on material gathered for her book, was published in the fall 1994 issue of The Journal of Popular Film & Television.

ALEC: I had this, like a radon shield. . . .
STUART: Well, when you love someone, you just have to let it down.
ALEC: Yeah. I tried that once and I got a rabbit punch in the stomach.

All My Children,
11 April 1994

RIDGE: I'm talking about sharing. . . . Not what's mine is yours. But . . .
    the more open you can be with the person you love, the more risk
    you take. But, if you can do it, it's the greatest feeling. . . .
TAYLOR: I've taught you that?
RIDGE: Yes.

The Bold and the Beautiful,
11 April 1994

On the eve of Mac Scorpio's wedding to Felicia Jones on *General Hospital* (4 February 1994), Mac and his men friends gathered for a poker game at the home of one of the show's mentors, Port Charles Police Commissioner Sean Donely. Cigars were passed around; Sean said he had gotten permission from his wife, Tiffany, to smell up the apartment. The men joshed about wives and freedom, and young Mac looked thoughtful. Dr. Tony Jones was there, warm yet strong, the ace family man. Dr. Steve Hardy was also there—a patriarch, but as respectful as he is loving of Audrey, his wife, chief of nurses at General Hospital. Luke Spencer, the guy of guys, dropped in. Luke, with Mac's help, rousted the card-cheat Ryan Chamberlain. In between this action, Luke and Sean, who, because of the past, don't trust each other, reminisced for the others about old poker games with Mac's older brother, Robert Scorpio. These memories brought back the moment in the early 1980s—the best moment among men in soap operas—when Robert and Sean, then adversaries, were struggling on a ski lift. Sean, who could have gotten away by pushing Robert off the lift, could not do it, and so became the first badguy-become-good because of—not romance, the usual reason—friendship.

The best part about *General Hospital*'s men is that they seem to like each other. Men's friendships have an uncommon history on *General Hospital*, as friendships do in general. In my count of friendships for my book, *"It's Time for My Story": Soap Opera Sources, Structure, and Response, General Hospital* came in first, which is surprising because in the late 1980s and early 1990s, *General Hospital* was known as the "action" soap. Perhaps in the 1990s it will lead the way as it did with "Luke and Laura," this time in integrating men-men relationships into a soap story.

In the history of soap opera, men have been women's objects of focus, but women, the prime audience, are the creators' focus. Because the genre is thought of as a woman's story, the makers of soap operas, even the men, have always written men with the peculiar mixed emotions women traditionally show men in life. It is like the familiar soap opera shot in which one character is in the foreground and another is in the background, and the focus moves back and forth from one to the other, blurring the unfocused one. Men in soap operas are both the loved/hated focus and the (maliciously) forgotten. Yet, like everything and everyone in soap opera (and popular art in general), the men also reflect the times. Today, the image shows some things that give hope for more equal—and more humane—relations between men and women and among men, and it also shows, more subtly, shadows of the era of sexual depression that is also our time.

4   Not uncommon today, soap opera men are so politically correct—*so horn-swaggled*—they are zombies. The emblem is Max Holden of *One Life to Live*. Max, a Texan, used to be 100 percent a man's and a woman's man, a randy roisterer. Now he rests blissfully in the loving hands of Luna Moody Holden, priestess of the New Age "Goddess" whose magical force, through Luna, has already saved Max twice from "death" (once, personified as a literal femme fatale). The new Max is soft, jolly. Worse, Luna is absolutely righteous, never wrong. But not the sign of the times: Max and his actor, James De Paiva, are at the top of the polls of Most Popular Soap Males. (Finally, Max became so dull, he rebelled in spring 1994; but, of course, a gambling addiction only made him a victim.)

At their liveliest, these gentle soap opera men seesaw. Because this is drama, they have to do *something*. But when the men act, the wary writers are remembering their political correctness, and the men are clearly manipulated by the women. If the writers forget, fans call them on it. Letters to the shows and fan magazines excoriate any forceful male love scene.

But the letters become fewer because, almost always, when a situation triggers a politically correct response, the writers make the right choice, loud and clear. For example, the 10 January 1994 *Days of Our Lives* showed (unusual these days) a bed sex scene, complete with décolleté lace negligee on her and bare hairy chest on him. Kristin Blake, wanting to forget her real love, John Black, tried to make love with her fiance, Tony DiMera. She failed because she flashed John making love to her (today's soap heroine is monogamous); afterwards, she and Tony outdid each other in politeness. "Did I do something wrong?" Tony begged. "No, no, no. You were 'perfect.' I'm so sorry, Tony. I did this to you," Kristin replied.

Like Tony DiMera, today's safe soap men often seem the women's creatures—very like the old days of radio and early television soap operas when Stella Dallas, Portia Manning, et al. adventured while their husbands (or eternal fiances, like Helen Trent's Gil Whitney) were Nazi prisoners (Walter Manning in *Portia Faces Life*) of nursed wounds (as *Mary Noble, Backstage Wife* solved the crime).[1] James Thurber's comical exposé of the "emasculated" soap opera male in the *New Yorker* in 1948 was on target then. Thurber noted how often soap males suffered crippling diseases or injuries, particularly below the waist, and called the male in the wheelchair a "symbol of the American male's subordination to the female" (220). Thurber would likely have written the same of males in 1950s television soaps, such as *Love of Life* (1951–1980), with its tomboyish heroine, Vanessa Dale (Peggy McKay, now the Brady matriarch, Caroline, in *Days of Our Lives*), and *The Secret Storm* (1954–1974) featuring in the 1950s a couple of harridans: Susan Ames

---

[1] See LaGuardia for Anne Elstner—Stella Dallas from 1938 to 1955—on her adventures in the Sahara and "trapped in a submarine at the bottom of the Suez Canal" (17). See chapter 1 on "The History of Electronic Story" in Williams.

Dunbar, a typical nag-bitch, and Pauline Rysdale, a Joan Collins type, both typically hiding hearts broken by men.[2] (It is difficult to trace but not hard to think that particularly Susan, the screeching, sad housewife, helped clarify "the feminine mystique" for '50s viewers.)

8   During the late 1970s and 1980s, soap opera changed. In a 1987 interview, soap opera writer Bill Asher told me confidently that "women want strong men because [they want] fantasy," and that because "soap opera is a woman's medium . . . you have to write men larger than life . . . so they don't come off weak." Perhaps the more assertive contemporary woman in the soap audience became more comfortable seeing her fantasies of Rhett Butler on the television screen. Perhaps American soaps in the 1980s reflected American men in reaction to women who seemed to them more competitive. Whatever the reason, the 1980s was the time of the raper, and then, because of his popularity, the raper redeemed (so he could stay on the show). Two of them, "Patch" (Steve) Johnson and Jack Devereaux, from *Days of Our Lives* were so redeemed (by women's love, of course) and were so popular that they could metamorphose into early forms of the '90s mellow men.

    What romance writers say of their heroes can as well be said of soap heroes. Because the heroine is "adventurous,"

> the hero must be part villain or else he won't be much of a challenge to a strong woman. . . . And the flat truth is that you don't get much of a challenge for a heroine from a sensitive, understanding, right-thinking "modern" man who is part therapist, part best friend, and thoroughly tamed from the start. You don't get much of a challenge for her from a neurotic wimp or a good-natured gentleman-saint who never reveals a core of steel. (Krentz 108–9)

    The hero described by romance novelist Jayne Ann Krentz is known as the "alpha" male in the romance trade (Krentz 107).[3]

    In this new age of (more) equality between women and men, soaps feature, besides the gentleman-saint or "beta" man, the old-fashioned male victims of women's wiles. Victims are needed because soaps are drama and, therefore, driven by irony: by lies and secrets shared with the audience but not with the protagonists. And because the soap fantasy is still generally for women, the victim is not always the woman, unlike in other genres, such as primetime television movies. But the extreme cowed male is as rare now as the authoritarian one; neither wimp nor macho plays. What does? Sometimes, confusion; always carefulness. But, at best, complexity.

12   Again, *One Life to Live* signifies the mixed-up times. Heroine Viki Buchanan—one of soapdom's superheroines, three-time Emmy winner Erika Slezak—

---

[2] The Museum of Broadcast Communications in Chicago has vintage episodes of *Love of Live, The Secret Storm, One Man's Family,* and other early TV soaps. *Secret Storm*'s director was Gloria Monty, in LaGuardia's words, "the most powerful woman executive in daytime television" in a time when directors "ran [the] show" (30–31). Today, writers and producers "run the show."

[3] Romance writer Mary Jo Putney put it succinctly: "A romance can survive a bland or even a bitchy heroine, but it cannot succeed with a weak hero" (100). I thank Emily Toth for putting me on to Krentz's collection.

unbelievably to most fans, dumped her big cowboy husband, Clint, for Sloan Carpenter, a genteel military scholar with wispy, pale hair, washed-out eyes, and a receding chin; he is even in remission from the old soap mystery disease. And yet, Carpenter's son, Andrew, is an example of the new soap man at his best. A minister, stereotypically sensitive, Andrew—with the help of actor Wortham Krimmer—is sensitive, but he is also strong and often courageous, especially in standing up to the homophobes, including his father. (*One Life to Live* may be the most rigidly correct soap opera because, for the last few years, it has been in the production hands of an outsider from primetime TV, Linda Gottlieb; its head writer, Michael Malone, was a novelist. Veteran soap writers tend to do complexity just because they are trying to please massively and for the long run.)

How do people cover up their insecurity? They wisecrack. This new age of "equality" between the sexes is marked most of all on the soaps by humor. Banter substitutes for soap opera's traditional (melo)dramatic tension. The popularity of *One Life to Live*'s twinkly Max—not even the male lead of the show—is significant. Today's supercouples are not Scarlett and Rhett; they are Nick and Nora Charles, e.g., *All My Children*'s Trevor, the smart, funny cop, and his "doll," the elegant and mischievous Natalie Dillon.

The big stars are not the Luke and Laura of the seduction-or-was-it-rape? scenario of a dozen years ago on *General Hospital*.[4] Today, Laura Spencer personifies the (controversial) feminine-feminist virtues popularized by psychologist Carol Gilligan's 1982 study, *In a Different Voice*. She can see all the sides; she empathizes. Laura's compassionate, almost magically instinctual wisdom is not only righter than Luke's louder, aggressive action; she is as active as he is, equally strong and equally courageous. Luke is hardly her plaything, but his actions in their comeback story in early 1994 controlled their lives—that is, his work for the mobster Frank Smith was frighteningly dangerous and violent, even to their 10-year-old son, Lucky. Laura was clearly in charge morally.

These new heroines and heroes explain why *All My Children*'s Erica Kane and Dmitri Marick did not click. They were overwrought. (Remember the history of Susan Lucci and Michael Nader that gave *All My Children* the idea of hiring Nader: They starred together in heavily melodramatic TV gangster flicks.) Fans agreed with critics and writers: Erica's best man was Jack Montgomery. (Again, note actor Walt Willey's other life as a stand-up comic.)

---

[4] McGarry cites the "anger" both Genie Francis and Anthony Geary (Laura and Luke, respectively) felt at the turn-around of the 1979–1980 *General Hospital* rape and rape-victim story and the ambivalence of the writers of the story. Sheri Anderson, an associate writer in 1979, said she would do the "acquaintance rape" story again, but she reflected today's confused times when she said of herself and Pat Falken Smith, *General Hospital*'s head writer then, that growing up "in the '60s—I can't say that we were all raped, but we experienced things as women . . . and accepted too often things that women don't accept now. . . . People say, 'Was it rape?' And I say no. And most people see it as—or, at the time, felt that rape was—purely a violent act. This was an act of . . . uncontrolled passion, which is equally devastating." Totally comfortable with his 1979 *General Hospital* rape story was its writer Frank Salisbury. Ironically, Salisbury was the author of the 1988 *Santa Barbara* parodic episode in which rape victim, Eden, attacks airheaded soap stars "Link" and "Laurie" who acted in a rape scene in "General Clinic" (Morse 98–99).

16   Erica's second best man was Edmund Grey, her abductor. John Callahan, who played Edmund, is one of today's hottest soap stars. Callahan's Edmund was even able to move from being a Pulitzer Prize writer—a younger Spencer Tracy to editor Brooke English's Katharine Hepburn in their own *Woman of the Year* romance—into madness, during which he kidnapped Erica, and then went back to normal. "Normal" was to love two women, Brooke and Dr. Maria Santos, at the same time, which he made understandable, not only to the audience, but to the women involved.

In an epitomic soap opera episode that shows today's soap man at his best, on 20 January 1994, *All My Children* paralleled climaxes in the Brooke-Edmund-Maria and the Erica-Dmitri stories. In both, the men shone in new ways. To fend off Tad's custody suit, Brooke claimed Edmund was the father of the child she was pregnant with. Maria, overhearing, thought Edmund was the father. Literally, physically, between the two women, Edmund convincingly pleaded his new love to Maria. With eloquent simplicity, he asked Brooke how, if they had loved each other as they had, she could now destroy his new happiness with her desperate lie. It might have been such melo-soap as to be parody, but not in the hands of these actors and writers, and not in these days of much more open, complex lives.

Erica, meanwhile, on the verge of trial for stabbing Dmitri (she had post-traumatically seen her husband as the man who had raped her at 14), came upon Dmitri in their old trysting place. He communicated to us his "hate" of the woman he clearly loved passionately. When he told her he hated himself because, at that moment, in spite of the stabbing, "I still *want* you," he was richly complex in his "new male" consciousness and openness. Erica leaped at once to seducing him. It was a telling moment, and Dmitri told Erica, "Sex. Whenever you are cornered, Erica, you turn to sex."

At the end of this rich day, Brooke was at the grave of her daughter, Laura, characteristically turning inward for insight. Equally characteristically, Erica reached outward, "rising" to the occasion of a press conference. For both women, recovery was temporary, but made for unusual purgation and quasiclosure for these unusual parallel, and therefore resonant, soap stories.

20   In his humor, as in his complexity, Edmund is the soap hero of today. But the '90s hero does not have to be humorous, which brings us to the shows of William Bell. *The Young and the Restless* has been first in the Nielsen ratings for daytime serials for six years; *The Bold and the Beautiful* is commonly in the top five. Humor may not be Bell's forte, as is often said, but male characters, it seems, are. In the 10 current daytime dramas, Bell's two soap operas have the largest proportion of men to women characters, by five in *The Young and the Restless* and by three in *The Bold and the Beautiful*.[5]

---

[5] These are main characters, analyzed in mid-1994. Such a breakdown of today's 10 daytime dramas, showing not only the number of male and female characters but also the hierarchy of ages from the patriarchs and matriarchs to the children, is a mirror pyramid, with fewest elders and youngsters and a bulge of men and women in their sexual prime. For a "woman's" genre, the relatively even number of men and women in the soaps may be a surprise.

There are potentially compelling men in the two series. In *The Young and the Restless,* the characters are Victor Newman; Jack Abbott and his father, John, who are former rivals now united against Victor; Brad Carlton, the maturing stud; Paul Williams, another ex-bad boy; and today's young bloods, Ryan McNeil and Neil Winters. But, like all of Bell's characters and more than on other soaps, these men seem glaringly manipulated by the storyteller. Why does Brad leave Lauren Fenmore, or Ashley Abbott, or Traci? Why does he come back? Is he after love, sex, or money and power? What these Bell men do does not seem to come from a mind and heart and history the audience knows.

Often, a soap's characters will get skewed when the show's writers change. With Bell's shows, paradoxically, perhaps the murky motivation comes about because there has been no upheaval of writers. Without writer changes, no one may think to clarify to new watchers what in the characters' histories makes them do what they do now. On *The Bold and the Beautiful,* the Bell dynasty of writers, producers, and so on may explain why the heroes, the Forrester men, have seemed untouched by characterization, endlessly moving from woman to woman, since the show's debut in 1987. Other male characters seem characterless and merely rivals to the Forrester men for their women. Maybe this is why the actors hired to play the Forrester rivals have been popular characters on other soaps (most recently, Michael Sabatino and Ian Buchanan came to *The Bold and the Beautiful* from hits on *Days of Our Lives* and *General Hospital,* respectively). It seems to be the actors' values Bell wants, rather than the best actor to create a new character.

But, how can one understand the popularity of *The Young and the Restless* and *The Bold and the Beautiful,* with all those male ciphers? Is it that the women in the audience are really throwbacks to Heathcliff-fantasizers? Perhaps. But, more likely, if we give art its due (which demands that we see soap opera as art), it is the acting (for example, *The Young and the Restless*'s Eric Braeden as Victor). Most of all, though, it seems to be the sureness of Bell's storytelling, which promises us that, when the time is right, we will understand Neil, or Ryan, or Brad. And, indeed, it happens, in the new inwardness of "ruthless" Victor, in love with blind Hope, and in *The Bold and the Beautiful*'s Ridge Forrester, the ex-playboy, finally growing up through seven years of loves lost and found. No one ever claimed that Bell's stories move fast. It seems to take forever for women to grow up on the shows, but the men, in the mid-'90s, spurred by changing times and a male-dominated production company, may be moving from obscurity to complexity.

24   In early 1994, the soap opera with the highest proportion of female characters was *Guiding Light* (six more women than men). *Guiding Light* and *General Hospital* (even men and women) seem currently to have the most interesting male characters. *General Hospital*'s male cast rivets attention today because of promising originality; *Guiding Light*'s because of overall complexity.

Clair Labine (creator of the much honored *Ryan's Hope*) took over as head writer of *General Hospital* in 1993, concurrent with the return after 10 years of the superstars Luke and Laura. Understandably, Labine, who had not watched *General Hospital,* concentrated on them. Her Luke is arguably the best male character of this new (feminist) age. The reason *General Hospital* has perhaps the best males in soap opera today is Luke Spencer, an adventurer, bold and foolhardy. Luke is passionately loving and wildly admiring of and empathetic with Laura. He is vulnerable and imperfect. But he listens, learns, gives credit; he wants a home and, passionately, to care for his family. On top of this, he is intelligent, always fun, and ever imaginative. He is, in short, complex.

But were the other *General Hospital* men shorted? From the poker scene, it seems not. The soap's writers have rich matter to work with in the Quartermaine men, dominated by the patriarch, Edward, and starring middle-aged Alan, who is complexly arrogant but insecure because he fears he is not worthy of those he loves and respects, especially his father and his wife, Monica.

In the wings, priming for the character development in which Labine specializes, are Damian Smith, the mobster's son, and Ned Ashton, a hungry Quartermaine scion. Particularly as acted by Leigh McCloskey and Wallace Kurth, respectively, Damian and Ned are arresting contemporary men: On the outside, they are cool connivers; on the inside, Damian is hurting for respectability and Ned is rebelling. Both characters ache to be free from their fathers. Most enigmatic is Maurice Benard's Sonny Corinthos, a young, ethnic hoodlum. Sonny loves the women, but he also loves the teenage Mike "Stone" Cates like a brother. Is Sonny streetwise or is he Mephisto? We do not know. Complexity of that caliber is both realistic and sexy.

28 Regularly cited by the industry as the best written soap, *Guiding Light*'s men are the most realistically complex. Correctly, one character, Buzz Cooper, said of Jenna Bradshaw, with whom he was in love, "[Yes], I have feelings for her, but none of them are simple" (19 January 1994). Eleni Cooper told her step-sister-in-law Lucy about the man Lucy loved: "Alan-Michael is many different things. He is not just one thing. He's constantly at war with himself" (14 January 1994). None of the *Guiding Light* men or women is "just one thing." Almost all are complex and each is different. The nuanced writing and the longevity of many of the characters turn the types—rich scion, poor boy—into individuals. Buzz is brilliantly layered, the Vietnam hero-deserter who abandoned his American wife and kids to try to save a buddy's Asian woman. When he returns to Springfield at age 40, he is still the hero who, sadly, hurts those who love him.

Ross Marler, introduced and played by Jerry ver Dorn since 1979, is a successful lawyer, as smooth as Buzz, the diner counterman, is awkward. Yet Ross, too, fears opening up, "giving" to a woman. Dr. Ed Bauer is the alcoholic for life, never "cured" and, since 1993, with more to feel guilty about since the death of his wife on whom he cheated. Billy Lewis is rich and lusty, but he too battles the demons of alcoholism and the feeling that he is not trusted by those he helplessly loves.

Guiding Light's younger men are a combination of aggression or charm and fears of holding back. For example, Nick McHenry, Alexandra's son, is an idealist who scorns her; yet he moves to her like a moth to a flame: Is he drawn by love, greed, or power? In the late 1980s, Philip Spaulding mightily combated his father, Alan. In the 1990s, the working-class son, Frank Cooper, tries but cannot wholly welcome home the father who abandoned him, Buzz.

Michael Zaslow's Roger Thorpe is *Guiding Light*'s "monster." In the 1990s, he is the show's protagonist: a *terrorist* of passion, a man with no seeming end to his destruction, often self-destruction, because he is hurting those he loves. Really, Roger is desperate for someone to love.

32   Looking at soap opera, it is clear that the "new" audience sophistication perceived by the industry is leading to some more realistically complex soap men, as well as soap women. And, the longer and closer one looks, the clearer it is how right the times and the soap opera story of today are for each other.

The soaps are self-consciously politically correct. As a feminist, I am more than willing to tolerate the lesser art of the new Kristin-Tony bed-talk. The general love story right now is the man's fear of opening up, of men torn, knotted, contradictory. It is the man's fear as much as the woman's.

The soap story is also the story of younger lovers rather than mature ones. It is, of course, the AIDS story. It is the story of sexual fear reflecting other experiences of love and loss—of parents, family, job, career, home, and even the world.

To look at soap opera today is, in sum, to look at the reflection of times in which how women and men feel about one another and how they treat each other are clouded, changing, and vastly new. As it always does, soap opera represents this current human story.

Works Cited

Gilligan, Carol. *In a Different Voice: Psychological Theory and Women's Development.* Cambridge: Harvard UP, 1982.

Krentz, Jayne Ann. "Trying to Tame the Romance: Critics and Correctness." *Dangerous Men and Adventurous Women: Romance Writers on the Appeal of the Romance.* Ed. Jayne Ann Krentz. Philadelphia: U of Pennsylvania P, 1992.

LaGuardia, Robert. *Soap World.* New York: Arbor House, 1983.

McGarry, Mark. "Did Luke Rape Laura?" *Soap Opera Weekly* 12 Oct. 1993: 44.

Morse, Susan. "*Santa Barbara* Attacks *General Hospital*." *Soap Opera Digest* 15 Nov. 1988: 98–99.

Putney, Mary Jo. "Welcome to the Dark Side." *Dangerous Men and Adventurous Women: Romance Writers on the Appeal of the Romance.* Ed. Jayne Ann Krentz. Philadelphia: U of Pennsylvania P, 1992.

Thurber, James. "Soapland." *The Beast in Me and Other Animals.* New York: Harcourt, Brace, 1948. 119–260.

Williams, Carol Traynor. "*It's Time for My Story*": *Soap Opera Sources, Structure, and Response.* New York: Praeger, 1992.

Personal Response

What do you think of the '90s soap opera men, as described in this essay?

Questions for Discussion

1. Explain the subtitle, "Signs of Fearful Times." You might begin by locating Williams' thesis and the paragraphs in which she elaborates on what she means by her subtitle.

2. Traynor repeatedly mentions "complexity" in her analysis of '90s soap opera males. What do you understand her to mean by that word? How does the complexity she discusses in '90s soap males differ from that of soap opera males in earlier decades? Which previous period of soap operas does Williams believe the decade of the '90s most closely aligns itself with and why?

3. Review Williams' explanation of why she says that Luke Spencer of *General Hospital* is "arguably the best male character of this new (feminist) age" (paragraph 25). To what extent do you agree with her that those characteristics make Luke and others like him "perhaps the best males in soap opera today."

4. Discuss this statement: "The soaps are self-consciously politically correct." What does Williams mean? Explain her reference to "the new Kristin-Tony bed-talk" (paragraph 33).

5. Explain the references to the fictional characters in these statements: "Today's supercouples are not *Scarlett and Rhett;* they are *Nick and Nora Charles*" (paragraph 13) and "Is it that women in the audience are really throwbacks to *Heathcliff* fantasizers?" (paragraph 23).

DO ASK, DO TELL

Joshua Gamson

Joshua Gamson is assistant professor of sociology at Yale University and the author of Claims to Fame: Celebrity in Contemporary America *(1994). This essay appeared in the Fall 1995 issue of* The American Prospect.

At the end of his 22 years, when Pedro Zamora lost his capacity to speak, all sorts of people stepped into the silence created by the AIDS-related brain disease that shut him up. MTV began running a marathon of *The Real World,* its seven-kids-in-an-apartment-with-the-cameras-running show on which Pedro Zamora starred as Pedro Zamora, a version of himself: openly gay, Miami Cuban, HIV-positive, youth activist. MTV offered the marathon as a tribute to Zamora, which it was, and as a way to raise funds, especially crucial since Zamora, like so many people with HIV, did not have private insurance. Yet, of course, MTV was also paying tribute to itself, capitalizing on Pedro's death without quite seeming as monstrous as all that.

President Clinton and Florida governor Lawton Chiles made public statements and publicized phone calls to the hospital room, praising Zamora as a heroic point of light rather than as a routinely outspoken critic of their own HIV and AIDS policies. The Clinton administration, in the midst of its clampdown on Cuban immigration, even granted visas to Zamora's three brothers and a sister in Cuba—a kindly if cynical act, given the realities of people with AIDS awaiting visas and health care in Guantánamo Bay.

Thus, according to *People* magazine, did Zamora reach a bittersweet ending. He was unable to see, hear, or speak, yet with his family reunited, "his dream had come true." Behind the scenes, one who was there for Zamora's last weeks told me, the family actually separated Zamora from his boyfriend—quite out of keeping with the "dreams" of Pedro's life. When Pedro had his own voice, he had spoken powerfully of how anti-gay ideology and policy, typically framed as "pro-family," contributed to teen suicides and the spread of HIV; when he died, those who spoke for him emphasized individual heroism and the triumph of the heterosexual family.

4   That others appropriated Zamora on his deathbed hardly tarnishes his accomplishment. As an MTV star, he had probably reduced suffering among lesbian and gay teenagers more, and affected their thinking more deeply, than a zillion social service programs. He spoke publicly to millions in his own words and with the backing of a reputable media institution, and he did not just tell them to wear condoms, or that AIDS is an equal-opportunity destroyer. Nor did he simply fill in the sexual blanks left by prudish government prevention campaigns. He also told them and showed them: Here is me loving my boyfriend; here is what a self-possessed gay man looks like hanging out with his roommates; here is what my Cuban family might have to say about my bringing home a black man; here is me at an AIDS demonstration, getting medical news, exchanging love vows.

To speak for and about yourself as a gay man or a lesbian on television, to break silences that are systematically and ubiquitously enforced in public life, is profoundly political. "Don't tell" is more than a U.S. military policy; it remains U.S. public policy, formally and informally, on sex and gender nonconformity. Sex and gender outsiders—gay men, transsexuals, lesbians, bisexuals—are constantly invited to lose their voices, or suffer the consequences (job loss, baseball bats) of using them. Outside of the occasional opening on MTV or sporadic coverage of a demonstration or a parade, if one is not Melissa Etheridge or David Geffen, opportunities to speak as a nonheterosexual, or to listen to one, are few and far between. Even if the cameras soon turn elsewhere, these moments are big breakthroughs, and they are irresistible, giddy moments for the shut up.

Yet, in a media culture, holding the microphone and the spotlight is a complicated sort of power, not just because people grab them back from you but because they are never really yours. If you speak, you must be prepared to be used. The voice that comes out is not quite yours: It is like listening to yourself on tape (a bit deeper, or more clipped) or to a version dubbed by your twin. It is you and it is not you. Zamora's trick, until his voice was taken, was to walk the line between talking and being dubbed. The troubling question, for the silenced and the heard alike, is whether the line is indeed walkable. Perhaps the best place to turn for answers is the main public space in which the edict to shut up is reversed: daytime television talk shows.

For lesbians, gay men, bisexuals, drag queens, transsexuals—and combinations thereof—watching daytime television has got to be spooky. Suddenly, there are renditions of you, chattering away in a system that otherwise ignores or steals your voice at every turn. Sally Jessy Raphael wants to know what it's like to pass as a different sex, Phil Donahue wants to support you in your battle against gay bashing, Ricki Lake wants to get you a date, Oprah Winfrey wants you to love without lying. Most of all, they all want you to talk about it publicly, just at a time when everyone else wants you not to. They are interested, if not precisely in "reality," at least not in fictional accounts. For people whose desires and identities go against the norm, this is the only spot in mainstream media culture to speak on their own terms or to hear others speaking for themselves. The fact that talk shows are so much maligned, and for so many good reasons, does not close the case.

8   The other day, I happened to tune into the *Ricki Lake Show*, the fastest-rising talk show ever. The topic: "I don't want gays around my kids." I caught the last 20 minutes of what amounted to a pro-gay screamfest. Ricki and her audience explicitly attacked a large woman who was denying visitation rights to her gay ex-husband ("I had to explain to a 9-year-old what 'gay' means"; "My child started having nightmares after he visited his father"). And they went at a young couple who believed in keeping children away from gay people on the grounds that the Bible says "homosexuals should die." The gay guests and their supporters had the last word, brought on to argue, to much audience whooping, that loving gays are a positive influence and hateful heterosexuals should stay away from children. The anti-gay guests were denounced on any number of grounds, by host, other guests, and numerous audience members: They are denying children loving influences, they are bigots, they are misinformed, they read the Bible incorrectly, they sound like Mormons, they are resentful that they have put on more weight than their exes. One suburban-looking audience member angrily addressed each "child protector" in turn, along the way coming up with a possible new pageant theme: "And as for you, Miss Homophobia . . ."

The show was a typical mess, with guests yelling and audiences hooting at the best one-liners about bigotry or body weight, but the virulence with which homophobia was attacked is both typical of these shows and stunning. When Lake cut off a long-sideburned man's argument that "it's a fact that the easiest way to get AIDS is by homosexual sex" ("That is not a fact, sir, that is not correct"), I found myself ready to start the chant of "Go, Ricki! Go, Ricki!" that apparently wraps each taping. Even such elementary corrections, and even such a weird form of visibility and support, stands out sharply. Here, the homophobe is the deviant, the freak.

Lake's show is among the new breed of rowdy youth-oriented programs, celebrated as "rock and roll television" by veteran Geraldo Rivera and denigrated as "exploitalk" by cultural critic Neal Gabler. Their sibling show, the older, tamer "service" programs such as *Oprah* and *Donahue*, support "alternative" sexualities and genders in quieter, but not weaker, ways. Peruse last year's *Donahue*: two teenage lesbian lovers ("Young, courageous people like yourself are blazing the way for other people," says Donahue), a gay construction worker suing his gay boss for harassment ("There's only eight states that protect sexual persuasion," his attorney reports), a bisexual minister, a black lesbian activist, and two members of the African-American theater group Pomo Afro Homos ("We're about trying to build a black gay community," says one), the stars of the gender-crossing

Priscilla, Queen of the Desert ("I have a lot of friends that are transsexuals," declares an audience member, "and they're the neatest people"), heterosexuals whose best friends are gay, lesbians starting families, gay teens, gay cops, gay men reuniting with their high school sweethearts, a gay talk show. This is a more diverse, self-possessed, and politically outspoken group of nonheterosexuals than I might find, say, at the gay bar around the corner. I can only imagine what this means for people experiencing sexual difference where none is locally visible.

Certainly *Donahue* makes moves to counter its "liberal" reputation, inviting right-wing black preachers and the widely discredited "psychologist" Paul Cameron, who argues that cross-dressing preceded the fall of Rome, that people with AIDS should be quarantined, and that sexuality "is going to get us." But more often than not, Donahue himself is making statements about how "homophobia is global" and "respects no nation," how "we're beating up homosexual people, calling them names, throwing them out of apartments, jobs." The "we" being asserted is an "intolerant" population that needs to get over itself. We are, he says at times, "medieval." In fact, Donahue regularly asserts that "for an advanced, so-called industrialized nation, I think we're the worst."

12   Oprah Winfrey, the industry leader, is less concerned with the political treatment of difference; she is overwhelmingly oriented toward "honesty" and "openness," especially in interpersonal relationships. As on Lake's show, lesbians and gays are routinely included without incident in more general themes (meeting people through personal ads, fools for love, sons and daughters you never knew), and bigotry is routinely attacked. But Winfrey's distinctive mark is an attack on lies, and thus the closet comes under attack—especially the gay male closet—not just for the damage it does to those in it, but for the betrayals of women it engenders.

On a recent program in which a man revealed his "orientation" after 19 years of marriage, for example, both Winfrey and her audience were concerned not that Steve is gay, but that he was not honest with his wife. As Winfrey put it, "For me, always the issue is how you can be more truthful in your life." One of Steve's two supportive sons echoes Winfrey ("I want people to be able to be who they are"), as does his ex-wife, whose anger is widely supported by the audience ("It makes me feel like my life has been a sham"), and the requisite psychologist ("The main thing underneath all of this is the importance of loving ourselves and being honest and authentic and real in our lives"). Being truthful, revealing secrets, learning to love oneself: These are the staples of Winfrey-style talk shows. Gay and bisexual guests find a place to speak as gays and bisexuals, and the pathology becomes not sexual "deviance" but the socially imposed closet.

All of this, however, should not be mistaken for dedicated friendship. Even when ideological commitments to truth and freedom are at work, the primary commitment of talk shows is, of course, to money. What makes these such inviting spots for nonconforming sex and gender identities has mostly to do with the niche talk shows have carved out for ratings. The shows are about talk; the more silence there has been on a subject, the more not-telling, the better a talk topic it is. On talk shows, as media scholar Wayne Munson points out in his book *All Talk* (Temple University Press, 1993), "differences are no longer repressed" but "become the talk show's emphasis," as the shows confront "boredom and channel clutter with constant, intensified novelty and 'reality.'" Indeed, according to Munson, Richard Mincer, *Donahue*'s executive producer, encourages prospective guests "to be especially unique or different, to take advantage of rather than repress difference."

While they highlight different sex and gender identities, expressions, and practices, the talk shows can be a dangerous place to speak and a difficult place to get heard. With around 20 syndicated talk shows competing for audiences, shows that trade in confrontation and surprise *(Ricki Lake, Jenny Jones, Jerry Springer)* are edging out the milder, topical programs *(Oprah, Donahue)*.

16   As a former *Jane Whitney Show* producer told *TV Guide*, "When you're booking guests, you're thinking, 'How much confrontation can this person provide me?' The more confrontation, the better. You want people just this side of a fistfight."

For members of groups already subject to violence, the visibility of television can prompt more than just a fistfight, as last year's *Jenny Jones* murder underlined. In March, when Scott Amedure appeared on a "secret admirer" episode of the *Jenny Jones Show,* the admired Jon Schmitz was apparently expecting a female admirer. Schmitz, not warming to Amedure's fantasy of tying him up in a hammock and spraying whipped cream and champagne on his body, declared himself "100 percent heterosexual." Later, back in Michigan, he punctuated this claim by shooting Amedure with a 12-gauge shotgun, telling police that the embarrassment from the program had "eaten away" at him. Or, as he reportedly put it in his 911 call, Amedure "fucked me on national TV."

Critics were quick to point out that programming that creates conflict tends to exacerbate it. "The producers made professions of regret," Neal Gabler wrote in the *Los Angeles Times* after the Amedure murder, "but one suspects what they really regretted was the killer's indecency of not having pulled out his rifle and committed the crime before their cameras." In the wake of the murder, talk show producers were likened over and over to drug dealers: Publicist Ken Maley told the *San Francisco Chronicle* that "they've got people strung out on an adrenaline rush," and "they keep raising the dosage"; sociologist Vicki Abt told *People* that "TV allows us to mainline deviance"; Michelangelo Signorile argued in *Out* that some talk show producers "are like crack dealers scouring trailer park America." True enough. Entering the unruly talk show world, one is apt to become, at best, a source of adrenaline rush, and at worst a target of violence.

What most reporting tended to ignore, however, was that most anti-gay violence does not require a talk show "ambush" to trigger it. Like the Oakland County, Michigan, prosecutor who argued that "*Jenny Jones*'s producers' cynical pursuit of ratings and total insensitivity to what could occur here left one person dead and Mr. Schmitz now facing life in prison," many critics focused on the "humiliating" surprise attack on Schmitz with the news that he was desired by another man. As in the image of the "straight" soldier being ogled in the shower, in this logic the revelation of same-sex desire is treated as the danger, and the desired as a victim. The talk show critics thus played to the same "don't tell" logic that makes talk shows such a necessary, if uncomfortable, refuge for some of us.

20   Although producers' pursuit of ratings is indeed, unsurprisingly, cynical and insensitive, the talk show environment is one of the very few in which the declaration of same-sex desire (and, to a lesser degree, atypical gender identity) is common, heartily defended, and often even incidental. Although they overlook this in their haste to hate trash, the critics of exploitative talk shows help illuminate the odd sort of opportunity these cacophonous settings provide. Same-sex desires become "normal" on these programs not so much because different sorts of lives become clearly visible, but because they get sucked into the spectacular whirlpool of relationship conflicts. They offer a particular kind of visibility and voice. On a recent *Ricki Lake,* it was the voice of an aggressive, screechy gay man who continually reminded viewers, between laughs at his own nasty comments, that he was a regular guy. On other days, it's the take-your-hands-off-my-woman lesbian, or the I'm-more-of-a-woman-than-you'll-ever-be transsexual. The vicious voice—shouting that we gay people can be as mean, or petty, or just plain loud, as anybody else—is the first voice talk shows promote. It's one price of entry into mainstream public visibility.

The guests on the talk shows seem to march in what psychologist Jeanne Heaton, co-author of *Tuning in Trouble* (Jossey-Bass, 1995), calls a "parade of pathology." Many talk shows have more than a passing resemblance to freak shows. Neal Gabler, for example, argues that guests are invited to exhibit "their deformities for attention" in a "ritual of debasement" aimed primarily at reassuring the audience of its superiority. Indeed, the evidence of dehumanization is all over the place, especially when it comes to gender crossing, as in the titles of various recent *Geraldo* programs; the calls of sideshow barkers echo in "Star-Crossed Cross-Dressers: Bizarre Stories of Transvestites and Their Lovers" and "Outrageous Impersonators and Flamboyant Drag Queens" and "When Your Husband Wears the Dress in the Family." As long as talk shows make their bids by being, in Gabler's words, "a psychological freak show," sex and gender outsiders arguably reinforce perceptions of themselves as freaks by entering a discourse in which they may be portrayed as bizarre, outrageous, flamboyant curiosities. (Often, for example, they must relinquish their right to defend themselves to the ubiquitous talk show "experts.")

      Talk shows do indeed trade on voyeurism, and it is no secret that those who break with sex and gender norms and fight with each other on camera help the shows win higher ratings. But there is more to the picture: the place where "freaks" talk back. It is a place where Conrad, born and living in a female body, can assert against Sally Jessy Raphael's claims that he "used and betrayed" women in order to have sex with them that women fall in love with him as a man because he considers himself a man; where months later, in a program on "our most outrageous former guests" (all gender crossers), Conrad can reappear, declare himself to have started hormone treatment, and report that the woman he allegedly "used and betrayed" has stood by him. This is a narrow opening, but an opening nonetheless, for the second voice promoted by the talk show: the proud voice of the "freak," even if the freak refuses that term. The fact that talk shows are exploitative spectacles does not negate the fact that they are also opportunities; as

Munson points out, they are both spectacle and conversation. They give voice to the systematically silenced, albeit under conditions out of the speaker's control, and in tones that come out tinny, scratched, distant.

These voices, even when they are discounted, sometimes do more than just assert themselves. Whatever their motivations, people sometimes wind up doing more than just pulling up a chair at a noisy, crowded table. Every so often they wind up messing with sexual categories in a way that goes beyond a simple expansion of them. In addition to affirming both homosexuality and heterosexuality as normal and natural, talk show producers often make entertainment by mining the in-between: finding guests who are interesting exactly because they don't fit existing notions of "gay" and "straight" and "man" and "woman," raising the provocative suggestion that the categories are not quite working.

24   The last time I visited the *Maury Povich Show,* for instance, I found myself distracted by Jason and Tiffanie. Jason, a large 18-year-old from a small town in Ohio, was in love with Calvin. Calvin was having an affair with Jamie (Jason's twin sister, also the mother of a three-month-old), who was interested in Scott, who had sex with, as I recall, both Calvin and Tiffanie. Tiffanie, who walked on stage holding Jamie's hand, had pretty much had sex with everyone except Jamie. During group sex, Tiffanie explained, she and Jamie did not touch each other. "We're not lesbians," she loudly asserted, against the noisy protestations of some audience members.

The studio audience, in fact, was quick to condemn the kids, who were living together in a one-bedroom apartment with Jamie's baby. Their response was predictably accusatory: You are freaks, some people said; immoral, said others; pathetically bored and in need of a hobby, others asserted. Still other aspects of the "discussion" assumed the validity and normality of homosexuality. Jason, who had recently attempted suicide, was told he needed therapy to help him come to terms with his sexuality, and the other boys were told they too needed to "figure themselves out." Yet much talk also struggled to attach sexual labels to an array of partnerships anarchic enough to throw all labels into disarray. "If you are not lesbians, why were you holding hands?" one women asked Tiffanie. "If you are not gay," another audience member asked Calvin, "how is it you came to have oral sex with two young men?"

This mix was typically contradictory: condemnation of "immoral sex" but not so much of homosexuality per se, openly gay and bisexual teenagers speaking for themselves while their partners in homosexual activities declare heterosexual identities, a situation in which sexual categories are both assumed and up for grabs. I expect the young guests were mainly in it for the free trip to New York, and the studio audience was mainly in it for the brush with television. Yet the discussion they created, the unsettling of categorical assumptions about genders and desires, if only for a few moments in the midst of judgment and laughter, is found almost nowhere else this side of fiction.

The importance of these conversations, both for those who for safety must shut up about their sexual and gender identities and for those who never think about them, is certainly underestimated. The level of exploitation is certainly not. Like Pedro Zamora, one can keep one's voice for a little while, one finger on the commercial megaphone, until others inevitably step in to claim it for their own purposes. Or one can talk for show, as freak, or expert, or rowdy—limits set by production strategies within the talk show genre.

28 Those limits, not the talk shows themselves, are really the point. The story here is not about commercial exploitation, but about just how effective the prohibition on asking and telling is in the United States, how stiff the penalties are, how unsafe this place is for people of atypical sexual and gender identities. You know you're in trouble when Sally Jessy Raphael (strained smile and forced tear behind red glasses) seems like your best bet for being heard, understood, respected, and protected. That for some of us the loopy, hollow light of talk shows seems a safe haven should give us all pause.

Personal Response

What is your opinion of talk shows in general? Do you view them? Why or why not?

Questions for Discussion

1. How does Gamson's title reflect his central purpose?

2. What function does the opening example of Pedro Zamora serve? How does it relate to Gamson's discussion of "voice"?

3. Gamson notes that the "primary commitment of talk shows is, of course, to money. . . . The more silence there has been on a subject, the more nottelling, the better a talk topic it is" (paragraph 14). Do you think limits should be placed on the topics television talk shows should be allowed to air, or should any subject be fair game as long as guests are willing to appear on the programs?

4. Explain what Gamson means when he writes that "talk shows can be a dangerous place to speak and a difficult place to get heard" (paragraph 15).

5. Gamson suggests that "the fact that talk shows are exploitative spectacles does not negate the fact that they are also opportunities; . . . they are both spectacle and conversation" (paragraph 21). Discuss the merits and drawbacks of television talk shows, including both those that intentionally court controversy and encourage heated confrontation and the tamer, more conservative talk shows. What value, besides entertainment, do such programs have?

MENACE TO SOCIETY

John Davidson

John Davidson is a writer living in Austin, Texas. He wrote this essay for the February 22, 1996, issue of Rolling Stone.

With three-quarters of Americans surveyed convinced that movies, television and music spur young people to violence, and politicians on the left and right blasting the entertainment industry for irresponsibility, the debate over violence in popular culture is likely to be a key issue in the presidential campaign.

Republican presidential front-runner Bob Dole, conservative guru William Bennett, black activist C. DeLores Tucker and liberal Democrat Sen. Paul Simon all have attacked portrayals of violence, treating the link between art and reality as gospel truth. They've found support for their claims from the American Psychological Association and the American Psychiatric Association, which have both issued reports stating that television violence causes aggression.

And a new controversy surrounding video games has been sparked by Lt. Col. Dave Grossman, a psychologist and Army Ranger. In his book *On Killing,* he claims that these games function like firing ranges, using the same type of conditioning employed to overcome soldiers' built-in inhibition to killing in the Vietnam War.

4   The research, however, is less clear. Most experts who have studied the issue believe there is *some* link—indirect, perhaps—between seeing violence and committing it, but there is no agreement on how strong that link is or how to measure it. What's more, even those who argue most persuasively that there is a case to be made for connecting violence and culture agree that the biggest problem may not be teenagers seeing *Natural Born Killers* or listening to the Geto Boys but small children watching Saturday morning cartoons.

For the last 40 years, social scientists have attempted to measure how media violence affects people, with the bulk of the research focused on television. One of the most influential studies was directed by George Gerbner. Beginning in 1967, Gerbner, who at that time was dean of the Annenberg School for Communication at the University of Pennsylvania, and his colleagues created a violence index that is still used to measure the percentage of network programs that have violence, the number of violent acts, the percentage of characters involved in violence and the percentage involved in killing. Their index doesn't reflect the increased amount of violent material made available through cable television and VCRs. (That count, according to the National Coalition on Television Violence, is that children in homes with cable TV and/or a VCR will see about 32,000 murders and 40,000 attempted murders by the time they're 18.)

Gerbner's group concluded that television acts as an electronic melting pot, which creates a national culture. Part of that culture is "the mean-world syndrome," which leads people to believe that they are more likely to be victims of violence than they are in reality. "People who watch the most television are usually the ones who have fewer options, less money and less education," says Nancy Signorielli, a professor of communication at the University of Delaware who worked on the Gerbner study. "Their views of the world reflect what they see on television, and they overestimate their chances of being involved in violence." Like the man in Louisiana who in 1992 shot and killed a Japanese exchange student looking for a Halloween party, people overreact to perceived threats and act violently.

Remarkably, Gerbner found that the indexes have remained relatively constant during the past two decades. Nonetheless, he's been accused of exaggerating the amount of violence by not taking context into consideration. A poke in the eye, as far as he's concerned, is basically a poke in the eye; his group counts *The Three Stooges* and Road Runner cartoons as violent programming.

8   A landmark study funded by the four major networks in response to congressional pressure and released this past fall attempted to correct that deficiency and qualify different types of violence by looking at time slot, parental advisory, duration, explicitness, relation to the story and consequences. Researchers at the Center for Communication Policy at the University of California at Los Angeles confirmed that context is crucial. In other words, a TV program that shows kids beating up a fellow student with impunity could have a more harmful effect than one that shows a couple of murderers who end up in jail. Even Signorielli acknowledges that context is important: "What we have in the U.S. is happy violence. In Japan, violence is much more graphic and much more realistic," she says. "There, television violence may actually work as a deterrent. But here, if someone's shot we don't see the wound. There's not much bleeding on U.S. television."

Leonard Eron, a research scientist at the University of Michigan, has taken another approach. He began by studying how aggression develops in children, never considering television to be important. "I thought television was just another version of the sort of things children were exposed to in the past—fairy tales, stories and movies," says Eron. "But television is different, if in no other way than [that programs are] repeated over and over again."

Eron and his colleagues tested 875 third-graders in New York's Columbia County and interviewed about 80 percent of their parents. To relieve tension in the interviews, Eron threw in a question about television viewing. What surprised him was the correlation between aggression and viewing habits. Children whose parents said they watched a lot of violent television turned out to be aggressive in school, and 10 years later, in the first of the follow-up studies, Eron discovered that what a child watched at 8 years old was "one of the best predictors" of adult aggression—more important than the parents' child-rearing habits or socioeconomic factors. "I could compare children over time," says Eron. "At 8, if the less aggressive of two children was watching more television violence, at 18, he would be the more aggressive of the two."

Eron's findings correspond with what psychologists believe about child development: Children are most vulnerable to television from ages 2 to about 8, when they become more capable of distinguishing what they see on the screen from reality. The conclusions also conform to what we know about the development of a child's moral sense: It is developed by age 9 at the latest.

12   Just how children learn from the media is the subject of competing theories. According to the simplest, the viewing of aggressive material triggers aggressive thoughts that influence subsequent actions. Kids imitate what they see, just as adults emulate styles of dress and behavior observed in movies and TV shows.

The theory is fine as far as it goes but doesn't take into account the child's expectations and comprehension—nor does it explain the cumulative effects of watching violence. Educators theorize that a child's response depends upon five variables: the child's intellectual achievement, social popularity, identification with television characters, belief in the realism of the violence and the amount of fantasizing about aggression. If a child identifies with the characters, for instance, then he tends to internalize "scripts" for future aggressive behavior. As a child becomes more aggressive, he becomes less popular and more troublesome in school. The more trouble he has with teachers and friends, the more likely it is he will turn to aggressive television for affirmation, thus establishing a vicious cycle.

What turned out to be the most startling result of Eron's study, however, was that a child's viewing beyond the age of 8 seems to have virtually *no* effect on his level of aggression: Once an 8-year-old's level of aggression is established, it tends to remain stable. If this is true, then most of the attacks on media are far off base. Children under the age of 8 are exposed to feature films but even with VCRs and cable, Hollywood movies are not staples in children's media diets in the same way that *Mighty Morphin Power Rangers* or *Teenage Mutant Ninja Turtles* are. In fact, the UCLA study singled out seven Saturday morning network shows including *Power Rangers* and *Ninja Turtles* for containing "sinister combat violence" or "violence for the sake of violence." The report warned that "the dark overtones and unrelenting combat in these shows constitute a fairly recent trend, which appears to be on the rise."

Of course, Eron's work is the subject of controversy. There are experts who warn against linking culture and violence at all. Jonathan Freedman, a psychology professor at the University of Toronto, says that after thoroughly reviewing all the existing studies on television and violence, he had to conclude that there was no convincing evidence that the media have an influence on real violence. "You always hear that there are 3,000 studies that prove that television contributes to violence," says Freedman, "but that's absolutely false. There are maybe 200 pertinent studies, and almost no one has read the literature. It sounds plausible that television causes violence, and everyone takes the word of the so-called experts. I was amazed at how different the studies were from what was being said about them."

16   Of those 200 studies, Freedman says, about 160 are lab studies, which he dismisses as "not totally irrelevant but not very meaningful." In typical lab studies, subjects are shown violent films, and then an attempt is made to measure their response. In one study, increased aggression was measured by showing children a balloon and asking if it would be fun to break it. In others, children were given plastic Bobo dolls that are designed to be hit. Freedman says that most experimenters get positive results because violent programs are simply more arousing than neutral programs and because children respond in the way they think the researchers expect them to. "All that these experiments show is potential effect," says Freedman. "But what is the real effect? In lab experiments they expose children to one kind of media, but in the real world no one watches just violence. You watch lots of different kinds of television. There's lots of different mediating stimuli."

Freedman finds the field studies equally disappointing. He thinks that Eron and his colleagues are true believers because they've devoted their careers to and built their reputations on the damaging effects of television violence. "Most people don't have the statistical and methodological expertise to read and evaluate the studies," Freedman explains. "Since [these study] committees all base their conclusions on the words of those few experts, naturally . . . they all conclude that television violence is harmful.

"People say that children are more aggressive," Freedman continues. "More aggressive than when? Not more than 1880. Somalia and Bosnia are worse than here, and Somalia doesn't have television."

The research on video games and rap music is even more inconclusive. A 1993 study of 357 seventh- and eighth-graders, for instance, found that 32 percent said fantasy violence was their favorite game category, while 17 percent chose human violence. But the study is small and doesn't draw conclusions between the games and aggression. As for rap, Peter Christiansen, a professor of communication at Lewis and Clark College, in Portland, Ore., says, "Seventy-six percent of rap is purchased by middle-class kids. For them, rap is a kind of cultural tourism. . . . They aren't turned on by the explicit lyrics."

20   Poverty, the easy accessibility of guns, domestic abuse, social instability and the like may all contribute more than the media do to the level of violence. Even researchers like Signorielli warn against drawing cause-and-effect conclusions. "You can't just blame TV for the problems of society," she says. "Television contributes to children's aggressiveness, but it's only one of the factors."

Unfortunately, the political debate tends to ignore the nuances and uncertainties contained in the research. In reaction to the wave of political pressure, Time Warner sold its interest in Interscope, which distributed some of rap's most inflammatory artists, and Time Warner Chairman Gerald Levin agreed to develop standards for the distribution and labeling of potentially objectionable music. Meanwhile, Jack Valenti, the president of the Motion Picture Association of America, has commented that the entertainment industry "must . . . act as if TV is indeed a factor in anti-social behavior," adding that the industry "has to be more responsible." Valenti, however, still questions the link between media and violence. A sociopath could be triggered by reading a Bible verse as easily as by watching a film. As Valenti says, "We can't create movies that are safe for deviants. Anything can set them off. We can't function at their level."

Fortunately, even the most fervent critics, like William Bennett, still shy away from advocating legislative remedies; Bennett declares he hopes to "shame" the industry into taking a more responsible stand. Meanwhile, the Democrats are still pushing for a federal law that will create a ratings system for all programs and require new TVs to have a V chip, which gives parents the power to shut off certain pornographic or violent channels.

With the presidential race heating up, however, the rhetorical battle isn't likely to cool down any time soon. Dole is demanding in his campaign ads that "Hollywood stop corrupting our children." He has said on the Senate floor: "Those who continue to deny that cultural messages can and do bore deep into the hearts and minds of our young people are deceiving themselves and ignoring reality."

24   Yet if Saturday morning cartoons are more a problem than Hollywood blockbusters or rap music, who's ignoring reality?

Personal Response

List the names of Saturday morning cartoons you remember watching as a child. Which of them do you recall as being violent? What forms did the violence take? Do you think the violence in cartoons shaped you or affected your behavior in any way?

Questions for Discussion

1. What is the "menace to society" that the title refers to?

2. What is it about media images of sex and violence that make them particularly likely targets of politicians during election years? What is your opinion of such attacks? Do you think there are other, more pressing issues politicians ought to address?

3. Summarize in your own words the debate over the link between the media and violence. Does Davidson seem to lean toward one side? Explain your answer.

4. Davidson mentions the push to get a federal law requiring new television sets to have a V chip that would allow parents to prevent their children from viewing programs they feel are too explicitly sexual or violent (paragraph 22). Discuss how effective you think such a chip would be.

BEATING THE SAME OLD DEAD HORSE

Joe Saltzman

Joe Saltzman is Associate Mass Media Editor of USA Today *and is a professor of journalism in the University of Southern California School of Journalism in Los Angeles. This essay appeared on the "Words & Images" page of the November 1993 issue of* USA Today Magazine.

Whenever everything looks the bleakest and there seems to be no political way out of the severe social and economic problems facing the nation, Congress always can be counted on to come up with a crusade against sex and violence on television. It has happened repeatedly for the last 40 years and undoubtedly will again in the future. It's a safe and popular subject, one that doesn't involve taking away benefits from voters or increasing taxes. It's foolproof, especially when wrapped in a patriotic campaign to save children. Everyone wants to do something good for the kids, to protect them from the evils that men and women do and no one but adults seem to know about.

Nobody seems to want violence or sex on television except the viewers. Humanists and moralists abhor violence because they say it inures young viewers to the pain and suffering of others, and they abhor sex because they say it promotes promiscuity and, in the age of AIDs, a dangerous lifestyle. Feminists say they hate both because they feel all of it is anti-female. Ministers and educators say they hate both because they believe TV should provide healthy, life-affirming experiences to the young, not sordid, vicious experiences. Publicly, Congressmen and women don't want sex or violence on TV for all of these reasons. Privately, they adore it because, for four decades, it has given them a safe port free from the real horrors—government taxes and spending, the deficit, health care, gun control, and crime prevention.

The latest wrinkle, labeling violent programming—and undoubtedly sexual programming in the future—is as absurd as the debate itself. All any kid who *really* wants to see sex and violence has to do is turn to cable, run down to the video store, or go to the movies.

4   Watching, a female police officer being attacked by a burglar on TV before she shoots him in the face is nothing compared to monsters murdering everyone in sight with axes, chain saws, butcher knives, sawed-off shotguns, and explosives. If you want real violence, take a look at the biggest-grossing action films: "Lethal Weapon" (and all of its sequels) or any Arnold Schwarzenegger, Sylvester Stallone, or Chuck Norris pectoral extravaganza. Want to really be grossed out? Take a look at any in the "Alien" or "Robocop" or "Terminator" series; those martial-arts films with soundtracks guaranteed to catch every breaking bone and body in sight; "Halloween" or Freddy Krueger in any of his vicious incarnations; or almost anything from Stephen King.

Watching a soap opera discreetly showing two naked bodies making love is nothing compared to the soft-core porn available on the big screen or late-night cable. Most movies have gone beyond a roll in the hay. Take a look at "Basic Instinct" or "Body of Evidence." They offer cleverly choreographed sexual violence, designed to titillate.

The debate over TV violence would be meaningless if it didn't distract legislators, entertainers, and the public from more serious issues at hand that can't be blown away with publicity and grandstanding. TV producers worry once again that a rating system labeling violence (and sex is sure to be next) will have a chilling effect on their creativity and provocative programming. That will only come about if television executives panic and kick some of their highest-rated programs off the air. But that won't happen. There may be more editing of violent and sexy theatrical films shown on TV, more blue penciling of strong violence or rough sexual behavior and language, but that too will pass. Maybe concerned producers even will hire writers to beef up story and character, and not rely on special effects and raunchy sex, but that too will pass because network executives want to keep their constituents happy.

Sex and violence always are good targets because, at first blush, everyone, publicly at least, wants them off TV. Privately, it's a different matter. Just look at the ratings. Many of the most popular programs of the past and present, whether they be "Hunter" or "Miami Vice," "Hill Street Blues" or "St. Elsewhere," "L.A. Law" or "Married . . . with Children" were and are popular because they pour(ed) on lots of action—physical or verbal violence or sex, or both. Sex and violence have been an intricate part of art and entertainment since recorded history because sex and violence involve the deepest and most absorbing parts of our being and history.

8   Reality programs and newsmagazines now dominate the networks' prime time as the genre of the day. They tell the same stories their fictional counterparts do, but cover them with the cloaks of actuality and authenticity. Like entertainment docudramas, most of the time these programs skillfully blend fact and fiction, but they're popular because they sell real sex and real violence perpetrated by real people. "Real" always has been more attractive than fiction. By focusing on the underbelly of the U.S., "America's Most Wanted," "Cops," and other reality shows offer the kind of programming young and old Americans always have liked best—stories involving violent and sometimes sexual events.

Isn't it time for responsible adults to quit beating a dead horse and get on with the important things in life? The human body always will be involved in some form of grappling, sexual or otherwise. Let it go at that. Turn off those programs you don't want your kids to watch. Don't let them go to the movies without your permission. Supervise what they read. And let the rest of us get on with our busy and sometimes desperate lives, where all that seems to make sense at the end of a hard day is to come home, kick off our shoes, grab a beer, and watch two gorgeous people making love or bashing each other into pulp. Freedom of choice—it's the American way.

Personal Response

Saltzman makes the point several times that "nobody seems to want violence or sex on television except the viewers" (paragraph 2). Do you agree with him?

Questions for Discussion

1. What especially bothers Saltzman about critics of television programming?

2. Why does Saltzman think that complaining about sex and violence on television is "beating a dead horse"? Do you find his reasoning sound?

3. Saltzman calls the proposal to label violent television programs "absurd." What reasons does he give for doubting the effectiveness of such a labeling system? What is your position on the issue of labeling television programs?

4. What do you think of the alternatives to crusading against sex and violence on television that Saltzman suggests in his last paragraph?

Suggestions for Writing About Television

1. With John Davidson's "Menace to Society" in mind, watch Saturday morning children's programs on television for several hours, paying particular attention to

the programs' violent component. Then write an analysis of the shows you watched. One approach to this assignment is to address your comments to a particular audience: parents of young children, the president of one of the major television networks, or the producers or sponsors of the programs you watched. If you find the violent component to be negligible, then focus on other aspects of the programs that you either liked or disliked, explaining why by citing examples from the programs.

2. Argue in support of or against a federal law requiring new television sets to have a V chip that would allow parents to prevent their children from viewing programs they feel are too explicitly sexual or violent.

3. Select several daytime talk shows such as those mentioned in Joshua Gamson's "Do Ask, Do Tell" and analyze the programs in terms of subject matter, audience reaction to the programs' guests, behavior of the guests, and attitude of the hosts toward the subject, the guests, and the audience. What conclusions can you draw from your brief survey of daytime talk shows?

4. Write an essay in which you respond to Joshua Gamson's suggestion in "Do Ask, Do Tell" that "the fact that talk shows are exploitative spectacles does not negate the fact that they are also opportunities" (paragraph 20). Explain what you understand him to mean by this statement and explain the degree to which you agree with him, stating reasons for your position.

5. Joe Saltzman in "Beating the Same Old Dead Horse" maintains that critics of television sex and violence should stop complaining because of the easy availability of movies that are much more violent or sexually explicit than television programs. Write an essay in which you explain your stand on this issue. Do you agree with Saltzman or with critics of television, or do you have an entirely different perspective on the subject?

6. If you are a regular viewer of television soap operas, respond to Carol Traynor Williams' description of the '90s soap opera male in her essay "Soap Opera Men in the '90s: Signs of Fearful Times." To what extent do you share her conclusions about their portrayal?

7. Watch at least several hours of the television soap operas that Carol Traynor Williams mentions in "Soap Opera Men in the '90s: Signs of Fearful Times," preferably over a period of several days or a week, for their portrayal of male characters. Summarize your findings and explain what conclusions you draw from them. To what extent does your assessment of soap opera males agree with that of Williams?

8. Research the portrayal of female characters or of contemporary social issues in soap operas such as those Carol Traynor Williams mentions in "Soap Opera Men in the '90s: Signs of Fearful Times."

9. Select a particular kind of television program such as situation comedy or drama and do an analysis of one aspect of television programming addressed in any of the essays in this section.

CHAPTER 7

ETHICS, MORALS, AND VALUES

Ethics, morals, and values are closely related in meaning and are often used interchangeably. According to the *American Heritage Dictionary, ethics* are the rules of standards governing the conduct of a person or members of a profession, as in *medical or legal ethics. Morals* also apply to rules of conduct but in a broader sense than ethics. Morals have to do with habits of conduct with regard to standards of right and wrong, as in *a person of loose morals* or *a decline in public morals.* Finally, *values,* in the context of ethics and morals, have to do with principles, standards, or qualities considered worthwhile or desirable, as in *family values.* The authors represented in this chapter are interested in exploring guidelines for ethical and moral behavior. Their essays focus on subjects that involve standards of conduct, standards of right and wrong, or standards of worthwhile behavior.

In the first piece, Ellen Goodman in "It's Failure, Not Success" takes exception to a definition of success advanced in a popular self-help book. Maintaining that it is not all right to be greedy or dishonest even if one becomes rich as a result, Goodman explains where she draws the line between what is morally acceptable and what is immoral. Next, Kurt Wiesenfeld, a physics professor at Georgia Tech, laments the behavior of students who disregard the connection between grades and performance by asking for a higher grade than they deserve at the end of the semester. In "Making the Grade," he explains the connection he sees among such student behavior, the superficial values of American society, an erosion in academic standards, and the potentially fatal effects of those things.

In "Woodstock's Message Is Still True," Steven Doloff explains his belief that the 1969 Woodstock Music Festival embodied the American dream of spiritual community. His essay suggests that a reconsideration of that 1960s music festival might serve the younger generation of the 1990s as a useful reminder of "the need to dream Walt Whitman's, the Rev. Dr. Martin Luther King's, and Woodie Guthrie's optimistic American dreams and to find their own Woodstocks."

Rabbi Joseph Telushkin addresses an issue of personal responsibility, the ethics of speech. In "Words That Hurt, Words That Heal: How to Choose Words Wisely and Well," he reminds us that the Golden Rule applies not just to behavior but to speech as well. On an entirely different topic but still addressing the importance of personal responsibility, Alan Thein Durning in "Can't Live

Without It" analyzes the global reach of advertisements and assesses both the environmental and cultural impact of the advertising industry. He is concerned about "earth-threatening consumption levels" and the role the advertising industry plays in encouraging behaviors that are potentially deadly: resource depletion, environmental pollution, and habitat degradation.

Three selections in this chapter provide differing viewpoints on the controversial matter of euthanasia, an act which many believe to have grave ethical and moral implications. Roger Rosenblatt in "The Quality of Mercy Killing" discusses the controversial case of Roswell Gilbert's mercy killing of his wife that received widespread news coverage and provoked heated public debate. He calls for passion and understanding in such tragic cases, while at the same time acknowledging the wrenching moral dilemmas they pose. Following Rosenblatt's short piece, Derek Humphrey, an active proponent of assisted suicide, explores in more detail and defends the actions of Roswell Gilbert in "Mercy Denied to Roswell Gilbert." Finally, Charles Krauthammer in "First and Last, Do No Harm," takes the position that allowing doctors to aid people in committing suicide is unconscionable.

The chapter ends with a short story by Albert Camus, the existential philosopher and writer born in Algeria when it was still a French colony and who later moved to France, where he joined the Resistance. During the Algerian war in the 1950s, his loyalties were divided between the Arab nationalists and the French colonists. His story "The Guest" reflects his personal conflict in its portrayal of the dilemma of a man trying to decide between conflicting responsibilities.

IT'S FAILURE, NOT SUCCESS

Ellen Goodman

Ellen Goodman was born in Boston and began her career as a reporter for Newsweek *after graduating with a bachelor's degree from Radcliffe College. She worked for the* Detroit Free Press *before becoming a columnist for the* Boston Globe *in 1967. Her column, "At Large," has been syndicated by the Washington Post Writers Group since 1976. In 1980 she won a Pulitzer Prize for distinguished commentary. She has published a study of human change,* Turning Points *(1979), and many of her columns have been collected in* Close to Home *(1979),* At Large *(1981),* Keeping in Touch *(1985), and* Making Sense *(1989). "It's Failure, Not Success" was published in the* Boston Globe *in 1987.*

I knew a man who went into therapy about three years ago because, as he put it, he couldn't live with himself any longer. I didn't blame him. The guy was a bigot, a tyrant and a creep.

In any case, I ran into him again after he'd finished therapy. He was still a bigot, a tyrant and a creep, *but* . . . he had learned to live with himself.

Now, I suppose this was an accomplishment of sorts. I mean, nobody else could live with him. But it seems to me that there are an awful lot of people running around and writing around these days encouraging us to feel good about what we should feel terrible about, and to accept in ourselves what we should change.

4   The only thing they seem to disapprove of is disapproval. The only judgment they make is against being judgmental, and they assure us that we have nothing to feel guilty about except guilt itself. It seems to me that they are all intent on proving that I'm OK and You're OK, when in fact, I may be perfectly dreadful and you may be unforgivably dreary, and it may be—gasp!—*wrong*.

What brings on my sudden attack of judgmentitis is success, or rather, *Success!*—the latest in a series of exclamation-point books all concerned with How to Make It.

In this one, Michael Korda is writing a recipe book for success. Like the other authors, he leapfrogs right over the "Shoulds" and into the "Hows." He eliminates value judgments and edits out moral questions as if he were Fanny Farmer and the subject was the making of a blueberry pie.

It's not that I have any reason to doubt Mr. Korda's advice on the way to achieve success. It may very well be that successful men wear handkerchiefs stuffed neatly in their breast pockets, and that successful single women should carry suitcases to the office on Fridays whether or not they are going away for the weekend.

8   He may be realistic when he says that "successful people generally have very low expectations of others." And he may be only slightly cynical when he writes: "One of the best ways to ensure success is to develop expensive tastes or marry someone who has them."

And he may be helpful with his handy hints on how to sit next to someone you are about to overpower.

But he simply finesses the issues of right and wrong—silly words, embarrassing words that have been excised like warts from the shiny surface of the new how-to books. To Korda, guilt is not a prod, but an enemy that he slays on page four. Right off the bat, he tells the would-be successful reader that:

- It's OK to be greedy.

- It's OK to look out for Number One.

- It's OK to be Machiavellian (if you can get away with it).

- It's OK to recognize that honesty is not always the best policy (provided you don't go around saying so).

- And it's always OK to be rich.

Well, in fact, it's not OK. It's not OK to be greedy, Machiavellian, dishonest. It's not always OK to be rich. There is a qualitative difference between succeeding by making napalm or by making penicillin. There is a difference between climbing the ladder of success, and macheteing a path to the top.

12   Only someone with the moral perspective of a mushroom could assure us that this was all OK. It seems to me that most Americans harbor ambivalence toward success, not for neurotic reasons, but out of a realistic perception of what it demands.

Success is expensive in terms of time and energy and altered behavior—the sort of behavior he describes in the grossest of terms: "If you can undermine your boss and replace him, fine, do so, but never express anything but respect and loyalty for him while you're doing it."

This author—whose *Power!* topped the best-seller list last year—is intent on helping rid us of that ambivalence which is a signal from our conscience. He is like the other "Win!" "Me First!" writers, who try to make us comfortable when we should be uncomfortable.

They are all Doctor Feelgoods, offering us placebo prescriptions instead of strong medicine. They give us a way to live with ourselves, perhaps, but not a way to live with each other. They teach us a whole lot more about "Failure!" than about success.

Personal Response

Explain your own position on Goodman's statement in paragraph 11 that "it's not always O.K. to be rich."

Questions for Discussion

1. How does Michael Korda's book *Success!* define "success"? What does Goodman find wrong with that definition and how would she define the word? How do you define "success"?

2. Summarize the complaints Goodman has about how-to-make-it books and the "me first" attitude they promote. What do you think she means in paragraph 15 when she writes: "They are all Doctor Feelgoods, offering us placebo prescriptions instead of strong medicine"?

3. Do you think Goodman anticipated an audience who buys the kind of book she is writing about or an audience already sympathetic to her view? How can you tell? What does Goodman's reference to "Machiavellian" (paragraphs 10–11) suggest about how she perceives her audience?

4. Describe the tone of this piece, as indicated by Goodman's word choice. For example, what effect do you think she wants to achieve when she uses figurative language such as "excised like warts" (paragraph 10) and "only someone with the moral perspective of a mushroom" (paragraph 12)? What level of diction is indicated by words like "creep" (paragraph 1) and "gasp!" (paragraph 4)?

5. Because this piece was originally written for a newspaper column, it has very short paragraphs. If you were evaluating Goodman's essay as if she were one of your classmates, where would you suggest she combine paragraphs to avoid so many one- or two-sentence paragraphs? Why do you think newspaper writing tends to use very short paragraphs while the kind of writing you do in your college work requires much longer paragraphs?

6. Besides being restricted to short paragraphs, newspaper columnists often do not have the space to fully develop their central ideas. If Goodman were writing this essay for a class assignment, where would you suggest that she expand or amplify her examples?

Giving students grades they don't deserve can have a negative effect on society

MAKING THE GRADE

Kurt Wiesenfeld

Kurt Wiesenfeld is a physicist who teaches at Georgia Tech in Atlanta. He wrote this essay for the "My Turn" column of the June 17, 1996, issue of Newsweek.

It was a rookie error. After 10 years I should have known better, but I went to my office the day after final grades were posted. There was a tentative knock on the door. "Professor Wiesenfeld? I took your Physics 2121 class? I flunked it? I wonder if there's anything I can do to improve my grade?" I thought: "Why are you asking me? Isn't it too late to worry about it? Do you dislike making declarative statements?"

experimental uncertain
for

After the student gave his tale of woe and left, the phone rang. "I got a D in your class. Is there any way you can change it to 'Incomplete'?" Then the e-mail assault began: "I'm shy about coming in to talk to you, but I'm not shy about asking for a better grade. Anyway, it's worth a try." The next day I had three phone messages from students asking *me* to call *them*. I didn't.

sorrow

Time was, when you received a grade, that was it. You might groan and moan, but you accepted it as the outcome of your efforts or lack thereof (and, yes, sometimes a tough grader). In the last few years, however, some students have developed a disgruntled-consumer approach. If they don't like their grade, they go to the "return" counter to trade it in for something better.

discontented/sulky

4   What alarms me is their indifference toward grades as an indication of personal effort and performance. Many, when pressed about why they think they deserve a better grade, admit they don't deserve one but would like one anyway. Having been raised on gold stars for effort and smiley faces for self-esteem, they've learned that they can get by without hard work and real talent if they can talk the professor into giving them a break. This attitude is beyond cynicism. There's a weird innocence to the assumption that one expects (even deserves) a better grade simply by begging for it. With that outlook, I guess I shouldn't be as flabbergasted as I was that 12 students asked me to change their grades *after* final grades were posted.

high-regard
astonish

That's 10 percent of my class who let three months of midterms, quizzes and lab reports slide until long past remedy. My graduate student calls it hyperrational thinking: if effort and intelligence don't matter, why should deadlines? What matters is getting a better grade through an unearned bonus, the academic equivalent of a freebie T shirt or toaster giveaway. Rewards are disconnected from the quality of one's work. An act and its consequences are unrelated, random events.

Their arguments for wheedling better grades often ignore academic performance. Perhaps they feel it's not relevant. "If my grade isn't raised to a D I'll lose my scholarship." "If you don't give me a C, I'll flunk out." One sincerely overwrought student pleaded, "If I don't pass, my life is over." This is tough stuff to deal with. Apparently, I'm responsible for someone's losing a scholarship, flunking out or deciding whether life has meaning. Perhaps these students see me as a commodities broker with something they want—a grade. Though intrinsically worthless, grades, if properly manipulated, can be traded for what has value: a degree, which means a job, which means money. The one thing college actually offers—a chance to learn—is considered irrelevant, even less than worthless, because of the long hours and hard work required.

In a society saturated with surface values, love of knowledge for its own sake does sound eccentric. The benefits of fame and wealth are more obvious. So is it right to blame students for reflecting the superficial values saturating our society?

8   Yes, of course it's right. These guys had better take themselves seriously now, because our country will be forced to take them seriously later, when the stakes are much higher. They must recognize that their attitude is not only self-destructive, but socially destructive. The erosion of quality control—giving appropriate grades for actual accomplishments—is a major concern in my department. One colleague noted that a physics major could obtain a degree without ever answering a written exam question completely. How? By pulling in enough partial credit and extra credit. And by getting breaks on grades.

But what happens once she or he graduates and gets a job? That's when the misfortunes of eroding academic standards multiply. We lament that schoolchildren get "kicked upstairs" until they graduate from high school despite being illiterate and mathematically inept, but we seem unconcerned with college graduates whose less blatant deficiencies are far more harmful if their accreditation exceeds their qualifications.

Most of my students are science and engineering majors. If they're good at getting partial credit but not at getting the answer right, then the new bridge breaks or the new drug doesn't work. One finds examples here in Atlanta. Last year a light tower in the Olympic Stadium collapsed, killing a worker. It collapsed because an engineer miscalculated how much weight it could hold. A new 12-story dormitory could develop dangerous cracks due to a foundation that's uneven by more than six inches. The error resulted from incorrect data being fed into a computer. I drive past that dorm daily on my way to work, wondering if a foundation crushed under kilotons of weight is repairable or if this structure will have to be demolished. Two 10,000-pound steel beams at the new natatorium collapsed in March, crashing into the student athletic complex. (Should we give partial credit since no one was hurt?) Those are real-world consequences of errors and lack of expertise.

But the lesson is lost on the grade-grousing 10 percent. Say that you won't (not can't, but won't) change the grade they deserve to what they want, and they're frequently bewildered or angry. They don't think it's fair that they're judged according to their performance, not their desires or "potential." They don't think it's fair that they should jeopardize their scholarships or be in danger of flunking out simply because they could not or did not do their work. But it's more than fair; it's necessary to help preserve a minimum standard of quality that our society needs to maintain safety and integrity. I don't know if the 13th-hour students will learn that lesson, but I've learned mine. From now on, after final grades are posted, I'll lie low until the next quarter starts.

Personal Response

Have you ever asked a teacher for a higher grade or received a grade you felt you did not deserve? If so, explain the circumstances.

Questions for Discussion

1. What bothers Wiesenfeld about students asking for a better grade?

2. Discuss this sentence: "The one thing college actually offers—a chance to learn—is considered irrelevant, even less than worthless, because of the long hours and hard work required" (paragraph 6).

3. What potential consequences does Wiesenfeld see of the erosion of academic standards and the emphasis some of his students place on grades, not education?

4. Wiesenfeld asks, "Is it right to blame students for reflecting the superficial values saturating our society?" (paragraph 7) and then answers, "Yes, of course it's right" (paragraph 8). Why does Wiesenfeld believe it is right to blame students for adopting society's values? To what extent do you agree with him?

5. Wiesenfeld seems to suggest that "gold stars for effort and smiley faces for self-esteem" are not worthwhile incentives or rewards for students (paragraph 4). What does he see as the effect of such rewards? Do you agree with him?

WOODSTOCK'S MESSAGE IS STILL TRUE

Steven Doloff

Steven Doloff is Associate Professor of English at Pratt Institute in New York City. His essays on culture and education have appeared in the New York Times, *the* Washington Post, *the* Philadelphia Inquirer, *the* Boston Globe, *and* The Chronicle of Higher Education. *This essay appeared in the August 8, 1991, edition of the* Philadelphia Inquirer.

Eleven years ago, when I asked a class of New York City college students a question about the Woodstock music festival, no one had even heard of it. While the 20th anniversary celebration in Bethel, N.Y., two summers ago of this rock concert may have provided today's teenagers with the fact of the event, I doubt that the celebration's recycling of baby boomer nostalgia left us with the most historically accurate or useful grasp of the festival.

As Woodstock's practically ignored 22d anniversary approaches (Aug. 15–17), commentary on the event continues to omit its multiple connections to the Vietnam War and the social reform of the time. Perhaps this is because these issues still fester unresolved in the American psyche. Perhaps this is also because the conservative habit, now over a decade old, of "kicking the '60s" for all of today's social ills has reduced the festival to a symbol of sybaritic self-indulgence. However, if Woodstock is to be recorded as some kind of sociological watermark of an era, it will be best understood as a response to its context of civil unrest and, what's more, as a timely reaffirmation of a national ideal.

Despite its commercial aspects, Woodstock momentarily embodied the deeply characteristic American dream of a spiritual community, of an emotionally harmonious, all-inclusive sense of "us." Perhaps the most romantic conception of this ideal was envisioned by the poet Walt Whitman 130 years ago, but its tradition reaches back to our Pilgrim beginnings. The novelty in the summer of 1969, however, was that this particular expression of the ideal became amplified and broadcast by the electronic media at unprecedented volume and speed to an already sensitized and self-conscious youth culture of unprecedented size.

4   In hindsight, the festival's sense of musical communion appears almost eerie. Rock-and-roll, itself derived from early black gospel music, became, not inappropriately, the emotionally unifying anthem for America's otherwise secularized youth. This may explain why Jimi Hendrix's Woodstock version of "The Star-Spangled Banner," as irony laden as it was, remains the most stirring rendition many of those present have ever heard.

This '60s community of the young, like the reach of the music, owed much to the media's enhanced powers. The baby boomers since birth were made conscious of their collective echo on the radio and reflection on the television. The street chant at the tumultuous 1968 Democratic convention in Chicago, "The whole world is watching," was simply the first self-aware cry of Marshall McLuhan's global village children exercising their discovered political clout.

So why so great a protestation of youthful community in the summer of 1969? As domestic strife over the Vietnam War and racial issues intensified, many of the middle-class boomers, on the brink of entering, if not the Army itself, then the ranks of a deeply divided and distressed American adulthood, innocently tried to hold off that entry by a kind of collective ritual at Woodstock and at innumerable lesser Woodstocks all over the country.

The "No rain! No rain!" chant sung by the crowd at Woodstock to ward off the storm spoke metaphoric volumes. Many of us wanted to believe we could will things better by fervently affirming and savoring our sense of community.

8   This psychological "Woodstock Nation," while initially nurtured by the media's attention, remained all too dependent upon the media's support. When media pundits used the violent December 1969 Altamont concert in California to declare a neat end to the ephemeral "Woodstock era" of peace and love, the bright reflection of youthful community rapidly disintegrated.

The depressing spiral of the early '70s and the Vietnam denouement were upon us, and the myth of Woodstock, like the decade's earlier Camelot of the Kennedy presidency, began to pass into the shining realm of nostalgia. "Bye, bye, Miss American pie."

This is the Woodstock that 22 years later I find myself attempting to explain to students in the abstracted, anecdotal and generally distorted form that such myths take on in classrooms. The final irony, I suppose, is the exasperation among some of today's younger generation with the recycling of '60s nostalgia in magazines, books, movies, etc. They complain that their youth is somehow overshadowed by that of their parents. They resent being told that they "missed" Woodstock. It's a legitimate complaint.

But it is also true that today's young share in culture and outlook much more with their middle-aged boomer parents than did the boomers with their parents. So a full and honest appraisal of the boomers' youthful idealistic aspirations may have some genuine social utility yet.

12   The America of the '90s is a nation still painfully divided by issues of race, sex, poverty and morality. The Persian Gulf war has in no way alleviated the host of American social problems and anxieties so intimately associated with what has become loosely referred to as the "Vietnam syndrome."

Among today's youth the prospect of entering adulthood in our society may well elicit as much apprehension as it did two decades ago. A fuller understanding of Woodstock, certainly, will not solve these problems. But it might serve as a useful reminder of our national ideal of a compassionate community, of the all-inclusive "us." Who knows, it may, even rekindle some enthusiasm for it among the disheartened of the boomer generation.

And how might reconsideration of a 22-year-old music festival serve today's youth, who while maybe more pragmatic and media savvy than their parents were, appear also more circumspect in their expectations of America? Perhaps, amid today's troubles, it will lead them to discover for themselves the need to dream Walt Whitman's, the Rev. Dr. Martin Luther King's and Woodie Guthrie's optimistic American dreams, and to find their own Woodstocks.

Personal Response

Explore your response to Doloff's comment in paragraph 10 that today's younger generation is exasperated "with the recycling of '60s nostalgia in magazines, books, movies, etc." How do you respond to his statement in paragraph 11 that today's youth have much more in common with their parents than their parents did with their own parents?

Questions for Discussion

1. According to Doloff, what did the 20th anniversary celebration of the Woodstock Music Festival fail to acknowledge?

2. Explain what Doloff means when he writes: "Despite its commercial aspects, Woodstock momentarily embodied the deeply characteristic American

dream of spiritual community" (paragraph 3)? To what extent do you agree with his assessment of this aspect of the American character?

3. What role does Doloff believe the media played in perpetuating the image of "the Woodstock nation"? What image does the phrase "the Woodstock nation" evoke for you?

4. What useful connections does Doloff believe can be made between the Woodstock generation and today's generation of young people? That is, how does he answer the question he poses at the beginning of his final paragraph: "And how might a reconsideration of a 22-year-old music festival serve today's youth"?

WORDS THAT HURT, WORDS THAT HEAL: HOW TO CHOOSE WORDS WISELY AND WELL

Joseph Telushkin

Joseph Telushkin received his rabbinical ordination from Yeshiva University and pursued graduate studies in Jewish History at Columbia University. He currently serves the Synagogue of the Performing Arts in Los Angeles. Telushkin is author of the Rabbi Winter mystery series as well as several books on Judaism, Jewish humor, Anti-Semitism, and Jewish history. His latest book is Words That Hurt, Words That Heal: How to Choose Words Wisely and Well *(1996). This selection was first presented as a speech during the September 1995 Center for Constructive Alternatives Seminar, "Fiction and Faith," at Hillsdale College and was subsequently published in* Imprimis.

Over the past decade, whenever I have lectured throughout the country on the powerful, and often negative, impact of words, I have asked audiences if they can go for twenty-four hours without saying any unkind words about, or to, anybody.

Invariably, a minority of listeners raise their hands signifying "yes," some laugh, and quite a large number call out, "no!"

I respond by saying, "Those who can't answer 'yes' must recognize that you have a serious problem. If you cannot go for twenty-four hours without drinking liquor, you are addicted to alcohol. If you cannot go for twenty-four hours without smoking, you are addicted to nicotine. Similarly, if you cannot go for twenty-four hours without saying unkind words about others, then you have lost control over your tongue."

4　　How can I compare the harm done by a bit of gossip or a few unpleasant words to the damage caused by alcohol and smoking? Well, just think about your own life for a minute. Unless you, or someone dear to you, has been the victim of terrible physical violence, chances are the worst pains you have suffered in life have come from words used cruelly—from ego-destroying criticism, excessive anger, sarcasm, public and private humiliation, hurtful nicknames, betrayal of secrets, rumors, and malicious gossip.

Testing Your Speech

There is no area of life in which so many of us systematically violate the Golden Rule. Thus if you were about to enter a room and heard the people inside talking about you, chances are what you would least like to hear them talking about are your character flaws and the intimate details of your social life. Yet, when you are with friends and the conversation turns to people not present, what aspects of their lives are you and your companions most likely to explore? Is it not their character flaws and the intimate details of their social lives?

If you do not participate in such talk, congratulations. But before asserting this as a definite fact, try monitoring your conversation for two days. Note on a piece of paper every time you say something negative about someone who is not present. Also record when others do so, as well as your reactions when that happens. Do you try to silence the speaker, or do you ask for more details?

To ensure the test's accuracy, make no effort to change the content of your conversations throughout the two-day period, and do not try to be kinder than usual in assessing another's character and actions.

8   Most of us who take this test are unpleasantly surprised.

Negative comments we make about absent companions is but one way we wound with words; we also often cruelly hurt those *to whom* we are speaking. For example, many of us, when enraged, grossly exaggerate the wrong done by the person who has provoked our ire. If the anger expressed is disproportionate to the provocation (as often occurs when parents rage at children), it is unfair, often inflicts great hurt and damage, and thus is unethical.

All too often, many of us criticize others with harsh, offensive words, turn disputes into quarrels, belittle or humiliate others, and inflict wounds that last a lifetime.

The Power of Words

One reason that many otherwise "good" people use words irresponsibly and cruelly is that they regard the injuries inflicted by words as intangible and therefore minimize the damage they can inflict. For generations, children taunted by playmates have been taught to respond, "Sticks and stones can break my bones, but words (or names) can never hurt me." But does anyone really think that a child exposed to such abuse believes it?

12   An old Jewish teaching compares the tongue to an arrow: "Why not another weapon—a sword, for example?" one rabbi asks. "Because," he is told, "if a man unsheathes his sword to kill his friend, and his friend pleads with him and begs for mercy, the man may be mollified and return the sword to its scabbard. But an arrow, once it is shot, cannot be returned."

The rabbi's comparison is more than just a useful metaphor. Because words can be used to inflict devastating and irrevocable suffering, Jewish teachings go so far as to compare cruel words to murder. A penitent thief can return the money he has stolen; a murderer, no matter how sincerely he repents, cannot restore his victim to life. Similarly, one who damages another's reputation through malicious gossip or who humiliates another publicly can never fully undo the damage.

Words, quite simply, are very powerful. Indeed, the Bible teaches that God created the world through words. At the beginning of Genesis we learn, "And God said, 'Let there be light,' and there was light." I would submit that human beings, like God, also create with words. Consider the fact that most, if not all, of us have had the experience of reading a novel and being so moved by the fate of a character that we have cried, even though the character who has so moved us doesn't exist. All that happened was that writer took a blank piece of paper, put words on it, and through words alone created a human being so totally real that he or she is capable of evoking our deepest emotions.

Words are powerful enough to lead to love, but they can also lead to hatred and terrible pain. We must be extremely careful how we use them.

16 A Jewish folktale, set in nineteenth-century Eastern Europe, tells of a man who went through a small community slandering the rabbi. One day, feeling suddenly remorseful, he begged the rabbi for forgiveness and offered to undergo any form of penance to make amends. The rabbi told him to take a feather pillow from his home, cut it open, scatter the feathers to the wind. The man did as he was told and returned to the rabbi. He asked, "Am I now forgiven?"

"Almost," came the response. "You just have to perform one last task: Go and gather all the feathers."

"But that's impossible," the man protested, "for the wind has already scattered them."

"Precisely," the rabbi answered.

20 The rabbi in this story understands that words define our place in the world. Once our place—in other words, our reputation—is defined, it is very hard to change, particularly if it is negative.

President Andrew Jackson who, along with his wife was the subject of relentless malicious gossip, once noted, "The murderer only takes the life of the parent and leaves his character as a goodly heritage to his children, while the slanderer takes away his goodly reputation and leaves him a living monument to his children's disgrace."

Considerate, fair and civilized use of words is every bit as necessary in the larger society as in one-on-one relationships. Throughout history, words used unfairly have promoted hatred and even murder. African Americans, for example, were long branded with words that depicted them as subhuman. Those who first described blacks in such terms hoped to enable whites to view them as different and inferior to themselves. This was important because, if whites perceived blacks as fully human, otherwise "decent" people could never have tolerated their persecution, enslavement, or lynching.

Similarly, when the radical Black Panther Party referred to police as "pigs" during the 1960s, its intention was not to hurt policemen's feelings but to dehumanize them and so establish in people's minds that murdering a policeman was really only like killing a dumb animal.

The Biblical Ethics of Speech

24   The biblical ethics of speech derive in large measure from a verse in Leviticus: "You shall not go about as a talebearer among your people" (19:16), which, not coincidentally, appears only two verses before the Bible's most famous law, "Love your neighbor as yourself" (19:18).

Because the commandment is so terse, it is difficult to know exactly what the Bible means by "talebearing." Does this law mean that it is forbidden to talk about any aspect of other people's lives (e.g., telling a friend, "I was at a party at Sam and Sally's house last night. It's absolutely gorgeous what they've done with their kitchen.")? Or does the verse only outlaw damning insinuations (e.g., "When Sam went away on that business trip last month, I saw his wife Sally at a real fancy restaurant with this good-looking guy. She didn't see me, because they were too busy making eyes at each other.")? Is it talebearing, for that matter, to pass on true stories (e.g., "Sally confessed to Betty she's having an affair. Sam ought to know what goes on when he's out of town.")?

The Bible itself never fully answers these questions. But for centuries Jewish teachers have elaborated upon the biblical law and formulated, in ascending order of seriousness, three types of speech that we should decrease or eliminate: non-defamatory and true remarks about others; negative, though true, stories that lower the esteem in which people hold the person being discussed (in Hebrew, *lashon ha-ra*); and slander—that is, lies or rumors that are negative and false (in Hebrew, *motzi shem ra*).

Non-Defamatory and True Remarks

The comment, "I was at a party at Sam and Sally's house last night. It's absolutely gorgeous what they've done with their kitchen," is non-defamatory and true. What possible reason could there be for discouraging people from exchanging such innocuous, even complimentary, information?

28   For one thing, the listener might not find the information so innocuous. While one person is describing how wonderful the party was, the other might well wonder, "Why wasn't I invited? I had them over to my house just a month ago."

But the more important reason for discouraging "innocuous" gossip is that it rarely remains so. Suppose I suggest that you and a friend spend twenty minutes talking about a mutual acquaintance. How likely is it that you will devote the entire time to exchanging stories about his or her niceness?

Maybe you will, that is if the person you are discussing is Mother Teresa. Otherwise the conversation will likely take on a negative tone. For most of us, exchanging critical news and evaluations about others is far more interesting and enjoyable than exchanging accolades. If I were to say to you, "Janet is a wonderful person. There's just *one thing* I can't stand about her," on what aspects of Janet's character do you think the rest of our conversation will most likely focus? The reason is that "Nobody ever gossips about other people's secret virtues," as British philosopher Bertrand Russell once noted. What most interests most people about others are their character flaws and private scandals.

Even if you do not let the discussion shift in a negative direction, becoming an ethical speaker forces you to anticipate the inadvertent harm that your words might cause. For example, although praising a friend might seem like a laudable act, doing so in the presence of someone who dislikes her will probably do your friend's reputation more harm than good. Your words may well provoke her antagonist to voice the reasons for his or her dislike, particularly if you leave soon after making your positive remarks.

32   Indeed, the danger of praise leading to damage is likely at the root of the Book of Proverbs' rather enigmatic observation: "He who blesses his neighbor in a loud voice in the morning, it will later be thought a curse" (27:14). Bible commentaries understand this to mean that fame and notoriety can ultimately damage a person's good name—or worse.

Negative Truths

As a rule most people seem to think that there is nothing morally wrong in spreading negative information about another as long as the information is true. But ordinary experience proves otherwise. The Jewish tradition also takes a very different view. Perhaps that is why the Hebrew term *lashon ha-ra* (literally "bad language" or "bad tongue") has no precise equivalent in English. For, unlike slander, which is universally condemned as immoral because it is false, *lashon ha-ra* is true. It is the dissemination of *accurate* information that will lower the status of the person to whom it refers; hence I translate it as "negative truths."

Jewish law forbids spreading negative truths about others unless the person to whom you are speaking needs the information. To do so is a very serious offense, one that has been addressed by many non-Jewish ethicists as well. Two centuries ago, the Swiss theologian and poet Jonathan K. Lavater offered a good guideline concerning the spreading of such news: "Never tell evil of a man if you do not know it for a certainty, and if you know it for a certainty, then ask yourself, 'Why should I tell it?'"

Intention has a great deal to do with the circumstances in which it is prohibited to speak negative truths. The same statement, depending on the context, can constitute a compliment or a mean-spirited attempt to diminish another person's status. For example, if you relate that a person known to have limited funds gave a hundred dollars to a certain charity, you will probably raise the person's stature because people will be impressed at his or her generosity. But, if you say of an individual known to be wealthy that he or she gave a hundred dollars to the same cause, the effect will be to diminish respect for the person; he or she will now be thought of as "cheap."

36   Unfortunately, this realization does not deter many people from speaking negative truths. Gossip often is so interesting that it impels many of us to violate the Golden Rule to "Do unto others as you would have others do unto you." Although we are likely to acknowledge that we would want embarrassing information about ourselves kept quiet, many of us refuse to be equally discreet concerning others' sensitive secrets.

Slander

The most grievous violation of ethical speech is, of course, the spreading of malicious falsehoods, what Jewish law calls *"motzi shem ra,"* or "giving another a bad name." To destroy someone's good name is to commit a kind of murder—that is why it is called "character assassination." Indeed, it has led to literal murder. During Europe's devastating fourteenth-century Black Plague, anti-Semites and others seeking scapegoats spread the lie that Jews had caused the Plague by poisoning village wells. Within a few months, enraged mobs murdered tens of thousands of Jews.

Too often, the victims of slanderous tongues suffer terribly. In Shakespeare's thirty-eight plays, there is no villain more vile than *Othello's* Iago, whose evil is perpetrated almost exclusively through words. At the outset, Iago vows to destroy the Moorish general Othello for bypassing him for promotion. Knowing Othello's jealous nature, Iago convinces him that his new wife, Desdemona, is having an affair with another man. The charge seems preposterous, but Iago repeats the accusation again and again, and he arranges the circumstantial evidence necessary to destroy Desdemona's credibility. Soon, Othello comes to believe the slander, and he murders his beloved, only to learn almost immediately that Iago's words were false. For Othello, "Hell," as an old aphorism teaches, "is truth seen too late."

What if we could share our consciousness of the power of words with many others—even the whole nation? I have proposed an annual "Speak No Evil" Day, starting on May 14, 1996. Senators Connie Mack (R-FL) and Joseph Lieberman (D-CT) have introduced a bipartisan resolution in the U.S. Senate that requires the co-sponsorship of fifty senators. This resolution would establish such a day, requesting that the President issue a proclamation calling on the American people to:

- Eliminate all hurtful and unfair talk for twenty-four hours;

- Transmit negative information only when necessary;

- Monitor and regulate how they speak to others;

- Strive to keep anger under control;

- Argue fairly, and not allow disputes to degenerate into name-calling or other forms of verbal abuse;

- And speak about others with the same kindness and fairness that they wish others to exercise when speaking about them.

40   A "Speak No Evil" Day would plant the seed of a more permanent shift in our consciousness. It would hopefully touch everyone—from journalists, politicians, activists, teachers, ministers, and businessmen to mothers, fathers, brothers, sisters, sons and daughters.

A rabbi once told me that his grandmother used to say, "It is not within everyone's power to be beautiful, but all of us can make sure that the words that come out of our mouths are." A "Speak No Evil" Day will be a twenty-four hour period of verbal beauty.

It will be a day when a young child frequently teased by his classmates, and called by an ugly nickname, can go to school confident no one will say a cruel word to him.

It will be a day on which an employee with a sharp-tongued boss can go to work without fearing that he or she will be verbally abused.

44   It will be a day on which that sharp-tongued boss, the type who says, "I don't get ulcers, I give them," might come to understand how vicious such a statement is and will say nothing that will cause pain to another.

It will be a day when a congressional candidate who suffered a nervous breakdown will not have to worry that his opponent will use this painful episode to publicly humiliate him.

It will be a day when a husband who always complains tells his wife what he loves about her.

It will be a day when a person of one race will see beyond the color of another person's skin.

48   It will be a day when people will use the words that heal others' emotional wounds, not those that inflict them.

Only on such a day will we will experience a taste of heaven on earth. A Jewish proverb teaches, "If you will it, it is no fantasy." If we only want it enough, a "Speak No Evil" Day is possible. Let us try.

Personal Response

Describe a time when you were deeply hurt because of what someone said to or about you. How would you answer Telushkin's question asking if you could "go for twenty-four hours without saying any unkind words about, or to, anybody" (paragraph 1)?

Questions for Discussion

1. Discuss Telushkin's statements about the power of words. How can words "define our place in the world" (paragraph 20)? How seriously do you take your own words?

2. Summarize the three categories of speech outlined by Jewish law. Which would be the most difficult to decrease or eliminate? What do you think of the comparison between slanderous speech and murder?

3. Discuss Telushkin's proposal for an annual "Speak No Evil" Day. How widely do you think such a day would be observed? Do you think that observing such a day annually would achieve the results Telushkin lists in the closing paragraphs?

4. Monitor your speech, following Telushkin's directions in paragraphs 6 and 7. Then compare the results with your classmates. Are you surprised at the results?

CAN'T LIVE WITHOUT IT

Alan Thein Durning

Alan Thein Durning is a senior researcher at Worldwatch Institute and author of How Much Is Enough? The Consumer Society and the Future of the World *(1992). This essay was written for the May–June 1993 issue of* World Watch.

Last January a single message was broadcast simultaneously in every inhabited part of the globe. The message was not "love thy neighbor" or "thou shalt not kill." It was "Drink Coke."

This first global advertisement was, on the face of it, simply a piece of technical showmanship—an inevitable one, considering the pace of change in telecommunications. On a symbolic level, however, it was something more. It was a neat encapsulation of the main trend in human communications worldwide: commercialization.

For better or for worse, almost all of humanity's 5.5 billion individuals, divided among 6,000 distinct cultures, are now soaking in the same gentle bath of advertising. The unctuous voices of the marketplace are insinuating themselves into ever more remote quarters of the globe and ever more private realms of human life.

4   Advertising has become one of the world's most premier cultural forces. Almost every living person knew the word "Coke," for example, long before the global ad. Two years ago, the trade journal *Adweek* published a two-page spread depicting Hitler, Lenin, Napoleon, and a Coke bottle. "Only one," read the caption, "launched a campaign that conquered the world. How did Coke succeed where history's most ambitious leaders failed? By choosing the right weapon. Advertising."

Aside from the arrogance of that statement, what is disturbing about it is its truth. Owing to a skillful and persistent marketing, Coke is sold in virtually every place people live. Go to the end of a rural road on any Third World continent, walk a day up a donkey trail to a hardscrabble village, and ask for a Coke. Odds are, you'll get one. This state of affairs—development workers call it "Coca-Colonization"—means that Coke's secret formula has probably reached more villages and slums than has clean drinking water or oral rehydration formula.

The point here is not to single out Coca-Cola—others would have circum-advertised the globe soon if the soft drink empire hadn't—but rather to question whether advertising has outgrown its legitimate role in human affairs. Advertisers maintain that their craft, far from being too widely practiced, is just beginning to achieve its destiny: to stimulate business growth, create jobs, and to unify humanity by eroding the ancient hatreds that divide us and joining us together in the universal fellowship of a Coke.

But from the perspective of the Earth's long-term health, the advertising industry looks somewhat different. Stripped to its essentials, contemporary advertising has three salient characteristics. It preys on the weaknesses of its host. It creates an insatiable hunger. And it leads to debilitating over-consumption. In the biological realm, things of that nature are called parasites.

8   If that rather pointed metaphor is apt, we are left with the sticky problem doctors face in treating any parasite: finding a medicine and a dosage that will kill the worm without poisoning the patient. How can we restrain the excesses of advertising without resorting to poisonous state censorship or curtailing the flow of information in society? Actions that are too heavy-handed, for example, could bankrupt the free—but advertising-dependent—press.

The Manufacture of Needs

The purpose of advertising, according to orthodox economic theory, is to provide us with information about the goods and services offered in the marketplace. Without that stream of information we consumers won't make informed choices, and Adam Smith's invisible hand will be not only invisible but also blind. We won't know when a better frozen dinner comes along, nor will we know where to get the best deal on a new car.

The contents of marketing messages themselves, however, show the simple-mindedness of that explanation. Classified ads and yellow page telephone directories would suffer if advertising were only about telling people who already want something where to get it and what it costs. Rather, advertising is intended to expand the pool of desires, awakening wants that would lie dormant otherwise—or, as critics say, manufacturing wants that would not otherwise exist.

Entire industries have manufactured a need for themselves. Writes one advertising executive, ads can serve "to make [people] self-conscious about matter of course things such as enlarged nose pores [and] bad breath." Historically, advertisers have especially targeted women, playing on personal insecurities and self-doubt by projecting impossible ideals of feminine beauty.

12   As B. Earl Puckett, then head of the department store chain Allied Stores Corporation, put it 40 years ago, "It is our job to make women unhappy with what they have." Thus for those born with short, skinny eyelashes, the message mongers offer hope. For those whose hair is too straight, or too curly, or grows in the

wrong places, for those whose skin is too dark or too light, for those whose body weight is distributed in anything but this year's fashion, advertising assures that synthetic salvation is close at hand.

Ads are stitched together from the eternal cravings of the human psyche. Their ingredients are images of sexual virility [sic], eternal youth, social belonging, individual freedom, and existential fulfillment. Advertisers sell not artifacts but lifestyles, attitudes, and fantasies, hitching their wares to the infinite yearnings of the soul.

They also exploit the desire individuals in mass societies feel to define a distinctive identity. Peter Kim, director of research and consumer behavior for the advertising agency J. Walter Thompson, says the role of brands in consumer society is "much akin to the role of myth in traditional societies. Choosing a brand becomes a way for one group of consumers to differentiate themselves from another."

Advertisers are extraordinarily sophisticated in the pursuit of these ends. The most finely wrought ads are masterpieces—combining stunning imagery, bracing speed, and compelling language to touch our innermost fears and fancies. Prime-time television commercials in the industrial countries pack more suggestion into a minute than anything previously devised.

16   From an anthropological perspective, ads are among the supreme creations of this era, standing in relation to our technological, consumer culture as the pyramids did to the ancients and the Gothic cathedrals to the medievals. Those structures embodied faith in the transcendent, acted out a quest for immortality, and manifested hierarchical social rankings. Advertisements, like our age, are mercurial, hedonistic, image-laden, and fashion-driven; they glorify the individual, idealize consumption as the route to personal fulfillment, and affirm technological progress as the motive force of density.

Advertising and the Earth

Of course, advertising is not the only force to promote consumption in today's world. That point is amply evident in the recent history of Eastern Europe. There where most advertising was illegal under the communist regimes of the past, popular desires for the Western consumer lifestyle were pervasive—indeed, they were among the forces that overthrew socialism. Communism had failed to deliver the goods.

Other forces driving the earth-threatening consumption levels of the world's affluent societies include everything from human nature's acquisitive streak to the erosion of informal, neighborhood sharing networks that has accompanied the rising mobility of our time. They include social pressures to keep up with the Joneses, the proliferation of "convenience" goods to meet the time-crunch created by rising working hours, national economic policies that favor consumption over savings and raw materials production over efficiency and recycling, and the prevailing trend in urban design—away from compact, human-scale cities toward anonymous, auto-scale malls and sprawl.

All these things—plus the weight of sheer purchasing power—define one of the world's most pressing environmental challenges: to trim resource consumption in industrial countries. Citizens of these nations typically consume 10 times as much energy as their developing country counterparts, along with 10 times the timber, 13 times the iron and steel, 14 times the paper, 18 times the synthetic chemicals, and 19 times the aluminum.

20   The consumer societies take the lion's share of the output of the world's mines, logging operations, petroleum refineries, metal smelters, paper mills, and other high-impact industrial plants. These enterprises, in turn, account for a disproportionate share of the resource depletion, environmental pollution, and habitat degradation that humans have caused worldwide. A world full of consumer societies is an ecological impossibility.

And even if advertising is not the sole force driving up consumption, it is an important one. It is a powerful champion of the consumer lifestyle, and is spreading its influence widely.

Commercializing the Globe

"Fifty years ago," wrote philosopher Ivan Illich in 1977, "most of the words an American heard were personally spoken to him as an individual, or to someone standing nearby." That certainly isn't true today. Most of the words an American—or a citizen of any industrial country—hears are sales pitches broadcast over the airwaves to us as members of a mass market. The text we read, the images we see, and the public places we visit are all dominated by commercial messages.

Take the example of commercial television, long the premier medium. Aside from sleeping and working, watching television is the leading activity in most consumer societies, from the United States and the United Kingdom to Japan and Singapore.

24   Commercial TV is advancing around the world, and everywhere it has proved exceptionally effective at stimulating buying urges. As Anthony J. F. Reilly, chief executive of the food conglomerate H. J. Heinz, told *Fortune* magazine, "Once television is there, people of whatever shade, culture, or origin want roughly the same things." Harnessed as an educational tool, TV can be powerful and effective, as in India and Africa, where lessons are beamed to teacherless villages. But the overwhelming trend in broadcasting almost everywhere is commercialization.

In 1985, the International Advertising Association rhapsodized: "The magical marketing tool of television has been bound with the chains of laws and regulations in much of the world, and it has not been free to exercise more than a tiny fraction of its potential as a conduit of the consumer information and economic stimulation provided by advertising. Those chains are at last being chiseled off."

During the 1980s, governments deregulated or privatized television programming in most of Western Europe. Public broadcasting monopolies splintered in Belgium, France, Italy, Germany, Norway, Portugal, Spain, and Switzerland—allowing advertising on a scale previously witnessed only in the United States. As the European Community became both a single market and a common broadcasting region this year, advertising time on European TV became a hot commodity, providing access to the region's 330 million consumers and $4 trillion of disposable income.

Meanwhile, commercial television is quickly spreading outside the industrial countries. In India, declares Gurcharan Das, chairman of Procter & Gamble India, "an advertiser can reach 200 million people every night" through television. India has gone from 3 million TVs in 1983 to more than 14 million today. Latin America has built or imported 60 million sets, almost one per family, since the early 1950s. All told, perhaps half the world's people have access to commercial television broadcasts.

28   The commercialization of television is just one part of the general expansion that includes magazines and newspapers, billboards and displays, catalogs, and other media. The overall growth stands out starkly in historical trends.

Total global advertising expenditures multiplied nearly sevenfold from 1950 to 1990; they grew one-third faster than the world economy and three times faster than the world population. They rose—in real, inflation-adjusted terms—from $39 billion in 1950 to $256 billion in 1990. (For comparison, the gross national product of India, the world's second most populous state, was just $256 billion that year.) In 1950, advertisers spent $16 for each person on the planet, in 1970 they spent $27, and in 1990, $48.

Americans are the most advertised-to people on earth. U.S. marketers account for nearly half of the world's budget, according to the International Advertising Association in New York, spending $468 per American in 1991. Among the industrial countries, Japan is second in the advertising league, dedicating more than $300 per citizen to sales pitches each year. Western Europe is close behind. A typical European is the target of more than $200 worth of ads a year. The latest boom is under way in Eastern Europe, a region that John Lindquist of the Boston Consulting Group calls "an advertising executive's dream—people actually remember advertisements."

Advertising is growing fast in developing countries as well, though it remains small-scale by Western standards. South Korea's advertising industry grew 35 to 40 percent annually in the late 1980s, and yearly ad billings in India jumped fivefold in the 1980s, surpassing one dollar per person for the first time.

Ad-ing Life

32   The sheer magnitude of the advertising barrage in consumer societies has some ironic results. For one thing, the clamor for people's attention means relatively few advertisements stick. Typical Americans are exposed to some 3,000 commercial messages a day, according to *Business Week*. Amid such a din, who notices what any one ad says?

To lend their messages greater influence, marketers are forced to deliver even higher-quality pitches—to seek new places to make them. They are constantly on the lookout for new routes into people's consciousness.

With the advent of the remote control, the mute button, and the video cassette recorder during the 1980s, people could easily avoid TV commercials, and advertisers had to seek out consumers elsewhere. Expanding on the traditional print and broadcast media, advertisers began piping messages into classrooms and doctors' offices, weaving them into the plots of feature films, posting them on chair-lift poles, printing them on postage stamps and board games, stitching them on Boy Scout merit badges and professional athletes' jerseys, mounting them in bathroom stalls, and playing them back between rings on public phones.

Marketers hired telephone solicitors, both human and computerized, to call people directly in their homes. They commissioned essays from well-known authors, packaged them between full-page ads fore the aft, and mailed them to opinion leaders to polish the sponsors' images. And they created ad-packed television programming for use at airports, bus stops, subway stations, exercise clubs, ski resorts, and supermarket checkout lines.

36   This creeping commercialization of life has a certain inevitability to it. As the novelty of each medium wears off, advertisers invent another one, relentlessly expanding the share of our collective attention span that they occupy with sales spiels.

Next, they will meet us at the mall, follow us to the dinner table, and shine down on us from the heavens. In shopping centers, they have begun erecting wall-sized video screens to heighten the frenzy of the shopping experience. Food engineers are turning the food supply into an advertising medium. The Viskase company of Chicago prints edible ad slogans on hot dogs, and Eggverts International is using a similar technique to advertise on thousands of eggs in Israel. Lighting engineers are hard at work on featherweight ways to turn blimps into giant airborne neon signs, and, demonstrating that not even the sky is the limit, Coca-Cola convinced orbiting Soviet cosmonauts to sip their soda on camera a couple of years ago.

The main outcome of this deadening commercialization is to sell not particular products, but consumerism itself. The implicit message of all advertising is the idea that there is a product to solve each of life's problems. Every commercial teaches that existence would be satisfying and complete if only we bought the right things. As religious historian Robert Bellah put it, "That happiness is to be attained through limitless material acquisition is denied by every religion and philosophy known to humankind, but is preached incessantly by every American television set."

Get 'Em While They're Young

The commercialization of space and time has been accompanied by the commercialization of youth. Marketers are increasingly targeting the young. One specialist in marketing to children told the *Wall Street Journal*, "Even two-year-olds are concerned about their brand of clothes, and by the age of six are full-out consumers." American children and teenagers sit through about three hours of television commercials each week—20,000 ads a year, translating to 360,000 by the time they graduate from high school.

40   The children's market in the United States is so valuable—topping $75 billion in 1990—that American companies spent $500 million marketing to kids in

1990, five times more than they spent a decade earlier. They started cartoons centered around toys and began direct-mail marketing to youngsters enrolled in their company-sponsored "clubs."

Such saturation advertising has allowed some firms to stake huge claims in the children's market. Mattel vice president Meryl Friedman brags, "Mattel has achieved a stunning 95 percent penetration with Barbie [dolls] among girls 3 to 11 in the United States."

Predictably, major retailers have opened Barbie departments to compete for the loyalty of doll-doting future consumers, and marketers pay premium prices to employ the dolls as an advertising medium. Barbies come equipped with Reebok shoes and Benetton clothes.

Madison Avenue's Paper Trail

Advertising's main ecological danger may be the consumption it inspires, but it also consumes heavily itself. Advertisers use a substantial share of the world's paper, particularly its heavily processed high-quality paper. Paper production involves not only forest damage but also large energy inputs and pollution outputs.

44   Ads pack the daily mail: 14 billion glossy, difficult-to-recycle mail-order catalogs plus 38 billion other assorted ads clog the post office each year in the United States. Most of those items go straight into the trash—including 98 percent of advertising letters sent in direct-mail campaigns, according to the marketing journal *American Demographics*.

Ads fill periodicals: most American magazines reserve 60 percent of their pages for advertising, and some devote far more. *Bride's* was so proud of its February/March 1990 edition that it submitted the issue to the *Guinness Book of World Records* and boasted in *Advertising Age*, "The Biggest Magazine in History. . . . It contains 1,040 pages—including 798 advertising pages."

Newspapers are no different; in the United States, they typically contain 65 percent, up from 40 percent half a century ago. Every year, Canada cuts 42,000 acres of its primeval forests—an area the size of the District of Columbia—just to provide American dailies with newsprint on which to run advertisements.

For big and immediate paper savings, newspapers could shift classified advertising—and telephone companies their directories—onto pay-per-use electronic databases accessible through phone lines. Still, advertising remains heavy in non-classified sections of newspapers. Trim out all the ads and most of the text would fit in a single section.

48   The problem in reducing the scale of advertising in the print media is that the financial viability of newspapers and magazines is linked to the number of advertising pages they sell. In the past two years of economic recession, for example, advertising pages have been harder to sell, and many periodicals have been forced to publish fewer articles. That is not good for the flow of information in democratic societies. To get less-commercialized information sources, subscribers may have to accept higher prices, as have the readers of *Ms.*, which dropped advertising three years ago.

The Industry of Needs

The needs industry—advertising—defends itself, ultimately, by claiming that advertising, whatever its social and cultural demerits, is an indispensable component of a healthy economy. As one Madison Avenue axiom counsels, "A terrible thing happens when you don't advertise. Nothing." Advertising, in this view, isn't the trim on the industrial economy, it's the fuel. Take out the ads, and the economy sputters to a halt; put in more ads, and the economy zooms. More ads equal more wants, more wants make more spending, and more spending makes more jobs.

Some promoters even call for governments to foster more advertising. The American Advertising Federation took out a full page in *Time* magazine last March to write, "Dear Mr. President . . . We respectfully remind you of advertising's role as an engine of economic growth. It raises capital, creates jobs, and spurs production. . . . It increases government revenues since jobs produce taxable income, and greater sales increase sales taxes. . . . Incentives to advertise are incentives for growth."

The validity of such claims is dubious, of course, but they cut to the heart of a critical issue. Even if advertising does promote growth, the question remains as to what kind of growth. Growth in numbers of second mortgages and third cars and fourth televisions may increase the money flowing around the economy without making us one bit happier. If much advertising is an exercise in generating dissatisfaction so that people will spend more and work harder, the entire process appears morally questionable. Several generations ago, Catholic theologian John Ryan dubbed this treadmill "squirrel cage progress."

52   Many of the areas in which the world needs growth most desperately—environmental literacy, racial and sexual equality, and political participation, for example—are not the stuff of advertising campaigns. "Civilization, in the real sense of the term," advised Gandhi, "consists not in the multiplication, but in the deliberate and voluntary reduction of wants."

Rechanelling Advertising

What legitimate role is there for advertising, then? In a substainable society, how much advertising would there be?

None! say some, as E. F. Schumacher commented in 1979: "What is the great bulk of advertising other than the stimulation of greed, envy and avarice . . . at least three of the deadly sins?" More succinctly, reader Charlotte Burrowes of Penacook, New Hampshire, wrote to *World Weekly* a year ago, "There'll be a special hell for advertisers."

In fairness, though, some advertising does provide useful information about products and services. The task for democratic societies struggling to restore balance between themselves and their ecosystems is to decide how much advertising to tolerate, and while respecting the right of individuals to speak their minds, to place appropriate limits on marketing.

56   The precise limits cannot yet be identified, but it may help define the issue to consider whether there are spaces that should be free of advertising. Churches?

Schools? Hospitals? Funeral homes? Parks? Homes? Workplaces? Books? Public libraries? Public swimming pools? Public buildings? Public buses? Public streets? Mail boxes? Newspapers? Television broadcasts? What about times of day, days of the week, and times of life? Early morning? Sundays? Childhood?

Restraining the excesses of marketers and limiting commercials to their legitimate role of informing consumers would require fundamental reforms in the industry, changes that will not come about without a well-organized grass-roots movement. The advertising industry is a formidable foe on the march around the world, and advertisers are masters at the slippery art of public relations. Madison Avenue can buy the best talents available to counter and circumvent reformers' campaigns, unless those campaigns are carefully focused and begin with the industry's vulnerabilities.

Advertising's Achilles heel is its willingness to push products demonstrably dangerous to human health, and this is the area where activists have been most successful and best organized. Tobacco ads are or soon will be banished from television throughout the Western democracies, and alcohol commercials are under attack as never before.

Another ready target for advertising-reform activists is the assault that marketers make on children. Public sentiment runs strongly against marketing campaigns that prey on youngsters. Action for Children's Television, a citizens' group based in Boston, won a victory in late 1990 when the U.S. Congress limited television commercials aimed at children. The same year, public interest organizations in the European Community pushed through standards for European television that will put strict limits on some types of ads.

60   The Australian Consumers' Association is attacking junk food ads, calling for a ban or tough restrictions on hawking unhealthful fare to youngsters. Of food ads aired during children's television programs, the association's research shows that 80 percent are for high-fat, high-salt, excessively packaged snacks. The American Academy of Pediatrics is similarly concerned. Noting the high proportion of advertisements for products that violate nutrition guidelines, the organization is urging Congress to ban food ads that target the young.

Alternatively, consumers could take aim at trumped-up corporate environmental claims. Since 1989, marketers have been painting their products "green" in an attempt to defuse citizen anger at corporate ecological transgressions. In 1990, for example, the oil company Texaco offered Americans "free" tree seedlings to plant for the good of the environment; to qualify, a customer had to buy eight or more gallons of gasoline. Unmentioned in the marketing literature was the fact that it takes a typical tree about four years to restore as much carbon dioxide as is released in refining and burning eight gallons of fuel, and that most tree seedlings planted by amateurs promptly die.

In the United States, one-fourth of all new household products introduced in 1990 advertised themselves as "ozone-friendly," "biodegradable," "recyclable," "compostable," or something similar—claims that half of all Americans recognize as "gimmickry." Environmentalists in the Netherlands and France have attempted to cut away such misinformation by introducing a 12-point environmental advertising code in their national legislatures. Ten state attorneys general are pushing for similar national standards in the United States. Meanwhile, official and unofficial organizations throughout Europe, North America, and Japan have initiated "green labeling" programs, aiming to steer consumers to environmentally preferable products.

Efforts to restrict advertising of tobacco and alcohol, to curtail advertising to children, and to regulate environmental claims of marketers are part of a broader agenda. The nonprofit Center for the Study of Commercialism in Washington, D.C., is calling for an end to brand-name plugs in feature films, for schools to declare themselves advertising-free zones, and for revision of the tax code so that money spent on advertising is taxable.

64   Just as the expanding reach of advertising is not going unchallenged, small networks of citizens everywhere are beginning to confront commercial television. In Vancouver, British Columbia, English teacher Michael Maser gets secondary students to study television production so they will be able to recognize techniques used to manipulate viewers' sentiments. Millions of young people could benefit from such a course, considering how many products are pitched to them on TV. Along the same lines as Maser's teaching, the Center for Media and Values in Los Angeles has been promoting media literacy since 1989, by furnishing parents throughout North America with tips on teaching their children to watch with a critical eye.

More boldly, some attempt to fight fire with fire. The Vancouver-based Media Foundation is building a movement aimed at using the same cleverness and humor evident in much commercial advertising to promote sustainable ends. Local groups raise funds to show the group's products on commercial television and in commercial magazines. TV spots have run in California, Ontario, and a half-dozen other states and provinces. Their "Tube Head" series of ads tell [sic] viewers to shut off the set. In one magazine ad, above a photo of a dark, sleek sports car, a caption purrs, "At this price, it will surely take your breath away." And below: "$250,000." In fine print, it explains, "U.S. sticker price based on individual share of social costs associated with automobiles in U.S. over average car life of 10 years. Does not include . . . oil spills at sea and on land; acid rain from auto emissions . . . environmental and health costs from global warming."

The premier spot in the Media Foundation's "High on the Hog" campaign shows a gigantic animated pig frolicking on a map of North America while a narrator intones: "Five percent of the people in the world consume *one-third* of the planet's resources. . . . Those people are us." The pig belches.

Imagine a message like *that* broadcast simultaneously to every inhabited part of the globe!

Personal Response

Durning says that the advertising industry creates consumerism. Are you and your friends driven to consume? Do you buy for the sake of buying, or do you buy only because of genuine need?

Questions for Discussion

1. How do advertisers manipulate their audiences?

2. Durning says that "historically, advertisers have especially targeted women" (paragraph 11). Why do you think women are prime targets of advertisers? Why do you think markets are increasingly targeting children?

3. According to Durning, why is advertising ecologically threatening? What aspects of advertising does Durning find morally questionable?

4. What "new routes to people's consciousness" have advertisers used?

5. How does Durning answer the questions he poses in paragraph 53? How would you answer those questions?

THE QUALITY OF MERCY KILLING

Roger Rosenblatt

Roger Rosenblatt has been a contributing editor for Time, Life, Family Circle, The New Republic, Vanity Fair, *and* Men's Journal. *He has written and performed two one-man off-Broadway shows and won Peabody and Emmy awards for his essays on PBS's* MacNeil/Lehrer News Hour. *His most recent collection of essays is* The Man in the Water *(1994). "The Quality of Mercy Killing" was first published in the August 1985 issue of* Time.

If it were only a matter of law, the public would not feel stranded. He killed her, after all. Roswell Gilbert, a 76-year-old retired electronics engineer living in a seaside condominium in Fort Lauderdale, Fla., considered murdering his wife Emily for at least a month before shooting her through the head with a Luger as she sat on their couch. The Gilberts had been husband and wife for 51 years. They were married in 1934, the year after Calvin Coolidge died, the year after Prohibition was lifted, the year that Hank Aaron was born. At 73, Emily had Alzheimer's disease and osteoporosis; her spinal column was gradually collapsing. Roswell would not allow her to continue life as "a suffering animal," so he committed what is called a mercy killing. The jury saw only the killing; they felt Gilbert had mercy on himself. He was sentenced to 25 years with no chance of parole, which would make him 101 by the time he got out. The Governor has been asked to grant clemency. Most Floridians polled hope that Gilbert will go free.

Not that there ever was much of a legal or practical question involved. Imagine the precedent set by freeing a killer simply because he killed for love. Othello killed for love, though his passion was loaded with a different motive. Does any feeling count, or is kindness alone an excuse for murder? Or age: maybe someone has to be 76 and married 51 years to establish his sincerity. There are an awful lot of old people and long marriages in Florida. A lot of Alzheimer's disease and osteoporosis as well. Let Gilbert loose, the fear is, and watch the run on Lugers.

Besides, the matter of mercy killing is getting rough and out of hand. No-body seems to use poison anymore. In Fort Lauderdale two years ago, a 79-year-old man shot his 62-year-old wife in the stairwell of a hospital; like Emily Gilbert, she was suffering from Alzheimer's disease. In San Antonio four years ago, a 69-year-old man shot his 72-year-old brother to death in a nursing home. Last June a man in Miami put two bullets in the heart of his three-year-old daughter who lay comatose after a freak accident. An organization that studies mercy killings says that nine have occurred this year alone. You cannot have a murder every time someone feels sorry for a loved one in pain. Any fool knows that.

4 Yet you also feel foolish watching a case like Gilbert's (if any case can be said to be like another) because, while both feet are planted firmly on the side of the law and common sense, both are firmly planted on Gilbert's side as well. The place the public really stands is nowhere: How can an act be equally destructive of society and wholly human? The reason anyone would consider going easy on Gilbert is that we can put ourselves in his shoes, can sit at his wife's bedside day after day, watching the Florida sun gild the furniture and listening to the Atlantic lick the beach like a cat. Emily dozes. He looks at her in a rare peaceful pose and is grateful for the quiet.

Or he dreams back to when such a scene would have been unimaginable: she, sharp as a tack, getting the better of him in an argument; he, strong as a bull, showing off by swinging her into the air—on a beach, perhaps, like the one in front of the condominium where old couples like themselves walk in careful slow motion at the water's edge. Since the case became a cause, photographs of the Gilberts have appeared on television, she in a formal gown, he in tails; they, older, in a restaurant posing deadpan for a picture for no reason, the way people do in restaurants. In a way the issue here *is* age: mind and body falling away like slabs of sand off a beach cliff. If biology declares war, have people no right to a pre-emptive strike? In the apartment he continues to stare at her who, from time to time, still believes they are traveling together in Spain.

Now he wonders about love. He loves his wife; he tells her so; he has told her so for 51 years. And he thinks of what he meant by that: her understanding of him, her understanding of others, her sense of fun. Illness has replaced those qualities in her with screams and a face of panic. Does he love her still? Of course, he says; he hates the disease, but he loves his wife. Or—and this seems hard—does he only love what he remembers of Emily? Is the frail doll in the bed an imposter? But no; this is Emily too, the same old Emily hidden somewhere under the decaying cells and in the folds of the painkillers. It is Emily and she is suffering and he swore he would always look after her.

He considers an irony: you always hurt the one you love. By what act or non-act would he be hurting his wife more? He remembers news stories he has read of distraught people in similar positions, pulling the plugs on sons and husbands or assisting in the suicides of desperate friends. He sympathizes, but with a purpose; he too is interested in precedents. Surely, he concludes, morality swings both ways here. What is moral for the group cannot always be moral for the individual, or there would be no individuality, no exceptions, even if the exceptions only prove the rule. Let the people have their rules. What harm would it do history to relieve Emily's pain? A little harm, perhaps, no more than that.

8   This is what we see in the Gilbert case, the fusion of our lives with theirs in one grand and pathetic cliché in which all lives look pretty much alike. We go round and round with Gilbert: Gilbert suddenly wondering if Emily might get better, if one of those white-coated geniuses will come up with a cure. Gilbert realizing that once Emily is gone, he will go too, since her way of life, however wretched, was their way of life. He is afraid for them both. In *The Merchant of Venice* Portia says that mercy is "twice blessed; / It blesses him that gives and him that takes." The murder committed, Gilbert does not feel blessed. At best, he feels he did right, which the outer world agrees with and denies.

Laws are unlikely to be changed by such cases: for every modification one can think of, there are too many loopholes and snares. What Gilbert did in fact erodes the whole basis of law, which is to keep people humane and civilized. Yet Gilbert was humane, civilized and wrong: a riddle. In the end we want the law intact and Gilbert free, so that society wins on both counts. What the case proves, however, is that society is helpless to do anything for Gilbert, for Emily or for itself. All we can do is recognize a real tragedy when we see one, and wonder, perhaps, if one bright morning in 1934 Gilbert read of a mercy killing in the papers, leaned earnestly across the breakfast table and told his new bride: "I couldn't do that. I could never do that."

Personal Response

What is your reaction to the jury's finding Roswell Gilbert guilty of murder? How do you feel about the issue of mercy killing?

Questions for Discussion

1. According to Rosenblatt, what is the dilemma posed by cases such as Gilbert's? What is the "riddle" mentioned in the last paragraph?

2. Where does Rosenblatt state the views of those opposed to leniency in cases such as Gilbert's?

3. In paragraph 8, Rosenblatt quotes from the play alluded to in his title, Shakespeare's *The Merchant of Venice*. The lines immediately before those he quotes are "The quality of mercy is not strained,/It droppeth as the gentle rain from heaven/Upon the place beneath." Explain the function of the allusion in the title and the lines Rosenblatt quotes in paragraph 8. What does the reference to Othello (paragraph 2) mean, and what purpose does it serve?

4. Do you think Rosenblatt's emotional appeal is too sentimental? Does the strong emotional appeal undercut his argument? What function do the closing sentences serve? Does Rosenblatt condone mercy killing? Does he imply that exceptions to the law should be made in some cases?

5. Rosenblatt writes in paragraph 5 that "in a way the issue here *is* age." In what sense might age be the issue?

MERCY DENIED TO ROSWELL GILBERT

Derek Humphrey

Derek Humphrey has written several books on euthanasia and assisted suicide, beginning with his book Jean's Way *(1978) describing his personal experience helping his terminally ill first wife die. He is author of* Let Me Die Before I Wake *(1981), the best-selling* Final Exit: The Practicalities of Self-Deliverance and Assisted Suicide for the Dying *(1990), and* Dying with Dignity: Understanding Euthanasia *(1992), from which the following chapter is taken. Derek Humphrey can be reached via e-mail at dhumphry@efn.org.*

Understanding mercy killing is difficult. It flies in the face of law and order, sanctity of life, and always earns that most barbed of comments: "It is done to benefit the life-taker: to make his or her life happier at the expense of another."

Trying to comprehend mercy killing does not mean I approve of it. Surely there is a better way to end suffering? Ever since I evoked a whirlwind of praise and criticism in 1978 for admitting that I helped my first wife commit suicide at the end of a long fight with terminal cancer, I have been studying similar cases, leading to two books.[1]

My action was not a mercy killing as was Roswell Gilbert's in Fort Lauderdale, Florida, on March 4, 1985. His action classically fell into that definition by being the *unrequested* taking of another person's life in order to save that person suffering. It is a desperate act of love by a person exhausted and unnerved: homicide laws and consequent severe punishments become, for him, irrelevant.

4   My action (a crime for which I could have received fourteen years imprisonment) was morally and legally "an assisted suicide." Had I been taken to court—which I was not—that would have been the indictment.

My "crime" differed from Mr. Gilbert's morally in that Jean, my wife, wanted to end her life. It was her idea; she laid the plan and chose the time. I was an accessory. She lifted the cup of poison (which I had provided) out of her own free choice.

But a mercy killer does not have the benefit of mutual forethought and choice. He or she is trapped by different circumstances into believing that he must act alone.

A mercy killer takes the life of a loved one who is incompetent—unable to think or act for himself or herself. Mrs. Gilbert had spoken of wishing to die but was too ill to make a rational decision about this or anything else. Prosecution is inevitable, and it is often endured by the offender in an attempt to resolve feelings of guilt and remorse.

---

[1] *Jean's Way* (1978) and *Let Me Die Before I Wake* (1981).

8   Peering under the layers of devotion and emotion in the Roswell Gilbert case is like reading a novel by Dostoevski or Franz Kafka. And because it is true, it has a greater effect on our psyche.

Here was a couple, Emily and Roswell, married back in 1936, now in the autumn years of their lives, taking off for Spain to live the good life which they had so richly earned. After four or five years, Roswell noticed his wife becoming forgetful. She often repeated herself seconds after making a statement. There were other moments of strange confusion.

In addition, Emily suffered considerable back pain. Eventually osteoporosis was diagnosed, a decrease in the bone mass, causing bones to snap easily, provoking excruciating pain. Between 1978 and her death this year, Emily's spine shortened by two and a quarter inches due to fractures. Many other bones broke over the years. Painkilling drugs helped, but also produced side effects, particularly severe constipation.

The Gilberts abandoned life in Spain, opting for better medical care in America. They bought a condominium in Fort Lauderdale in 1978. Alzheimer's disease, a progressive neurological disorder, was also diagnosed, which caused the personality change and forgetfulness. With Alzheimer's, death comes, but usually after, five, ten or fifteen years from general weakness of the body making it susceptible to infection.

12   During this time, Emily became totally dependent on Roswell. She was terrified that he would die or would desert her. She could not bear him out of her sight, always running after him minutes after agreeing to stay put in the living room.

Inexorably, she deteriorated mentally and physically. "Our friends stopped coming because she was so embarrassing," Roswell later told the court.[2]

Now isolated socially, tending a demented woman with a severe physical ailment, Roswell continued to look after Emily. Everyone who knew him testified to his total devotion, even up to the moment of the killing.

"They were inseparable," said a friend, Mrs. Joy Rhodes. "Ros adored and took care of Emily. I saw her a week before her death. She'd lost weight, her hair was falling out, her walk was slow and her expression changed. I noticed that the effect on Ros was devastating. He was tired and lost. He looked in a bad condition."

16   Emily told Joy, her friend since 1977: "I am not long for this world. I want to die."

In their last years together, Roswell had to bathe and dress Emily, floss her teeth, and wash her soiled underwear as incontinence developed. No one ever heard him grumble.

In court, Mr. Gilbert was criticized for not having put her in a nursing home. But do they really exist for Alzheimer's patients? (Heavy drug sedation is the norm for those in nursing homes.) Particularly one so demented as Emily, who also had breaking bones? Consider the weekend before she was shot:

---

[2] The author attended the jury trial as observer.

Emily complained of severe pains. The analgesics were not working. Her doctor hospitalized her, but she was so obstreperous she could neither be treated nor put to bed. Medication sedated her at night, but invariably, the next day, she was unmanageable and disruptive. When Mr. Gilbert realized that formal medical care was hopeless, he took her home. Although he never said so, it must have been the final blow.

20   He was by now unnerved and exhausted. He had had almost no sleep during the three nights before he shot Emily: one sleepless night, followed by half a night's sleep, followed by no sleep. He admits that it was then he began to think of taking her life.

On March 4 he went downstairs to a board meeting at the condominium complex, telling Emily he would soon return. Within minutes she followed him, making a scene, shouting, "I am so sick. I want to die."

Humiliated, drained, desperate, solitary, Roswell took her back to their apartment. When she was not looking, he put two bullets through her head.

Roswell Gilbert is not an emotional man, nor is he diplomatic in his language. Some remarks in the witness box could easily be misunderstood. "I was ice-cool when I shot her," he said. Perhaps he meant he was numb.

24   He used blunt language, such as "I terminated her suffering" and this apparently offended some jurors. He also said: "I figured I'd done the right thing. I still do. I'd do it again if I had to. What else could I have done? The only other choice was to stick her in a nursing home, which is like a warehouse."

The prosecutor succeeded in convincing the jury that Mrs. Gilbert was not dying, although she had two terminal illnesses. Alzheimer's and osteoporosis. He made great play with the fact that she went to lunch on the day she died, was cosmetically well made-up and smartly dressed.

The forewoman of the jury of ten women and two men was quoted afterwards as saying: "She was, in fact not terminal in our opinion. She was undoubtedly in pain, uncomfortable, but somebody who could make her face up like that the day she was shot! She was not ready to die; if we felt she was ready to die, it probably would not have been first degree murder."[3]

The jury could not or would not take account of the fact that Mrs. Gilbert looked so good because her husband helped her dress, and shepherded her about in the car. It is also well known that Alzheimer's sufferers vary in condition from day to day, have tremendous mood swings, and even sometimes manage to mask their dementia by displaying the social graces previously practiced all their lives.

28   From talking to Roswell Gilbert privately as well as hearing his testimony, I heard a voice which perhaps only those few of us who have been tested in helping a loved one to die can recognize. Mr. Gilbert was saying, in effect, that if people have been loving companions for a great length of time, there is a fusion of minds, where one assumes the burden of the other. The suffering is mutual, as is the responsibility of one to do something about it.

---

[3] *Newsday.* May 5, 1985.

Mr. Gilbert and the other mercy killers take a loved one's life as the ultimate act of love, however felonious that action may be. For them there is no alternative to action. *The rest of the world, at that point, does not exist.*

A man in Los Angeles who shot his sick mother told me: "When you take the life of someone you love, you take your own life. In this past year I've felt dead inside."

A woman in Arizona who suffocated her mother after a botched assisted suicide said: "I was willing to do this for her. I am not sorry I went through with it. I would do it again, even if things went wrong and she suffered horribly that last day, I probably spared her quite a long time of suffering."

32   Asked if she killed her mother to relieve her own suffering, this woman told me: "My motivations for doing things are never all one thing or the other. They're never all pure nor all malicious. They are always mixed."

Such is the dread of Alzheimer's disease today, that couples who are perfectly healthy sometimes tell me that they have private pacts giving advance permission to the other partner to kill them if one gets the disease and life becomes unbearable for both.

Unless they can carry this out without detection, there is going to be an epidemic of mercy killing cases like Mr. Gilbert's.[4]

The Alzheimer's victim cannot get *voluntary* euthanasia because there is no intellectual capacity for decision making. In these special circumstances, there may have to be a family decision, in conjunction with doctors, to help the victim to die at a late stage of the disease—but only if the sufferer had firmly expressed such a wish while healthy, through a Living Will and a detailed statement.

36   In the national debate on the case triggered by the refusal of clemency, the pro and con arguments on the Gilbert case, which reflect on many other cases, were as follows:

> Emily Gilbert was not dying, nor ready to die. State Attorney Hancock described her as a "well functioning human being."

Alzheimer's and osteoporosis, both terminal illness, had been diagnosed seven years earlier. Both diseases were well advanced. Prosecution evidence that she was seen out of doors fleetingly does not discount the evidence of her suffering during the rest of the twenty-four-hour cycle.

> Mrs. Gilbert did not ask to die.

With her brain largely destroyed from Alzheimer's, Mrs. Gilbert could not make a legally informed and competent decision. Apart from her husband's statements that she wanted to die, corroborating evidence came from friends and neighbors of her request.

---

[4] The case is now under appeal. If the appeal is rejected, Mr. Gilbert can again ask the governor for clemency.

Mr. Gilbert "snuck up behind her" and shot her not once, but twice. This showed premeditation.

He never denied he intended to do it. Was it mercy-aforethought or malice-aforethought? The second bullet was fired because Mr. Gilbert was ignorant of the fact that vital signs continue in a human for some minutes after a bullet has passed through the brain. Records show that almost all mercy killers use several bullets; this has not stopped them from getting light sentences.

He should have put his wife in a nursing home.

40   About the only way to cope with Alzheimer's victims in a health facility is through heavy sedation. Mr. Gilbert did not want that for Emily. Her dementia took the form of excessive dependence on him. If they were separated it would have been necessary to pacify her through drugs.

He should have brought in a resident nurse.

Their apartment was not big enough. As it was, Mr. Gilbert usually slept on the sofa in the living room because his wife's pain and discomfort were too great to be able to share the same bedroom.

He should have joined a support group.

Nobody has claimed that there was one near to him. Anyway, he thought he was coping. Nobody told him he was not. Mr. and Mrs. Gilbert had always been a self-sufficient couple, comfortably off financially, and they tried to live out their lives privately.

He shot her to relieve himself of the burden of caring for her.

Mr. Gilbert *thought* he was managing all right until, in the final week, things became so bad that, through desperation, he lost his previous self-control and killed her. Anyway, he knew he was breaking the law when he acted, and would receive life imprisonment as his penalty, which can hardly be considered "relief."

If he is given clemency, then the floodgates will open and people will start shooting the dying relative for whom they are caring.

44   In 1920 Frank Roberts, in Michigan, received life imprisonment for aiding his wife's suicide. Since then many "mercy killers" up until the Gilbert case (fifty-three of them) have received probationary sentences. Other communities have not found a rash of carbon copy mercy killers after dealing with such offenders leniently.

According to the Scriptures, Mr. Gilbert deserved to be executed. (The born-again Christian view.)

We used to execute unhappy and unstable people who tried and failed to commit suicide. We used to imprison children for petty theft. We used to pull apart (draw and quarter) traitors. Today's more thoughtful and caring society finds better ways to treat malefactors, and "mercy killing" deserves that same tolerance and understanding, too.

Conclusion

If nothing else, the Roswell Gilbert case has fueled two important debates:

> *One.* Is the nation spending enough time and money on its sick and elderly?
> *Two.* Has the time arrived for lawful voluntary euthanasia?

48

Note: In 1990 Mr. Gilbert was granted clemency by Florida's governor. He had served five years in a maximum security prison.

Personal Response

What is your opinion of the Gilbert Roswell case after reading Humphrey's account of the Roswells' lives together?

Questions for Discussion

1. Humphrey writes that Roswell Gilbert felt that it was his responsibility as a loving companion to relieve his wife of her suffering (paragraph 28) and that "mercy killers take a loved one's life as the ultimate act of love" (paragraph 29). What is your opinion of this view about mercy killing as an act of love?

2. Discuss the pros and cons on the mercy killing argument that Humphrey lists in paragraphs 36 to 45. With which side are you more sympathetic?

3. Humphrey begins this selection by saying that understanding mercy killing does not mean that he approves of it. Has Humphrey increased your understanding of mercy killing or changed your opinion in any way?

4. Humphrey ends by noting two debate questions the Roswell Gilbert case has raised (paragraph 46). Hold a class debate on one or both of those questions, or hold small group or class discussions on them.

FIRST AND LAST, DO NO HARM

Charles Krauthammer

Charles Krauthammer has had a varied career as a political scientist, psychiatrist, journalist, speech writer, and television talk show panelist. Since 1983, he has written essays for Time *magazine. He is also a contributing editor to* The New Republic *and, since 1985, he has contributed a weekly syndicated column to the* Washington Post. *In 1981, he won a Pulitzer Prize for commentary on politics and society. He has published one book,* Cutting Edges: Making Sense of the Eighties *(1985). This commentary appeared in the April 15, 1996, issue of* Time, *when the Second Circuit Court of Appeals struck down a New York State law that prohibited physicians from helping their patients die. The Ninth Circuit Court in San Francisco made a similar ruling in the month before the New York ruling.*

"I will give no deadly medicine to anyone if asked."
The Hippocratic Oath

"Did you ask for your hemlock?" Thanks to appeals-court judges in New York and California, this question will now be in your future.

You will be old, infirm and, inevitably at some point, near death. You may or may not be in physical distress, but in an age of crushing health-care costs, you will be a burden to your loved ones, to say nothing of society. And thanks to courts that back in 1996 legalized doctor-assisted suicide for the first time in American history, all around you thousands of your aging contemporaries will be taking their life.

You may want to live those last few remaining weeks or months. You may have no intention of shortening your life. But now the question that before 1996 rarely arose—and when it did arise, only in the most hushed and guilty tones—will be raised routinely: Others are letting go; others are giving way; should not you too?

4   Of course, the judges who plumbed the depths of the Constitution to find the "right" to physician-assisted suicide—a right unfindable for 200 years—deny the possibility of such a nightmare scenario. Psychological pressure on the elderly and infirm to take drugs to hasten death? Why, "there should be none," breezily decrees the Second Circuit Court of Appeals.

King Canute had a better grip on reality. This nightmare scenario is not a hypothesis; it has been tested in Holland and proved a fact. Holland is the only jurisdiction in the Western world that heretofore permitted physician-assisted suicide. The practice is now widespread (perhaps 2,000 to 3,000 cases a year; the U.S. equivalent would be 40,000 to 60,000) and abused. Indeed, legalization has resulted in so much abuse—not just psychological pressure but a shocking number of cases of out-and-out *involuntary* euthanasia, inconvenient and defenseless patients simply put to death without their consent—that last year the Dutch government was forced to change its euthanasia laws.

Judge Roger Miner, writing for the Second Circuit, uncomprehendingly admits the reality of the nightmare: "It seems clear that some physicians [in the Netherlands] practice nonvoluntary euthanasia, although it is not legal to do so." Well, why would such things occur in the Netherlands? Are the people there morally inferior to Americans? Are the doctors somehow crueler and more uncaring?

Of course not. The obvious reason is that doctors there were relieved of the constraint of the law. The absolute ethical norm established since the time of Hippocrates—that doctors must not kill—was removed in the name of compassion, and the inevitable happened. Good, ordinary doctors, in their zeal to be ever more compassionate in terminating useless and suffering life, began killing people who did not even ask for it. Once given power heretofore reserved to God, some exceeded their narrow mandate and acted like God. Surprise.

8   In America the great moral barrier protecting us from such monstrous God-doctoring is the one separating passive from active euthanasia. Pulling the plug for the dying is permitted. Prescribing death-dealing drugs to those who are quite self-sustaining is not. It is this distinction that the judges are intent on destroying.

"Physicians do not fulfill the role of 'killer' by prescribing drugs to hasten death any more than they do by disconnecting life-support systems," writes Judge Miner. This is pernicious nonsense. There is a great difference between, say, not resuscitating a stopped heart—allowing nature to take its course—and actively killing someone. In the first case the person is dead. In the second he only wishes to be dead. And in the case of life sustained by artificial hydration or ventilation, pulling the plug simply prevents an artificial prolongation of the dying process. Prescribing hemlock initiates it.

The distinction is not just practical. It is also psychological. Killing is hard to do. The whole purpose of this case is to make it easier. How? By giving doctors who actively assist in suicide the blessing of the law and society.

After all, why did we need this ruling in the first place? In New York State, where this case was brought, not a single physician has been penalized for aiding a suicide since 1919. For 77 years, one can assume, some doctors have been quietly helping patients die. Why then the need for a legal ruling to make that official, a ruling that erases a fundamental ethical line and opens medical practice to unconscionable abuse?

12   The need comes from the modern craving for "authenticity." If you are going to do it, do it openly, proudly, unashamedly. But as a society, do we not want this most fearful act—killing—to be done fearfully? If it must be done at all—and in the most extreme and pitiable circumstances it will—let it be done with trembling, in shadow, in whispered acknowledgment that some fundamental norm is being violated, even if for the most compassionate of reasons.

No more. These judges have now liberated us from the hypocrisy of the unenforced law. Damn them. Lack of enforcement is an expression of compassion, but the law is the last barrier to arrogance. And God knows that in this age of all-powerful medicine, arrogance is the greater danger. Every grandparent will soon know that too.

Personal Response

Krauthammer asks, "Why did we need this ruling in the first place?" (paragraph 11). Are you convinced that the Second Circuit ruling is necessary, or do you share Krauthammer's reservations?

Questions for Discussion

1. In the matter of terminally ill patients, it was already legal for doctors to withhold or withdraw treatment at the patient's request, but the New York

and California rulings allow a doctor to prescribe a lethal dose of medicine as long as the patient is in the final stages of a terminal disease, is mentally competent, and is able to take the medicine on his or her own. What dangers does Krauthammer see in the rulings? Do you believe his fears are reasonable?

2. What distinction does Krauthammer draw between what doctors were previously allowed to do under the law and what they are now legally free to do in New York and California?

3. Krauthammer calls the opinion of Judge Miner in the Second Circuit Court ruling "pernicious nonsense" (paragraph 9). What is your opinion of Judge Miner's statement? Do you agree with Krauthammer?

4. Discuss Krauthammer's comment that the ruling "erases a fundamental ethical line and opens medical practice to unconscionable abuse" (paragraph 11).

THE GUEST

Albert Camus

Albert Camus (1913–1960) was a writer and philosopher whose novels The Stranger *(1942),* The Plague *(1947), and* The Fall *(1956), along with his collection of philosophical essays* The Myth of Sisyphus *(1942), established him as one of the leading speakers for existential philosophy. He won the Nobel Prize for literature in 1957 for his major philosophical work,* The Rebel: An Essay on Man in Revolt *(1954), which explores his attempts to find a reasonable middle position in his divided loyalties between the Arab Nationalists in Algeria and the French colonists there. "The Guest" is reprinted from Camus' collection of short stories,* Exile and the Kingdom *(1957).*

The schoolmaster was watching the two men climb toward him. One was on horseback, the other on foot. They had not yet tackled the abrupt rise leading to the schoolhouse built on the hillside. They were toiling onward, making slow progress in the snow, among the stones, on the vast expanse of the high, deserted plateau. From time to time the horse stumbled. Without hearing anything yet, he could see the breath issuing from the horse's nostrils. One of the men, at least, knew the region. They were following the trail although it had disappeared days ago under a layer of dirty white snow. The schoolmaster calculated that it would take them half an hour to get onto the hill. It was cold; he went back into the school to get a sweater.

He crossed the empty, frigid classroom. On the blackboard the four rivers of France, drawn with four different colored chalks, had been flowing toward their estuaries for the past three days. Snow had suddenly fallen in mid-October after eight months of drought without the transition of rain, and the twenty pupils, more or less, who lived in the villages scattered over the plateau had stopped coming. With fair weather they would return. Daru now heated only the single room that was his lodging, adjoining the classroom and giving also onto the plateau to the east. Like the class windows, his window looked to the south too. On that side the school was a few kilometers from the point where the plateau began to slope toward the south. In clear weather could be seen the purple mass of the mountain range where the gap opened onto the desert.

Somewhat warmed, Daru returned to the window from which he had first seen the two men. They were no longer visible. Hence they must have tackled the rise. The sky was not so dark, for the snow had stopped falling during the night. The morning had opened with a dirty light which had scarcely become brighter as the ceiling of clouds lifted. At two in the afternoon it seemed as if the day were merely beginning. But still this was better than those three days when the thick snow was falling amidst unbroken darkness with little gusts of wind that rattled the double door of the classroom. Then Daru had spent long hours in his room, leaving it only to go to the shed and feed the chickens or get some coal. Fortunately the delivery truck from Tadjid, the nearest village to the north, had brought his supplies two days before the blizzard. It would return in forty-eight hours.

4   Besides, he had enough to resist a siege, for the little room was cluttered with bags of wheat that the administration left as a stock to distribute to those of his pupils whose families had suffered from the drought. Actually they had all been victims because they were all poor. Every day Daru would distribute a ration to the children. They had missed it, he knew, during these bad days. Possibly one of the fathers or big brothers would come this afternoon and he could supply them with grain. It was just a matter of carrying them over to the next harvest. Now shiploads of wheat were arriving from France and the worst was over. But it would be hard to forget that poverty, that army of ragged ghosts wandering in the sunlight, the plateaus burned to a cinder month after month, the earth shriveled up little by little, literally scorched, every stone bursting into dust under one's foot. The sheep had died then by thousands and even a few men, here and there, sometimes without anyone's knowing.

In contrast with such poverty, he who lived almost like a monk in his remote schoolhouse, nonetheless satisfied with the little he had and with the rough life, had felt like a lord with his whitewashed walls, his narrow couch, his unpainted shelves, his well, and his weekly provision of water and food. And suddenly this snow, without warning, without the foretaste of rain. This is the way the region was, cruel to live in, even without men—who didn't help matters either. But Daru had been born here. Everywhere else, he felt exiled.

He stepped out onto the terrace in front of the schoolhouse. The two men were now halfway up the slope. He recognized the horseman as Balducci, the old gendarme he had known for a long time. Balducci was holding on the end of a rope an Arab who was walking behind him with hands bound and head lowered. The gendarme waved a greeting to which Daru did not reply, lost as he was in contemplation of the Arab dressed in a faded blue jellaba, his feet in sandals but covered with socks of heavy raw wool, his head surmounted by a narrow, short chèche. They were approaching. Balducci was holding back his horse in order not to hurt the Arab, and the group was advancing slowly.

Within earshot, Balducci shouted: "One hour to do the three kilometers from El Ameur!" Daru did not answer. Short and square in his thick sweater, he watched them climb. Not once had the Arab raised his head. "Hello," said Daru when they got up onto the terrace. "Come in and warm up." Balducci painfully got down from his horse without letting go the rope. From under his bristling mustache he smiled at the schoolmaster. His little dark eyes, deep-set under a tanned forehead, and his mouth surrounded with wrinkles made him look attentive and studious. Daru took the bridle, led the horse to the shed, and came back to the two men, who were now waiting for him in the school. He led them into his room. "I am going to heat up the classroom," he said. "We'll be more comfortable there." When he entered the room again, Balducci was on the couch. He had undone the rope tying him to the Arab, who had squatted near the stove. His hands still bound, the _chèche_ pushed back on his head, he was looking toward the window. At first Daru noticed only his huge lips, fat, smooth, almost Negroid; yet his nose was straight, his eyes were dark and full of fever. The _chèche_ revealed an obstinate forehead and, under the weathered skin now rather discolored by the cold, the whole face had a restless and rebellious look that struck Daru when the Arab, turning his face toward him, looked him straight in the eyes. "Go into the other room," said the schoolmaster, "and I'll make you some mint tea." "Thanks," Balducci said. "What a chore! How I long for retirement." And addressing his prisoner in Arabic: "Come on, you." The Arab got up and, slowly, holding his bound wrists in front of him, went into the classroom.

8   With the tea, Daru brought a chair. But Balducci was already enthroned on the nearest pupil's desk and the Arab had squatted against the teacher's platform facing the stove, which stood between the desk and the window. When he held out the glass of tea to the prisoner, Daru hesitated at the sight of his bound hands. "He might perhaps be untied." "Sure," said Balducci. "That was for the trip." He started to get to his feet. But Daru, setting the glass on the floor, had knelt beside the Arab. Without saying anything, the Arab watched him with his feverish eyes. Once his hands were free, he rubbed his swollen wrists against each other, took the glass of tea, and sucked up the burning liquid in swift little sips.

"Good," said Daru. "And where are you headed?"

Balducci withdrew his mustache from the tea. "Here, son."

"Odd pupils! And you're spending the night?"

12   "No. I'm going back to El Ameur. And you will deliver this fellow to Tinguit. He is expected at police headquarters."

Balducci was looking at Daru with a friendly little smile.

"What's this story?" asked the schoolmaster. "Are you pulling my leg?"

"No, son. Those are the orders."

16   "The orders? I'm not . . ." Daru hesitated, not wanting to hurt the old Corsican. "I mean, that's not my job."

"What! What's the meaning of that? In wartime people do all kinds of jobs."

"Then I'll wait for the declaration of war!"

Balducci nodded.

20   "O.K. But the orders exist and they concern you too. Things are brewing, it appears. There is talk of a forthcoming revolt. We are mobilized, in a way."

Daru still had his obstinate look.

"Listen, son," Balducci said. "I like you and you must understand. There's only a dozen of us at El Ameur to patrol throughout the whole territory of a small department and I must get back in a hurry. I was told to hand this guy over to you and return without delay. He couldn't be kept there. His village was beginning to stir; they wanted to take him back. You must take him to Tinguit tomorrow before the day is over. Twenty kilometers shouldn't faze a husky fellow like you. After that, all will be over. You'll come back to your pupils and your comfortable life."

Behind the wall the horse could be heard snorting and pawing the earth. Daru was looking out the window. Decidedly, the weather was clearing and the light was increasing over the snowy plateau. When all the snow was melted, the sun would take over again and once more would burn the fields of stone. For days, still, the unchanging sky would shed its dry light on the solitary expanse where nothing had any connection with man.

24   "After all," he said, turning around toward Balducci, "what did he do?" And, before the gendarme had opened his mouth, he asked: "Does he speak French?"

"No, not a word. We had been looking for him for a month, but they were hiding him. He killed his cousin."

"Is he against us?"

"I don't think so. But you can never be sure."

28   "Why did he kill?"

"A family squabble, I think. One owed the other grain, it seems. It's not at all clear. In short, he killed his cousin with a billhook. You know, like a sheep, *kreezk!*"

Balducci made the gesture of drawing a blade across his throat and the Arab, his attention attracted, watched him with a sort of anxiety. Daru felt a sudden wrath against the man, against all men with their rotten spite, their tireless hates, their blood lust.

But the kettle was singing on the stove. He served Balducci more tea, hesitated, then served the Arab again, who a second time, drank avidly. His raised arms made the jellaba fall open and the schoolmaster saw his thin, muscular chest.

32   "Thanks, kid," Balducci said. "And now, I'm off."

He got up and went toward the Arab, taking a small rope from his pocket.

"What are you doing?" Daru asked dryly.

Balducci, disconcerted, showed him the rope.

36   "Don't bother."

The old gendarme hesitated. "It's up to you. Of course, you are armed?"

"I have my shotgun."

"Where?"

40   "In the trunk."

"You ought to have it near your bed."

"Why? I have nothing to fear."

"You're crazy, son. If there's an uprising, no one is safe, we're all in the same boat."

44 "I'll defend myself. I'll have time to see them coming."

Balducci began to laugh, then suddenly the mustache covered the white teeth.

"You'll have time? O.K. That's just what I was saying. You have always been a little cracked. That's why I like you, my son was like that."

At the same time he took out his revolver and put it on the desk.

48 "Keep it; I don't need two weapons from here to El Ameur."

The revolver shone against the black paint of the table. When the gendarme turned toward him, the schoolmaster caught the smell of leather and horseflesh.

"Listen, Balducci," Daru said suddenly, "every bit of this disgusts me, and first of all your fellow here. But I won't hand him over. Fight, yes, if I have to. But not that."

The old gendarme stood in front of him and looked at him severely.

52 "You're being a fool," he said slowly, "I don't like it either. You don't get used to putting a rope on a man even after years of it, and you're even ashamed—yes, ashamed. But you can't let them have their way."

"I won't hand him over," Daru said again.

"It's an order, son, and I repeat it."

"That's right. Repeat to them what I've said to you: I won't hand him over."

56 Balducci made a visible effort to reflect. He looked at the Arab and at Daru. At last he decided.

"No, I won't tell them anything. If you want to drop us, go ahead; I'll not denounce you. I have an order to deliver the prisoner and I'm doing so. And now you'll just sign this paper for me."

"There's no need. I'll not deny that you left him with me."

"Don't be mean with me. I know you'll tell the truth. You're from hereabouts and you are a man. But you must sign, that's the rule."

60 Daru opened his drawer, took out a little square bottle of purple ink, the red wooden penholder with the "sergeant-major" pen he used for making models of penmanship, and signed. The gendarme carefully folded the paper and put it into his wallet. Then he moved toward the door.

"I'll see you off," Daru said.

"No," said Balducci. "There's no use being polite. You insulted me."

He looked at the Arab, motionless in the same spot, sniffed peevishly, and turned away toward the door. "Good-by, son," he said. The door shut behind him. Balducci appeared suddenly outside the window and then disappeared. His footsteps were muffled by the snow. The horse stirred on the other side of the wall and several chickens fluttered in fright. A moment later Balducci reappeared outside the window leading the horse by the bridle. He walked toward the little rise without turning around and disappeared from sight with the horse following him. A big stone could be heard bouncing down. Daru walked back toward the prisoner, who, without stirring, never took his eyes off him. "Wait," the schoolmaster said in Arabic and went toward the bedroom. As he was going through the door, he had a second thought, went to the desk, took the revolver, and stuck it in his pocket. Then, without looking back, he went into his room.

64   For some time he lay on his couch watching the sky gradually close over, listening to the silence. It was this silence that had seemed painful to him during the first days here, after the war. He had requested a post in the little town at the base of the foothills separating the upper plateaus from the desert. There, rocky walls, green and black to the north, pink and lavender to the south, marked the frontier of eternal summer. He had been named to a post farther north, on the plateau itself. In the beginning, the solitude and the silence had been hard for him on these wastelands peopled only by stones. Occasionally, furrows suggested cultivation, but they had been dug to uncover a certain kind of stone good for building. The only plowing here was to harvest rocks. Elsewhere a thin layer of soil accumulated in the hollows would be scraped out to enrich paltry village gardens. This is the way it was: bare rock covered three quarters of the region. Towns sprang up, flourished, then disappeared; men came by, loved one another or fought bitterly, then died. No one in this desert, neither he nor his guest, mattered. And yet, outside this desert neither of them, Daru knew, could have really lived.

When he got up, no noise came from the classroom. He was amazed at the unmixed joy he derived from the mere thought that the Arab might have fled and that he would be alone with no decision to make. But the prisoner was there. He had merely stretched out between the stove and the desk. With eyes open, he was staring at the ceiling. In that position, his thick lips were particularly noticeable, giving him a pouting look. "Come," said Daru. The Arab got up and followed him. In the bedroom, the schoolmaster pointed to a chair near the table under the window. The Arab sat down without taking his eyes off Daru.

"Are you hungry?"

"Yes," the prisoner said.

68   Daru set the table for two. He took flour and oil, shaped a cake in a frying-pan, and lighted the little stove that functioned on bottled gas. While the cake was cooking, he went out to the shed to get cheese, eggs, dates, and condensed milk. When the cake was done he sat it on the window sill to cool, heated some condensed milk diluted with water, and beat up the eggs into an omelette. In one of his motions he knocked against the revolver stuck in his right pocket. He set the bowl down, went into the classroom, and put the revolver in his desk drawer. When he came back to the room, night was falling. He put on the light and served the Arab. "Eat," he said. The Arab took a piece of the cake, lifted it eagerly to his mouth, and stopped short.

"And you?" he asked.

"After you. I'll eat too."

The thick lips opened slightly. The Arab hesitated, then bit into the cake determinedly.

72   The meal over, the Arab looked at the schoolmaster. "Are you the judge?"

"No, I'm simply keeping you until tomorrow."

"Why do you eat with me?"

"I'm hungry."

76   The Arab fell silent. Daru got up and went out. He brought back a folding bed from the shed, set it up between the table and the stove, perpendicular to his own bed. From a large suitcase which, upright in a corner, served as a shelf for papers, he took two blankets and arranged them on the camp bed. Then he stopped, felt useless, and sat down on his bed. There was nothing more to do or to get ready. He had to look at this man. He looked at him, therefore, trying to imagine his face bursting with rage. He couldn't do so. He could see nothing but the dark yet shining eyes and the animal mouth.

     "Why did you kill him?" he asked in a voice whose hostile tone surprised him.

The Arab looked away.

"He ran away. I ran after him."

80   He raised his eyes to Daru again and they were full of a sort of woeful interrogation. "Now what will they do to me?"

     "Are you afraid?"

He stiffened, turning his eyes away.

"Are you sorry?"

84   The Arab stared at him openmouthed. Obviously he did not understand. Daru's annoyance was growing. At the same time he felt awkward and self-conscious with his big body wedged between the two beds.

     "Lie down there," he said impatiently. "That's your bed."

The Arab didn't move. He called to Daru:

"Tell me!"

88   The schoolmaster looked at him.

"Is the gendarme coming back tomorrow?"

"I don't know."

"Are you coming with us?"

92   "I don't know. Why?"

     The prisoner got up and stretched out on top of the blankets, his feet toward the window. The light from the electric bulb shone straight into his eyes and he closed them at once.

     "Why?" Daru repeated, standing beside the bed.

     The Arab opened his eyes under the blinding light and looked at him, trying not to blink.

96   "Come with us," he said.

In the middle of the night, Daru was still not asleep. He had gone to bed after undressing completely; he generally slept naked. But when he suddenly realized that he had nothing on, he hesitated. He felt vulnerable and the temptation came to him to put his clothes back on. Then he shrugged his shoulders; after all, he wasn't a child and, if need be, he could break his adversary in two. From his bed he could observe him, lying on his back, still motionless with his eyes closed under the harsh light. When Daru turned out the light, the darkness seemed to coagulate all of a sudden. Little by little, the night came back to life in the window where the starless sky was stirring gently. The schoolmaster soon made out the body lying at his feet. The Arab still did not move, but his eyes seemed open. A faint wind was prowling around the schoolhouse. Perhaps it would drive away the clouds and the sun would reappear.

During the night the wind increased. The hens fluttered a little and then were silent. The Arab turned over on his side with his back to Daru, who thought he heard him moan. Then he listened for his guest's breathing, become heavier and more regular. He listened to that breath so close to him and mused without being able to go to sleep. In this room where he had been sleeping alone for a year, this presence bothered him. But it bothered him also by imposing on him a sort of brotherhood he knew well but refused to accept in the present circumstances. Men who share the same rooms, soldiers or prisoners, develop a strange alliance as if, having cast off their armor with their clothing, they fraternized every evening, over and above their differences, in the ancient community of dream and fatigue. But Daru shook himself; he didn't like such musings, and it was essential to sleep.

A little later, however, when the Arab stirred slightly, the schoolmaster was still not asleep. When the prisoner made a second move, he stiffened, on the alert. The Arab was lifting himself slowly on his arms with almost the motion of a sleepwalker. Seated upright in bed, he waited motionless without turning his head toward Daru, as if he were listening attentively. Daru did not stir; it had just occurred to him that the revolver was still in the drawer of his desk. It was better to act at once. Yet he continued to observe the prisoner, who, with the same slithery motion, put his feet on the ground, waited again, then began to stand up slowly. Daru was about to call out to him when the Arab began to walk, in a quite natural but extraordinarily silent way. He was heading toward the door at the end of the room that opened into the shed. He lifted the latch with precaution and went out, pushing the door behind him but without shutting it. Daru had not stirred. "He is running away," he merely thought. "Good riddance!" Yet he listened attentively. The hens were not fluttering; the guest must be on the plateau. A faint sound of water reached him, and he didn't know what it was until the Arab again stood framed in the doorway, closed the door carefully, and came back to bed without a sound. Then Daru turned his back on his and fell asleep. Still later he seemed, from the depths of his sleep, to hear furtive steps around the schoolhouse. "I'm dreaming! I'm dreaming!" he repeated to himself. And he went on sleeping.

100   When he awoke, the sky was clear; the loose window let in a cold, pure air. The Arab was asleep, hunched up under the blankets now, his mouth open, utterly relaxed. But when Daru shook him, he started dreadfully, staring at Daru with wild eyes as if he had never seen him and such a frightened expression that the schoolmaster stepped back. "Don't be afraid. It's me. You must eat." The Arab nodded his head and said yes. Calm had returned to his face, but his expression was vacant and listless.

The coffee was ready. They drank it seated together on the folding bed as they munched their pieces of the cake. Then Daru led the Arab under the shed and showed him the faucet where he washed. He went back into the room, folded the blankets and the bed, made his own bed and put the room in order.

Then he went through the classroom and out onto the terrace. The sun was already rising in the blue sky; a soft, bright light was bathing the deserted plateau. On the ridge the snow was melting in spots. The stones were about to reappear. Crouched on the edge of the plateau, the schoolmaster looked at the deserted expanse. He thought of Balducci. He had hurt him, for he had sent him off in a way as if he didn't want to be associated with him. He could still hear the gendarme's farewell and, without knowing why, he felt strangely empty and vulnerable. At that moment, from the other side of the schoolhouse, the prisoner coughed. Daru listened to him almost despite himself and then, furious, threw a pebble that whistled through the air before sinking into the snow. That man's stupid crime revolted him, but to hand him over was contrary to honor. Merely thinking of it made him smart with humiliation. And he cursed at one and the same time his own people who had sent him this Arab and the Arab too who had dared to kill and not managed to get away. Daru got up, walked in a circle on the terrace, waited motionless, and then went back into the schoolhouse.

The Arab, leaning over the cement floor of the shed, was washing his teeth with two fingers. Daru looked at him and said: "Come." He went back into the room ahead of the prisoner. He slipped a hunting-jacket on over his sweater and put on walking-shoes. Standing, he waited until the Arab had put on his *chèche* and sandals. They went into the classroom and the schoolmaster pointed to the exit, saying: "Go ahead." The fellow didn't budge. "I'm coming," said Daru. The Arab went out. Daru went back into the room and made a package of pieces of rusk, dates, and sugar. In the classroom, before going out, he hesitated a second in front of his desk, then crossed the threshold and locked the door. "That's the way," he said. He started toward the east, followed by the prisoner. But, a short distance from the schoolhouse, he thought he heard a slight sound behind them. He retraced his steps and examined the surroundings of the house; there was no one there. The Arab watched him without seeming to understand. "Come on," said Daru.

They walked for an hour and rested beside a sharp peak of limestone. The snow was melting faster and faster and the sun was drinking up the puddles at once, rapidly cleaning the plateau, which gradually dried and vibrated like the air itself. When they resumed walking, the ground rang under their feet. From time to time a bird rent the space in front of them with a joyful cry. Daru breathed in deeply the fresh morning light. He felt a sort of rapture before the vast familiar expanse, now almost entirely yellow under its dome of blue sky. They walked an hour more, descending toward the south. They reached a level height made up of crumbly rocks. From there on, the plateau sloped down, eastward, toward a low plain where there were a few spindly trees and, to the south, toward outcroppings of rock that gave the landscape a chaotic look.

104   Daru surveyed the two directions. There was nothing but the sky on the horizon. Not a man could be seen. He turned toward the Arab, who was looking at him blankly. Daru held out the package to him. "Take it," he said. "There are dates, bread, and sugar. You can hold out for two days. Here are a thousand francs too." The Arab took the package and the money but kept his full hands at

chest level as if he didn't know what to do with what was being given him. "Now look," the schoolmaster said as he pointed in the direction of the east, "there's the way to Tinguit. You have a two-hour walk. At Tinguit you'll find the administration and the police. They are expecting you." The Arab looked toward the east, still holding the package and the money against his chest. Daru took his elbow and turned him rather roughly toward the south. At the foot of the height on which they stood could be seen a faint path. "That's the trail across the plateau. In a day's walk from here you'll find pasturelands and the first nomads. They'll take you in and shelter you according to their law." The Arab had now turned toward Daru and a sort of panic was visible in his expression. "Listen," he said. Daru shook his head: "No, be quiet. Now I'm leaving you." He turned his back on him, took two long steps in the direction of the school, looked hesitantly at the motionless Arab, and started off again. For a few minutes he heard nothing but his own step resounding on the cold ground and did not turn his head. A moment later, however, he turned around. The Arab was still there on the edge of the hill, his arms hanging now, and he was looking at the schoolmaster. Daru felt something rise in his throat. But he swore with impatience, waved vaguely, and started off again. He had already gone some distance when he again stopped and looked. There was no longer anyone on the hill.

Daru hesitated. The sun was now rather high in the sky and was beginning to beat down on his head. The schoolmaster retraced his steps, at first somewhat uncertainly, then with decision. When he reached the little hill, he was bathed in sweat. He climbed it as fast as he could and stopped, out of breath, at the top. The rock-fields to the south stood out sharply against the blue sky, but on the plain to the east a steamy heat was already rising. And in that slight haze, Daru, with heavy heart, made out the Arab walking slowly on the road to prison.

A little later, standing before the window of the classroom, the schoolmaster was watching the clear light bathing the whole surface of the plateau, but he hardly saw it. Behind him on the blackboard, among the winding French rivers, sprawled the clumsily chalked-up words he had just read: "You handed over our brother. You will pay for this." Daru looked at the sky, the plateau, and, beyond, the invisible lands stretching all the way to the sea. In this vast landscape he had loved so much, he was alone.

Personal Response

What do you think of Daru's decision to let the Arab make his own choice about going to prison or walking toward freedom? Would you want Daru for a friend? Explain your answer.

Questions for Discussion

1. Characterize Daru, considering among other things his attitude toward being isolated, his attitude toward firearms, his relationship with Balducci, and his treatment of the Arab.

2. What choices does Daru make? Which choice forms the climax of the story?

3. Describe the environment in which this story is set and the role it plays.

4. Discuss the ending of the story. What are the implications of the writing on the blackboard? Has Daru really betrayed his "brother"?

5. Existentialism is a philosophy that emphasizes the uniqueness and isolation of the individual experience in a hostile or indifferent universe, regards human existence as unexplainable, and stresses freedom of choice and responsibility for the consequences of one's acts. What elements of this story reflect that philosophy?

Suggestions for Writing About
ETHICS, MORALS, AND VALUES

1. Drawing on Ellen Goodman's "It's Failure, Not Success," explain your position on the Machiavellian philosophy that any means you have to use to get to the top are justifiable.

2. Define "success" or "failure" by using the example of a person (or persons) you know personally or have read about. It might be that one person illustrates how you define the term, or it may be that several people represent different kinds of success. Is it possible for one person to be both a success and a failure?

3. With Ellen Goodman's "It's Failure, Not Success" in mind, explore the moral aspects of success by considering to what degree morality or ethics might be an issue in certain careers or professions.

4. Write to the editor of *Time* magazine in response to either Kurt Wiesenfeld's "Making the Grade" or Charles Krauthammer's "First and Last, Do No Harm."

5. Write your own "My Turn" column on the subject of grades, teachers, and jobs, using Kurt Wiesenfeld's "Making the Grade" as a starting point for your thinking and discussion. Consider whether you believe that grades and the job they lead to are more valuable or important than getting a good education. Consider, too, the matter of incentives such as the gold stars and smiley faces Wiesenfeld mentions. In what ways have teachers you have had rewarded you for effort, not results?

6. Interview your parents or other people who were young adults in the 1960s about what they recall of their hopes, fears, formative values, and moral options. Then write an essay describing the results of your interviews and the conclusions you draw from them. Consider, for instance, the ways in which the experiences and beliefs of the people you interviewed are similar to and different from your own.

7. Define an abstract quality like justice, honor, integrity, honesty, or moral responsibility by using specific examples to illustrate your general statements.

8. Drawing on Alan Thein Durning's "Can't Live Without It," select several advertisements in any medium and analyze them in terms of the dreams they sell or the values they promote and whether you consider their tactics ethical.

9. Select an advertisement that appeals to you and analyze what you like about it and how it makes you want whatever it is selling, or do an analysis of an advertisement you find particularly offensive or irritating.

10. Drawing on Roger Rosenblatt's "The Quality of Mercy Killing," Derek Humphrey's "Mercy Denied to Roswell Gilbert," and Charles Krauthammer's "First and Last, Do No Harm," write an opinion paper on mercy killing. Include the example of the Gilbert case or of another mercy killing case you know of. Consider whether mercy killing is ever justified and, if so, under what circumstances it might be.

11. Write an analysis of Albert Camus' "The Guest" by explaining the ways in which it reflects certain elements of existential philosophy.

12. Taking into account what some of the writers in this chapter say about individual responsibility, moral or ethical choices, and positive values, write an analysis of the character Daru in Albert Camus' "The Guest."

13. Examine the issue of an individual's right to act according to conscience when the act would violate the law. Under what circumstances, aside from mercy killing, might such a dilemma occur? When might the issue of individual freedom take precedence over the law, or should the law always be obeyed?

14. Explain how a specific person, institution, book, or course in school has had a strong effect on the formation of your own values.

CHAPTER 8

PREJUDICE AND DISCRIMINATION

Despite civil rights struggles and the women's movement, despite legislation to ensure equal treatment under the law and the creation of agencies to monitor and punish discriminatory practices, prejudice and discrimination remain real problems in American society. Many people, particularly young adults, believe that the problems faced by women and minorities in the past have been eradicated and that such things are no longer issues. However, statistics demonstrate that women and minorities have not achieved equity with white males, nor has discrimination on the basis of sex, race, or ethnicity disappeared. Indeed, as some of the selections in this chapter demonstrate, prejudice and discrimination are still very much a part of the American fabric.

In "Prejudice, Conflict, and Ethnoviolence," Joan C. Weiss argues that, despite civil-rights legislation of the 1960s, America is still a highly segregated society. Citing examples of racism and violence motivated by bigotry, Weiss explains what the National Institute Against Prejudice and Violence, of which she is executive director, does in its efforts to deal with such problems. Next, Michel Wieviorka in "The Ruses of Racism" examines the conditions under which racial violence as a means of oppression is encouraged to grow.

Speaking from personal experience, Mary Crow Dog tells of her involvement in the 1970s' conflict between Native Americans and federal troops at Wounded Knee in "A Woman from He-Dog." The selection is the first chapter of her autobiography *Lakota Woman*. The book documents "a story of death, of determination against all odds, and of the cruelties perpetrated against American Indians during the last several decades. It is also a deeply moving account of a woman's triumphant struggle to survive in a hostile world."

The focus shifts to a consideration of discrimination of another sort in Daniel Meier's "One Man's Kids." Meier discusses the difficulty he has had with other people accepting his choice of profession—teaching first grade. He has found that reactions vary, but people are often not only surprised but suspicious when

331

they find out what he does for a living. His essay explains some of the perceived differences between traditionally male and traditionally female occupations.

The last three essays address the subject of affirmative action and equitable treatment, particularly in employment, of everyone regardless of sex or race. Stephen Steinberg explains in "The Affirmative Action Debate" how affirmative action policies were developed and why he believes they are still needed. Marilyn Webb in "Why Women Don't Get Paid What They're Worth" points out that despite its being over thirty years since a law was passed requiring men and women to be paid the same salaries for the same work, women are still lagging far behind men in earnings. Finally, Pico Iyer in "The Masks of Minority Terrorism" argues against affirmative action, despite his being a member of a minority group himself.

PREJUDICE, CONFLICT, AND ETHNOVIOLENCE: A NATIONAL DILEMMA

Joan C. Weiss

Joan C. Weiss is executive director of the National Institute Against Prejudice and Violence in Baltimore, Maryland. In its efforts to achieve its purpose of reducing prejudice and violence in our nation, the Institute monitors incidents of racial and ethnic violence and seeks ways to prevent such conflicts in the future. This 1989 article is reprinted from USA Today Magazine.

"The United States Constitution provides us with the tools we need to deal with racism," Pres. Reagan claimed in the spring of 1988 in a speech in which he compared human rights in the U.S. with those in the Soviet Union. While the Constitution is far-reaching and timeless beyond even the vision of its framers, providing us with a legal framework which enables us to attack many racist practices, laws do not solve problems. One of the great myths in this country is that civil rights were guaranteed with the passage of a few laws in the 1960's. Therefore, the logic proceeds, if people still are suffering the effects of racism, it is either because the laws are not being enforced adequately or because not enough time has passed. In other words, 25 years is a relatively short time and, in fact, strides have been made—we just need to be patient.

It is true that there is not adequate enforcement of civil and human rights statutes, and strides have been made. No one would argue with the fact that blacks and other minorities have entered mainstream America in a visible way. The number of black elected officials in this country is testimony to that, as are the number of minority-owned businesses, Jesse Jackson's candidacy, and a host of other measures one could choose.

However, it is easy to let these facts obscure reality. I recently participated in a conference in Jackson, Miss., sponsored by the U.S. Department of Housing and Urban Development in honor of the 20th anniversary of the passage of the Fair

Housing Laws. After 20 years, according to the findings of a variety of recent studies, we continue to live in a highly segregated society.

4   Both institutionalized discrimination and individual prejudices are still at work. Government policies virtually have eliminated low-income housing and, since minorities are disproportionately poor, the impact on them is devastating. Furthermore, minorities still are turned away from the rental of apartments and the purchase of homes. The methods of discrimination are just more subtle, more sophisticated than they used to be, so much so that black testers are sometimes unaware that prejudice has been at work until they see the test results.

The percentage of black high school graduates who go to college has declined since 1976, as has the proportion of blacks in graduate schools, which reached a new low in 1986. Housing and education are but two areas in which discrimination and prejudice are still problems.

Economic disparities between minorities and non-minorities persist, maintained by institutionalized discrimination. For example, 1986 figures indicate that poverty rates among blacks and Hispanics are nearly three times that for whites, according to a report by the Commission on Minority Participation in Education and American Life, which was formed by the American Council on Education and the Education Commission of the States. It adds that, "In education, employment, income, health, longevity and other basic measures of individual and social well-being, gaps persist—and in some cases are widening—between members of minority groups and the majority population."

Other factors compound the existing prejudice and discrimination, creating an environment ripe for intergroup tension. There has been a lack of planning with regard to the influx of immigrants, contributing to misunderstandings and conflict stemming from cultural differences among groups. We have seen a backlash to major social changes such as the women's and gay rights movement, as well as to the institution of affirmative action programs. The elimination of Federally funded social programs has sent an anti-authority message to the community. We also are affected by political and social events around the world. In this time of media satellites and instant news, we should understand fully what happens in South Africa, the Middle East, or Central America has a profound impact on intergroup relations in this country.

Bigotry Begets Violence

8   These factors have created fertile ground for violence motivated by bigotry. There are extraordinary numbers of violent incidents based on someone's race, religion, ethnic background, and sexual orientation occurring around the country: harassment of victims day in and day out as they leave their homes; attacks on children as they go to school; bricks and gunshots through windows of homes, businesses, churches, and synagogues; crosses burned; death threats; racist graffiti; swastika paintings; arson; physical assaults; and murder. These acts

of bigotry are happening in communities, schools, and workplaces all across the nation. No area is immune.

Nobody knows exactly how many crimes motivated by bigotry are committed because there is no accurate system of national data collection. We know from research at the National Institute Against Prejudice and Violence, however, that the problem is persistent, pervasive, and serious. Thousands of ethnoviolent incidents occur each year. In addition to the Institute's files, a number of other sources confirm the seriousness of this matter.

In Maryland, one of only eight states in the country with data collection legislation, between 350 and 500 incidents based on race, religion, and ethnicity were reported to the State Human Relations Commission each year from 1981 through 1986. The other states with data collection legislation—Connecticut, Illinois, Maine, Minnesota, Oklahoma, Pennsylvania, and Virginia—have not had their laws in effect long enough to have multi-year data available. However, the police in New York and Boston both have collected data for approximately eight years. The New York City police documented between 172 and 286 incidents each year from 1981 until 1986. Then, in 1987, in the wake of the Howard Beach racial attack, they documented 463 incidents. In Boston, the police department recorded over 2,700 incidents from 1978 through 1987.

Other sources include the Center for Democratic Renewal, which documented almost 3,000 incidents in the country from 1980 to 1987; the Anti-Defamation League of B'nai B'rith, which recorded 1,018 anti-Semitic incidents in 1987; and the National Gay and Lesbian Task Force, which documented over 7,000 instances of anti-gay violence in 1986. On the local level, human relations commissions in Montgomery County, Md., and Los Angeles County, Calif., as well as citizens' groups such as the North Carolinians Against Racist and Religious Violence, consistently have recorded dozens, sometimes hundreds, of incidents in their communities in the last few years. As high as the figures are, we know that they represent only a portion of the crimes that occur. Institute research findings show that one-third of victims never report their incidents to any official agency.

12   Campus violence has received considerable attention during the last two years. In our study of violence on the University of Maryland's Baltimore County campus, we learned that one out of five minority students had been the victim of some form of harassment during the academic year. Based on accounts in the print media alone, the Institute recorded the occurrence of ethnoviolence at 155 different institutions of higher education between September, 1986, and May, 1988.

In addition, the white supremacist groups are alive and well. Though small in numbers, they have been responsible for a spate of violent crimes in recent years. Perhaps even more frightening are the youth groups which have sprung up. The Aryan Youth Movement and various Skinhead factions have been recruiting alienated teens and young adults, capturing their loyalty, playing on their fears, and fueling their anger until it erupts into violence, sometimes murder. However, too much attention to hate groups diverts us from the most serious issue: most perpetrators of crimes of prejudice are unaffiliated with hate groups. They are our neighbors and our neighbors' children.

I'd like to share with you a few of the images in my head from interviewing victims as part of the data-gathering process for the Institute's seven-state study of the impact of incidents on victims.

- I'm listening to a middle-aged Laotian woman, talking through a translator, tell of being attacked at noon while walking to her English class. She never returned to school.

- I see the face of a young black father, his wife sitting next to him, his two-year-old son smiling, making friends with everyone in the room. The father is speaking fast and angrily about the repeated attacks on his home since he moved into a white neighborhood—trash on his lawn, windows broken, arson, and death threats. He finally bought a gun. Quietly, he says, "I'm afraid of what I might do if I catch one of them. I'm damned if I don't protect my family and damned if I do. Either way, I'll lose with the system."

- I hear the voice of a 16-year-old son of an interracial couple, victims of harassment over a period of three years and, finally, a cross-burning. He says, wistfully, "My mom used to walk and talk to people. Now she's afraid. She just sits inside and reads all the time."

The effects of incidents on victims are traumatic and long-lasting. They experience fear and isolation, never knowing what future act awaits them. Their sense of personal violation is similar to that of a rape victim. They lose sleep. They fear for their lives and those of their children. Some change jobs. Some move away from communities, looking for a safe place. They cannot live in peace.

What Can Be Done?

16 A reporter came into my office recently to discuss what the National Institute Against Prejudice and Violence does. After I briefly explained its programs, he asked, "What is the solution to the problem? There has been violence based on prejudice since the beginning of time. Do you really think you can do anything which will make any difference?" On one level, his cynicism is understandable. On another level, it is sad, because there *are* ways in which we can make a difference, and believing otherwise means giving up and giving in.

The Institute has a multifaceted approach to the problem of violence motivated by bigotry. We maintain a clearinghouse of information about incidents, as well as programs to prevent and respond to them. We publish a newsletter, educational materials, and reports of our research. We have a legislative manual of federal and state civil and criminal remedies, and recently published a report on bigotry and cable TV. The latest publication discusses the legal and community issues involved in the use of cable television by racist and anti-Semitic groups.

We provide consultation and technical assistance on preventing and handling incidents and responding to activities of the Ku Klux Klan, neo-Nazis, and other hate groups. We have been asked for advice and assistance by the U.S. Department of Housing and Urban Development, the U.S. Department of Justice, state and local human relations commissions, and community groups.

We conduct original research on the causes and nature of incidents, their impact on victims, and the effectiveness of different methods of response. We are conducting research on ethnoviolence in the workplace and are about to embark on the first major national survey of victimization in the general population.

20   Our educational efforts include convening national and regional conferences, conducting trainings and seminars, assisting educators in developing programs and curricular materials, and providing information to media.

Over the last few years, a variety of positive responses has emerged around the country. People of good will, responsible state and local agencies, and community organizations have formed coalitions and task forces. States have passed laws which proscribe activities of hate groups and increase penalties for hate crimes. The Institute increasingly has been asked to train community leaders, police officers, and human rights officials to identify, monitor, and respond to ethnoviolence. Victim assistance programs have been established, and a few creative criminal justice systems are utilizing alternative programs in the adjudication of crimes committed by juveniles.

The needed programs of prevention have been slower in coming, in part because we don't know enough about intervening in the direction of an individual's life to avert a course of violence, let alone violence motivated by prejudice. While we need more research in the area, we do know that intergroup relations and cross-cultural issues need to be addressed from the beginning of kindergarten through high school.

We also know that, until the economic disparities among different groups in our society are rectified and basic needs such as housing and employment are met, it will be impossible for us to deal effectively with intergroup tension. These needs create a barrier to educating youth, to dispelling the ignorance and fear and anger which erupt into violence.

24   We must educate public officials and citizens that ethnoviolence is not an isolated phenomenon. Laws need to be passed. Law enforcement officials need to be trained. Victims need assistance and treatment. Curriculum materials need to be developed. Research needs to be done. We also must speak out—not to do so is to condone the pain and suffering which is going on all around us.

I shared all of these thoughts with the cynical reporter, but there is more. Underlying all that we do should be a commitment to social justice and human equality, and the realization that the inequities, injustice, and pain resulting from prejudice in our society hurt us all and sap the strength that we need as a nation to build a better future.

William Schwartz, a professor of social work, wrote of the importance of "lending a vision" to a group. In order to find solutions, we all must have a vision and lend it to those we meet in our communities, schools, and workplaces. This vision is one which gives rise to activism that changes what is. It is a vision that can see beyond the injustices of today to the possibility of a more just society tomorrow. Such a vision requires not only a depth of commitment to a set of ideals, but also the conviction that one's effort *can* make a difference and the belief that even small changes can be important.

Bigotry and Ethnoviolence in the Workplace

San Francisco, Calif.—A former employee of the Board of Public Utilities testified in Federal court that a one-time president and current member of the board had made disparaging remarks about black workers. When discussing giving employees a holiday on Martin Luther King, Jr.'s birthday, he had joked, "Shoot four more of them and give them a week off."

Fort Lauderdale, Fla.—"Nigger Squad" was spray-painted on the window of the Police Department's executive office, to which four black officers were assigned.

Annapolis, Md.—Alderman Carl Snowden, an outspoken black community leader, received hate mail at his City Hall office, including a photograph of a black man hanging from a tree with a caption warning Snowden of a similar fate.

Portland, Ore.—An employee of a transport company was harassed racially and fired. His supervisor called him a "fat Mexican," a "taco bender," a "wetback," and a "spic."

Seattle, Wash.—A black head janitor of an elementary school found dead animals, including a cat, opossum, squirrel, and raccoon, near her office.

Bensalem, Pa.—In a Federal court suit, a Jewish man claimed that a supervisor in the company where he worked made anti-Semitic remarks, including one in which he said the owner was "going to manufacture a special microwave oven just to put you in."

Lima, Ohio—A black foreman in a General Dynamics weapons plant found a burning cross suspended from one of his work cranes.

New York City—A white supervisor who supported black workers' demands for equal promotions received threatening letters addressed to "Race Traitor."

Chicago, Ill.—A U.S. District Court judge ruled that a black employee at an industrial tape plant was a victim of racial discrimination when, on separate occasions, he found a dead rat with its neck slit on his desk, oil in his shoes, worms near his lunch, and garbage on his desk.

Philadelphia, Pa.—The president of a branch of the NAACP found "Kill Niggers" scribbled on a doorjamb of his headquarters.

Cincinnati, Ohio—Dressed in mock Ku Klux Klan robes, a group of workers assaulted a black employee. They made a cross of paper, set it on fire, and attempted to put it between his legs.

Personal Response

What response did Weiss's descriptions of racism in America evoke in you?
What kinds of harassment or acts of violence have you witnessed? What was
your reaction to such incidents?

Questions for Discussion

1. What evidence does Weiss supply to support her argument that, despite the
   civil-rights legislation of the 1960s, ours is still a highly segregated society?
   What evidence does she provide to support her contention that "bigotry
   begets violence" (paragraph 8)?

2. Describe the audience Weiss seems to have in mind. Do you think she antic-
   ipates an audience opposed to her viewpoint or one that will be sympathetic?
   Explain your answer.

3. Summarize the various approaches that the National Institute Against Prejudice and Violence has taken toward solving the problem of violence based on
   prejudice. Comment on the effectiveness of those strategies.

4. What actions does Weiss call for in order to deal with the problem of
   prejudice-motivated violence? How likely do you think that those actions
   will be carried out?

5. The section entitled "Bigotry and Ethnoviolence in the Workplace" was
   originally featured in a box following the conclusion of the article. Does
   setting this information off from the rest of the text seem a more effective
   strategy to you than including the examples in the body of the article? Why
   or why not?

THE RUSES OF RACISM

Michel Wieviorka

*Michel Wieviorka is a French sociologist, a lecturer at the University of Paris-
Dauphine, and assistant director of the Centre d'Analyse et d'Intervention So-
ciologiques in Paris. He is co-author, with Dominique Wolton, of* Terrorisme à
la Une *(1987) and author of* Sociétés et Terrorisme *(1988) and* The Making of Terrorism *(1993). This essay is reprinted from the February 1993 UN-
ESCO Courier.*

Racism is not always overtly, brutally violent—it does not always kill. Racial discrimination, expressions of prejudice and racist tracts can all carry ominous overtones of violence, but they cannot be ranked alongside the physical violence
perpetrated in pogroms, lynchings, immigrant-bashing, murders and other types of
assault, which is what I wish to discuss.

What is more, the most violent forms of racism do not necessarily grow out of other varieties of racism. Contrary to popular belief, prejudice does not invariably and inevitably lead on to acts of violence. Deep-seated racism may be widespread in societies where there is no outward sign of naked violence.

For racist violence to erupt, a certain set of conditions must exist. One conditioning factor is the attitude of those in authority: what they are willing and able to do in order to deal with those who engage in racist acts. When a government is weak or remote, or even tinged with racism itself, it encourages political groups and forces wishing to turn their message of hatred, contempt, subordination and rejection into deeds. It may even become actively racist itself or manipulate racist violence, as happened in the Russian Empire at the turn of the century, where the Czarist regime was largely instrumental in setting off the pogroms.

4   But there are other factors. Some institutions—particularly the legal system and the police—may use methods which, although not deliberately or explicitly racist in themselves, nevertheless contribute to the spread of serious outbreaks of violence. Many official enquiries have found that when police behaviour has exacerbated ethnic and social tensions instead of defusing them, it has often led to an escalation of violence in which racism occupies a prominent place.

Yet another factor is the existence of political forces capable of providing racist violence with an organized structure and an ideological foundation. As long as such forces do not exist or are relegated to the sidelines of society, violence is always possible and sometimes erupts, but it crops up in the form of sudden outbursts and short-lived explosions, in other words of acts which, numerous though they may be, are not linked by any apparent unifying principle.

When such forces do gain a political foothold, however, the violence for which they provide a structure, even if it is not directly organized by them, nonetheless becomes more cold-blooded, methodical, and active. It becomes a matter of schemes and strategies; it channels popular feelings of hatred and hostility towards the group marked out as a racial target, but does not allow them to be expressed spontaneously. It may even prevent them from being expressed at all, on the political grounds that any act of violence should be consistent with the aims and thinking of the party or organization.

This is why the emergence of a political force with a racist ideology and plans does not necessarily mean that there will be an immediate increase in violence, for violence may actually be detrimental to its attempts to achieve legitimate political status. Violence may create an image of disorder and accordingly be played down until the movement achieves power, when it will be able to indulge in violence in its most extreme forms. Conversely, there may be an increase in violence when the power of a racist force or party is on the wane, because some of its members may take a harder line if they feel they have no political future. The end of apartheid in South Africa is providing scope not for more racism but for more racial violence.

8   Since the beginning of the modern era, racism has been linked to patterns of domination, especially those of colonialism set against the background of empire-building. But it has also informed trends in thinking which, from the nineteenth

century onwards, influenced aspects of physical anthropology and other doctrinaire intellectual movements. When the term "racism" emerged in the period between the two World Wars, some of the theories from the past were refurbished. Above all, racist attitudes spread all over the world in the wake of the social upheavals that are at the root of various forms of racial violence.

Racial violence is no longer only the crude expression of colonial-type domination. It may also stem from an economic crisis, in which a deprived group, threatened with a decline in social status or exclusion from the mainstream, turns against another group in an attempt to oust it, on racial grounds, from a shrinking job market. The racism of the poor whites, which led to the lynching of blacks in the southern United States in the first half of the twentieth century, came about when the whites saw their black neighbours as dangerous competitors on the industrial job market.

But racial violence may also occur among more affluent classes, which want to maintain the gap separating them from the less privileged. The method they use is a combination of social and racial segregation, which may in fact lead to more cold-blooded and calculated forms of violence. At the beginning of the century, well-to-do white citizens in the southern United States organized lynching parties to punish black men accused of raping white women or theft.

However, racist violence does not always stem solely or directly from social factors. It may originate in a real or imagined threat to the identity of a group, or it may accompany the expansion of a state or religion, sometimes claiming to represent universal values, as often happened during the colonial period.

12   The urge to uphold a particular identity can lead to unlimited violence, fuelled either by an obsessive fear of "racial intermingling" or by reference to an absolute difference that prohibits all social intercourse and all contact between races except in war. Such forms of racism are intended to keep others at bay, to ensure that they are segregated or even expelled or destroyed. The aim is not so much to establish the inferior status of a group on the grounds of its physical attributes as to ensure that a community remains homogeneous or a nation remains pure, or to justify their unimpeded expansion.

Identity-related racism and the violence that goes with it can have three quite distinct motivations.

In some cases, this form of racism is founded on the affirmation of an identity that claims to be universal and seeks to crush everything that opposes it. The history of colonialism contains many instances of this phenomenon. Conversely, it may be based on the resistance of a nation or community to the modern world, in which case the chosen target is a group that is seen as the incarnation of evil, intrusion, or the corruption of culture or traditional values. The Jews have long been denounced and attacked as representatives of a hated modernity. The explosive violence of the pogroms and the more methodical violence of the gas chambers largely grew out of criticisms, phantasms and rumours that reproached the Jews on the grounds of their cosmopolitanism, wealth, political power and influence in the media.

Thirdly, this identity-related racism may flare up as a result of a clash between two or more communities within the same political entity or multiracial or multicultural society. In such cases, violence results from strained relations between communities, from a process of interaction in which one group's real or imagined attempt to assert itself prompts reactions from other groups and triggers off a spiralling power struggle that may end in an outburst of violence and political chaos. The civil war in Lebanon and the breakup of Yugoslavia are recent examples of conflicts where overt or implied references to race can be sensed behind rhetorical appeals to the nation or to the cultural, confessional and historical community.

16   When violence is associated with racism, therefore, it is governed by various conditions that dictate the course it takes and is rooted in a wide range of social and identity-related factors. But the important thing about violence is that it compresses into a single action factors that may be not only different but contradictory. Perpetrators of racist violence may wish, for example, to exclude a specific group from their society so as to exploit it. This happens frequently in industrialized countries, where immigrants are employed to do low-grade jobs and rejected on account of their culture. Or to take another case, in Czarist Russia and central Europe at the beginning of the present century, it was the rich, assimilated Jew, symbol of modernity, who was regarded as an intolerable threat, yet the victims of the pogroms were the culturally conspicuous and poverty-stricken Jewish masses.

This is the paradox of violence: not only is it unembarrassed by its inherent contradictions, it also creates its own logic and its own dynamics, so that in the end it alters the conditions that allowed it to emerge in the first place.

Personal Response

Wieviorka offers a number of reasons from a sociological perspective to account for the emergence and growth of racial violence. What are your personal observations or thoughts on the subject?

Questions for Discussion

1. What factors, according to Wieviorka, are necessary in order for racial violence to erupt?

2. Explain in your own words what Wieviorka means when he says that when a political force with a racist ideology emerges, there is not necessarily an increase in racial violence (paragraph 7). When is a racist force or party likely to increase its use of violence, according to Wieviorka?

3. Summarize the sociological causes of racial violence that Wieviorka identifies. What examples of the kinds of violence he is discussing does Wieviorka give?

4. State in your own words what you understand Wieviorka to mean by identity-related racial violence.

5. Summarize the three distinct motivations for identity-related racism that Wieviorka identifies.

6. Explain the title.

A WOMAN FROM HE-DOG

Mary Crow Dog

Mary Crow Dog grew up on a South Dakota reservation, living in a one-room cabin without running water or electricity. She became active in the Native American tribal pride movement in the 1960s and 1970s and married the movement's chief medicine man. "A Woman from He-Dog" is the first chapter of Mary Crow Dog's autobiography Lakota Woman *(written with Richard Erdoes and published in 1990).*

> A nation is not conquered until
> the hearts of its women
> are on the ground.
>   Then it is done, no matter
> how brave its warriors
> nor how strong their weapons.
>   *Cheyenne proverb*

I am Mary Brave Bird. After I had my baby during the siege of Wounded Knee they gave me a special name—Ohitika Win, Brave Woman, and fastened an eagle plume in my hair, singing brave-heart songs for me. I am a woman of the Red Nation, a Sioux woman. That is not easy.

I had my first baby during a firefight, with the bullets crashing through one wall and coming through the other. When my newborn son was only a day old and the marshals really opened up on us, I wrapped him up in a blanket and ran for it. We had to hit the dirt a couple of times, I shielding the baby with my body, praying, "It's all right if I die, but please let him live."

When I came out of Wounded Knee I was not even healed up, but they put me in jail at Pine Ridge and took my baby away. I could not nurse. My breasts swelled up and grew hard as rocks, hurting badly. In 1975 the feds put the muzzles of their M-16s against my head, threatening to blow me away. It's hard being an Indian woman.

4   My best friend was Annie Mae Aquash, a young, strong-hearted woman from the Micmac Tribe with beautiful children. It is not always wise for an Indian woman to come on too strong. Annie Mae was found dead in the snow at the bottom of a ravine on the Pine Ridge Reservation. The police said that she had

died of exposure, but there was a .38-caliber slug in her head. The FBI cut off her hands and sent them to Washington for fingerprint identification, hands that had helped my baby come into the world.

My sister-in-law, Delphine, a good woman who had lived a hard life, was also found dead in the snow, the tears frozen on her face. A drunken man had beaten her, breaking one of her arms and legs, leaving her helpless in a blizzard to die.

My sister Barbara went to the government hospital in Rosebud to have her baby and when she came out of anesthesia found that she had been sterilized against her will. The baby lived only for two hours, and she had wanted so much to have children. No, it isn't easy.

When I was a small girl at the St. Francis Boarding School, the Catholic sisters would take a buggy whip to us for what they called "disobedience." At age ten I could drink and hold a pint of whiskey. At age twelve the nuns beat me for "being too free with my body." All I had been doing was holding hands with a boy. At age fifteen I was raped. If you plan to be born, make sure you are born white and male.

8   It is not the big, dramatic things so much that get us down, but just being Indian, trying to hang on to our way of life, language, and values while being surrounded by an alien, more powerful culture. It is being an iyeska, a half-blood, being looked down upon by whites and full-bloods alike. It is being a backwoods girl living in a city, having to rip off stores to survive. Most of all it is being a woman. Among Plains tribes, some men think that all a woman is good for is to crawl into the sack with them and mind the children. It compensates for what white society had done to them. They were famous warriors and hunters once, but the buffalo is gone and there is not much rep in putting a can of spam or an occasional rabbit on the table.

As for being warriors, the only way some men can count coup nowadays is knocking out another skin's teeth during a barroom fight. In the old days a man made a name for himself by being generous and wise, but now he has nothing to be generous with, no jobs, no money; and as far as our traditional wisdom is concerned, our men are being told by the white missionaries, teachers, and employers that it is merely savage superstition they should get rid of if they want to make it in this world. Men are forced to live away from their children, so that the family can get ADC—Aid to Dependent Children. So some warriors come home drunk and beat up their old ladies in order to work off their frustration. I know where they are coming from. I feel sorry for them, but I feel even sorrier for their women.

To start from the beginning, I am a Sioux from the Rosebud Reservation in South Dakota. I belong to the "Burned Thigh," the Brule Tribe, the Sicangu in our language. Long ago, so the legend goes, a small band of Sioux was surrounded by enemies who set fire to their tipis and the grass around them. They fought their way out of the trap but got their legs burned and in this way acquired their name. The Brules are part of the Seven Scared Campfires, the seven tribes of the Western Sioux known collectively as Lakota. The Eastern

Sioux are called Dakota. The difference between them is their language. It is the same except that where we Lakota pronounce an L, the Dakota pronounce a D. They cannot pronounce L at all. In our tribe we have this joke: "What is a flat tire in Dakota?" Answer: "Bdowout."

The Brule, like the Sioux, were a horse people, fierce riders and raiders, great warriors. Between 1870 and 1880 all Sioux were driven into reservations, fenced in and forced to give up everything that had given meaning to their life—their horses, their hunting, their arms, everything. But under the long snows of despair the little spark of our ancient beliefs and pride kept glowing, just barely sometimes, waiting for a warm wind to blow that spark into a flame again.

12   My family was settled on the reservation in a small place called He-Dog, after a famous chief. There are still some He-Dogs living. One, an old lady I knew, lived to be over a hundred years old. Nobody knew when she had been born. She herself had no idea, except that when she came into the world there was no census yet, and Indians had not yet been given Christian first names. Her name was just He-Dog, nothing else. She always told me, "You should have seen me eighty years ago when I was pretty." I have never forgotten her face—nothing but deep cracks and gullies, but beautiful in its own way. At any rate very impressive.

On the Indian side my family was related to the Brave Birds and Fool Bulls. Old Grandpa Fool Bull was the last man to make flutes and play them, the old-style flutes in the shape of a bird's head which had the elk power, the power to lure a young girl into a man's blanket. Fool Bull lived a whole long century, dying in 1976, whittling his flutes almost until his last day. He took me to my first peyote meeting while I was still a kid.

He still remembered the first Wounded Knee, the massacre. He was a young boy at that time, traveling with his father, a well-known medicine man. They had gone to a place near Wounded Knee to take part in a Ghost Dance. They had on their painted ghost shirts which were supposed to make them bulletproof. When they got near Pine Ridge they were stopped by white soldiers, some of them from the Seventh Cavalry, George Custer's old regiment, who were hoping to kill themselves some Indians. The Fool Bull band had to give up their few old muzzle-loaders, bows, arrows, and even knives. They had to put up their tipis in a tight circle, all bunched up, with the wagons on the outside and the soldiers surrounding their camp, watching them closely. It was cold, so cold that the trees were crackling with a loud noise as the frost was splitting their trunks. The people made a fire the following morning to warm themselves and make some coffee and then they noticed a sound beyond the crackling of the trees: rifle fire, salvos making a noise like the ripping apart of a giant blanket; the boom of cannon and the rattling of quick-firing Hotchkiss guns. Fool Bull remembered the grown-ups bursting into tears, the women keening: "They are killing our people, they are butchering them!" It was only two miles or so from where Grandfather Fool Bull stood that almost three hundred Sioux men, women, and children were slaughtered. Later grandpa saw the bodies of the slain, all frozen in ghostly attitudes, thrown into a ditch like dogs. And he saw a tiny baby sucking at his dead mother's breast.

I wish I could tell about the big deeds of some ancestors of mine who fought at the Little Big Horn, or the Rosebud, counting coup during the Grattan or Fetterman battle, but little is known of my family's history before 1880. I hope some of my great-grandfathers counted coup on Custer's men, I like to imagine it, but I just do not know. Our Rosebud people did not play a big part in the battles against generals Crook or Custer. This was due to the policy of Spotted Tail, the all-powerful chief at the time. Spotted Tail had earned his eagle feathers as a warrior, but had been taken East as a prisoner and put in jail. Coming back years later, he said that he had seen the cities of the whites and that a single one of them contained more people than could be found in all the Plains tribes put together, and that every one of the wasičuns' factories could turn out more rifles and bullets in one day than were owned by all the Indians in the country. It was useless, he said, to try to resist the wasičuns. During the critical year of 1876 he had his Indian people keep most of the young men on the reservation, preventing them from joining Sitting Bull, Gall, and Crazy Horse. Some of the young bucks, a few Brave Birds among them, managed to sneak out trying to get to Montana, but nothing much is known. After having been forced into reservations, it was not thought wise to recall such things. It might mean no rations, or worse. For the same reason many in my family turned Christian, letting themselves be "whitemanized." It took many years to reverse this process.

16   My sister Barbara, who is four years older than me, says she remembers the day when I was born. It was late at night and raining hard amid thunder and lightning. We had no electricity then, just the old-style kerosene lamps with the big reflectors. No bathrooms, no tap water, no car. Only a few white teachers had cars. There was one phone in He-Dog, at the trading post. This was not so very long ago, come to think of it. Like most Sioux at that time my mother was supposed to give birth at home, I think, but something went wrong, I was pointing the wrong way, feet first or stuck sideways. My mother was in great pain, laboring for hours, until finally someone ran to the trading post and called the ambulance. They took her—us—to Rosebud, but the hospital there was not yet equipped to handle a complicated birth, I don't think they had surgery then, so they had to drive my mother all the way to Pine Ridge, some ninety miles distant, because there the tribal hospital was bigger. So it happened that I was born among Crazy Horse's people. After my sister Sandra was born the doctors there performed a hysterectomy on my mother, in fact sterilizing her without her permission, which was common at the time, and up to just a few years ago, so that it is hardly worth mentioning. In the opinion of some people, the fewer Indians there are, the better. As Colonel Chivington said to his soldiers: "Kill 'em all, big and small, nits make lice!"

I don't know whether I am a louse under the white man's skin. I hope I am. At any rate I survived the long hours of my mother's labor, the stormy drive to Pine Ridge, and the neglect of doctors. I am an iyeska, a breed, that's what the white kids used to call me. When I grew bigger they stopped calling me that, because it would get them a bloody nose. I am a small woman, not much over five feet tall, but I can hold my own in a fight, and in a free-for-all with honkies I can become rather ornery and do real damage. I have white blood in me. Often I have wished to be able to purge it out of me. As a young girl I used to look at myself in the mirror, trying to find a clue as to who and what I was. My face is very Indian, and so are my eyes and my hair, but my skin is very light. Always I waited for the summer, for the prairie sun, the Badlands sun, to tan me and make me into a real skin.

The Crow Dogs, the members of my husband's family, have no such problems of identity. They don't need the sun to tan them, they are full-bloods—the Sioux of the Sioux. Some Crow Dog men have faces which make the portrait on the buffalo Indian nickel look like a washed-out white man. They have no shortage of legends. Every Crow Dog seems to be legend in himself, including the women. They became outcasts in their stronghold at Grass Mountain rather than being whitemanized. They could not be tamed, made to wear a necktie or go to a Christian church. All during the long years when practicing Indian beliefs was forbidden and could be punished with jail, they went right on having their ceremonies, their sweat baths and sacred dances. Whenever a Crow Dog got together with some relatives, such as those equally untamed, unregenerated Iron Shells, Good Lances, Two Strikes, Picket Pins, or Hollow Horn Bears, then you could hear the sound of the can gleska, the drum, telling all the world that a Sioux ceremony was in the making. It took courage and suffering to keep the flame alive, the little spark under the snow.

The first Crow Dog was a well-known chief. On his shield was the design of two circles and two arrowheads for wounds received in battle—two white man's bullets and two Pawnee arrow points. When this first Crow Dog was lying wounded in the snow, a coyote came to warm him and a crow flew ahead of him to show him the way home. His name should be Crow Coyote, but the white interpreter misunderstood it and so they became Crow Dogs. This Crow Dog of old became famous for killing a rival chief, the result of a feud over tribal politics, then driving voluntarily over a hundred miles to get himself hanged at Deadwood, his wife sitting beside him in his buggy; famous also for finding on his arrival that the Supreme Court had ordered him to be freed because the federal government had no jurisdiction over Indian reservations and also because it was no crime for one Indian to kill another. Later, Crow Dog became a leader of the Ghost Dancers, holding out for months in the frozen caves and ravines of the Badlands. So, if my own family lacks history, that of my husband more than makes up for it.

20   Our land itself is a legend, especially the area around Grass Mountain where I am living now. The fight for our land is at the core of our existence, as it has been for the last two hundred years. Once the land is gone, then we are gone too. The Sioux used to keep winter counts, picture writings on buffalo skin, which told our people's story from year to year. Well, the whole country is one vast winter count. You can't walk a mile without coming to some family's sacred vision hill, to an ancient Sun Dance circle, an old battle-ground, a place where something

worth remembering happened. Mostly a death, a proud death or a drunken death. We are a great people for dying. "It's a good day to die!" that's our old battle cry. But the land with its tarpaper shacks and outdoor privies, not one of them straight, but all leaning this way or that way, is also a land to live on, a land for good times and telling jokes and talking of great deeds done in the past. But you can't live forever off the deeds of Sitting Bull or Crazy Horse. You can't wear their eagle feathers, freeload off their legends. You have to make your own legends now. It isn't easy.

Personal Response

Does this selection give you any insights or new perspectives on the experience of Native Americans?

Questions for Discussion

1. Identify the reference to Wounded Knee in paragraph 1.

2. What evidence does Mary Crow Dog offer to support her assertion that it is not easy being an Indian woman? What does this selection tell you about life today for Indian men?

3. What does Crow Dog mean when she refers to things "it was not thought wise to recall" (paragraph 15).

4. In paragraph 17, Crow Dog says that she used to look into the mirror as a young girl to try to "find a clue as to who and what [she] was." What does this selection tell you about who she is? What aspects of her character does she reveal?

5. What contrasts does Crow Dog draw between how Native Americans live now and how they once lived? In what ways do Crow Dog and other Native Americans keep alive "the little spark of [their] ancient beliefs and pride" (paragraphs 11 and 18)?

ONE MAN'S KIDS

Daniel Meier

Daniel Meier earned a master's degree from the Harvard Graduate School of Education in 1984. He taught first grade in Brookline, Massachusetts, from 1985 to 1988 and now teaches in an elementary school in Boston. His thoughts on teaching have been published in a variety of journals and magazines. This essay first appeared in the "About Men" series of the New York Times Magazine *in 1987.*

I teach first graders. I live in a world of skinned knees, double-knotted shoelaces, riddles that I've heard a dozen times, stale birthday cakes, hurt feelings, wandering stories, and one lost shoe ("and if you don't find it my mother'll kill me"). My work is dominated by 6-year-olds.

It's 10:45, the middle of snack, and I'm helping Emily open her milk carton. She has already tried the other end without success, and now there's so much paint and ink on the carton from her fingers that I'm not sure she should drink it at all. But I open it. Then I turn to help Scott clean up some milk he has just spilled onto Rebecca's whale crossword puzzle.

While I wipe my milk- and paint-covered hands, Jenny wants to know if I've seen that funny book about penguins that I read in class. As I hunt for it in a messy pile of books, Jason wants to know if there is a new seating arrangement for lunch tables. I find the book, turn to answer Jason, then face Maya, who is fast approaching with a new knock-knock joke. After what seems like the 10th "Who's there?" I laugh and Maya is pleased.

4   Then Andrew wants to know how to spell "flukes" for his crossword. As I get to "u," I give a hand signal for Sarah to take away the snack. But just as Sarah is almost out the door, two children complain that "we haven't even had ours yet." I stop the snack mid-flight, complying with their request for graham crackers. I then return to Andrew, noticing that he has put "flu" for 9 Down, rather than 9 Across. It's now 10:50.

My work is not traditional male work. It's not a singular pursuit. There is not a large pile of paper to get through or one deal to transact. I don't have one area of expertise or knowledge. I don't have the singular power over language of a lawyer, the physical force of a construction worker, the command over fellow workers of a surgeon, the wheeling and dealing transactions of a businessman. My energy is not spent in pursuing, climbing, achieving, conquering, or cornering some goal or object.

My energy is spent in encouraging, supporting, consoling, and praising my children. In teaching, the inner rewards come from without. On any given day, quite apart from teaching reading and spelling, I bandage a cut, dry a tear, erase a frown, tape a torn doll, and locate a long-lost boot. The day is really won through matters of the heart. As my students groan, laugh, shudder, cry, exult, and wonder, I do too. I have to be soft around the edges.

A few years ago, when I was interviewing for an elementary-school teaching position, every principal told me with confidence that, as a male, I had an advantage over female applicants because of the lack of male teachers. But in the next breath, they asked with a hint of suspicion why I chose to work with young children. I told them that I wanted to observe and contribute to the intellectual growth of a maturing mind. What I really felt like saying, but didn't, was that I loved helping a child learn to write his name for the first time, finding someone a new friend, or sharing in the hilarity of reading about Winnie the Pooh getting so stuck in a hole that only his head and rear show.

8   I gave that answer to those principals, who were mostly male, because I thought they wanted a "male" response. This meant talking about intellectual

matters. If I had taken a different course and talked about my interest in helping children in their emotional development, it would have been seen as closer to a "female" answer. I even altered my language, not once mentioning the word "love" to describe what I do indeed love about teaching. My answer worked; every principal nodded approvingly.

Some of the principals also asked what I saw myself doing later in my career. They wanted to know if I eventually wanted to go into educational administration. Becoming a dean of students or a principal has never been one of my goals, but they seemed to expect me, as a male, to want to climb higher on the career stepladder. So I mentioned that, at some point, I would be interested in working with teachers as a curriculum coordinator. Again, they nodded approvingly.

If those principals had been female instead of male, I wonder whether their questions, and my answers, would have been different. My guess is that they would have been.

At other times, when I'm at a party or a dinner and tell someone that I teach young children, I've found that men and women respond differently. Most men ask about the subjects I teach and the courses I took in my training. Then, unless they bring up an issue such as merit pay, the conversation stops. Most women, on the other hand, begin the conversation on a more immediate and personal level. They say things like "those kids must love having a male teacher" or "that age is just wonderful, you must love it." Then, more often than not, they'll talk about their own kids or ask me specific questions about what I do. We're then off and talking shop.

12   Possibly, men would have more to say to me, and I to them, if my job had more of the trappings and benefits of more traditional male jobs. But my job has no bonuses or promotions. No complimentary box seats at the ball park. No cab fare home. No drinking buddies after work. No briefcase. No suit. (Ties get stuck in paint jars.) No power lunches. (I eat peanut butter and jelly, chips, milk, and cookies with the kids.) No taking clients out for cocktails. The only place I take my kids is to the playground.

Although I could have pursued a career in law or business, as several of my friends did, I chose teaching instead. My job has benefits all its own. I'm able to bake cookies without getting them stuck together as they cool, buy cheap sewing materials, take out splinters, and search just the right trash cans for useful odds and ends. I'm sometimes called "Daddy" and even "Mommy" by my students, and if there's ever a lull in the conversation at a dinner party, I can always ask those assembled if they've heard the latest riddle about why the turkey crossed the road. (He thought he was a chicken.)

Personal Response

How do you view Meier's decision to teach first grade? Do you think it is as reasonable a career choice as any other, or do you feel, as Meier indicates some people do, "a hint of suspicion" about why a man would want to work with young children?

Questions for Discussion

1. What do you think Meier's purpose in this essay is; that is, what do you think he hopes to accomplish with it? Notice that Meier does not state his central idea until paragraph 5. What function do you think is served by the first four paragraphs? What difference would it have made had Meier put his fifth paragraph first?

2. Do you think Meier anticipated a sympathetic or a skeptical audience? How can you tell? What is the tone of the essay? Does Meier sound defensive?

3. Why isn't Meier's work "traditional male work" (paragraph 5)? Locate the series of adjectives Meier uses to describe "male work" and the adjectives he uses to describe what he does. What is Meier implying about the difference between "male work" and his work?

4. The central part of Meier's essay contrasts what he says are male activities and attitudes with female activities and attitudes. Summarize what Meier sees as the differences between males and females. Do you agree with him?

5. What benefits does Meier get from being a first-grade teacher? Would those benefits give you the same pleasure that they give Meier?

THE AFFIRMATIVE ACTION DEBATE

Stephen Steinberg

Stephen Steinberg, a sociologist, is a professor in the Urban Studies Department at Queens College and at the Graduate School and University Center of the City University of New York. His most recent book is Turning Back: The Retreat from Racial Justice in American Thought and Policy *(1995). This selection is from the March 1996 UNESCO Courier.*

The civil rights revolution in the United States was primarily a struggle for liberty, not equality. It sought to dismantle the system of official segregation that had been erected in the aftermath of slavery and to secure full rights of citizenship for African Americans. The abiding faith of the movement was that once the walls of segregation came tumbling down, blacks would be free to assume their rightful place in American society.

No sooner were the historic Civil Rights Acts of 1964 and 1965 passed, however, than it became clear that legislation alone would not address the deep-seated inequalities that were the legacy of two centuries of slavery and another century of Jim Crow. This was acknowledged by President Lyndon Johnson in a commencement address at Howard University in Washington, D.C., in June 1965, the very month that the Voting Rights Act received Congressional approval. As he told the graduating class:

"Freedom is not enough. You do not wipe away the scars of centuries by saying: 'Now you are free to go where you want, do as you desire, choose the leaders you please.' You do not take a person who for years has been hobbled by chains and liberate him, bring him to the starting line and then say, 'You are free to compete with all the others,' and still justly believe that you have been completely fair. We seek not just freedom but opportunity, not just equality as a right and a theory but equality as a fact and as a result."

Passive and Active Policies

4 Johnson's oratory was punctuated by the outbreak of racial violence in the Watts section of Los Angeles only two months later. In the ensuing years there were scores of other "riots" that threw American society into a deep political crisis, one that forced the nation to confront the issue of equality as well as liberty. This is the historical context in which affirmative action evolved as national policy.

Affirmative action has never been formulated as a coherent policy, but evolved incrementally through a series of presidential executive orders, administrative policies and court decisions. Partly for this reason, the term itself is so fraught with ambiguity that it is not always clear what advocates and opponents are squabbling about. Let us therefore make several crucial distinctions.

First, affirmative action must be distinguished from policies of non-discrimination. Although both seek racial justice in the workplace, policies of non-discrimination merely enjoin employers not to practice discrimination in the recruitment, hiring and promotion of workers. It is essentially a passive injunction *not* to discriminate. Affirmative action, on the other hand, commits employers to go a decisive step beyond non-discrimination and to *actively* seek out protected groups in employment. In this form—essentially "outreach" programmes reliant on the good faith efforts of employers—affirmative action arouses little or no opposition.

There is another form of affirmative action, however, that goes a decisive step beyond outreach and involves granting "preference" to minority applicants in order to guarantee the desired result. This is where controversy begins. For example, in his confirmation hearings to the Supreme Court in 1991, Clarence Thomas spoke passionately of his support for outreach programmes to extend opportunity to women and minorities, but he was equally adamant in his opposition to affirmative action programmes that involve preference.

8 These three forms an anti-discrimination are not mere abstractions, but are anchored in history. Let us briefly review how social policy evolved from non-discrimination, to outreach, to preference.

Occupational Apartheid

Africans were originally imported to the United States to provide labour in the South's evolving plantation economy. In the century after slavery, when tens of

millions of immigrants from Europe were rapidly absorbed into the North's bur-
geoning industries, a colour line excluded blacks from employment in the entire
industrial sector, with the exception of a few menial and low-paying jobs. When
the Southern economy finally underwent modernization, blacks were still confined
to "negro jobs"—servile and undesirable jobs that were reminiscent of slavery itself. As late as the 1960s, even as the civil rights movement reached its triumphant
climax, the United States had, in effect, a system of occupational apartheid that excluded blacks from entire job sectors. Most black men worked as unskilled labour-
ers; most black women as low-level service workers, especially domestics.

   This racial division of labour went virtually unchallenged until the Second
World War, when the black union leader A. Philip Randolph threatened a march
on Washington unless blacks were given access to jobs in defence industries.
This also led to the establishment of a Fair Employment Practices Committee.
Even though the FEPC had few resources and virtually no power to enforce non-
discrimination, it was quickly engulfed in controversy and disbanded as soon as
the war was over. Here was an early sign that attempts to enforce compliance
with non-discriminatory policies would encounter enormous resistance.

   In the 1940s and 1950s a second FEPC, along with other federal and state
agencies, preached non-discrimination, but with meagre results at best. Indeed,
this is precisely what eventually led to a shift from non-discrimination to affirmative action. A major turning point occurred in 1961 when President John F.
Kennedy, again in response to rising protest from the black community, issued Executive Order 10925, which required federal contractors to take "affirmative action" to desegregate their work force. Unlike similar declarations in the past, the
presidential edict established specific sanctions, including termination of contract,
to be applied against contractors who were not in compliance. Three years later
Title VII of the 1964 Civil Rights Act proscribed employment discrimination on the
basis of race, colour, religion, sex or national origin. A year later President Johnson
issued Executive Order 11246 that put further teeth into affirmative action by requiring federal contractors to develop specific goals and timetables for increasing
the employment of women and minorities.

Corporate Inertia

12   One might think that these developments would have dealt a fatal blow to America's system of occupational apartheid. This was hardly the case. In 1973—nine
years after the passage of the 1964 Civil Rights Act—a telephone company which
was the nation's largest corporate employer and a major government contractor
still had a highly segregated workforce. The company employed 165,000 persons
in low-paying operator classifications—99.9 percent of whom were female. Of
190,000 higher-paying craft workers, 99 percent were male. Virtually no women
were in management positions, and even supervisory personnel in "female" departments were male.

   The company, furthermore, could boast of "equal opportunity" policies that
had increased black employment from 2.5 percent in 1960 to 10 percent in 1970,

but this mainly reflected the hiring of black women as operators to replace white women who were experiencing a high rate of turnover. There were virtually no black males in craft jobs and even fewer in management. This was the context in which the Federal Communications Commission opposed a rate increase on the grounds of the company's discriminatory employment practices.

Eventually this resulted in a landmark consent decree with the Equal Employment Opportunity Commission (EEOC), the Department of Justice, and the Department of Labor in which the company paid monetary damages to aggrieved classes and agreed to change its employment policies and meet employment targets for women and minorities. According to a study on the impact of the consent decree, the programme got off to a poor start but by 1976, 99 percent of its short-term targets had been reached. Furthermore, these gains occurred in the context of a declining labour force due to the impact of new technology.

What's at Stake

As this case illustrates, good-faith efforts to increase minority representation were generally ineffective until they were backed up by specific "goals and timetables" that, in effect, gave preference to minority applicants who met basic qualifications but might not have been hired or promoted without affirmative action mandates. Critics, of course, complain that this amounts to a system of de facto quotas. Like Clarence Thomas, they raise no objection to affirmative action so long as it involves "outreach," but reject affirmative action as soon as it involves "preference."

What these critics overlook, however, is that decades of preaching nondiscrimination produced little or no change in the system of occupational apartheid. Indeed, this is why affirmative policy shifted from outreach to preference in the first place.

Unfortunately, no systematic body of evidence exists that would permit a precise accounting of what has been achieved under affirmative action. This much is clear, however: the occupational spheres where blacks have made the most notable progress—in government service, in major blue-collar occupations, in corporate management, and in the professions—are all areas where vigorous affirmative action programmes have been in place over the past two decades. Before affirmative action, the black middle class consisted of a small number of professionals and businessmen anchored in the ghetto economy. Most of the progress that we celebrate—particularly the emergence of a large black middle class with roots in mainstream economic structures—is a direct product of affirmative action.

Thus, much is at stake in the current debate over the future of affirmative action. In recent years there has been a rising chorus of criticism against affirmative action programmes, and it has not come only from whites who feel that they are being asked to pay the price for crimes that they did not commit. Criticism also has been levelled by legal scholars who challenge the constitutionality of affirmative action and see it as betraying the cardinal principle of the civil rights movement itself: a color-blind society. A new genre of black conservatives have denounced affirmative action as patronizing to blacks and subversive of black self-esteem. Even some liberals who say they support affirmative action in principle have concluded that it is self-defeating because it triggers a popular backlash that only serves their political enemies.

These are powerful arguments, based as they are on legal and moral principles as well as on political pragmatism. However, they fail to recognize the lesson of history: that even laws proscribing discrimination and well-intentioned efforts to increase minority representation were never effective until they were backed up with specific affirmative action mandates.

20   Thus, the problem is stated falsely when it is suggested that we must choose between merit or preference, or between the rights of individuals and the rights of groups, or between a color-blind or a color-conscious society. Rather, the paramount choice is between racial progress or returning to the status quo ante: the period before affirmative action when we salved our national conscience with laws on the books that did little or nothing to reverse centuries of occupational apartheid.

Personal Response

What is your opinion of affirmative action?

Questions for Discussion

1. How do affirmative action and policies on nondiscrimination differ?

2. Define "occupational apartheid."

3. In your own words, explain what led to the development of affirmative action policies.

4. Summarize the arguments in support of and against affirmative action. Where do you position yourself in the debate?

WHY WOMEN DON'T GET PAID WHAT THEY'RE WORTH

Marilyn Webb

Marilyn Webb teaches journalism at Columbia University and is the former editor-in-chief of Psychology Today. *This article appeared in the June 1993 issue of* Ladies Home Journal.

Frantic phone calls come in regularly to the New York City Police Department's 911 switchboard. And when they do, the dispatchers there mobilize the real-life version of TV's *Rescue 911*.

Most of the emergencies they respond to are routine: fires, car crashes, bomb scares, street muggings and medical crisis. But sometimes, the 911 dispatchers have to switch into higher gear. Once, they spent six hours coordinating emergency operations after a thirty-five-ton crane toppled on a woman who'd been walking past a construction site. "We saved her life," says Linda Scotti, a 911 supervisor at the time.

As Scotti sees it, the work requires a high level of responsibility. So, when she learned that dispatchers at the city's fire department were earning higher salaries than the 911 workers, she was outraged. After all, their jobs were nearly identical. "The only difference was that our department was ninety percent female and the fire department was ninety percent male," she says.

4   When she first became aware of the difference in 1981, Scotti says the starting salary for 911 workers was $19,000 a year; for fire dispatchers, it was $24,000. The gap grew larger higher up the salary scale.

Armed with those figures, Scotti rallied her co-workers. Thwarted in their efforts to change things internally, they contacted an attorney. In 1989, the parties reached an out-of-court settlement. The 911 workers ended up with eight years of back pay, and a raise that brought their hourly wage to an equal level.

"The average person's salary went up a minimum of $5,000, some much more," Scotti says happily.

This month marks the thirtieth anniversary of the Equal Pay Act of 1963, a federal law that makes it illegal for employers to pay women less than men for equal work. And it's been nearly as long since Title VII of the 1964 Civil Rights Act made equal-employment laws more stringent.

8   Yet, as Scotti's experience shows, women are still fighting an uphill battle for fair wages. "A generation of workers has been born, gone to school, gotten married and had children, and it still isn't equal," says Susan Bianchi-Sand, executive director of the National Committee on Pay Equity, in Washington, D.C.

According to the latest U.S. Census figures, full-time working women make only 70 percent of what men do. That's not much of an increase over the 60 percent of male salaries that women were earning when the equal-pay law took effect. And the increase has come only in the past fourteen years.

Actually, the complete picture is probably even grimmer than the official numbers suggest. These census figures are based on full-time employment, and many women work on a part-time or temporary basis. "Part-time employees are not covered by the Equal Pay Act or any equal-pay legislation," says Ellen Bravo, national director of 9to5, the National Association of Working Women, based in Cleveland, Ohio. "We see pay equity here as one of the goals for the 1990s."

Explaining the Gap

Why, if laws have been around for so long, are women still not getting equal pay? There are many reasons: There are big gaps in the laws, and the ones that exist aren't stringently enforced. Beliefs prevail that a woman's job isn't crucial to family survival. Cultural conditioning causes many women to devalue their work and not demand more. "We have to recognize that law doesn't change attitudes," says Bianchi-Sand. "The myth is that women's work isn't important, that it's just extra."

12   Even if it was ever true that women worked for "pin money," that's hardly the case anymore. Studies repeatedly show that most women who work do so because they need the income.

Unfortunately, though, most women work in jobs that don't pay as well as the jobs in male-dominated fields. Sixty-two percent of women hold secretarial or clerical positions or work in the sales or service fields, according to the U.S. Bureau of Labor Statistics. And even though those jobs may require the same level of training and responsibility as, say, a truck driver or a construction worker, wages are considerably lower. "Women's work has always been undervalued," says Bianchi-Sand.

Over the past decade, attempts have been made to correct this. Advocates have been promoting a "pay equity" system, whereby employers would be required by law to reevaluate salaries for jobs traditionally held by women: With an established formula as a guideline, each job would be allotted points on the basis of skill, experience and responsibility level. Salaries would be adjusted to compare with male-dominated jobs of an equal point value. (This is called "pay equity" and is not the same as "equal pay," which means identical wages for identical work.) Advocates believe that pay-equity policies would begin to close the gap between salaries in traditionally female and traditionally male fields.

Some suggest that another factor preventing women from getting equal pay is that women tend to take time off or to curtail their work schedules during their childbearing years. But advocates say that's not the reason. Most women reenter the workforce within the first six months after having children, says Heidi Hartmann, director of the Institute for Women's Policy Research, in Washington, D.C. In addition, she says that when women do take longer leaves, their salary levels jump right back very quickly after they return. The real culprits, she believes, are more insidious: discrimination and prejudice.

"Devastating, Humiliating"

16   Prejudice hit Wilma Burton, fifty-five, of Neoga, Illinois, hard. For ten years, she had been the warranty administrator at Effingham Truck Sales, processing claims for tractor trailers that may have had defects. For most of that time, she was a divorced mother of five.

"Around January 1991, my boss called me in and said they wanted to hire another person, and wanted me to train him," Burton explains. She says the company hired a thirty-six-year-old man and paid him $7.60 an hour to start. Burton's hourly wage was $5.95. But she was also earning a commission on the warranties she administered. With that commission, Burton's earnings were roughly equal to the new man's.

Six months later, though, the man asked for more money. The boss decided he should get it, and told Burton that, in the future, all her earnings from the warranty commissions would have to be split with the man, she says. "That would have meant reducing my annual income about $4,000 a year," Burton says. She told her boss that if she had to split the commissions, her hourly wage should be raised. It wasn't.

Frustrated, Burton resigned and got another job. "I'm making $5,000 less a year in my new job, I lost my health coverage and life-insurance policy, my vacation was reduced from three weeks to one week a year, and I have no profit sharing anymore," she says. Burton has filed a lawsuit in federal court seeking compensation for her lost earnings.

20   Effingham Truck Sales denies the allegations but refuses to comment further because, it says, the case is in litigation.

For Burton, the experience has been traumatic. "It's not just the money. It's devastating, humiliating," she says. "Except for losing my mother, this is the worst thing that's ever happened to me. The women I know are the most loyal employees, and they're also the most underpaid. Someone had to say it wasn't right, so why not me?"

As Burton knows well, it's difficult to challenge the status quo. Though salaries of government workers are public information, there is no law requiring private employers to disclose what they pay to employees, so it is often hard to ferret out pay differences. Lawsuits can be time-consuming and costly. And women who stir things up risk losing their jobs.

Some avenues have been opened to make challenging unequal pay easier. The federal Equal Employment Opportunity Commission (EEOC), created in 1964, allows workers to file complaints, and, if evidence of discrimination is found, the EEOC sues the offending companies at public expense. But critics say, the commission has not been very aggressive, particularly under the administration of former President Ronald Reagan.

24   Though complaints continued to pour in to the EEOC, the number that resulted in lawsuits dropped from seventy-nine in 1980 to just two in 1992, the National Committee on Pay Equity reports.

Enforcement has also been weak in other areas. Many states have created local human-rights commissions, designed to hear grievances. Those have varied in their effectiveness, but underfunding has been a chronic problem.

The Good News

A glimmer of hope is buried in all this bad news. Though we're not there yet, women are slowly inching their way toward equal pay. And some important victories have been won. In recent years, major American corporations—IBM and AT&T among them—have implemented pay-equity policies.

And pay-equity laws have been adopted by six states. In Minnesota, some 8,500 state employees received pay raises averaging $2,200 a year after jobs were reevaluated.

28   For Mary Martin, forty-eight, that meant being able to buy her first house. "When my pay raise came through, I was really surprised," says Martin, a secretary in the state's education department. "Now I make $23,000 a year. That pay-equity adjustment allowed me to qualify [for a mortgage]."

Women have also begun making inroads into higher-paying professions tradi-tionally dominated by men. And in younger age groups, the salary gap between genders appears to be narrowing. The Institute for Women's Policy Research, in Washington, D.C., reports that women aged twenty-five to thirty-four make 80 percent of what men make, compared to the 60 percent made by women in the forty-five to fifty-four age group. Some experts predict that, as these women grow older, they will maintain their gains.

Advocates are guardedly optimistic. "I'm always torn," says Hartmann. "Is the glass half empty or half full? If you're too negative, it doesn't mark our prog-ress. So, it's not all better, but it's better than it was. And what we do know is this: Each generation of women has done better than the one before."

THE WAGE GAP AT A GLANCE
MEDIAN WAGES FOR FULL-TIME,
YEAR-ROUND WORKERS

Educational Level	Men	Women	Wage Gap (%)
High-school graduate	$26,218	$18,042	69
College graduate	$39,894	$27,654	69
Master's degree	$47,002	$33,122	70

Source: The National Committee on Pay Equity, based on U.S. Census Bureau figures.

Personal Response

Explain your view of women like Linda Scotti, the 911 supervisor who brought suit against the city because fire department dispatchers, mostly male, were earning more money for essentially the same work. Do you think women should be paid as much as men for the same work?

Questions for Discussion

1. What is "pay equity"? How does it differ from "equal pay"? What is your po-sition on the subject of pay equity?

2. Webb asks, "Why, if laws have been around for so long, are women still not getting equal pay?" What are some of the factors that explain why women's earnings are not the same as men's?

3. Discuss other factors you think might account for the gap between men's and women's wages.

THE MASKS OF MINORITY TERRORISM

Pico Iyer

Pico Iyer was born in England to Indian parents and studied at Oxford and Harvard Universities. His books include Video Night in Kathmandu: And Other Reports from the Not-So-Far-East *(1988),* The Lady and the Monk: A Season in Kyoto *(1991),* Falling Off the Map: Some Lovely Places of the World *(1994), and* The Contagion of Innocence *(1991). "The Masks of Minority Terrorism" was first published in the September 3, 1990, issue of* Time.

When Actors' Equity briefly decided three weeks ago that the part of a Eurasian in the play *Miss Saigon* could not be taken by a European, its board members provided some of the best entertainment seen on Broadway recently. It was not just that they were asserting an Orwellian principle: All races are equal, but some are more equal than others. Nor even that they were threatening to deprive thousands of playgoers of a drama that promised to shed some light on precisely such cross-cultural nuances; nor even that they were more or less ensuring—if the principle were to be applied fairly—that most Asian-American actors would have to sit around in limbo and wait for the next production of *The Mikado.* They were also raising some highly intriguing questions. How can John Gielgud play Prospero when Doug Henning is at hand? Should future Shakespeares—even future August Wilsons—stock their plays with middle-class whites so as to have the largest pool of actors from which to choose? And next time we stage *Moby Dick,* will there be cries that the title part be taken by a card-carrying leviathan?

The quickly reversed decision, which effectively proclaimed that actors should do everything but act, was a short-running farce. But when the same kind of minority terrorism is launched offstage, as is more and more the case, the consequences are less comical. Jimmy Breslin, long famous as a champion of the dispossessed, speaks thoughtlessly and finds himself vilified as a "racist." Spike Lee, an uncommonly intelligent filmmaker whenever he remains behind the camera, maintains that films about blacks should be directed by blacks (what does this mean for *The Bear,* one wonders, or for *Snow White and the Seven Dwarfs?*). Lee in turn becomes an irresistible target for charges of anti-Semitism. And others contend that Marion Barry is being hounded because he is black, as if to suggest that he be excused because he is black.

The problem with people who keep raising the cry of "racism" is that they would have us see everything in terms of race. They treat minorities as emblems, and everyone as typecast. And in suggesting that a white cannot put himself in the shoes, or soul, of a half-white, or a black, they would impose on us the most stifling form of apartheid, condemning us all to a hopeless rift of mutual incomprehension. Taken to an extreme, this can lead to a litigious nation's equivalent of the tribal vendetta: You did my people wrong, so now I am entitled to do you wrong. A plague on every house.

4   Almost nobody, one suspects, would deny that equal rights are a laudable goal and that extending a hand to the needy is one of the worthiest things we can do. Reserving some places in schools, or companies, or even plays for those who are less privileged seems an admirable way of redressing imbalances. But privilege cannot be interpreted in terms of race without making some damningly racist assumptions. And rectifying the injustices of our grandfathers is no easy task, least of all in a country made up of refugees and immigrants and minorities of one, many of whom have lived through the Holocaust, the Khmer Rouge, the unending atrocities of El Salvador. Sympathy cannot be legislated any more than kindness can.

The whole issue, in fact, seems to betray a peculiarly American conundrum: the enjoyment of one freedom means encroachment on another; you can't school all of the people all of the time. Older, and less earnest, countries like Britain or Japan live relatively easily with racial inequalities. But America, with its evergreen eagerness to do the right thing, tries to remedy the world with an innocence that can become more dangerous than cruelty. All of us, when we make decisions—which is to say, discriminations—judge in part on appearances. All of us treat Savile Row–suited lawyers differently from kids in T shirts, give preference to the people that we like—or to the people that are most like us—and make differing assumptions about a Texan and a Yankee. To wish this were not so is natural; to claim it is not so is hypocrisy.

But state-sponsored favoritism is something different. As an Asian minority myself, I know of nothing more demeaning than being chosen for a job, or even a role, on the basis of my race. Nor is the accompanying assumption—that I need a helping hand because my ancestors were born outside Europe—very comforting. Are those of us lucky enough to be born minorities to be forgiven our transgressions, protected from insults and encouraged to act as if we cannot take responsibility for our actions (it wasn't my fault I failed the exam; society made me do it)? Are we, in fact, to cling to a state of childlike dependency? As an alien from India, I choose to live in America precisely because it is a place where aliens from India are, in principle, treated no better (and no worse) than anyone else. Selecting an Asian actor, say, over a better-qualified white one (or, for that matter, a white over a better-qualified Asian, as is alleged to happen with certain university admissions) does nobody a service: not the Asian, whose lack of qualifications will be rapidly shown up; not the white, whose sense of racial brotherhood is hardly likely to be quickened by being the victim of discrimination himself; not the company, or audience, which may understandably resent losing quality to quotas.

Affirmative action, in fact—so noble in intention—is mostly a denial: a denial of the fact that we are all born different; a denial of a person's right to get the position he deserves; a denial of everyone's ability to transcend, or live apart from, the conditions of his birth. Most of all, it is a denial of the very virtues of opportunity and self-determination that are the morning stars of this democracy.

People around the world still long to migrate to America because it is a place, traditionally and ideally, where people can say what they think, become what they dream and succeed—or fail—on the basis of their merits. Now, though, with more and more people telling us not to say what we think and to support everyone except the majority of Americans, the country is in danger of becoming something else: the land of the free, with an asterisk.

Personal Response

Does the fact that Pico Iyer is an Asian minority opposed to affirmative action in any way affect your own view of affirmative action? Does it make you more inclined to favor his view of it?

Questions for Discussion

1. What does Iyer mean by the term "minority terrorism"?

2. What point does Iyer make with the series of questions at the end of paragraph 1?

3. What does Iyer mean when he writes, "But privilege cannot be interpreted in terms of race without making some damningly racist assumptions" (paragraph 4)? Do you agree with him?

4. Why does Iyer say that "the whole issue . . . seems to betray a peculiarly American conundrum" (paragraph 5)?

5. What does Iyer have against affirmative action? Do you agree with him?

Suggestions for Writing About
PREJUDICE AND DISCRIMINATION

1. Drawing on Joan C. Weiss's "Prejudice, Conflict, and Ethnoviolence: A National Dilemma," offer a possible solution to the problem of bigotry and ethnoviolence in America.

2. Drawing on some of the readings in this chapter, develop a theory about why people hold prejudices against others whose skin color, religion, nationality, or the like is different from their own. Where do stereotypes and prejudices come from? What aspects of American culture reinforce or even perpetuate stereotypes? How can you personally work against stereotyping and prejudice?

3. Apply Michel Wieviorka's analysis in "The Ruses of Racism" of the identity-related causes of racial violence to a specific area of the world now in conflict over racial or ethnic issues.

4. Referring to Michel Wieviorka's "The Ruses of Racism" where relevant, explain your own theory on the conditions that encourage the growth of racial violence in America.

5. If you, like Daniel Meier in "One Man's Kids," have chosen a career that is often perceived as not typical for your sex, explain why you chose it, what kind of opposition you might expect (or have already had), and the potential benefits you anticipate from it.

6. Support or oppose Daniel Meier's contention in "One Man's Kids" that people still very much think of certain careers or behaviors as either masculine or feminine. Draw on your own personal experience or observations for your supporting evidence.

7. Narrate your first experience with prejudice, discrimination, or bigotry, as either witness to or victim of it. Describe in detail the incident and how it made you feel.

8. Explore the personality of bigots. Are there particular characteristics, such as income, education, or geographical location, that bigots have in common? Under what circumstances does personal preference or opinion become prejudice?

9. Drawing on Stephen Steinberg's "The Affirmative Action Debate," Marilyn Webb's "Why Women Don't Get Paid What They're Worth," and Pico Iyer's "The Mask of Minority Terrorism," argue your position on the subject of affirmative action in education or employment.

10. Argue your position on the proposition that funding and facilities for men's and women's college sports should be equal.

11. Drawing on the selections in this chapter, explore the question of whether racial or sexual discrimination is a thing of the past. Consider including interviews of people who lived through the 1950s, 1960s, and 1970s about what they remember of segregation, the civil-rights movement, or the women's liberation movement.

12. Show the effects of one kind of prejudice—racial, religious, sexual, or the like—on a person or a group of people with whom you are familiar.

13. Drawing on Daniel Meier's "One Man's Kids" and Marilyn Webb's "Why Women Don't Get Paid What They're Worth" as well as your own observations, write an essay on the subject of sex-role stereotyping or sex discrimination in employment.

14. Stephen Steinberg in "The Affirmative Action Debate" and Pico Iyer in "The Masks of Minority Terrorism" both use the word "apartheid." Analyze their use of that term, consider how they use it, if they differ in the way they use it, and whether they have a common definition of the word.

15. Drawing on the Steinberg and Iyer essays, analyze some specific aspect of the system of apartheid: what the system is, how it benefits those in power, what its effect is on those oppressed by it, how those in power maintain it, or what is being done now to end it.

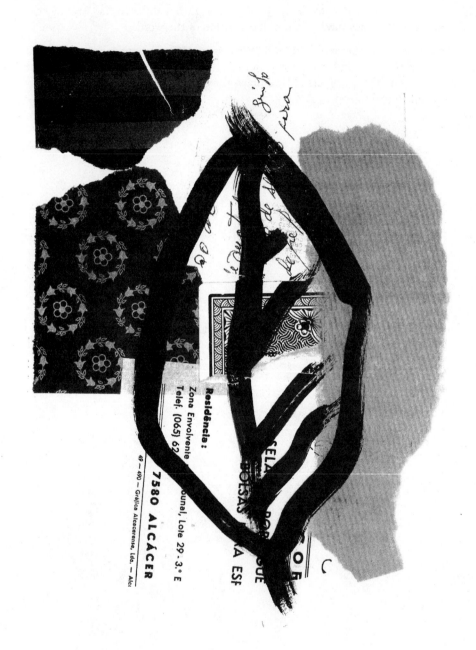

CHAPTER 9

POLITICAL CORRECTNESS

The term "political correctness" refers to the views of those opposed to speech that smacks of racism, sexism, ageism, or other "isms" potentially demeaning to selected groups. In their efforts to make American culture more inclusive and to eradicate discrimination, for instance, feminists, blacks, Hispanics, Asians, gays and lesbians, disabled persons, and similar groups object to language that excludes, belittles, or demeans them. Their attempts to monitor both written and spoken words have led some people to criticize them for being overly sensitive and extreme in their recommendations for change. The controversy has engendered much heated debate between those in favor of politically correct language and their critics, who find the need for the designation silly and even obnoxious, as the selections in this chapter suggest.

First is Gerald F. Kreyche's commentary "Have We Lost Our Sense of Humor?" Writing for a monthly feature of *USA Today* magazine called "Parting Thoughts," Kreyche devotes the first half of his essay to political correctness, maintaining that "political correctness is making cowards of almost everyone" and that "people have become thin-skinned, touchy, [and] overly sensitive." He provides many examples of jokes to illustrate his belief that virtually any group is subject to being joked about and that such humor is harmless. Next, Peggy Noonan explains in "Toward Candor and Courage in Speech" why she would like to "rescue" some words and "return them to their true meanings." In her essay, Noonan discusses some of the words that have lost their original meanings in the name of political correctness.

Providing a different perspective on the subject of language and political correctness, Rebecca Thomas Kirkendall protests the belittling of rural people in her commentary, "Who's a Hillbilly?" As a person who grew up in the Ozarks, she objects to the unflattering stereotypes evoked by the word "hillbilly" and suggests that the current national interest in all things country does nothing to dispel the negative image of the word. In a similar vein, Gloria Naylor in "Mommy, What Does 'Nigger' Mean?" explores the way in which the word "nigger" is used in both derogatory and positive ways, depending on who is saying the word. Both essays raise the question of the appropriateness or inappropriateness of certain words, depending on the context in which they are used.

Next is a piece by Nat Hentoff, who often writes about and publicly debates First Amendment issues. In "'Insensitive Language' and the New HUAC Mentality," Hentoff demonstrates his absolute belief in freedom of speech and his ardent opposition to any attempts to limit that freedom. For many of the same reasons as Hentoff's, Michiko Kakutani takes exception to political correctness as well. In "The Word Police," she explains her objections to "the methods and fervor of the self-appointed language police." Finally, concluding the chapter is Barbara Ehrenreich's "Teach Diversity with a Smile." In this essay, Ehrenreich criticizes both sides of the political correctness debate and urges them both to lighten up.

HAVE WE LOST OUR SENSE OF HUMOR?

Gerald F. Kreyche

Gerald F. Kreyche is emeritus professor of philosophy at DePaul University in Chicago and American Thought Editor of USA Today *magazine. This commentary appeared in the "Parting Thoughts" column of the May 1994 issue of that magazine.*

Philosophers claim that only humans are risible, meaning that we can laugh at a joke or a funny situation and appreciate the comical. In short, humor is a peculiarly human trait requiring insight and intelligence. Often, it gives us perspective and helps get us through crisis situations. Our tendency always is to get overly serious, and humor puts a helpful brake on this. It is a truism that the person who can laugh at himself has a firm grip on his world.

Seeming to acknowledge the importance of humor in our country, the U.S. Post Office put out a series of stamps honoring comedians such as Jack Benny, Red Skelton, Sid Caesar, and even ventriloquist Edgar Bergen's dummy, Charlie McCarthy. Talk show hosts such as Jay Leno and David Letterman try to keep up the tradition. However, all is not well with humor in America.

Actress-comedienne Whoopi Goldberg recently charged that the nation is losing its sense of humor, as she was criticized for a "blackface" skit she wrote for Ted Danson, former star of "Cheers" and her boyfriend at the time. The occasion was a "roasting" of Goldberg at the Friars Club in New York. While it unquestionably was an example of poor taste, the resulting furor proved again that political correctness is making cowards of almost everyone.

4   People have become thin-skinned, touchy, overly sensitive—"underhumored," as one commentator put it. Foremost among those killing a sense of humor are the deadly serious feminists. The fact is that *they* just don't get it! Everyone is on edge today, ready to charge bias, a lack of respect, or harassment of some imagined type or another. Ethnic jokes used to abound, and the ethnic group itself enjoyed them more than anyone. Jews, for instance, delighted in telling jokes on and about themselves, usually connected with business, Jewish mothers, or one-upmanship. Now, anyone uttering a joke about Jews is deemed anti-Semitic.

For years, there have been a rash of so-called "Polish" jokes (in different parts of the country, other nationalities are the butt). For instance: Chicago is the largest Polish city outside of Warsaw. It seems that the Polish aldermen there were getting fed up with Polish jokes and decided to send an entourage to Washington to protest to Congress. They all got on a plane and landed in . . . Seattle! Now how can one take umbrage at that? Everyone knows that Poland has a rich intellectual and musical heritage, producing a Copernicus, a Chopin, a Pope John Paul II, and a Paderewski. Nevertheless, such jokes have become taboo, and the world is worse off for it.

It is interesting that jokes often seem to have national traits. Take the story of an Englishman, German, and Frenchman being put into a library and told to write about the elephant. After a while, the Englishman came out with a slim treatise, entitled *The Elephant and the Queen*. The Frenchman emerged with his book, *The Sex Life of the Elephant*. The German then revealed his *opus magnus* of six volumes, *Introduction to the Study on the Elephant*.

As a rule, English humor tends to be cryptic and clever. It is not so much what is said, but the *way* it is said that matters. For example: One Englishman was talking to another and mentioned, "I say, I passed your house last night." Replied the other, "Thank you." Again, one Englishman was visiting another in the latter's new home and declared, "I thought your house was bigger than it is." The reply came, "How could it be?" Obviously, these are intellectual in genre and require quick-wittedness.

8 Gallic humor shares the wittiness of English. Apocryphally, the story is told that, when Charles DeGaulle was preparing for his death, he visited the undertaker to make final arrangements. When asked what size mausoleum the famous general would desire to mark his resting place, DeGaulle shrugged his shoulders and replied, "None, Monsieur. After all, it will be for only three days."

A little laughter goes a long way in today's world. There are clever, often caustic, "one-liners" that also serve as "put-downs." Examples: He kept up his end of the conversation to the point of being perpendicular. Or, consider Mark Twain's remark: "He was a good man—in the worst sense of the term."

Surely "cornball" must be another category. Did you hear about the modern man who turned on the radio and thought he went blind? Or about the chameleon who landed on a Scotch plaid blanket and blew up? Then there were two doctors who made an incision into a patient's stomach. When a bunch of butterflies flew out, one surgeon said to the other, "What do you know? He was right!"

Animal jokes make up a very large category. A billy goat got loose in a Hollywood film studio and ate a reel of "Gone with the Wind." Another goat asked him how he liked it. Replied the first: "I thought the book was better." Then there was the farmer who mated a cow with an octopus. Asked what the result was, the farmer replied: "I don't know, but it is able to milk itself."

12 Many jokes revolve around a play on words. Punsters, such as Lou Rukeyser of "Wall Street Week," would appreciate the following: A contest between two southern debaters ended in a drawl. A male Christmas shopper was looking for a gift for his beloved and asked the saleswoman, "Do you have any notions?"

"Yes," she answered, "but we're not allowed to express them during business hours." When a dinghy came to rescue two men who had fallen into the water, the rescuer said he only could pick up one at a time. He asked the one still in the water, "Can you float alone?" "Yes," was the response, "but this is no time to talk business!"

Although trite, the old adage still is true. "Laugh and the world laughs with you. Cry and you cry alone."

Personal Response

What do you think people should do when they hear a joke they believe is offensive, for whatever reason? What do you do in such situations, especially if no one else but you seems to be bothered by it?

Questions for Discussion

1. Discuss Kreyche's observations that "political correctness is making cowards of almost everyone" (paragraph 3) and that "people have become thin-skinned, touchy, [and] overly sensitive" (paragraph 4). Explain whether you agree or disagree with him and why.

2. What is Kreyche's central purpose? Do the examples he gives support that purpose?

3. Discuss the question of how to distinguish between what is funny and what is in poor taste.

4. Share a joke you have heard about a particular group of people and examine it in terms of the political correctness issue. Is the joke offensive? Is it funny? Should you repeat the joke? What do you think is a tactful way to handle a situation in which someone has told an offensive joke?

TOWARD CANDOR AND COURAGE IN SPEECH

Peggy Noonan

Peggy Noonan is a former speech writer for Ronald Reagan and journalist whose articles have appeared in such publications as the New York Times, *the* Wall Street Journal, *the* Washington Post, *and* Vanity Fair. *Her books include* What I saw at the Revolution *(1992) and* Life, Liberty, and the Pursuit of Happiness *(1994). This selection from her monthly column "Looking Forward" appeared in the September 1996 issue of* Good Housekeeping.

"It was so gay," my elderly friend says of a party. "Not homosexual," she quickly adds, "but happy." She laughs, and I wonder which was more embarrassing for her: that she had introduced a sexual reference or that she had, once again, been caught being old-fashioned in her usage. For 50 years of her life, *gay* meant "lighthearted and joyous." Now it means "homosexual." It's hard for her to adjust.

I know how she feels. I miss a lot of words, too—the ones that were hijacked by political movements and lost in the vapors of the politically correct universe. I wish we could rescue them and return them to their true meanings, not in the name of bigotry or narrow-mindedness, but in the name of candor, courage, and coherence.

Gay was a good word because it sounded like what it meant—"merry and bright." But as a word meaning "homosexual" it makes little sense. I know gays who are almost never happy, and I know straights who are truly twisted. Really, why call heterosexuals *straight*? *Straight* means "having an unchanging direction"; it means "honest and trustworthy" too. Why not use it that way?

4   When you politicize language you leave it not liberated, but jailed. We have not become clearer and more direct—but less. There are phrases we used in the old America that are not used now, and I would challenge anyone to tell me how their disuse led to any kind of progress.

Up until 20 years ago, we spoke of children whose parents were divorced as coming from "a broken home," a good phrase because it was honest: Divorce *does* break families in two. We stopped using it because we wanted to be non-judgmental. And the phrase did carry a stigma: We all know that whole things are better than broken things. Now we say "single-parent families," which is not only stigma-free, but also makes the parents sound heroic. Many of them are. But I doubt it's a complete accident that in the years since we removed the stigma, the incidence of divorce increased dramatically.

We once called children born out of wedlock—another phrase considered quaint—*illegitimate*. That was a word blunt enough to make you shudder, and it, too, carried a stigma. It was society's way of saying that it gave greater honor and legitimacy to parents who had married before having children than to parents who didn't. Society understood that through marriage a man and woman declare that they will assume responsibility for their offspring. We stopped speaking of illegitimacy when we decided it was cruel aimed at children. It was. But even crueler to children is the breathtaking rise of illegitimacy—and its attendant hardships—that have followed removal of the stigma.

Housewife has also come under fire. It's a good short word that means "I am a woman, a wife, a mother, and I run the house." What could be more honorable than that? Was it liberation to make *housewife* seem like an insult, as some intellectuals have tried to do?

8   Now brace yourself: I do not miss but I do respect the terms *Caucasian* and *Negro*. They were better at least than what replaced them. When I was a little girl, the polite word for *black* was *colored*, which is why black reformers called their group the National Association for the Advancement of Colored People. During the most passionate days of the civil rights era, young blacks decided

colored was prissy. They embraced *black* and obediently we all trudged along, though it's still hard to see how this was linguistic progress. For no one is black and no one is white, though many are brown and many are beige.

Now *black* is out; *people of color* is on its way in, and there is also the new designation *African-American*. The problem with that, as I see it, is that *African-American* sets apart and marginalizes. It is not *inclusive* but exclusive; it says, "you are different, not one of us." It's also a throwback to the days of hyphenated Americans. I am Irish and American but when people ask me what nationality I am, I tell them American, because it's the truth. African-Americans are Americans too.

We ought to get braver and be blunter. We should be *short* and not "height-impaired," *handicapped* and not "physically challenged." We should be less timid in our speech, more honest. I wonder if all of us—homosexuals, heterosexuals, housewives, the whole lot of us—shouldn't stage a little rebellion and start talking like people again. I'd certainly like to. Just thought I'd say it.

Personal Response

How do you feel about the use of the words and terms Noonan discusses? Do you find the terms *gay* and *straight* more appropriate or meaningful than homosexual and heterosexual? What about *single-parent families* for *broken homes?* Should we start using the terms *illegitimate, Caucasian,* and *Negro* again?

Questions for Discussion

1. Discuss Noonan's statement that "when you politicize language you leave it not liberated, but jailed" (paragraph 4). Do you agree with her?

2. Noonan implies that there is a causal relationship between the removal of the stigma of certain terms and an increase in the behavior the term describes (paragraphs 5 and 6). Do you think her point is valid? What other reasons account for the increases in the numbers of divorces and births to unwed mothers? How much do you think removing the stigma has contributed to those increases?

3. Comment on Noonan's suggestion that *housewife* is a good and honorable word (paragraph 7). Why do some people oppose its use?

4. Respond to Noonan's discussion in paragraphs 8 and 9 of the terms *Negro, colored, black,* and *African-American.*

5. What do you think of Noonan's suggestion in her closing paragraph that "we ought to get braver and be blunter" in our speech? Do you agree, for instance, that it would be better to use certain terms that are now considered politically incorrect?

WHO'S A HILLBILLY?

Rebecca Thomas Kirkendall

Rebecca Thomas Kirkendall was a doctoral student at the University of Missouri when she wrote this essay for the "My Turn" column of the November 27, 1995, issue of Newsweek.

I once dated a boy who called me a hillbilly because my family has lived in the Ozarks in southern Missouri for several generations. I took offense, not realizing that as a foreigner to the United States he was unaware of the insult. He had meant it as a term of endearment. Nonetheless, it rankled. I started thinking about the implications of the term to me, my family and my community.

While growing up I was often surprised at the way television belittled "country" people. We weren't offended by the self-effacing humor of "The Andy Griffith Show" and "The Beverly Hillbillies" because, after all, Andy and Jed were the heroes of these shows, and through them we could comfortably laugh at ourselves. But as I learned about tolerance and discrimination in school, I wondered why stereotypes of our lifestyle went unexamined. Actors playing "country" people on TV were usually comic foils or objects of ridicule. Every sitcom seemed to have an episode where country cousins, wearing high-water britches and carrying patched suitcases, visited their city friends. And movies like "Deliverance" portrayed country people as backward and violent.

As a child I laughed at the exaggerated accents and dress, never imagining that viewers believed such nonsense. Li'l Abner and the folks on "Hee Haw" were amusing, but we on the farm knew that our work did not lend itself to bare feet, gingham bras and revealing cutoff jeans.

4 Although our nation professes a growing commitment to cultural egalitarianism, we consistently oversimplify and misunderstand our rural culture. Since the 1960s, minority groups in America have fought for acknowledgment, appreciation and, above all, respect. But in our increasingly urban society, rural Americans have been unable to escape from the hillbilly stigma, which is frequently accompanied by labels like "white trash," "redneck" and "hayseed." These negative stereotypes are as unmerciful as they are unfounded.

When I graduated from college, I traveled to a nearby city to find work. There I heard wisecracks about the uneducated rural folk who lived a few hours away. I also took some ribbing about the way I pronounced certain words, such as "tin" instead of "ten" and "agin" for "again." And my expressed desire to return to the country someday was usually met with scorn, bewilderment or genuine concern. Co-workers often asked, "But what is there to *do?*" Thoreau may have gone to Walden Pond, they argued, but he had no intention of staying there.

With the revival of country music in the early 1980s, hillbillyness was again marketable. Country is now big business. Traditional country symbols—Minnie Pearl's hat tag and Daisy Mae—have been eclipsed by the commercially successful Nashville Network, Country Music Television and music theaters in Branson,

MO. Many "country" Americans turned the negative stereotype to their advantage and packaged the hillbilly legacy.

Yet with successful commercialization, the authentic elements of America's rural culture have been juxtaposed with the stylized. Country and Western bars are now chic. While I worked in the city, I watched with amazement as my Yuppie friends hurried from their corporate desks to catch the 6:30 line-dancing class at the edge of town. Donning Ralph Lauren jeans and ankle boots, they drove to the trendiest country bars, sat and danced together and poked fun at the local "hicks," who arrived in pickup trucks wearing Wrangler jeans and roper boots.

8   Every summer weekend in Missouri the freeways leading out of our cities are clogged with vacationers. Minivans and RVs edge toward a clear river with a campground and canoe rental, a quiet lake resort or craft show in a remote Ozark town. Along these popular vacation routes, the rural hosts of convenience stores, gift shops and corner cafés accept condescension along with personal checks and credit cards. On a canoeing trip not long ago, I recall sitting on the transport bus and listening, heartbroken, as a group of tourists ridiculed our bus driver. They yelled, "Hey, plowboy, ain't ya got no terbacker fer us?" They pointed at the young man's sweat-stained overalls as he, seemingly unaffected by their insults, singlehandedly carried their heavy aluminum canoes to the water's edge. That "plowboy" was one of my high-school classmates. He greeted the tourists with a smile and tolerated their derision because he knew tourism brings dollars and jobs.

America is ambivalent when it comes to claiming its rural heritage. We may fantasize about Thomas Jefferson's agrarian vision, but there is no mistaking that ours is an increasingly urban culture. Despite their disdain for farm life—with its manure-caked boots, long hours and inherent financial difficulties—urbanites rush to imitate a sanitized version of this lifestyle. And the individuals who sell this rendition understand that the customer wants to experience hillbillyness without the embarrassment of being mistaken for one.

Through it all, we Ozarkians remind ourselves how fortunate we are to live in a region admired for its blue springs, rolling hills and geological wonders. In spite of the stereotypes, most of us are not uneducated. Nor are we stupid. We are not white supremacists, and we rarely marry our cousins. Our reasons for living in the hills are as complex and diverse as our population. We have a unique sense of community, strong family ties, a beautiful environment and a quiet place for retirement.

We have criminals and radicals, but they are the exception. Our public-education system produces successful farmers, doctors, business professionals and educators. Country music is our favorite, but we also like rock and roll, jazz, blues and classical. We read Louis L'Amour, Maya Angelou and the *Wall Street Journal*. And in exchange for living here, many of us put up with a lower standard of living and the occasional gibe from those who persist in calling us "hillbillies."

Personal Response

Explain your understanding of the word "hillbilly." Do you think of people from the Ozarks and other parts of the rural South as "hillbillies"? Is there a stereotypical image of people from your geographical region?

Questions for Discussion

1. Kirkendall says that certain television shows when she was growing up "belittled 'country' people" (paragraphs 2 and 3). Does television still portray people from rural areas in a comic, stereotypical way?

2. Kirkendall asserts that Americans "consistently oversimplify and misunderstand our rural culture" (paragraph 4). Discuss the extent to which you agree with her on this point.

3. In her introduction, Kirkendall says that she began "thinking about the implications of the term ['hillbilly']" to herself, her family, and her community. Summarize what the implications of that term are for her. What is her response to those implications?

4. Discuss what you think are the implications of such terms as not only "hillbilly" but also "white trash," "redneck," and "hayseed" for the people to whom those labels are applied. Then extend your discussion to consider the nature of stereotypes and labels in general. For instance, where do they come from and what harm do they do?

MOMMY, WHAT DOES "NIGGER" MEAN?

Gloria Naylor

Gloria Naylor, who holds a master's degree in Afro-American Studies from Yale University, is a writer. She has worked as a columnist for the New York Times *and has been a visiting professor and writer in residence at a number of universities, including Princeton University, the University of Pennsylvania, Boston University, and Brandeis. Her first novel,* The Women of Brewster Place *(1980), won an American Book Award and served as the basis for a highly acclaimed television movie. Her other novels are* Linden Hills *(1985) and* Mama Day *(1988). This essay first appeared in the* New York Times Sunday Magazine *in 1986.*

Language is the subject. It is the written form with which I've managed to keep the wolf away from the door and, in diaries, to keep my sanity. In spite of this, I consider the written word inferior to the spoken, and much of the frustration experienced by novelists is the awareness that whatever we manage to capture in even the most transcendent passages falls far short of the richness of life. Dialogue achieves its power in the dynamics of a fleeting moment of sight, sound, smell and touch.

I'm not going to enter the debate here about whether it is language that shapes reality or vice versa. That battle is doomed to be waged whenever we seek intermittent reprieve from the chicken and egg dispute. I will simply take the position that the spoken word, like the written word, amounts to a nonsensical arrangement of sounds or letters without a consensus that assigns "meaning." And building from the meanings of what we hear, we order reality. Words themselves are innocuous; it is the consensus that gives them true power.

I remember the first time I heard the word nigger. In my third-grade class, our math tests were being passed down the rows, and as I handed the papers to a little boy in back of me, I remarked that once again he had received a much lower mark than I did. He snatched his test from me and spit out that word. Had he called me a nymphomaniac or a necrophiliac, I couldn't have been more puzzled. I didn't know what a nigger was, but I knew that whatever it meant, it was something he shouldn't have called me. This was verified when I raised my hand, and in a loud voice repeated what he has said and watched the teacher scold him for using a "bad" word. I was later to go home and ask the inevitable question that every black parent must face—"Mommy, what does 'nigger' mean?"

4   And what exactly did it mean? Thinking back, I realize that this could not have been the first time the word was used in my presence. I was part of a large extended family that had migrated from the rural South after World War II and formed a close-knit network that gravitated around my maternal grandparents. Their ground-floor apartment in one of the buildings they owned in Harlem was a weekend mecca for my immediate family, along with countless aunts, uncles and cousins who brought along assorted friends. It was a bustling and open house with assorted neighbors and tenants popping in and out to exchange bits of gossip, pick up an old quarrel or referee the ongoing checkers game in which my grandmother cheated shamelessly. They were all there to let down their hair and put up their feet after a week of labor in the factories, laundries and shipyards of New York.

Amid the clamor, which could reach deafening proportions—two or three conversations going on simultaneously, punctuated by the sound of a baby's crying somewhere in the back rooms or out on the street—there was still a rigid set of rules about what was said and how. Older children were sent out of the living room when it was time to get into the juicy details about "you-know-who" up on the third floor who had gone and gotten herself "p-r-e-g-n-a-n-t-!" But my parents, knowing that I could spell well beyond my years, always demanded that I follow the others out to play. Beyond sexual misconduct and death, everything else was considered harmless for our young ears. And so among the anecdotes of the triumphs and disappointments in the various workings of their lives, the word nigger was used in my presence, but it was set within contexts and inflections that caused it to register in my mind as something else.

In the singular, the word was always applied to a man who had distinguished himself in some situation that brought their approval for his strength, intelligence or drive:

"Did Johnny really do that?"

8 "I'm telling you, that nigger pulled in $6,000 of overtime last year. Said he got enough for a down payment on a house."

When used with a possessive adjective by a woman—"my nigger"—it became a term of endearment for husband or boyfriend. But it could be more than just a term applied to a man. In their mouths it became the pure essence of manhood— a disembodied force that channeled their past history of struggle and present survival against the odds into a victorious statement of being: "Yeah, that old foreman found out quick enough—you don't mess with a nigger."

In the plural, it became a description of some group within the community that had overstepped the bounds of decency as my family defined it: Parents who neglected their children, a drunken couple who fought in public, people who simply refused to look for work, those with excessively dirty mouths or unkempt households were all "trifling niggers." This particular circle could forgive hard times, unemployment, the occasional bout of depression—they had gone through all of that themselves—but the unforgivable sin was lack of self-respect.

A woman could never be a "nigger" in the singular, with its connotation of confirming worth. The noun girl was its closest equivalent in that sense, but only when used in direct address and regardless of the gender doing the addressing. "Girl" was a token of respect for a woman. The one-syllable word was drawn out to sound like three in recognition of the extra ounce of wit, nerve or daring that the woman had shown in the situation under discussion.

12 "G-i-r-l, stop. You mean you said that to his face?"

But if the word was used in a third-person reference or shortened so that it almost snapped out of the mouth, it always involved some element of communal disapproval. And age became an important factor in these exchanges. It was only between individuals of the same generation, or from an older person to a younger (but never the other way around), that "girl" would be considered a compliment.

I don't agree with the argument that use of the word nigger at this social stratum of the black community was an internalization of racism. The dynamics were the exact opposite: the people in my grandmother's living room took a word that whites used to signify worthlessness or degradation and rendered it impotent. Gathering there together, they transformed "nigger" to signify the varied and complex human beings they knew themselves to be. If the word was to disappear totally from the mouths of even the most liberal of white society, no one in that room was naïve enough to believe it would disappear from white minds. Meeting the word head-on, they proved it had absolutely nothing to do with the way they were determined to live their lives.

So there must have been dozens of times that the word "nigger" was spoken in front of me before I reached the third grade. But I didn't "hear" it until it was said by a small pair of lips that had already learned it could be a way to humiliate me. That was the word I went home and asked my mother about. And since she knew that I had to grow up in America, she took me in her lap and explained.

Personal Response

If you have ever been called something you found belittling, offensive, or demeaning, explain the circumstances and how you felt at the time. How do you feel about the incident now?

Questions for Discussion

1. Naylor opens her essay with the statement that "language is the subject." What is the central conflict posed by the subject of language? What is Naylor's main point about language?

2. Naylor writes that "words themselves are innocuous; it is the consensus that gives them true power" (paragraph 2). Explain in your own words what that statement means. Do you agree with Naylor?

3. At the end of paragraph 3, Naylor says that she asked her mother "the inevitable question that every black parent must face," and at the end of the essay, she says that her mother "took [Naylor] in her lap and explained." What do you think Naylor's mother told her about the word "nigger"? What other "inevitable question[s]" do you think black parents must face? What questions do you suppose children of other minority groups inevitably ask their parents?

4. Explain whether you agree with Naylor that the use of the word "nigger" by blacks is not "an internalization of racism" (paragraph 14). Does Naylor convince you that the word has no power in the black community?

5. Make a list of derogatory words and phrases that you have heard applied to members of minority groups and discuss their implications. Which do you feel are particularly derogatory? Are any of the words used by members of the group themselves and, if so, do the words lose their power, as Naylor says "nigger" does when used by the black community?

"INSENSITIVE LANGUAGE" AND THE NEW HUAC MENTALITY

Nat Hentoff

Nat Hentoff is a syndicated columnist for the Village Voice *and the* Washington Post *and author of* Free Speech for Me But Not for Thee: How the American Left and Right Continually Censor Each Other. *This article first appeared in the January 1990 issue of* Playboy.

The ever-smiling Jerry Falwell, in closing down the Moral Majority, explained that its work had been accomplished—its values had become part of the American mainstream. He was right, in one respect. For years, the Moral Majority worked zealously to banish "bad speech," targeting "offensive" books in school libraries, as well as "socially harmful" magazines on newsstands.

Now, on American college campuses, there is a new, rapidly growing legion of decency also devoted to punishing bad speech. Its list of indefensible words is different from Falwell's. Expressions of racism, sexism, homophobia, anti-Semitism and prejudice against the handicapped are to be outlawed. But the basic principle is precisely that of Falwell: A decent society requires limits to free expression, and if that means diminishing the First Amendment, the will of the majority must rule.

Accordingly, on a number of prestigious campuses, a majority of students and faculty have concluded that censorship must be integral to higher education. As Canetta Ivy—one of the heads of student government at Stanford University—says, "We don't put as many restrictions on freedom of speech as we should."

4   A quarter of a century after the Free-Speech Movement began at UC Berkeley, helping fuel the anti-war and civil rights campaigns, some of the brightest of today's students are marching in the other direction.

This neoconservatism among liberals and radicals, Blacks and feminists, and even a number of law professors, has its roots in the very real racism existing on a number of campuses. At Brown, for instance, fliers were distributed, reading: "Things have been going down hill since the kitchen help moved into the classroom." At Smith, four Black women received vicious racist letters. At Yale, the Afro-American Cultural Center's building was emblazoned with a WHITE POWER sign and a swastika.

In reaction, Black students and many white students have joined to insist on the creation of codes not only of student conduct but also of student speech. Administrators, often enthusiastically, have yielded to those demands.

There are now various codes of forbidden speech at Emory University, the University of Wisconsin, the University of California, the University of Buffalo Law School and New York University Law School, among others.

8   The codes which have been adopted are not limited to epithets. On most campuses, a student can be disciplined—or even expelled—for words which create an intimidating, hostile or demeaning environment for educational pursuits.

Or a student may be put on trial for "racist or discriminatory comment . . . or other expressive behavior directed at an individual"—if the speaker "intentionally" set out to "demean the race, sex or religion" of the aggrieved complainant (University of Wisconsin).

These thou-shalt-not-speak codes are so vague and broad that just a disagreement on such issues as Affirmative Action or an independent Palestinian state can lead to a verdict that a particularly vehement student is guilty of discriminatory harassment against Blacks or Jews.

Who will judge the defendants? Administrators will, or a panel of administrators and students. And if they are ideologues and find the controversial political views of the defendant repellent, the student can miss a semester or more for being under the illusion that the university is a place of free inquiry.

12   While the presidents of the universities of Michigan and Wisconsin, among others, have hailed these codes as prohibited speech, Donald Kennedy, president of Stanford, is resisting the notion that students are best taught to think for themselves by being told what they can't say. When you tell people what they can't say, Kennedy has emphasized, they will begin to suppress what they think.

Already, in classrooms at some American colleges where language is monitored—as it is at Chinese universities—there are students afraid to explore certain lines of thought lest they be considered racist or sexist. At New York University Law School, for example, where heresy hunters abound in the student body, the atmosphere in some classes is like that of the old-time House Un-American Activities Committee. One student describes "a host of watchdog committees and generally hostile classroom reception regarding any student comment right of center."

At Stanford, the student organizations insistently demanding a code of forbidden language include the Asian Law Students Association, the Black Law Students Association, and the Asian-American Students Association. From these groups and from NYU Law School will come some of the judges of the next decades, and maybe even a Supreme Court justice or two.

The First Amendment is always fragile—witness the frenzy to amend the Bill of Rights after the Supreme Court ruled in June that the First Amendment protected flag burning. But with students at prestigious colleges now intent on limiting speech for a greater social good, the First Amendment will become even more vulnerable to attack in the years ahead.

16   But shouldn't there be some punishment of especially hurtful, insulting, infuriating words? When he was mayor of Chicago, Harold Washington was asked to punish those responsible for inflammatory language which had gone out over a city radio station. According to his former press secretary, he refused, saying, "If I scratch one word, where do I stop?"

The current college codes began in response to crude racial and sexist scrawls. But now the language being scratched out extends to any words that create a hostile atmosphere or any language that "involves an express or implied threat to an individual's academic efforts"—whatever that may mean.

There is also the damaging effect of these protective regulations on the very people who are insisting they be safeguarded. Malcolm X used to talk about the need for young people to learn how language works, how to dissect it, how to use it as both a shield and a sword. Above all, he thought, Blacks should not be fearful of language. They should not let it intimidate them but rather should fight back when words are used against them with more powerful words of their own.

If you read Malcolm X's collected speeches and listen to his recordings, it is clear he was an extraordinarily resilient, resourceful, probing master of language. Can you imagine his asking to be protected from somebody else's—anybody else's—words?

20   I've debated Black students about these speech codes. They are highly articulate and quick with polemical counterpoint. And I've asked them why on earth

they are running away from language when they can turn a campus into a continuing forum on racism by using the vicious racist language directed at them to illuminate what's going on there.

Moreover, by turning to censorship instead of challenge, these students can well cut off the expression of speech they themselves want to hear.

On ABC-TV's "Nightline" some time ago, debating Barbara Ransby (a Ph.D. student at the University of Michigan and founder of the United Coalition Against Racism), I posed this quite possible scenario: A group of Black students invite Louis Farrakhan to lecture in a political science class. He comes and says, "I want to explain what I said about Judaism being a gutter religion. I meant it, but I want to give you the context in which I said it."

There are Jewish students in the class and they claim that—according to the university's code—Farrakhan has created a hostile atmosphere. In my view, Farrakhan ought to be able to speak anywhere he chooses, and certainly on a college campus. As long as the students have the right to question him and argue with him, they'll have something to gain from the experience. But under the speech codes at more and more colleges, Farrakhan—having created a hostile atmosphere—would quite likely not be permitted on campus again.

24   Is that what the Black students pressing for speech codes want? To have Black speakers they invite on campus rejected because of what they say and how they say it? Do female students want radical feminist Andrea Dworkin barred because of possible charges that she creates a hostile environment for male students?

Also overlooked by students concerned with artistic expression is that a hostile atmosphere can be created by a painting or a piece of sculpture, because expression can be graphic as well as verbal. When the University of Wisconsin's code was being debated before the state's board of regents, E. David Cronon— then dean of UW-Madison's College of Letters and Science—testified that the code would, indeed, chill students' rights to artistic expression.

For example, some years ago, I was lecturing at the University of Wisconsin when a fierce fight broke out over a student's exhibition of paintings in a university building. Feminists claimed his work was outrageously sexist and demanded that the paintings be removed. The administration gingerly upheld the artist and the very core of a university's reason for being: the right to freedom of expression. But under the university's new code of propriety, that exhibition would be scrapped as fast as you can say "Edwin Meese" [conservative U.S. Attorney General under President Reagan].

Furthermore—and this is a poignant dimension of the rush to virtuous censorship—it won't do a bit of good. Let us suppose these codes were in place on every campus in the country. Would racism go away? No, it would go underground, in the dark, where it's most comfortable.

28   The language on campus could become as pure as bottled water, but racist attitudes would still fester. The only way to deal with racism is to bring it out into the open—not suppress it.

One approach is to examine particular incidents on a particular campus and get people—and that includes Blacks—to talk about their own racist attitudes. This approach won't work wonders, but, depending on the honesty and the incisiveness of the faculty and the students leading these probes, whatever happens will be a lot more useful than squashing expression. And it may lead to specific, durable changes on campus, which will also be a lot more productive than quibbling over who created a hostile atmosphere and whether or not it was done intentionally.

But the way the lemmings—administrators as well as students—are going, the anti-free-speech movement may intimidate and harass students for some time to come. And it's scary. As Lee Dembart—a former *New York Times* reporter who is now a student at Stanford Law School—said in the *Times:*

"It is distressing that the 'politically correct' view on campus these days seems to favor curtailment of speech. Oddly, defense of the First Amendment is now an anti-progressive view. Yes, speech is sometimes painful. Sometimes it is abusive. That is one of the prices of a free society. Unfortunately, this is a lesson which has to be learned over and over again. No victory endures."

32   Yet Dembart's views are held by only a besieged minority. The voice of the regulatory majority is that of Sharon Gwyn, 1989 graduate of Stanford who wrote this in the *New York Times.*

"As a Black woman attending Stanford University, I feel that no one should be allowed to promote racially derogatory ideas on this campus."

And beginning with that simple preliminary statement, campuses are being caught in a web of such restrictions as these from Emory University:

Forbidden is "discriminatory harassment," which "includes conduct (oral, written, graphic or physical) directed against any person or group of persons because of their race, color, national origin, religion, sex, sexual orientation, age, handicap or veteran's status and that has the purpose or reasonably foreseeable effect of creating an offensive, demeaning, intimidating or hostile environment for that person or group of persons."

36   Anything you say can and will be used against you.

As an indication of the degree to which America's colleges have retreated from their reason for being, there is a section from the 1975 Report of the Committee on Freedom of Expression at Yale (the celebrated C. Vann Woodward report):

"If expression may be prevented, censored or punished because of its content or the motives attributed to those who promote it, then it is no longer free. It will be subordinated to other values that we believe to be of lower priority in a university."

Yale has not reaffirmed the thrust of that report, but it is incomprehensible to too many colleges and universities.

40   I lecture at colleges and universities around the country every year, and I intend to say what I think about these shameful speech codes. At some schools, I may thereby be creating a hostile atmosphere in lecture halls where there are students who say they crave censorship.

And that is precisely my intention: to create an atmosphere hostile to suppression of speech—for any reason.

Recently, friends of the First Amendment were given reason for hope when a federal district court in Michigan struck down the University of Michigan's restrictions on student speech as unconstitutional. They are too vague and over-broad, said Judge Avern Cohn, and therefore in violation of the First Amendment. The suit was brought by the American Civil Liberties Union.

This is the first court decision on university suppression of speech, and since it is so clear, it may influence other courts in other parts of the country to remind colleges and universities that they are in the business of free thought, not regulated thought.

Personal Response

How do you feel about speech codes on university campuses? Would you restrict the right of someone else to be verbally abusive to you, for instance?

Questions for Discussion

1. What parallels does Hentoff draw between conservatives and campus liberals on the issue of speech codes? What do you think of his aligning these two groups?

2. Explain the title by first identifying HUAC. What do you think of Hentoff's comparing the attempts of university administrators and students to prohibit speech to the activities of the House Un-American Activities Committee?

3. What problems does Hentoff see with the speech codes being adopted by many university campuses? What does Hentoff suggest as an alternative way of dealing with racist and other derogatory comments? Do you think his suggestion would be more effective than prohibiting speech?

4. Where does Hentoff use loaded language (words weighted to clearly indicate the writer's attitude)? What does he mean when he compares administrators and students to lemmings in paragraph 30? What is the effect of such language in an argument?

5. How convincing do you find Hentoff's argument? Do you find his reasoning logical?

THE WORD POLICE

Michiko Kakutani

Michiko Kakutani is the leading book reviewer for the New York Times, *where "The Word Police" was first published in the January 31, 1993, issue. The reference to "this month's inaugural festivities" that begins the essay is to the 1993 inauguration of President Clinton.*

This month's inaugural festivities, with their celebration, in Maya Angelou's words, of "humankind"—"the Asian, the Hispanic, the Jew/The African, the

Native American, the Sioux,/The Catholic, the Muslim, the French, the Greek/The Irish, the Rabbi, the Priest, the Sheik,/The Gay, the Straight, the Preacher,/The privileged, the homeless, the Teacher"—constituted a kind of official embrace of multiculturalism and a new politics of inclusion.

The mood of political correctness, however, has already made firm inroads into popular culture. Washington boasts a store called Politically Correct that sells pro-whale, anti-meat, ban-the-bomb T-shirts, bumper stickers and buttons, as well as a local cable television show called "Politically Correct Cooking" that features interviews in the kitchen with representatives from groups like People for the Ethical Treatment of Animals.

The Coppertone suntan lotion people are planning to give their longtime cover girl, Little Miss (Ms?) Coppertone, a male equivalent, Little Mr. Coppertone. And even Superman (Superperson?) is rumored to be returning this spring, reincarnated as four ethnically diverse clones: an African-American, an Asian, a Caucasian and a Latino.

4   Nowhere is this P.C. mood more striking than in the increasingly noisy debate over language that has moved from university campuses to the country at large—a development that both underscores Americans' puritanical zeal for reform and their unwavering faith in the talismanic power of words.

Certainly no decent person can quarrel with the underlying impulse behind political correctness: a vision of a more just, inclusive society in which racism, sexism and prejudice of all sorts have been erased. But the methods and fervor of the self-appointed language police can lead to a rigid orthodoxy—and unintentional self-parody—opening the movement to the scorn of conservative opponents and the mockery of cartoonists and late-night television hosts.

It's hard to imagine women earning points for political correctness by saying "ovarimony" instead of "testimony"—as one participant at the recent Modern Language Association convention was overhead to suggest. It's equally hard to imagine people wanting to flaunt their lack of prejudice by giving up such words and phrases as "bull market, "kaiser roll," "Lazy Susan," and "charley horse."

Several books on bias-free language have already appeared, and the 1991 edition of the Random House Webster's College Dictionary boasts an appendix titled "Avoiding Sexist Language." The dictionary also includes such linguistic mutations as "womyn" (women, "used as an alternative spelling to avoid the suggestion of sexism perceived in the sequence m-e-n") and "waitron" (a gender-blind term for waiter or waitress).

8   Many of these dictionaries and guides not only warn the reader against offensive racial and sexual slurs, but also try to establish and enforce a whole new set of usage rules. Take, for instance, "The Bias-Free Word Finder, a Dictionary of Nondiscriminatory Language" by Rosalie Maggio (Beacon Press)—a volume often indistinguishable, in its meticulous solemnity, from the tongue-in-cheek "Official Politically Correct Dictionary and Handbook" put out last year by Henry Beard and Christopher Cerf (Villard Books). Ms. Maggio's book supplies the reader intent on using kinder, gentler language with writing guidelines as well as a detailed listing of more than 5,000 "biased words and phrases."

Whom are these guidelines for? Somehow one has a tough time picturing them replacing "Fowler's Modern English Usage" in the classroom, or being adopted by the average man (sorry, individual) in the street.

The "pseudogeneric 'he,'" we learn from Ms. Maggio, is to be avoided like the plague, as is the use of the word "man" to refer to humanity. "Fellow," "king," "lord" and "master" are bad because they're "male-oriented words," and "king," "lord" and "master" are especially bad because they're also "hierarchical, dominator society terms." The politically correct lion becomes the "monarch of the jungle," new-age children play "someone on the top of the heap," and the "Mona Lisa" goes down in history as Leonardo's "acme of perfection."

As for the word "black," Ms. Maggio says it should be excised from terms with a negative spin: she recommends substituting words like "mouse" for "black eye," "ostracize" for "blackball," "payola" for "blackmail" and "outcast" for "black sheep." Clearly, some of these substitutions work better than others: somehow the "sinister humor" of Kurt Vonnegut or "Saturday Night Live" doesn't quite make it; nor does the "denouncing" of the Hollywood 10.

12   For the dedicated user of politically correct language, all these rules can make for some messy moral dilemmas. Whereas "battered wife" is a gender-biased term, the gender-free term "battered spouse," Ms. Maggio notes, incorrectly implies "that men and women are equally battered."

On one hand, say Francine Wattman Frank and Paula A. Treichler in their book "Language, Gender, and Professional Writing" (Modern Language Association), "he or she" is an appropriate construction for talking about an individual (like a jockey, say) who belongs to a profession that's predominantly male—it's a way of emphasizing "that such occupations are not barred to women or that women's concerns need to be kept in mind." On the other hand, they add, using masculine pronouns rhetorically can underscore ongoing male dominance in those fields, implying the need for change.

And what about the speech codes adopted by some universities in recent years? Although they were designed to prohibit students from uttering sexist and racist slurs, they would extend, by logic, to blacks who want to use the word "nigger" to strip the term of its racist connotations, or homosexuals who want to use the word "queer" to reclaim it from bigots.

In her book, Ms. Maggio recommends applying bias-free usage retroactively: she suggests paraphrasing politically incorrect quotations, or replacing "the sexist words or phrases with ellipsis dots and/or bracketed substitutes," or using "sic" "to show that the sexist words come from the original quotation and to call attention to the fact that they are incorrect."

16   Which leads the skeptical reader of "The Bias-Free Word Finder" to wonder whether "All the King's Men" should be retitled "All the Ruler's People"; "Pet Sematary," "Animal Companion Graves"; "Birdman of Alcatraz," "Birdperson of Alcatraz"; and "The Iceman Cometh," "The Ice Route Driver Cometh"?

Will making such changes remove the prejudice in people's minds? Should we really spend time trying to come up with non-male-based alternatives to "Midas touch," "Achilles' heel," and "Montezuma's revenge"? Will tossing out Santa

Claus—whom Ms. Maggio accuses of reinforcing "the cultural male-as-norm sys-tem"—in favor of Belfana, his Italian female alter ego, truly help banish sexism? Can the avoidance of "violent expressions and metaphors" like "kill two birds with one stone," "sock it to 'em" or "kick an idea around" actually promote a more har-monious world?

The point isn't that the excesses of the word police are comical. The point is that their intolerance (in the name of tolerance) has disturbing implications. In the first place, getting upset by phrases like "bullish on America" or "the City of Brotherly Love" tends to distract attention from the real problems of prejudice and injustice that exist in society at large, turning them into mere questions of semantics. Indeed, the emphasis currently put on politically correct usage has un-canny parallels with the academic movement of deconstruction—a method of textual analysis that focuses on language and linguistic pyrotechnics—which has become firmly established on university campuses.

In both cases, attention is focused on surfaces, on words and metaphors; in both cases, signs and symbols are accorded more importance than content. Hence, the attempt by some radical advocates to remove "The Adventures of Huckleberry Finn" from curriculums on the grounds that Twain's use of the word "nigger" makes the book a racist text—never mind the fact that this American classic (written in 1884) depicts the spiritual kinship achieved between a white boy and a runaway slave, never mind the fact that the "nigger" Jim emerges as the novel's most honorable, decent character.

20   Ironically enough, the P.C. movement's obsession with language is accom-panied by a strange Orwellian willingness to warp the meaning of words by placing them under a high-powered ideological lens. For instance, the "Dictio-nary of Cautionary Words and Phrases"—a pamphlet issued by the University of Missouri's Multicultural Management Program to help turn "today's journal-ists into tomorrow's multicultural newsroom managers"—warns that using the word "articulate" to describe members of a minority group can suggest the op-posite, "that 'those people' are not considered well educated, articulate and the like."

The pamphlet patronizes minority groups, by cautioning the reader against using the words "lazy" and "burly" to describe any member of such groups; and it issues a similar warning against using words like "gorgeous" and "petite" to describe women.

As euphemism proliferates with the rise of political correctness, there is a spread of the sort of sloppy, abstract language that Orwell said is "designed to make lies sound truthful and murder respectable, and to give an appearance of solidity to pure wind." "Fat" becomes "big boned" or "differently sized"; "stu-pid" becomes "exceptional"; "stoned" becomes "chemically inconvenienced."

Wait a minute here! Aren't such phrases eerily reminiscent of the eu-phemisms coined by the Government during Vietnam and Watergate? Remember how the military used to speak of "pacification," or how President Richard M. Nixon's press secretary, Ronald L. Ziegler, tried to get away with calling a lie an "inoperative statement"?

24   Calling the homeless "the underhoused" doesn't give them a place to live; calling the poor "the economically marginalized" doesn't help them pay the bills. Rather, by playing down their plight, such language might even make it easier to shrug off the seriousness of their situation.

Instead of allowing free discussion and debate to occur, many gungho advocates of politically correct language seem to think that simple suppression of a word or concept will magically make the problem disappear. In the "Bias-Free Word Finder," Ms. Maggio entreats the reader not to perpetuate the negative stereotype of Eve. "Be extremely cautious in referring to the biblical Eve," she writes; "this story has profoundly contributed to negative attitudes toward women throughout history, largely because of misogynistic and patriarchal interpretations that labeled her evil, inferior, and seductive."

The story of Bluebeard, the rake (whoops!—the libertine) who killed his seven wives, she says, is also to be avoided, as is the biblical story of Jezebel. Of Jesus Christ, Ms. Maggio writes: "There have been few individuals in history as completely androgynous as Christ, and it does his message a disservice to overinsist on his maleness." She doesn't give the reader any hints on how this might be accomplished; presumably, one is supposed to avoid describing him as the Son of God.

Of course the P.C. police aren't the only ones who want to proscribe what people should say or give them guidelines for how they may use an idea; Jesse Helms and his supporters are up to exactly the same thing when they propose to patrol the boundaries of the permissible in art. In each case, the would-be censor aspires to suppress what he or she finds distasteful—all, of course, in the name of the public good.

28   In the case of the politically correct, the prohibition of certain words, phrases and ideas is advanced in the cause of building a brave new world free of racism and hate, but this vision of harmony clashes with the very ideals of diversity and inclusion that the multicultural movement holds dear, and it's purchased at the cost of freedom of expression and freedom of speech.

In fact, the utopian world envisioned by the language police would be bought at the expense of the ideals of individualism and democracy articulated in the "The [sic] Gettysburg Address": "Forescore and seven years ago our fathers brought forth on this continent a new nation, conceived in liberty and dedicated to the proposition that all men are created equal."

Of course, the P.C. police have already found Lincoln's words hopelessly "phallocentric." No doubt they would rewrite the passage: "Fourscore and seven years ago our foremothers and forefathers brought forth on this continent a new nation, formulated with liberty, and dedicated to the proposition that all humankind is created equal."

Personal Response

With whom are you more sympathetic, those who advocate politically correct language or those who believe the P.C. movement carries its reform efforts too far?

Questions for Discussion

1. Explain what Kakutani means when she writes of P.C. that it "both under-scores Americans' puritanical zeal for reform and their unwavering faith in the talismanic power of words" (paragraph 4).

2. What in particular does Kakutani object to in the P.C. movement? What effect do you think she intends to achieve by calling proponents of P.C. "the word police"?

3. Select specific words that Kakutani uses as examples of unreasonable substitutions for offensive language suggested by Rosalie Maggio in her book *The Bias-Free Word Finder.* What is Kakutani's objection to the proposed alternatives? What does Maggio find unacceptable in the language she proposes substitutions for?

4. Kakutani suggests that one problem with the P.C. movement is that it lends itself so easily to parody and even mockery. Bring to class both a book advocating changes, such as Maggio's *The Bias-Free Word Finder,* and a book that parodies political correctness, such as the *Official Politically Correct Dictionary and Handbook.* Read aloud selected passages from each. Do you and your classmates find the suggestions in the politically correct book reasonable? Do you find the parody funny?

TEACH DIVERSITY WITH A SMILE

Barbara Ehrenreich

Barbara Ehrenreich is the author of seven books, including a critique of the 1980s, The Worst Years of Our Lives: Irreverent Notes from a Decade of Greed *(1990), and a study of the middle class,* Fear of Falling *(1989). Her essays appear regularly in such periodicals as* Ms., *the* Atlantic Monthly, *the* New Republic, *and the* New York Times. *This essay was first published in the April 8, 1991 issue of* Time.

Something had to replace the threat of communism, and at last a workable substitute is at hand. "Multiculturalism," as the new menace is known, has been denounced in the media recently as the new McCarthyism, the new fundamentalism, even the new totalitarianism—take your choice. According to its critics, who include a flock of tenured conservative scholars, multiculturalism aims to toss out what it sees as the Eurocentric bias in education and replace Plato with Ntozake Shange and traditional math with the Yoruba number system. And that's just the beginning. The Jacobins of the multiculturalist movement, who are described derisively as P.C., or politically correct, are said to have launched a campus reign of terror against those who slip and innocently say "freshman" instead of "freshperson," "Indian" instead of "Native American" or, may the Goddess forgive them, "disabled" instead of "differently abled."

So you can see what is at stake here: freedom of speech, freedom of thought, Western civilization and a great many professional egos. But before we get carried away by the mounting backlash against multiculturalism, we ought to reflect for a moment on the system that the P.C. people aim to replace. I know all about it; in fact it's just about all I *do* know, since I—along with so many educated white people of my generation—was a victim of monoculturalism.

American history, as it was taught to us, began with Columbus' "discovery" of an apparently unnamed, unpeopled America, and moved on to the Pilgrims serving pumpkin pie to a handful of grateful red-skinned folks. College expanded our horizons with courses called Humanities or sometimes Civ, which introduced us to a line of thought that started with Homer, worked its way through Rabelais and reached a poignant climax in the pensées of Matthew Arnold. Graduate students wrote dissertations on what long-dead men had thought of Chaucer's verse or Shakespeare's dramas; foreign language meant French or German. If there had been high technology in ancient China, kingdoms in black Africa or women anywhere, at any time, doing anything worth noticing, we did not know it, nor did anyone think to tell us.

4   Our families and neighborhoods reinforced the dogma of monoculturalism. In our heads, most of us '50s teenagers carried around a social map that was about as useful as the chart that guided Columbus to the "Indies." There were "Negroes," "whites" and "Orientals," the latter meaning Chinese and "Japs." Of religions, only three were known—Protestant, Catholic and Jewish—and not much was known about the last two types. The only remaining human categories were husbands and wives, and that was all the diversity the monocultural world could handle. Gays, lesbians, Buddhists, Muslims, Malaysians, Mormons, etc. were simply off the map.

So I applaud—with one hand, anyway—the multiculturalist goal of preparing us all for a wider world. The other hand is tapping its fingers impatiently, because the critics are right about one thing: when advocates of multiculturalism adopt the haughty stance of political correctness, they quickly descend to silliness or worse. It's obnoxious, for example, to rely on university administrations to enforce P.C. standards of verbal inoffensiveness. Racist, sexist and homophobic thoughts cannot, alas, be abolished by fiat but only by the time-honored methods of persuasion, education and exposure to the other guy's—or, excuse me, woman's—point of view.

And it's silly to mistake verbal purification for genuine social reform. Even after all women are "Ms." and all people are "he or she," women will still earn only 65¢ for every dollar earned by men. Minorities by any other name, such as "people of color," will still bear a hugely disproportionate burden of poverty and discrimination. Disabilities are not just "different abilities" when there are not enough ramps for wheelchairs, signers for the deaf or special classes for the "specially" endowed. With all due respect for the new politesse, actions still speak louder than fashionable phrases.

But the worst thing about the P.C. people is that they are such poor advocates for the multicultural cause. No one was ever won over to a broader, more inclusive view of life by being bullied or relentlessly "corrected." Tell a 19-year-old white male that he can't say "girl" when he means "teen-age woman," and he will most likely snicker. This may be the reason why, despite the conservative alarms, P.C.-ness remains a relatively tiny trend. Most campuses have more serious and ancient problems: faculties still top-heavy with white males of the monocultural persuasion; fraternities that harass minorities and women; date rape; alcohol abuse; and tuition that excludes all but the upper fringe of the middle class.

8   So both sides would be well advised to lighten up. The conservatives ought to realize that criticisms of the great books approach to learning do not amount to totalitarianism. And the advocates of multiculturalism need to regain the sense of humor that enabled their predecessors in the struggle to coin the term P.C. years ago—not in arrogance but in self-mockery.

Beyond that, both sides should realize that the beneficiaries of multiculturalism are not only the "oppressed peoples" on the standard P.C. list (minorities, gays, etc.). The "unenlightened"—the victims of monoculturalism—are oppressed too, or at least deprived. Our educations, whether at Yale or at State U, were narrow and parochial and left us ill-equipped to navigate a society that truly is multicultural and is becoming more so every day. The culture that we studied was, in fact, *one* culture and, from a world perspective, all too limited and ingrown. Diversity is challenging, but those of us who have seen the alternative know it is also richer, livelier and ultimately more fun.

Personal Response

Describe your own education in terms of multiculturalism. Has it been inclusive or exclusive? Would advocates of multiculturalism praise your education or criticize it?

Questions for Discussion

1. Explain in your own words what Ehrenreich means when she writes that she was "a victim of monoculturalism" (paragraph 2). What does she mean when she says that such victims are oppressed too (paragraph 9)?

2. Explain what Ehrenreich finds reasonable in the positions of those on both sides of the political correctness debate.

3. Ehrenreich writes that "both sides would be well advised to lighten up" (paragraph 8). Find examples of language in the essay that suggest that Ehrenreich has taken her own advice.

4. Hold a classroom debate on the issue of political correctness, taking into consideration not only Ehrenreich's position but the positions of the other writers in this chapter.

Suggestions for Writing About
POLITICAL CORRECTNESS

1. Write a response to Gerald F. Kreyche's observations in "Have We Lost Our Sense of Humor?" that "political correctness is making cowards of almost everyone" and that "people have become thin-skinned, touchy, [and] overly sensitive."

2. Explain your position on the subject of Peggy Noonan's "Toward Candor and Courage in Speech" by commenting on the words and phrases she discusses as well as on similar examples with which you are familiar.

3. If you belong to a group that is often stereotyped, explore the implications of that stereotype for you personally as well as for your friends and family, as Rebecca Thomas Kirkendall does in "Who's a Hillbilly?"

4. Argue your own position on Nat Hentoff's assertion in "'Insensitive Language' and the New HUAC Mentality" that there should be absolutely no restrictions on speech on college campuses.

5. Compare what Gloria Naylor in "Mommy, What Does 'Nigger' Mean" has to say about the power of words with what Peggy Noonan in "Toward Candor and Courage in Speech" and Rebecca Thomas Kirkendall in "Who's a Hillbilly?" have to say about the subject.

6. Michiko Kakutani writes in "The Word Police" that "the utopian world envisioned by the language police would be bought at the expense of the ideals of individualism and democracy articulated in *The Gettysburg Address*" (paragraph 29). Explain in detail what Kakutani means by that statement and your reasons for agreeing or disagreeing with her.

7. Write an analysis of the differing opinions on the subject of political correctness as represented by the readings in this chapter. Consider, for instance, on which points the writers agree and disagree and what their underlying assumptions seem to be. Conclude by explaining your own position on the subject.

8. Focus on a First Amendment issue, such as pornography, obscenity in art or the media, campus speech codes, or political correctness, and explain the extent to which you think there should be limits on freedom of expression. Consider where you would draw the line, if at all, between what is allowable under the First Amendment and what is intolerable by standards of decency. Where does the matter of social responsibility as opposed to creative freedom come into play?

CHAPTER 10

VIOLENCE

America has the highest violent crime rate in the world. The number of murders and rapes in some areas of the country is at an all-time high, while muggings, armed robbery, and drug trafficking make contemporary life perilous for people of all age groups, ethnic backgrounds, and socioeconomic levels. The essays in this chapter focus on selected aspects of this very real problem.

The first three offer examples of crimes against women and speculate on reasons to account for such crimes. Susan Baker and Tipper Gore in "Some Reasons for 'Wilding'" begin with the violent rape and beating of a woman jogger in New York's Central Park and go on to suggest that certain media and music messages are factors that contribute to such crimes. Similarly, Caryl Rivers is interested in the relation of rock music to violent behavior. In "Rock Lyrics and Violence Against Women," she registers her protest against lyrics that depict violence against women on the grounds that they legitimize such behavior. Finally, Carol Lynn Mithers in "The War Against Women" surveys the alarming statistics on violent crimes against women, offers reasons to account for such crimes, and suggest ways to stop this "war against women."

In the next selection, "Violence Against Whom?", Warren Farrell offers a different perspective by suggesting that the real war is against men. While not discounting violence done to women, Farrell insists that too much is made of such violence at the expense of males, who make up a much larger percentage of violent crime victims. Legislation to make acts of violence against women hate crimes and violations of their civil rights, he maintains, is legislation of sexual inequality.

The next four selections focus on guns in America. The authors of these pieces are not particularly interested in entering the debate over gun control. Rather, they are alarmed at the widespread availability of guns and the human toll of crimes involving firearms. According to statistics gathered by a number of sources including the Bureau of Alcohol, Tobacco, and Firearms; the National Center for Health; FBI Uniform Crime Reports; and the U.S. Justice Department, as of 1993, 67 million Americans own handguns, 640,000 violent crimes are committed with handguns annually, and the estimated total cost to the U.S. economy of firearm injuries is $14 billion. Handgun murders in the United

States number over 12,000 annually (*Time*, "The New Arms Race," 20 Dec. 1993, pp. 20–21).

Anna Quindlen, in "Old Enough to Kill?", tells the story of Cameron Kocher, who killed a neighbor girl when he was nine years old. Quindlen expresses dismay at the increasingly lower ages at which children commit violent crimes and wonders what to do with such children. Next, Gail Buchalter explains her decision to purchase a handgun, a decision she did not make lightly, as you will see when you read "Why I Bought a Handgun." Next, Matthew Maranz in "Guns 'Я Us" explains how an American citizen can purchase an automatic submachine gun. The occasional ironic tone of Maranz's essay reveals his astonishment at how simple the process really is. The final piece in this group of essays on guns is Nicholas Von Hoffman's "Gun Crazy." In his brief essay, Von Hoffman makes some pointed observations on the ready availability of guns and the atmosphere of fear that today's young people live in.

The last essay in this chapter is an excerpt from Martin Luther King, Jr.'s 1958 book *Stride Toward Freedom*. In "Pilgrimage to Nonviolence," King defines his concept of nonviolent resistance, a strategy he advocated for resisting oppression and gaining true equality. As you read, consider how effective you believe his strategy to be and whether you think King's philosophy is appropriate as a response to today's social problems.

SOME REASONS FOR "WILDING"

Susan Baker and Tipper Gore

Susan Baker and Tipper Gore are cofounders of Parents' Music Resource Center (PMRC), located in Arlington, Virginia. PMRC was founded in 1985 to address the issue of popular-music lyrics that glorify sex and violence and glamorize the use of drugs and alcohol. Baker and Gore often collaborate, as in this article, which was first published in Newsweek *magazine in May 1989.*

"Wilding." It's a new word in the vocabulary of teenage violence. The crime that made it the stuff of headlines is so heinous, the details so lurid as to make them almost beyond the understanding of any sane human being.

When it was over, a 28-year-old woman, an investment banker out for a jog, was left brutally beaten, knifed and raped by teenagers. She was found near an isolated road in New York's Central Park, covered with mud, almost dead from brain damage, loss of blood and exposure.

"It was fun," one of her suspected teenage attackers, all between 14 and 17 years old, told the Manhattan district attorney's office. In the lockup, they were nonchalantly whistling at a policewoman and singing a high-on-the-charts rap song about casual sex: "Wild Thing."

4 Maybe it's the savagery, the remorseless brutality that brought the national attention to this crime. We all heard about this one, either directly or from a friend or family member who would end the story with an "I can't believe it."

Believe it. Because it's happening elsewhere too.

In 1987, in Brooklyn, N.Y., three teenagers methodically set fire to a homeless couple. When at first rubbing alcohol wouldn't ignite the couple, they went to a local service station for gasoline. It worked.

In 1988, in rural Missouri, three teenagers killed a friend—partly out of curiosity! They just wanted to know what it would feel like to kill someone. One of the teenagers claimed the fascination with death began with heavy-metal music. When the victim asked "Why?" over and over as his friends brutally attacked with baseball bats, the answer was "Because it's fun."

8
In 1988 a record 406 people died in the county of Los Angeles alone in teen-gang-related attacks. One victim who survived was a pregnant woman who was shot, allegedly by a 16-year-old as a gang initiation rite.

This is truly a "generation at risk." Indeed, the statistics reflect its pain and confusion:

- The three leading causes of death among adolescents are drug- and alcohol-related accidents, suicide and homicide.

- Every year 1 million teenagers run away from home.

- Every year 1 million teenagers get pregnant.

- Every year over half a million—600,000 teenagers—attempt suicide; 5,000 succeed.

- Alcohol and drug abuse are so prevalent among the young that a *Weekly Reader* survey recently reported that 10-year-olds often feel pressure to try alcohol and crack.

- According to the Department of Education, 81 percent of the victims of violent crime are preteens and teenagers, 19 or younger. For the first time, teenagers have topped adults in the percentages of serious crimes committed per capita.

There are many complex reasons for this sad litany. Divorce and working parents strain the family's ability to cope. Latchkey kids are the rule more than the exception. Our schools and neighborhoods have become open-air drug markets. But it is not enough to excuse these children as products of a bad environment.

As a society, we must take full responsibility. Our music, movies and television are filled with images of sexual violence and killing. The message to our kids is: it's OK to enjoy brutality and suffering: "It's fun."

12
The American Academy of Pediatrics released a national policy statement on the impact of rock lyrics and music videos on adolescents last November. In it, they noted that some lyrics communicate potentially harmful health messages in a culture beset with drug abuse, teenage pregnancy, AIDS and other sexually transmitted diseases.

The No. 2 album in the country this week is "GN'R Lies" from the very popular group, Guns N' Roses. This band is a favorite of 6th through 12th graders. It contains the following lyrics: "I used to love her but I had to kill her, I had to put her six feet under, and I can still hear her complain."

Teen "slasher" films, featuring scenes of graphic, sadistic violence against women are so popular that characters like Jason from "Friday the 13th" and Freddie from "Nightmare on Elm Street" are considered cult heroes, and now there are spinoff television shows.

As parents, it is our responsibility to teach our children to make wise decisions. This responsibility is not only to feed and clothe their bodies, but also to feed and nurture their spirits, their minds, their values. The moral crisis facing our nation's youth requires that we *all* share the responsibility, parents and the entertainment industry.

16   Too often, those who produce this violence evade any discussion of their own responsibility by pretending the entire debate begins and ends with the First Amendment. We are strong advocates of its protections of free speech and free expression. We do not and have not advocated or supported restrictions on those rights; we have never proposed government action. What we are advocating, and what we have worked hard to encourage, is responsibility.

For example, producers and songwriters don't consider putting out songs, movies or videos that would portray racism in a positive way. They could. The First Amendment provides that freedom. But they don't. In part, perhaps it's because they think those products wouldn't sell. But in part, they recognize it would be irresponsible. Why is there no similar reticence when the issue is glorifying violence, generally against women?

The same sense of responsibility should be brought to a marketplace so saturated with violence that it legitimizes it for our children. It's time to stop the spilling of blood both as "entertainment" and in real life.

Personal Response

Do you think that Baker and Gore are overreacting to the dangers they see in certain rock music and teenage slasher films, or do they have a legitimate basis for complaint? Explain your answer.

Questions for Discussion

1. What do you think of the connection Baker and Gore make between "wilding" and media and music images of sexual violence? What is your position on the subject?

2. How effective do you find the examples that Baker and Gore offer to illustrate the brutality of crimes committed by young people? Are you convinced that today's youth are "truly a 'generation at risk'" (paragraph 9)?

3. What do you think of the actions Baker and Gore call for in order to address what they see as "the moral crisis facing our nation's youth" (paragraph 15)?

4. According to Baker and Gore, what reasons or excuses do song writers and film makers give to defend the violence in their products? Do you think

Baker and Gore make a convincing case in their argument against violence in music? If not, what would make it more effective?

ROCK LYRICS AND VIOLENCE AGAINST WOMEN

Caryl Rivers

Caryl Rivers is a professor of journalism at Boston University and has written many newspaper and magazine articles. Her novels include Virgins *(1984) and* Intimate Enemies *(1987); her most recent nonfiction book is* Slick Spins and Fractured Facts: How Cultural Myths Distort the News *(1997). This essay first appeared in the* Boston Globe *in 1985 and has been widely reprinted.*

After a grisly series of murders in California, possibly inspired by the lyrics of a rock song, we are hearing a familiar chorus: Don't blame rock and roll. Kids will be kids. They love to rebel, and the more shocking the stuff, the better they like it.

There's some truth in this, of course. I loved to watch Elvis shake his torso when I was a teenager, and it was even more fun when Ed Sullivan wouldn't let the cameras show him below the waist. I snickered at the forbidden "Rock with Me, Annie" lyrics by a black Rhythm and Blues group, which were deliciously naughty. But I am sorry, rock fans, that is not the same thing as hearing lyrics about how a man is going to force a woman to perform oral sex on him at gunpoint in a little number called "Eat Me Alive." It is not in the same league with a song about the delights of slipping into a woman's room while she is sleeping and murdering her, the theme of an AC/DC ballad that allegedly inspired the California slayer.

Make no mistake, it is not sex we are talking about here, but violence. Violence against women. Most rock songs are not violent—they are funky, sexy, rebellious, and sometimes witty. Please do not mistake me for a Mrs. Grundy. If Prince wants to leap about wearing only a purple jock strap, fine. Let Mick Jagger unzip his fly as he gyrates, if he wants to. But when either one of them starts garroting, beating, or sodomizing a woman in their number, that is another story.

4   I always find myself annoyed when "intellectual" men dismiss violence against women with a yawn, as if it were beneath their dignity to notice. I wonder if the reaction would be the same if the violence were directed against someone other than women. How many people would yawn and say, "Oh, kids will be kids," if a rock group did a nifty little number called "Lynchin'," in which stringing up and stomping on black people were set to music? Who would chuckle and say, "Oh, just a little adolescent rebellion" if a group of rockers went on MTV dressed as Nazis, desecrating synagogues and beating up Jews to the beat of twanging guitars?

I'll tell you what would happen. Prestigious dailies would thunder on editorial pages; senators would fall over each other to get denunciations into the *Congressional Record*. The president would appoint a commission to clean up the music business.

But violence against women is greeted by silence. It shouldn't be.

This does not mean censorship, or book (or record) burning. In a society that protects free expression, we understand a lot of stuff will float up out of the sewer. Usually, we recognize the ugly stuff that advocates violence against any group as the garbage it is, and we consider its purveyors as moral lepers. We hold our nose and tolerate it, but we speak out against the values it proffers.

8   But images of violence against women are not staying on the fringes of society. No longer are they found only in tattered, paper-covered books or in movie houses where winos snooze and the scent of urine fills the air. They are entering the mainstream at a rapid rate. This is happening at a time when the media, more and more, set the agenda for the public debate. It is a powerful legitimizing force—especially television. Many people regard what they see on TV as the truth; Walter Cronkite once topped a poll as the most trusted man in America.

Now, with the advent of rock videos and all-music channels, rock music has grabbed a big chunk of legitimacy. American teenagers have instant access, in their living rooms, to the messages of rock, on the same vehicle that brought them Sesame Street. Who can blame them if they believe that the images they see are accurate reflections of adult reality, approved by adults? After all, Big Bird used to give them lessons on the same little box. Adults, by their silence, sanction the images. Do we really want our kids to think that rape and violence are what sexuality is all about?

This is not a trivial issue. Violence against women is a major social problem, one that's more than a cerebral issue to me. I teach at Boston University, and one of my most promising young journalism students was raped and murdered. Two others told me of being raped. Recently, one female student was assaulted and beaten so badly she had $5,000 worth of medical bills and permanent damage to her back and eyes.

It's nearly impossible, of course, to make a cause-and-effect link between lyrics and images and acts of violence. But images have a tremendous power to create an atmosphere in which violence against certain people is sanctioned. Nazi propagandists knew that full well when they portrayed Jews as ugly, greedy, and powerful.

12   The outcry over violence against women, particularly in a sexual context, is being legitimized in two ways: by the increasing movement of these images into the mainstream of the media in TV, films, magazines, albums, videos, and by the silence about it.

Violence, of course, is rampant in the media. But it is usually set in some kind of moral context. It's usually only the bad guys who commit violent acts against the innocent. When the good guys get violent, it's against those who deserve it. Dirty Harry blows away the scum, he doesn't walk up to a toddler and say, "Make my day." The A Team does not shoot up suburban shopping malls.

But in some rock songs, it's the "heroes" who commit the acts. The people we are programmed to identify with are the ones being violent, with women on the receiving end. In a society where rape and assaults on women are endemic, this is no small problem, with millions of young boys watching on their TV screens and listening on their Walkmans.

I think something needs to be done. I'd like to see people in the industry respond to the problem. I'd love to see some women rock stars speak out against violence against women. I would like to see disc jockeys refuse air play to records and videos that contain such violence. At the very least, I want to see the end of the silence. I want journalists and parents and critics and performing artists to keep this issue alive in the public forum. I don't want people who are concerned about this issue labeled as bluenoses and bookburners and ignored.

16   And I wish it wasn't always just women who were speaking out. Men have as large a stake in the quality of our civilization as women do in the long run. Violence is a contagion that infects at random. Let's hear something, please, from the men.

Personal Response

Do you agree or disagree with the argument Rivers makes about rock lyrics? Explain your answer.

Questions for Discussion

1. What distinction does Rivers draw between the lyrics of music she enjoyed when she was younger and the lyrics she is opposed to now? What distinction does Rivers draw in *any* music between what she finds tolerable and intolerable in lyrics? What is your opinion of the distinctions she draws?

2. What examples does Rivers use to back up her argument about sexual violence in today's rock music? Do you think she is overreacting, or does she have enough evidence to support her point?

3. Where does Rivers present the views of those opposed to her own? Does acknowledging those opposing views make her argument more effective?

4. According to Rivers, what is the difference between the depiction of violence in movies and the news media and the depiction of violence in some rock lyrics and rock videos? Do you agree with her that depicting violence against women legitimizes it?

5. What action does Rivers call for in addressing the problem of violent rock lyrics? Do you find Rivers' closing paragraph effective? Explain your answer.

THE WAR AGAINST WOMEN

Carol Lynn Mithers

Carol Lynn Mithers is a freelance journalist whose works have appeared in such publications as the New York Times, Gentlemen's Quarterly, California, *and the* Village Voice. *This selection appeared in 1989 in* Ladies' Home Journal, *where Mithers is a contributing editor.*

The story was the kind that gives women nightmares. A teenage girl was abducted from a bus station in downtown Los Angeles and repeatedly raped. After several days, she managed to escape into the street, flag down a car and ask the men inside for help. Instead, they raped her. Yet in 1989, it was not the sheer horror of those facts that made reading them so difficult—it was that we had already confronted so many similar cases:

- The infamous gang rape and near-fatal beating of a jogger in New York City's Central Park. The attack on the woman, a Wall Street investment banker, was so savage that it induced brain injury; the victim, who has a graduate degree from Yale, has had to relearn even the simplest reading and math skills.

- The reported hour-long sexual assault on a mentally impaired girl by five teenage boys in the affluent suburb of Glen Ridge, New Jersey, while eight others were present. The girl, who was allegedly raped with a miniature baseball bat and a broomstick, was said to have known most of the youths since childhood.

- The killing of a respected judge in Grand Rapids, Michigan, by her estranged husband, a police officer, who was convicted only of manslaughter. "Everybody," said a male juror, "felt that he was provoked by his wife to do this."

- And for every rape and assault reported by the news media, there were thousands that were not. "He started to come on to me, and when I refused, he pulled a knife and made me strip," recalls Bonnie, twenty-eight, an Iowa student who was raped by the relative of a friend. "When I went to the hospital to report it," she says, starting to cry at the memory, "the doctor was so rough I felt I'd been raped a second time."

Like physical violence, cultural violence against women suddenly seemed to be everywhere this year—in misogynistic rock-music videos; in sadomasochistic comic books and men's magazines; in "slasher" films; in sick and ugly jokes by popular comedians; and even on the computer screen, with an obscene software program.

The more one saw and read in 1989, the more it seemed that, despite decades of crusades against rape and other assaults, sexual rage was not only not abating, it was getting worse. Many women felt a higher level of hostility, a thickening miasma of menace that ranged from degrading imagery to casual insults to overt attacks.

4   Says Nancy Biele, past president of the National Coalition Against Sexual Assault, in Minneapolis, "I've been doing this kind of work for fifteen years, and it feels more dangerous out there to me now."

"We're seeing a culture in which it has become a little more okay to hate women," says Jennie Balise, of the Los Angeles Commission on Assaults Against Women.

Even President Bush, hardly a radical feminist, was moved to give a name to the growing problem. "We must," he declared, "halt this war against women."

A New Level of Violence

And a war it often seems to be, fought on every front. It is raging on the streets. According to the FBI, a woman is raped every six minutes, and one in ten will be raped in her lifetime. Since many attacks are not reported, the true figures may be considerably higher; Nancy Biele believes that as many as one woman in three may become a rape victim.

8   Nor is home a safe harbor. A woman is beaten every fifteen seconds, and each day at least four women are killed by their batterers, according to federal statistics. "Battery," says former Surgeon General C. Everett Koop, "is the single most significant cause of injury to women in this country."

Most troubling of all, perhaps, is the reported rise in levels of sexual hostility among our young. Some rape counselors fear that overexposure to violently anti-female images is creating a kind of emotional numbness. Mary Beth Roden, of the rape treatment center at Santa Monica Hospital, in Santa Monica, California, says, "A few years ago, we'd show high school students a taped interview with a rape victim, and kids would be saying, 'Wow, that was terrible.' Now many of them are less shocked. I don't know any other word to use but *desensitization.*"

Male college students, in particular, seem to have become more abusive. "Between 75 and 90 percent of campus women have experienced at least one incident with campus men that made them feel insulted or degraded," says Bernice R. Sandler, of the Association of American Colleges, in Washington, D. C. "When one university held an anti-pornography march, for instance, the women marching were taunted with cries of 'gang rape, gang rape' and 'I'll take that one.'"

Far too often, male students do not confine themselves to verbal assaults: According to a survey of six thousand students at thirty-two campuses by Mary Koss, Ph.D., a professor in the psychiatry department at the University of Arizona, one in twelve men admitted to having forced, or tried to force, a woman to have intercourse.

12   Incredibly, many men see nothing out of the ordinary about such attacks. "A 'nice' guy I was seeing decided he was tired of me saying no to sex," says Kelly, a musician from Seattle. "He had forcible, very painful intercourse with me. I fought, but he was a very large man. Afterward, he seemed to have no idea that he'd done anything wrong."

More shocking still are statistics on mere boys provided by Elizabeth Holtzman, district attorney for the borough of Brooklyn, in New York City. In the last two years, there has been an astounding increase of 200 percent in rape arrests of boys under thirteen in New York City, she says, while rape arrests of boys under eighteen went up 27 percent.

The comments of one of those youths provide a chilling insight into an attacker's motives. "She was weak. She couldn't do nothing," the boy says of his victim. "I was a dominant force over her."

Certainly, that need for power is a factor in sexual violence, and the current wave of sexual rage may be caused at least in part by a backlash against the challenges to traditional male power that have been posed by the women's movement. "[Some men] may be uncomfortable dealing with strong women," say

Bernice Sandler and Jean O'Gorman Hughes in a report on campus harassment. "Lashing out at these and other women by harassing them is a way to alleviate their discomfort."

16   Many men have been deeply shaken by the social upheaval in the years since the women's movement became mainstream, according to J. William Gibson, Ph.D., an assistant professor of sociology at Southern Methodist University, in Dallas. "From the mid-sixties through the late seventies, many traditional social relationships for men were significantly altered," Gibson says. "A lot of the culture that has emerged in the eighties, such as the increased popularity of movies and novels that present men as warriors, has been a symbolic attempt to restore a more traditional world."

The Heart of the Matter

Then again, some cultural traditions do stand—especially the definition of a "real" man. "Unfortunately," says Holtzman, "we have the idea that men prove themselves by being physically stronger than someone else or even harming that person physically."

Since many boys are also taught that manhood can only be conferred on them by other men, women are seen primarily as "the other"—and the appropriate victims on whom to prove oneself.

And these days, such time-dishonored stereotypes are more widely disseminated than ever. The misogynistic images appear everywhere:

- *Computer software.* MacPlaymate, a program that has found its way into both college dorms and executive suites, has graphics that display a nude, spread-eagled woman who is, according to a personal computing magazine, "ready to entertain your wildest electronic fantasies." The author of the program, Mike Saenz, a twenty-nine-year-old from Chicago, cheerfully admits that the program is "sexist as hell." Prudence Baird, a Los Angeles executive who is conducting an informal campaign against the program, says "I call it 'MacRape.'"

- *Comic books.* Many titles in the $300-million-per-year industry focus with disturbing frequency on the theme of sexual violence. One comic, "Black Orchid," begins with a woman being tied up and set afire; another, "Displaced Paranormals," shows an attractive female "mutant" being suspended from the ceiling and tortured.

- *Men's magazines.* Violent sexual themes such as rape and bondage are often depicted in mainstream publications, says Neil Malamuth, Ph.D., professor of communications at UCLA. In the book *Pornography and Sexual Aggression* (Academic Press, 1984), Malamuth writes of the negative effects of the "coupling of sex and aggression in these portrayals."

- *"Slasher" films.* Box-office attractions like *The Tool Box Murders* and the *Friday the 13th* series customarily show "independent women" being killed "in a sadistic, highly sexualized way," says Pauline Bart, Ph.D., a sociology professor at the University of Illinois, Chicago.

- *Popular music.* An uncomfortably high percentage of the music bought by teenagers emphasizes violence, especially sexual violence against women. Examples: A song by the band Guns 'n' Roses that contains the line *I used to love her, but I had to kill her;* and one by the group Poison, "I Want Action," that contains the lyric *If I can't have her I'll take her and make her.* Still another performer, the rapper Slick Rick, has released a record called "Treat Her Like a Prostitute."

- *Comedy.* Some of the most unabashed contempt for women can be found in the routines of popular performers like Eddie Murphy ("Remember the good old days, when you could beat up on women?"), Sam Kinison ("I don't condone wife beating . . . I *understand* it"), and Andrew Dice Clay, who, said one reviewer, portrays women as "a series of pliant orifices accompanied by a plaintive nagging voice."

20   Such cracks are no joke. One Los Angeles woman who saw Clay's show called it "forty of the most upsetting minutes I've ever experienced." Routines like Clay's clearly reflect how common some ugly attitudes are; his shows habitually draw raucous approval from hundreds of male fans.

A Dreadful Price

The toll taken by the war against women is clear and devastating. For the millions who've been the victims of sexual assault, life will never be the same. According to a study co-authored by Susan Sorenson, Ph.D., a clinical psychologist at UCLA, victims of rape and other sexual assaults are much more likely than nonvictims to suffer from major depression, alcohol or drug dependence, or anxiety disorders such as phobias and panic attacks. "The rape rules my life; I couldn't stop thinking about it," says Bonnie, the Iowa student. She was unable to work for eight months after the attack, and even today, she speaks haltingly of her ordeal. "It's taken a long time for me to come to terms with it, and I still don't trust men at all."

Kelly, the Seattle woman who was raped by her date, says, "I completely stopped going out with men for a while. But even after I started dating again, I wouldn't go to a man's apartment alone for any reason. I was sure that something awful would happen."

The same kind of fear often grips women even if they have escaped an attack. "I'm completely afraid of being alone anywhere for more than a few minutes," says Alice, thirty-two, a nurse who fought off an attacker on a deserted Northern California beach. "And I'm still furious at the guy, whoever he was. How could he believe he had the right to do that to me?"

24   For women who have become accustomed to independence, the loss of control they experience after an attack can be almost as frightening as the incident itself: Bonnie had been living on her own at the time she was raped, but she moved back to her parents' home the day of the attack "I felt terrified," she explains.

Nora, a thirty-five-year-old computer executive from Dallas, was raped in an underground parking lot. Now, she thinks, she will be looking fearfully behind her for the rest of her life. "I had gotten careless," she says. "But you can't ever let your guard down."

And one New York City woman, who was verbally harassed four times in the space of a block late one night, says the incidents have made her more wary of traveling by herself. "I used to think I could go pretty much anywhere at any time," she says. "Now I'm not so sure. I have to start thinking like a victim. No woman should have to do it, but that's reality."

Fighting the Violence

Although the war against women may seem unwinnable, there are some specific defensive steps that can be taken. "We need to have more effective enforcement of existing laws, and in some cases, strengthening of them," says Elizabeth Holtzman. "We also need to have counseling and training programs *within* the criminal justice system—we still find judges who reflect attitudes that women who are raped are responsible for it."

28   Unquestionably, though, the most important changes to be made are cultural. "This isn't a problem that can be fixed with a little psychotherapy and a few more prisons," says Diana Russell, Ph.D., professor of sociology at Mills College, in Oakland, California. "The real issue is the way men are brought up to view women and to see manhood."

At home, parents should be aware of the messages their children may be getting from the music they listen to and the videos they see. If those messages are exploitative, parents should reasonably discuss the issue with their kids: It is of the utmost importance that children not think of sexual violence as entertainment.

Holtzman says, "Speaking out against violence in media and particularly violence against women is crucial. I also think we need to address issues of discrimination against women, so we can strengthen the notion of the humanity of women."

It's essential, too, for men to understand that sexual harassment, even if it is not violent, is part of the spectrum that has rape and murder at its farthest end. "Sexual harassment is not a lunchtime sport," says Bonnie Lynn, forty-eight, an insurance claims adjuster from New York City. Lynn was outraged by a humorous *New York Times* article that appeared last April, one week after the Central Park rape, on "good-natured" men in the Wall Street area who volubly judged passing women on their appearance. "In its extreme, the idea that women are fair game leads to the kind of animal violence that was demonstrated against the woman in Central Park."

32   Most important of all, perhaps, is teaching boys that being a real man does not have to mean being violent or aggressive. It is here, says Jane Hood, associate professor of sociology at the University of New Mexico at Albuquerque, that parents can play an especially significant role. "We need to encourage children of both sexes to play together so that by the time they're teenagers, boys will learn to see girls as friends and not just sex objects," she says. "We don't need to en-

courage them to fight all their battles physically. I know these are hard changes to make, but they are ones we must think about."

Nancy Biele agrees. "If we can stop at a generational level and teach boys and girls differently, we can break through this. A world that is truly equal," she says, "would be a world without sexual violence."

Personal Response

How would you account for the high rate of violent crimes against women? Are your reasons the same as those of Mithers? Can you think of others besides those she names?

Questions for Discussion

1. Where does Mithers get the title of her essay? Do you think it an appropriate metaphor for the social problem Mithers describes?

2. Why do you think Mithers begins with five extended examples of violent crimes against women? Do you think that strategy is more effective than if she had begun with the federal statistics she cites in paragraphs 7 and 8? Why do you suppose Mithers quotes the reactions of some of the victims of violent crimes (paragraphs 21 through 25)?

3. Besides rape and murder, what other behaviors does Mithers include as evidence of the "war against women"? What seems to be a key factor in sexual violence?

4. What does Mithers suggest is the effect of the kinds of misogynistic images she lists in paragraph 19? Do you agree with her?

5. What do you think of Mithers' suggestions of possible ways to end the "war against women"? Can you suggest other ways?

VIOLENCE AGAINST WHOM?

Warren Farrell

Warren Farrell has been a spokesman for men since the 1970s. Advocating neither a women's nor a men's movement, he speaks in favor of a gender transition movement, in which men and women engage in dialogue that leads to mutual understanding and equitable treatment for both sexes. A former teacher at the School of Medicine at the University of California at San Diego, he also taught at Georgetown University, Rutgers University, and Brooklyn College. His books include The Liberated Man *(1974),* Why Men Are the Way They Are *(1986), and* The Myth of Male Power: Why Men Are the Disposable Sex *(1993), from which the following is excerpted.*

Item. For every woman who is murdered, three men are murdered.[1]

Item. With the exception of rape, the more violent the crime, the more likely the victim is a man.[2]

Item. Males are the primary victims of all violent crimes except rape. These violent crimes (excluding rape) have increased by 36 percent.[3] Rape, the one violent crime in which females are the primary victims, has *decreased* by 33 percent.[4]

4   *Item.* Forcible rape constitutes less than 6 percent of all violent crimes; violent crimes of which men are the primary victims constitute the remaining 94 percent.[5]

Item. The average American has 1 chance in 153 of being murdered; a black man has 1 chance in 28 of being murdered.[6]

Item. When the Department of Justice conducted a nationwide survey, it found that Americans rated a wife stabbing her husband to death as 41 percent less severe than a husband stabbing his wife to death.[7]

---

[1] The latest data available in 1991 are that 74.6 percent of all murder victims are male (13,632 males versus 4,611 females). U.S. Department of Justice, Federal Bureau of Investigations, *Crime in the United States, 1988,* p. 11, table titled "Age, Sex, and Race of Murder Victims, 1988."

[2] U.S. Department of Justice, Office of Justice Programs, Bureau of Justice Statistics, *Criminal Victimization in the United States, 1987,* publication #NCJ-115524, June 1989, table 3, "Personal Crimes, 1987," p. 16. Per 1,000 population, males are 1.7 times more likely than females to be victims of violent crimes. This statistic includes rape, but excludes murder, of which males are 3 times more likely to be victims.

[3] U.S. Department of Justice, Federal Bureau of Investigation, Uniform Crime Reports, *Crime in the United States: 1990,* pp. 15 and 51. Excluding forcible rape, the numbers of violent crimes are:

1981	*1990*
1,267,316	1,718,575

[4] The *rape rate decreased from 1.8 per 1,000 in 1973 to 1.2 per 1,000 in 1988.* See the U.S. Bureau of Justice, Bureau of Justice Statistics, National Crime Survey Report, *Criminal Victimization in the United States, Annual (1973–1988),* p. 15. This figure comes from a national sampling of households. It is considered a more reliable comparison of rates than reports of rapes to the police, since reports of rape to the police have increased as public awareness of rape has increased and as the definition of rape has broadened (e.g., to include ignoring a verbal "no") in the last decade. But even here there has been a 9 percent increase in rapes reported to the police between 1981 and 1990 versus a 36 percent increase in violent crimes of which men are the primary victims that were reported to the police between 1981 and 1990. For the source of the 9 percent increase, see ibid.

[5] *Crime in the United States: 1990,* op. cit. The exact figures are 102,555 forcible rapes and 1,757,572 violent crimes (murder, robbery, and aggravated assault, excluding forcible rapes).

[6] U.S. Department of Justice, *Crime in the United States, 1981.* As cited in Mark L. Rosenberg, M.D., M.P.P., and James A. Mercy, Ph.D., "Homicide: Epidemiologic Analysis at the National Level," *Bulletin of the New York Academy of Medicine,* 1986, vol. 62, no. 5, p. 389.

[7] U.S. Department of Justice, Federal Bureau of Investigation, Bureau of Justice Statistics, *National Survey of Crime Severity* (Washington, D.C.: US-GPO, 1985), #NCJ-96017; conducted by Marvin E. Wolfgang, Robert M. Figlio, Paul E. Tracy, and Simon I. Singer from the Center for Studies in Criminology and Criminal Law, the Wharton School, University of Pennsylvania.

Item. Wives report that they were *more* likely to assault their husbands than their husbands were to assault them. (This according to the National Family Violence Survey's nationwide random sampling of households.[8])

8   *Item.* Blacks are six times more likely than whites to be victims of homicides.[9] Forty-five percent of black males will become victims of violent crime three or more times.[10]

Aren't Men the Perpetrators of This Violence, and Isn't This Violence a Reflection of Male Power?

We have no problem seeing this last Item as a reflection of black powerlessness; but we rarely see *men's* greater likelihood of being victims of violence as a reflection of male powerlessness. When we hear men are the greater victims of crime, we tend to say, "Well, it's men hurting other men." When we hear that blacks are the greater victims, we consider it racist to say, "Well, it's blacks hurting blacks." The victim is a victim no matter who the perpetrator was.

But why do men commit most of the violent crime? Is it a reflection of male power? Hardly. Blacks do not commit proportionately more crimes than whites because blacks have more power. Flint, Michigan, gives us a clue.

In the mid-1980s, Flint was faced with the closing of a number of General Motors plants, forcing 30,000 auto workers to leave the area and leaving numerous others unemployed.[11] By 1985, a town formerly low in its crime rate reported huge increases not only in suicides and alcoholism, but in spouse abuse, rape, and murder. Flint soon had a higher rate of violent crime than New York City. And it reported 285 rapes in 1985, a staggering figure for a city of 150,000.

12   What does this tell us? It gives us a hint that murder, rape, and spouse abuse, like suicide and alcoholism, are but a minute's worth of superficial power to compensate for years of underlying powerlessness. They are manifestations of hopelessness committed by the powerless, which is why they are acts committed disproportionately by blacks and by men.

Crime, especially crime involving money, reflects the gap between the *expectation* to provide and the *ability* to provide.[12] Thus women who work and earn enough to meet their expectations rarely commit crimes. But women who are working and not meeting expectations do commit more crime.

---

[8] Murray A. Straus and Richard J. Gelles, "Societal Change and Change in Family Violence from 1975 to 1985 as Revealed by Two National Surveys," *Journal of Marriage and the Family,* vol. 48, August 1986, pp. 465–79.

[9] U.S. Department of Health and Human Services, National Center for Health Statistics, *Monthly Vital Statistics Report,* vol. 38, no. 5, supplement, September 26, 1989, p. 6, table D, "Ratio of Age-Adjusted Death Rates for the 15 Leading Causes of Death by Sex and Race: United States, 1987."

[10] *Criminal Victimization in the United States, 1987,* op. cit., p. 1.

[11] David Zeman, Knight-Ridder Newspapers, "Father, Martyr, Fraud?" *Detroit Free Press,* May 25, 1990, p. 1-F.

[12] Robert Gramling, Craig Forsyth, and Jeff Fewell, University of Southwestern Louisiana, "Crime and Economic Activity: A Research Note," *Sociological Spectrum,* vol. 8, no. 2, 1988, pp. 187–95.

If we really want men to commit crime as infrequently as women, we can start by not expecting men to provide for women more than we expect women to provide for men. . . .

The "War Against Women"?

> . . . attitudes toward women help breed violent crimes against them and can rob them of full equality in American life. . . . It is unthinkable that my granddaughters not have the same opportunity as my grandsons. . . . This war against women must stop.
>
> President Bush, June 26, 1989, to the American Association of
> University Women[13]

The headlines after President Bush's speech read "The War on Women Must Stop."[14]

Imagine President Clinton delivering the following speech to an American Association of University *Men* (which, of course, would no longer be allowed to exist):

> My fellow Americans . . .

> . . . attitudes toward boys help breed violent boys who become violent dads and husbands. So Hillary and I are asking, "Why do we cheer for our sons to be violent and then put them in jail when they grow up to be violent?"

> It is immoral to use our education dollars to train our sons to play "smash face," er, pardon me, football, in junior high school.[15] To tell boys this age we will applaud for you if you mutilate yourselves is not education, it is child abuse. And to give that message only to boys is sexism that deprives our sons of the right to choose. When Hillary and I see how our cheers encourage boys to swallow their fears and repress their tears, we realize it is time to repress our cheers so our boys can express their fears.

> Football scholarships are mutilation scholarships. If cheerleaders were as likely as football players to have herniated disks and dislocated shoulders, fractured vertebrae and damaged knees that haunted them into old age, would we be using taxpayer money to support cheerleading? Even Hillary doesn't think so.

> We feel it is immoral to teach our sons to increase their sex appeal by increasing their risk of concussions. Would we encourage girls to increase their sex appeal by using their bodies—by having sex on the fifty-yard line with boys from another school? Which of us would yell, "First of ten, do it again"? Oh, my . . . Our men will become gentler when cheerleaders are shouting, "First and ten, be *gentle* again."

> Hillary and I realize football is only a metaphor for preparing our sons to be sixteen times as likely as our daughters to die at work; for preparing only

---

[13] Associated Press, "War on Women Must Stop—Bush," *Los Angeles Times,* June 27, 1989.

[14] Ibid.

[15] 1991–92 *Handbook* of the National Federation of State High School Associations, Kansas City, Missouri.

your 18-year-old son to register for the draft. We realize we can no longer claim to favor equality between the sexes and then make your sons the disposable sex.

So I am introducing today the ELA: the Equal Life Amendment. None of us can tolerate being part of a country that robs men of an equal life.

This war against our sons must stop. It is America's longest war. And it is preparation for nuclear war. It is our most unrecognized domestic violence. And it is preparation for future domestic violence.

President Clinton, June 26, the future American
Association of University *Men* convention

When Violence Against Men Does Become Visible, Do We Still Ignore It?

Item. When a female jogger in Central Park in 1989 was raped and brutalized,[16] "Take Back the Night" demonstrations were nationwide. The solution? A headline in an Ellen Goodman column read "Safety for Women? Try Removing Men."[17]

Item. When a male jogger in Central Park in 1989 was hospitalized after being brutally beaten on the head with a club, he reported the incident to the police.[18] Coincidentally, he had witnessed two similar incidents of men being kicked, punched, or beaten in Central Park within the previous month. He had also reported both of those incidents to the police. He later called the police to see how many such attacks had occurred in the previous two months. He was told there had been none at all.

Our anger toward men as victimizers blinds us to men as victims. The attacks the male jogger reported—all attacks on men—were never acknowledged as even having occurred. If a woman had reported three separate rapes to the police and not a single one was even acknowledged as having been reported—much less investigated—it would be hard to imagine the degree of outrage. When crimes against women are more readily recorded, crimes against women become more readily visible.

20   Violent crimes against innocent women create distrust toward innocent men. Every man who invites a woman back to his home has to risk rejection not only because he is expected to be the one doing the asking but because the rape she just read about or heard about adds to her likelihood of rejecting him. He is tainted with suspicion even if he himself has also been victimized by other men or been injured while protecting women. . . .

---

[16] Editorial:"The Jogger and the Wolfpack," *New York Times,* April 26, 1989.
[17] Ellen Goodman, "Safety for Women? Try Removing Men," *Santa Barbara News-Press,* Tuesday, January 9, 1990.
[18] Gerald Galison, Letter-to-the-Editor, *New York Times,* May 7, 1989.

What Are We Doing to Stop This Violence Against Men?

The sexist perception that violence by anyone against only women is antiwoman while violence by a woman against only men is just generic violence creates a political demand for laws that are even more protective of women. For example, when we publicized studies of battered women but ignored a dozen studies pointing to equal numbers of battered men,[19] we felt justified in legislating a "battered woman syndrome," but didn't even think of a "battered man syndrome." Soon, the battered woman syndrome became but one of twelve defenses potentially available for a woman who killed, but not available for a man who killed. Now, if the media even *simulates* violence against women, we might call it a civil rights violation while *real-life* violence against men in football and wrestling is called education.

Although men are more likely than women to be victims of all violent crime except rape, the U.S. Senate is sponsoring a Violence Against *Women* Act—an act which makes violence against women a hate crime and a violation of women's civil rights, but not violence against men a hate crime and an act against men's civil rights. In brief, it legislates sexual *inequality*. The only way such an act could be constitutional is if women were subject to much more violence than men. Because it is men who are subject to much more violence, not only is a Violence against Women Act unconstitutional, but a Violence against Men Act might well be constitutional.

The Violence against Women Act provides $300 million for the protection of women against violent crimes, but nothing to protect men; $75 million for women's shelters, but none for men's shelters. Its subtitles tell the story: Safe Streets *for Women,* Safe Homes *for Women* (emphasis supplied) . . .

24   By law, all governmental acts are molded and modified based on testimony before the relevant congressional committee. The testimony is supposed to reflect all sides of an issue. But in this case, only women testified—fifteen women and no men—before the Committee on the Judiciary.[20] No man who requested permission to testify was permitted.

What can we do to stop violence against both sexes? We can start by decreasing the expectation on men to be our killers and protectors—from our personal bodyguards to our nation's bodyguards. And we can stop electing legislators who feel they must protect women and forget men. The process starts with remembering that legislators cannot hear what we do not say.

---

[19] For example, two nationwide studies of both sexes that are among the 14 two-sex studies are reported in Straus and Gelles, op. cit.

[20] U.S. Senate, "Women and Violence Hearing before the Commission on the Judiciary, U.S. Senate," part I, June 20, 1990, and part II, August 29, 1990, and December 11, 1990 (Order #J-101-80). Almost all of the fifteen women were feminist oriented (NOW, etc.). Jon Ryan and other men were refused permission to testify.

Personal Response

Explore your reactions to Farrell's insistence that the problem of violence against women is not nearly as great as that of violence against men and that in focusing on women exclusively, we do a grave disservice to men.

Questions for Discussion

1. What do you make of the statistics that Farrell begins this selection with, especially in relation to those provided by Susan Baker and Tipper Gore ("Some Reasons for 'Wilding'"), Caryl Rivers ("Rock Lyrics and Violence Against Women"), and Carol Lynn Mithers ("The War Against Women")?

2. How does Farrell answer the question posed at the end of the initial list of items, "Isn't this violence a reflection of male power?" What is your opinion of the answer he gives?

3. In the hypothetical speech by President Clinton (paragraph 16), Farrell raises some issues that bear discussion. For instance, what do you make of the statements that "it is time to repress our cheers so our boys can express their fears," "football scholarships are mutilation scholarships," and "it is immoral to teach our sons to increase their sex appeal by increasing their risk of concussions"? Find other statements in the speech that you would like to discuss.

4. What do you think of Farrell's comparison of violent crimes against women to football and wrestling in this statement: "If the media even *simulates* violence against women, we might call it a civil rights violation while *real-life* violence against men in football and wrestling is called education" (paragraph 20).

5. Discuss Farrell's suggestions for stopping violence in the closing paragraph. How successful do you think such efforts would be?

OLD ENOUGH TO KILL?

Anna Quindlen

Anna Quindlen began her journalism career at the New York Post *and then became deputy metropolitan editor of the* New York Times. *In 1986, she began her syndicated column "Life in the Thirties" and a few years later "Public and Private," for which she won a Pulitzer Prize in 1992. Her columns are collected in* Living Out Loud *(1988) and* Thinking Out Loud *(1992). She has written two novels,* Object Lessons *(1991) and* One True Thing *(1994). Quindlen frequently addresses difficult moral and ethical issues, as in this 1990* Times *syndicated article.*

Later this year, when the forsythia on the mountain slopes here has turned from yellow to green, Cameron Kocher will stand trial for killing Jessica Carr. Late May or early June, his lawyer says, unless there is some kind of plea bargain. The timing is fortunate; the defendant will not miss much of fifth grade.

He was 9-years-old when the shooting of the little girl took place, and Cameron Kocher, Cub Scout and only child, could well become the youngest person in this century tried as an adult in a homicide case. The defense has entered a plea of not guilty. The prosecutor has not asked for the death penalty. He says a primary goal in this prosecution is psychiatric, not punitive, and that the decision to try Cameron as an adult was influenced by the seriousness of the crime. You have to wonder how it was influenced by an atmosphere of frustration and disillusionment, an atmosphere in which we have had it with criminals and we no longer believe in childhood.

In our big cities and our little burgs, people have become enraged by a criminal justice system they think favors the bad guys. The rehabilitative prison model is dead; mention it to legal experts and they laugh, a mirthless chuckle. "Lock 'em up and throw away the key" is a constant refrain, and the death penalty is the Big Daddy of solutions. When crack gangs are populated by 12-year-olds, and rapists are high-school sophomores, the rage is keener, and tinged with something more personal. It's 10 o'clock; do you know where your children are?

4   They're living in a fearsome world. It's become a truism that they are too early adult, that they learn about abortion and AIDS at the same time that they're learning to read. The bright line between child and adult, drawn in the past by knowledge and privilege, has faded. We judge them grown up by the things they do, and unkindest cut of all, by the things that are done to them.

"I'd like information on the 7-year-old who was raped," I said to a sergeant in the Bronx sex crimes unit recently. "Which one?" he replied. It is self-protection for adults to think of children growing up in such a world as more mature than they truly are.

Oh, the children themselves have provided ample evidence of corruption. When the infamous Willie Bosket, New York State's most incorrigible inmate, said he had committed 2 murders and 25 stabbings by the time he was 15, it seemed incredible. No more. Age down, severity up.

The National Center for Juvenile Justice reports that in the last decade more than two-thirds of the states have got tougher with juveniles. Some make younger kids more culpable; some pick out certain crimes as outside any possible boundary of childhood. If you are 13 in New York, you are a juvenile unless you commit murder. Murder is a grown-up crime.

8   Prosecutors say Cameron Kocher acted in a grown-up fashion a year ago. They say he got the key to his father's gun cabinet from the base of a lamp, unlocked the cabinet and the ammunition drawer, loaded the gun, and removed a screen before he fired from a second-story window, hitting the 7-year-old in the back as she rode on a snowmobile. There is speculation that he did so because she boasted of being better at Nintendo.

Is that horrible scenario an answer, or a question? At what age does a child realize that death is not a video game, that only on television do people get up after they are shot, that actions have permanent consequences? Nine? Eleven?

Fourteen? Are we past the point where we care? A witness says that after the shooting, Cameron said to his playmates, "If you don't think about it, you won't be sad."

Kids who commit crimes rob adults of illusions. We enshrine the years when our children are young, at least until we first read "Lord of the Flies." The easiest way to respond to child criminals is to say that they are somehow not children at all. We think of them as children without childhood, growing up on streets crunchy with hypodermic needles and crack vials.

Not Cameron Kocher. He will go on trial in a town with a Main Street and a courthouse square, a neighborly place that might as well be the Bedford Falls of "It's a Wonderful Life." He made the honor roll, has no history of behavioral problems, and can't go to jail. He's even too young for a juvenile facility; if he were convicted and given a custodial sentence, he would have to be sent initially to some private institution.

12   This prosecution is essentially an exercise. The defense attorney says it is an exercise in futility. He hints at a tragic accident and says this is not the way to proceed if his client needs help. The prosecutor talks of diagnosis, and rehabilitation. Let's hope so. If we stick with rehabilitation for anyone, it should be for the young, if not out of compassion, then out of pragmatism. They'll be around for a long, long time.

This is also an exercise in self-definition. On the day this trial begins in the Monroe County courthouse, we will be a nation that believes it is right to try a fifth-grader for murder.

Personal Response

What is your reaction to reading that a nine-year-old boy had killed someone, apparently deliberately? What is your opinion of the explanations Quindlen gives for how such a thing could happen?

Questions for Discussion

1. How does the prosecutor's description of the Cameron Kocher case as an "exercise in futility" (paragraph 12) reinforce Quindlen's central point? In what way, according to Quindlen, is this case "an exercise in self-definition" (paragraph 13)?

2. What effect do you suppose Quindlen wanted to achieve in the opening paragraph? That is, why does she start with references to forsythia on mountain slopes and the timing of Cameron Kocher's trial?

3. Quindlen reports that the prosecution in the Kocher case wants to try the boy as an adult because of the seriousness of the crime. What other possible reasons does Quindlen offer for the decision to prosecute Kocher as an adult? What examples does Quindlen give to support her reasons?

4. Explain Quindlen's statement in paragraph 4 that "the bright line between child and adult, drawn in the past by knowledge and privilege, has faded." What does she mean when she writes: "Kids who commit crimes rob adults of illusions" (paragraph 10)?

5. Explain the allusions to *Lord of the Flies* (paragraph 10) and *It's a Wonderful Life* (paragraph 11) and discuss what purpose you think they serve.

WHY I BOUGHT A GUN

Gail Buchalter

Gail Buchalter was a staff writer for People *magazine in the mid-1980s and is now a freelance writer living in New York. A regular contributor to* Parade, *she has just finished writing a mystery book. This essay was first published in* Parade *magazine in 1988.*

I was raised to wear black and cultured pearls in one of Manhattan's more desirable neighborhoods. My upper-middle-class background never involved guns. If my parents felt threatened, they simply put another lock on the door.

By high school, I had traded in my cashmere sweaters for a black arm band. I marched for Civil Rights, shunned Civil Defense drills and protested the Vietnam war. It was easy being 18 and a peacenik. I wasn't raising an 11-year-old child then.

Today, I am typical of the women whom gun manufacturers have been aiming at as potential buyers—and one of the millions who have succumbed: Between 1983 and 1986, there was a 53 percent increase in female gun-owners in the U.S.—from 7.9 million to 12.1 million, according to a Gallup Poll paid for by Smith & Wesson, the gun manufacturer.

4   Gun enthusiasts have created ad campaigns with such snappy slogans as "You Can't Rape a .38" or "Should You Shoot a Rapist Before He Cuts Your Throat?" While I was trying to come to a rational decision, I disliked these manipulative scare tactics. They only inflamed an issue that I never even dreamed would touch me.

I began questioning my beliefs one Halloween night in Phoenix, where I had moved when I married. I was almost home when another car hit mine head-on. With the speed of a New York cabbie, I rolled down my window and screamed curses as the driver passed me. He instantly made a U-turn, almost climbing on my back bumper. By now, he and his two friends were hanging out of the car windows, yelling that they were going to rape, cut and kill me.

I already had turned into our driveway when I realized my husband wasn't home. I was trapped. The car had pulled in behind me. I drove up to the back porch and got into the kitchen, where our dogs stood waiting for me. The three men spilled out of their car and into our yard.

My adrenaline was pumping faster than Edwin Moses' legs clearing a hurdle. I grabbed the collars of Jack, our 200-pound Irish wolfhound, and his 140-pound malamute buddy, Slush. Then I kicked open the back door—I was so scared that

I became aggressive—and actually dared the three creeps to keep coming. With the dogs, the odds had changed in my favor, and the men ran back to the safety of their car, yelling that they'd be back the next day to blow me away. Fortunately, they never returned.

8   A few years and one divorce later, I headed for Los Angeles with my 3-year-old son, Jordan (the dogs had since departed). When I put him in preschool a few weeks later, the headmistress noted that I was a single parent and immediately warned me that there was a rapist in my new neighborhood.

I called the police, who confirmed this fact. The rapist had no *modus operandi*. Sometimes he would be waiting in his victim's house; other times he would break in while the person was asleep. Although it was summer, I would carefully lock my windows at night and then lie there and sweat in fear. Thankfully, the rapist was caught, but not before he had attacked two more women.

Over some time, at first imperceptibly, my suburban neighborhood became less secure. A street gang took over the apartment building across from my house, and flowers and compact cars gave way to graffiti and low-riders.

Daytime was quiet, but these gang members crawled out like cockroaches after dark. Several nights in a row they woke me up. It was one of the most terrifying times in my life. I could hear them talking and laughing as they leaned against our fence, tossing their empty beer cans into our front yard. I knew that they were drinking, but were they also using violence-inducing drugs such as PCP and crack? And if they broke in, could I get to the police before they got to me?

12   I found myself, to my surprise, wishing that I had a loaded pistol under my pillow. In the clear light of day, I found this reaction shocking and simply decided to move to a safer neighborhood, although it cost thousands of dollars more. Luckily, I was able to afford it.

Soon the papers were telling yet another tale of senseless horror. Richard Ramirez, who became known as "The Walk-In Killer," spent months crippling and killing before he was caught. His alleged crimes were so brutal and bizarre, his desire to inflict pain so intense, that I began to question my beliefs about the sanctity of human life—his, in particular. The thought of taking a human life is repugnant to me, but the idea of being someone's victim is worse. And how, I began to ask myself, do you talk pacifism to a murderer or a rapist?

Finally, I decided that I would defend myself, even if it meant killing another person. I realized that the one-sided pacifism I once so strongly had advocated could backfire on me and, worse, on my son. Reluctantly, I concluded that I had to insure the best option for our survival. My choices: to count on a cop or to own a pistol.

But still I didn't go out and buy a gun. Everything about guns is threatening. My only exposure to them had been in movies; owning one, I feared, would bring all that violence off of the screen and into my home.

16   So, instead, I called up my girlfriend (who has begged to remain nameless) and told her I had decided to buy a gun. We were both surprised that I didn't know she already had one. She was held up at gunpoint several years ago and

bought what she said was a .37. We figured out it must be either a .38 or a .357. I was horrified when she admitted that not only had she no idea what type of gun she owned, but she also had never even shot it. It remains in her drawer, loaded and unused.

Upset, I hung up and called another friend. He was going to the National Rifle Association convention that was being held in Reno and suggested I tag along. My son's godmother lives there, so I figured I could visit her and kill two birds with one stone.

My first night in Reno, I attended the Handgun Hunters' Awards dinner and sat next to a contributing editor for one of the gun magazines. He bitterly complained that killing elephants had been outlawed, although there were thousands still running around Africa. Their legs, he explained, made wonderful trash baskets. I felt like Thumper on opening day of the hunting season, and my foot kept twitching under the table.

The next day at the convention center, I saw a sign announcing a seminar for women on handguns and safety. I met pistol-packing grandmas, kids who were into competitive shooting and law-enforcement agents. I listened to a few of them speak and then watched a video, "A Woman's Guide to Firearms." It explained everything from how guns worked to an individual's responsibilities as a gun owner.

20   It was my kind of movie, since everything about guns scares me—especially owning one. Statistics on children who are victims of their parents' handguns are overwhelming: About 300 children a year—almost a child a day— are killed by guns in this country, according to Handgun Control, Inc., which bases its numbers on data from the National Safety Council. Most of these killings are accidental.

As soon as I returned to Los Angeles, I called a man I had met a while ago who, I remembered, owned several guns. He told me he had a Smith & Wesson .38 Special for sale and recommended it, since it was small enough for me to handle yet had the necessary stopping power.

I bought the gun. That same day, I got six rounds of special ammunition with plastic tips that explode on impact. These are not for target practice; these are for protection.

For about $50, I also picked up the metal safety box that I had learned about in the video. Its push-button lock opens with a touch if you know the proper combination, possibly taking only a second or two longer than it does to reach into a night-table drawer. Now I knew that my son, Jordan, couldn't get his hands on it while I still could.

24   When I brought the gun home, Jordan was fascinated by it. He kept picking it up, while I nervously watched. But knowledge, I believe, is still our greatest defense. And since I'm in favor of education for sex, AIDS and learning to drive, I couldn't draw the line at teaching my son about guns.

Next, I took the pistol and my son to the target range. I rented a .22 caliber pistol for Jordan. (A .38 was too much gun for him to handle.) I was relieved when he put it down after 10 minutes—he didn't like the feel of it.

But that didn't prevent him from asking me if he should use the gun if someone broke into our house while I wasn't home. I shrieked "no!" so loud, we both jumped. I explained that, if someone ever broke in, he's young and agile enough to leap out of the window and run for his life.

Today he couldn't care less about the gun. Every so often, when we're watching television in my room, I practice opening the safety box, and Jordan times me. I'm down to three seconds. I'll ask him what's the first thing you do when you handle a gun, and he looks at me like I'm a moron, saying for the umpteenth time: "Make sure it's unloaded. But I know I'm not to touch it or tell my friends about it." Jordan's already bored with it all.

28   I, on the other hand, look forward to Mondays—"Ladies' Night" at the target range—when I get to shoot for free. I buy a box of bullets and some targets from the guy behind the counter, put on the protective eye and ear coverings and walk through the double doors to the firing lines.

Once there, I load my gun, look down the sights of the barrel and adjust my aim. I fire six rounds into the chest of a life-sized target hanging 25 feet away. As each bullet rips a hole through the figure drawn there, I realize I'm getting used to owning a gun and no longer feeling faint when I pick it up. The weight of it has become comfortable in my hand. And I am keeping my promise to practice. Too many people are killed by their own guns because they don't know how to use them.

It took me years to decide to buy a gun, and then weeks before I could load it. It gave me nightmares.

One night I dreamed I woke up when someone broke into our house. I grabbed my gun and sat waiting at the foot of my bed. Finally, I saw him turn the corner as he headed toward me. He was big and filled the hallway—an impossible target to miss. I aimed the gun and froze, visualizing the bullet blowing a hole through his chest and spraying his flesh all over the walls and floor. I didn't want to shoot, but I knew my survival was on the line. I wrapped my finger around the trigger and finally squeezed it, simultaneously accepting the intruder's death at my own hand and the relief of not being a victim. I woke up as soon as I decided to shoot.

32   I was tearfully relieved that it had only been a dream.

I never have weighed the consequences of an act as strongly as I have that of buying a gun—but, then again, I never have done anything with such deadly repercussions. Most of my friends refuse even to discuss it with me. They believe that violence begets violence.

They're probably right.

Personal Response

How do you feel about Buchalter's decision to buy a handgun? Would you buy one if you were in her place? Could you shoot another human being?

Questions for Discussion

1. Summarize Buchalter's reasons for buying a gun. Why was it so hard for her to make that decision?

2. What does Buchalter imply about her unnamed woman friend's ignorance of her own gun? How does her own attitude toward gun ownership and her frankness with her son contrast with the attitude of her friend?

3. How did Buchalter's experiences at the National Rifle Association convention help in her decision to buy a gun?

4. Why do you think Buchalter includes the information about her conversation with the man sitting next to her at the 'Handgun Hunters' Awards dinner (paragraph 18)? Explain what she means when she says she felt like "Thumper on opening day of hunting season."

5. Why do you think Buchalter ends her essay as she does? Do you think she still doubts her reasons for buying a gun, despite her many reasons for doing so?

GUNS 'Я' US

Matthew Maranz

Matthew Maranz was a student at the Columbia School of Journalism when he wrote the following essay, which first appeared in The New Republic *in 1989.*

I am over 21 years of age. I am a citizen of the United States. I have not been convicted of a felony. And I have not been treated or confined for drug addiction, drunkenness, or mental illness. According to the National Firearms Act of 1934, I thus qualify to purchase a fully automatic machine gun capable of firing hundreds of bullets with a single squeeze of the trigger. A few months ago, I decided to try.

As far as the federal government is concerned, private citizens have always had the right to purchase machine guns—at a price. The Firearms Act, passed by Congress to curb mob warfare, added a $500 manufacturers tax and $200 transfer tax to the cost. And in May 1986, Congress effectively doubled the price by banning the future manufacture of machine guns for private sale, making them an increasingly scarce commodity. Also, prospective machine-gun buyers must go through a lengthy (one to three months) licensing process, including fingerprinting, that helps the FBI do a background check. But provided I pass muster on the federal (and state) level, a MAC-10 or Uzi can be mine.

In order to apply for a machine-gun permit, I have to specify exactly what make of machine gun I want. So I walked down to my local newsstand to consult the machine-gunners equivalent of *Consumer Reports*. *Assault Rifles* carried the definitive work on the .223 controversy—"Can it Measure up to the 7.62 on the Battlefield?" (rest easy, it can). *Firepower* ran a full-page color ad for "Rock n' Roll #3: Sexy Girls and Sexy Guns," a mail-order home video. It starred Dottie/Uzi, Tani Jo/MAC-10, Rosie/MP-5, and Lillian/MP-K and sold for $59.95 plus $3 shipping. Then I came upon an article referring to the Ingram M-11 LISP. The M-11 is a tiny machine pistol that fires 1,200 rounds per minute and fits neatly in a single hand. The CIA used to favor it as a weapon for operations behind enemy lines. That sounded like the gun for me.

4   Taking names from the advertisers' index, I started calling some of the nation's 3,530 licensed machine-gun dealers. My first call reached an answering machine: "Hello. This is SWD Incorporated. Our offices are closed for the holidays. M-11-9 semi-auto pistols and carbines are in stock. M-11-9, M-11-380, and M-10-45 submachine-guns are also in stock in limited quantities. All SMG [submachine-gun] orders must be prepaid to ensure you receive yours. We will ship semi-autos on a c.o.d. basis. Have a joyous holiday season."

The first dealer I actually contacted told me that federal law requires machine-gun purchases to be in-state transactions. He suggested I locate a local machine-gun shop. If it didn't have the gun I wanted, an out-of-state dealer would then sell the M-11 to the in-state dealer, who would sell it to me. Turning to "Guns" in the Yellow Pages, I found a local machine-gun salesman. I called and asked about the M-11.

"I won't sell it to you," he insisted.

I understood. Surely the Second Amendment wasn't meant to cover weapons used to mow down hundreds of innocent bystanders in the streets of our inner cities.

8   "It's a piece of junk," he continued. "Try the MAC-10."

The MAC-10 is capable of firing 900 rounds every 60 seconds. The .45 version is a mere 10½ inches long and weighs 6.25 pounds. With telescope and silencer, it grows to 22 inches. Critics frown on its unreliability past 30 yards, but the MAC-10 remains an immensely popular weapon. One reason is that buyers don't just get a gun; they get a piece of history. The MAC-10 was one of the ancestors of the Uzi, arguably today's hippest machine gun. The CIA, FBI, DEA, and Special Forces endorse the MAC-10. So do the Crips and Bloods of Los Angeles gang war fame. And so did Tani Jo in "Rock n' Roll #3: Sexy Girls and Sexy Guns." Good enough for Tani Jo, good enough for me. I became a MAC-10 convert.

Now I was ready to apply for a state and federal machine-gun permit. How difficult that is depends on where you live. Some 14 states prohibit private ownership of machine guns; others like Texas, Virginia, and Ohio are notorious for their loose gun laws. In Massachusetts, gun laws are tight. Before going through the cumbersome federal process, I had to think of a subtle way to ask a boss and a friend to provide letters of reference certifying my ability to be a responsible owner of a machine gun. I had to obtain three 1.5 by 1.5 pictures of myself to attach to the handgun application that's required for a machine-gun license. I also had to deal with a policy sergeant manning the licensing table who was understandably hostile to civilians seeking machine guns. I persevered.

But the eternally curious federal bureaucracy almost stopped me in my tracks. They sent me a slew of white Form 4's and yellow Form 7's required by the Bureau of Alcohol, Tobacco and Firearms, which keeps track of the number of machine guns in private circulation (191,857 as of December 1988). No one, not the National Rifle Association, the local gun dealer, my friends at work, my mother, even the people I called at the Bureau of Alcohol, Tobacco and Firearms, could decipher them. paperwork is America's tightest means of gun control.

12   There had to be an easier, yet legal, way to evade the bureaucracy. I went back to my magazines and found Automatic Weaponry of Brentwood, Tennessee, "America's Foremost Supplier of Title II Firearms [machine guns and silencers]."

The man at Automatic Weaponry said they specialized in simplifying the federal licensing process. I give Automatic Weaponry basic biographical information over the phone. I send them a 50 percent deposit that's refundable except for a $100 processing fee. They mail me an order form, the already completed white Form 4 and two FBI Fingerprint Applicant Cards. I sign the forms, affix a recent 2 by 2 photograph, and declare a purpose for purchasing a machine gun ("don't put down 'to kill human beings,'" he suggested). I take them to my local chief law enforcement officer, who fingerprints me and verifies my identity and age. He also conducts a National Crime Information Center search for felony convictions (misdemeanors OK). He signs the forms. I mail the paperwork back to Automatic Weaponry. I pay the balance. (Automatic Weaponry accepts personal and business checks, and all major credit cards.) They ship the weapon to an in-state gun dealer via United Parcel Service. Seventy to 90 days after I first contact Automatic Weaponry, I pick up my machine gun. A MAC-10 .45 caliber in mint condition costs $1,295 plus the $200 federal machine-gun transfer tax (Tani Jo not included).

For those with less time, money, and respect for the law, there's an easier way. A semi-automatic MAC-10 retails for as little as $350 and is sold under the same federal regulatory guidelines as a rifle—no fingerprinting or background check required, just proof that you are a U.S. citizen over 18, are not a convicted felon, and have never been confined or incarcerated for drunkenness, drug addiction, or mental illness. In some states I could walk into a gun shop, fill out a few forms, plunk down some cash, and leave with gun in hand. True, like all semi-automatics it would fire only one bullet with each squeeze of the trigger. But if I wanted to risk a 20-year jail term and $20,000 fine, I could convert my semi- into a fully-automatic 900-round-a-minute weapon. A matchstick is all that's needed to convert some guns. The MAC-10 is more sophisticated: one gun dealer I spoke with said he's used a nickel. A guy at the NRA boasted it would take him 15 minutes. But what about someone like me, with zero mechanical ability? He asked if I could change a spark plug. Probably, I replied. Don't worry, he said, you could do it in an hour.

Personal Response

While the process Maranz describes is not quick and simple, it is relatively easy for almost anyone to buy a machine gun. Does that surprise you? Why do you think so many people want to own such weapons? Would you want to own one?

Questions for Discussion

1. Point out passages that indicate Maranz's point of view toward his subject. Does he approve or disapprove of the relative ease with which Americans can

purchase submachine guns? What resources are available to assist the potential machine-gun buyer in selecting a model for purchase?

2. Why do you suppose Maranz included the information about requirements for purchasing a machine gun according to the National Firearms Act of 1934 and the restrictions or changes that were added to that act by Congress in 1986 (paragraphs 1 and 2)?

3. Maranz says that at one stage of this process he almost quit. What stage was that and how did he solve the problem? How long does the process of becoming a machine-gun owner ordinarily take?

4. In his conclusion, Maranz explains the ways people can illegally convert their semi-automatic machine guns into automatic weapons. What point do you think Maranz wants to make with that information?

5. What is the implication of the closing sentences? What effect do you suppose Maranz wanted to achieve by concluding this way?

GUN CRAZY

Nicholas Von Hoffman

Nicholas Von Hoffman is a writer whose works have appeared in a number of publications. He wrote the following essay for The New Yorker *in 1993.*

In the early fifties, when I went to Forham Prep, a small high school in the Bronx run by a band of intrepid Jesuits, the only violence was an occasional cuff delivered by a faculty member to the head of a particularly dimwitted student. It was a small school, attended mostly by the sons of blue-collar families. Many of us, including me, were first-generation immigrants, but we had no difficulty mastering English as a second language without the benefit of a federally funded program. We were there to apply ourselves and to do what we were told.

So we were profoundly shaken when we heard that an algebra teacher in a nearby public high school had been shot and killed by a student. In that bygone Truman–Eisenhower era, such crimes were unheard of in any school. The murder weapon was a zip gun. A zip gun was of home manufacture, consisting of a piece of ordinary pipe, a wooden handle kept in place by string or wire wrapping, and a rubber-band-like firing mechanism similar to a slingshot's. The thing was wildly inaccurate and unpredictable, so the teacher was incredibly unlucky to have fallen victim to it.

It is a testament to our rising standard of living that today's high-school kids don't have to depend on such crudely unreliable weaponry. When I was in high school, handguns were rare and next to unobtainable. But, progress being what it is, the 1993 high schooler has a car, a CD player, and an Uzi. A Louis Harris poll published last week tells us that, among pupils in grades six through twelve, nine percent have taken a shot at another human being and eleven percent have had a shot taken at them by another human being. Nearly sixty percent said they would know where to get a gun if they needed one. Not surprisingly, more than a third of the children attending our Sarajevo-like institutions of instruction believe there is a good possibility that they will die before they reach threescore and ten. Fifty-five per cent of these young academic-combat veterans also said they would like to see metal detectors installed at school entrances. This Dodge City, check-your-guns-at-the-door approach to the problem might go some way to achieving a cease-fire in the classroom, but it wouldn't silence the gunfire out-of-doors.

4   Patrick Daly, a Brooklyn elementary-school principal, was killed in crossfire last December when he was out on the street looking for a missing student. How can young people keep their minds on quadratic equations when they know that something similar could happen to them when they come down the front steps after school? The more advanced centers of education are now training their pupils to deal with the kind of battlefield conditions that prevail in, say, Somalia or the former Yugoslavia. To be prepared for a life of scholarship, students are now being taught to use condoms and to ignore the crump of distant artillery. The militarily challenged child is also being taught how to apply a tourniquet without depositing bodily fluids on hard-to-come-by textbooks.

In my day, Mother packed a banana in your lunchbox, and you had to use that as a pistol or to fake it when attempting a heist or a mugging. Today, it seems, the box contains Teflon-coated .38-calibre specials along with the trail gorp. This is certainly an advance of a sort, for at least today's students no longer have to depend on zip guns.

Personal Response

How accurately do the Harris Poll results Von Hoffman mentions describe the high school you attended (paragraph 3)? How would you answer the questions in the poll?

Questions for Discussion

1. What contrasts between his own high school and today's high schools does Von Hoffman imply in his introductory paragraph? How does the story of the murdered algebra teacher contribute to Von Hoffman's central idea?

2. Find passages in which Von Hoffman is being ironic. What does he mean by "Sarajevo-like institutions of instruction" (paragraph 3)?

3. What purpose does the reference to the death of Patrick Daly serve (paragraph 4)?

4. Besides the ready availability of guns, what other danger of contemporary life does Von Hoffman refer to? Do you think Von Hoffman makes a valid point about the dangers facing today's young people, or is he overstating the problem?

5. Discuss the measures your own high school takes to regulate student behavior, particularly its rules regarding fights and/or carrying weapons. Does the school have metal detectors at entrances? Do you think schools should have them?

PILGRIMAGE TO NONVIOLENCE

Martin Luther King, Jr.

Martin Luther King, Jr. was born in Atlanta, Georgia, in 1929. At age 18 he was ordained a Baptist minister in his father's church, the same year that he earned his undergraduate degree from Morehouse College. He earned his B.D. from Crozer Theological Seminary in 1951 and his Ph.D. from Boston University in 1954. In 1955 King organized a successful boycott of the Montgomery, Alabama, bus system and became the leader of the civil rights movement. By the time he founded the Southern Christian Leadership Conference in 1957, he had become internationally known for his philosophy of nonviolent resistance. King was Time *magazine's Man of the Year in 1963, and in 1964 he was awarded the Nobel Peace Prize. He was assassinated in Memphis, Tennessee, in 1968. This selection is from his book* Stride Toward Freedom *(1958).*

When I went to Montgomery as a pastor, I had not the slightest idea that I would later become involved in a crisis in which nonviolent resistance would be applicable. I neither started the protest nor suggested it. I simply responded to the call of the people for a spokesman. When the protest began, my mind, consciously or unconsciously, was driven back to the Sermon on the Mount, with its sublime teachings on love, and the Gandhian method of nonviolent resistance. As the days unfolded, I came to see the power of nonviolence more and more. Living through the actual experience of the protest, nonviolence became more than a method to which I gave intellectual assent; it became a commitment to a way of life. Many of the things that I had not cleared up intellectually concerning nonviolence were now solved in the sphere of practical action.

Since the philosophy of nonviolence played such a positive role in the Montgomery Movement, it may be wise to turn to a brief discussion of some basic aspects of this philosophy.

First, it must be emphasized that nonviolent resistance is not a method for cowards; it does resist. If one uses this method because he is afraid or merely because he lacks the instruments of violence, he is not truly nonviolent. This is why Gandhi often said that if cowardice is the only alternative to violence, it is better to fight. He made this statement conscious of the fact that there is always another alternative: no individual or group need submit to any wrong, nor need they use violence to right the wrong; there is the way of nonviolent resistance. This is ultimately the way of the strong man. It is not a method of stagnant passivity. The phrase "passive resistance" often gives the false impression that this is a sort of "do-nothing method" in which the resister quietly and passively accepts evil. But nothing is further from the truth. For while the nonviolent resister is passive in the sense that he is not physically aggressive toward his opponent, his mind and emotions are always active, constantly seeking to persuade his opponent that he is wrong. The method is passive physically, but strongly active spiritually. It is not passive nonresistance to evil, it is active nonviolent resistance to evil.

4   A second basic fact that characterizes nonviolence is that it does not seek to defeat or humiliate the opponent, but to win his friendship and understanding. The nonviolent resister must often express his protest through noncooperation or boycotts, but he realizes that these are not ends themselves; they are merely means to awaken a sense of moral shame in the opponent. The end is redemption and reconciliation. The aftermath of nonviolence is the creation of the beloved community, while the aftermath of violence is tragic bitterness.

A third characteristic of this method is that the attack is directed against forces of evil rather than against persons who happen to be doing the evil. It is evil that the nonviolent resister seeks to defeat, not the persons victimized by evil. If he is opposing racial injustice, the nonviolent resister has the vision to see that the basic tension is not between races. As I like to say to the people in Montgomery: "The tension in this city is not between white people and Negro people. The tension is, at bottom, between justice and injustice, between the forces of light and the forces of darkness. And if there is a victory, it will be a victory not merely for fifty thousand Negroes, but a victory for justice and the forces of light. We are out to defeat injustice and not white persons who may be unjust."

A fourth point that characterizes nonviolent resistance is a willingness to accept suffering without retaliation, to accept blows from the opponent without striking back. "Rivers of blood may have to flow before we gain our freedom, but it must be our blood," Gandhi said to his countrymen. The nonviolent resister is willing to accept violence if necessary, but never to inflict it. He does not seek to dodge jail. If going to jail is necessary, he enters it "as a bridegroom enters the bride's chamber."

One may well ask: "What is the nonviolent resister's justification for this ordeal to which he invites men, for this mass political application of the ancient doctrine of turning the other cheek?" The answer is found in the realization that unearned suffering is redemptive. Suffering, the nonviolent resister realizes, has tremendous educational and transforming possibilities. "Things of fundamental importance to people are not secured by reason alone, but have to be purchased with their suffering," said Gandhi. He continues: "Suffering is infinitely more powerful than the law of the jungle for converting the opponent and opening his ears which are otherwise shut to the voice of reason."

8   A fifth point concerning nonviolent resistance is that it avoids not only external physical violence but also internal violence of spirit. The nonviolent resister not only refuses to shoot his opponent but he also refuses to hate him. At the center of nonviolence stands the principle of love. The nonviolent resister would contend that in the struggle for human dignity, the oppressed people of the world must not succumb to the temptation of becoming bitter or indulging in

hate campaigns. To retaliate in kind would do nothing but intensify the existence of hate in the universe. Along the way of life, someone must have sense enough and morality enough to cut off the chain of hate. This can only be done by projecting the ethic of love to the center of our lives.

In speaking of love at this point, we are not referring to some sentimental or affectionate emotion. It would be nonsense to urge men to love their oppressors in an affectionate sense. Love in this connection means understanding, redemptive good will. Here the Greek language comes to our aid. There are three words for love in the Greek New Testament. First, there is *eros*. In Platonic philosophy *eros* meant the yearning of the soul for the realm of the divine. It has come now to mean a sort of aesthetic or romantic love. Second, there is *philia*, which means intimate affection between personal friends. *Philia* denotes a sort of reciprocal love; the person loves because he is loved. When we speak of loving those who oppose us, we refer to neither *eros* nor *philia*; we speak of love which is expressed in the Greek word *agape*. *Agape* means understanding, redeeming good will for all men. It is an overflowing love which is purely spontaneous, unmotivated, groundless, and creative. It is not set in motion by any quality or function of its object. It is the love of God operating in the human heart.

Agape is disinterested love. It is a love in which the individual seeks not his own good, but the good of his neighbor (I Cor. 10:24). *Agape* does not begin by discriminating between worthy and unworthy people, or any qualities people possess. It begins by loving others *for their sakes*. It is an entirely "neighbor-regarding concern for others," which discovers the neighbor in every man it meets. There, *agape* makes no distinction between friend and enemy; it is directed toward both. If one loves an individual merely on account of his friendliness, he loves him for the sake of the benefits to be gained from the friendship, rather than for the friend's own sake. Consequently, the best way to assure oneself that love is disinterested is to have love for the enemy-neighbor from whom you can expect no good in return, but only hostility and persecution.

Another basic point about *agape* is that it springs from the *need* of the other person—his need for belonging to the best in the human family. The Samaritan who helped the Jew on the Jericho road was "good" because he responded to the human need that he was presented with. God's love is eternal and fails not because man needs his love. St. Paul assures us that the loving act of redemption was done "while we were yet sinners"—that is, at the point of our greatest need for love. Since the white man's personality is greatly distorted by segregation, and his soul is greatly scarred, he needs the love of the Negro. The Negro must love the white man, because the white man needs his love to remove his tensions, insecurities, and fears.

12   *Agape* is not a weak, passive love. It is love in action. *Agape* is love seeking to preserve and create community. It is insistence on community even when one seeks to break it. *Agape* is a willingness to sacrifice in the interest of mutuality. *Agape* is a willingness to go to any length to restore community. It doesn't stop at the first mile, but it goes the second mile to restore community. It is a willingness to forgive, not seven times, but seventy times seven to restore community. The

cross is the eternal expression of the length to which God will go in order to restore broken community. The resurrection is a symbol of God's triumph over all the forces that seek to block community. The Holy Spirit is the continuing community creating reality that moves through history. He who works against community is working against the whole of creation. Therefore, if I respond to hate with a reciprocal hate I do nothing but intensify the cleavage in broken community. I can only close the gap in broken community by meeting hate with love. If I meet hate with hate, I become depersonalized, because creation is so designed that my personality can only be fulfilled in the context of community. Booker T. Washington was right: "Let no man pull you so low as to make you hate him." When he pulls you to the point of working against community; he drags you to the point of defying creation, and thereby becoming depersonalized.

In the final analysis, *agape* means a recognition of the fact that all life is interrelated. All humanity is involved in a single process, and all men are brothers. To the degree that I harm my brother, no matter what he is doing to me, to that extent I am harming myself. For example, white men often refuse federal aid to education in order to avoid giving the Negro his rights; but because all men are brothers they cannot deny Negro children without harming their own. They end, all efforts to the contrary, by hurting themselves. Why is this? Because men are brothers. If you harm me, you harm yourself.

Love, *agape*, is the only cement that can hold this broken community together. When I am commanded to love, I am commanded to restore community, to resist injustice, and to meet the needs of my brothers.

A sixth basic fact about nonviolent resistance is that it is based on the conviction that the universe is on the side of justice. Consequently, the believer in nonviolence has deep faith in the future. This faith is another reason why the nonviolent resister can accept suffering without retaliation. For he knows that in his struggle for justice he has cosmic companionship. It is true that there are devout believers in nonviolence who find it difficult to believe in a personal God. But even these persons believe in the existence of some creative force that works for universal wholeness. Whether we call it an unconscious process, an impersonal Brahman, or a Personal Being of matchless power and infinite love, there is a creative force in this universe that works to bring the disconnected aspects of reality into a harmonious whole.

Personal Response

How appropriate do you think King's philosophy of nonviolent resistance is to today's social problems? In what circumstances would it work? In what circumstances would it not work?

Questions for Discussion

1. Comment on King's opening paragraph. How well does it introduce his subject?

2. Do you think King has in mind an audience opposed to or in favor of his philosophy? Explain your answer.

3. What characteristics of King's style reflect the fact that he was a minister?

4. King frequently alludes to other people and events. Who was Gandhi (paragraph 1)? What was the Sermon on the Mount (paragraph 1)? Who was the Samaritan (paragraph 11)? Who was Booker T. Washington (paragraph 12)?

5. Find passages in which King says what nonviolent resistance and *agape* are *not* (as opposed to those in which he says what they *are*). Why do you suppose King uses the strategy of saying what things are not when his purpose is to define what they are? Would such an approach work for all definitions?

6. Explain in your own words what you understand King to mean by both nonviolent resistance and *agape*.

———

Suggestions for Writing About VIOLENCE

1. Taking into consideration the comments of Carol Mithers in "The War Against Women," Caryl Rivers in "Rock Lyrics and Violence Against Women," and Susan Baker and Tipper Gore in "Some Reasons for 'Wilding,'" explore the question of what would have to change in American society before the rate of violent crimes against women can be reduced.

2. Compare and contrast Warren Farrell's "Violence Against Whom?" with Carol Lynn Mithers' "The War Against Women."

3. Gail Buchalter in "Why I Bought a Gun," Matthew Maranz in "Guns 'Я' Us," and Nicholas Von Hoffman in "Gun Crazy" all touch on the issue of gun control. Taking into consideration Buchalter's reasons for buying a hand gun, Maranz's success at purchasing an automatic machine gun, and Von Hoffman's lament about students with guns, argue for or against stricter gun control laws.

4. Argue for or against Carol Mithers' contention in "The War Against Women" that misogynistic images in popular culture have a causal relationship to the high rate of violent crimes against women.

5. Drawing from the lyrics of selected popular rock songs, support or argue against Caryl Rivers' contention in "Rock Lyrics and Violence Against Women" that such lyrics legitimize and even promote violence against women. Alternatively, analyze the content of several MTV videos that depict violence against women. What messages do they send? Consider whether what you observe supports Caryl Rivers' argument or not.

6. Argue for or against extending the First Amendment's freedom of speech to include violent lyrics in rock music. Consider how far you think the First Amendment's protection of free speech should be allowed to go.

7. Focusing on teenage "slasher" films, argue for or against Baker and Gore's position in "Some Reasons for 'Wilding'" that such movies send morally wrong messages to children. Use specific examples of scenes in movies to support your argument.

8. Write an essay addressed to Martin Luther King, Jr., in which you either support or argue against the practicality of his philosophy of nonviolent resistance.

9. Illustrate the concept of *agape* by showing how it is practiced by community groups, organizations, or individuals you know, particularly in the context of violence in society.

10. Anna Quindlen says that children are living in "a fearsome world" ("Old Enough to Kill?" paragraph 4). Define what you think this "fearsome world" is. Or, explore ways in which certain everyday realities of our world push children into adulthood too early. If possible, use children you know as examples to support your observations.

11. Examine one aspect of a social problem that is often accompanied by or leads to violence, such as teenage drug abuse, teenage run-aways, or teenage pregnancy. Or, examine one cultural cause often cited as a factor to explain why people commit violent crimes.

12. Write an essay on violent children, that is, children who murder, rape, or commit other violent crimes. Focus on just one aspect of that subject, such as how widespread it is, how to account for its increase, possible explanations for it, or possible solutions to it. Or, for an even more manageable subject, write about one particular case, as Anna Quindlen does in "Old Enough to Kill?"

13. Given that the United States has the highest violent crime rate in the industrialized world, offer one possible approach to reducing the level of crime in America. Refer to any of the readings in this chapter where appropriate.

14. If you have been the victim of a crime, narrate what happened and describe the effects of the crime. If you personally have not been a victim but someone you know well has, describe the experience of that person and the effects of the crime.

15. Argue for or against the position that the Second Amendment right to bear arms extends to the right of citizens to own semi-automatic machine guns.

PERMISSIONS AND ACKNOWLEDGMENTS

Baker, Russell. "Deems" from *The Good Times* by Russell Baker. Copyright © 1989 by Russell Baker. Reprinted by permission of William Morrow & Company, Inc.

Baker, Susan, and Tipper Gore. "Some Reasons for 'Wilding,'" from *Newsweek*, May 29, 1989. Reprinted by permission of Parents' Music Resource Center.

Bambara, Toni Cade. "The Lesson" from *Gorilla, My Love* by Toni Cade Bambara. Copyright © 1972 by Toni Cade Bambara. Reprinted by permission of Random House, Inc.

Beathard, Ron. "Over 40 and Unmarried" from *Newsweek*, June 3, 1996. Copyright © 1996, Newsweek, Inc. All rights reserved. Reprinted by permission.

Berry, Wendell. "Men and Women in Search of Common Ground" from *Home Economics* by Wendell Berry. Copyright © 1987 by Wendell Berry. Reprinted by permission of North Point Press, a division of Farrar, Straus & Giroux, Inc.

Buchalter, Gail. "Why I Bought a Gun," first published in *Parade* magazine in 1988. Reprinted by permission of author.

Camus, Albert. "The Guest," from *Exile and the Kingdom* by Albert Camus, trans., J. O'Brien. Copyright © 1957, 1958 by Alfred A. Knopf, Inc. Reprinted by permission of the publisher.

Chan, Sucheng. "You're Short, Besides!" Copyright © 1989 by Sucheng Chan. Reprinted from *Making Waves* by permission of the author.

Conroy, Frank. "Think About It: Ways We Know, and Don't." Copyright © 1988 by *Harper's Magazine*. All rights reserved. Reprinted from the November 1988 issue by special permission.

Crichton, Jennifer. " 'Who Shall I Be?' The Allure of a Fresh Start" from *Ms.* Magazine, 1994. Reprinted by permission of the author.

Crow Dog, Mary. "A Woman from He-Dog," from *Lakota Woman* by Mary Crow Dog with Richard Erdoes. Copyright © 1990 by Mary Crow Dog and Richard Erdoes. Used by permission of Grove/Atlantic, Inc.

Davidson, John. "Menace to Society," from *Rolling Stone*, February 22, 1996. Copyright © 1996 by John Davidson. Reprinted by permission of Straight Arrow Publishers Company, Ltd, 1996.

Davis, Katherine. "I'm Not Sick, I'm Just in Love" from *Newsweek*, July 24, 1995. Copyright © 1995, Newsweek, Inc. All rights reserved. Reprinted by permission.

Delaney, Paul. "Gangsta Rappers vs. the Mainstream Black Community." Reprinted from *USA Today Magazine*, January 1995, Copyright © 1995 by the Society for the Advancement of Education.

Doloff, Steven. "Woodstock's Message Is Still True," from *The Philadelphia Inquirer,* August 8, 1991. Reprinted by permission of the author.

Durning, Alan Thein. "Can't Live Without It" appeared in *World Watch* magazine, Washington, D.C., May/June 1993. Reprinted by permission.

Ehrenreich, Barbara. "Teach Diversity with a Smile," from *Time* magazine, April 8, 1991. Copyright © 1991 Time Inc. Reprinted by permission.

Farrell, Warren. "Violence Against Whom?" Reprinted with the permission of Simon & Schuster from *The Myth of Male Power: Why Men are the Disposable Sex* by Warren Farrell. Copyright © 1993 by Warren Farrell, Ph. D.

Fisher, Scott. "Lessons from Two Ghosts," from *The Chronicle of Higher Education,* June 14, 1996. Reprinted by permission of the author.

Ford, Richard. "An Urge for Going," first published in *Harper's,* February 1992. Copyright © 1992 by Richard Ford. Reprinted by permission of International Creative Management.

Gage, Nicholas. "The Teacher Who Changed My Life," first published in *Parade,* December 17, 1989. Reprinted by permission of the author.

Gallant, Emilie. "White Breast Flats," from *A Gathering of Spirits,* edited by Beth Brant. Firebrand Books, Ithaca, New York. Copyright © 1984 by Beth Brant.

Gamson, Joshua. "Do Ask, Do Tell," reprinted by permission from *The American Prospect,* Fall 1995. Copyright New Prospect, Inc.

Golding, William. "Thinking as a Hobby," from *Holiday* magazine, 1961. Copyright © 1961 by William Golding. Reprinted by permission of Faber and Faber Ltd.

Goodman, Ellen. "It's Failure, Not Success," Copyright © 1987, The Boston Globe Newspaper Company/The Washington Post Writers Group. Reprinted by permission.

Hentoff, Nat. "'Insensitive Language' and the New HUAC Mentality," appeared in *Playboy* magazine in January 1990. Reprinted by permission of the author.

Humphrey, Derek. "Mercy Denied to Roswell Gilbert," from *Dying with Dignity: Understanding Euthanasia* by Derek Humphrey. Copyright © 1992 by Derek Humphrey. Published by arrangement with Carol Publishing Group. A Biorch Lane Press Book.

Hurston, Zora Neale. "How It Feels to be Colored Me," first published in *The World Tomorrow* in 1928. Permission provided by Lois Hurston Gaston for the Estate of Zora Neale Hurston.

Iwata, Edward. "Race Without Face," appeared in *San Francisco Focus,* May 1991. Reprinted by permission of the author.

Iyer, Pico. "The Masks of Minority Terrorism," from *Time* magazine, September 3, 1990. Copyright © 1990 Time Inc. Reprinted by permission.

Kakutani, Michiko. "The Word Police," Copyright © 1993 by the New York Times Co. Reprinted by permission.

King, Martin Luther, Jr. "Pilgrimage to Nonviolence," from *Stride Toward Freedom.* Reprinted by arrangement with The Heirs to the Estate of Martin Luther King, Jr., c/o Writers House, Inc. as agent for the proprietor. Copyright © 1963 by Martin Luther King, Jr., Copyright renewed 1991 by Coretta Scott King.

Kirkendall, Rebecca Thomas. "Who's a Hillbilly?" from *Newsweek,* Nov. 27, 1995. Copyright © 1995, Newsweek, Inc. All rights reserved. Reprinted by permission.

Krauthammer, Charles. "First and Last, Do No Harm," from *Time* magazine, April 15, 1996. Copyright © 1996 Time Inc. Reprinted by permission.

Kreyche, Gerald F. "Have We Lost Our Sense of Humor?" Reprinted from *USA Today Magazine,* May 1994, Copyright © 1994 by the Society for the Advancement of Education.

Landale, Zoë. "Remembering Karen," from *Saturday Night,* May 1993. Reprinted by permission of the author.

Layng, Anthony. "Tracing the Roots of Sexual Discrimination." Reprinted from *USA Today Magazine,* September 1993, Copyright © 1993 by the Society for the Advancement of Education.

Mairs, Nancy. "On Being a Cripple," from *Plaintext* by Nancy Mairs, by permission of the University of Arizona Press, Copyright © 1986.

Maranz, Matthew. "Guns 'Я' Us," The New Republic, January 23, 1989. Reprinted by permission of *The New Republic,* Copyright © 1989, The New Republic, Inc.

Medved, Michael. "A Sickness in the Soul," from the chapter entitled "Sleaze and Self-Indulgence" in *Hollywood vs. America: Popular Culture and the War on Traditional Values* by Michael Medved. Copyright © 1992 by Michael Medved. Reprinted by permission of HarperCollins Publishers, Inc.

Meier, Daniel. "One Man's Kids" from "About Men" column, *The New York Times Magazine,* November 1, 1987. Copyright © 1987 by the New York Times Co. Reprinted by permission.

Mithers, Carol Lynn. "The War Against Women," first appeared in *Ladies Home Journal,* October 1989. Copyright © 1989, Meredity Corporation. All rights reserved. Reprinted by permission of Ladies Home Journal® magazine.

Mora, Pat. "To Gabriela, a Young Writer," from *Nepantla* by Pat Mora, Copyright © 1993. Reprinted by permission of the University of New Mexico Press.

Morris, David. "Rootlessness," from *Utne Reader,* May/June 1990. Reprinted by permission of the author.

Naylor, Gloria. "Mommy, What Does 'Nigger' Mean?" Reprinted by permission of Sterling Lord Literistic, Inc. Copyright © 1986 by Gloria Naylor.

Noble, Robert C. "There Is No Safe Sex," reprinted by permission of the author.

Noonan, Peggy. "Toward Candor and Courage in Speech," from her "Looking Forward" column, *Good Housekeeping.* September 1996. Reprinted by permission of the author.

Orwell, George. "Shooting an Elephant" from *Shooting an Elephant and Other Essays* by George Orwell. Copyright © 1950 by Sonia Pitt-Rivers. Reprinted by permission of Harcourt Brace and Company.

Ozick, Cynthia. "On Excellence" from *Metaphor and Memory* by Cynthia Ozick. Copyright © 1989 by Cynthia Ozick. Reprinted by permission of Alfred A. Knopf, Inc.

Paley, Grace. "The Loudest Voice" from *The Little Disturbances of Man* by Grace Paley. Copyright © 1956, 1957, 1958, 1959 by Grace Paley. Used by permission of Viking Penguin, a division of Penguin Books USA Inc.

Parenti, Michael. "Political Entertainment," from *Make-Believe Media: The Politics of Film and Television* by Michael Parenti. Copyright © 1991 by Michael Parenti. Reprinted by permission of St. Martin's Press Incorporated.

Perrin, Noel. "The Androgynous Man" from "About Men" column, *The New York Times Magazine,* February 5, 1984. Copyright © 1984 by the New York Times Co. Reprinted by permission.

Quindlen, Anna. "Old Enough to Kill?" from *The New York Times,* April 1, 1990. Copyright © 1990 by the New York Times Co. Reprinted by permission.

Randall, Lynn. "Grandma's Story" from *A Gathering of Spirits,* edited by Beth Brant. Firebrand Books, Ithaca, New York. Copyright © 1984 by Beth Brant.

Rivers, Caryl. "Rock Lyrics and Violence Against Women," first published in *The Boston Globe,* 1985. Reprinted by permission of the author.

Rodriguez, Richard. "Complexion" from *Hunger of Memory.* Reprinted by permission of David R. Godine, Publishers, Inc. Copyright © 1982 by Richard Rodriguez.

Rose, Tricia. "Rap Music and the Demonization of Young Black Males." Reprinted from *USA Today Magazine,* May 1994, Copyright © 1994 by the Society for the Advancement of Education.

Rosenblatt, Roger. "The Quality of Mercy Killing," from *Time* magazine, August 26, 1985. Copyright © 1985 by Time Inc. Reprinted by permission.

Rothman, Stanley. "Is God Really Dead in Beverly Hills? Religion and the Movies." Reprinted from *The American Scholar,* volume 65, number 2, Spring 1996. Copyright © 1996 by the author.

Saltzman, Joe. "Beating the Same Old Dead Horse." Reprinted from *USA Today Magazine,* November 1993, Copyright © 1993 by the Society for the Advancement of Education.

Sharrett, Christopher. "Movies, Morality, and Conservative Complaints." Reprinted from *USA Today Magazine,* September 1993. Copyright © 1993 by the Society for the Advancement of Education.

Showalter, Julie. "Vows," first published in *Other Voices,* a publication of the University of Illinois at Chicago, Spring 1996. Reprinted by permission of the author.

Simmins, Marjorie. "Trips from There to Here," from *Saturday Night,* May 1993. Reprinted by permission of the author.

Steinberg, Stephen. "The Affirmative Action Debate," reprinted from the *UNESCO Courier,* March 1996.

Tammaro, Thom. "*Italianità* in a World Made of Love and Need" from *Two Worlds Walking: Short Stories, Essays, and Poetry by Writers with Mixed Heritages.* Eds. Diane Glancy and C. W. Truesdale. Minneapolis: New River Press, 1994. Reprinted by permission of the author.

Tan, Amy. "Mother Tongue," from *The Threepenny Review.* Copyright © 1990 by Amy Tan. Reprinted by permission.

Tannen, Deborah. "Sex, Lies, and Conversation," from *The Washington Post,* June 14, 1990. Copyright © 1990 by Deborah Tannen. Reprinted by permission.

Tavris, Carol. "Love Story," reprinted with the permission of Simon & Schuster from *The Mismeasure of Woman* by Carol Tavris. Copyright © 1992 by Carol Tavris.

Telushkin, Joseph. "Words That Hurt, Words That Heal: How to Choose Words Wisely and Well," reprinted by permission from *IMPRIMIS,* the monthly journal of Hillsdale College. Copyright © 1996.

Toth, Susan Allen. "Cabin Fever" first appeared in *The Minneapolis-St. Paul Magazine*, April 1989. Reprinted by permission of the author.

Von Hoffman, Nicholas. "Gun Crazy" first appeared in the August 2, 1993, issue of *The New Yorker*. Reprinted by permission of the author.

Wallace, Michele. "When Black Feminism Faces the Music, and the Music Is Rap" from *The New York Times*, July 29, 1990. Copyright © 1990 by the New York Times Co. Reprinted by permission.

Watson, Larry. "Silence." Reprinted by permission of the author.

Webb, Marilyn. "Why Women Don't Get Paid What They're Worth," first published in *Ladies Home Journal*, June 1993. Copyright © 1993, Meredith Corporation. Reprinted from *Ladies Home Journal* by permission of the author.

Weiss, Joan C. "Prejudice, Conflict, and Ethnoviolence." Reprinted from *USA Today Magazine*, May 1989, Copyright © 1993 by the Society for the Advancement of Education.

Wiesenfeld, Kurt. "Making the Grade" from *Newsweek*, June 17, 1996. Copyright © 1996, Newsweek, Inc. All rights reserved. Reprinted by permission.

Wieviorka, Michel. "The Ruses of Racism," reprinted from the *UNESCO Courier*, February 1993.

Wilkins, Roger. "I Became Her Target," reprinted by permission of author.

Williams, Carol Traynor. "Soap Opera Men in the '90s: Signs of Fearful Times," from the *Journal of Popular Film & Television*, fall 1994. Reprinted by permission of author.

Wu, Shanlon. "In Search of Bruce Lee's Grave," Copyright © 1990 by Shanlon Wu. All rights reserved.